The Cambridge Companion to
the Italian Renaissance

The Renaissance in Italy continues to exercise a powerful hold on the
popular imagination and on scholarly inquiry. This *Companion* presents
a lively, comprehensive, interdisciplinary, and current approach to the
period that extends in Italy from the turn of the fourteenth century
through the latter decades of the sixteenth. Addressed to students,
scholars, and non-specialists, it introduces the richly varied materials
and phenomena as well as the different methodologies through which
the Renaissance is studied today both in the English-speaking world
and in Italy. The chapters are organized around axes of humanism,
historiography, and cultural production, and cover a wide variety
of areas including literature, science, music, religion, technology,
artistic production, and economics. The diffusion of the Renaissance
throughout Italian territories is emphasized. Overall, the *Companion*
provides an essential overview of a period that witnessed both a
significant revalidation of the classical past and the development
of new, vernacular, and increasingly secular values.

MICHAEL WYATT is an independent scholar. His work is engaged
with the pre-modern cultural histories of Italy, England, and France,
particularly questions of translation as both a textual practice and a
socio-political phenomenon. He is the author of *The Italian Encounter
with Tudor England: A Cultural Politics of Translation* (2005) and co-edited
(with Deanna Shemek) *Writing Relations: American Scholars in Italian
Archives – Essays for Franca Nardelli Petrucci and Armando Petrucci* (2008).
He is currently working on a second monograph, *John Florio and the
Circulation of Stranger Cultures in Early Stuart Britain*, a critical edition of
Florio's 1603 translation of Montaigne, *The Essayes or Morall, Politike
and Millitarie Discourses*, and he is an associate-editor of *The Encyclopedia of
Renaissance Philosophy*.

Cambridge Companions to Culture

Recent titles in the series

The Cambridge Companion to
the Italian Renaissance

Edited by
MICHAEL WYATT

CAMBRIDGE
UNIVERSITY PRESS

University Printing House, Cambridge CB2 8BS, United Kingdom

One Liberty Plaza, 20th Floor, New York, NY 10006, USA

477 Williamstown Road, Port Melbourne, VIC 3207, Australia

314-321, 3rd Floor, Plot 3, Splendor Forum, Jasola District Centre, New Delhi - 110025, India

79 Anson Road, #06-04/06, Singapore 079906

Cambridge University Press is part of the University of Cambridge.

It furthers the University's mission by disseminating knowledge in the pursuit of education, learning and research at the highest international levels of excellence.

www.cambridge.org
Information on this title: www.cambridge.org/9780521699464

© Cambridge University Press 2014

First published 2014

A catalogue record for this publication is available from the British Library

Library of Congress Cataloging in Publication data
The Cambridge companion to the Italian Renaissance / edited by Michael Wyatt.
 pages cm. – (Cambridge companions to culture)
Summary: "The Renaissance in Italy continues to exercise a powerful hold on the popular imagination and on scholarly enquiry.
ISBN 978-0-521-87606-3 (Hardback) – ISBN 978-0-521-69946-4 (Paperback)
1. Renaissance–Italy. 2. Italy–Civilization–1268-1559. 3. Italy–Intellectual life–1268-1559. 4. Italy–Social conditions–1268-1559. I. Wyatt, Michael, 1956-
DG533.C36 2014
945'.05–dc23 2013024948

ISBN 978-0-521-87606-3 Hardback
ISBN 978-0-521-69946-4 Paperback

For Jacques Grès-Gayer

Contents

Illustrations

Contributors

GIOVANNA BENADUSI is Professor of History at the University of South Florida. She is the author of *A Provincial Elite in Early Modern Tuscany: Family and Power in the Creation of the State* (1996), has co-edited (with Judith Brown) *Medici Women: The Making of a Dynasty in Grand Ducal Tuscany* (forthcoming), and is completing a book manuscript, *Vision of the Social Order: Women's Last Wills, Notaries, and the State in Baroque Tuscany.*

JUDITH C. BROWN has served as Professor of History at Stanford University, Dean of the School of Humanities at Rice University, and Vice President for Academic Affairs and Provost at Wesleyan University, where she is now Professor Emerita. She is the author of *In the Shadow of Florence: Provincial Society in Renaissance Pescia* (1982) and numerous articles on women, gender, and the economy in Renaissance Italy. She has co-edited (with Robert C. Davis) *Gender and Society in Renaissance Italy* (1998), and (with Giovanna Benadusi) *Medici Women: The Making of a Dynasty in Grand Ducal Tuscany* (forthcoming).

MAURIZIO CAMPANELLI is Assistant Professor in the Department of Greek, Latin, and Italian Studies at the University of Rome, "La Sapienza." His wide-ranging research interests span medieval and humanist Latin literatures and their reception. He has published *Polemiche e filologia ai primordi della stampa: Le 'Observationes' di Domizio Calderini* (2001), and an edition of Marsilio Ficino's translation of Mercurio Trismegisto, *Pimander sive de potestate et sapientia Dei* (2011). He is Principal Investigator for the Australian Research Council project "The Invention of Rome: Biondo Flavio's *Roma triumphans* and its Worlds" (2013–15).

STEPHEN J. CAMPBELL is Henry and Elizabeth Wiesenfeld Professor and Chair of the Department of the History of Art at Johns Hopkins University. He specializes in Italian art of the fifteenth and sixteenth centuries with a particular focus on the artistic culture of North Italian courts. In addition to studies of Giorgione, the Carracci, Bronzino, Michelangelo, and Rosso Fiorentino, his books include *Cosmè Tura of Ferrara: Style, Politics and the Renaissance City 1450–1495* (1997), and *The Cabinet of Eros: Renaissance Mythological Painting and the Studiolo of Isabella d'Este* (2006). His co-authored and edited books include *Cosmè Tura: Painting and Design in Renaissance Ferrara* (exhibition catalogue, 2002), *Artistic Exchange and Cultural Translation in the Italian Renaissance City* (2004), *Artists at Court: Image Making and Identity 1300–1550* (2004), and (with Michael Cole), *Renaissance Art in Italy 1400–1600* (2011).

KATHLEEN WREN CHRISTIAN is Lecturer in Art History at the Open University, Milton Keynes, UK, having previously taught in the Department of History of Art and Architecture at the University of Pittsburgh. She is the author of *Empire without End: Antiquities Collections in Renaissance Rome c. 1350–1527* (2010) and co-edited (with David Drogin) *Patronage and Italian Renaissance Sculpture* (2010). She is currently co-editing *The Muses and their Afterlife in Post-Classical Europe.*

FRANCESCA FIORANI is Professor of Art History and Chair of the Art Department at the University of Virginia, Charlottesville. An expert on the relationship between art and science in early modern Europe, she has written extensively on the representation of space, cartography, mapping, art theory, and Leonardo da Vinci. She is the author of *The Marvel of Maps: Art, Cartography and Politics in Renaissance Italy* (2005), and the co-author of *Bartolo di Fredi's 'Adoration of the Magi': A Masterpiece Reconstructed* (2012, with Bruce Boucher) and *Leonardo da Vinci and Optics: Theory and Pictorial Practice* (2013, with Alessandro Nova). She is currently completing a book on Leonardo da Vinci's shadows considered from the point of view of artistic practice, optics, philosophy, and culture.

GIUSEPPE GERBINO is Associate Professor and Chair of the Department of Music at Columbia University. His research interests include the Italian madrigal, the relationship between music and language in the early modern period, early opera, and Renaissance theories of cognition and sense perception. His publications have appeared in the *Journal of Musicology*, the *Journal of Medieval and Early Modern Studies*, the *Musical Quarterly, Studi Musicali*, and *Il Saggiatore Musicale*. His book *Music and the Myth of Arcadia in Renaissance Italy* (2009) won the Lewis Lockwood Award of the American Musicological Society.

MARK JURDJEVIC is Associate Professor of History at Glendon College of the University of York in Toronto. He studies the political and intellectual history of Renaissance Florence and is the author of *Guardians of Republicanism: The Valori Family in the Florentine Renaissance* (2008), *A Great and Wretched City: Promise and Failure in Machiavelli's Florentine Political Thought* (forthcoming).

RONALD L. MARTINEZ is Professor of Italian Studies at Brown University, having previously taught at the University of Minnesota, Twin Cities. He teaches and has published extensively on a wide range of medieval and Renaissance Italian literature and cultural history. He is co-author (with Robert Durling) of *Time and the Crystal: Studies in Dante's Rime Petrose* (1990), and co-editor with Durling of a bilingual edition with translation and commentary of Dante's *Commedia*: *Inferno* (1996), *Purgatorio* (2003), and *Paradiso* (2011). He is currently preparing a book-length study of Dante's appropriation of medieval Catholic liturgy for narrative and linguistic aspects of the *Commedia*.

KATHARINE PARK, the Samuel Zemurray, Jr. and Doris Zemurray Stone Radcliffe Professor of the History of Science at Harvard University, works on the cultural, social, and intellectual history of science and medicine in the European Middle Ages and Renaissance. She is the author of *Doctors and Medicine in Early Renaissance Florence* (1985) and *Secrets of Women: Gender, Generation, and the Origins of Human Dissection* (2006), winner of the Margaret W. Rossiter History of Women and Science Prize of the History of Science Society in 2007, and co-author (with Lorraine Daston) of *Wonders and the Order of Nature, 1150–1750* (1998), winner of the Pfizer Award of the HSS for the best book in the history of science in 1999. She and Daston also co-edited volume 3 of *The Cambridge History of Science* (2006), dedicated to science in early modern Europe.

CONCETTA PENNUTO is Assistant Professor at the Centre d'Études Supérieures de la Renaissance of the Université François-Rabelais in Tours, where she teaches the history of medicine and neo-Latin language. Her research is dedicated to the history of Renaissance medicine, with a particular focus on contagious diseases, astrological medicine, sports medicine, women's health, and surgical knowledge. The author of *Simpatia, fantasia e contagio: il pensiero medico e il pensiero filosofico di Girolamo Fracastoro* (2008), she has also edited the first volume of Antonio Vallisneri's *Quaderni di osservazioni*, Girolamo Mercuriale's *De arte gymnastica* (2008), and Fracastoro's *De sympathia et antipathia rerum* (2008).

DIEGO PIRILLO is Assistant Professor of Italian Studies at the University of California, Berkeley, having previously taught at the Scuola Normale Superiore and the University of Pisa. His research focuses on early modern philosophy, heterodoxy, and political thought, with special attention to the history of books and reading. He is the author of *Filosofia ed eresia nell'Inghilterra del tardo Cinquecento: Bruno, Sidney e i dissidenti religiosi italiani* (2010) and the editor (with Olivia Catanorchi) of *Favole, metafore, storie: seminario su Giordano Bruno* (2007). He is currently working on a monograph on the Italian Protestant reformers of the sixteenth and seventeenth centuries.

ADRIANO PROSPERI is Professor Emeritus of Modern History at the Scuola Normale Superiore, and earlier taught at the University of Calabria, the University of Bologna, and the University of Pisa. Among his vast critical output are *Tribunali della coscienza: inquisitori, confessori, missionari* (1996), *L'eresia del Libro Grande: storia di Giorgio Siculo e della sua setta* (2000), and *Il seme dell'intolleranza: Ebrei, eretici, selvaggi* (2011). He has edited his teacher Delio Cantimori's *Eretici italiani del Cinquecento e altri scritti* (1992), the six-volume *Storia del mondo moderno e contemporaneo* (with Paolo Viola, 2004), the *Colloquia* and *Scritti religiosi e morali* of Erasmus (both with Cecilia Asso, 2002 and 2004), and the four-volume *Dizionario storico dell'Inquisizione* (with Vincenzo Lavenia and John Tedeschi).

PATRICIA L. REILLY is Associate Provost and Associate Professor of Art History at Swarthmore College, Pennsylvania. In addition to articles and essays, including "Raphael's Fire in the Borgo and the Italian Pictorial Vernacular" (2010) and "Drawing the Line: Benvenuto Cellini's *On the Principles and Method of the Learning the Art of Drawing* and the Question of Amateur Education" (2004), she is the co-editor (with Roberta Olson and Rupert Shepherd) of *The Biography of the Object in Late Medieval and Renaissance Italy* (2006). She has completed a book manuscript dealing with Giorgio Vasari's re-envisioning of Leonardo, Raphael, and Michelangelo on the walls of the Palazzo Vecchio in Florence, and her current project is a study of the stylus drawings of Leonardo da Vinci.

BRIAN RICHARDSON is Emeritus Professor of Italian Language at the University of Leeds, UK, and a Fellow of the British Academy. His publications include *Print Culture in Renaissance Italy: The Editor and the Vernacular Text, 1470–1600* (1994), *Printing, Writers and Readers in Renaissance Italy* (1999), an edition of Giovan Francesco Fortunio's *Regole grammaticali della volgar lingua* (2001), and *Manuscript Culture in Renaissance Italy* (2009). From 2003 to 2013 he was general editor of the *Modern Language Review*.

He is currently the Principal Investigator of *Oral Culture, Manuscript and Print in Early Modern Italy, 1450–1700*, a project funded by the European Research Council (2011–15).

DEANNA SHEMEK is Professor of Literature at the University of California, Santa Cruz, where she also directs the program in Italian Studies. She is the author of *Ladies Errant: Wayward Women and Social Order in Early Modern Italy* (1998); co-editor (with Dennis Looney) of *Phaethon's Children: The Este Court and its Culture in Early Modern Ferrara* (2005) and (with Michael Wyatt) of *Writing Relations: American Scholars in Italian Archives – Essays for Franca Nardelli Petrucci and Armando Petrucci* (2008); and editor and co-translator (with Robert de Lucca) of Adriana Cavarero, *Stately Bodies: Literature, Philosophy, and the Question of Gender* (2002). She is currently working on an edition of the letters of Isabella d'Este and on a monographic study of this correspondence.

JON R. SNYDER is Professor of Italian Studies and Comparative Literature at the University of California, Santa Barbara. He has taught at the University of California in San Diego, and Los Angeles, as well as at the Università degli Studi di Torino and the Università degli Studi di Macerata. He is the author of *Writing the Scene of Speaking: Theories of Dialogue in the Late Italian Renaissance* (1989), *L'estetica del Barocco* (2005), *Dissimulation and the Culture of Secrecy in Early Modern Europe* (2009), and a bilingual edition/ translation of Giovan Battista Andreini's *Amor nello specchio/Love in the Mirror* (2009). He is co-editor of *California Italian Studies* and is completing a translation/edition of Torquato Accetto's *Della dissimulazione onesta*.

MICHAEL WYATT is an independent scholar. He has taught at Stanford University, the Università degli Studi di Trento, Wesleyan University, and Northwestern University, and he has served as the Associate Director of the Stanford Center for Medieval and Early Modern Studies. His work is engaged with the pre-modern cultural and intellectual histories of Italy, England, and France, particularly questions of translation as both a textual practice and a socio-political phenomenon. He is the author of *The Italian Encounter with Tudor England: A Cultural Politics of Translation* (2005) and co-editor (with Deanna Shemek) of *Writing Relations: American Scholars in Italian Archives – Essays for Franca Nardelli Petrucci and Armando Petrucci* (2008). He is currently working on a second monograph, *John Florio and the Circulation of Stranger Cultures in Early Stuart Britain*, a critical edition of Florio's 1603 translation of Montaigne, *The Essayes or Morall, Politike and Millitarie Discourses*, and he is an associate-editor of *The Encyclopedia of Renaissance Philosophy*.

Preface

The idea for a volume of essays dedicated to the Italian Renaissance first occurred to me fifteen years ago when I was teaching the literature and cultural history of the period to American undergraduates. My students and I were frequently in need of a synthetic presentation of subjects critical for understanding the texts or objects being studied but which were outside either the scope of their preparation or my expertise, and there was at the time no up-to-date resource pitched at the right level that might have helped to address these lacunae. Since then several useful books have appeared that examine many of the central concerns of the Italian Renaissance, some written by single authors and others organized as collections of essays (see "Renaissances," my introduction to this volume), each bearing the disciplinary imprint of their authors or editors. This *Companion* reflects the literary, linguistic, and historical interests of its editor, but the aim here has been to provide a broad framework for the interdisciplinary study of the Italian Renaissance, with contributions from scholars at various stages of their careers who represent the disparate traditions of Anglo-American and Italian scholarship. The volume has been conceived with advanced undergraduate and graduate students in the English-speaking world in mind, but as these essays are more than mere summaries of existing scholarship it is hoped that they will have something to offer both to professionals working in Italian Renaissance studies and related fields and to general readers interested in the period.

While the initial impetus for this *Companion* arose from teaching, the actual form the book has taken owes a great deal to the enormously stimulating environment of Villa I Tatti, the Harvard University Center for Italian Renaissance Studies in Florence, where I and many of this volume's authors have had the privilege and pleasure of being fellows.

Constituted by a widely diverse and ever-expanding global community of scholars, I Tatti has played a crucial role over the last fifty years in the promotion and renewal of Italian Renaissance studies through its fellowship program for junior scholars, sabbaticals for senior scholars and museum curators, publications, conferences, concerts, and innovative initatives such as the one that brought sixteen Chinese scholars to Florence in the summer of 2013 for a three-week seminar examining the "Unity of the Arts in Renaissance Italy." I owe a particular debt to Katharine Park, who as Acting Director of I Tatti during the second half of my fellowship year patiently worked through several versions of the initial proposal for this *Companion*, greatly improving it in countless ways large and small. Thanks are also due to former Director Joseph Connors for encouraging me to apply (and reapply) for an I Tatti fellowship in the first place; and to current Director Lino Pertile for his advice with regard to this project, and for the hospitality he and Anna Bensted so generously extend to former fellows. Michael Rocke and his excellent staff have built the unparalleled library collection at I Tatti into the finest dedicated resource anywhere in the world for the study of the Italian Renaissance.

Collaborative ventures pose particular challenges to all involved, and this *Companion* has seen its fair share of difficulties and delays. I am especially grateful for the forbearance and understanding of both my contributors and Sarah Stanton, our editor at Cambridge University Press. Thanks also to Fleur Jones, Rebecca Taylor, Anna Lowe, and Jonathan Ratcliffe at Cambridge and to our copy-editor Anna Hodson for their attentive work in producing the volume; thanks as well to Rebecca Frankel for her assistance in preparing the index, and to Eugenio Refini for his diligent editing of it. For their help, advice, recommendations and/or moral support with regard to various aspects of this project, I would also like to thank Dario Tessicini, Frances Andrews, Monica Calabritto, Agata Pincelli, Alessandra Petrina, Massimo Scalabrini, Paul Gehl, Gerry Milligan, David Lummus, Mary Therese Martinez, Nancy Durling, Jacqueline Marie Musacchio, Raúl Martinez-Martinez, Daniel Zolli, Louise George Clubb, Lucinda Byatt, Ilaria Andreoli, Giovanni Carlo Federico Villa, and Maria Luisa di Rinaldis. Special thanks are due to Giorgio Alberti; and to Stephen Orgel, my best editor and most exigent critic, who has carefully read the entire manuscript (some parts of it more than once).

Note on money

It is difficult to provide precise modern equivalents for earlier monetary values. The tangle of currencies and unstable economic markers resulting from the political and administrative fragmentation of the Italian peninsula and its islands in the period of the Renaissance make the task particularly problematic. But some sense of what the principal instruments of financial exchange were worth at the time is useful for understanding the costs of goods and services mentioned in the essays in this volume and its bibliography.

Coins were struck all over Italy in *zecche* [mints] regulated by the particular authority to which they were accountable, whether republics, duchies, lordships, and feudal principalities, the Papal States, or the kingdoms of Naples, Sicily, and Sardinia.[1] Gold coins were primarily used in large transactions, while silver-based and billon coins (like the *soldo di piccioli* in Florence) were mainly used for smaller everyday payments. However, over the course of the sixteenth century exchange rates between gold and silver coins fluctuated constantly. There were also virtual systems of coinage, moneys of account based on the *lira* and made up of 20 *soldi*, 240 *denari*. These "ghost moneys" only appeared in account books and never in anyone's purse.[2] The gold coins most commonly cited here are the Venetian *ducato*, the Florentine *florin* (replaced by the *scudo* in 1530),[3] and the papal *scudo*,[4] each with its own fixed local value that fluctuated with time. In Venice between 1517 and 1573, for instance,

---

[1] Travaini (2007). Notwithstanding the close controls, counterfeit was a constant worry, or seen from another perspective, a tempting opportunity.
[2] Goldthwaite (2009) 611.
[3] Cipolla (1989) 61.
[4] Guidi Bruscoli (2007) xiii.

1 gold *ducato* varied in value from roughly 6 to 8 *lire*;[5] and in Florence throughout the sixteenth century 1 *florin* was worth 140 *soldi*, although its real purchasing power was halved over the same period.[6]

To translate these figures into more easily understandable terms: 1 Florentine *florin* would have provided fourteen days of an unskilled worker's stipend in 1500, but only seven days in 1600;[7] "in 1536 [1] *scudo* would buy twenty-eight chickens or fifty kilograms of flour and represented one week's wages for a master builder";[8] a document from Pavia in 1547 specifies that the rent of a house for the eight-month academic year accommodating five students, meals, and the wages and maintenance of two servants cost 192 *lire* (28 Venetian *ducati*) per student;[9] an unbound copy of the first edition of Ludovico Ariosto's *Orlando furioso* (1516) cost 1 *lira*; and the total labor costs for the construction of Villa Farnese at Caprarola (completed in the 1570s) was 25,855.80 *scudi*.[10]

Acknowledgment

Thanks to Lucy Byatt for her suggestions and improvements to this note.

---

[5] Birnbaum (2003) 121.   [6] Goldthwaite (2009) 612.   [7] *Ibid.*
[8] Hollingsworth (2004) xii.   [9] Grendler (2002) 167–68.
[10] See in this volume, respectively, Richardson, "Publication," Chapter 7, 171; and Wyatt, "Technologies," Chapter 5, 130.

Timeline

1282	War of the "Sicilian Vespers" drives French Angevin colonizers from Sicily; they are replaced by Aragonese rulers, the first sign of the Spanish presence in Italy that will come to dominate the territory in the latter period of the Renaissance.
1297–1323	Reform of the Venetian *Maggior Consiglio*, the principal political organ of the city–republic responsible for electing the Doge, magistrates, and other civic officials, and consisting exclusively of all male members of the aristocracy.
1303–05	Dante Alighieri writes *De vulgari eloquentia* (incomplete); Giotto and his workshop fresco the Cappella Scrovegni in Padua.
1309–77	Papacy moves its seat to Avignon, in southern France.
1327–74 (*c.*)	Petrarch writes and rewrites his cycle of vernacular poems, the *Canzoniere* (also known as *Le rime sparse* or the *Rerum vulgarium fragmenta*).
1340s (*c.*)	First recorded use of gunpowder-based firearms, imported from Asia, in Italy.
1341	Petrarch crowned Poet Laureate in Rome, after a three-day examination conducted by Robert of Anjou, King of Naples.
1347–53	Black Death ravages Europe, killing roughly one-third of the population of the continent.
1347–80	Catherine of Siena, Dominican mystic, fought for the reformation of the church and return of papacy to Rome.
1347–51	Cola di Rienzo is acclaimed Tribune in Rome in an attempt to re-establish a form of ancient republican government in the city.
1349–74	Giovanni Boccaccio writes his vernacular *Decameron* and, among many other works in Italian and Latin, compiles his encyclopedia of classical mythology, the *Genealogia deorum gentilium*.
1365–80	Giovanni Dondi designs and builds his "planetarium."

1377–1417	Great (Western) Schism, which saw the papacy divided into two, and then three, competing factions.
1395–1402	Gian Galezzo Visconti is Duke of Milan.
1397	Giovanni di Bicci de' Medici, a banker with close ties to the papacy, returns to Florence from Rome to establish the bank that would guarantee the future wealth and status of his descendants.
1401	Lorenzo Ghiberti awarded commission to cast doors for the baptistery of cathedral in Florence.
1417	Poggio Bracciolini "rediscovers" a manuscript of Lucretius' *De rerum natura*.
1420–36	Filippo Brunelleschi plans and constructs the dome of the cathedral in Florence.
1420	Pope Martin V (Ottone Colonna) brings the papacy back to Rome.
1423	Vittorino da Feltre establishes his Latin grammar school in Mantua.
1424–27	Masaccio and Masolino fresco the Church of the Carmine in Florence.
1429	Cosimo de' Medici inherits the family bank and begins the consolidation of Medici power in Florence.
1432–1502	The "Ufficiali di notte," a tribunal established in Florence to adjudicate accusations of homosexual sodomy.
1434	Pope Eugene IV (Gabriele Condulmer) forced to abandon Rome due to local political instability; he manages to bring the papacy definitively back to Rome only in 1443.
1440	Lorenzo Valla writes *De falso ementita Costantini donatione declamatio* – exposing the document claimed for centuries to justify the church's temporal authority as a forgery; Donatello casts his bronze David for the courtyard of Palazzo Medici in Florence.
1442	Alfonso V of Aragon is crowned Alfonso I, King of Naples, linking the political destinies of Sicily and the Kingdom of Naples to the Spanish Aragonese.
1443–57	Leon Battista Alberti writes his architectural treatise, *De re aedificatoria*.
1447	Francesco Sforza seizes power in Milan; election of Pope Nicholas V (Tommaso Parentucelli), who initiates the monumental reconstruction of Rome.
1452–71	Construction of the *Triumphal Arch of Alfonso I* at Castel Nuovo in Naples.
1453	Ottoman conquest of Constantinople, after which many Greek-speaking intellectuals immigrate to Italy together with their libraries.
1458	Election of Pope Pius II (Enea Silvio Piccolomini).
1465–82	Luciano Lauredana and Francesco di Giorgio Martini build the Palazzo Ducale for Federico da Montefeltro in Urbino.

1465–67	Germans Conrad Sweynheym and Arnold Pannartz establish first known printing press in Italy, at the Benedictine monastery of Subiaco outside of Rome.
1465–77	Francesco di Giorgio Martini compiles his reflections on technologal developments, the *Codicetto*.
1469	Lorenzo de' Medici, "The Magnificent," assumes control of his family's interests, and, de facto, those of Florence.
1471	Election of Pope Sixtus IV (Francesco della Rovere). Major building continues in Rome, including the Sistine Chapel and the Vatican Library (formally constituted in 1475).
1474	Isabella d'Este born in Ferrara; Flavio Biondo publishes his geography of Italy, *Italia illustrata*; and Marsilio Ficino completes his *Theologia platonica* (published in 1482).
1472–75 (*c.*)	Andrea Mantegna paints his *Lamentation over the Dead Christ*.
1478	"Pazzi Conspiracy" in Florence that wounded Lorenzo de' Medici and killed his brother Giuliano.
1480 (*c.*)	Piero della Francesca writes his treatise on visual perspective, *De prospectiva pingendi*.
1480	Angelo Poliziano's version of the Orpheus myth, *Orfeo*, staged with designs by Leonardo da Vinci in Mantua (an earlier date, 1473, has been suggested by some scholars).
1480s	Gubbio *Studiolo* realized by the workshop of Giuliano da Maiano after designs by Francesco di Giorgio Martini.
1480–81	Ottoman siege of Otranto that threatened a Muslim invasion of the Italian peninsula, repelled by various Italian contingents and troops of the Hungarian humanist king Matthias Corvinus, cut short by the premature death of the sultan Mahomet II.
1482	Francesco Berlinghieri publishes his *Septe giornate della geografia*, the first comprehensive effort to modernize Ptolemy's ancient geography; Sixtus IV authorizes the dissection of human cadavers for medical research.
1486	Pico della Mirandola publishes his controversial 900 theses dedicated to philosophical questions.
1491–1507	Giovanni Pontano, Neapolitan humanist, publishes his five *Dialogi* (*Charon, Antonius, Actius, Aegidius,* and *Asinus*).
1492	Election of Pope Alexander VI (Rodrigo Borgia); Columbus sails west; death of Lorenzo de' Medici.
1494	Descent into Italy of the French King Charles VIII, initiating a period of extreme political instability on the Italian peninsula that would last until 1559 with the Peace of Cateau-Cambrésis; Luca Pacioli publishes his mathematical treatise *Summa de arithmetica, geometria, proportioni e proportionalità e della divina proportione*.
1494–98	Dominican friar Girolamo Savonarola becomes effective leader of Florence, at the end of which time he is publicly hanged and burned as a heretic.

1495	Matteo Maria Boiardo's incomplete *Orlando innamorato* published posthumously.
1495–98	Aldus Manutius publishes in Greek the complete works of Aristotle in Venice.
1497–1502	Filippino Lippi frescoes the Strozzi Chapel in the Church of Santa Maria Novella, Florence.
1498	Leonardo da Vinci paints his *Last Supper* in the refectory of the Convent of Santa Maria delle Grazie in Milan.
1498–1512	Florentine Republic re-established; Niccolò Machiavelli appointed secretary to the Second Chancellery (for internal and military affairs).
1499	The *Hypnerotomachia Poliphili*, an anonymous prose romance (Francesco Colonna may be the author) written in a hybrid language and among the most highly prized books of the early period of Italian printing, published by Aldus Manutius' press in Venice.
1501	Ottaviano Petrucci publishes the *Harmonice Musices Odhecaton*, a collection of ninety-six polyphonic pieces, a landmark in the printing of music.
1501–04	Michelangelo's *David*, originally intended for the roofline of the Florence cathedral, placed in front of the administrative seat of the Florentine republic, Palazzo Vecchio.
1503	Election of Pope Julius II (Giuliano della Rovere).
1504	Amerigo Vespucci publishes *Mundus novus*, an account of his four journeys to the West Indies and Brazil; the Kingdom of Naples assimilated into the Spanish Hapsburg empire.
1506	The ancient Hellenistic monumental statue-set of *Laocoön and his Sons* unearthed in Rome.
1506–1615	St. Peter's Basilica in Rome rebuilt by numerous architects.
1507–24	Baldassare Castiglione writes his treatise of the ideal courtly life, *Il libro del cortegiano* (published in 1528).
1508	Bologna conquered by Julius II.
1508–09	Ludovico Ariosto writes his vernacular comedies *Cassaria* and *I suppositi*, modeled after works of the ancient Roman playwrights Plautus and Terence.
1508–12	Michelangelo frescoes ceiling of the Sistine Chapel.
1509	Republic of Venice defeated in the Battle of Agnadello by the League of Cambrai consisting of the papacy allied with the major European powers, exposing vulnerabilities in Venetian control over its mainland territories.
1509–11	Raphael frescoes the Vatican *Stanza della Segnatura*.
1512–14 (*c.*)	Giovanni Bellini paints the *Feast of the Gods*.
1513	Machiavelli begins work on the *Discorsi* (finished by 1519 but not printed until 1531) and writes *Il principe* (printed in 1532); election of Pope Leo X (Giovanni de' Medici), following the restitution of the Medici in Florence the previous year.

1516	First edition of Ludovico Ariosto's *Orlando furioso*, subsequently enlarged and published in a second edition in 1521, further expanded and adapted in the now-standard Tuscan dialect and issued definitively in 1532; Giovan Francesco Fortunio publishes his *Regole grammaticali della volgar lingua*, the first printed Italian grammar; Pietro Pomponazzi publishes *De immortalitate animae*, arguing against the immortality of the soul.
1521	Teofilo Folengo publishes his macaronic mock-epic *Baldus*.
1521–36	Gian Giacomo Acaya transforms the feudal settlement of Segine (near Lecce) into the fortified town of Acaya.
1523–34	Papacy of Clement VII (Giulio de' Medici).
1524	Marcantonio Raimondi publishes his erotic engravings (subsequently destroyed on order of Clement VII) known as *I modi* after (lost) images of Giulio Romano for which Pietro Aretino wrote accompanying sonnets.
1525	Battle of Pavia between France and the Holy Roman Empire, after which French claims on Italy end with the French king Francis I taken prisoner; Pietro Bembo publishes *Le prose della volgar lingua*.
1525–26	Aldine press in Venice publishes the ancient medical texts of Galen and Hippocrates in Greek.
1527	Sack of Rome by troops of Hapsburg Holy Roman Emperor Charles V.
1530	The Paduan physician Girolamo Fracastoro publishes his poem dealing with syphilis, *Syphilis sive Morbus Gallicus*, a disease that had first appeared in Europe in the late fifteenth century and may have been brought to Italy with the French invasion in the 1490s.
1534	Election of Pope Paul III (Alessandro Farnese).
1534–35	Lorenzo Lotto paints his *Annunciation* for the Confraternity of Merchants in Recanati.
1536–41	Michelangelo frescoes *The Last Judgment* in the Sistine Chapel.
1538	Vittoria Colonna's *Rime* printed.
1542	Creation of the Holy Office, the administrative center of the Roman Inquisition.
1543	First edition of *Il beneficio di Cristo* (issued anonymously but written by Benedetto Fontanini) – the most influential text of the Italian "Reformation" – published in Venice.
1545–63	Council of Trent, the Catholic counter-offensive to the Protestant Reformation.
1547	Tullia d'Aragona publishes her *Rime*.
1549	Giovanni della Casa, Papal Nuncio to the Republic of Venice, compiles the first Italian Index of Forbidden Books (his treatise on social customs, *Il Galateo*, is published posthumously in 1558); Laura Terracina publishes her chivalric romance in dialogue with Ariosto, the *Discorso sopra tutti i primi canti dell' "Orlando furioso."*

1550	Giorgio Vasari publishes the first edition of his survey of the Italian visual arts, the *Vite de' più eccellenti pittori, scultori e architettori* (expanded and reissued in 1568).
1550s (c.)	Cristoforo Sabbadino writes his treatise dealing with the technological and ecological challenges facing the Venetian lagoon, the *Trattato delle acque* (unpublished in the period).
1550–59	Gian Battista Ramusio publishes the three volumes of his collection of accounts of the voyages of discovery, *Navigazioni et viaggi*, from Marco Polo through Vespucci and including the exploration of Africa (printed together with maps of Giacomo Gastaldi).
1551	Leandro Alberti publishes his *Descrittione di tutta Italia*, the first geography of Italy to include Sicily and Sardinia.
1552	Giovanni Filippo Ingrassia, a Sicilian physician and public health official, publishes *De tumoribus praeter naturam*, documenting his earlier discovery that the human brain could host tumors.
1554	First three parts of Matteo Bandello's *Novelle*, the most important collection of short narrative fiction since Boccaccio's *Decameron*, published (a fourth part was issued posthumously in 1573).
1555	Election of Pope Paul IV (Gian Pietro Carafa).
1556–73	Vignola (Jacopo Barozzi) designs and builds Villa Farnese at Caprarola.
1558	Gioseffo Zarlino publishes his influential treatise of music theory, the *Istitutioni harmoniche*.
1559	Papal Index of Forbidden Books established; first anthology of verse by women poets, the *Rime diverse d'alcune nobilissime et virtuosissime donne*, published in Lucca; Cosimo I de' Medici, Duke of Florence since 1537, named Grand Duke of Tuscany by Pope Pius IV (Giovanni Angelo Medici di Marignano).
1560	Giovanni della Porta founds the "Academia Secretorum Naturae" in Naples, one of the earliest learned societies in Europe dedicated to the natural sciences; Laura Battiferri publishes the *Primo libro dell'opere toscane*, a collection of her own poetry and that of a group of male correspondents.
1561	Alessandro Citolini publishes his encyclopedic dictionary of the knowledge of the world, *La tipocosmia*; posthumous publication of Francesco Guicciardini's *Historia d'Italia*, a devastating critique of Italian politics between 1492 and 1532.
1562	Isabella Andreini, the most famous actress of the "Commedia dell'arte" and a prolific poet, born in Padua.
1564	Death of Michelangelo.
1566	Election of Pope Pius V (Antonio Ghislieri).
1569	Girolamo Mercuriale publishes his treatise on physical exercise, *De arte gymnastica*.

1570	Andrea Palladio publishes his architectural treatise, the *Quattro libri di architettura*.
1571	Battle of Lepanto in which for the first time a league of European Christian allies prevailed over Turkish forces at sea.
1574	Stefano Guazzo publishes *Della civil conversazione*, a "courtesy" manual dealing with education, family life, and social practices.
1575	Veronica Franco publishes her colletion of poems, *Terze rime*.
1580–81	Torquato Tasso publishes *Aminta*, a widely imitated pastoral play, and his equally influential epic poem, *La Gerusalemme liberata*.
1580–83	Ignazio Danti supervises the painting of frescoes of maps of Italian territories in the Vatican Gallery of Maps.
1582–85	Renegade Dominican friar Giordano Bruno writes and publishes in London six Italian dialogues dealing with a wide range of controversial philosophical and cosmological issues, including the heliocentric universe and the infinity of worlds.
1584	Installation of the Fontana Pretoria in Palermo, originally built by Francesco Camilliani in 1554 for the Florentine villa of Don Pedro di Toledo.
1585	Inauguration of the Teatro Olimpico, designed by Andrea Palladio, in Vicenza.
1588	Giovanni Botero publishes his treatise on cities, *Della grandezza e magnificenza delle città*.
1589	Elaborate musical *intermezzi* staged between the acts of Girolamo Bargagli's comedy *La pellegrina* in a theater constructed within the Uffizi Palace in Florence for the wedding celebrations of Grand Duke Ferdinand I and Christine of Lorraine.
1593	Antonio Possevino's *Biblioteca selecta* forcefully reasserts the relationship of Aristotelianism and Catholic doctrine, subordinating all philosophical thinking to the teaching magisterium of the church.
1598	John Florio, son of an Italian religious exile, publishes in London *A Worlde of Words*, an Italian–English dictionary and the most comprehensive lexicon of the Italian language to date (a second, greatly expanded edition, *Queen Anna's New World of Words*, is published in 1611); Ferrara loses its independence to the papacy.
1600	Giordano Bruno executed by the Roman Inquisition.

MICHAEL WYATT

Renaissances

The Renaissance in Italy continues to exercise a powerful hold on scholarly inquiry and on the popular imagination, and the essays in this volume seek to provide an introduction to the richly varied materials and phenomena as well as the different methodologies through which the period – here considered as extending from the turn of the four-teenth century to the end of the sixteenth – is studied today both in the English-speaking world and in Italy. No single discipline has been privileged in either the choice or placement of essays in the volume; its objective is to provide a series of tools with which any one of the matters addressed (some of which would not have occurred to earlier gener-ations of scholars as being relevant to the period as they conceived it) might be further contextualized. In a volume that includes essays on science and medicine, technologies, artists' workshops, and economies, the absence of a chapter dedicated to a subject as fundamental to the Italian Renaissance as humanism might seem incongruous but for the fact that humanists and their questions are central to all but a few of the essays here. Humanism was never considered an autonomous field during the period in which its practices were first developed, and treating it as an organic dimension of the culture of the Italian Renaissance demonstrates the significant ways in which the energies driving that culture were effectively bilingual and interdisciplinary.[1] Similarly, the important issues raised by gender studies inform a number of the contributions here but are not addressed in a separate

---

[1] See the *Cambridge Companion to Renaissance Humanism*, Kraye (1996), for an excellent introduction to humanism considered in its broader European development.

essay.[2] Each of the chapters of this *Companion* provides a select, but by no means exhaustive, survey of the principal questions, genres, and practices evoked in their titles. Every effort has been made to provide a relevant and up-to-date bibliography, primarily in English and Italian, and especially with regard to matters necessarily touched upon only briefly.

To be sure, Jacob Burckhardt would barely recognize today the Renaissance that he has been variously praised and castigated for having "invented" in his influential study *Die Kultur der Renaissance in Italien* [The Civilization of Italy in the Renaissance], published in Basel in 1860. Burckhardt's Renaissance was largely an intellectual and political phenomenon, a burst of energy the likes of which the world had not seen since the twilight of the classical world, the standard-bearer of a cultural history that identified in fourteenth- through sixteenth-century Italy the harbinger of modernity.[3] This sense of an inevitable historical trajectory has proved to be one of the more controversial elements of Burckhardt's project, linked as it was to a golden age that emerged from a "backward" period called the Middle Ages and followed by a similarly "retrograde" era defined as the Counter-Reformation. Anglo-American historiography of the last several decades has grown increasingly suspicious and dismissive of such value-laden periodization, and Burckhardt's Renaissance has thus been endlessly "contested," "decentered," "reframed," and even "hopelessly shattered" in scholarly debates and conferences, monographs, and collections of essays that have aimed to redefine for our own era the parameters, content, and significance of these distant centuries.[4] But as unsatisfied as so many are with the very idea of the Renaissance, it stubbornly refuses to go away, and efforts to supplant the term with the apparently less loaded but clearly more indeterminate "early modern" have failed to dislodge its place in scholarly and institutional practices, and in popular representations of it.[5]

---

[2] See Cox/Ferrari (2012) 7–29 for a discussion of the relatively slow assimilation of gender within Italian studies in general, and Italian academic culture in particular; and see 33–100 for a provocative series of essays and responses to them relevant to the period of the Renaissance.

[3] Woolfson (2005) 9–26 provides a balanced account of Burckhardt's argument, its sources, merits, and limitations.

[4] See, respectively, Caferro (2011); Burke (2005); Farago (1995) 1–20; and Ruggiero (2002) 3.

[5] See Findlen/Gowens (1998); Starn (2007); and Bowd (2010) 1–9. For general studies of the period, see Ruggiero (2002); Reinhardt (2004); MacKenney (2005); Brotton (2006); Crouzet-Pavan (2007); Gardini (2010); and Goody (2010).

Burckhardt would be surprised both by his alleged paternity of the Renaissance and by the rancor that his particular interpretation of the period has provoked. Many of the canonical figures of Italian Renaissance culture – Leon Battista Alberti, Flavio Biondo, Niccolò Machiavelli, and Giorgio Vasari – had already articulated from within the period in which they lived and worked a sense that something new, or newly possible, was afoot. And among Burckhardt's predecessors and contemporaries – Friedrich Otto Mencke, Étienne-Jean Delécluze, William Roscoe, Jules Michelet, Georg Voigt, and John Addington Symonds – a number of Renaissances emerged that differed in many ways from the one articulated in the *Kultur*.[6] Too often unacknowledged in critiques of Burckhardt is his avoidance of dogmatism, and the fact that he himself left the door wide open to interpreting the material that drives his narrative in an entirely different light. And it is also worth noting that the *Kultur* was not a runaway success from the very beginning. Only in the late 1920s, when the work was finally out of copyright, did it begin to exert the influence against which so much recent scholarship has sought to distance itself.[7]

To a great extent history is made by historians, not by those who live through the events that come to define the patterns which later emerge in accounts of them. To recognize the mediated character of historical knowledge is not, of course, to deny that there is such a thing as concrete historical data or that certain singular events are experienced by their subjects as epochal, but rather to see that even the most apparently unambiguous game-changer is subject to widely divergent views of it, both in its immediate wake and longer term, and depending on one's own position in relation to it. This is as much the case concerning the collapse of Soviet-bloc communism in the late 1980s or the events of September 11, 2001 as it is with the conjunction of a series of milestones in the mid fourteenth century in Italy, the moment Italian historiography has traditionally associated with the beginning of the Renaissance: Petrarch's engagement with Roman antiquity in the early 1340s; the Black Death that wiped out a third of the population of Italy (and elsewhere in Europe) beginning in 1348, and Giovanni Boccaccio's

---

[6] For the best survey of these various Renaissances, see Gardini (2010) 21–80. On Roscoe, see Fletcher (2012); for Symonds' seven-volume *Renaissance in Italy* (1875–86), the first systematic effort in English to deal with the period, see Quondam (2003).

[7] See Milner (2005) 15–16; and Starn (2007). On the reception of the Italian Renaissance in the twentieth century, see the essays in the volume edited by Grieco *et al.* (2002).

Decameron (1349–52), the great Italian vernacular prose testament to that pandemic's devastation; and the appearance in Italy in precisely these years of gunpowder-based weapons that would forever change the future course of armed conflict. If caution and a sensitivity to multiple points of view are requirements for understanding even recent history that has played itself out within a world familiar to us, so much more necessary then is a healthy sense of the difficulty of connecting the dots of earlier periods whose social, political, and cultural coordinates were so vastly different from our own. What will always be true of historical analysis is its contingency: the material and conceptual conditions that determine our understanding of the past shape that past no less than earlier and differing factors influenced previous historical narratives.[8]

Timelines are useful for seeing the frequently surprising juxtaposition of historical events, but it is crucial to bear in mind that history is not equivalent to linear chronology, and the boundaries between what have come to be defined as historical periods are, in fact, extraordinarily malleable. Filippo Brunelleschi and Leon Battista Alberti, paragons of Italian Renaissance architectural style, greatly admired the medieval Romanesque aesthetic; and Dante Alighieri, the first Italian to write a substantial verse work in his mother-tongue, *La commedia* [The Divine Comedy] – a poem that resists classification in its employment of classical, medieval, and proto-Renaissance literary conventions in a wide variety of linguistic registers – also composed a theoretical treatise, *De vulgari eloquentia* [On Vernacular Eloquence], in a Latin yet untouched by the philological revolution that would define fifteenth-century humanism but which nevertheless proposed ideas about language that anticipated in a number of respects the "linguistic turn" of contemporary post-structural criticism.[9]

The Middle Ages – a nearly thousand-year period following the collapse of the Roman empire, whose heterogeneous cultures were geographically dispersed throughout Europe – is perhaps the most knotty legacy of Renaissance boundary-setting, a designation associated with the emergence of humanism in the late thirteenth and early fourteenth centuries, and particularly with the figure of Petrarch, who sought to

---

[8] For a fascinating discussion of how such issues are addressed by a widely diverse group of art historians working on the Italian Renaissance today, see Elkins/Williams (2008), consisting of pre-circulated essays, the transcribed exchanges of a subsequent full-day seminar at the University of Cork, and a series of follow-up assessment papers.

[9] See Cestaro (2003); and Ascoli (2008) 130–74.

forge a direct link to the ancient Roman world by effectively erasing all that had occurred in the intervening millennium.[10] In spite of his undisputed importance for the recuperation of ancient Latin literature and the corresponding renewal of the Latin language, Petrarch is something of a tabula rasa in terms of defining Renaissance values: did he achieve a brilliant synthesis of "pagan" Latin culture and early Christianity; or was his sense of the normative character of ancient Roman culture and history too "easily displaced by the perspective of eternity"?[11] The Latin address that Petrarch gave on the Capitoline Hill in Rome in April 1341 on the occasion of his crowning as Poet Laureate would not seem to support either view in its lofty, apparently secular, sense of the classical scholar and the poet in direct communion with Roman antiquity, an ambitious effort at cultural re-enactment and self-promotion.[12] But such a utopic and ahistorical operation was fraught with contradictions, not least of which was Petrarch's considerable investment in his own vernacular poetry, and by much of his subsequent reflection on the priority of ethics over the veneration of the past.[13] Petrarch's peculiar sense of history would seem to encompass only the golden age of imperial Rome, relegating late antiquity and practically the entire successive medieval period to a sort of limbo outside of the history that mattered. Here there was little room for Dante, whose *Commedia* does not correspond to the limited definition of poetry as the representation through "subtle figures" of "things that have really come to pass" that Petrarch offered in his coronation address.[14] Nor is there any space for recognition of earlier moments of renewal – "Renaissances" in the ninth, tenth, and twelfth centuries nurtured by courts in northern and southern Europe as well as by the University of Paris – that provided a significant amount of the raw material upon which the later Italian Renaissance would draw (roughly three-quarters of the manuscripts "discovered" or "rediscovered" by humanists in the fourteenth and fifteenth centuries, for instance, were copied in Carolingian *scriptoria* in the ninth century),[15]

---

[10] See Witt (2000) 281–87.

[11] See, respectively, Lee (2012); and Witt (2000) 291.

[12] On Petrarch's oration, the *Collatio laureationis*, as a template for Renaissance poetic invention, see Petrina (2010); for a general introduction to the text, see Looney (2009) 131–40.

[13] Witt (2000) 239–60.   [14] Petrarca (1955) 306.

[15] See Witt (2012) 29 n. 52, and in general for a comprehensive survey of European intellectual life between the Carolingian era and the late thirteenth century.

or against which it would position itself (most notably the tradition of Scholastic philosophy, stemming from the work of St. Thomas Aquinas).

Considerably more sensitive to the potential for cultural renewal through recognizing and exploiting historical continuities was Petrarch's friend and slightly younger contemporary Boccaccio. His *Genealogia deorum gentilium* [The Genealogy of the Pagan Gods, 1360–74] is among the most remarkable texts of the early Italian Renaissance given the huge arc of its subject matter, extending well beyond its ostensible purpose of cataloguing the mythology of the ancient world in 728 entries of varying length and complexity, and in its generous embrace of the possibilities inherent in cultural exchange.[16] Rather than Petrarch's exclusive privileging of the Latin literature of ancient Rome, Boccaccio is keenly aware in the *Genealogia* of Roman culture's enormous debt to Greece, and of Greece's ties to both the larger Medietteranean world and an even more remote archaic past. Though Boccaccio's knowledge of Greek was limited, the *Genealogia* was the first humanist text to take ancient Greek language and literature seriously – there are forty-five passages from Homer cited in Greek besides hundreds of others in translation or paraphrased from a wide variety of sources – and the range and depth of its learning provided access to a wealth of ancient literature that had remained largely inaccessible to Western European readers since the end of the Roman empire.[17] But in addition to the massive appropriation of classical culture in the *Genealogia*, Boccaccio also incorporated Greek and Arabic natural philosophy as well as Tuscan vernacular poetry in the service of a "holistic vision of culture that nonetheless reflects historical difference ... a divergent model [from that of Petrarch] for overcoming the historical isolation of the modern world."[18] The amassing of information here anticipates the development of extra-monastic libraries in the fifteenth and sixteenth centuries (Petrarch had tried, unsuccessfully to bequeath his books to the city of Venice in order to create a library open to scholars), and it reflects an analogous and growing interest in the "collection, creation, and celebration of objects" that redefined

---

[16] For the first of three volumes of the very first English translation of the entire text together with the original Latin, with an introduction by the translator, Jon Solomon, see Boccaccio (2011).

[17] See Solomon in *ibid*. xiii–xv.

[18] Lummus (2012) 103, and in general on the significance of the *Genealogia* as an innovative account of the generation of culture.

in Renaissance Italy what it meant to "possess the past."[19] Among the most striking novelties in Boccaccio's text is its employment of perspective, a long historical view meant to establish the web of relationships that unite diverse cultures across vast spatial and temporal limits, an approach that Boccaccio would have had long acquaintance with in other media: through the technical revolution in painting initiated by Giotto and his followers in central and northern Italy; and in the carefully planned perspectival geometries of the public spaces of Florence.[20]

Perspective was also a key element in one of the most significant insights of subsequent Italian Renaissance intellectual culture: that language itself has a history. In *De vulgari eloquentia*, Dante attempted to articulate an idea of the historicity of the Italian vernacular over against the prevailing medieval understanding of an immutable Latin, but more than a century would pass before Lorenzo Valla applied a method that led to a radical rethinking of the nature of all languages. In *De falso credita et ementita Constantini donatione declamatio* [On the Donation of Constantine, 1440], Valla showed how the Latin employed in the document long used by the Church to justify its temporal authority did not date to the fourth century CE – when the Emperor Constantine was believed to have ceded the Western empire to the papacy – but from a period almost five hundred years later. Others had earlier questioned the authenticity of the Donation, but with his extensive knowledge of the culture and language of late antique Rome Valla was the first to expose the document's lexical and stylistic anachronisms and accordingly demonstrate through the incipient tools of philology that it was indeed a forgery. While the church was predictably slow to address Valla's withering critique, the careful philological analysis employed in it opened up yet another way of thinking about history and provided a template for the reconstruction and editing of ancient texts perfected by Angelo Poliziano and other humanists later in the fifteenth and early sixteenth centuries, work that took on increasing urgency with the rapid spread of the printed book and an ever-increasing interest in ancient authors such as Vitruvius and

---

[19] Findlen (1998) 86, and in general on Renaissance collecting. On libraries, see Connors/ Dressen (2010).
[20] See, respectively, Edgerton (1991); and Trachtenberg (1997).

Lucretius, whose works had survived only in poorly copied or badly preserved manuscripts.[21]

In addition to its impact on the transmission of classical literature, humanist philology had a decisive influence on the editing of the Bible and the texts of the Latin and Greek church fathers. As with Valla's treatise, this renewed corpus of Christian literature raised troubling questions about the contemporary shape and direction of the church just at the moment that the papacy was beginning to reassert its primacy in Italy again, following its fourteenth-century sojourn in Avignon, the schism that erupted at the end of that period and lasted until 1417, and local Roman political infighting that only allowed for the definitive return of the pope to the Eternal City in 1443. The papal curia was filled with humanists from that point forward – Alberti and Valla among them – but the great paradox of their presence there was that even as they assisted in the creation of a monumental papal culture fashioned after the image of imperial Rome they contributed to the refinement of philological tools that would lead in the early sixteenth century to the great war of words that became the Reformation.[22] The failed effort at an internal reform of the Church in Italy is one of the least studied elements of Italian Renaissance history in Anglo-American scholarship of the period (several of the most influential Italian historians of the last century either began or defined their careers working on Italian reform: Benedetto Croce, Federico Chabod, Delio Cantimori, and Luigi Firpo), but it is crucial for understanding the tightening of cultural and political controls that led to the Council of Trent (1545–63) and its aftermath, and for the blossoming of Italian vernacular culture and its transmission abroad.[23]

The process of education in Renaissance Italy – crucial to the advancement of humanist learning, but also for the acquisition of professional skills in an expanding range of fields – can only be partially situated within the context of formal academic institutions in the period. While the innovations of humanist practices exercised a radical reform within the context of the elementary schools – Latin-based for

---

[21] See Valla (2007) for a concise introduction to and translations of both Valla's text and the forgery; Black (1995) on Valla's importance for the development of a specifically Renaissance idea of history; and Grafton (1977) on Poliziano's philological work. Passannante (2011) 8 on Lucretius provides a brilliant account of what it means "for a text, a poem, a philosophy to be reborn."

[22] See Celenza (2010b).   [23] See Wyatt (2005) 84–98.

the university-bound, and vernacular *abbaco* [abacus] schools with a more pragmatic focus – they had a less permanent effect on the structure of the universities of the period.[24] The recovery of and insistence upon classicizing Latin, a thorough and lasting achievement of the humanists, together with the recovery of important ancient texts on education, meant that elementary classroom materials had to be re-examined and new ones devised.[25]

The progress of humanism meant that local political leaders felt the need for a Latin-educated citizenry and these initiatives multiplied in the later sixteenth century, where they were joined by an entirely new form of school, those of Christian Doctrine, aimed not at Latin but at broader literacy.[26] The case of the universities, however, was different because of institutional inertia and professional conservatism. The medieval universities – in Italy and elsewhere in Europe – persisted in their traditional disciplinary pursuits, and the newer institutions founded by territorial princes tended to follow suit.[27] Some humanists were employed as university professors in the the fifteenth century, but if their presence in the lecture hall was limited the impact of humanist philology on a great number of the texts used throughout the university curriculum was more important.[28] Law and medicine, together with related scientific disciplines, were the most significant fields taught in Italian universities of the Renaissance – the former strongly marked by medieval scholastic analysis, and the latter by their medieval Aristotelian inheritance – while theology, so important in northern European universities, was a late and not particularly important entry in the curricular mix.[29] Though universities were not crucial to the development of the Renaissance they were certainly important to its diffusion,

[24] For the best concise survey of schools, see Black (2004); for more comprehensive studies, see Grendler (1989) and Black (2001); and for studies of schools in different regions, see Gehl (1993); Vecce (2006); Black (2007); and Carlsmith (2010)

[25] See Kallendorf (2002) and (2013); Percival (2004); and Gehl (2008). See Richardson, "Publication," Chapter 7 in this volume, 173, for a primer intended for learners outside the school system.

[26] See Carlsmith (2010) 145–69; on the question of literacy in Renaissance Italy, see Burke (1987).

[27] See Grendler (2002); Terlizzo (2010); and Rundle/Petrina (2013) on Italian universities in the period.

[28] See Grendler (2002) 510. In this volume, see Campanelli, "Languages," Chapter 6, 145–46; and Perillo, "Philosophy," Chapter 12, 266–70.

[29] On the law curriculum, see Grendler (2002) 430–73. On medicine, see Wear *et al.* (1985); and Park/Penutto, "Science and Medicine," Chapter 17 in this volume, 366, 368–73.

and northern European students who came to study in Italy were among the Italian university system's most significant legacy.[30] Much of the innovative intellectual foment of the period occurred in other forums, allowing not only for the exploration of topics and practices outside of the purview of schools and universities, but also permitting the active participation of women.[31]

One of the most problematic issues in confronting the period of the Renaissance in Italy is the question of Italy itself. After the gradual disintegration of the ancient Roman empire, Italy would not again be unified as a political entity until 1870, and the geographical area of the Italian peninsula and its islands in the fourteenth through sixteenth centuries was fragmented into a great number of states of varying sizes, the entire area convulsed by foreign invasions beginning in 1494 and lasting though 1559. A recent map representing each of the administrative units mentioned in the treaty known as the Lega Italica in 1455 (an alliance of almost all of the recognized Italian political actors active at that time) provides a striking picture of the situation: though five political authorities commanded the greater part of the territory – the Kingdom of Naples (including the Kingdom of Sicily), under Spanish rule after 1442; the Duchy of Milan; the Republics of Venice and Florence; and the Papal States – the remaining states scattered throughout Italy numbered over 115 (some of them obviously quite small), a figure that does not include several others such as Rimini and the Republic of Genoa, not party to the agreement.[32] Works from the period such as Flavio Biondo's *Italia illustrata* [Italy Expounded, 1474] and Leandro Alberti's *Descrittione di tutta Italia* [Description of All of Italy, 1551] proposed accounts of Italian unity based on geography (Alberti was the first to situate Sicily and Sardegna in Italy; and Ignazio Danti supervised the painting of the frescoed maps of the territory painted in the Vatican Gallery of Maps in 1580–83), while the *Historia d'Italia* [History of Italy, 1561] by Francesco Guicciardini paints a pessimistic picture of the peninsula between 1492 and 1534,

---

[30] See Woolfson (1998) and (2013).
[31] See below in this chapter, 14 n. 43; Grafton/Jardine (1986); Stevenson (2005) 141–76; Sanson (2011); and Shemek, "Verse", Chapter 8 in this volume, 185–86, 200.
[32] See the map in Somaini (2012) facing 112, and 51–60 for his discussion of it. For a general history of Italy in this period, including a significant examination of the middle and lower social classes, see the introduction and essays in Najemy (2004); and for more detailed considerations of the Italian states, see Gamberini/Lazzarini (2012).

wracked by internal political conflicts (especially by the machinations of the papacy) and besieged by foreign invaders. This devastating analysis of Italy's ills, together with Guicciardini's equally hard-hitting *Ricordi* [Remembrances, published only in 1576], offers little hope for its future prospects. But Giorgio Vasari's entirely different idea of Italy in his *Vite de' più eccellenti pittori, scultori e architettori* [Lives of the Most Excellent Painters, Sculptors, and Architects, 1550 and 1568] recounts a series of exemplary careers along the classical model of the "illustrious life" taken up by Boccaccio and the humanist tradition, a "nation" (heavily weighted toward Florence as its center) constituted as such through its cultural excellence.

However construed, the variously configured equations of the Italian Renaissance have left considerable dimensions of its history untold. As recently as two decades ago, one of the most important American scholars of Italian Renaissance architecture could still maintain that "Naples [was] the only southern city affected by the Renaissance."[33] But as one of the most cosmopolitan cities of Europe well into the nineteenth century, Naples was also the capital of the largest single political territory in Renaissance Italy, the state with the strongest foreign imprint (initially that of Angevin France and later of Aragonese and imperial Spain), and the nexus of a vast network of cultural exchange that extended from what is now the central Adriatic region of the Marche to the western islands of Sicily.[34] The complex cultural coordinates of Naples, the Magna Grecia (encompassing the area now called Salento in the south-eastern "boot" of the peninsula across to southern Calabria, where Greek was still widely spoken through at least the fourteenth century), Sicily, and Sardinia go a long way in explaining why these "peripheral" areas do not easily fit within the parameters of Italian studies as institutionalized in Anglo-American universities and the scholarship that they have until quite recently promoted.[35] The dialects spoken in these areas were marked by their proximity to Mediterranean influences less evident in central and northern Italy, though everywhere in the Italian territories where dialects were (and in some cases still are) prominent they reflect a complex stratification

---

[33] Ackerman (1994) 344.
[34] For the best introduction to Renaissance Naples, see Bentley (1987).
[35] On the Renaissance in southern Italy, see Abulafia (2004) and (2005). Ceserani (2012) 17–37 argues that fifteenth-century humanists were the first to consider the Magna Grecia an Italian territory.

of earlier linguistic practices that established unique local languages particularly important for communitarian identity given both the political fragmentation of Italy and the occasional or permanent subjugation by foreign powers of many of its constituent parts.[36] And while Tuscan originated as only one among a number of central-northern dialects of Italian (Dante discusses fourteen of them in De vulgari eloquentia), once it was codified as the normative Italian vernacular in the early sixteenth century original dialect literature as well as translations into dialect emerged as one of the principal means of contesting linguistic and cultural hegemony (a tendency particularly pronounced in the south, where over one hundred dialect authors were active between Naples, Calabria, and Sicily in the sixteenth and seventeenth centuries).[37]

It is undeniably the case that what has been most studied, and therefore, valorized in Italian Renaissance culture, is strongly conditioned by what has survived in the prosperous regions of central and northern Italy, with their better-preserved urban cores, libraries, archives, and museums.[38] Natural disasters, earlier wars, and the bombardment by Allied air forces in the Second World War – to say nothing of the relentless assault on civic life and the natural environment propagated by organized crime – have deprived huge areas of the south of a priceless and irrecuperable cultural heritage. The fate of Alfonso II's villa at Poggioreale is typical: built in the late 1480s and early 1490s just outside the walls of Naples, its gardens and waterworks were considered to be the most extraordinary anywhere in Italy. A Tuscan architect, Giuliano da Maiano, initiated the project, but it was completed after his death by other, probably local, engineers and is known to have incorporated Islamic elements from Spanish and Sicilian gardens. The villa was abandoned soon after its completion, however, when Alfonso fled to Sicily at the time of the invasion of Naples by the French King Charles VIII in 1494, and though enough of its previous splendor was still in evidence

---

[36] On the question of dialects in general, see Dionisotti (1967) 25–54; Burke (1987); and Stussi (1994).

[37] For literature in dialect, see Haller (1999); and Antonelli et al. (2010), with a series of statistical tables and a map showing the geographical extension of dialect authors throughout Italy.

[38] Though the radical reduction in Italian public financing for cultural institutions, the university system, and research initiatives over the last generation has had a devastating effect in all parts of the country, and given the cumulative damage it is difficult at this point to see a way out of this profoundly disturbing situation.

when Cosimo de' Medici visited in 1535 – Poggioreale's technological innovations would serve as the model for the garden of the Medici villa at Castello and the Boboli Gardens in Florence – the further decline of the complex was unstoppable, and all that remains of it are a few drawings and several written descriptions.[39]

In his magisterial history of the Mediterranean basin in the sixteenth century, Fernard Braudel situated Sicily at the center of a polyglot and multicultural world,[40] but the incorporation of Sicily into the narrative of the Italian Renaissance has been very slow in coming. The curators of a revelatory exhibition of the paintings of Antonello da Messina in Rome in 2006 argued persuasively that though the artist had traveled in northern Italy, and perhaps to Provence and points farther north, it was the specific context of his early training in Naples and rootedness in Messina – a crucial gateway from the eastern and southern Mediterranean to the rest of Europe – that provided this most important Sicilian painter of the period his aesthetic and technical bearings.[41] Costantino Lascaris, among the greatest Byzantine scholars of Greek in Renaissance Italy, spent the majority of his career in Messina and had a decisive impact on the development of learned culture in Sicily and beyond (Pietro Bembo studied with him in Messina from 1492 through 1494); the earliest version of Lascaris' Greek grammar was the first book published in Italy in Greek (in 1476, in Milan), and numerous subsequent editions of the full text were published throughout Europe well into the sixteenth century (Raphael Hythloday takes one of them along to the citizens of Thomas More's *Utopia* in order to teach them Greek).[42] The most distinguished scholar formed in the circle of Lascaris was Francesco Maurolico; expert in optics, astronomy, and mathematics, he also published histories of Sicily in both Italian and Latin. The Dominican friar Tommaso Fazello in his *De rebus Siculis* [On the History of Sicily, 1558] provided the first comprehensive account of the island that encompassed topography (identifying the ancient Greek cities of Selinunte, Agrigento, and Heraclea Minoa) and anthropology as well as its ancient, medieval, and contemporary history. Palermo hosted two literary academies in the sixteenth century: the anti-aristocratic *Solitari* [Loners], founded in 1549 by the *letterato* and judge Paolo Caggio, an

---

[39] See Edelstein (2004).   [40] See Braudel (1972).
[41] See the catalogue of the exhibition, Lucco (2006).
[42] On Lascaris, see Cesera (2004); there is not, as of yet, any book-length study.

active promoter of the Tuscan literary tradition in Sicily who also wrote about the economic and social conditions of the island; and the *Accesi* [Ardent], established in 1568 under the patronage of the Spanish Viceroy and the watchful eye of the island's Chief Inquisitor.[43] Sicily played a central role in the religious currents that swept through the Italian peninsula in the 1530s and 1540s, and the Benedictine community of San Martino delle Scale just outside Palermo hosted in these years three of the protagonists of this season of reform: Benedetto Fontanini, author of the most influential text of the Italian "evangelicals," the *Beneficio di Cristo* [Benefit of Christ, 1543]; Giorgio Siculo, whose defense of Nicodemism – the public adherence to Catholic doctrine on the part of privately confessing Protestants – led to his trial and execution by the Inquisition in Ferrara in 1551; and Teofilo Folengo, most famous for his macaronic epic poem *Baldus* (1521) but also the author of a number of religious works that skirted the boundaries of Catholic orthodoxy, arousing the concern of his monastic superiors and the later admiration of the Neapolitan arch-heretic Giordano Bruno.[44]

The image that adorns the cover of this volume, the *Annunciation* of Lorenzo Lotto, was commissioned by the Confraternity of Merchants for their chapel in Recanati in the Marche and realized in 1534–35 (it is now housed in the Museo Civico there).[45] The painting is among the most original artistic treatments of the episode recounted in the Gospel of Luke 1.26–38, when Mary learns that while still a virgin she is to give birth to the son of God. Set in a simple but elegant bedroom marked by a classicizing arched portal and a mullioned window that gives onto a loggia and garden beyond, the carefully calibrated perspectival coordinates of the scene are at one and the same time contiguous with and interrupted by the sudden eruption into it of the angel Gabriel and God the father: supreme representatives of the laws of nature that govern the created world, these unexpected divine

---

[43] On Maurolico, Fazella, Caggio, and the academies, see Zaggia (2003) vol. 1, 307–45; and in general for the most comprehensive recent political and cultural history of sixteenth-century Sicily. The Palermitan academies were similar to hundreds of others that sprang up everywhere in Italy in the period as centers for the promotion of new ideas and practices in a broad array of disciplines, independent from universities and courts, and in which men and women from across the social spectrum participated; see *The Italian Academies 1525–1700*, an online project directed by Jane Everson: http://italianacademies.org

[44] On Bruno and Folengo, see Gulizia (2006–09).

[45] See Francescutti (2011) for a concise history and reading of the painting.

visitors momentarily disrupt the symmetries of this patently domestic scene in order to announce the even more portentous reconfiguration of the natural order to come with the birth of Christ. Mary is portrayed here as the very young woman that she would have been, her face and posture betraying surprise, wonder, or possibly fear. Objects of her daily life placed atop and hanging from a shelf on the wall between the bed and doorway – books, a candelabra, an inkwell (this is a Virgin who writes as well as reads), a sleeping cap, and a hand-towel – establish the lived-in character of the space, while the hourglass below measures out the temporal progression of a life now irrevocably penetrated by the timeless. Shadows cast by both the angel and the frightened cat draw attention to Lotto's singular use of light, one of the most powerful of the technical elements that the artist learned from the Netherlandish painters he had encountered in Venice and that marked his own work with its particular emotional timbre. Cats are almost as ubiquitous in Renaissance Annunciations as is the lion in paintings of St. Jerome[46] – Lotto would have been familiar with the cat in Jacopo Sansovino's Annunciation bas-reliefs on the exterior of the Holy House in Loreto, only several kilometers distant from Recanati – but here the feline's unusual position at the center of the image, positioned along the perspectival grid between Mary and the divine figures, suggests that its presence is something more than the domestic furnishing or allegorical symbol that art historians have been inclined to see it as. Cats are now widely acknowledged to have empathic qualities, and though they were until quite recently considered to be dangerous to pregnant women – undoubtedly a legacy of their association with witchcraft – they are known to be particularly sensitive to the physiological changes that accompany pregnancy. For an increasingly sophisticated medical and scientific culture that in the period of the Renaissance did not yet eschew elements of folk wisdom relevant to its questions, and in a human world lived in close proximity to animals of all kinds, Lotto's privileging of the Virgin's cat in his Recanati *Annunciation* might perhaps be explained through looking for clues in this direction. Lotto was in many respects a counter-cultural figure: the only Venetian artist invited to work in the Vatican of Julius II, he spent the greater part of his career in Bergamo and the small towns of the

---

[46] On the prevalence of cats in Annunciation paintings, see Bobis (2000) 161–66.

Marche, disconnected from the powerful church and state networks of patronage that supported his contemporaries Michelangelo, Raphael, and Titian; and the idiosyncratic visual language that he developed sought to express the interior lives of his subjects, establishing an immediacy in its impact on the viewer.[47] Like Pontormo, another artist who made his own unorthodox career choices, Lotto was attracted by the reformed religious thinking that emanated from north of the Alps and the Italian south, and such sentiments may well be reflected in the sense of an intimate encounter that so much of his work suggests.[48] Long excluded from the canons of Italian Renaissance culture, Lotto is emblematic of the possibilities opened up by a more expansive view of the various Renaissances, and their intersecting trajectories, represented in this collection of essays.

[47] In a 1548 letter, Pietro Aretino backhandedly wrote to Lotto that he was a second-rate artist who wisely recognized his own limits. Vasari was more appreciative, but Bernard Berenson was the first to argue forcefully for Lotto's originality; see Berenson (1895).
[48] See M. Firpo (2006).

1

Artistic geographies

The idea of cultural rebirth or *rinascità* was linked by Renaissance commentators to the visual arts as an index of progress and change.[1] "I do not know," wrote Lorenzo Valla in the mid fifteenth century, "why the arts most closely approaching the liberal arts – painting, sculpture in stone and bronze, and architecture – had been in so long and so deep a decline and almost died out together with literature itself; nor why they have come to be aroused and come to life again in this age; nor why there is now such a rich harvest both of good artists and good writers."[2] Not only was "Renaissance art" to be understood and defined as a process unfolding in time, it also made historical change intelligible, making visible what can be called a process of cultural "modernization." Artists such as Lorenzo Ghiberti and Leonardo da Vinci understood their own achievements in relation to more than a century of progress beginning with Giotto in the late thriteenth century. The most ambitious and influential version of this historical paradigm is, of course, Giorgio Vasari's *Vite de' più eccellenti pittori, scultori e architettori* [Lives of the Most Excellent Painters, Sculptors, and Architects, 1550 and 1568], in which artistic production along the entire peninsula was explained in three phases of historical evolution, beginning with the first steps of Giotto and his followers, followed by the diligent problem-solving craftsmen of the fifteenth century, and culminating in the triumph of the *maniera moderna* [modern manner], with its effortless mastery of beauty and conquest of technical difficulty.[3]

---

[1] For a classic study, see Gombrich (1966) 1–10.
[2] Lorenzo Valla, *Elegantiae linguae latinae* (*c.* 1440), cited in Weisinger (1943) 164.
[3] On Vasari's historical scheme, see Rubin (1995); Campbell (2008); and Burioni (2010).

No less influential than Vasari's view of history, however much it continues to be resisted and revised, is his view of geography. The dynamic of historical change was linked to the supremacy of a handful of major centers – Rome, Florence, and Venice – possessing both cultural and political distinction.[4] All three were capitals of independent territorial states of a peninsula increasingly dominated from the 1520s by Hapsburg rule. The city of Florence plays a particularly prominent role in the *Lives* as the place of birth or training of practically all the most important artists from Giotto to Michelangelo (including Vasari himself): "Tuscan intellects have always been exalted and raised high above all others because they are far more devoted to the labors and studies of every skill than any other people of Italy."[5] Vasari's geographical bias at times even threatened to overwhelm his historical periodization: he admitted that he had considered including Donatello in his third phase, as a pioneer of the modern manner, while Andrea Mantegna, an artist whom others ranked the equal of Leonardo and Michelangelo, was consigned (with strenuous arguments) to the second period.[6] Vasari's geography, in other words, is primarily ideological rather than topographical, where a principle of what Pierre Bourdieu characterizes as "cultural capital" is yoked to political and economic prominence. Vasari wrote as the subject of a modernizing territorial state – the new duchy of Tuscany – with a bureaucratic and military apparatus centered around a sovereign: this apparatus included a top–down organization of culture, with an academy for the promotion of Tuscan language and literature, and one for the visual arts.[7] Vasari, along with Venetian writers such as Ludovico Dolce and the Venice-based Pietro Aretino (born in Vasari's hometown of Arezzo) elaborated "Venice" and "Rome" as rival systems of artistic values. Vasari's promotion of Tuscan–Roman art and genius paralleled the highly contentious creation of literary canons and prescriptive theories of Italian language and literature centered in the Tuscan vernacular tradition

[4] The geographical consequences of Vasari's history of art have been taken up in many contexts; a sustained treatment is provided in Bologna (1982), especially 81–94.

[5] Vasari (1996) vol. 2, 642.

[6] Vasari's life of Donatello is examined in Rubin (1995) 321–55; on Vasari's treatment of Mantegna, see Agosti (1995) 61–89.

[7] On the Academia del Disegno, of which Vasari himself was a founder in 1563, see Wazbinski (1987); and Barzman (2000).

of Dante, Petrarch, and Boccaccio, especially on the part of the Venetian humanist, later cardinal, Pietro Bembo.[8]

The geographical consequences of Vasarian historiography, with its effective marginalization or erasure of artistic production throughout much of the peninsula, continue to demand critical attention. His initiative had real consequences for how sixteenth-century Italians would assess the importance of art and artists: it established an artistic canon dominated by centrally located Italians which effectively "peripheralized" artistic production in places "off the axis." The Brescian Girolamo Romanino, who had produced important works throughout northern Italy, was attacked in 1557 by a colleague whose work he had been asked to evaluate; the indicting artist claimed that Romanino was insufficiently qualified, since he did not appear in recent rankings of leading artists by *celebri scriptori* [famous writers] like Ariosto, or in histories (i.e., Vasari's) of *valenti pictori* [worthy painters] through the ages.[9] That canon was already emerging in Rome and Venice from at least the third decade of the sixteenth century, as artistic production in those cities was increasingly dominated by, respectively, Raphael, Titian, and their followers. Vasari, moreover, is only part of a larger shift in spatial mentality that occurs in Italy during the late fifteenth and into the sixteenth century, a hierarchical dynamic of what can be called regional identity formation that leaves its imprint deep into the present. This chapter cannot do justice to the whole complex of historical factors that shaped this geographical mentality but will seek instead to outline its effects in the history of art and the continuing challenge it presents for the interpretation of early modern visual culture. That challenge is to produce alternative geographical models that do not simply reproduce the artistic hegemony of Rome–Florence–Venice as if inevitable, but recognize the independence of artists working elsewhere, and, on occasion, their overt contestation of this urban axis. But we also need a historical model that does not treat "regional," "off-the-axis," production as entirely localized, marginal phenomena. Such an inquiry requires consideration of the nature of place, or rather its understanding, in the Renaissance, and how art both manifests and informs that understanding. In order to

---

[8] On the "questione della lingua", see Campanelli, "Languages," Chapter 6 in this volume, 155–63.
[9] Nova (1994) 33, 50 n. 9; in his 1550 edition, Vasari does actually refer briefly to Romanino, in the *Vita* of Carpaccio.

lay out the problem of the regional and to assess its methodological consequences for the study of the history of Italian art in the period, a useful starting point is the revisionist model of "center" and "periphery" developed by Enrico Castelnuovo and Carlo Ginzburg in 1979 (revised in 1981; I cite from the 2009 English translation of the latter).[10]

These authors – one an art historian specializing in late medieval art in northern Italy, the other a pioneering scholar of "microhistory" – offered an alternative to the historical schema wherein art produced in some cities and territories was classed as provincial, because artists either embraced the "influence" of the major centers, or by not doing so further marginalized themselves. The "periphery," in their account, was not just the passive provincial deposit of powerful influences imported from a "center," but a place with the potential for critical distance, oppositionality, and innovation. Artistic style in sites "off the axis" could speak not just of the inevitable diffusion of Vasari's modern manner, but of real alternatives.

The weight given to style and to artistic intentions is a notable feature of Castelnuovo/Ginzburg's use of the "center/periphery" model, which they formulated with terminology from the social sciences.[11] What will require some critical examination here is the idea of "place" in this account – more specifically, how does its political/economic understanding of the "center" allow the definition and recognition of a "periphery," and what kind of place is a "periphery"?

A "center" is carefully defined by Castelnuovo/Ginzburg as "a place characterized by the presence of a large number of artists and of important groups of patrons who, moved by various motivations – be it their family or self-pride, their wish for hegemony, or their quest for eternal salvation – are ready to invest part of their wealth in works of art."[12] They add the qualification that a "center" is also characterized by the production of surplus wealth which can be invested in art, and the

---

[10] Castelnuovo/Ginzburg (2009).

[11] Terms derived from Shils (1961) have also been influential among historians of Italy; see for example G. Benzoni (1992). Kauffmann (2004) 97–100 and 223–35 observes that a form of the model operated in the work of George Kubler on Spanish Colonial art, and in that of Jan Bialostocki on Eastern Europe. Bock (2008a) provides an important critique of Castelnuovo/Ginsburg and of Kauffmann, drawing on the work of social scientists Saskia Sassen and Ulf Hannerz on "world cities"; see also Bock (2008b). For an approach that usefully addresses the psychological or imaginary aspects of center/periphery see Summers (2003) 194–97.

[12] Castelnuovo/Ginzburg (2009) 9.

more original perception that "only an extra-artistic center of power, be it political and/or economic and/or religious, may be an artistic center." The mere concentration of art in one site is not enough: there has to be a market, a degree of professional organization, and an additional source of legitimation ("cultural capital").

"Periphery" is a more fluid and even elusive term in the Castelnuovo/ Ginzburg account, even as the two scholars clearly saw the characterization of "periphery" as being at the very heart of their enterprise. In general, a "periphery" is the opposite of a "center": it lacks the combined continuity of patronage, institutions, and public sphere that sustain the artistic culture of a city like Florence. It is a provincial site, a place of "delayed development," characterized by artists edged out by competition in the urban markets, such as the Umbrian towns where Perugino worked after 1512, when demand for his work receded in Florence and Rome. But it is also a place of real potential, "the place of alternative production ... side stepping." The periphery is a place for artists like Lorenzo Lotto or Tanzio da Varallo who want to pursue "experimental" approaches not welcome in the centers.[13]

According to the examples Castelnuovo/Ginzburg provide, "periphery" encompassed a rather considerable variety of working situations for artists. Sometimes it is an extended region as opposed to a city – the Marche traversed by Lotto in the last decades of his career, or the Piedmont of Defendente Ferrari. It might be a city of diminished political importance, such as the ducal capital of Urbino to which Federico Barocci withdrew in the midst of a successful career in Rome, or a provincial town like Valescio, in which Tanzio da Varallo settled after years in Milan.

More surprisingly – and as the authors admit, problematically – a major political and administrative capital like Avignon is also classed as a "peripheral" site for the "resistance to Giotto" demonstrated there by Italian artists such as Matteo Giovanetti and Simone Martini. It becomes apparent that the "periphery" might finally have nothing to do with space or distance: Florence in the sixteenth century is revealed to contain its own "periphery," in the person of Pontormo

---

[13] On Tanzio da Varallo, who worked in Milan and Rome as well as small centers in Lombardy, Piedmont, and Abruzzo, see Bologna (2000). Among studies of Lotto's "regional" commissions, see Zampetti/Sgarbi (1980); *Omaggio a Lorenzo Lotto* (1984); and Mozzoni (2009).

(Jacopo Carucci) and "anti-classical" artists, who "operated in rather eccentric conditions, or used weapons [against classicism] imported from a peripheral culture such as [that of] German[y]."[14]

Whereas the "center" is seen to be defined with a cartographic degree of certainty, the "periphery" in this relativist account is inchoate not only in geographical terms but conceptually. In subsequent art history that invokes the Castelnuovo/Ginzburg paradigm, we find a persistent multiplicity in the characterization of the "periphery":

1. Most commonly, it is a generally rural region that imports its artistic expertise from elsewhere, usually from a major center.
2. A minor urban center supporting a *longue durée* of artistic practice not strongly motivated by imperatives of progress or modernization.
3. A provincial town supporting a local workshop tradition, from which art and artists may be exported to a major center: e.g., Bassano, Pordenone, or Treviso in relation to Venice.
4. A major city which has been subordinated by a large territorial state, often with a flourishing artistic culture of its own: Bologna and Ferrara, incorporated by the Papal States in 1508 and 1598 (and with markedly different results on local artistic production in each case).
5. A dissident or heterodox practice within a major center: Castelnuovo/ Ginzburg's example of Pontormo in Florence.[15]

Most Italian art in the period could be fitted to one or another of these "peripheral" categories. The impression given is that the dynamic of Italian art from the fourteenth to the seventeenth centuries is a process of "peripheralization" in relation to Florence, Rome, or Venice, so much so that even polemical alternative histories of art which appeared from the sixteenth well into the eighteenth centuries were unable to dislodge Vasari's view of where important art originated. At the same time, the problematic association of Avignon with the category of "periphery" by Castelnuovo/Ginzburg, and the ambiguous and undefined status of Genoa or Naples, might make it appear that the

[14] Castelnuovo/Ginzburg (2009) 20.
[15] On these diverse "peripheries," see Argan (1984); and Kroegel (2005). Benzoni (1995) addresses Bassano as *periferia*; Ambrosini (2000), local production in Tuscan towns such as Cortona, Volterra, Pistoia, Lucca, Poggibonsi, Arezzo, and Montepulciano; Humfrey (2001) gives an overview of the importation of Venetian altarpieces into one region of the *terraferma*; Ricci (2001) deals with Bologna; and Talignani (2005) with Parma – all of which correspond, in other words, to what Italian scholars in the wake of Roberto Longhi have referred to as the "eccentric" or "anti-classical" tradition.

term "periphery" is doing far too much work, that its usefulness is compromised through overextension.

A modification of terminology is therefore necessary, above all a less transhistorical application of concepts such as "center" and "periphery." There is not, for instance, any contemporary term for "center," nor is there a linguistic distinction between a major urban settlement ("city") and a smaller one ("town") in Latin or Italian.[16] While the idea of "center" might be said to exist, it has to be addressed through terms such as *caput mundi* – an expression used by the ancient historian Livy to convey Rome's importance as the seat of a universal empire. Yet Rome as *caput mundi* provided other cities in pre-modern Italy with a powerful model of political and cultural pre-eminence, reinforcing the self-promotion of several different polities as *altera Roma* or 'new Rome' – often with significant consequences for art and architectural patronage and for city planning.[17] It could be said that ancient Rome provided the model for a kind of cosmopolitan and even multicultural "world city" long before the re-emergence of Rome alongside other "centers" during the Renaissance – a model destined, however, to give place to other, newer paradigms.

Models of the center

The idea of the "world city" has provided the grounds for an important critique of the "center/periphery" paradigm by a group of art historians whose research addressed the general neglect of the city and Kingdom of Naples in the history of art – a marginalization reflected in the city's indeterminate status in Castelnuovo/Ginzburg's essay. Naples, one of the largest cities of the Mediterranean in the fourteenth and fifteenth centuries, was a hugely important locus of artistic patronage and production, and it would continue to be so even as a subject city of the Hapsburg empire.[18] In part its marginalization rested not only on the loss of much of its pre-Hapsburg artistic patrimony and the destruction of archival records, but also on the perception of its dependency on

---

[16] On the problem of defining an *urbs* or *civitas* [city] in the Middle Ages, and its persistence into the present, along with a critique of the economic orientation of urban history, see Maxwell (2007), especially 6–12.
[17] On the theme of *altera Roma*, see Hammer (1944); and Beneš (2011).
[18] For a still-useful overview of art under the viceroyalty of Naples, see Whitfield/Martineau (1982); and the essays collected in Bock (2008a).

imported artistic expertise: Angevin Naples in the fourteenth century supported a polyglot court culture, where Provençal, Catalan, French, and Tuscan influences were all important; in terms of art, within a single generation the court employed (or imported works by) the Florentine Giotto, the Roman Pietro Cavallini, and the Sienese Simone Martini and Tino da Camaino, in addition to supporting local producers.[19] In fifteenth-century Naples, the invading dynasty of the Aragonese pursued this tradition even more vigorously, importing art and artists from throughout Italy, Spain, the Dalmatian coast, and northern Europe. Such artistic all-inclusiveness was consistent with the expansionist ambitions, in Italy and the wider Mediterranean basin, of King Alfonso V of Aragon (who ruled Naples as Alfonso I from 1442 to 1458) and his successors. Alfonso acquired works by Jan Van Eyck, Rogier Van der Weyden, Filippo Lippi, Donatello, Desiderio da Settignano, and Mino da Fieole, along with tapestries from the Netherlands; the painter and medallist Pisanello joined his household in 1448. Migrant sculptors employed by the Aragonese kings include Francesco Laurana from Dalmatia, the Lombard Pietro da Milano, and Domenico Gagini from Lugano; and Francesco di Giorgio from Siena was employed by Alfonso II in 1492. The work of most leading Florentine sculptors of the later *Quattrocento* was represented in the kingdom, as well as the painters Matteo di Giovanni of Siena, Andrea Mantegna of Padua, and the Vivarini of Venice.[20] Scholarship has tended to overemphasize the "Florentinization" of Neapolitan artistic culture in the later fifteenth century, manifest especially in the commissioning of monumental sculpture from Florentine workshops.[21] Yet for Nicolas Bock, a proper social history of art needs to "discard the narrow view of artistic production functioning independently within a national framework of pure economics, and propose instead an analysis of the city within an international cultural web." It would differentiate "between the economics of production and the establishment of cultural standards," whereby "the importation of foreign artists and works of art is ... not primarily a sign

[19] On the House of Anjou and its patronage, see Bologna (1969); and Leone De Castris (1986).
[20] On Aragonese patronage, see Warr/Elliott (2010); and Mele/Senatore (2011a) and (2011b). On artistic exchanges between the Medici and the Aragonese see also Cagliotti (2007).
[21] A critique of "Florentinization" with regard to Neapolitan architecture is provided by De Divitiis (2008).

of cultural weakness but a sign of an intentional cultural enrichment and an essential foundation for freedom of choice, which is one of the criteria defining a centre ...".[22]

"World cities" pursued artistic distinction and demonstrated political, economic, and cultural centrality by importing artistic producers as well as media and materials – along with other symbolic capital – from other places. But Bock's invocation of Immanuel Wallerstein's "world city" model to define Naples and the court centers of Italy has broader implications. First of all, such cosmopolitan centers long precede the rise of "Renaissance" cities like Florence which embraced an "orthogenetic" and proto-nationalist idea of artistic production. Venice could be taken as another pre-modern example: the basilica of San Marco, largely built and decorated between the eleventh and fourteenth centuries, exhibits *spolia* [spoils] and a rich array of colored stone from throughout the Mediterranean world as well as the work of Byzantine mosaicists; similarly, the fifteenth-century Doge's palace displays architectural motifs translated from Byzantine, Ottoman, and Mameluke cultures, by means of which the republic expressed something quite different from cultural dependency.[23] An analogous cosmopolitan character is evident in the city of Avignon during the papal residency there in the fourteenth and early fifteenth centuries, as it was also in cities without courts (such as Genoa) implicitly consigned to a kind of limbo according to the Castelnuovo/Ginzburg model.[24] Venice in the sixteenth century, despite its diminishing sphere of influence in the Mediterranean and the eclipse of its imperial ambitions by globalizing Hapsburg and Ottoman empires, continued to promote itself as the city where "the world" was on display.[25] Giovanni Battista Tiepolo, the last great painter of the Venetian republic, was still trafficking in the spectacular multiethnic pageantry of Venetian cosmopolitanism in the eighteenth century.

Florence presents a clear contrast. Although by no means closed to foreign artistic expertise in the fourteenth century, from the fifteenth century on Florence promoted itself as a self-sufficient polity which exported home-grown artistic work as a distinctive and superior

---

[22] Bock (2008b) 591–92.   [23] Howard (2000).
[24] Castelnuovo/Ginzburg (2009) 31 characterize Genoa as "a kind of relay center," although it is not clear why this is a useful distinction from a center proper.
[25] Wilson (2005), especially 1–33.

product.[26] The example of Giotto, active in Florence and abroad, cast a long shadow over subsequent Florentine artistic production and established a continuity and consistency of artistic practice. It has been argued that Giotto's prestige was precisely a result of the recognition and honors he had received from the court of Naples – the mercantile and republican city could be itself touched by royal charisma, albeit at a safe distance.[27] The mythical figure of Giotto (and, for several generations, his style) stood as a bearer of Florentine memory and identity, and his revival or promotion by various regimes over the fifteenth and sixteenth centuries had the force of a cult of origins.[28] Florence by the fifteenth century had begun to identify with a patrimony largely created outside itself – through migrants and exiles like Dante, Petrarch, and Giotto as well as noted warriors and prelates – and to reappropriate it for the city on the Arno.[29] The orthogenetic model is sustained through the fifteenth century by the systematic promotion of Florentine art abroad, especially by the Medici regime, and by writer–practitioners like Lorenzo Ghiberti, whose mid-fifteenth-century *Commentaries* celebrate the revival of the arts in "Etruria," a name designating pre-Roman ancient central Italy. In particular, the Medici promoted Florentine art in its maintenance of relations with foreign courts, from Naples to Budapest. Subsequently, Florentine painters and sculptors were extensively patronized at the papal court under Sixtus IV (reigned 1471–84) and his successors. Diplomatic relations between the Medici and the Sforza rulers of Milan were facilitated by a supply of Florentine artistic expertise – and the architects Filarete, from 1451 through 1465, and Michelozzo in 1456 and again in 1462 – although there was little interest in Florentine painting there before the 1490s.[30]

Naples and Florence, then, help to articulate the distinction between two models of artistic center – the pre-modern "world city" and the

---

[26] Siena – a significant point of reference for early Florentine artists – only 46 miles from Florence, was in the period considered "foreign." On Florence's growing sense of autonomy, see Bologna (1982), especially 25–29, 40–45.

[27] Warnke (1993) 9; see also Fleck (2008).

[28] On the Renaissance cult of Giotto, see Bologna (1982) 25–32; Previtali (1989) 5–8; and Rubin (1995) 287–321.

[29] See, for instance, Borsook (1980) 76, on the 1393 plan to erect marble monuments in the Duomo to eight heroes of the republic.

[30] For Budapest see Farbaky/Waldman (2011). On the role of art in the relations between the Medici and the Sforza rulers of Milan, see D. Kent (2000) 348–54; and with regard to the relatively limited impact of Florentine art in late-fifteenth-century Milan, see Shell (1998).

proto-modern orthogenetic "cultural producer" – but also their systemic *interdependence*. Each legitimates the other's centrality through
exchanging different kinds of "symbolic capital": through Giotto's
association with Naples, Florence found a means of non-political affiliation with a regal system founded on transnational authority, while
Naples could command the services of an individual who epitomized
the best of what a foreign city such as Florence had to offer, enhancing
its own international character.

The republic of Venice also valued the special aura that came of
serving foreign monarchs:

> At the request of Mehmed, King of the Turks, Gentile [Bellini] was
> sent all the way to Byzantium, where, demonstrating clearly by his
> skill and talent what Venetian blood is capable of, he both shed a
> marvelous glory on Venetian painting and, rewarded with the rank of
> knight ... brought back to his homeland gold in the form of a wreath,
> the reward for his powers.[31]

These two models of the city's extension across space through cultural
and artistic means coexist in the fifteenth and sixteenth centuries.
Especially before the French and Spanish invasions of Italy, the princely
"Naples model" of commandeering the best of everything defines
the process of artistic exchange in Italy between a network of cities
with courts, such as Ferrara, Mantua, Bologna, Urbino, and Rimini.
Pisanello, Piero della Francesca, Francesco Laurana, Sperandio, Caradosso,
Girolamo da Cremona, and Francesco di Giorgio all moved on this
courtly circuit, as did portable works of art created by court artists
such as Mantegna and Cosmè Tura who enjoyed more stable patronage.
So too did new typologies of princely architecture and urban design,
often strikingly independent of Florence.

Rome in the fifteenth and sixteenth centuries was a special case.
Perhaps because in many respects the city epitomizes the very idea of
"center," there is no other place so uniquely privileged in fulfilling both
sets of criteria. Following the re-establishment of the papacy in Rome in
1420, the papal court and the city drew almost all of its most important
artists from elsewhere. Such was also the case by the time of Raphael's
death in 1520, but by then Rome was the major point of diffusion for
the increasingly normativized *maniera moderna* and hence for the very

---

[31] Francesco Negro, *Peri archon* (*c.* 1493–98), cited in Chong (2005) 116.

idea of Renaissance art (an important circumstance was the Roman print trade and the trans-European dissemination of prints after Raphael).[32] Even by the seventeenth century "Roman style," as a phenomenon diffused outwards through academic normalization, was a creation of non-Roman artists who made their mark in the "center": Barocci and the Zuccari brothers from Urbino, Girolamo Muziano from Brescia, the Carracci from Bologna, Caravaggio (Michelangelo Merisi) from Milan, Peter Paul Rubens from Antwerp. Luigi Lanzi, whose comprehensive history of art (1792 and 1796; definitive edition in 1809) pioneered the division of Italian art into regional schools with distinguishable characteristics, admitted that the "Roman School" contained a variety of styles and nationalities, but insisted that only a few of these – the followers of Raphael and the Carracci – properly pertained to it.[33]

Rome's emergence as a center of artistic distinction in the later fifteenth century followed upon several centuries of attempts by rulers of other states to appropriate Rome's supreme embodiment of "centrality" for themselves. Artistic references to Roman antiquity in cities like Florence, Siena, Padua, Naples, Venice, and Mantua sometimes appear governed by ideas of the *translatio imperii*, or relocation of the Imperial Center.[34] Genealogical myths invoking Rome were particularly important at points of historical rupture, such as the establishment of a new regime by an invading power, as with Naples under Alfonso of Aragon. The portal to the Castel Nuovo in Naples, known as the *Arco aragonese* (built in two phases between 1452 and 1471), celebrates the city of Naples and its implicit "refoundation" under the new dynasty (Fig. 1.1).[35] Just as Alfonso was the first Renaissance ruler to stage a triumphal entry in the ancient manner after his conquest of the city in 1443, so the monumental gateway is a recasting of motifs from Roman triumphal arches, reliefs, and other statuary in the city of Rome.

---

[32] On Raphael's involvement with printmakers, see Pon (2004); and for the later Roman print trade, Bury (2001).

[33] See the useful discussion in De Mambro Santos (2012), especially 47–55. On Lanzi's *Storia pittorica*, see also Bologna (1982); and Rossi (2006).

[34] On Padua's competitive self-fashioning as a second Rome in the late thirteenth and fourteenth centuries, see Berrigan (1990); for Siena's appropriation of Roman symbols of civic origin, see Caciorgna/Guerrini (2005); and on Mantua's claim to be the birthplace of Virgil, enabling an artistic ideology of *translatio* around 1500, see Campbell (2004).

[35] Hersey (1973).

Fig. 1.1 *Triumphal arch of Alfonso I* (1443, Castel Nuovo, Naples).

Dynamics of regionalization

Perceptions of the relation between a great city and its art were changing in the sixteenth century, and in ways that proponents of the Neapolitan challenge to the "center/periphery" model have not addressed. We began with remarks by Lorenzo Valla on art as a sign of cultural rebirth, probably composed in Naples in the mid fifteenth century when he was in the service of King Alfonso. In 1524, the Neapolitan humanist Pietro Summonte addressed the same criteria to his own city in response to a query about art in Naples from the Venetian connoisseur Marcantonio Michiel, but in a strikingly more pessimistic vein:

> King Rene was also a skilled painter and was very keen on the study of the discipline, but according to the style of Flanders. He ruled [Naples] for a very short period of time, since he was expelled by King Alfonso I. The other kings of the past, who can be considered as belonging to the Italian nation, and were keen to send for painters, sculptors, architects, and all kinds of glorious artists, were, I regret to

say, ruined and removed from power at a very early stage, so that they could not leave behind any good monument.[36]

The marginalization of Naples in the history of art, notwithstanding the quantity and quality of work produced there, is still ascribed to Vasari's scathing account of the ignorance of its ruling classes and its history of political instability.[37] Yet here, a quarter century before Vasari, we have a local writer laying out a similarly despondent view of the fortunes of art in Naples, deploring its catastrophic discontinuity, the philistinism of its rulers, and the dependency on foreign talent. According to Summonte, since the time of Giotto there had been no good painters working in Naples before the emergence of Colantonio, who painted like King Rene "in the style of Flanders." Alfonso I's great Hall of the Barons in Castelnuovo is considered a mighty work by Summonte, "but it is Catalan [in style], having nothing whatsoever to do with ancient architecture." Summonte already has a particular model of a legitimating relationship between a place and its artistic production, to which Naples clearly fails to measure up. It was Florence that provided the standard: the Tuscan city maintained a coherent tradition of largely native artists; it was a source or origin which exported its cultural and artistic merit: "Florence should not be deprived of [that] praise due to her, because there began not only painting, sculpture, architecture and the other honored mechanical arts, but also the study of letters."

Vasari's promotion of a topography of cultural importance is thus an element of a greater process, in large part shaped by the domination of the peninsula by non-Italian powers in the sixteenth century. And Vasari's institutionally supported promotion of Tuscan–Roman supremacy in his painting and his writing is paralleled by initiatives in the Venetian state. His identification with the centralizing process of Tuscan state formation could be seen in terms of what Castelnuovo/ Ginzburg call "symbolic domination," a kind of colonization-by-art

---

[36] For the full text of Summonte's letter to Michiel, see Nicolini (1925); this translation is from Richardson *et al.* (2007) 194–96. The best discussion of the letter is Bologna (1982) 74–79.

[37] Loconte (2008), which despite an evident prejudice against Vasari takes no account of the Neapolitan Summonte's negative view of art in his native city. Summonte's letter is also unaddressed in Bock's counter-Vasarian claim of a flourishing cosmopolitan economy of artistic production in Naples.

which often follows but may even be quite independent of political annexation. Even before he became the chief artistic ideologue of the Medici rulers, Vasari drew upon the network provided by the Camaldo-lite and Olivetan religious orders as well as other other elite contacts to export his version of the Florentine *maniera moderna* to sites as far afield as Venice, Bologna, Rimini, Ravenna, and Naples in addition to sites in Tuscany. In the decade which saw the establishment of the state-sponsored Accademia del Disegno (1562), Vasari and his shop sent works to Città di Castello, Livorno, Arezzo, Pisa, Pistoia, and Prato, though the process was not necessarily one-sided. There was no coercion involved in the non-Medici commissions: local interests collaborating with the centralized state tended to order works of art from the capital, even as they maintained or negotiated limited autonomy in trade and administration.[38] Florentine art appeared to hold sway even further afield as Vasari was sought out for papal commissions in Rome and Lombardy by Pius V in 1567. The leading artists of Venice appeared to accept the legitimating force of the Florentine Accademia, and peti-tioned for membership in 1566. Florentine centrality in matters of art was again affirmed when King Philip of Spain consulted with the insti-tution about the design of the Escorial in 1567.[39]

There had been a fairly constant demand for Venetian painting throughout northern Italy over the fourteenth century with Jacopo Bellini supplying works to Brescia and Verona, Antonio Vivarini and Giorgio d'Allemagna to Bologna, Giovanni Bellini to Vicenza and Pesaro, and Cima da Conegliano to Parma and Treviso. The difference in the sixteenth century is the relative consistency of Venetian style as it is represented in the *terraferma* works of Titian and Veronese. Titian exported altarpieces to Treviso (1517), Ancona (1520 and 1558), Brescia (1522), and Verona (1536). Before moving to Venice in 1553, Veronese had already produced an altarpiece for Mantua (1552), and several of his *terraferma* works were for the network of Benedictine houses linked to Santa Giustina in Padua, including commissions for SS. Nazaro e Celso

---

[38] See, for instance, Krohn (2004) and Milner (2004) on the political factors at work in commissioning or not commissioning work from Florentine artists in the cities of San Gimignano and Pistoia. In an essay on the Tuscan territorial state under the Medici principate, Guarini (1995) 82 demonstrates that local interests often became stronger, in a kind of trade-off for the recognition of Florentine domination.

[39] Barzman (2000) 56–59.

in Verona (1556), three altarpieces for San Benedetto Po near Ferrara (1561–62), and the monastery of Praglia (1562). Altarpieces for private and corporate donors outside Venice include one for Montagnana cathedral (1555), Lendinara near Ferrara in 1563 and again in 1581, San Paolo and San Giorgio in Braida in Verona (1565), Latisana near Udine (1566), Vicenza (1572), Padua (1574), and Ostuni in Puglia (1574).[40] Veronese adaptated his Venetian manner in response to prominent local works: in Mantua, he emulated Giulio Romano; in Lendinara, he modeled his altarpiece for the Petrobelli family on Cosmè Tura's 1475 Roverella altarpiece; and the altarpiece for San Giorgio in Braida was conceived in dialogue with the Brescian Romanino's paintings (1540) in the same church.[41] From the 1560s, just as Vasari and his followers dominated artistic production from Bologna to Rome, the Venetian workshop of Paolo Veronese supplied further altarpieces for numerous sites in and around Venetian territory on the *terraferma*, as well as paintings that circulated as diplomatic gifts at the courts of Spain, the Hapsburg empire, and Savoy. More than Tintoretto and even Titian, although drawing judiciously on both of them, the artist from Verona formulated what would be recognized through modern times as the key principles of a Venetian manner: following his death in 1588, his successor as purveyor of Venetian art for the *terraferma* was Palma Giovane. "Peripheralization" can be seen in terms of an ideological process, the marking of hierarchies of artistic value between a city and a wider territory – and it can be challenged.

Castelnuovo/Ginzburg had little to say about the manifestations of resistance by artists in the periphery, but some scholars in recent decades have pointed to several artist-centered initiatives. Thus Romanino's 1526 altarpiece of the *Resurrection* for the rural church of Capriolo outside Brescia has been seen not as a provincial eccentricity but as a rejoinder, even as a point-by-point refutation, of the qualities associated with Titian and Venetian style, manifest in the 1522 polyptych of the *Resurrection* for SS. Nazaro e Celso in Brescia.[42] With its atmospheric nocturnal landscape with varied lighting effects, its emotionally charged energy in the figures, this was a manifesto-like proclamation both of the Venetian modern manner and of its domination by Titian.

[40] See Cocke (2001).
[41] For Veronese's practice of adaptation in Lendinara, see Salomon (2009) 86–87.
[42] See Campbell (2009) 297–300.

Romanino's grimacing Christ is brutish and lumpen rather than ephebic; he stands solidly on the edge of the sarcophagus rather than surging upwards with supernatural energy. The whole has a deliberately primitive character, flaunting its indifference to perspective and to protocols of imitating other art characteristic of Rome in the wake of Raphael. Examples of a resistance to Rome and Raphael by artists in "peripheral" locations might also be represented by Polidoro da Caravaggio in his coarsely expressionistic *Christ Carrying the Cross* for SS. Annunziata in Messina (1533), and Lorenzo Lotto in his 1511 *Lamentation* for the town of Jesi in the Marche.[43]

It was in Venice that the critical principles of an opposition to Vasari, Michelangelo, and the hegemony of Tuscan/Roman style were first formulated, and the critical terms of a distinctively Venetian art were articulated. The treatises of Paolo Pino (1548) and Ludovico Dolce (1557) paved the way for two centuries of polemical anti-Vasarianism in other regional centers, and the rise of a preoccupation with regional difference in the new critical literature of art.[44] In the later *Cinquecento* and beyond, however, the initially Venetian challenge to Vasari's Florence-centrism would be taken up in the polemics of writers who proclaimed the existence of a Cremonese, a Bolognese, a Venetian, a Genoese, a Lombard, or a Neapolitan artistic heritage, decrying Vasari's ignorance or prejudice.[45] The result was a kind of self-enclaving, a fetishizing of the local also manifest in the development of dialect literatures from the sixteenth century onwards.[46] Deliberate or intransigent provincialism had become a recognizable phenomenon by mid-century: it had already been a *topos* in Vasari's *Vite* (that of Correggio, for instance, as well as those of Garofalo, Marco Cardisco, and Cola dell'Amatrice) and was taken to the point of caricature by the Milanese painter Gian Paolo Lomazzo in the self-consciously provincial Accademia dei Facchini della Val di Blenio in which Lomazzo and his friends parodied the analogy of regional art to regional forms of the Italian language by publishing burlesque poems in an uncompromising rural dialect. The ironic

---

[43] On Polidoro's altarpiece for Messina, see Leone de Castris (2001) 343–356; and for Lotto's Jesi *Lamentation*, Mozzoni (2011). Cosgrove (1993) 70–84, writes of "townscape as cultural struggle" in his analysis of the cultural rivalry between Venice and its subject city of Vicenza.

[44] Bologna (1982) 94–102.   [45] Bologna (1982) 123–59; and Previtali (1989) 39–67.

[46] On dialect in early modern Italian linguistic usage, see Wyatt, "Renaissances," in this volume, 11–12.

intention was made only more pointed by the fact that several of the poems paid facetious tribute to famous artists who had achieved fame and success in the international arena, far from their place of birth: Rosso Fiorentino, Marco Pino from Siena, and the Bolognese Camillo Procaccini.[47] Yet Lomazzo would become the advocate for a transpeninsular account of Italian painting, devising a theoretical basis for practice based on the example of Mantegna, Leonardo, Michelangelo, Raphael, Polidoro da Caravaggio, Titian, and Gaudenzio Ferrari – an alternative canon that implicitly opposes Vasari's.[48]

Otherwise, insularity replaced polycentrism. In reaction to Rome/ Florence/Venice, Italy became a mosaic of endless peripheries. Even Luigi Lanzi's recognition of the regional "schools" of Italian painting as an alternative to Vasari's biographical approach in his *Storia pittorica della Italia* [History of Painting in Italy] seems driven by a dialectic of endless and bewildering variation *between* and *within* regions and the "timeless" Renaissance ideal of Raphael, Annibale Carracci, and their followers: the Roman (or Roman–Bolognese) school, which Lanzi identified with criteria inspired by the eighteenth-century German art historian and archeologist Johann Joachim Winckelmann.[49]

It is the Carracci family of painters, active in Bologna from the 1580s, that best illustrates the dilemma of regional versus central identification. These artists – two brothers and an older cousin – correspond to the most vehement and influential resistance to Vasari's historiography and artistic practice, founding an academy dedicated to an alternative and superior formulation of the modern manner based on Correggio, Veronese, and north Italian models.[50] Yet the Carracci differed in their estimation of the regional dimension of their reformed style. While Ludovico was adamant that the Carracci reform would remain anchored in Bologna, his cousins Annibale and Agostino staked a claim for its universality by introducing it to Rome in a series of spectacular commissions that laid the groundwork for the academic ideal of painting in Europe: a new, universal Roman modern manner drawing not just on

---

[47] On the Accademia dei Facchini, see Bora *et al.* (1998); and for the burlesque poetry produced in this circle, see Lomazzo (1993).

[48] See Kemp (1987); and also the edition of Lomazzo's writing on art, Lomazzo (1973–75).

[49] De Mambro Santos (2012) 47–55.

[50] See Dempsey (2000). For Ludovico's polemical aversion to Rome, a major theme of Carlo Cesare Malvasia's 1678 biography of the family of painters, see Malvasia (2000), especially 54, 84–85, and 175–77.

the "Lombards" but on Venetian and central Italian traditions. For Ludovico, the reformed style was a regional challenge to Rome from a culturally insubordinate city of the Papal States; according to the Carracci biographer Carlo Cesare Malvasia, Ludovico believed that his cousin Annibale had merely adulterated the force of the style by incorporating Raphael and Roman antiquity into it. Ludovico was drawing on the example of Correggio, whom he believed to have resisted the allure of Rome. The difference of outlook between Ludovico and Annibale corresponds to a fundamental distinction between a "secessionist" model of regionalism and one that seeks legitimation through the symbolic authority of Rome.

Mentalities

Case studies of artists or sites both outside and within the principal centers have too often been self-provincializing, stressing the particular as opposed to the structural or comparative dimension; old hierarchies of priority in the study of Italian art – the assumed pre-eminence of Florence, for instance – are left in place and unchallenged. There is already a long tradition of writing on art that celebrates and even romanticizes the provincial and the marginal in the person of say, Lorenzo Lotto, or Girolamo Romanino, or Cosmè Tura.[51]

The prevailing question for art history now is how to address the local, wherever it might be identified, and to characterize the local in terms of *relations* within an overall field of artistic production which is increasingly marked by *centralization*. Works assigned to the "periphery," by Vasari or by modern art history, might in fact be inscribing themselves into an alternative affiliation – the persistence of an older "network" model, and implicitly or explicitly contesting the force of an axis defined in political and hegemonic terms. Castelnuovo/Ginzburg assert that Pontormo, without leaving Florence, "chose" the periphery, a choice that "went together with a true material self-exclusion from his artist friends and colleagues."[52] This is to invest heavily in Vasari's own deeply prejudiced account of Pontormo, who has been shown to be far less professionally marginal than Vasari's life of the artist would suggest.[53] Pontormo's self-peripheralization is manifest in his choice of

---

[51] See, for example, Testori (1975) and (1995).   [52] Castelnuovo/Ginzburg (2009) 20.
[53] See Pilliod (2001), especially 1–43, 187–212.

models from what Vasari saw as an artistically marginal culture – the prints of Albrecht Dürer and Lucas van Leyden. Yet in so doing, Pontormo could equally have been locating his own artistic enterprise on a much broader transregional network, one that linked contemporaries such as Polidoro in Messina, Lotto in the Marche and in Lombardy, Pordenone (Giovanni Antonio Licinio) in Lombardy and the Veneto, and Gaudenzio Ferrari in the region between Milan and Turin. Pontormo's gravitation to this polycentric aggregate of nomadic artists (specially noteworthy for an artist who scarcely left Florence) need not be as extreme as a rejection of the values of Florentine art, but rather be seen to manifest a desire for the broadening of artistic norms in Florence, away from Rome and towards a more expanded field of practice.

In the past decade, new modes of conceptualizing artistic exchange have emerged which further call into question the "center/periphery" paradigm. Studies of "artistic transfer" – a method emerging so far mainly in French medieval studies – have challenged the idea that imported artistic models are necessarily perceived by their local beholders as transmissions of authority located in a "center," whether defined in political, economic, religious, or artistic terms.[54] Artists and their styles are not indelibly tagged with visible signs of their place of origin: the works that they create away from home may enter into a visual continuum with works in another locale. Cesare da Sesto's imposing altarpiece for Messina (c. 1513–15) (Fig. 1.2), with its Leonardesque *sfumato*, its Giorgione-like interest in lustrous surfaces, and its Mantegnesque antiquarian detail looks like a demonstration of the principles of north Italian painting which could serve both to represent the congregation of Genoese merchants who commissioned it, and to emulate the local prestige of Antonello, the most esteemed painter of Messina.[55] On the other hand, the presence of Milanese artists is tellingly minimal in Florence and Venice where style increasingly served the ends of a politicized cultural identity.

There are no indications that the styles of the Venetians Carlo Crivelli or Lorenzo Lotto, both of whom spent large parts of their careers working in the Marche, were perceived to be "from" Venice more than anywhere else. Their styles do not bear signs of such "regional coding." As commissions led to further commissions, the artist was more likely

[54] See the useful overview Guillouët (2009).   [55] On Cesare da Sesto, see Carminati (1994).

Fig. 1.2 Cesare da Sesto, *Madonna and Child with St. John the Baptist and St. George* (*c.* 1513–15, Fine Arts Museums of San Francisco).

held to the standard set by his own earlier works in the area. Lotto came to Bergamo having already worked in Rome alongside Raphael in the Vatican palace, and he had produced monumental altarpieces at Jesi and Recanati in the Papal States, where some of Bergamo's merchant community (including Marchetto Angelini, patron of Lotto's next major work) had business interests. In the scale of the figures relative to the monumental architecture, the Colleoni Martinengo altarpiece of 1513–16 (Fig. 1.3) has no precedent in Venetian painting.[56] The crossing of the church evokes rather Raphael's *School of Athens*, with the flood of light from the open dome above. *Romanitas* is manifest also in the display of the hieroglyphic emblem of Pope Leo X, the yoke with the legend SUAVE [sweet, gentle, or soft]. Beyond its cosmopolitan Roman references, the painting enters into a continuum with artistic models that would be familiar to Bergamask clients: the Virgin's gesture

[56] Humfrey (1997) 48–53; and Rossi (2001) 29.

Fig. 1.3 Lorenzo Lotto, *Virgin and Child with Saints* (1513–16, Church of
S. Bartolommeo, Bergamo).

resonates with Leonardo's *Virgin of the Rocks* in nearby Milan, with
Mantegna's *Virgin of the Victories* in Mantua, with Correggio's exactly
contemporary *Virgin of St. Francis* for Parma, while the architectural
setting recalls Bramante's choir at Santa Maria presso San Satiro in
Milan.

We need, furthermore, to be more historically relativist in our understanding of what considerations gave value to a place in pre-modern
Italy: landscapes and non-urban locations can possess in some cases
greater pre-eminence than centers of economic or political might or
princely charisma.[57] According to the criteria of Castelnuovo/Ginzburg,
for instance, the Sacro Monte of Varallo is a site on the "periphery"
of a major cultural, economic, and political metropolis, the city of
Milan – yet it displays its importance in completely other terms: it is

[57] A still growing field in cultural geography, from a historical and a philosophical
perspective; see Casey (1993), Cosgrove (1993), and Walsham (2011).

nothing less than a replication of Jerusalem, even equaling and replacing it as a sacred pilgrimage destination. And the artistic involvement of Gaudenzio Ferrari, and later of Tanzio da Varallo, together with the patronage of powerful figures such as Archbishop Carlo Borromeo, places the relegation of the Sacro Monte to the "periphery" under serious strain.

The pilgrimage site of Loreto perhaps epitomizes this alternative constitution of a center: the prosperous trading cities of the region were all invested in its production as a charismatic spiritual center which was precisely not defined as a place of economic or political influence. From the mid fifteenth century, the social orders of Italy began to array themselves as donors, pilgrims, and supplicants around the shrine of Our Lady of Loreto in the Marche, a frontier alternative to the venality of Rome. But the stylistic dialogism and heterogeneity of the Marche has led to its marginal status in an art history that has been so heavily invested in the coherence of regional styles, itself a legacy of a dynamic of regionalization that began in the sixteenth century with the reaction to Vasari (and was implicit even earlier). The challenge for art history is what kind of narrative we can provide for the Marche and for other regions (such as Lombardy–Veneto in the 1500s), and how we can give shape to a complex dynamic of artistic migration and exchange without recourse to the notion of "influence" percolating from the centers.[58]

However much the distinction between "centers" and "peripheries" might usefully describe political or economic reality, I have primarily been concerned here with the "center" as mental construct or fiction, and I am correspondingly skeptical about identifying the "periphery" with any specific geographical locale. Thus, resistance to the domination of the great centers might mean, on one hand, the bid to constitute a regional alternative *locus*, and on the other, the negation of the very principle of a geometric, circumscribable territory. "Center/ periphery" have here been regarded less as a binary model of objective description and analysis than as a dynamic of historical thought and practice, as an ideology which artists might extend, transform, or undermine through their work.

---

[58] On the Marche, see Zampetti (1988); De Marchi (2002) and (2005); and Lightbown (2004) 23–67.

2

Antiquities

In the fourteenth century, Petrarch called for the return of ancient Roman *virtus* [virtue, excellence] in the hopes that a distant, seemingly better antique past could inspire moral and political reform in the present. The rise of communal governments had begun to stir up nostalgic memories of Roman antiquity, an illustrious, native culture that seemed superior to that of the "barbaric" North. As the cult of antiquity attracted a wider following in the following century, its advocates would imagine that the ancient past had been reborn in the present, creating the myth of the death, sudden rebirth, and gradual flowering of the antique in Italy that continues to obscure the rich afterlife of classical art in the so-called Middle Ages. Traditionally, art historians have defined the Renaissance of antiquity as a gradual shift in style, one that took place as patrons and artists resuscitated a glorious ancient past. Now, however, it is widely acknowledged that the "Renaissance" of the visual arts was not sudden, progressive, or unitary. Nor was the integration of frequently inscrutable, often erotically charged pagan images into Christian culture a straightforward or intellectually cohesive process. Nevertheless, the effects of a reorientation towards the antique in so many aspects of Italian visual culture – in civic and religious spheres, in public and private life – were undeniably profound and wide-ranging. Although a short survey can only begin to introduce such vast and complex topics,[1] it will consider

---

[1] More comprehensive discussions of the recovery of the antique in Renaissance Italy can be found in: Panofsky (1965); Weiss (1969); Settis (1984–86); and Dacos (1994). The *Census of Antique Works Known to the Renaissance* (www.census.de) is a database of images, documents, and bibliography related to the topic.

some of the more significant moments in the recovery and reinvention of the ancient past and discus recent approaches to the reception of antiquity in Italy.

Painting and sculpture: *Quattrocento* to *Cinquecento*

The most important history of antique art known in the Renaissance was found in Pliny the Elder's *Natural History*, written in the first century CE. Pliny's text described the wondrous inventions of Greek masters such as Lysippus, Apelles, and Praxiteles, artists who had been the subjects of laudatory biographies in their own lifetimes. The artistic biography was a Greek genre that had flourished in the fourth century BCE and then quickly died out, ensuring that these few masters were the only famous artists in Pliny's time and, indeed, for centuries thereafter. In the fourteenth century, Dante still wrote of Polycleitus' sculptures as paradigms of artistic achievement; but at the same time, Dante also introduced new names to the canon when he commented on his own contemporaries, the painters Cimabue and Giotto. These became the first artists of the post-classical era to become famous, earning this status not only because of the perceived rebirth of a classical golden age through their successes, but also thanks to their promotion by literati who were well versed in classical texts.

Long before Giotto's day, in every region of Italy, patrons and artists had invested the remains of the antique past with complex political and aesthetic meanings, from sarcophagi reused as Christian tombs, to antique columns built into medieval churches, to the *Mirabilia* of Rome, the awe-inspiring ruins and statues that towered over the Christian city, described as wonders of the world in contemporary pilgrims' guides. Yet in the *Trecento* and early *Quattrocento* artists and writers began to evoke pagan antiquity in new contexts and in a more conspicuous and self-conscious manner. Civic art recalled the legendary "famous men" of ancient history, while humanist authors touted the lessons that could be learned from the ancients through the perfection of Greco-Roman arts and letters. Notably, late *Trecento* and early *Quattrocento* Florence witnessed a confluence of the artistic, literary, and civic revival of the antique, one which contemporaries mythologized as the beginning of a glorious revival. Around 1391–1405, anonymous Florentine artists carved *all'antica* [ancient style] nudes on the Porta della Mandorla of the Florentine cathedral, where a figure of Hercules appeared in classical

Fig. 2.1 Donatello, *St. Mark* (1411–13, Orsanmichele, Florence).

guise as both an *exemplum* of Christian virtue (Fortitude) and an emblem of Florence. Around the same time the quotation of antique sculpture in Brunelleschi's and Ghiberti's competition panels for the bronze Baptistery doors, cast in 1401–03, reflected new standards of antiquarianism among the guilds who commissioned public monuments. Another conspicuous allusion to Florence's antique origins came in the first three decades of the fifteenth century, when the city guilds decorated the exterior of Orsanmichele with over-life-sized statues in niches, taking their cue from the antique practice of setting up honorific statues in civic forums. Donatello's *St. Mark* (Fig. 2.1), made for Orsanmichele in 1411–13, assumes a *contrapposto* stance [in which the figure's upper torso twists away from the lower body], while its drapery folds seem to mimic the flutes of an antique column.

Artists began to theorize a revival of the antique in accordance with their own professional aspirations. When Leon Battista Alberti arrived in Florence in 1434, he wrote the *De pictura*, the first theoretical treatise on the visual arts to appear since antique times. Reflecting the importance of the humanist movement as an inspiration for artistic change, Alberti urged artists to associate with poets and orators to learn the art of invention, taking the ancients as their models: Apelles had painted his *Calumny*, for example, with the ingenuity of a rhetorician, and modern-day artists should follow his lead. In the 1440s, Lorenzo Ghiberti echoed Alberti's ambitions in his own manifesto, the *Commmentarii*. Like Alberti, Ghiberti drew upon Pliny and upon Vitruvius' *De architectura*, the only artistic treatise of any kind to have survived from antiquity, to praise the ancient painters and sculptors and condemn the destruction of their works in the Christian era. With the loss of precious antique artworks and theoretical writings, Ghiberti declared that *"finita fu l'arte,"* artistic know-how had died. Ghiberti took heart, however, in the notion that the arts had recently come back to life with Giotto, a fellow Tuscan who seemed equipped with not only marvelous *ingegno* [talent], but also the diligence and skill needed to master the *doctrina* [teaching] of the ancients.[2]

For Ghiberti, the artistic knowledge of the ancients largely consisted of the mastery of proportion and human anatomy. From Pliny the Elder, he and his fellow artists knew that the ancient Greek sculptor Polycleitus had written a treatise on the proportions of the body and that the ancient masters had greatly valued the symmetry and geometric harmony of the human figure (Pliny, *Natural History* 34.55, 34.58, and 34.65). Presumably it was in the 1440s that Alberti penned his *De statua* [On Sculpture], a direct response to Polycleitus' lost treatise, which was principally concerned with human proportions. Afterwards one sees a new interest in drawing nude figures, as artists even positioned models in the poses of antique statues. From the second half of the fifteenth century, model books filled with drawings of figural antiquities – mostly those visible in churches and public places in Rome – circulated widely in Tuscan workshops. Around 1450, one such drawing inspired Andrea del Castagno to quote one of the *Quirinal Horsetamers* (a colossal statue then attributed to Pheidias) in a figure of *David* he painted on a parade shield (*c.* 1450–55; Washington, DC, National Gallery of Art).

When the Medici commissioned a statue of *David* from Donatello for the courtyard of their new *palazzo*, the sculptor created an inventive

---

[2] Ghiberti (1998) 83–85.

image inspired by the nude, ephebic youths he would have seen in antique art. Donatello's *David* (1440s?; Florence, Bargello) could hardly be mistaken for an classical statue, yet it restates what were then considered to be paradigms of antique art: it was a nude figure in the round, made in bronze, and charged with the eroticism of an ancient Satyr or Cupid. Likewise Antonio Pollaiuolo's large engraving known as *The Battle of Nude Men* (*c.* 1470–75) celebrated the figural nude, recapturing the energy of an antique battle sarcophagus without quoting any one source too literally. As was typical of *Quattrocento* artists, Pollaiuolo followed Seneca's recommendation that sources not be merely copied, but instead mutate and change within the creative process, as the bee gathers pollen from many flowers and "transforms nectar into honey" (Seneca, *Epistles* 84). It was common practice for artists to combine antique and non-antique visual models freely and creatively, borrowing from *all'antica* statuettes and plaquettes as well as genuinely antique models.[3]

Closer ties between writers and artists in the *Quattrocento* also effected profound changes in the style and subject matter of Florentine painting. Artists followed the lead of the poets in creating the new genre of the mythological *favola*, a type of visual invention that used the imagery of antique mythology to access recondite topics. It seems that it was the patronage of Lorenzo de' Medici – an intellectual as deeply engaged in both poetry and the visual arts as he was in the political life of Florence – that inspired the most daring experiments in the genre. The *Primavera* by Botticelli (*c.* 1482; Florence, Uffizi) weaves together erudite references to the classical texts studied in Lorenzo's circle. While the Venus of the *Primavera* is dressed in contemporary festival garb, aligning the antique narrative with the themes of vernacular love poetry celebrated in Medici spectacle and in Lorenzo's own poetry,[4] the Venus in Botticelli's *Birth of Venus* restores the nude *Venus Pudica* to life in an energetic narrative that challenges Apelles' painting of the "foam-born" Venus. Botticelli would again rival Apelles in his *Allegory of Calumny* (1495; Florence, Uffizi), another reinterpretation of a famous antique painting. Other artworks from the circle of Lorenzo de'

---

[3] For imitation generally, see Gombrich (1966c); Gardini (1997); and Ackerman (2000).
For workshop practices, see Fusco (1982); and Reilly, "Artists' workshops," Chapter 4 in this volume, pp. 91–93.

[4] Dempsey (1992).

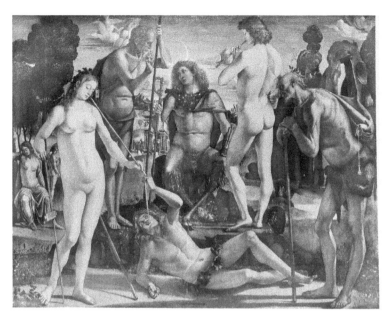

Fig. 2.2 Luca Signorelli, *Court of Pan* (*c.* 1484, formerly in Berlin but destroyed in 1945).

Medici engaged scholarly topics using mythological subject matter. Luca Signorelli's *Court of Pan* (*c.* 1484; now destroyed) (Fig. 2.2), a painting probably made for Lorenzo, borrows the visual formula of the altarpiece, yet replaces Christian imagery with an entirely pagan philosophical allegory.

Given the central position of Tuscan art in art-historical scholarship, the Florentine love affair with the figural nude is one of the reasons why artistic response to life-sized antique statues has been the overwhelming focus of scholarly attention. One finds a persistent under-valuation of *all'antica* art that precedes or differs from the styles of central Italy, or of antiquarian traditions centered on genres of antique art that are different from the life-sized figural marbles valued in the collections of Rome in the era of Raphael and Michelangelo. In northern Italy, artists and their patrons were often inspired by antique works such as medals, gems, sarcophagus reliefs, or antique inscriptions, yet their regard for smaller, two-dimensional images rather than free-standing statues in no way limited them, as has often been assumed. Indeed, the most sophisticated discussion of pagan nudity surviving from the mid *Quattrocento* is found not in Alberti's artistic treatises, but in a dialogue from the court of Ferrara inspired by Leonello d'Este's collection of ancient gems.[5]

Long before he had ever set foot in Rome, the Paduan artist Mantegna's knowledge of antique culture was remarkably broad. His training in the antique – like that of other northern Italians – came largely through collaboration with *eruditi* in the creation of antiquarian albums, the most remarkable example of which is the Paris album of his father-in-law Jacopo Bellini (*c.* 1450; Louvre), which includes many polished drawings of funerary altars, inscriptions, and coins on vellum sheets. Mantegna is known to have had access to a sketchbook filled with "pictures of certain antique sculpture, most of which are battles of centaurs, fauns and satyrs,"[6] and he advertised his ability to reinvent these ancient reliefs with engravings of bacchanals and battling sea gods.

Southern Italy is another region that has often been marginalized in the history of Renaissance antiquarianism, despite the importance of the *all'antica* architecture and antiquities collections of *Quattrocento* Naples and the vast array of surviving antique remains thoroughout Puglia, Basilicata, Sicily, and Campania. Ciriaco d'Ancona traveled throughout the South in the early *Quattrocento* recording antique inscriptions and also sketching ruins, while later travelers observed a wide array of epigraphic and statuary remains visible in public and private settings.[7] The use of ancient *spolia* [spoils] in churches, bell-towers, and private residences was a ubiquitous practice throughout the Kingdom of Naples as can still be seen, for example, in Capua and Benevento. Local barons sometimes led coordinated efforts to excavate and reuse antiquities; the *Quattrocento* revival of Nola near Naples under the Orsini, for example, is chronicled in Ambrogio Leone's *De Nola* of 1514. The outstanding survival from Nola's renaissance is the Palazzo Orsini built *c.* 1470 by the *condottiere* Orso Orsini. The façade, inscribed with a lengthy homage to Orso's fictive antique ancestor, Ursus, is constructed from smooth ashlar blocks taken from a nearby amphitheater and rearranged

---

[5] Baxandall (1963).

[6] Letter of 1476 from Angelo Tovaglia to Ludovico Gonzaga cited in Lightbown (1986) 83.

[7] The majority of the manuscript volumes of Ciriaco's transcriptions of ancient epigrams, gathered *in situ* throughout italy and the eastern Mediterranean, disappeared in the fire that destroyed the Sforza library in Pesaro in 1514. A collection of his letters, with English translations, and reproductions of some of his drawings, can be found in Cyriac of Ancona (2003).

in the *opus isodomum* [regularly patterned masonry] style recommended by Vitruvius, an example of the technique which predates the much more celebrated example of *opus isodomum* at Palazzo Riario (the Cancelleria) in Rome.[8] Following widespread practice in the Kingdom of Naples, antique statues and inscriptions were often gathered together in *seggi*, assembly rooms attached to open-air *loggie* which served various social and legal functions, such as the drawing up of notarial acts. Some of the more famous examples of the antiquities displayed in front of these *seggi* or in their *loggie* include the recumbent statue of Nile now in front of Sant'Angelo a Nilo in Naples or the Colossus of Barletta in Puglia, a statue that was widely admired in the fifteenth and sixteenth centuries as one of the most important surviving examples of large-scale antique statuary in bronze.[9]

While knowledge of antique painting and stuccowork seems to have been limited in most regions of Italy, archeological explorations in Rome during the second half of the *Quattrocento* led to the rediscovery of these genres. After torchlit expeditions to the underground chambers of Nero's *Domus Aurea* [Golden House] brought to light their colorful, playful forms, these *grotteschi* [grotesques] began to appear in the work of painters, sculptors, and woodcarvers who used them to decorate slim, vertical spaces such as pilasters and frames. The decoration on the painted *all'antica* pilasters in Filippino Lippi's *Strozzi Chapel* (1497–1502; Florence, Church of Santa Maria Novella), for example, relies upon the grotesques that circulated in pattern-books and prints in the fifteenth century. The theatrical temple in Lippi's *Expulsion of a Daemon from the Temple of Mars* (Fig. 2.3) recalls the type of imagery inspired by stage sets that the artist could have seen in Roman wall paintings. The Perugian Pinturicchio was one among many artists who scratched his name onto the ceiling of the *Domus Aurea*, and in the 1480s and 1490s he also became a specialist in the genre of the grotesque, decorating the ceilings of cardinals' palaces with the antique griffins, satyrs, and demigods he had discovered underground.

By the last three decades of the fifteenth century collecting antique sculpture had become widely popular in Florence and Rome, as these

---

[8] Clarke (1996).
[9] De Divitiis (2007); see also the website of the project *Historical Memory, Antiquarian Culture, Artistic Patronage: Social Identities in the Centres of Southern Italy between the Medieval and Early Modern Period* (http://histantartsi.eu/project.php) for which De Divitiis serves as Principal Investigator.

Fig. 2.3 Filippino Lippi, *Strozzi Chapel, The Expulsion of a Daemon from the Temple of Mars in Hierapolis* (1497–1502, Santa Maria Novella, Florence).

objects were more assiduously excavated.[10] In the 1480s and 1490s, Lorenzo de' Medici's sculpture garden at the convent of San Marco became a training ground for the restoration and close imitation of antiquities. The custodian of the sculpture garden, Bertoldo di Giovanni, created relief sculpture and table bronzes that closely resembled antique prototypes. In the same spirit of emulation, Michelangelo mastered the genre of the antique sarcophagus in his *Battle of the Centaurs* (c. 1492; Florence, Casa Buonarroti) (Fig. 2.4), and recreated the Hellenistic Eros in his lost *Sleeping Cupid*. Michelangelo's biographers tell us that Cardinal Raffaele Riario in Rome bought this *Cupid* as a genuine antique work and eventually lured the sculptor to Rome. Michelangelo's closest ally there was Riario's banker, Jacopo Galli,

[10] Christian (2010).

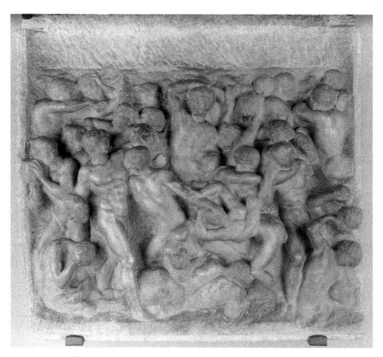

Fig. 2.4 Michelangelo, *Battle of the Centaurs* (*c.* 1492, Casa Buonarroti, Florence).

who hosted Michelangelo in his house and granted him access to his own personal collection of antiquities. The artist's skill was advertised by the display of his *Bacchus* (1496–97; Florence, Bargello) in the midst of Galli's classical sculptures, as if the statue could fool unwary visitors into thinking it was a genuine antiquity. Upon Michelangelo's return to Florence in 1501, the results of his novel artistic training – which seems to have been the first to privilege the close study of ancient sculpture over traditional workshop exercises – would be seen and judged on a public stage. Michelangelo's lost cartoon for the *Battle of Cascina* (1504) was a tour de force of the male nude and a monumentalization of the ancient battle-sarcophagus. Michelangelo's *David* (1501–04; Florence, Accademia) famously represents the adolescent hero as an antique colossus. Although this rhetorical and architectural figure diverges considerably from the models of classical sculpture, the ancient *Quirinal Horsetamers* were the only works known at the time that were comparable in their scale and forthright nudity.

In his preface to the third part of the *Vite de' più eccellenti pittori, scultori e architettori* [Lives of the Most Excellent Painters, Sculptors, and Architects, 1550 and 1568], Vasari wrote that when artists "saw rise from the earth certain classical works mentioned by Pliny, among the most famous, the Laocoön, the Hercules, the powerful Torso Belvedere, the Venus, the Cleopatra, the Apollo [all statues in the Vatican Belvedere] and numberless others, and these, from their softness and precision, their contours full-fleshed and observed from the greatest beauties of real life … caused the disappearance of that dry, rude, and cutting manner."[11] While grossly oversimplifying the history of archeological discoveries in Rome and their impact on visual artists, Vasari alludes here to a notable shift in central Italian art away from a Pollaiuolo-esque rendition of the body, where muscles are decorative embellishments to weightless bodies, and towards the plasticity and movement of antique sculpture in the round. The shift occurred as discoveries of antique sculpture coincided with the enthusiastic reception of Leonardo's figural style and its emphasis on *invenzione* [invention], *contrapposto*, and variety.[12] Elite audiences soon began to favor the *grazia* [grace] of Raphael's interpretation of the antique and the physical potency of Michelangelo's, conceived in opposition to one another. In these years antique torsos in Roman collections were an important impetus for figural invention; their curved backs and twisted waists inspired artists to recreate them as vigorous, action-charged bodies. Hellenistic sculptures rediscovered among the ruins of the city were also especially prized for their emotional pitch and figural torsion. Thus when the *Laocoön*, a masterpiece of the Hellenistic Baroque, came to light in January 1506, its discovery seemed providential. The statue group was a work of unparalleled prowess, it was discovered in a near-perfect state of completion, and Pliny had even mentioned it by name in his *Natural History*. The *Laocoön* became the most famous antiquity in all of Europe and was widely copied in bronze statuettes, prints, and plaquettes. Michelangelo was said to have called the work "a singular miracle of art" and prized it and the *Torso Belvedere* as ideal examples of the powerful male body in motion.

---

[11] Translation and citation from Panofsky (1965) 32.
[12] On these concepts, see Summers (1981). For the artistic response to antique sculpture, see Haskell/Penny (1981); Bober/Rubinstein (1987); and Barkan (1999).

Raphael's approach to antique sculpture was different, as he tended to find inspiration in androgynous or female bodies. As soon as the artist arrived in Rome, he began to model his female figures on the Belvedere *Cleopatra*. In his *Alba Madonna* (*c.* 1510; Washington, National Gallery of Art) the artist imitates the antique statue's sandals and adopts the elegant rotation of its limbs, a technique that he repeated in the graceful figure of *Sappho* painted in the *Parnassus* (*c.* 1511; Vatican Apartments). With greater exposure to Roman antiquities, Raphael's interest in antique sculpture broadened considerably. A profound, even systematic study in Rome's antiquities collections by the artist and his workshop is evident not so much from the drawings after the antique they have left behind – only a handful have survived – but through the quotations and reinterpretations that appear everywhere in their work. In the stuccoes and frescoes of the Vatican *Loggie* (*c.* 1515–19), the *stufetta* of Cardinal Bernardo Dovizi da Bibbiena (1516), and the Villa Madama (from 1517), the Raphael workshop defined a new mode of *all'antica* wall decor, inspired by the study of antique sculpture and the intensified exploration of the *Domus Aurea*.[13] Although Raphael was never appointed papal "superintendent of antiquities" as is often stated, his studies of the city's antique monuments was so profound that he could even distinguish between the late antique and imperial-era carvings on the Arch of Constantine. His approach stemmed from the antiquarian strands of research that had developed around the goal of reconstructing the appearance of ancient Rome using textual and visual remains, first fully articulated in Flavio Biondo's *Roma instaurata* [Rome Renewed, begun in the 1440s]. This project gained momentum through Raphael's own plans – cut short by his early death – to map the Roman ruins, but was only realized in part in 1561 with the publication of Pirro Ligorio's *Antiquae urbis imago*, an engraving that purported to show ancient Rome in its full splendor.[14]

---

[13] Dacos (1986).

[14] Over several decades Ligorio wrote and illustrated thirty manuscript volumes of an encyclopedia of the Italian ancient world that catalogues monuments, epigraphs, coins, and illustrious lives. Though only one early volume of this work was published in Ligorio's lifetime, *Delle antichità di Roma, nel quale si tratta de' circi, theatri, et anfitheatri* [On Roman Antiquities, dealing with Stadiums, Theaters, and Amphitheaters, 1553], there is a national edition of Ligorio's works under way, for which see www.culturaimmagineroma.it. On Ligorio in general, see Gaston (1998); and Coffin (2004).

In Venice, the revival of antiquity brought about radical innovations in style and subject matter. Tullio Lombardo produced works like the half-length relief known as a *Portrait of the Artist and his Wife* (*c.* 1495; Venice, Ca' d'Oro). The sculpture inventively combines the form of the antique funerary relief with the open-mouthed, emotionally anxious expressions found in Hellenistic sculpture.[15] At the same time, the female nudity in Lombardo's relief is astonishing, especially if it is – as has been suggested – a double portrait. Such transgressions remind us that antiquity had become an agent of change and an ideal conduit of artistic *fantasia*. With the reinvention of antique models, painters and sculptors could redefine themselves as super-artists, supreme creative agents who had the fame and stature to pick their own commissions and subjects. While Giovanni Bellini spent most of his career as a painter of devotional images, he ended it as a painter of mythologies, where the free exercise of his own faculties of invention trumped all other concerns. Even the demanding patron Isabella d'Este was happy to leave content up to Bellini, "just so that he paints some story or antique fable, or he invents something out of his own imagination that is antique."[16] The career of Bellini marks a period of extraordinary transition in the visual arts, when artists had become "idea men" and patrons were much more eager to collect *all'antica* fantasies. In the next generation, Giorgione catered almost exclusively to this type of patron, making lush landscapes of ancient pastoral and the erotic female nude the subjects of his inventive canvases. His *Sleeping Venus* (*c.* 1507–10, completed by Titian; Dresden, Gemäldegalerie) and *Tempest* (*c.* 1509; Venice, Accademia) celebrate alluring topics drawn from the world of classical mythology and establish the new genre of the erotic fable. Giorgione's paintings are also particularly concerned with the representation of transitory, atmospheric phenomena on the model of the ancient master Apelles, who could, as Pliny wrote, "paint the unpaintable: thunder, lightning, and stormbursts" (Pliny, *Natural History* 35.96).

While some artists and patrons resisted the lure of Rome – in Ludovico Sforza's Milan, for example, the artists Giovanni Antonio Amadeo and Bramantino continued local traditions by choosing to imitate *all'antica* prints or the antique coins and gems available in local collections – in the

---

[15] Luchs (1995).   [16] C. M. Brown (1976).

sixteenth century the antiquities of the "Eternal City" gained increasing aesthetic authority in Italy and beyond.[17] Greater interest in Rome's antiquities led to a high demand for casts, statuettes, and classicizing bronze plaquettes that copied the most famous sculptures. Such objects appealed to the growing numbers of collectors outside of Rome who found it difficult to get their hands on genuinely ancient works. Although Isabella d'Este, driven by what she described as a "hunger for antiquities," had agents in Rome and Greece looking for ancient marbles, her success was limited.[18] Instead Isabella collected small-scale bronze reproductions of the statues of Rome, such as the canonical works displayed in the Vatican Belvedere. An important catalyst for elite taste of the early *Cinquecento* was the reproductive print, especially those by Marcantonio Raimondi, which made Rome's ancient statues even more famous and brought the inventions of Raphael and Michelangelo to an international audience.

Around 1505 Isabella's brother, Duke Alfonso d'Este of Ferrara, conceived of a painting gallery – his *camerino* – decorated with canvases by the greatest artists of his day, each illustrating a different classical myth. After a trip to Rome, however, Alfonso required that his paintings be not only *all'antica*, but also *alla Romana*. The *pentimenti* [changes, or second thoughts] to Bellini's *Feast of the Gods* made *c.* 1512–14 (Washington, National Gallery of Art) reveal that the artist lowered the necklines of his goddesses, eroticizing the work and bringing it closer to Raphael's female types and to antique sculpture.[19] No matter how earnestly Bellini studied the sources available to him, however, he could never imitate the powerful, expressive figural types that Duke Alfonso had seen in Rome. For the completion of the *camerino* in a more heroic manner, Alfonso relied on Titian, a master well versed in both Venetian *colorito* [coloring] and in the figural types most highly prized in Rome. The sumptuous *Bacchus and Ariadne* created for Alfonso's *camerino* in 1520–23 (London, National Gallery) (Fig. 2.5) is Titian's homage to both Raphael and the antique: some of its figures look to Raphael's cartoon for a tapestry in the Sistine Chapel, the satyr wrestling with a snake quotes the *Laocoön*, while other details, such as the bronze vase lying at the feet of Ariadne, put the antiquarian credentials of painter and patron fully in evidence.

[17] Schofield (1992).   [18] C. M. Brown (1976).   [19] D. A. Brown (1993).

Fig. 2.5 Titian, *Bacchus and Ariadne* (1520–23, National Gallery, London).

The painting also catered to a new sort of viewer who could, after extended looking, decode multiple references to antique and contemporary art and literature in order to grasp the full extent of the artist's originality in recombining these sources.[20] It was the type of work that Titian would later call a *poesia*, a visual work that rivals poetry in its density of allusion and visibility of invention. For centuries to come, such painted poems would continue to be written in the aristocratic lingua franca of antique mythology and classical statues.

The Renaissance and antiquity

The subject of this volume is the "Renaissance," a term that calls to mind an all-embracing, gradually expanding recovery of the antique past.

[20] Shearman (1992) 227–61.

The notion of an artistic Renaissance of antiquity was most clearly and influentially articulated in Vasari's *Lives of the Artists*. The concept was subsequently developed by Jacob Burckhardt and other nineteenth-century historiographers, rejected by medievalists who thought the Renaissance had invented nothing new, and then largely re-established in the influential work of Erwin Panofsky. Panofsky nuanced Vasari's historical model, however, by contrasting a truly innovative Italian Renaissance with the presumably less important renascences that had come before it.[21] For Panofsky, the Renaissance revival of antiquity was unique, since it was the first time that "correct" classical forms had been successfully reunited with classical content. In recent decades, however, scholars have questioned the ability of sweeping theories to describe the complex and diverse transformations of this era. They have also questioned the notion that the "classical" is a timeless ideal that could ever have been correctly and authentically restored. In the 1980s, Panofsky's model was seriously challenged by the *Memoria dell'antico*, a series of essays edited by Salvatore Settis. Rather than imagining the rebirth of the antique in a series of greater or lesser revivals, the *Memoria* emphasized the sense of continuity between pagan and Christian culture guaranteed, above all, by the enduring physical presence of antiquity's remains.[22] Such an approach recognizes that the notion of an Italian Renaissance that begins with Cimabue and Giotto is a Florentine myth of origins. It also takes full account of Aby Warburg's theories on the survival of antiquity, and indeed, since the publication of the *Memoria*, Warburg's influence has been profound. The search for the classical sources of Renaissance style, itself a hallmark of formalist art history, has been overshadowed by a more interdisciplinary approach to the reception of the antique. In this broader context, patrons and collectors, as well as artists, can be regarded as creative agents.

Just as the concept of a "Renaissance" has become more complex, so too has "antiquity." For Vasari, antiquity was a native "Golden Age" that added a sense of coherence to his own notion of history. It has become increasingly clear, however, that antiquity was not such a well-defined concept in this era, before the categories of ancient, late antique, or medieval became the separate fields of study that they are today. Alexander Nagel and Christopher Wood's work has criticized the

---

[21] Panofsky (1965).
[22] Settis (1984–86), especially the "Nota dell'editore" in vol. 1, xxiii–xxvii.

evolutionary, stratified, and objective sense of time which – especially since Erwin Panofsky's *Perspective as Symbolic Form* – has been thought to characterize the period as a whole, pointing instead to the "instable temporalities" that are evident in Renaissance artworks.[23] Recent research has also shed light upon the different antiquities in operation contemporaneously in Renaissance Italy: Rome's past could be either Republican or Imperial, while alternatives to Roman antiquity could be found in the Greek, Hebrew, Etruscan, and illustriously old Egyptian past.[24] For Venice, the Byzantine empire was its own sort of "antiquity," a prestigious but not-so-distant past – Constantinople fell to the Turks only in 1453 – and had the advantage of being Christian.[25] Throughout Italy, antiquity was a concept tailor-made made to fit the requirements of families, social groups, or local communities. Individuals often traced their ancestry back to well-chosen antique heroes, while cities invented and celebrated their presumed ancient founders. In the Marche, the native antique population was the Piceni, a Latin tribe that had settled on the Adriatic coast before the Romans arrived and who had resisted Roman conquest.[26] In southern Italy, Renaissance Naples looked back with great pride to its origins as a Greek colony and honored the nymph Parthenope, a tragic figure mentioned in Homer's *Odyssey* whose tomb monument had supposedly been built on the Neapolitan coast.[27]

One of the enduring myths about the Italian Renaissance is that Italy formed its modern, national identity in this period through the revival of its antique past. Yet adding to the problem of the diversity of the "antique" discussed above is the fact that by the early sixteenth century the study of Italy's ancient monuments had become a pan-European phenomenon. Curiosity about Italy's classical ruins spread through the wide availability of guidebooks and prints, fostering cross-cultural discussions both inside and outside of Italy that were focused in particular on the ruins of Rome. The invention of archeological methods and the revival of the antique arts in Italy owe much to the imagination of foreign artists and patrons (such as Maarten van Heemskerck and Cardinal Jean du Bellay) who were just as deeply invested in Rome's antique past as the locals were.

By now, the Renaissance revival of the antique has lost its aura of innocence as scholars have probed the question of how the "high"

---

[23] Nagel/Wood (2010).   [24] Curran (2007).   [25] C. M. Brown (1976).
[26] Fanelli (1979).   [27] Beyer (2000); and De Divitiis (2007).

culture of the ruling elite operated in political terms. In the *Trecento*, the revival of antiquity had been by and large a civic phenomenon, as when the famous men of the Republican era were celebrated in fresco cycles painted in town halls. Over time, however, antiquity became largely the purview of the wealthy, who invented the idea of the antiquities collection and the private art gallery decorated with mythological artworks. Civic governments sometimes took measures to stop the privatization of the antique. In the 1480s, for example, the Brescian *comune* founded a museum of classical inscriptions in their Piazza della Loggia, declaring that inscriptions discovered in the city's salt market should not be sold to private collectors, but preserved for public display.[28] Yet attempts to reserve the language of antiquity for the public, civic sphere proved to be futile. As antique objects grew more scarce, a jealousy system transformed their possession into a universally recognized mark of prestige and power. In the hands of aristocratic patrons, the evocation of antiquity could help assert their right to rule, as when antique mythology, evoked in festival celebrations or triumphal entries, allowed patrons to represent themselves as quasi-divine figures presiding over mythical realms. The *all'antica* visual culture of the ruling classes in Renaissance Italy was often an unapologetically misogynistic expression of male power and dominance. It is telling in this regard that one of the more popular antiquarian motifs in sixteenth-century painting is that of a sleeping female nude approached by a lusty satyr, an image that catered to the sexual fantasies of male spectators.

In recent years Warburgian topics such as pagan magic and astrology have attracted attention.[29] So too has the fear of pagan idolatry in Renaissance culture, unease about which was common – despite the growth of collecting and artistic reuse of antiquities – as is witnessed by the success of the Dominican preacher Girolamo Savonarola in Florence, or by the imagery seen in Lippi's *Expulsion*, begun in the years of Savonarola's influence (see Fig. 2.3, above).[30] An explosion of literature on the topic of artistic inspiration has, furthermore, underscored the role of ancient visual culture in transforming the nature of the creative process itself in this period. As artists allied themselves with the classic locus of invention, poetry, they more frequently engaged the

---

[28] Passamani (1979).   [29] Cole (2002).   [30] Helas/Wolf (2009).

antique *topoi* of divine inspiration – the dream, the Bacchic frenzy, or the impassioned state of poetic *furor* [frenzy].[31] Given the unfamiliarity of much antique art and the fact that it often reappeared by chance excavation, fragmented and out of context, the reception of antique works demanded enormous invention on the part of Renaissance artists and viewers. Leonard Barkan's work on the fragment has seen a greater investment in creative interpretation as a by-product of antiquity's revival: when incomplete and unfamiliar objects arose from the ground, they invited reinvention by creative minds, making visual decipherment a "fundamental hermeneutic" of Renaissance culture.[32] The unbounded range of meaning contained within such a concept as open-ended as the "antique" was what made it so appealing and susceptible to so many transformations in the Renaissance. It also ensures that our own interpretations of Renaissance revival will be just as fluid.

---

[31] For example, Ruvoldt (2004).
[32] Barkan (1999).

3

Mapping and voyages

Fundamentally human is the need to know the places that we
inhabit and to dominate them through mapping. In the process of
mastering the geography of our world, we define our place within it
and our relations to others. If the need to represent the surrounding
space is universal, how to map it, what to include and what to omit, is
always a selective cultural process that involves choices, reductions,
and distortions. Renaissance mapping is traditionally associated with
the beginning of modern cartography, and its history has often been
reduced to documenting the gradual conquest of mathematical accuracy
in the representation of a world of expanding borders. Early European
voyages beyond the Columns of Hercules (at Gibraltar) and the rediscovery of Ptolemy's *Geographia* [Geography], the foundational text for
locating places precisely on a cartographic grid, date from the late
fourteenth century. But Ptolemy's mathematical geography, which
has become the dominating concern of modern cartography, coexisted
in the Renaissance with the verbose descriptions of places that other
ancient authors had presented in their geographical texts and which
have disappeared from modern maps. As cultural artifacts, maps
participated in major cultural trends of the period, from humanism
to the exploration of trading routes and the emergence of the printing
press as well as in the planning of religious expeditions and the
formation of overseas dominions. Their techniques and conventions
of representation emerged in relation to the intentions of their makers
and the expectations of their patrons and users. In this process of
defining the practices of Renaissance mappings and the conventions

of cartographic representations, humanists, courts, and cities of the Italian peninsula played a significant role.[1]

In the Renaissance, mapping was not an independent discipline or a distinct profession but an integral component of geography, the study of the Earth's globe. A laborious endeavor, mapping required the skills of such diverse disciplines and crafts as philology, surveying, computation, mathematics, geometry, drawing, painting, engraving, printing, the making of instruments, and knowledge of Greek and Latin. Because only rarely did one single person master the full array of skills required to make maps, Renaissance mapping resulted from the close collaboration of humanists, artists, merchants, and printers, who were all obsessed with the measurement of the universe, the visualization of the Earth's globe, the philological exegesis of ancient texts, and the trade of exotic goods. Based in Florence, Venice, Ferrara, Rome, Genoa, Naples, and Mantua as well as in Paris, Seville, Lisbon, Nuremberg, and later also in London, Antwerp, and Amsterdam, these heterogeneous groups of mapmakers operated within a European network of relations that often intersected with the network of the republic of letters, the courts of rulers, the councils of the church, the associations of merchants and bankers, and the mercenary armies of European powers. Each center and group was under a different rule, pursuing cartography with different gains in mind and often keeping news of travels and lands jealously from others, but nonetheless legal and illegal exchanges abounded in cartographic matters. Typical were the interactions that brought a Genoese sailor to lead an expedition sponsored by the Spanish king, a Florentine engraver to print maps in Venice, an Italian diplomat to smuggle nautical charts from Lisbon to Ferrara, a Venetian monk to make maps for the Portuguese king, or a Vicentine sailor to search for a north-west passage to China on behalf of the French king.

Images destined for a restricted public in the Middle Ages, maps became one of the most favored forms to represent the world in the Renaissance. By the end of the sixteenth century millions of maps representing the whole world, continents, individual countries, regions,

---

[1] For a cultural approach to Renaissance cartography see: Cosgrove (1999); Fiorani (2005); and the introduction to Woodward (2007); this latter volume includes important essays on various aspects of Renaissance cartography, including cosmography, nautical charts, star maps, cadastral maps, city views, maps and literature, printing, collecting, mapmaking techniques, and projections.

and cities were produced in Europe.[2] The emergence of the printing press contributed to this unprecedented diffusion of maps, which were sold as individual prints but also used as illustrations in bibles, history books, classics, and contemporary texts. Editions of such famous books as Pliny's *Natural History*, Ariosto's *Orlando furioso*, Petrarch's *Opere volgari*, and Dante's *Divine Comedy* contained maps, while Renaissance authors started to use the space of maps as an inspiration for their literary compositions.[3] Maps came to be used for a variety of purposes. Objects of learning and delectation, they were collected and displayed in audience halls, libraries, and studies. In Italy they were also painted in city residences, villas, and princely palaces. They were used as visual aids in estimating the daily reports on European wars and in establishing merchandising franchises. Some were visual aids to study the Bible and the classics, to learn history, or to facilitate the contemplation of the divine through the study of nature.

The burst of activity that characterized Renaissance cartography was due to a set of concomitant factors. It built on the long-standing western tradition of representing the Earth visually and verbally.[4] Although ancient maps were unknown until the late fifteenth century, medieval maps of the world, the Mediterranean, and the Holy Land were well documented and continued to be made throughout the sixteenth century. Medieval *mappaemundi* [world maps] represented the three continents of Europe, Africa, and Asia schematically, placing Jerusalem at the center of the globe, and were mainly intended as memory-images to visualize and recall encyclopedic knowledge. Charts of the Mediterranean recorded coastlines, ports, and directions of navigation (rhumb lines); their origin is still hotly debated but it is plausibly due to the interactions of Islamic, Pisan, Genoese, and Venetian sailors and map-makers in the thirteenth century. Maps of the Holy Land, the first area of the world to be represented individually in Western maps, served for biblical studies but also for planning pilgrimages, crusades, and commercial expeditions. Also popular were geographical descriptions of the world and its regions included in ancient texts, among which Pliny's

---

[2] It has been calculated that only a few thousand maps existed in the years 1400–72, but that their number jumped to about 56,000 from 1472 to 1500, while millions of maps were produced from 1500 to 1600; see Woodward (2007) 11.

[3] On the relation between cartography and literature, see Conley (2007).

[4] On medieval maps, see Campbell (1987); Harvey (1987); Woodward (1987); Scafi (2006); and Edson (2007).

Natural History, Macrobius' *Commentarius in somnium Scipionis* [Commentary on the Dream of Scipio], Solinus' *Collectanea rerum memorabilium* [Collection of Remarkable Things], and Martianus Capella's *De nuptiis Philologiae et Mercurii* [On the Marriage of Philology and Mercury] held authoritative status, while the fourteenth-century travel report written by the Venetian Marco Polo about his journey to Cathay was favored reading of early humanists, nobles, clergy, and bankers across Europe.

Equally important for the diffusion of maps in the Renaissance was the rediscovery of ancient geographical texts by Pomponius Mela, Ptolemy, and Strabo, and the journeys of European travelers beyond the Columns of Hercules and in central Africa. The recovery of these geographical texts coincided with defining moments in the early history of humanism, while the texts themselves rapidly generated a widespread interest that exemplifies the different motivations coexisting in Renaissance mapping and the wide-ranging cultural relations from which it emerged. More importantly, these texts were systematically read against each other, in the effort to reconcile their contradictory information on the shape of the world, the size of continents, and the extension of oceans. They were also read in conjunction with modern travel reports from northern Europe, the Atlantic, and Africa, which related that although these lands were situated beyond the world known by the ancients, they were inhabited. Initially the recovery of ancient geographical knowledge and early travels were independent pursuits, carried out by different people for different purposes. Eventually they came to interact in such significant ways that by the late fifteenth century the study of ancient geography and the recording of modern voyages became part and parcel of Renaissance mapping. Indeed, the Renaissance notion of mapping as a mathematical and descriptive record of the entire world emerged from the practice of comparing ancient texts to modern voyages.

The first-century CE author Pomponius Mela enjoyed a long-standing reputation in geographical matters, given Pliny's praise of him in the *Natural History*. But no text by Mela was known until the 1330s, when Petrarch discovered his *De chorographia* [On Chorography, or Descriptive Geography] in Avignon.[5] Petrarch was fascinated with

---

[5] Romer (1998). Mela did not include a map in his text, but it has been suggested that he had in mind the map of the known world that Agrippa had started and Augustus completed. Displayed in the Porticus Vipsania in Rome, this map was known as *chorographia*, a name possibly recalled by the title of Mela's text.

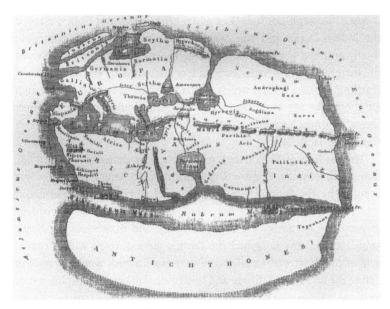

Fig. 3.1 Pomponius Mela, *World Map*, from *P. Bertij tabvlarvm geographicarvm contractarvm libri septem* (Tracy W. McGregor Library of American History, Albert and Shirley Small Special Collections Library, University of Virginia, Charlottesville). The Earth's globe is surrounded by water and divided into five climatic zones, of which only one is inhabited. The two polar zones are too cold, the central zone is too torrid, and the southern temperate zone is unknown. The northern temperate zone corresponds to the known world and it is divided into three continents, Europe, Africa, and Asia.

Mela's brief and engaging text and had copies made for fellow human-ists, including Giovanni Boccaccio, facilitating the wide circulation of the manuscript for almost a century, until it was printed in Milan in 1471. Mela conceived the Earth's globe as a sphere surrounded by water and divided into five climatic zones, of which only the *orbis situm* [northern temperate zone] was known and inhabited (Fig. 3.1), and he describes a journey across the *orbis situm*, which started and ended at the Columns of Hercules. Typical of ancient authors who regarded geog-raphy and ethnography as intertwined, Mela's description includes reports on geographical features along with information on peoples, plants, animals, marvels, and legends. In addition, Mela imagines a circumnavigation of the entire globe through the outer waters sur-rounding the Earth. Starting at the Columns of Hercules, this sea journey proceeded along the Atlantic coast of Spain and Britain;

it passed through northern Europe, northern Asia and China, reached the Indian Ocean and the Arabic Sea, circumnavigated Africa, and finally returned to Gibraltar. Mela's fictive circumnavigation captivated the imagination of Renaissance readers fascinated by the possibility of reaching the East Indies, which Marco Polo had done by land, through an alternative sea route. Such a novel route would have given direct access to spices and exotic goods, eliminating the onerous taxes of traditional land routes.

The reading of Mela's text acquired a new dimension in the late fourteenth century, when a Greek copy of Ptolemy's *Geography* was brought by the Byzantine scholar Manuel Chrysoloras to Florence.[6] Ptolemy's text was not an easy read, however, requiring knowledge of geometry, mathematics, and astronomy, and mastery of the Greek language. Ptolemy imagined the Earth's globe covered with a spatial grid of coordinates of parallels and meridians, which would be used to define the degrees of latitude and longitude (Fig. 3.2). He explains how to connect terrestrial locations to astronomical observations and shows how to make projections that maintain proportional distance between the roundness of the Earth and the flatness of the map. Ptolemy's theoretical geography was difficult, but his discussion of the differences between geography and chorography was quite accessible and indeed resonated with Renaissance readers. Geography aimed at representing large areas of the Earth with its general features, while chorography recorded small places pictorially. Consequently, the geographer dealt with the quantitative values of positions and distances while the chorographer dealt with the qualitative details of individual places. The geographer made schematic drawings representing a coast with a line and a city with a point, while the chorographer, a skilled draftsman, portrayed the likeness of a place illusionistically. Ptolemy's work is only geographical, and the bulk of his manual is a dry list of latitudinal and longitudinal coordinates for roughly 8,000 places of the known world. Although Ptolemy's *Geography* had arrived without maps, its Renaissance editors eventually provided a general map of the world along with twenty-six regional maps (ten maps of Europe, four of Africa, and twelve of Asia).

---

[6] Ptolemy (2000). On the diffusion of Ptolemy's *Geography* in the Renaissance, see Dalché (2007). On Renaissance interpretations of Ptolemy's geographical theory, see Milanesi (1984); Cosgrove (1992); and Fiorani (2005) 93–108.

Fig. 3.2 Ptolemy, *World Map* (first half of fifteenth century, illuminated manuscript on vellum, Florence, Biblioteca Medicea Laurenziana). The known world is divided into three continents, Europe, Africa, and Asia. It extends from the equator to the 50th degree of latitude and from the Atlantic coast of Europe and Africa to China. The Earth's globe is covered with an imaginary grid of parallels and meridians.

In spite of its difficulties, Ptolemy's *Geography* enjoyed a rapid circulation in manuscript form, and from 1477 also in print. To make the text available to a larger readership Chrysoloras himself started a Latin translation which his pupil Jacopo d'Angelo da Scarperia completed before 1410. Many scholars cooperated in collating, emending, and interpreting the text, and in making the maps. Palla Strozzi, the richest Florentine of the early fifteenth century and a discerning patron of art and architecture, owned one of the oldest copies. The bibliophile and antiquarian Niccolo Niccoli produced lavishly illuminated manuscript copies for illustrious patrons, including Cosimo de' Medici, Carlo Marsuppini, Leonardo Bruni, Poggio Bracciolini, and Paolo dal Pozzo Toscanelli, a circle of patrons and friends who often met at the monastery of Santa Maria degli Angeli in Florence to discuss geographical matters. Francesco Rosselli illuminated maps for Vespasiano da Bisticci to which his brother, the painter Cosimo, contributed cartoons for the heads of the winds. The study of Ptolemy's *Geography* spread from Florence to the courts of Ferrara, Mantua, and Naples and the republic of Venice, while interest in Ptolemy arose also in Paris and Vienna. D'Angelo dedicated his translation first to Pope Gregory XII and then to Alexander V (this was the moment of the Great Schism, with rival claimants to the papal throne) and brought the text to Rome, which became a center of cartographic studies. The first edition of Ptolemy with maps was printed there in 1478.

Ancient geographical knowledge was further enriched by Strabo's *Geographia* [Geography], a text written in the first century CE that had been completely ignored by the major geographers of imperial Rome and Alexandria and was thus completely unknown in the early Renaissance.[7] A Greek version of Strabo arrived in Florence in 1439 with the Byzantine philosopher George Gemistus Plethon who, while attending the Council of Florence, also delivered influential philosophical lectures on Plato and Aristotle that initiated the study of Platonic philosophy in Florence. Like Mela, Strabo's encyclopedic description of the world combines geography and ethnography, but it also contains the welcome novelty of articulating the relation between geography and history. For Strabo, history studies human actions in time, while geography describes the same actions in space. Thus geography was considered a

---

[7] Strabo (1917–32). On Strabo's geography, see Clarke (1999).

philosophical enterprise with the political and ethical mission of edu-
cating statesmen and commanders in the government of the world. The
humanist Guarino Guarini, who translated Strabo's text into Latin in
1458, shared this notion of geography and regarded the text as suitable
reading for his aristocratic students, the future rulers of the Gonzaga,
d'Este, and Montefeltro dynasties. Strabo might have consulted maps
during the compilation of his work or imagined his readers as familiar
with a map of the known world, yet he was not concerned with the
visual description of the Earth's globe, let alone with its measurement.

The wide Renaissance success of these ancient geographical texts
can be ascribed to different, albeit compatible, reasons. Humanists cherished the recovery of ancient texts and painstakingly tried to restitute
them to their original form. Antiquarians enthusiastically embraced the
reconstruction of the ancient world with an accuracy that was unimagin-
able before. Ptolemy's list of names and coordinates was invaluable to
identify and locate cities, mountains, rivers, and lakes mentioned in
ancient sources, while Mela's and Strabo's descriptions added specificity
and details of peoples, flora, and fauna. Scholars of mathematics and
geometry welcomed a geographical theory that assured the univocal
correspondence of places on Earth and places on the map. Philosophers
and theologians, but also merchants and bankers, compared Ptolemy,
Mela, and Strabo, trying to reconcile the shape and measurement of the
Earth's globe that they proposed as well as their different ways of
describing it. For Renaissance mapmakers, Ptolemy offered a system to
fix the position of places mathematically and to measure distances,
while Mela and Strabo provided vivid descriptions of geographical
features, people, animals, natural resources, and marvels. Unwilling to
discard "the mass of reports about the characteristics of people and
places" that Ptolemy wished to exclude from geography,[8] Renaissance
mapmakers chose instead to blend geography with chorography, combining Mela and Strabo's literary tradition with Ptolemy's mathematical
geography. Their expanded notion of geographical description came to
include not only the mathematical location of a place, as Ptolemy had
suggested, but also whatever that place contained, as Mela and Strabo
had done. It is this wider notion of geography that informed Renaissance
mapping.

---

[8] Ptolemy (2000) II.1, 95.

Parallel to the elaboration of geography as a mathematical and verbal description of places were the early voyages by Europeans who ventured beyond the Columns of Hercules, along the west coast of Africa and into the Atlantic Ocean.[9] Portuguese sailors, who were the first Europeans to travel along the Atlantic coast of Africa, certainly did not plan their voyages with Mela's descriptions in mind. They had no knowledge of Ptolemy's mathematical geography and, as far as one can tell, did not carry maps on board. In the fourteenth and early fifteenth centuries, sailing beyond Gibraltar never involved losing sight of the coast for more than a couple of days. As with the Mediterranean, early Atlantic navigation was based exclusively on first-hand experience and indigenous knowledge of currents, winds, and coastal landmarks, which were recorded in written travel reports known as portolans. Using portolans, information gathered from local travelers, and motivated by the search for mercantile trading routes, Portuguese sailors reached the Madeira Islands in 1419, the Azores in 1427, the Canaries in 1434, and the Cape Verde Islands in 1460. They sailed along the coast of Guinea in 1434 and crossed the Tropic of Cancer the following year. In 1473 they crossed the equator, two years later they found the island of São Tomé and Príncipe in the Gulf of Guinea, and in 1488 they rounded the Cape of Good Hope, opening a sea route to the East Indies. Just as the Atlantic islands acquired a fixed position on the world map, the Atlantic Ocean shrank in size reaching an extension that was imaginable to sail across. As voyages became longer and moved farther into the ocean, sailors had to learn new ways to adjust directions of navigation, which were increasingly affected by the curvature of the Earth. With no coastal landmarks visible, sailors resorted to astronomical observations to record their position at sea and the locations of the places they visited. Ancient geographical knowledge became increasingly useful, and coupled with advanced knowledge of Atlantic navigation it might well have encouraged inclined patrons to underwrite longer expeditions. Mela's shape of the world suggested that the Indian Ocean could be reached either by circumnavigating Africa or by sailing across the Atlantic, while Ptolemy's geographical theory made it possible to estimate distances. The relations between ancient geography and modern voyages remain sketchy, but some occasions of direct contact are well

[9] On Portuguese and Spanish travels and maps see Brotton (1997). On the use of nautical charts in the Renaissance, see Dalché (2007) 327–33; and Astengo (2007).

documented. The humanist text *Imago mundi* [Image of the World] written by Pierre d'Ailly, bishop of Cambrai, around 1410, was a comparative reading of Mela and Ptolemy on the issue of the Earth's inhabitability, shape, and measurement, and deals with a possible voyage to reach the southern temperate zone that Ptolemy did not map and that Mela considered deserted. Among d'Ailly's Renaissance readers was Christopher Columbus, who filled his own manuscript copy – extant today in Seville – with comments and observations on the feasibility of such a voyage and on the size of the oceans.

Sailors and merchants from the Italian peninsula were quick to seize the commercial opportunities offered by Portuguese ventures, and they wrote extensively about their voyages in letters and travel reports, contributing to the growing genre of travel literature.[10] Among the first Italians to board Portuguese ships were the Genoese, followed by Florentines and Venetians. Antonio Malfante went to Segelmessa in Africa in 1447, Antoniotto Usodimare was in Gambia and Guinea in 1455, and Antonio da Noli sailed to the Cape Verde Islands in 1460. The Florentine merchant Benedetto Dei visited north Africa, going as far as Timbuktu. The Venetian Alvise Cadamosto traveled to Senegal, sailed to the Madeira and Canaries Islands and led the first Portuguese expedition to the Cape Verde Islands in 1456. Cadamosto wrote a travel report, which was used by his fellow citizen, Grazioso Benincasa, to make maps in 1467 and which was printed in Milan in 1507–08. The Venetian Andrea Bianco, a sailor and mapmaker, worked extensively for the Portuguese and later collaborated with Fra Mauro (about whom see below). Independent from Portuguese voyages was the travel of the Franciscan friar Alberto da Sarteano who, in 1441, was sent by Pope Eugene IV to convert Ethiopia to the Roman church. Upon his return, he reported that central Africa was populated, even if located outside Ptolemy's known world, shattering traditional views of the Earth's inhabitability and initiating the universalizing scope of cartography for religious, political, and commercial purposes.[11]

Other Italians joined Spanish ships, most notably the Genoese Christopher Colombus, who had resided in Lisbon from 1476 but convinced the Spanish king to sponsor an unprecedented, westward expedition to

---

[10] On Italian travelers, mapmakers, map printers, and writers of geography, see the essays by Woodward, Sereno, Quaini, Casti, Rombai, Valerio, and Cachey Jr. in Woodward (2007).

[11] On globalism and Renaissance mapping, see Cosgrove (2003); and Headley (2008) 9–62.

the East Indies. In 1492 his ship landed on one of the Bahamas that he named San Salvador; he was convinced he had arrived in the East Indies.[12] In 1500, the Florentine Amerigo Vespucci led another expedition for the Spanish king. In his travel report of 1505, *Mundus Novus* [New World], he was the first to understand that Columbus had not reached Asia, but rather a different land that was as extended as a continent.[13] In 1519, Antonio Pigafetta from Vicenza, Leone Pancaldo from Savona, and Giovanni Battista da Poncevera from Genoa joined the first circumnavigation of the globe sponsored by the Spanish king and led by the Portuguese Ferdinand Magellan. While Magellan never made it back to Spain – he died in Mactan – Pigafetta returned and wrote the voyage's official account, the *Viaggio attorno al mondo* [First Voyage around the World], a colorful account that became popular reading across Europe.[14] In 1524, the Florentine Giovanni da Verrazzano led a French expedition in search of a mythical north-west passage to China that would avoid circumnavigating South America. He thought he had found it and made his discovery public in a famous letter addressed to King Francis I, while his brother published a travel report and a map documenting the passage.[15] Soon it became clear that Verrazzano had mistaken the Outer Banks in North Carolina for the mythical north-west passage, but the "Sea of Verrazzano" continued to appear in maps for many years, including the popular charts and atlases made by Battista Agnese. Seizing on public enthusiasm for travel reports and maps, Italian authors and printers specialized in a new kind of publication: collections of miscellaneous texts and selected maps relating to modern voyages around the world. The unquestionable best-seller among travel collections was Gian Battista Ramusio's three-volume *Navigazioni et viaggi* [Navigations and Voyages], published in Venice in 1550–59 and illustrated with maps by the cartographer Giacomo Gastaldi.[16] Also conspicuously Italian was the creation of the *isolario* [island book], a new literary genre of texts and maps of the world's islands. Started by the Florentine monk Cristoforo Buondelmonti around 1420 and followed by Henricus Martellus Germanus, a German engraver who resided in Florence in the 1480s, and by the Venetian Bartolomeo delli Sonetti, a shipmaster who wrote his descriptions of

---

[12] Cohen (1969); and Columbus (1989).   [13] Vespucci (1992) and (2012).
[14] Pigafetta (2007).   [15] Verrazzano (1970).
[16] Ramusio (1970); see also Milanesi (1984); and Headley (2008).

islands in verses around 1485, the *isolario* culminated with the printed works by the Paduan illuminator Benedetto Bordone (1528) and the Venetian *letterato* Tommaso Porcacchi (1572).[17]

Printers and editors engaged in fierce competition to publish the most updated maps and travel reports. Armed with this rich baggage of ancient geographical knowledge and news from recent voyages, Renaissance editors, scholars, and mapmakers aimed at completing the work of ancient geographers: to map the world that ancient geographers did not know, and to describe the entire globe of the Earth both mathematically and pictorially. This process of integrating ancient geography with modern voyages was pervasive in Renaissance mapping, affecting many different kinds of manuscript and printed maps made both for the wider public and selected viewers. Maps that differed in terms of purpose, medium, context, and technique shared nonetheless a syncretistic approach to their visual and verbal cartographic sources. This kind of syncretism, rather than the search for cartographic accuracy, characterized Renaissance mapping, as it can be elucidated through the analysis of Italian printed editions of Ptolemy's *Geography*, manuscript nautical charts, and printed world maps.

Between 1477 and 1561, Ptolemy's *Geography* was printed in twenty-five editions in Latin, Greek, and Italian, making it one of the most successful printed books of the Renaissance. These editions varied in format, from luxurious folio formats with hand-painted maps to pocket editions in the vernacular. The great success of this text was due to the fact that its Renaissance – and particularly Italian – editors regarded it not only as an ancient text to be restituted to its pristine form, but also as the repository of the mapping of the modern world. They interpreted the newly discovered lands as extensions of the Ptolemaic continents and made maps illustrating northern Europe, central and south Africa, south-east Asia, and the West Indies. When later sailors, scholars, and mapmakers realized that the West Indies were physically separated from Asia, they added a fourth continent to the traditional three, thus expanding the canonical number of Ptolemaic maps to represent the world that Ptolemy had not known.

The process of integrating Ptolemaic and modern maps, which started in the 1420s when the French Cardinal Guillaume Fillastre

---

[17] On island books, see Tolias (2007).

added a map of northern Europe to his manuscript of the *Geography*, became routine for Renaissance manuscripts and editions prepared in Florence. In the 1460s, Nicolaus Germanus made copies for Borso d'Este and Pope Paul II that included modern maps of Spain, Italy, northern Europe, France, and the Holy Land, introducing also a trapezoid projection that was widely adopted later. In the 1470s, the Florentine painter and miniaturist Pietro del Massaio added six modern maps – Spain, Italy, Tuscany, the Peloponnesus, Crete, and Egypt – to the copies prepared in his workshop as well as nine city views of Milan, Venice, Florence, Rome, Constantinople, Damascus, Jerusalem, Cairo, and Alexandria. Later city views developed as individual prints and as illustrations in books of cities, another popular cartographic genre.[18] Particularly significant in this process was Francesco Berlinghieri's *Septe giornate della geografia* [Seven Days of Geography], published in Florence in 1482, which contained twenty-seven Ptolemaic maps and six modern maps of northern Europe, the British Isles, Spain, France, Italy, and Palestine. Using Ptolemy's original text as a springboard for a personal, poetic description of the world written in Italian and composed in verse, Berlinghieri effectively synthesized the Renaissance notion of geography. Modeled after Mela and Strabo, his text was an engaging description of places and their ornaments – peoples, animals, plants, rocks, historical and mythological events – while his maps, made according to Ptolemy's grid, represented ancient and modern places mathematically.[19]

As time passed, modern maps increased steadily from edition to edition, eventually outnumbering the Ptolemaic maps, while at the same time Ptolemy's text was complemented with modern commentaries conveying new information regarding projections, instruments, travels, and lands. Unlike northern editors of the sixteenth century, such as Willibald Pirckheimer, Desiderius Erasmus, and Gerhard Mercator, who regarded Ptolemy's text as historical and thus deleted modern commentaries and maps from their editions, Italian scholars regarded their editions as a *summa* of modern geography. Giacomo Gastaldi and Girolamo Ruscelli, who published editions in Venice in 1548 and 1561, respectively, with over a hundred modern maps, produced not only the earliest translations into any vernacular language but also the earliest map books that intercalated Ptolemaic and modern maps. Unlike earlier

---

[18] On city views, see Nuti (1994); and Ballon/Friedman (2007).   [19] See Roberts (2013).

editors who had published modern maps as a separate appendix at the end of the book, Gastaldi and Ruscelli placed them in correspondence with the pertinent Ptolemaic map, so that the modern map of northern Europe followed Ptolemy's maps of the old continent, the map of the newly discovered Moluccas islands completed Ptolemy's maps of Asia, and so forth (Figs. 3.3 and 3.4). By intercalating the modern maps with the Ptolemaic maps these late-sixteenth-century editors integrated, graphically and conceptually, Ptolemy's authority with modern cartography. They made explicit that the mapping of the modern world was accommodated within the study of ancient geography, indeed it was structured according to Ptolemy's authority, just as the natural world was organized according to Pliny, and architecture was measured according to Vitruvius.

Another way to integrate ancient and modern geography is exemplified by the magnificent world map that the Camaldolese monk Fra Mauro made in Venice in the mid fifteenth century (Fig. 3.5). Although Fra Mauro was well informed about ancient and modern geography and certainly knew Ptolemy's text – it is quoted repeatedly here – he chose to disregard Ptolemy's cartographic grid and instead modeled his map after medieval *mappaemundi*. He represented the three continents circled by the oceans and filled his map with inscriptions pertaining to trading routes, spices, luxury goods, wonders, botany, zoology, ethnography, and religious beliefs and practices. He surrounded the globe with cosmographical diagrams and boldly moved Paradise outside the Earth's geographical perimeter. In addition to the wide range of ancient geographical literature available to him through the rich libraries of his monastic order, Fra Mauro had easy access to first-hand information from merchants and sailors who often visited him in the monastery of San Marco on the island of Murano; and his friend and collaborator, the mapmaker and traveler Andrea Bianco, brought him Portuguese charts from which he learned about the shape of the African coast, the Atlantic islands, and northern Europe. Arab maps provided the inverted orientation for Fra Mauro's map, with south at the top, and they showed him that the Indian Ocean was an open sea filled with islands. With the help of the painter Francesco da Cherso, Fra Mauro combined these heterogeneous elements on a large parchment sheet about 6 feet square, and the resulting map visualized the new and the old worlds so effectively that the king of Portugal, owner of the most up-to-date maps, commissioned a copy for the considerable sum of 62 ducats.

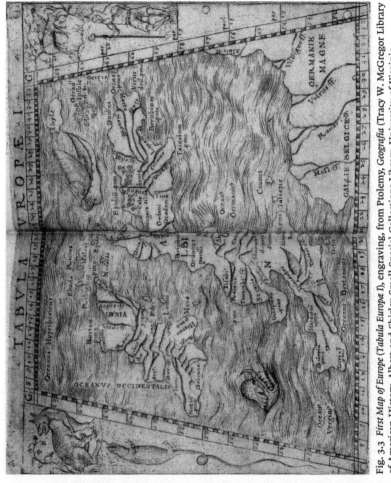

Fig. 3.3 *First Map of Europe* (*Tabula Europe I*), engraving, from Ptolemy, *Geografia* (Tracy W. McGregor Library of American History, Albert and Shirley Small Special Collections Library, University of Virginia, Charlottesville).

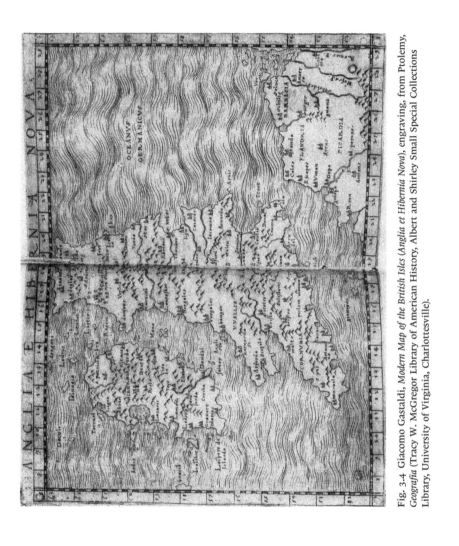

Fig. 3.4 Giacomo Gastaldi, *Modern Map of the British Isles* (*Anglia et Hibernia Nova*), engraving, from Ptolemy, *Geografia* (Tracy W. McGregor Library of American History, Albert and Shirley Small Special Collections Library, University of Virginia, Charlottesville).

Fig. 3.5 Fra Mauro, *World Map* (1459, illuminated manuscript on vellum, Venice, Biblioteca Nazionale Marciana).

The most reliable information regarding voyages and mercantile trading routes was found in nautical charts made for the Portuguese and Spanish kings. Treated as secret documents and jealously kept from public view, these maps have not survived and are known only indirectly, through the illegal copies commissioned by other European rulers. One of the most accurate and spectacular of these was made in Lisbon for Alberto Cantino, the Ferrarese ambassador at the Portuguese court, who paid 12 gold ducats for it (Fig. 3.6). Cantino was well aware that this smuggled nautical chart would have been highly appreciated by Duke Ercole d'Este, whose ancestors had recognized the importance of geography and the prestige associated with map ownership since the early fifteenth century. In 1435–37, Borso d'Este had commissioned

Fig. 3.6 The *Cantino Map* (1502, Biblioteca Estense Universitaria, Modena).

Guglielmo Capello to update the long didactic poem *Dittamondo*, a popular travelogue of an imaginary journey around Europe and Africa written in Dantean tercets by the Florentine Fazio degli Uberti, but left unfinished at its author's death in 1367. Around 1450, Borso was able to acquire a precious Catalan world map (now in Modena) thanks to his familial and political connections with the Aragonese king of Naples; and following his father's lead, Ercole d'Este had his children's tutor, the humanist Guarino Guarini, translate Strabo into Latin.

Based on secret Portuguese charts and travel reports, the *Cantino Map* was never intended for navigation but rather as a presentation map, and its cartographic features declare its princely destination. Rhumb lines coexist with the equator and the tropics, which are proper to medieval *mappaemundi* and Ptolemaic maps; coastlines and port names, typically recorded in sea charts, mingle with city views and landscape details in bright color, useless for sailors but extremely informative for armchair travelers. Notable are the trees and parrots along the coast of Brazil. They are represented in an odd, albeit effective, perspective that combines the plan-view of the general chart with the perspective-view of the trees as they would appear from a moving ship. Elaborate legends inform about the richness of West Africa: gold, slaves, pepper, and other highly valued items. An inscription situated near Sumatra asserts its identification with Taprobana, the mythical island described by Ptolemy as rich in "gold, silver, precious stones, and pearls and very big and fine rubies and all kind of spices and silks and brocades,"[20] that Renaissance mapmakers had difficulty in placing on their maps. Clearly marked is the line of Tordesillas that the Spanish Pope Alexander VI established to divide Portuguese and Spanish conquests overseas, while the same nations' flags mark their respective dominions of ports, lands, and trade routes throughout the world. Mathematically and chorographically, the *Cantino Map* charted new lands, overseas dominions, and exotic goods.

Typical of the maps that reached the wider public is the small copper engraving made by the Florentine Francesco Rosselli in Venice in 1507, possibly in relation to a pocket edition of Ptolemy's *Geography* which was never realized (Fig. 3.7).[21] Conceived as a Ptolemaic map based on

---

[20] Brotton (1997) 22–26. On the *Cantino Map*, see also Baldacci (1993) 53–57; and Caraci Luzzana (1996–99) 478–80.

[21] Woodward (2001); and Boorsch (2004).

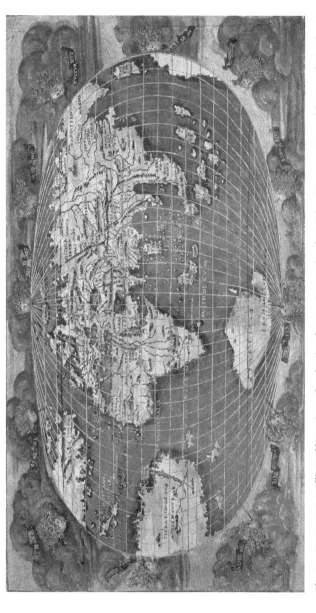

Fig. 3.7 Francesco Rosselli, *World Map* (1507, hand-painted engraving, National Maritime Museum, Greenwich, United Kingdom).

a cartographic grid, it recorded modern discoveries much more approximately than the *Cantino Map*, but its aim was to reach a large international public, as suggested by its Latin inscriptions. An illuminator, engraver, and the owner of a successful print shop in Florence, Francesco Rosselli created a new projection for his world map, that made it possible to represent the globe with minimal distortion. This globe is divided into two hemispheres, one representing Europe and Africa, the other Asia and America. The first hemisphere is represented at the center of the map, while the second is divided into two crescents, each of them attached to the sides of the first hemisphere. The resulting image is an unbroken panorama of the Earth from America to Asia, an unprecedented image of the globe offered to the human eye from a point of view that no one, not even God, could enjoy from the heavens. Like Fra Mauro's world map and the *Cantino Map*, Rosselli's panoramic view of the world was also based on heterogeneous sources: modern travel reports, ancient texts, and religious writings. A masterful synthesis from different sources is the label that Rosselli used to identify the West Indies, *Terra Sancta Crucis sive Mondus Novus* [The Holy Land of the Cross or the New World]. The traveler Pedro Alvares Cabral, who landed in Brazil in 1500, had named it *Terra Crucis* [Land of the Cross]; Cabral's patron, King Manuel of Portugal, added the adjective *Santa* [Holy]; while the alternative name *Mundus Novus* [New World] referred to the title of Vespucci's printed travel report of 1504 (or 1505), in which he had suggested that Brazil was on a different continent. Rosselli's ambivalence about the status of the West Indies appears throughout his map. Unable to decide whether the West Indies were in Asia, as Columbus believed, or on a different continent, as Vespucci suggested, he combined both options in his map: he accepted Vespucci's name *Mundus Novus*, but he also labeled places in Asia with the names that Columbus had assigned to the new lands he "discovered," which were on the new continent but which Columbus believed throughout his life were located in Asia. Finally, in this newly discovered land, Rosselli placed four large rivers, which perhaps represent schematically the large rivers of South America but which, in their symmetrical convergence, recall too closely the four rivers of Paradise. Indeed, having lost its place in the old world, Paradise seems to have been relocated in the newly discovered one.

A culminating synthesis of Renaissance cartography is Giacomo Gastaldi's *Cosmographia universalis* [Universal Cosmography], published in Venice in 1561, a magnificent nine-sheet woodcut representing the

Earth's globe (Fig. 3.8).[22] The Piedmontese Gastaldi worked as a civic
engineer for the Venetian republic and acquired a solid reputation for
both the maps of his 1548 edition of Ptolemy's *Geography* and Ramusio's
collections of geographical writings. For his world map he adopted
Rosselli's oval projection, complementing it with other images. At the
top, portraits of Strabo and Ptolemy stand symbolically for descriptive
and mathematical geography, the two branches of ancient geography
that were reunited in Renaissance maps, while personifications of cosmography and astronomy hold their respective instruments, an armil-
lary sphere and a globe. Terrestrial globes and celestial charts adorn the
corners, relating geography to cosmography. Gastaldi ordered this
cosmographical representation of the world around the city of Venice,
represented with an allegorical personification and the lion of St. Mark,
the symbol of the city's patron saint. Compiled from a multitude of
published and unpublished sources Gastaldi had obtained from his
friend Ramusio, this map made available to a large public coasts and
islands mapped by Portuguese and Spanish sailors, relating them to
ancient geographical knowledge. Similarly to Fra Mauro, Gastaldi
filled his world map with a plethora of qualitative details. Philip II's
imperial ship crosses the Atlantic, marking Spanish ownership of
Atlantic trade routes, while the Strait of Anian, a fictional sea passage
between Asia and Africa, is prominently displayed for the first time
(it will reappear in many later maps). Legends, cartouches, and inscriptions inform the viewer about the main geographic features of the
mapped territory, the coordinates of its major cities, the main rivers
and lakes, the mountain chains and the flat lands as well as the ethnography and history of their diverse peoples, their habits and beliefs, and
the look of their dwellings and their costumes. These descriptive elements are represented on a larger scale than the mapped territory itself
and are represented in perspective rather than in orthographic view.
Gastaldi's map was ostensibly different from Ptolemy's maps, but the
difference involved not so much the cartographic accuracy of the
mapped places or the extent of the known world (this would hardly
be surprising), but rather its very content, which was both mathematical and descriptive.

---

[22] On G. Gastaldi's *Cosmographia universalis* (Venice, 1561), see Shirley (1983) 122–23; and
Karrow (1993) 240–41. Gastaldi's world map is known only through a seventeenth-
century reprint, now at the British Library in London, though it was accompanied by a
booklet that survives in numerous copies.

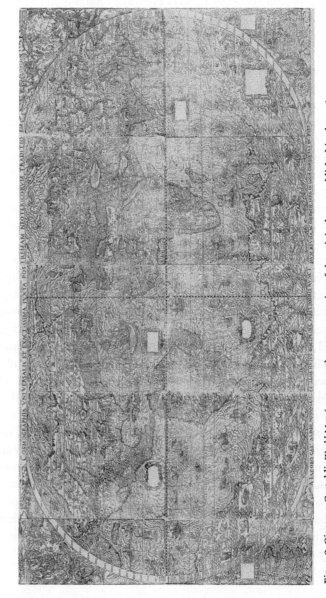

Fig. 3.8 Giacomo Gastaldi, *World Map* (seventeenth-century reprint of the original map published in the 1561 *Cosmographia universalis*, The British Library, London).

The maps we have examined embodied the comprehensive Renaissance notion of geography. They effectively combined in one single image different systems of representation: the orthographic grid; the bird's-eye prospect; and the perspective view. While maintaining the Ptolemaic grid of coordinates, they also included additional qualitative descriptions of places in the form of lengthy legends, lively vignettes, and proliferating inscriptions, which were not mere embellishments of the cartographic content but rather an integral part of the map. These maps reflected Renaissance knowledge of geography and place-names (toponymy), but they also illustrated the history of a territory and its inhabitants, integrating geographical descriptions with historical, mythological, botanical, and zoological details. Ptolemy's Taprobana had to find a place on modern maps, and – conversely – newly found lands had to be located in relation to Ptolemy's coordinates. To please the expectations of their audience of kings, merchants, and humanists, Renaissance mapmakers made their maps according to Ptolemy's grid and then filled them with descriptions of marvelous details ransacked from Strabo, Mela, Pliny, and the Bible. As contradictory as it may seem to us, Renaissance cartographers were convinced that the shape of the modern world could emerge only by combining modern measurements with classical texts, mathematical geography with humanistic philology. As skilled mathematicians but also as experts on ancient cultures, dealers in antiquities, philologists, or, at the very least, friends of accomplished scholars, the cartographers compiled comparative lists of ancient and modern place-names, made historical maps and discussed ancient geography in the legends of their maps. Systematically intermingling Renaissance geography with traditional and mythical toponymy, features, and legends, Renaissance mapmakers constructed a complex image of a place. The cultural value of their maps resided precisely in such a syncretistic approach to different sources in terms of accuracy, chronology, and origin. For Renaissance mapmakers and their public, a map came to be an encyclopedic description of the world projected onto an accurate geographical framework.

4

Artists' workshops

The workshop was at the heart of the thriving craft industries in the Italian Renaissance. Carpenters, coopers, bakers, shoemakers and painters, sculptors, bronze-casters, ceramicists, goldsmiths, and architects – all were *artigiani* [craftsmen].[1] In the Renaissance the term *artista* [artist] applied only to the student of the seven liberal arts: the *trivium* of grammar, logic, and rhetoric and the *quadrivium* of arithmetic, geometry, music, and astronomy.[2] While artists, as we will anachronistically refer to them here, aspired to the status enjoyed by liberal artists, very few achieved it. They were craftsmen and like their fellow craftsmen they produced functional and decorative products in a workshop setting. In cities such as Florence where the craft industries were particularly vital, this workshop environment became an integral part of the social and economic structure.[3] Each firm was headed up by a *maestro del bottega* [workshop master] who had been vetted by his colleagues as knowledgeable in his craft and capable of training others in the same. He was skilled in assessing materials, negotiating with vendors and patrons, in training and managing employees, entering into contracts, paying the bills, and investing the profits. His ability to manufacture quality products in a timely and cost-efficient manner ensured his success and that of his workshop.

The artist's products were meant to serve a broad range of purposes, from the facilitation of devotion to the inspiration of love or desire, from the production of awe, admiration, and obedience to the construction

---

[1] On the artist as craftsman see Wackernagel (1981); Cole (1983); Thomas (1995); and Burke (1999).
[2] Hughes, (1986) 59.   [3] Rubin/Wright (1999) 82.

of personal and political agendas. A group of nuns, for instance, might commission an altarpiece for their convent chapel with the intent of inspiring devotion and honoring a patron saint. A successful merchant might purchase a ready-made image of the Virgin and Child for his home in order to provide his sons with an example of the obedient and devoted child. Or a notary might commission a painter to embellish his home with painted bedstand, chairs, bed-curtains, and wainscoting to impress his extended family. Yet another patron might commission a goldsmith to design and engrave a silver chalice to donate to a church or hire a painter to draw embroidery patterns for a liturgical garment. A recently betrothed man might commission a carpenter to build a set of fine chests to present to his new bride and then engage a painter to ornament these with stories of virtuous and chaste women of biblical fame. And a banker might engage a painter and sculptor to embellish his private family chapel in order to publicly demonstrate his piety and simultaneously celebrate his wealth and family name.[4]

Images were also commissioned by governing bodies and individuals. In a republic, oligarchs would engage a sculptor to carve an image of the city's patron saint, employ a painter to fresco the walls of the hall of state, and hire an architect to design fortifications for the city walls. A duke, too, would employ artisans to these ends and others that brought honor to his person and reputation. This might include commissioning a goldsmith to create a medal adorned with his likeness or hiring an architect to design a spectacular villa and garden. Rulers and republics as well as wealthy families and small corporations would employ painters, woodworkers, architects, and sculptors to design images that were also portable, ephemeral, or both. Indeed, artists would design and create things that we might not consider art objects today: painted pennants, draperies, wooden shields, engraved silver helmets, and horse trappings for tournaments, for instance, or full-scale arches, carts, stage sets, and costumes for triumphal processions.[5] Groups such as confraternities, too, would commission objects such as painted cloth banners to carry as they processed through the streets on the feast-day of their patron saint.

---

[4] For artistic patronage in general, see Chambers (1971); and for an interesting series of documents related to the patronage of artists, see Gilbert (1980).
[5] See Goldthwaite (1993).

We get a fuller idea of the images artists were asked to create when we look at the contracts they drew up with their patrons.[6] We are fortunate that Florence was a city of notaries, merchants, bankers, and businessmen – all of whom shared a penchant for documentation.[7] As a result, the Florentine archives are rich with contracts which tell us that most patrons were concerned with four things. In painting contracts, the first of these indicated what was to be painted; the second, the payment amount and terms. In some cases this was contingent upon an appraisal of the work by the patron or by a committee of artists. Also stated in many contracts was the date the work was to be completed or delivered, often followed by a provision for levying a penalty upon the artist if the deadline was not met. The third concern of most contracts was for the value and amount of materials to be used. The gold and ultramarine used in most panel paintings in the fifteenth century, for instance, was the topic of many a clause stipulating quality, quantity, and price. Patrons also included in these contracts a fourth stipulation that the most important elements of an image were to be executed by the master alone and not by his assistants. At the beginning of the fifteenth century the patron's concern for the quality and price of precious materials took precedence over his concern for which parts of the painting would be executed by the hand of the master. By the end of the century, this priority was reversed. Patrons were more interested in making known their ability to purchase the skilled hand of the master than in the costly materials he manipulated.[8] For the painter's part, the main concerns as reflected in these contracts were for enough assistants and materials, workshop space, and room and board if the work was to be executed on site. However, there is also a great deal about the relationship between artists and patrons that contracts cannot tell us, primarily about the oral communication that must have occurred between them and that would have been so important in determining the finished product. Here, in this more elusive interaction between artist and patron, much of the creative relationship likely occurred.

---

[6] See O'Malley (2005).

[7] Many of the examples used in this chapter are Florentine, for which there is good reason: a large proportion of the extant documents dealing with Italian artists' workshops and training come from Florentine archives and, as a result, much of the scholarly research on this topic has been centered on the artists and practices of this city. Where possible, I include examples from other geographical regions in this account. For Genoa and Bologna, for example, see respectively Lukehart (1993) and Feigenbaum (1993).

[8] See Baxandall (1972) 1–29; and Glasser (1977).

The artist's workshop was a physical site as well as a commercial enterprise and the manufacture of objects required ample space to house materials, tools, products, and workers as well as plentiful natural light to facilitate production. These spaces were sometimes associated with the master's living quarters but were more often set up outside the home in districts occupied by fellow craftsmen. For larger or site-specific projects, an artist would often set up a workshop in a space provided by the patron since it was easier to move the master, tools, and workers to the materials and site than the other way around. This was the case for the Florentine sculptor Donatello, who was assigned a chapel in the city's Duomo as his workspace when commissioned to execute sculptures for the church exterior.

The workshop was also the place where the master trained his apprentices and assistants, the majority of whom had been born to the trade rather than called to it through creative impulse. The Florentine bronze-caster and sculptor Lorenzo Ghiberti, for instance, belonged to a family firm that was founded by his father and spanned five generations. The Venetian painters Marietta, Domenico, and Marco Tintoretto were also trained in the workshop of their renowned father.[9] The Florentine ceramic sculptor Andrea della Robbia learned the trade under the tutelage of his famous uncle, Luca della Robbia, who ultimately bequeathed to him his workshop; in turn, Andrea trained his sons in the family business and bequeathed it to them. This practice of keeping the business in the family had several economic advantages. In Venice, for example, stone-carvers could avoid the limit normally imposed on the number of apprentices they could have if these apprentices were family members.[10] In many cases artists would marry into artist families, even if they weren't born into them. This was a normal custom for artisans of any trade, allowing them to consolidate equipment and clientele and sometimes gain a skilled partner in the process. The Paduan painter and printmaker Andrea Mantegna, for instance, married the daughter of the Venetian painter Jacopo Bellini, and the Sienese painter Simone Martini wed the daughter of his compatriot, Memmo di Filipuccio, each of them gaining a painter brother-in-law in the process.

---

[9] Girls rarely apprenticed in the workshops of artists, and those who did were the daughters of the masters who ran them; see Frick *et al.* (2007).

[10] Further, sons who trained in the workshops of their fathers did not have to pay an entrance fee to the guild; see Connell (1988) 55. For documents related to workshop practices in Venice, see Chambers *et al.* (1992).

Those who entered the artist's workshop from outside a family structure were more likely motivated by parental dictate than by aptitude or desire. Their fathers, most of whom were craftsmen in other trades, considered arts such as painting, sculpting, and printmaking to be solid occupations and contracted with artists to teach their youngsters the skills of the trade. The Florentine painter Andrea del Sarto, for instance, was placed in an apprenticeship by his father, a tailor; Mantegna, by his father, a carpenter; the Florentine sculptor and painter Andrea del Verrocchio, by his father, a brickmaker; the painter Piero della Francesca from Borgo San Sepolcro, by his father, a tanner; and the Florentine painter Francesco Salviati, by his father, a weaver. Of course, well-known artists such as these were exceptionally talented, but it is important to note that natural talent was not a requisite for becoming an apprentice. Skills in painting, sculpting, and metalwork could be taught. If a youngster brought natural talent to the endeavor, all the better. In Florence, youths who were wards of the Ospedale degli Innocenti, or foundling home, were also placed as apprentices in the workshops of local craftsmen. As administrator of the Innocenti, the historian and philologist Vincenzo Borghini saw it as part of his civic and humanitarian mission to apprentice these youths in Florentine *botteghe*. A friend to many of the painters in Florence, he placed these wards in apprenticeships with such important practitioners as Agnolo Bronzino, Giorgio Vasari, and Alessandro Allori.[11]

The average age of a beginning apprentice was thirteen. At this age most boys would have had some primary schooling and thus would have known how to read and write in the vernacular language and some would have attended abacus school where they would have learned how to cipher well enough to succeed in the merchant class.[12] Very few, however, went to grammar school where they would have learned how to read and write in Latin. Apprenticeships could range from several months to several years, but the average was about three years, the amount of time specified in a contract drawn up in 1469 between the woolworker Agostino di Luca and the Florentine painter Neri di Bicci, himself the son and grandson of a painter. Here, Neri agrees to train Agostino's son and to pay him 88 lire, an amount he would disburse to the boy in gradually increasing sums over the

---

[11] Pilliod (2001).   [12] Ames-Lewis (2000).

three years.[13] Often masters would feed, clothe, and shelter their apprentices in addition to, or in lieu of, paying them a small wage. There was one type of apprentice, however, who did not receive a wage, and this was the slave. Although we might not imagine that Renaissance Italians had slaves, documents indicate that, at least in Venice, there were indeed slaves in artisan workshops. Susan Connell cites one example of the Venetian stone-carver Martino, who in a will of 15 July, 1405 was freed by his owner Gerardo di Mainardo to work as a stonemason in his own right.[14]

Parental dictate and slavery aside, most apprentices who were not born into an artisan family came to the task more or less freely and many formed such a strong attachment to the master and his family that they ultimately took his surname as their own. Once a youth entered a workshop he would learn a specific set of skills based upon the arts practiced there. This tradition was one that developed in the medieval workshop and continued with gradual modification into the Renaissance.[15] In the workshops of potters and ceramic sculptors, for instance, *discepoli* [beginners] started out performing elementary tasks such as straining clay to remove chalk, shell, and other impurities.[16] In a painter's workshop, they would begin as errand boys, bringing in the firewood to heat the workshop, grinding pigments on a marble slab, collecting eggs to create tempera paint, and plucking hairs from the pelts of boars to make paintbrushes. As his training advanced, the apprentice would learn and perform more skill-based tasks. In the painter's workshop these would include mixing the gesso, or plaster, that would be used to coat the strips of linen that covered the panels used in painting as well as burnishing these strips with the tooth of a carnivorous animal.

These workshop practices and others were codified by the painter Cennino Cennini in the earliest known Italian treatise on the art of painting, *Il libro dell'arte* [The Book of Art] (*c.* 1390).[17] A recipe-book of sorts for "the use and good and profit of anyone who wants to pursue this art,"[18] this work, as Anabel Thomas has observed, often describes

---

[13] Thomas (1995) 71.
[14] Connell (1988) 71, 88. On slavery in Renaissance Italy, see Epstein (1996) and (2001).
[15] See Dempsey (1980).   [16] Piccolpasso (1980).
[17] For an analysis of the late medieval painting practices described by Cennini, see Bomford *et al.* (1989).
[18] Translation slightly modified from Cennini (1960).

the painter's methods in terms associated with cooking and baking.[19] In his instructions for making the gesso used in panel painting, for instance, Cennini instructs the painter to:

> Take a new casserole, which is not greasy; and if it is glazed, so much the better. Take the loaf of this gesso, and with a penknife cut it thin, as if you were cutting cheese; and put it into this casserole. Then pour some of the size [a glutinous thinner] over it; and proceed to break up this gesso with your hand, as if you were making a batter for pancakes, smoothly and deftly, so that you do not get it frothy. Then have a kettle of water, and get it quite hot, and place this casserole of tempered gesso over it. And this keeps the gesso warm for you; and do not let it boil, for if it boiled it would be ruined.[20]

In many such recipes, in fact, the painter is advised to use the same materials as cooks and bakers as well as the same methods. In Cennini's instructions on how to make the crushed-bone powder used to coat boxwood drawing tablets, he instructs the beginner to use "bone from the second joints and wings of fowls, or of a capon" adding that "the older they are the better." How old depended on how often the floor was swept, for the reader is here advised to look for these bones under the dining table.[21]

Some of the ingredients required in these recipes would have made even the most adventurous of cooks balk. In a recipe for glue used to temper colors, thicken gessos, and fasten pieces of wood, for instance, Cennini advises the painter to use clippings from the muzzles, feet, and sinews of goats. After bringing these to a boil and reducing the water to almost half, he states, the painter should strain the mixture into "flat dishes, like jelly molds or basins" and let it stand overnight. In the morning, "an ideal glue will result," he states, if the gelatinous mixture is cut "with a knife into slices like bread; [and] put...on a mat to dry in the wind."[22]

In a sixteenth-century treatise on sculpture, the goldsmith and sculptor Benvenuto Cellini also takes the cook's approach to preparing some less than savory ingredients. In a recipe for making the plaster for casting molds he advises the sculptor to add a moist solution of strained and washed horse dung to a mixture of gesso and ground oxen horn.[23]

[19] Thomas (1995) 149ff.   [20] Cennini (1960) 72.   [21] Ibid. 5.
[22] Ibid. 67.   [23] Cellini (1967) 112.

In treatises such as these two, the emphasis is on the mundane working practices that originated in the medieval workshop. In most Renaissance treatises on the arts, however, a theoretical approach was more common than a practical one, suggesting that the concept of the artist's training was expanding to include the liberal arts, a concept that will be explored more fully below.

As the apprentice advanced in his training he moved from preparing raw materials to acquiring the skills of imitation. For virtually all artists this meant learning how to draw. The draftsman's education – whether that of the painter, woodworker, marble sculptor, ceramicist, engraver, or architect – began with copying drawings or tracing them with a piece of parchment oiled especially for this purpose. The fifteenth-century apprentice would begin by copying from workshop model-books, bound collections of silverpoint drawings filled with pictorial motifs drawn from other works of art. More popular in the aristocratic courts of the north than the merchant cultures of the south, these books were filled with lifeless, stock images of animals, figures, and antique motifs that artists sometimes literally copied into paintings.[24]

Cennini recommended that the fifteenth-century draftsman first take up silverpoint, a form of drawing executed by dragging a silver stylus over a boxwood tablet coated with a mixture of pulverized bone and saliva.[25] The fine residue of silver left by the stylus on this coating would oxidize to create lines much like those created by a hard graphite pencil. Shading was achieved through making parallel strokes, or hatching, that would combine to create areas of modulated tonal density. The problem with silverpoint drawing was that it was virtually impossible to erase. The two advantages it offered the beginning draftsman, however, outweighed this liability. The first was that silverpoint required careful and controlled movements, just the kind called for by a hand in training. The second was that the coated surface of the panel could be scraped down and recoated again and again.[26] In a period when paper (made from cloth rags) was expensive and difficult to come by, silverpoint drawing was an economic means of providing the beginning draftsman the materials he needed to practice his skills.

In the late fifteenth and early sixteenth centuries, the use of model-books gave way to more experimental drawing practices. The artist in

---

[24] Ames-Lewis/Wright (1983) 43, 99.   [25] Cennini (1960) 4–5.   [26] *Ibid.* 44.

training copied instead from loose sketches, figure studies, sketch-books, and prints. Indeed, with the availability of paper in the sixteenth century, metalpoint drawing was abandoned in favor of charcoal, a medium that was much easier to manipulate and that could be erased with a brush of the hand, a feather, or with *midolle*, the small pieces of soft bread that were most commonly used for this purpose. Charcoal was also a medium that encouraged experimentation. It was more fluid and spontaneous and its impermanence made it useful for sketching out preliminary forms and compositions that could be worked over in other media.

The most permanent of these media was pen and ink made from oak-gall, a medium that would have been particularly familiar to hands trained to write and calculate with a quill pen. Ink was also used in relief drawing, the imitation of three-dimensional forms through monochro-matic constructions of light and shadow. In the workshop, most of these three-dimensional forms were plaster casts of antique sculptural frag-ments which the apprentice would imitate with brush and ink or with chalk, another drawing medium embraced in the sixteenth century for its ability to provide tonal depth and range. For the beginning painter, learning to imitate forms in this manner provided the first step in learning the art of painting itself.

Relief drawing was also important to the training of the sculptor and many a three-dimensional image was first conceived on a two-dimensional surface. Not all sculptors, however, were adept at the more traditional methods of drawing. It was for this reason that Giorgio Vasari, in the technical introduction to his *Vite de' più eccellenti pittori, scultori e architettori* [Lives of the Most Excellent Painters, Sculptors, and Architects, 1550 and 1568], advised those "sculptors who have not much practice in lines and contours, and therefore cannot draw on paper," to create the same effects by sketching "in clay or wax, fashioning men, animals, and other things in relief."[27] Such three-dimensional sketches, or *bozzetti*, were constructed out of beeswax, paraffin, or clay and were often built over an armature of gesso or metal rods. Created in partial or full scale, these three-dimensional sketches were used by sculptors, painters, goldsmiths, and architects alike to arrive at a form, demonstrate a conception to a prospective patron, or guide the efforts of a workshop.

---

[27] Translation slightly modified from Vasari (1960) 206.

The draftsman's training took place outside the workshop as well as in it, in the churches, hospitals, squares, gardens, and public buildings that housed some of the most important works of the time. In Florence, for instance, aspiring and experienced artists alike would go out to copy works such as Masaccio's frescoes in the Brancacci chapel, Leonardo's cartoon in the Palazzo Vecchio, or Michelangelo's sculptures in the Medici chapel. Once Pope Sixtus IV approved the practice of dissecting human bodies in a papal brief of 1482, they would also go out to practice anatomical drawing, witnessing public dissections and conducting anatomies in local hospitals.[28] Drawing the anatomized body allowed artists to understand better the substructure of sinews, bones, muscles, and tendons that produced the contours, shadows, and lights they saw on the surface of the human form. One of the most talented anatomical draftsmen of the sixteenth century, Allori, was so devoted to the practice of anatomical drawing that he performed it in his workshop and stored partially dissected limbs under the beds of his apprentices. One such youth, Lodovico Cigoli, was so overwhelmed by the odor of decay that he took ill and was forced to temporarily retire from his studies.

More often, however, the student of drawing found himself sketching from live bodies, usually those of other apprentices posed as shepherds, the Virgin, or even suspended from the ceiling by ropes in the guise of angels. Apprentices and masters alike would draw these figures in their entirety as well as in parts, refining their skills through detailed studies of heads, hands, feet, and limbs. Life-drawing was encouraged by many artists, including Leonardo, who advised the young painter to carry a *taccuino* or sketchbook with him so that he could record the natural movements of men in their daily labors.[29] Workshop drawing exercises also included drawing from the nude, a practice that developed in the fifteenth century and quickly became the foundation of drawing activities in the shop.[30] In most workshops, custom dictated that these nudes were male and many of the female bodies we see in Renaissance paintings and drawings started out as such. Leon Battista Alberti, the author of the first theoretical treatise on the art of painting, considered the study of the nude to be fundamental to the painter's practice. In his *De pictura* [On Painting] (1435) – which he translated from the original Latin into the vernacular a year later – he advises the painter

---

[28] See Schultz (1985); and Cazort (1996).   [29] Leonardo (2001a) 198–99.
[30] Ames-Lewis/Wright (1983) 178.

to draw upon his knowledge of anatomy and the nude to construct figures from the inside out, starting with the bones, clothing these with flesh, and, finally, attiring this fleshed-out form with draperies.[31] Not surprisingly, chalk – red and black – was the favored medium for imitating the contours and tonal modulations found on the surface of these nude and clothed human forms.

Drawing from direct observation of the natural world taught apprentices how to record in a graphic language what they saw and understood of the world around them. Indeed, line was not to be found in nature but was something the artist superimposed upon the visual world to structure and record it. The importance of this ability to control and convey information through line may well be the reason why so many artists chose to train in the workshops of Florentine goldsmiths. There they found the "rigorous training in draughtsmanship and design" that they needed to pursue most any art.[32] Among the many painters and sculptors that began their careers in the workshops of goldsmiths were Botticelli, Ghirlandaio, Verrocchio, and Antonio del Pollaiuolo. The Florentine architects Filippo Brunelleschi and Michelozzo di Bartolomeo were also trained in the workshops of goldsmiths. Indeed, since architecture was not viewed as a separate craft in the Renaissance, architects were by necessity trained in other media.

In addition to learning how to master the art of drawing, the advancing apprentice would learn how to manipulate the tools of his chosen art(s).[33] For painters, this meant learning to control a brush loaded with pigment suspended in water, oil, or egg yolk, and to calculate the viscosity and drying time of these materials in order to produce the desired effect. For marble sculptors this entailed learning how to use different saws, hammers, and claws in order to block out the figure, as well as how to employ chisels, drills, files, and abrasives to bring it to completion. For wood sculptors, this involved learning how to wield an ax and mallet as well as use a plane and chisel, and for the ceramicist this would have required learning how to control the foot-driven potter's wheel or build an armature for a terracotta sculpture. These skills would have been different yet again for the bronze-caster, and would have

---

[31] Alberti (1966a) 11. By the end of the fifteenth century Alberti's own translation of *De pictura* had fallen out of circulation and was not available again until Lodovico Domenichi published his Italian translation of the original Latin text in 1547.

[32] Rubin/Wright (1999) 86.

[33] On artists' materials and a good relevant bibliography, see Welch (1997).

included learning how to chase the rough areas of a cast bronze and engrave details into its surface with a burin (a steel cutting-tool).

Perhaps the most important part of an apprentice's training, however, was copying the drawings and works of the master in order to acquire his manner. Once he had subsumed his own hand to that of the master the apprentice was ready to contribute to the works being produced by the shop. In the painter's workshop, this likely would have begun with enlarging the master's original compositional drawing to the same scale as the intended image. This was done by squaring, a process that involved drawing a grid over the original design so that it could be transferred square by square onto a larger drawing, also divided by a grid. These full-scale drawings, called cartoons and made up of several pieces of paper glued together, would be placed over the surface to be painted. The image would then be transferred onto this surface in one of several ways. One was by rubbing the back of the cartoon with charcoal and then tracing over the contours on the front in order to transfer these lines onto the surface below. Another was by pricking small holes along the contours of the cartoon and then tapping them with a bag of powdered charcoal or chalk so that the dust would leave a dotted underdrawing on the surface beneath it.[34] Yet another was to trace over the contour lines of the cartoon with a stylus, leaving indentations in the surface below.

At around this point in his career the artist in training would likely move from the position of apprentice to that of salaried assistant. In this capacity he would regularly contribute to the actual production of works.[35] In a painter's workshop this would often be in the form of adding in the background or landscape elements to a work or applying the extremely thin sheets of gold to halos and other elements. Later, as a more advanced assistant, he would contribute to the construction of the most important elements of the workshop's productions, perhaps painting the face and hands of an important figure or the draperies of another. Although most workshops were structured in this top–down manner some were less so. In the workshop of Raphael, at least, there was a creative and collaborative graphic dialogue that went all the way up the hierarchical ladder.[36]

[34] On cartoons, design transfer, and pouncing, see Bambach (1999).
[35] On artistic collaboration, see Sheard/Paoletti (1978); and Ladis/Wood (1992).
[36] See Ames–Lewis (1986); and Talvacchia (2005).

To matriculate from apprentice to master an artist had to submit a masterpiece to a board of guild masters. Guilds were the trade organizations that monitored standards of production, the setting of wages, and the training of apprentices. They also moderated disputes between artists and patrons if they arose. In addition, they instituted protectionist policies to prevent foreign artists from entering into the local market. Guilds and their associated confraternities also provided for the care of members and their families, providing burial expenses for the deceased as well as dowries for unmarried daughters. In Florence, painters belonged to the *Arte dei Medici e Speziali* [guild of physicians, apothecaries, and spice dealers] because the *speziali* supplied artists with some of the basic materials with which they prepared their work surfaces. The use of common materials was also the reason that goldsmiths belonged to the guild of gold beaters and gold-thread spinners; and shared materials *and* tools explains why wood-, stone-, and marble-carvers belonged to the same guild as carpenters.

Once an artist was vetted – and once he had paid the significant guild fees – he was considered a master and free to open his own firm. Many, however, did not have the capital to open up a practice of their own and instead formed temporary partnerships with other newly matriculated masters in order to share the costs of setting up shop. Still others worked for wages in the shops of established masters as collaborators or assistants. In some instances they would contract to use the facilities with the agreement that they would share a percentage of any profits they earned while doing so.[37] Those artists who did establish their own workshops were faced with an expensive proposition. They needed to have the resources to rent or purchase a building and equipment, and to pay apprentices and assistants. If he was fortunate, a newly minted master would have learned from his own master the administrative, fiscal, and management skills that he would need to have in order to survive. As we have seen, these included knowing how to assess the quality of materials, negotiate with vendors and patrons, manage employees, enter into contracts, pay the bills, and invest the profits. If he was particularly fortunate, he would also have shared in the established reputation and clientele of the master with whom he trained.

[37] Thomas (1995) 76.

As grounded as artists were in the manual activities of producing objects, some of them sought to graft conceptual terms onto their traditional practices by equating their activities with the liberal arts. One of the primary ways in which they did so was through writing about their art in a theoretical manner. Cennini, for instance, stated that painting was the most learned of all the crafts and should be ranked among the arts and sciences. The first to undertake this project in earnest, however, was Alberti. Trained in the liberal arts himself at the university at Bologna, Alberti attempted to equate the painter with the liberal artist by emphasizing the importance of geometry to the painter's art and by describing the constituent elements of painting – drawing, composition, and coloring – in terms traditionally used to describe the parts of oratory.[38] Since Alberti was aware that most artists did not have the skills to access the classical Latin texts upon which he himself drew, he advises them to "associate with poets and orators who have many embellishments in common with painters and who have a broad knowledge of many things."[39]

The bronze-caster and goldsmith Lorenzo Ghiberti also attempted to elevate the status of his art through the format of a treatise. In his *Commentarii* [Commentaries], begun around 1447 and left incomplete at his death, Ghiberti constructed a venerable history of sculpture from antiquity to the present.[40] Drawing upon antique texts such as Vitruvius' *On Architecture* and Pliny's *Natural History*, Ghiberti also stressed the importance of having knowledge of the liberal arts as well as anatomy, medicine, and proportion.[41] Unlike Alberti, however, he includes in his work the first artist's biography – his own. Traditionally reserved for the lives of emperors, saints, kings, and popes, the genre of biography enabled Ghiberti to position the artist among the ranks of great men.

It was in the hands of the painter and architect Vasari, however, that the power of biography to elevate the status of the artist was fully realized. By the sixteenth century, artists, like merchants and bankers, were becoming more learned. The Florentine sculptors Benedetto and Giuliano da Maiano, for instance, owned numerous books including the Bible, lives of the emperors, contemporary and ancient histories, and

---

[38] Alberti (1966a) 89.   [39] *Ibid.* 90.
[40] Alberti, too, later embarked on the same endeavor for the arts of sculpture and architecture in, respectively, his *De statua* and *De architettura*.
[41] Ghiberti (1998) 46.

works by Dante and Boccaccio.[42] Vasari also read works such as these and drew upon them to construct an image of the artist as conceptual thinker in the *Lives*. He does this even in the technical introduction to the work, defining the art of *disegno* [both design and drawing], as "having its origins in the intellect" and concluding that it is nothing less than "a visible expression and declaration of our inner conception and of that which others have imagined or given form to in their idea."[43] Here, and in the earlier treatises of Alberti and Ghiberti, the artist as craftsman was being transformed into the artist as individual, intellectual, and creative agent.

As indicated by the fact that Alberti first published his *De pictura* in Latin, these treatises – often dedicated to wealthy, educated patrons first and fellow artists second – were written primarily to educate and entertain an audience of potential patrons. Although aspiring and established artists alike read them, the knowledge they gleaned from treatises was not the same as the knowledge they gained in the workshop. What they learned from reading was how to represent and conduct themselves in a manner that would enrich their art and lives, and obtain favor with patrons and fame among their countrymen. Instruction in the skills of their craft would remain in the workshop. This was the case even after a group of prominent Florentine artists, Vasari among them, founded the artists' Accademia del Disegno in 1562.

The term "academy" was first applied to the school of Plato, and in the Renaissance it was used to describe the many philosophical and literary societies that developed during this period. By using the term academy to describe their organization, Vasari and his colleagues hoped to invoke the prestige of the well-established literary and philosophical academies in Florence and to suggest that the three arts of *disegno* – painting, sculpture, and architecture – ranked among the liberal rather than the manual arts. As did the other academies, the Accademia del Disegno sponsored public lectures, in this case on topics such as mathematics, and offered instruction on life-drawing, drapery studies, and anatomy.[44] In the 1590s in Rome, under the leadership of the painter Federico Zuccaro, the Accademia di San Luca also developed a curriculum of drawing instruction and learned debates. It was not until the seventeenth century, however, that this curriculum was more than occasionally implemented.

---

[42] Burke (1999) 59ff.   [43] Vasari (1960) 205.   [44] Barzman (2000).

The sporadic instruction, lectures, and competitions organized by these academies may well have augmented a workshop education, but they by no means replaced it. Despite the best efforts of these and other Renaissance academicians of art, the artist's training would remain firmly grounded in the workshop tradition until well into the nine-teenth century. For the vigorously successful community of artists in the Renaissance, the workshop tradition was far from broken. It made no sense to try to fix it.

MICHAEL WYATT

5

Technologies

In the dedication of his *De divina proportione* [On Divine Proportion] to Ludovico Sforza in 1498, Luca Pacioli writes in a passage praising ancient and modern "machines and instruments" that "Federico da Montefeltro, illustrious Duke of Urbino, ordered that the base of the entire edifice of his noble and splendid palace in Urbino be covered with a stone frieze [worked by the] hands of most worthy stone-cutters and sculptors."[1] Even if Pacioli slightly exaggerates – the frieze extended over only the northern end of the long eastern façade that gives onto what is today called Piazza Rinascimentale, and continued along the north- and east-facing walls on Piazza Duca Federico, the *facciata ad ali* [L-shaped facade] and the principal entrance to the building – he draws attention to one of the least studied of the decorative details that once graced this building, widely regarded at the time and since to be among the supreme expressions of an Italian Renaissance architectural aesthetic: a series of seventy-two carved stone panels celebrating the mechanical arts associated with warfare and other technological achievements ancient and modern. Though educated in the noted humanist school of Vittorino da Feltre in Mantua, Federico made his name and fortune as a *condottiere*, a for-hire military commander active throughout central and northern Italy in the middle decades of the fifteenth century. The palaces he constructed in Urbino and Gubbio were meant to reflect the Duke's sophisticated culture, but the stone frieze in Urbino – removed from its original position in the mid eighteenth century – would also have served as a conspicuous public display of the means through which Federico had

<hr/>

[1] Pacioli (2009) 7^r.

achieved his power, similar in its conception, if not consistently in its realization, to the more private marriage of Renaissance technological and humanist cultures celebrated in the Duke's *studioli* [small studies] discussed below.

The stone *formelle* [panels] represent a broad range of combat and civil technologies as well as a series of panoplies and symbolic tableaux: various kinds of catapults; a *bastia* (or "Arab machine"), an assault vehicle in the form of a winged dragon that spews fire, mounted on axles connected by ropes and pulleys which permit it to be moved; both a trireme and quinquereme (Fig. 5.1), the ancient sailing ships; portable drawbridges; the *balista*, a mechanism resembling a crossbow with a screw-driven widget for launching arrows; several different kinds of watermill; a revolving crane (similar to one Filippo Brunelleschi used in the construction of the *cupola* [dome] of the Florence cathedral, and later drawn by Leonardo); a clock-bell mechanism; a water-driven saw; and a hoist for a pyramid consisting of four large nuts and vertically situated screws which when turned lift the object's support-planks, a device that may reflect the interest of Renaissance popes and their engineers in the displacement of such objects as they reconstructed Rome in their own images (Leonardo had a plan for raising the level of the Florence Baptistery with a similar device).[2]

There are earlier such sculptural depictions of technologies-in-action – the capitals of the *paratici* [tradesmen] in the cathedral of Piacenza, for instance – but the creators of such work were generally anonymous and the expertise that produced it was bound by the custom of medieval guilds jealous to guard their professional practices.[3] Realized in the mid 1470s, the Urbino frieze represents a singular effort at rendering visible a wide variety of technologies, but in addition to Federico's active role in the project we also know the names of its designers: initially Roberto Valturio, author of a famous treatise on ancient military practices (about which see below), illustrations for which served as the basis for

---

[2] The most complete study of the frieze is Bernini Pezzini (1985), but better reproductions of forty of the best-preserved panels are in Dal Poggetto (2003) 292–308; here the *formelle* – each measuring just under 3′ by 2′ – are arranged in a conjectural configuration of their original positions.

[3] See Long (2001) 88–96. Florentine exceptions to the usual anonymity of these artists are Andrea Pisano, who made the stone panels featuring technologies for Giotto's Campanile, and Nanni di Banco, who carved the panel of the *quattro coronati* [four martyrs] represented as sculptors for Orsanmichele.

Fig. 5.1 Ambrogio Barocci (after designs by Francesco di Giorgio Martini), *Quinquereme*, sailing ship with five oars (after 1475, Palazzo Ducale, Urbino).

many of the panels; and subsequently Francesco di Giorgio Martini, the Sienese painter, sculptor, and architect. Both based their work on earlier drawings of Taccola (Mariano di Jacopo). We also know who executed the work: Ambrogio Barocci, the sculptor and architect responsible for the elegant stone door and window jambs of the Urbino ducal palace, assisted by Giacomo Cozzarelli, apprentice and then assistant of Francesco di Giorgio, later an expert bronze-caster.

The Urbino frieze was a collaborative project realized under the aegis of a powerful patron and drew on a number of new or newly invigorated disciplines (geometry and perspective, for instance, come into play). As such, it serves as a paradigmatic example of the technological practices of Renaissance Italy for which antiquarian interests, hands-on experience, and experimentation were joined to the arts of exposition. Though a few of the figures we shall encounter in this survey of Italian Renaissance technologies were university-educated and some were employed, at least part-time, as professors, the university system's standardized curriculum was largely unprepared to promote the experimentation that rendered technological breakthroughs possible,[4] and the majority of innovators and their initiatives were supported instead by patrons associated with the Italian courts and states as well as by ecclesiastics and church institutions.

Prior to the eighteenth century the work that we think of "engineers" and "architects" as performing autonomously was more often than not carried out by the same professional together with a group of assistants, and single treatises addressing a broad array of technological practices were the norm through the middle of the sixteenth century. The term "technology" as we understand it appeared in the principal European vernaculars only in the seventeenth century, but one of the meanings of its ancient Greek root τέχνη [téchne] was "an art or craft; a set of rules, system or method of making or doing, whether of the useful arts, or of the fine arts."[5] "Technology" thus implied both the the practice itself, whether artistic or utilitarian, and the thinking behind it. But apart from the elaboration of specific technologies, there was also a growing sense in the fifteenth and sixteenth centuries of the linkage of technological progress to its application for both civil and military purposes. The study of technological developments, both in their material manifestations and in their social and political implications, thus constitutes one of the fundamental components for consideration of the meaning and impact of the Renaissance in Italy and beyond.

"Innovation" is a loaded term with regard to the markers of what we have come to regard as historical periods, and it is important to recognize that "the actual technology of a society is separable from, and more important than, the technological literature produced by that society."[6] Thus while technological thinking in Renaissance Italy might have reached its apex in treatises and other forms of exposition – some of it far ahead of its time and consequently left unrealized in the period (this true not only of a number of Leonardo da Vinci's inventions, but also of many of the machines projected by Taccola and others) – it is often difficult to determine how completely new the knowledge conveyed through these means was, and to what extent significant threads of continuity remained with the advances of preceding centuries, passed

---

[4] Medicine was a notable exception, for which see in this volume Park/Penuto, "Science and medicine," Chapter 17, 370–71, 382–85.
[5] Liddell/Scott (1996) 1784–85; and see Tafuri (2006) 41–52.
[6] Shelby (1975) 471.

along orally through guilds and workshops and in their continuous practices. This is not, of course, to minimize the most extraordinary feats of engineering in the period – Brunelleschi's *cupola* is the iconic example – but rather to recall that such achievements themselves have long and complex histories.[7] What was entirely new was that written Renaissance technological works – and, later, printed editions of ancient texts such as the *De architectura libri decem* [Ten Books on Architecture, *c.* 30–20 BCE] of Marcus Vitruvius Pollio – employed *disegno*: they were illustrated. The Neapolitan painter, antiquarian, and architect Pirro Ligorio wrote in the later sixteenth century that he had learned mathematics and drawing "not in order to make myself proficient in the art of painting, but in order to be able to express antique objects or buildings in perspective and profile."[8] And as Paolo Galuzzi has noted, "the success of Renaissance engineers depended in great measure on drawing. Illustrated collections of their 'know-how' were formidable communicative tools."[9] For Leonardo da Vinci, reflection on and resolution of technological questions depended on images through which he worked out his ideas.[10]

But the ability of potential patrons, individual or communal, to read a *disegno* could not always be taken for granted, and architects in particular turned to three-dimensional models to explain their ideas (a century after the engineers, Sebastiano Serlio was the first Italian architect to illustrate fully an original architectural treatise, *Regole generali di architettura* [General Rules for Architecture; later Book 4 of the *Sette libri di architettura*] in 1537). Antonio da Sangallo the Younger's monumental wooden model for the new St. Peter's in Rome demonstrates the extremes to which a sixteenth-century architect might go in order that his project be understood in detail: built at a scale of 1 : 30, 23′ 5″ long, 19′ 4″ wide, and 15′ high, it weighed 6 tons, cost the massive sum of over 5,500 scudi, and took seven years (from 1539 to 1546) to build. But such efforts did not by any means guarantee success – Michelangelo drastically cut back on Sangallo's plan when

---

[7] For an overview of the web of questions regarding the planning and construction of the *cupola*, see Trachtenberg (1983); and Di Pasquale (2002).

[8] Cited in Coffin (2004) 46; on the move from words to images between Vitruvius and Vignola (Jacopo Barozzi), see Carpo (2009).

[9] Galluzzi (2002) 28.

[10] See Mariane Schneider's introduction to Leonardo (2001b) 14–16. For his inventory of extant ancient Roman antiquities, Raphael developed a form of orthographic projection still used by architects today; see Di Teodoro (2003).

he took over the project in 1546, and the church we see today bears little resemblance to the most magnificent architectural model of the Italian Renaissance.[11]

This chapter will explore the intertwined trajectories of a number of disciplines – civil and military architecture, technologies associated with natural resources, the sciences of measurement, the study of cities – following their evolution through the period. Architecture occupies a privileged place in these considerations because it is the field in which a wide array of technologies were incorporated, integrating and representing the new possibilities. It is, besides, the discipline that produced what were at the time – and still are – among the most visible and influential effects of Renaissance innovation. The non-canonical buildings examined here emerge from the course of the argument, but they also serve to illustrate that the accomplishments of Italian Renaissance τέχνη are more far-reaching in their scope than any single example, however famous or well-studied, can establish on its own.

Vitruvius and his progeny

Vitruvius is the starting point for any consideration of technologies in Renaissance Italy. *De architectura* exercised consistent influence on both technological developments and architectural theory and practice in the period that stretched from Leon Battista Alberti in the first half of the fifteenth century through Andrea Palladio in the later sixteenth, though the extent to which Vitruvius' Renaissance heirs understood his text varied enormously.[12] Vitruvius had invented not only the comprehensive architectural/engineering treatise, drawing on and synthesizing earlier Greek and Latin works (most now lost), but also a good deal of the language he utilized to describe the various technologies which contribute to the planning and construction of buildings and other

---

[11] Sangallo's model was the centerpiece of an extraordinary exhibit dedicated to thirty-one surviving Renaissance architectural models at Palazzo Grassi in Venice in 1994. For the catalogue of the exhibit together with an illuminating series of essays, see Millon/ Magnago Lampugnani (1994); about the model of St. Peter's, see Connors (1995).

[12] For useful summaries of each of the principal architectural treatises in the period, see Hart/Hicks (1998). Payne (1999) provides insightful readings of the *trattati* and their relationship to Vitruvius; and Clarke (2002) gives a concise account of the arc of Vitruvius' impact in Italian Renaissance architectural theory. For general introductions to Italian Renaissance architecture, see Heydenreich (1996) for the *Quattrocento*; Lotz (1995); and Rowe/Satkowski (2002) for the *Cinquecento*.

enterprises involving mechanics, importing terms from Greek into a Latin that alternates between the "high" style of Cicero for the prefaces to each book, a "middle" register for anecdotes, and demotic language more fitting for the technical explanations which make up the bulk of the text. Given the important role he came to play for the development of Renaissance technologies, Vitruvius seems to have built very little himself – he discusses only the Basilica at Fano, no longer extant[13] – and he apparently exercised little influence in the ancient world, but his treatise had never entirely disappeared from view. There was some knowledge of it during the Carolingian period (751–987); a copy annotated by Petrarch is now in the Bodleian Library at Oxford; and Boccaccio regularly draws on Vitruvius in his *Genealogia deorum gentilium* [Genealogy of the Pagan Gods, 1350–74].[14] But the manuscript of the text that Poggio Bracciolini famously "rediscovered," probably in 1416, would have been in poor condition: its Greek neologisms corrupted through centuries of misunderstanding and faulty transcription; numbers for both weights and measures had been changed, partially obscured, or dropped; and the few geometrical diagrams originally provided had long since disappeared.[15] Scholars spent decades sorting out these problems before the first authoritative Latin edition was edited by Giovanni Sulpicio da Veroli and published in Rome in 1486 (together with Julius Sextus Frontinus' late-first-century CE report on the system of Roman aqueducts, *De aquae ductu*). Francesco di Giorgio Martini had partially translated Vitruvius into Italian earlier in the 1480s, around the same time that he was working in Urbino; the first Latin edition with illustrations was published by Fra Giovanni Giocondo in 1511; and the first complete Italian translation, with an extensive series of woodcuts, was issued by Cesare Cesariano in 1521.[16]

But in the meantime, through their circulation in manuscript and by word of mouth, Vitruvian ideas worked their way into both the emerging technological and architectural practices of fourteenth-century Italy and the treatises that promoted them. One of the primary

---

[13] For a reconstruction of which, and in general on Vitruvius see the Italian/English website of the Centro Studi Vitruviani (www.centrostudivitruviani.org). See also Pagliara (1988) on the development of Vitruvius' Renaissance profile.

[14] See Kruft (1994) 30–40.

[15] On the difficulties Vitruvius' treatise poses for both interpretation and translation, see Rowland (1998b) 107–08, and Vitruvius (1999) xiii–xiv.

[16] On Francesco di Giorgio's translation of Vitruvius, see Biffi (2002); and on Renaissance editions of Vitruvius in Latin and Italian, see Rowland (1998b).

aims of Vitruvius' interpreters was to translate the ancient Roman's prescriptions – nothing in *De architectura* can really be considered a complete design[17] – into tangible, workable forms. The first *Quattrocento* treatises dedicated to technologies, Giovanni Fontana's *Bellicorum instrumentorum liber* [Book of Military Machinery, *c.* 1420–40] and Taccola's *De ingeneis* [On Engineering, *c.* 1427–33] and *De machinis* [On Machines, *c.* 1430–49], consist almost entirely of drawings supplemented by textual explanations (those in Fontana are in cipher).[18] These works were conceived at just the time when a renewed interest in Vitruvius' account of ancient technologies began to register in Italy, and Taccola, closely tied to humanist circles in Siena, was particularly eager to engage with the ancient Roman's not always entirely intelligible recommendations. Fontana, a medical doctor, draws on a wide range of ancient Greek, Latin, and Arab–Latin literature, illustrating an impressive collection of machines and devices, including a mobile tower equipped with a battering ram, a mechanical organ, and a variety of water works, the whole subtly interwoven with references to mathematics, natural history, and poetry;[19] while Taccola's drawings encompass an array of military and civil technologies including the chain transmission system, the compound crank with connecting rod, water provisioning and regulation as well as the reclamation of swamps (the water-delivery system created in the thirteenth century, the *bottini*, that he helped to expand and maintain in Siena was still in use until several decades ago), a mask for breathing under water, and a sketch for the aqualung later elaborated by Leonardo.[20] Taccola's drawings of devices for hoisting heavy weights reflect his close relationship with Brunelleschi – some of these are images of the machines used in the construction of the *cupola* – and they (together with the *Zibaldone* of Bonaccorso Ghiberti) provide a window onto Brunelleschi's practices.[21]

Leon Battista Alberti's *De re aedificatoria* [On the Art of Building, 1443–52] is the most comprehensive fifteenth-century effort to respond

---

[17] See Dewar in Vitruvius (1999) xvi.
[18] See Fontana (1984), including folio-page reproductions of about half of the drawings, the Latin text deciphered and translated into Italian; and Taccola (1972), for images, commentary, and a complete English translation alongside the original Latin of *De ingeneis*.
[19] See Muccillo (1997) 674.
[20] See Doti (2008) 328.
[21] For the construction of the dome along with reconstructions of the technologies employed, see Galuzzi (1996) 93–116. The complete extant documentation regarding the project, including drawings, is available online, for which see Haines (2009).

to Vitruvius. Although he initially conceived it as a commentary, Alberti soon realized that an entirely new treatise, more persuasively argued, better organized, and written in a more elegant Latin was necessary to fully assimilate the sometimes fragmentary and often confusing information in *De architectura*.[22] But while maintaining the ten-book format of his model, Alberti focuses almost exclusively in his treatise on the elements of civil architecture – only three short sections of Book Five deal with military encampments, siegeworks, and ships – though in other written works and built projects he took up a number of the remaining technological matters that Vitruvius had addressed.[23] Alberti dedicates books to the separate parts of buildings and their contexts; building materials; structural theory; different types of buildings; and their maintenance. But crucial to his architectural aesthetic is *ornamentum* [ornament or embellishment], a concept that is explored over four entire books (Six through Nine) and encompasses the wide range of features that not only distinguish the outer appearance of buildings but also express, according to Alberti, something essential to their function and meaning. A hierarchy of values thus allows for the finest and most elaborate decoration in what for Alberti is the highest form of civil architecture, the church, and he recommends a considerably simpler style for private homes, suggesting, for instance, that country villas and farmhouses be organized entirely on one level, eliminating the need for stairs. Alberti wrote for a learned readership and provided no illustrations to accompany his text, but unlike Vitruvius – who described buildings which either have no other testimony or have not survived – Alberti's theorizing could (and can still) be judged against the buildings he realized in Rimini, Mantua, and Florence.[24]

The Tempio [Temple] that Matteo de' Pasti, Agostino di Duccio, and Alberti conceived for Sigismondo Pandolfo Malatesta, *condottiere* and lord of Rimini, is arguably the most surprising building of *Quattrocento* Italy (Fig. 5.2).[25] Leon Battista's involvement with the project most

---

[22] For a summary of the contents of Vitruvius' treatise, see Rowland (2002).

[23] On Alberti, technologies, and building see Borsi (1977); Grafton (2000) 71–109, 261–92; Grassi/Patetta (2005); and Trachtenberg (2010) 357–81. For the Latin edition of the *De re aedificatoria* with facing Italian translation, see Alberti (1966b); and for the most recent English translation, Alberti (1988).

[24] See Rykwert (1998) 50.

[25] For overviews of Alberti's project, see Burns (1998) 129–34; Tavernor (1998) 49–77; and Cassani (2005). And for excellent reproductions of the building and its rich decorative detail, along with a separate volume of essays, see Paolucci (2010).

Fig. 5.2 Leon Battista Alberti, Il Tempio Malatestiano (*c.* 1450–60, Rimini).

likely dates from 1453, just when he would have been completing work
on his treatise, though de' Pasti and Duccio were to remain its principal
on-site managers. It is generally agreed that Alberti had little or nothing
to do with the refashioning of the interior of the structure, initially
intended only to add a Malatesta family chapel but subsequently
expanded to encompass the entire space of the older church, Sigismondo having effectively expropriated the building from its Franciscan
tenants in order to create a monument to himself, his family, and
associates, and the singularly pre-Christian culture that distinguishes
the Tempio's extraordinarily refined decorative scheme. Alberti created
a shell of white Istrian stone to enclose the original church, with a base
and decorative frieze that would have originally extended along the
entire lower portion of its perimeter. The principal mass of the façade
evokes a number of elements of the nearby Arch of Augustus in Rimini:
it is demarcated above the base by four composite half-columns and
entablatures; situated within these are two arches on either side of the
central door and a slightly larger arch framing it; a triangular tympanum is centered over the door, below a semicircular field of polychro-
matic marble likely plundered from Ravenna and recalling the *opus sectile*
[inlaid stone] of imperial Rome; oculi surrounded by wreaths punctuate
the upper and lower orders of the façade as well as the sides of the

building. Visible in the gap between two unfinished half-columns and the beginnings of another arch in the upper order of the façade (left unfinished when the project was abandoned after a downturn in Sigismondo's fortunes in the early 1460s) is the medieval gable; and just beneath the trabeation is an inscription bearing the names of Sigismondo and his father, and the date 1450 that "for the typology and proportion of its letters as well the reinvigorated technique of its carving, is the very first [post-classical] example of public writing based on ancient models."[26] The flanks of the Tempio consist of a series of identical arches supported by piers (the Gothic windows of the church are still in evidence behind them); those on the south-west side of the structure host tombs of several of Sigismondo's humanist collaborators as well as the neo-Platonist scholar Georgius Gemistus Pletho, whose remains Malatesta brought back with him from Mystras after fighting in the Venetian republic's war against the Ottomans in the Peloponnesus from 1464 to 1466 (identical Greek inscriptions on the piers closest to the façade on both sides of the edifice note Sigismondo's desire to build it and to celebrate his roles as patron and *condottiere*).

While the aesthetic language that the Tempio speaks is monumental its actual realized dimensions differ little from many other churches built in the period throughout the peninsula. Its ambitions were, nevertheless, as huge as they were audacious: an unabashed celebration of a "pagan" world with which Sigismondo strongly identified (inside, Duccio's graceful bas-reliefs of frolicking *putti*, Olympian divinities, the signs of the zodiac, and the liberal arts depict a world untouched by Christianity, though the Hebrew prophets Micah and Isaiah are positioned together with the Sibyls), and the structure demonstrates the first material fruits of Alberti's reinvention of Vitruvius. Sigismondo had wanted a dome for his *Tempio* that would have rivaled the Roman Pantheon – a medal cast by de' Pasti in 1450 clearly shows such a structure looming behind the yet-to-be-realized façade, and Alberti discusses its form and dimensions in his only extant letter to de' Pasti regarding the building. But surely what Alberti and company managed to achieve is of far greater interest: for the equilibrium the Tempio achieves, despite its heterogeneity and its incomplete state; and for its failure to erase the signs of its medieval origins. In this it is significantly

---

[26] Petrucci (1985) 92.

unlike Alberti's later façade and lateral decoration for the Church of Santa Maria Novella in Florence, where the Renaissance overlay self-consciously presents itself as such, a spectacular but two-dimensional stage set that coexists with the church's medieval character.

Buried in one of the external tombs of the *Tempio* is the humanist Roberto Valturio, active in the Malatesta circle in Rimini in these years, but also, as we noted earlier with regard to the Urbino frieze, involved with Federico da Montefeltro. Though there is no documentary evidence of their relationship, Valturio would have been an associate of Alberti's in the papal curia during the decade Pope Eugene IV spent between Florence and Bologna after fleeing a Roman civil insurrection in 1434. Valturio dedicated his *De re militari* [On Military Matters] to Sigismondo. Written between 1430 and 1455, Valturio's text circulated extensively in various manuscripts before being printed in Verona in 1472, only the second book to be published in Italy containing illustrations; it and an ancient text dealing with technological matters and warfare, the *De re militari* of Publius Flavius Vegetius Renatus, published in 1471, were among the biggest publishing successes of the first generation of printing in Italy (running to four and eight editions, respectively, before 1500).[27] Valturio's *De re militari* is not, however, a technological treatise, but rather an erudite account of the values and practices of ancient warfare for which technologies were a basic tool. Among the topics addressed are the qualities of the perfect *condottiere* (here, obviously, Sigismondo Malatesta); the strategies of successful military leaders; a detailed presentation of the ancient Roman "arts" of war; accounts of military formations and their movements; arms and war machines; naval battles and the equipment required to stage them; and military honorifics. While Valturio was trained as a classical rhetorician and his text is organized accordingly, it completely ignores contemporary military practices. The images by Matteo de' Pasti which accompany Valturio's text were meant to represent up-to-date technologies, though even they only fleetingly demonstrate the firearms which were revolutionizing warfare in the period. As had been the case with Fontana and Taccola, there is a high degree of untethered invention in the military technology represented in fifteenth-century treatises:

---

[27] For a facsimile reprint of the 1472 edition, together with a volume of essays dedicated to the text, see Valturio (2006).

stuck in a distant past – "dead letters, material for the conception of huge fascinating monsters of wood, twigs, leather, or rigging more appropriate for theatrical stage apparatus than for fighting off assaults or conquering cities"[28] – or unconcerned about the unrealizable nature of their more experimental proposals. Even Alberti, with his ship gang-plank sporting retractable porcupine quill-like pikes, was not immune to the temptation.[29] Nevertheless, Valturio's text was in the libraries of Leonardo and Niccolò Machiavelli, and through a series of gifts recorded in annotations to a copy of the 1472 edition now in the library of the Fondazione Cini in Venice we know that this book was in the baggage of one of the German soldiers who took part in the 1527 Sack of Rome.[30]

Francesco di Giorgio Martini was an entirely different kind of engineer and architect, his antiquarian interests and experimentation entirely pragmatic. He proved to be the ablest operator among the technological polymaths of fifteenth-century Italy, successfully negotiating an increasingly complex political scene as he moved between his native Siena and Florence, the Montefeltro court in Urbino and its surrounding territories, Milan and Pavia under the Sforza, papal Rome, and the Aragonese-ruled Kingdom of Naples. The scope of his technological activities exceeded that of any of his predecessors, and the extensive and eclectic body of his built work was scattered from north to south across the entire peninsula. Most of his important civil buildings survive – in Cortona, Urbino, Gubbio, Jesi, and possibly Siena – as do several imposing fortresses in Montefeltro territory (now the northern Marche and southern Emilia Romagna).[31]

Francesco's early training was in painting and sculpture, but also in the Sienese waterworks which Taccola had overseen, and he seems early on to have acquired technical and organizational skills which made him a natural manager of building sites and workshops. Evident in Francesco's first written/drawn work, the so-called *Codicetto* [Little Codex] compiled between 1465 and 1477, is a minute interest in machines and the mechanics behind them, many of which are re-elaborated and improved versions of elements in Taccola (there are annotations in

[28] Cardini, F. (2006) 13.   [29] See Alberti (1988) 137.
[30] See Dolza (2007) 122–25.
[31] For the best survey of Francesco di Giorgio's architectural work, see Fiore/Tafuri (1993); and for a concise picture of Francesco's career, see Fiore (1998).

Francesco's hand in Taccola's autograph manuscript of *De ingeneis* I–II, demonstrating the direct access he had to them).[32] Francesco wrote here and elsewhere in Italian, and he introduces new systems and devices which if not necessarily invented by him are first recorded in the *Codicetto*, among which "the worm-screw that engages a ratchet both for the transmission of movement and the proportional reduction of force" used for lifting or moving enormous weights (columns, obelisks, towers), a significant improvement with regard to efficiency when compared to Taccola's conventional gear wheels, bobbins, and pulleys.[33]

A restless sense of exploration coupled with a rigorous effort to push technology in new directions emerges from the successive group of manuscripts which register Francesco's work, "concluding syntheses" in mechanical engineering, military technologies, and civil architecture "that expose [both] to us [and] to his contemporaries a complex thinking process"[34] (a notable difference from Alberti's definitively magisterial text). Vitruvius remained a constant point of reference throughout Francesco's career: long passages of *De architectura* translated literally (and not always accurately) with detailed accompanying illustrations in the first redaction of Francesco's principal treatise dealing with military and civil architecture lead in the second version of the work to both a greater understanding of ancient models and an imperative to modernize them. The material organized into seven books in this second *trattato* addresses the principal areas of technological concern that were to be developed by Francesco's successors in sixteenth-century Italy: requirements and conditions for building (Francesco was the first Renaissance architect to demonstrate what we would call a site-specific sensibility), with a discussion of materials; the construction of private homes and palaces, along with methods for locating sources of water; military fortresses and city planning; sacred buildings; fortifications; harbors; and transportation. It might appear surprising that such an innovator would have been completely ignored by the early printing press, but the interplay of text and image resulting in complex graphic forms on the pages of Francesco's theoretical works would have posed enormous challenges for the new technology of moveable print, and in the end these drawn texts enjoyed a continuing life of their own, circulating

---

[32] For a useful discussion of the "Sienese engineers," see Galluzzi (1996) 24–46.
[33] Galluzzi (1991) 202, and 380–89 for Francesco's drawings of this mechanism at work.
[34] Fiore (1998) 72; and Payne (1999) 89.

Fig. 5.3 Francesco di Giorgio Martini, Palazzo della Signoria (1486–1666, Jesi). Drawing from F. Mariano and M. Agostinelli, *Francesco di Giorgio e il Palazzo della Signoria di Jesi* (1986).

in manuscript well into the following century and influencing techno-logical practitioners from Leonardo (whose annotations adorn the manuscript now in the Biblioteca Laurenziana in Florence) through the mid seventeenth century.[35]

The graceful town hall in Jesi, in the Marche, is a good example of Francesco's mature architectural style (Fig. 5.3). The original project was first conceived in 1486, but its history illustrates the multiple hands that contributed to pre-modern buildings often represented as the work of a single artistic imagination (St. Peter's in Rome is only

[35] See Biffi (2002).

the most obvious instance, where Michelangelo's involvement was just one part of a very long and by no means harmonious continuum). Created not for a territorial lord such as Federico da Montefeltro with forceful ideas of his own but for a town with a *Consiglio comunale* [town council] under the direct control of the papacy after 1447 following centuries of relative independence as a small republic, the project was unfinished at the time of Francesco's death, and the loss of the model that illustrated his original design has made it difficult to understand fully his contribution to certain elements of it.[36] Work progressed slowly due to financial constraints and problems with the original local contractors, but these were replaced by a team from Varese in 1497, and the first meeting of the town council was held in the completed building in July 1503. Andrea Sansovino subsequently put his own stamp on the interior courtyard; Milanese stonemasons provided all the ornamental and lapidary work as well as the window and door jambs (though the central door giving onto the piazza in front of the building following a model closer to the principles of Serlio or Vignola (Giacomo Barozzi) was added in 1586, just as the town conceded the palazzo as the residence of the papal governor of the area);[37] and a clock built in Faenza was mounted on a dispropor-tionately high tower consisting of three orders built between 1511 and 1551 that constituted the most radical modification of the original project, entirely reconfiguring the interior of the south-west corner of the structure. But that tower was poorly supported, and after a moderate earthquake destroyed it in 1657 the more modest tower in one single order that we see today was finished by 1666.

Earth sciences

Much of the territory of the Italian peninsula and its islands is seismic-ally active, but until the early sixteenth century there had been little attention paid by engineers or architects to planning and building with this eventuality in mind. Several devastating earthquakes in the sixteenth century prompted the first theoretical considerations of the

[36] For succinct discussions of the Jesi *Palazzo della Signoria*, see Mariano (1993); and Fiore/ Tafuri (1993). Agostinelli/Mariano (1986) provides a complete analysis of the building, with splendid fold-out plates.
[37] On Vignola, see Tuttle (1998).

matter by Filippo Beroaldo, Agricola (Georg Bauer), Girolamo Cardano, and Lucio Maggio.[38] But the most intriguing contribution to the question was provided later in the century by Pirro Ligorio, the architect and hydraulic engineer responsible for monumental projects in and near Rome in the 1550s and 1560s such as Villa d'Este in Tivoli and the Vatican Cortile del Belvedere (he briefly succeeded Michelangelo as superintendent of the new St. Peter's in 1564). Ligorio lived through the series of earthquakes that shook Ferrara between November 17, 1570 and February 1571 (aftershocks continued for several years), and his unfinished *Libro di diversi terremoti* [Book of Various Earthquakes, 1571] was written in the midst of the resulting catastrophe. Largely a survey of history's most destructive earthquakes and volcanic eruptions, Ligorio's work also gives an eyewitness account of the damage inflicted upon Ferrara's medieval core by the ongoing tremors (the "Addizione erculea," the northern addition to the city initiated by Duke Ercole I in 1492, remained largely intact). Because he faulted poor construction for the widespread devastation, Ligorio furnishes specific, if somewhat simplistic, recommendations to protect against future loss in drawings for an earthquake-resistant house constructed of brick secured with the best mortar and iron or stone ties, built on a solid foundation on one level consisting of perfectly perpendicular thick outer walls, with huge corner piers in each of its six rooms, and double-arches situated over all wall openings (citing Pliny the Elder and Vitruvius, Ligorio notes the testimony of surviving ancient structures fitted with them).[39] Like many of his contemporaries, Ligorio believed that earthquakes were the direct result of divine retribution for human sinfulness, but he parted with most of them in also viewing seismic events as unpredictable natural phenomena.

Aristotle's theory of earthquakes – caused by the build-up of winds inside the Earth that at a critical moment break violently free, rushing through vast underground chambers and provoking the movement of the Earth's outer surface – was still widely held in the sixteenth century, and Ferrara was thought to be situated over a series of such caverns. Because of his relatively liberal policy toward Jews and

---

[38] See Emanuela Guidoboni's introduction to Ligorio (2005) xiii–xxxi for a general presentation of the work (in both Italian and – unfortunately, uncorrected – English).
[39] See Coffin (2004) 111; and Guidoboni in Ligorio (2005) xix, xxix.

"heretics" in Este territories, Duke Alfonso II was blamed by Pope Pius V for provoking the earthquakes. But closer to home he was also criticized for the drainage of marshlands surrounding the city, thus contributing to the expansion of the abyss believed to underlie it, and in December 1570 a group of "experts" recommended flooding the reclaimed land along with the city in order to stop the Earth from shaking.[40] Alfonso, of course, did nothing of the sort – dubious science aside, the project had begun in 1559 and would continue through 1580, involved a pan-Italian group of investors, and in the end yielded roughly 75,000 cultivable acres[41] – but the episode draws attention to one of the most pressing technological concerns of the period: the marshaling and regulation of water for both civil and military purposes.

A little-known chapter in the otherwise brilliant career of Filippo Brunelleschi illustrates the potential risks of hydraulic engineering in the period: the project he oversaw, together with Michelozzo di Bartolomeo, to flood Lucca in the spring of 1430 in what was to have been the final blow of an offensive operation against that city–republic in one of the recurring efforts of Florence to incorporate Lucca into its expanding Tuscan state. The plan was to construct an embankment over four miles long, south, east, and west of the city walls, creating a basin on lower-lying ground which together with the varying ground levels north of the walls was meant to completely isolate the city when flooded. Water diverted from the river Serchio – lying just north of the city, on slightly higher ground – was supposed to be released into the new basin via one or more locks newly built into a pre-existing trench, but in the event something went seriously wrong (scholars are divided about the cause, though the hasty one-month construction schedule must have contributed to it), and rather than flooding the city the water breached the dyke and washed the Florentine encampment away.[42] Leonardo da Vinci may have known about the episode,[43] but at any rate his fascination with the often unbridled power of water and the enormous uses to which it might be put is well documented. A projected treatise on the topic was never completed,

[40] *Ibid.* xiv–xvii, xxv–xxix.   [41] See Ciracono (2007) 454.
[42] For an account of the project, with a reconstructed map of its key elements, see Benigni/ Ruschi (1980).
[43] See Fara (1997).

but its planned chapters dealing with various aspects of the science of water were to be followed by specific technological applications aimed at channeling and controlling water's potential for destruction into an element beneficial for defense, industry, agriculture, and civil society. One such project, a system of canals and pumps to drain the coastal Pomptine marshes south of Rome, was abandoned at the death of Leonardo's Roman patron, Giuliano de' Medici (younger brother of Pope Leo X, Giovanni de' Medici) in 1516, but as with so many of Leonardo's intuitions the essential elements of this plan formed the basis for subsequently successful interventions in the region. Scattered throughout the drawings and writing produced over the course of his working life, Leonardo produced the most innovative body of thinking on hydraulics in the period.[44]

The city of Venice had a clearly vested interest in developing effective hydraulic systems, but the conflicting demands of the lagoon and those of the Venetian republic's mainland territories (demands that corresponded, respectively, to international sea-based and local agricultural commerce) required solutions which were often mutually exclusive. The drainage of the marshes nearest Venice and the redirection of rivers on the mainland, for example, put the delicate ecology of the lagoon at extreme risk, and Cristoforo Sabbadino was the first to understand in scientific terms the environmental consequences of unconstrained development in the area. As Venetian *proto* [principal engineer] of waters, he was in a powerful position to influence political debate with regard to questions about the use and safe-keeping of the lagoon (the *proto*'s responsibilities also involved making a number of related environmental evaluations, such as assessing the impact of new building within the city, or giving an opinion about the construction of a mainland canal).[45] Venetian hydraulics drew in the sixteenth century upon the knowledge accumulated from medieval Arab and Iberian practices which had passed into the region with the Spanish occupation of Lombardy. Sabbadino represented a nexus between the knowledge of a variety of fields – mechanics and physics, mathematics, geometry, physical geography, meteorology,

---

[44] For a collection of his writings on water, see Leonardo (2001b). For analyses of Leonardo's hydraulic science, see Gombrich (1976); Di Teodoro (2002); and Pfister *et al.* (2009).

[45] For an introduction to Sabbadino's work and the frequently contentious climate in which it was exercised, together with the two texts he left unedited at his death in 1560, see Sabbadino (2000), which I follow closely here.

geology – and that of the *genii loci*, those who worked the waters (fisherman, sailors, etc.), with whom he was on good terms. Sabbadino fought against three fundamental problems: the effects of rivers flowing into the lagoon, carrying with them both earth and fresh water; the frequently unpredictable incursions of the sea; and Venetians themselves, intent on exploiting the lagoon but unconcerned about the consequences. Unlike his fiercest critics, Sabbadino recognized the essential work of cleansing that the ebb and flow of the sea's tides accomplished even in the most remote channels of the lagoon, areas which would have been isolated, for instance, by his compatriot Alvise Cornaro's plans for an extensive system of embankments. And even if he can now be criticized for having misread some aspects of the earlier history of the lagoon and for not having fully understood certain issues which only later hydraulics were able to illuminate, Sabbadino was a trailblazer in defending the complexities of a unique ecosystem whose waters were, as he put it, Venice's *cinta muraria* [defensive bastion] and were to be maintained as scrupulously as any such defensive construction.

But Venice could not live by the sea alone, and the agricultural production that served as one of Italy's primary economic resources until the mid twentieth century attracted a great deal of attention in the Serene Republic, as it did throughout Italian territories. In the period of the Renaissance "the values of the earth and the earth as a value registered a significant turning point,"[46] and the agricultural treatises produced in Italy from the late fourteenth through the mid sixteenth centuries, largely for the benefit of landholders, but also addressed to the interested authorities of the states in which their properties were situated, went far beyond the Greek and Latin texts which inspired them. Over two-thirds of these ancient treatises were published in Venice between 1450 and 1550 – some 262 titles between editions and re-editions of fifteen authors, among whom Cato, Pliny the Elder, Columella, and the anonymous Byzantine author of the *Geoponica* [Agricultural Pursuits]; in the same period, forty-one

---

[46] Zaninelli (1995) xiii; here, in addition to later works, four agricultural treatises written between 1489 and the 1560s – by the Tuscan Michelangelo Tanaglia (in *terza rima* verse, the interlocking three-line rhymed form adopted by Dante), the Sicilian Antonio Venuto, and the Brescians Agostino Gallo (the first to write about the cultivation of rice) and Camillo Tarello – are reproduced either whole or in significant extracts, with informative introductions.

contemporary authors were represented by 100 titles (again between editions and re-editions), half of these issued in Venice, the remainder by presses in Tuscany, Lombardy, Emilia, Lazio, Campania, and Sicily.[47] Ancient authors dealt with agriculture in general terms, while also discussing hunting and fishing, horticulture, gardening, the breeding of animals, and dairying; the *Geoponica* added bee-keeping, the care of olive trees, and viticulture. The influential treatise of Pietro de' Crescenzi, a Bolognese magistrate, written in the thirteenth century and first published in Augsburg in 1471 (it was printed in Venice in 1495) was the first to promote the benefits of sorghum, previously uncultivated in Europe and which came to dominate grain production in the reclaimed marshes of the Po valley in the sixteenth century.[48] Subsequent Italian treatises addressed the breeding of silkworms; applied economic sciences with particular attention to rural building and farm management, agricultural hydraulics, agrarian mechanics, and the rotation of crops (particularly cereals).[49] Renaissance authors of agricultural treatises delimited their interventions by acknowledging local particularities of soil, topography, customs of planting and cultivation, and climate while at the same time accommodating other perspectives, "experienced first-hand or through books, the exchange of letters, or reported accounts which conveyed new knowledge, some of it accepted, [often] not, but always with an eye to enriching the tradition."[50] One of the central preoccupations of these treatises through the mid sixteenth century was the relation of the landowner to those who worked the land for him, illiterate peasants here generally taken to be dishonest and in need of strict oversight and correction. The well-run farm was thus seen as a microcosm of the properly functioning state, agricultural practices presented with a strongly moralizing overlay and framed within a narrative that celebrated the *otium* [leisurely delight] of country life and/or the pleasures of reading itself.

---

[47] See *Ibid*. xiv–xv.
[48] See Gaulin (2007) 161, and in general for an introduction to the genre of the agricultural treatise.
[49] The technologies associated with silk production were first developed in Italy between the tenth and eleventh centuries in Calabria and eastern Sicily thanks to the Arab and Byzantine Greek presence in the region, from where it spread north in the following centuries (Venice acquired the cultivation of silkworms directly from the Byzantines in the thirteenth century); see Battistini (2003) 33–34, and in general on the early modern silk industry.
[50] Gaulin (2007) 160.

Fig. 5.4 Andrea Palladio, Villa Poiana (*c.* 1546–63, Poiana).

Camillo Tarello's *Ricordo d'agricoltura* [Agricultural Record, 1567] broke definitively with the ethical and aesthetic elements of this tradition in dealing only with pragmatic matters presented in a relatively short work arranged from "A to Z" and meant to address one specific issue: how to increase profits.

Unlike his grander and more famous villas, Andrea Palladio's Villa Poiana wears its identity as the home of a gentleman-farmer on its sleeve (Fig. 5.4). Here there is considerably less of the culture of *otium* associated with the great villas of antiquity or those represented in pastoral Renaissance literature from Boccaccio to Bembo, and more of the no-nonsense character of the working farm whose residence it was.[51] Situated on fertile land that was once the Venetian republic's bread-basket, about 20 miles south of Vicenza and just west of the volcanic Euganean Hills, the building was originally one of a "conglomerate of villas [near the village of Poiana], each with its own agricultural courtyard, gardens, enclosed orchards, and annexes, the whole surrounded by a solid wall."[52] Initiated by Palladio in 1546,

---

[51] On the siren call of the ancient villa, see Rowland (1995).
[52] Burns (2010) 483; this extended essay is the best introduction to the culture of the Italian Renaissance villa, with an excellent bibliography.

building at the site continued for more than a decade but was never completed according to his design (only one of two service wings evident in Palladio's drawing of the villa in his *Quattro libri dell'architettura* [Four Books of Architecture, 1570] was ever realized; the wing linking it to the villa was added in the seventeenth century). The possession of agricultural lands on the part of individuals who for the most part lived in nearby cities was the sure sign of having achieved a certain financial independence, for farming was widely considered to be a sound investment (in mountainous regions of Renaissance Italy, villas – such as Michelozzo's for the Medici in Cafaggiolo – served as the residential and administrative anchors for business ventures in herding, the marshaling of water resources, timber, and mining).[53] But in spite of its apparently modest yeoman's service, the Villa Poiana marks an important turning point in Palladio's career: its architectural language is at once classical and contemporary: the interrupted tympanum on the façade is a citation of the Baths of Diocletian in Rome, and underneath it the pier-supported *serliana* [a semicircular arch – here two arches with five oculi situated between them – and two symmetrical vertical apertures at its sides] recalls the portico of the Teatro di Marcello and both Donato Bramante's nymphaeum in Genazzano and his unrealized project for the drum of the dome of St. Peter's in Rome. While other architects had previously managed to bridge the ancient–modern divide, here Palladio also found solutions for the back of his free-standing villa (mirroring the façade, with slight variations) and its sides which overcame the awkward compromises he and his predecessors had earlier adopted; it became a model for domestic architecture for centuries to come. But "Palladio thought through interior space as well as external appearance, and he thought carefully about how his patrons would live in his buildings."[54] Here the principal living spaces are all located on the main floor – recalling Alberti's recommendation about country residences – and an ample granary, other storage areas, and quarters for servants are located above the lateral rooms on either side

[53] *Ibid.* 492. On the technologies associated with forestry and mining in the period, see respectively, Morelli (2007) and Vergani (2007). The most important mining treatise of the period, Agricola's *De re metallica* (1556), circulated widely in Italy in its 1563 Italian translation by Michelangelo Florio; on Agricola and his treatise, see Long (2001) 183–86.

[54] Rowland (2009). Rybczynski (2002) 225–49 describes a month the author spent living in the Villa Saraceno, built around the same time as the Villa Poiana.

of the high, vaulted central *sala* that runs from the loggia at the front to the back of the house. The *Villa Poiana*'s materials are straightforward – stucco-covered brick, only the window jambs are stone (the statuary was added in the seventeenth century) – its quiet, unadorned elegance wedding a harmonious aesthetic vision to practical functionality.[55]

Figures and numbers

"Harmony" is a concept that has been much contested in recent Renaissance scholarship, but as an ideal there is no denying that a great number of humanists, artists, architects, poets, and musicians sought to achieve it in the varied forms in which they worked, regardless of how near or far we may judge that they came in achieving the goal. The thinking of the ancient Greek philosopher and mathematician Pythagoras – known to us only through what his near-contemporaries and their ancient interpreters wrote about him – came to embody this principle for Italian Renaissance aesthetics,[56] and it is no coincidence that one of the primary foci of architectural treatises in the period concerned the proper disposition of the "orders" most evident in the forms of columns recuperated from antiquity via Vitruvius and in the remains of ancient buildings scattered throughout Italy.

For Vitruvius, most measurements were to be derived from the proportions of the single parts of a building, usually from the diameter of its columns, and Alberti refined this practice, providing "a [diachronic] method, itemizing the steps in a process … that, if carefully carried out, generate[d] the right proportional relations among the parts."[57] This procedure was entirely geometrical, consisting of a sequence of identical operations in which segments were divided into proportionally related parts: the dimensions of the different sections of the base of the Doric column Alberti describes in Book Seven of *De re aedificatoria*, for example, are determined by dividing and subdividing a segment derived initially from the diameter of the column at its base: the proper proportions of the plinth, upper and lower toruses, scotia, and fillets emerge

[55] *Ibid.* 65–73, 85–93 provides a lively discussion of the Villa Poiana.
[56] On the importance of Pythagoras for architecture in Renaissance Italy, see Joost-Gaugier (2009) 145–239.
[57] Carpo (2003) 450; and in general for what follows here on the shift from geometry to mathematics in Renaissance architectural theory and practice.

clearly from this method of division. But while Alberti implies fractions here, the Roman numerals he employed in his treatise were incapable of performing as such (Hindu–Arabic numbers had been known in Europe since at least the twelfth century but were not readily adopted until the sixteenth, and the decimal point was not introduced until the end of that century).[58] The process did not require numbers and could have been done by anyone capable of using a ruler and a pair of geometrical compasses, a system that did not depend upon drawings and that was transmissible orally. Most buildings and technological innovations in Italy were realized in this way through the middle of the sixteenth century.

Among the most striking achievements of the interplay between geometry and technologies in Renaissance Italy is the *studiolo* planned by Francesco di Giorgio and executed by the Florentine workshop of Giuliano da Maiano for Federico da Montefeltro's palace in Gubbio (now in the Metropolitan Museum of Art in New York) (Fig. 5.5). Completed in the 1480s after the duke's death (an earlier *studiolo* had been created by the same workshop for his Urbino palace) and reconstructed in New York to correspond precisely to its original placement in an asymmetrical space in Gubbio, the *studiolo* is what one of the directors of its most recent restoration calls "a total environment."[59] It encompasses in its illusionistic *intarsia* [inlaid-wood paneling] a distillation of Italian Renaissance cultures. The room represents an idealized scholar's study, all of its intricate detail worked out through the juxtaposition of different woods (some of them cured for long periods in order to render exactly the color or timbre desired), thinly cut into a seemingly infinite and infinitesimal variety of shapes and sizes, and arranged in a carefully worked-out perspective program. Federico's presence is evoked by his honorifics and devices (among which the Order of the Garter, conferred upon him by the English King Edward IV in 1474), and in objects associated both with his learned court and the mercenary war-making that financed it: scientific and musical instruments; books, including a manuscript of the *Aeneid* open on a lectern; a rebec and its bow, ceremonial armor, Federico's ducal

---

[58] See Crosby (1997) 111–18.

[59] Raggio/Wilmering (1999) vol. 1, 83, and vol. 1 in general on the history and cultural context of Federico's *studioli* as well as the earlier *intarsie* in the north sacristy of the Florence cathedral; vol. 2 provides a full account of the technologies of *intarsia* work, and of the complex process of restoring the Gubbio *studiolo*.

Fig. 5.5 Workshop of Giuliano da Maiano (after designs by Francesco di Giorgio Martini), *Studiolo* (1480s, Gubbio; now in The Metropolitan Museum of Art).

sword, an ivory hunting-horn; tools for writing and reading; an hour-glass. Twelve cabinets form the principal divisions of the *intarsia* panels, each separated by classical pilasters and entablatures, their latticed shutters partially open to reveal the varied objects contained within (most are organized according to like use; one cabinet contains only a caged parakeet, with delicately colored fillets for its plumage). Above the *intarsia* panels, a frieze utilizing letters similar to those Alberti had employed for the façade of the Tempio Malatestiano spells out an enco-mium to the liberal arts as its runs around the entire perimeter of the space. This is capped by a cornice and elaborate coffered ceilings at two heights, the lower of which is situated over the skewed perpendicular alcove at the right of the space, reiterating some of the symbolic details of the *intarsie* below (paintings of the liberal arts would have originally been placed on what are here blank walls above the cornice). Every element of the *studiolo* – from the form and placement of each object to the lettering of the frieze – is determined geometrically, but one item in particular underscores the proportional character of the space, the *mazzocchio* centered atop the bench represented along the long left wall

Fig. 5.6 Workshop of Giuliano da Maiano (after designs of Francesco di Giorgio Martini), *Mazzocchio*, detail of *Studiolo* (1480s, Gubbio; now in The Metropolitan Museum of Art).

(Fig. 5.6), whose "circular form ... echoes that of the 'porphyry' roundel behind it and of the garter above." Used by hat-makers to shape the *cappuccio*, a popular headpiece, the *mazzocchio* was also employed to teach perspective, as Piero della Francesca notes in his treatise on the subject *De prospectiva pingendi* [On Perspective in Painting, *c.* 1480]. There called a *torculo*, it was utilized to show how "to proportionally foreshorten column bases and capitals in perspective," a technique meant "for architects as well as painters,"[60] and *intarsia*-workers frequently used the *mazzocchio* to demonstrate their skill in employing perspectival effects. Its central position in the Gubbio *studiolo* (whose panels were realized over 100 miles from the irregular site where they were to be installed) as well as in the *Quattrocento* transmission of knowledge regarding perspective renders the *mazzocchio* emblematic of the geometrical practices that it demonstrates in both.[61]

[60] *Ibid.* vol. 1, 122.
[61] See Kemp (1999) on the perspectival scheme of the space; and Camerota (2006) in general on the theory and practice of Renaissance perspective.

Equivalent to the valorization of images in technological treatises of the fifteenth century was the move toward mathematical measurement in sixteenth-century architectural treatises written specifically for the medium of print. In Raphael's Vatican fresco *The School of Athens* (1509–10), Euclid is given Bramante's features, and as such the ancient father of geometry is made to serve as a crucial transitional figure for the evolving architectural language of Renaissance Italy. It was Bramante who most forcefully determined the sense of classical style embraced by his sixteenth-century successors, and it was he "who in casual conversation with Raphael and others may have given us our concept of the classical orders, Doric, Ionic, and Corinthian."[62] But it was Serlio, Vignola, and Palladio who first used numbers to quantify those orders, though measurements expressed in Hindu–Arabic integers were only fully incorporated into images in Vignola's *Regola delli cinque ordini d'architettura* [Rule for the Five Architectural Orders], first published in 1562 (Serlio used Roman numbers throughout the text of his treatise but not in its drawings).[63] Vignola's drawn Doric base differs only slightly from Alberti's, but very few words are used to describe it.[64] Here narrative gives way to quantification, precise numerical measurements inserted into the image itself, and with this shift toward quantification came detailed architectural drawings. Still, numeracy was not yet widespread among those in the building trade (even Michelangelo apparently had difficulty with two-digit multiplication, a real problem given the need for architects to estimate and keep track of building costs),[65] and it was essential that a precisely drawn design could be "copied, enlarged, or diminished to any other scale with a pair of compasses and without any knowledge of geometry or algorism."[66] Palladio hedged his bets in the *Quattro libri* by providing most of his instructions for single elements in all three media simultaneously – words, images, and numbers – though there is occasionally some discrepancy between the results each produce.

While the subtle technologies of the Gubbio *studiolo* are compressed into a space of just over 200 square feet, the project that Vignola

---

[62] Rowland (2010) 84.
[63] Serlio's treatise was conceived in seven books, the first five of which were published out of sequence during his lifetime, between 1537 and 1545; the seventh appeared posthumously in 1575; and the sixth was not printed until 1966.
[64] See plates VIIII–XIIII of the *Regola* in Vignola (1985).
[65] Carpo (2003) 469 n. 54.   [66] *Ibid.* 456.

planned for the Farnese dynasty at Caprarola after 1556 was hugely expansive. The Villa Farnese imposed itself on both its rugged natural environment – an extensive forest spread over several hills, already partially developed as a massive pentagonal fortification by Baldassare Peruzzi and Antonio da Sangallo the Younger between 1521 and 1534 – and an existing village that had to be entirely reconfigured (also by Vignola) in order to accommodate the most grandiose private residence ever constructed in Renaissance Italy. Michel de Montaigne visited the villa in September 1581, only several years after its completion, and while he has often been taken to task for paying little attention to art or architecture while on his Italian tour (Michelangelo is the only artist noted in the *Journal de voyage* (once), and the Ducal Palace in Urbino was found wanting both inside and out), at Caprarola his eye was trained on both its gigantic scale and technological marvels, particularly its waterworks, among the most sophisticated in later sixteenth-century Italy.[67] The spectacular 1608 engraving of Jacques Lemercier (the future architect of the Palais Royal and Sorbonne in Paris) entitled *Scenografia generale del Palazzo di Caprarola* [General View of the Palace of Caprarola] (Fig. 5.7) presents the villa as the centerpiece of a monumental stage set: a 72° cutaway exposes the interior arrangement of its ceremonial rooms, central spiral staircase, and circular inner court; outside, the lower semicircular and upper double-ramp stairs ascending toward the villa on either end of the trapezoidal piazza demarcate the "public" character of this space, open to all – Cardinal Alessandro Farnese as well as Pope Gregory XIII, who visited in 1578, addressed crowds here from the loggia (now enclosed) at the center of the façade on the *piano nobile* [principal floor] – while the gardens on the left and right behind were "private" areas for the cardinal, his family, and their guests, accessible via a bridge at the far side of the villa, below its single tower. "Stratified and superimposed projects of different architects, different models and typologies,"[68] Caprarola's built world is in stark contrast to the wild landscape subdued to create it, evident in the unruly, precipitous topography depicted at the right and left extremes of Lemercier's drawing.

[67] See Pertile (1973).
[68] Fagiolo (2007) 108, and in general on Caprarola. See Fagliari Zeni Buchicchio (2002) for drawings by Peruzzi, Sangallo, Vignola as well as the subsequent engravings of Villa Farnese by Lemercier and others.

Fig. 5.7 Jacques Lemercier, *Scenografia generale del Palazzo di Caprarola* (1608).

Though Lemercier's engraving bears no numerical indications, its geometrical coordinates are extraordinarily precise – the roundel on the right of the engraving notes that every inch of the palace had been meticulously measured but also that Vignola's drawings had been consulted (possibly originals, as Lemercier would have had ready access to the Farnese collection during the years he studied in Rome) – a demonstration of the precedence of Vignolan numeracy over Albertian narrative. The turn registered with Caprarola was further refined by Palladio: the choice of arithmetical operations to express the dimensions of a project allowed for the conception, design, and construction of buildings of enormous complexity.[69] Print contributed significantly to the success of this new system: documents, drawings, and entire projects now could be easily reproduced and circulated, rendering obsolete the older technologies linked to oral transmission and memory just at the time that moveable type consolidated the rapid spread of Hindu–Arabic numbers. A drawing thus synchronically calibrated on the page presented the builder with the precise measurements he needed to do

---

[69] See Carpo (2003) 465: "if we design buildings prior to building them, we can only build what we can measure."

his work. From here onward, the drawn project would become the norm for architectural practice.

Of a piece with Caprarola's architectural grammar, its interior decoration encompasses in its three grandest *piano nobile* rooms a glorification of Farnese exploits, a celebration of the feats of Hercules, and maps of the Heavens and the Earth as they were increasingly coming to be known through scientific and navigational exploration in the period (this latter room also features portraits of famous explorers). Caprarola thus presents the Farnese as masters not only of this particular piece of Roman territory, but of the known and expanding world, worthy companions of the greatest hero of ancient mythology for their derring-do, the entire complex a "vortex of moral connotations, admonitions, instructions, but above all the sign of the astral distance that separates the Farnese from common humanity."[70] The effort and expense involved in the creation of this "world apart" as well as its impact on the social fabric of the village of Caprarola was without equal anywhere in Europe in the period. Caprarola's rich extant documentation reveals that labor costs for construction of the villa alone amounted to the mind-boggling sum of 25,855.80 *scudi*, and the cost of a great deal of the initial infrastructure work (including the diversion of water for the gardens) was borne by the village.[71] Vignola cut an appropriately scenographic street right through the center of Caprarola, necessitating the destruction of a number of homes and businesses, but the upshot was not entirely bad for the community: in addition to the capital that flowed into the area – first in relation to such an ambitious building project, and then with the moneyed courtiers attached to the Farnese court – new houses for the displaced, a hospital, and church were constructed, and Vignola oversaw a hydraulic project in the area surrounding the nearby Lago di Vico that produced a significant amount of reclaimed land put at the disposal of townspeople for their own agricultural uses.

Cities, ideal and otherwise

As manifestations of human ingenuity, technologies find their greatest expression in cities, where humans are most concentrated, and the first

[70] Fagiolo (2007) 115.
[71] Partridge (1970) 82 n. 3, and in general on these records, "probably the most fully documented Renaissance monument presently known."

to argue for this connection was Giovanni Botero in a chapter of his *Della grandezza e magnificenza delle città* [On the Causes of the Greatness and Magnificence of Cities, 1588]. Drawing on both ancient and contemporary examples from throughout the known world, Botero argues that the promotion of "human industry" and the "multitude of the arts" for purposes which run the gamut from necessity to pleasure are among the basic elements that constitute the "civil life" exemplified in cities. The natural building blocks of technologies – wool, silk, mined metals and minerals, quarried stone and clay, trees – are made usable through the "industries" present in cities. For Botero, the prince is well advised to cultivate and patronize the most talented "artificers," even luring them from foreign countries, in order that his city be populous and prosperous, "because a numerous population is what makes the land fertile, and by means of its skills and hands endows raw materials with a thousand forms."[72] Botero's treatise establishes a sort of early modern urban sociology as it examines the formation of cities through linking environment, demographics, technologies (including transportation networks), economic growth, and institutions of learning and law.[73] Real cities, in other words, such as Palermo, where Botero was sent to study by the Jesuits in 1559 at the age of fifteen, and whose technological marvels – one of the grandest avenues in all of Italy and a splendid harbor – he still remembered vividly thirty years later (he did not stay long enough to see the most remarkable of the city's Renaissance wonders, the fountain originally built by Francsco Camilliani in Florence for the Spanish brother-in-law of Duke Cosimo I, moved to Palermo and installed there in Piazza Pretoria by 1584).[74]

"Ideal" cities, or utopias, have long been the object of interest to scholars of Renaissance Italy and beyond, but while the idea has roots in Greek antiquity and the medieval period the first treatise to employ the term was published only at the end of the sixteenth century: Giorgio Vasari il Giovane's *La città ideale, piante di chiese, palazzi e ville di Toscana e d'Italia* [The Ideal City, Plans of Churches, Palaces, and Villas in Tuscany and Elsewhere in Italy, 1598].[75] Recent historians of the architecture of Renaissance Italy have engaged in a debate about the merits of the

---

[72] Botero (2012) 46, and in general the section on "Industry," 41–46.
[73] See L. Firpo (1971) 356.
[74] See Botero (2012) 67–68 on Palermo; and Arnoldi (1974) on the Fontana Pretoria. For the best general overview of the Italian Renaissance city, see Adams/Nussdorfer (1994).
[75] On sixteenth-century literary formulations of the utopic city, see Bolzoni (1993).

concept and its applicability to a handful of fifteenth- and sixteenth-century planned cities, most of them located in the center and north of the peninsula.

Three celebrated fifteenth-century paintings of ideal cities, each inconclusively attributed to various central-Italian painters active in the period 1480–90 (now in museums in Urbino, Baltimore, and Berlin), set a standard against which any city, ideal or otherwise, could scarcely hope to compete.[76] Pictured in each is a central square worked out with geometrical precision, flanked by classicizing buildings which could have been designed by Alberti or Bramante, the whole conceived to guide the viewing eye to a perfect perspectival vanishing point. Though the setting of each of the panels is quite distinct, there is enough similarity between them to suggest that they were produced if not by the same painter at least within the same artistic environment, possibly Urbino during the final period of construction of the Palazzo Ducale. Federico's Urbino might thus be considered a model Renaissance city, reflecting in the elegant proportions of its newly constructed civic core – palazzo, cathedral, surrounding residences, and other ecclesiastical buildings – the latest architectural language (conceived by the Dalmatian Luciano Laurana as early as 1465 and brought, almost, to completion by Francesco di Giorgio by the time of Federico's death in 1482), the "ideal" container for the enlightened humanist values the duke sought to showcase in his court. But the palace, situated at the edge of a steep crag that would have involved significant engineering to ready it to support such an ambitious building, suggests the achievement of a controlled heterogeneity that respects the natural contours of the site (the *facciata ad ali* that originally hosted the majority of the *formelle* dedicated to technologies, for instance, sits slightly askew the piazza onto which it faces) rather than the geometrical symmetry of an imagined *città ideale*.

Pienza, the Tuscan hill town 40 miles south-east of Siena willed into being by Pope Pius II (Enea Silvio Piccolomini), and constructed between 1459 and 1464, has been at the center of the debate over "ideal" cities. Built on the site of a pre-existing village, Corsignano, where

---

[76] For reproductions of the three panels and a discussion of the most recent scholarship dealing with them, see the catalogue for the exhibit *La Città Ideale*, held in the Urbino Palazzo Ducale in 2012: Marchi/Valazzi (2012) 110–26.

Piccolomini had been born into noble but reduced circumstances in 1405, its sudden transformation into a papal retreat reconfigured the social and economic coordinates of an agrarian village (similar to but smaller than Caprarola) as cardinals and others attached to the Roman curia were compelled to invest in properties there. But when the real estate market skyrocketed with this influx of foreign capital, the pope was obliged to construct homes for the displaced poor; he also invested funds for the recruitment of artisans to live in the town, bought a building to be developed into a hospice, and financed the restoration of a number of house façades. Even more than Urbino, Pienza fails to correspond to a single harmonious aesthetic, though many of its new buildings were designed by one architect, Bernardo Rossellino. Several of these are more Gothic than Renaissance in inspiration (the residence of the French Cardinal Jouffroy mixes a number of distinct styles), and there is little classicizing evident in any of them apart from the *all'antica* façade of the cathedral (for which Piccolomini had indicated that he wanted a German-inspired design; a number of likely models have been identified in Bavarian churches) – and the uneven trapezoidal shape of its central piazza resists any attempt to fit it within a congruent perspectival grid. There are, to be sure, many carefully constructed pleasures to be had in Pienza – well-conceived buildings slowly revealing their details as one approaches them, the surprise of the expansive views of the Val d'Orcia that suddenly open up on either side of the cathedral (earlier obscured by fortified walls) – but the impression of a perfectly ordered Renaissance utopia is not one of them.[77] Piccolomini's premature death in 1464, at any rate, put an abrupt end to whatever such aspirations may have guided the project.

The plan that Filarete (Antonio di Pietro Averlino) developed for Sforzinda, explained in a fictitious extended dialogue with a princely patron (a thinly veiled Francesco Sforza) in his *Libro architettonico* [Book of Architecture, *c.* 1460–66] does propose a geometrically perfect form for his planned city: an eight-point star created by rotating one square 45° over another, thus creating a perimeter of sixteen segments with watchtowers situated at each of its outer points and gates at the inner ones; streets lead rectilinearly from the gates into the city's central square

---

[77] Smith (1992) and Adams (1998) support this more heterogeneous reading of Pienza, while C. R. Mack (1987), rich in documentary evidence about the planning and construction of the city, represents the "ideal" view of it.

around which the lord's residence, cathedral, state institutions, and its principal market were to be situated (basic geometrical shapes form the building blocks for everything in the city as well as the relations of every element in it); a circular moat surrounds the city walls, and a system of canals linked to the river outside them alternates with radial streets within. Though never built, several of the buildings Filarete describes in detail in his treatise bear some resemblance to structures he did succeed in constructing elsewhere (the Ospedale Maggiore in Milan, for example). The shape of the city can be seen to reflect idealized images of medieval Milan, and at the end of the sixteenth century it came to provide the blueprint for Palmanova, a nine-point star-shaped city intended as a defensive bastion against Ottoman expansion. But its Friulian site (now near the border with Slovenia) never proved popular with the Venetian citizens for whom it was intended, and though it served as a model for future city–fortresses throughout Europe well into the eighteenth century, Palmanova as a socially and commercially viable city never lived up to the expectations generated by the huge investment of Venetian financial resources and talent in it.[78]

It is no accident that treatises on the fortification of cities preceded those about cities themselves, and the consequences of the 1527 Sack of Rome suggest one possible explanation: cities are unstable receptacles of peoples and their cultures, in need not only of organization, develop-ment, and maintenance, but above all of protection.[79] The defensive strategy behind Palmanova had earlier informed the planning and con-struction of two well-known city–fortresses, Sabbioneta (near Mantua) and Terra del Sole (just outside of Forlì). But Acaya, at the south-eastern extreme of the peninsula, 6 miles from Lecce and roughly 2 miles from the Adriatic Sea, preceded them all. Redesigned between 1521 and 1536

---

[78] On the geometry of Sforzinda, see Filarete (1972) vol. 1, xxi–xxiii; and for a concise discussion of this "ideal city," see Giordano (1998) 64–65. For Palmanova, see Pollak (2010) 155–69; and Howard (2011) 193–211.

[79] On the extensively illustrated treatise of Girolamo Maggi and Giacomo Castriotto, *Della fortificazione delle città* [On the Fortification of Cities] originally published in 1564, see Hale (1985) 37–38; and for Giacomo Aconcio's *Trattato sulle fortificazioni* [Treatise on Fortifications] – translated into English in 1573 after circulating in England in both Italian and a Latin translation by the author (both lost), a sign of the long reach of Italian military engineering in the period – see Aconcio (2011). Tafuri (2006) 157–79 examines the ambiguous afterlife of the Sack, the single greatest trauma suffered by an Italian city since the mid-fourteenth-century Black Death; and Pearson (2011) provides a new reading of Alberti and the city, previously seen as tending toward the "ideal" but here considerably more ambivalent.

on the site of Segine, a medieval town first developed in the later thirteenth century by the Anjou rulers of the Kingdom of Naples, Acaya is the earliest Renaissance Italian town to incorporate up-to-date defensive and urban planning in an integrated project. Francesco di Giorgio had previously built fortresses throughout the Montefeltro territories of central-eastern Italy that were the first to factor firearms into their design; and other engineer–architects in the first half of the sixteenth century such as Michele Sanmicheli, the Sangallo family, and Baldassare Peruzzi developed massive fortifications contiguous with the pre-existing walls of large cities intended to safeguard urban areas from increasingly invasive gunpowder-based artillery (the Fortezza da Basso in Florence, for example). The crucial element in these later fortifications, and in treatises that promoted them, was the pentagonal angle bastion that has been described by John Hale as "the most significant of all architectural forms evolved during the Renaissance,"[80] effective both in reinforcing the segments of a defensive, or "curtain," wall otherwise overly exposed to enemy fire and in permitting a highly effective lateral defense from the narrow recessed flanks connecting the bastion's two principal faces to the "curtain." This axonometric map of Acaya as it remains today shows how essential the angle bastion was to the town's reconfiguration, three of them dominating its north-west, north-east, and south-east corners as well as the south-east portion of the castle (which, unusually, retains its two earlier, effectively outdated, circular defensive towers) (Fig. 5.8). Planned by the feudal lord of the area, the mathematician and military architect Gian Giacomo Acaya (later responsible for initiating or completing fortifications in Lecce, Crotone, Capua, Cosenza, and at the Castel Sant'Elmo in Naples), the town of Acaya balances exigencies of defense and those of an agricultural village situated at a strategic point for Italian push back against potential Ottoman incursions (the Battle of Otranto had been fought only 20 miles away in 1480–81). There is nothing particularly revolutionary about the design of the town: houses and shops all built originally on one level were situated on a grid of six north–south streets (a seventh was added later) and three west–east ones, with three *piazze* facing the castle, church, and

---

[80] Hale (1965) 466. See Adams (2002) on the new architectural forms elicited by the shift from *armi bianche* [pointed, blunt, or bladed weapons] to gunpowder-based ones; on the development of gunpowder itself, see Panciera (2007); and on the new artillery, see Belhoste (2007).

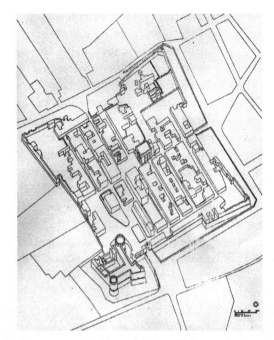

Fig. 5.8 Antonio Monte, *Axonometric Map of the Fortified-Town of Acaya*, 1:500 scale (1988).

Franciscan convent intersecting the urban space diagonally. But the scale of Acaya, from the relatively modest size of the ruling family's defensive castle to the generous dimensions of its town-houses – most of them comprising several rooms, a courtyard, basement, and access from streets on both sides of the block – everything realized unostentatiously in local stone and with sparing use of *ornamentum*, is in sharp contrast to many other Italian town-planning projects of the period, in which the needs of ordinary citizens were more often than not an afterthought.[81]

Perhaps the most telling detail of the Baltimore *città ideale* panel – the only one of the three to include recognizable buildings (such as the Roman Colosseum) – are the human figures who dot its exacting perspectival sight lines. Absent from the other two paintings, they appear to lend a welcome touch of realism to its otherwise sharply defined representation of a built environment whose every element seems to be almost too perfectly in place. But ultrasound research on the panel has

---

[81] On Acaya, see Monte (1996); D'Ercole (1999); and Mele (2012).

revealed that these figures were a subsequent addition, and their absence from the original painting confirms the distance that separates "ideal" cities from the practical imperatives of a world in the course of rapid transformation in the fifteenth and sixteenth centuries.

In the ninth canto of Ludovico Ariosto's epic poem *Orlando furioso* [Orlando Gone Mad, 1532], its eponymous hero hurls into the sea the gun he has just seized from Cimosco, a cruel tyrant who had aimed his fire at Orlando but instead killed the paladin's horse. The soundscape that Ariosto creates to evoke the effect of the gun firing, full of sibilant 's'es and 'z's in Italian, serves as a striking marker for the history of technologies in Renaissance Italy:

> There was a flash from behind like lightning, and from the front a roar like thunder in the air. The walls shuddered, and the ground underfoot; the heavens echoed to the dreadful sound. The fiery bolt, which smashes and annihilates whatever it meets and spares no one, hissed and screeched [IX.74].[82]

The sound would have been all too familiar to Ariosto's first readers, who in the early decades of the sixteenth century lived through one of the most destructive periods of warfare the Italian peninsula had endured since the end of the Roman empire. But firearms had appeared in Europe only in the first half of the fourteenth century, and their anachronistic introduction into a narrative poem situated in the tenth-century reign of Charlemagne suggests one of the many ways in which Renaissance literature appropriated the past in order to reflect contemporary concerns. In Cimosco's gun, Orlando recognizes a challenge to a whole range of values – individual, social, political, and cultural – which Ariosto's poem both celebrates and calls into question. Casting the offending weapon (together with its gunpowder and bullets) into the watery depths, however, turns out to be a Pyrrhic gesture, for it is rediscovered only two cantos later by a sorcerer, handed over to Germans who perfect the technology, and then – unleashed in all its potential destructiveness – lays waste to the poet's world.[83] Having added this episode to the poem in the course of its final redaction, Ariosto's attitude here was shaped by the Sack of Rome which occurred only 5 years

---

[82] Ariosto (1998) 90.
[83] See Murrin (1994) 123–30 for a discussion of Ariosto and artillery. Francesco di Giorgio, expert in explosives, expressed reservations about their use, see L. and P. G. Molari (2006) 15.

before its publication, but elsewhere in his poem he shows himself to be more amenable to a wide array of other technological innovations in the period, among them cartography and its sister sciences that contributed to ever more accurate maps of the world the *Orlando furioso*'s protagonists endlessly traverse. Cimosco's gun is, nevertheless, a powerful reminder that technological innovation is anything but neutral, its promise of progress counterbalanced by the real possibility of other outcomes and a signpost of both the limits and foresight of Jacob Burckhardt's idea of the Italian Renaissance as the precursor of modernity.

Acknowledgment

Thanks to Giovanni Fara, Emanuela Ferretti, Ingrid Rowland, and Giorgio Alberti for their invaluable help with this essay.

6

Languages

Humanism inherited from the late Middle Ages an idea of the Latin language that was completely different from ours. Late medieval artists, authors, and scholars imagined the ancient world as largely similar to theirs. Language was no exception, for they were convinced that Latin coexisted with vernacular languages in antiquity just as it did for them. This idea seemed to be supported by the biblical account of the tower of Babel: Latin would thus have been created as an artificial language in order to make possible an exchange of ideas among learned people, after the human race had lost its original common language and was forced to speak different languages (the vernaculars), without any possibility of under-standing each other. Latin, with its complex morphology and syntax, was thus considered a creation of scholars, not subject to alteration over time; it represented a realm of stability, whereas vernaculars were the domain of mutability and disorder. The word *grammatica* [grammar], therefore, came to be synonymous with Latin, in the belief that vernaculars were essentially bereft of grammatical rules. Similarly the word *litteratus* was used to denote someone who knew Latin, the only language considered suitable for proper writing. This theory of Latin and vernaculars was expounded by Dante Alighieri in his *De vulgari eloquentia* [On Vernacular Eloquence]. Differences between the Latin of ancient authors and the Latin of the moderns did not, of course, pass unnoticed by medieval scholars, but they thought that these differences were confined to vocabulary and that the morphological and grammatical structure of the language was unchanging.[1]

[1] See Rizzo (2002) 15–27; and Celenza (2005). For a broad overview, see Mazzocco (1993). The best and most up-to-date study in English on the debate regarding Latin in fifteenth-century Italy is Celenza (2009).

Humanists – scholars or students of classical literature and the disciplines associated with it – initially gave no particular priority to theoretical issues. Their unprecedented project of patterning culture and society on a world that had disappeared more than a thousand years earlier was carried out starting from the ground up, through rescuing and restoring texts which kept the memory of the ancient world alive. The first decades of the fifteenth century were spent in scouring remote, inhospitable ecclesiastical libraries for long-abandoned manuscripts. When a "new" author was discovered, the humanist hastened to copy out the text, either alone or with the aid of scribes, sometimes making corrections during or just after transcription, and then immediately circulated it among friends. Ancient authors were thus brought back to life as they entered into the continuum of contemporary culture. But the first and fundamental step of this *restitutio in integrum* [full recovery] of ancient literature was the repristination of its language and style, a humanist manifesto aimed at erasing the "barbarisms" of medieval Latin.

The battle for the new Latin was soon won on the literary front and over the course of the fifteenth century the classical Latin of the *auctores* [authors, but also authorities] that the humanists had made newly fashionable extended its reach – not, however, without fierce opposition – into disciplines which were hitherto strongholds of medieval Latin, such as medicine, philosophy, and law. This rapid success was due not so much to the intrinsic value of the cultural project that lay behind it, but rather to the support that the humanists managed to gain from the power-brokers of fifteenth-century Italy. The reasons for this phenomenon were multifaceted and varied between the different centers of Italian humanism, but its constitutive element was the growing importance of propaganda. The Italian peninsula was subject in this period to persistent and burdensome political instability, and recourse to either religious or imperial ideologies became increasingly problematic. A program presenting itself in such a situation as heir to the Roman political tradition – power nourished on higher moral and cultural values – was a potentially decisive weapon for the ruling class. The Medici in Florence, the Este in Ferrara, cardinals and popes in Rome, the former mercenary soldier Federico da Montefeltro in Urbino, and even a king with scarce humanist interests, Alfonso of Aragon ("il Magnanimo") in Naples, gathered together teams of humanists whose principal function was to represent the image and express the views of their patrons in the new Latin, a language favored by its wide circulation and its apparent resistance to change. The letters, orations, treatises, and histories that humanists produced while working for the various Italian courts and oligarchic republics established humanist Latin as the language of political power in fifteenth-century Italy.

As the first and most significant period of the rediscovery of texts drew to a close, the thesaurus of ancient Latin literature was greatly expanded. Humanists could then contemplate the new landscape as they began to reflect on the language that they had renewed. In the spring of 1435 a dispute developed in the antechamber of pope Eugene IV – then resident in Florence – on a topic that had already been debated at length: in which language had the Romans given their orations?[2] Leonardo Bruni (together with Antonio Loschi and Cencio de' Rustici) argued that the Romans used a vernacular in which the orators delivered their speeches, and that they subsequently rewrote the texts for posterity *in grammaticam Latinitatem* [in proper Latin]. Flavio Biondo, Poggio Bracciolini, and Andrea Fiocchi had completely different opinions about the matter, and Biondo recounts the dispute in his *De verbis Romanae locutionis* [On the Words of the Latin Language], dated April 1, 1435, and addressed to Leonardo Bruni. For Biondo, everyone in ancient Rome had spoken Latin, and differences within the large Latin-speaking community were due only to a varying degree of refinement in its language usage. Relying on the *Orator* of Cicero, Biondo distinguished three separate registers of Latin: one for poetry, determined by metrics; one for oratory, characterized by the use of specific quantitative clauses; and one for the vernacular, that did not follow any fixed rules. According to Biondo, the Romans initially had only the latter, common to all; subsequently, a restricted elite perfected the language, creating both poetry and oratorical prose. Orators thus spoke in more or less refined Latin, and comedies were performed in it. Finally, basing his analysis on Cicero's *Brutus*, Biondo claims that Latin was a living language, already subject to historical evolution before Cicero's time, and that after the northern invasions it was gradually replaced by the vernacular. It is noteworthy that the evidence Biondo proffers in support of his thesis is entirely derived from the *Brutus*, a work rediscovered in Lodi in 1421 which Biondo transcribed in his own

---

[2] For the story of the debate and the related humanist texts see Tavoni (1984); Rizzo (2002) 75–85; Celenza (2009) 213–22; and Ferrente (2010).

hand the following year. His thesis could never have been formulated without the recovery of this ancient text.

Bruni replied to Biondo posing a general problem: whether during the lifetime of Plautus and Terence commoners and the educated in Rome would all have spoken in the same way. Bruni's thesis was still strongly marked by the medieval tradition: two languages coexisted in the ancient world just as in the present: one grammar-less, that of unlearned people; the other Latin, the prerogative of the learned, with its highly structured grammar. Public speakers thus addressed an audience formed mainly of the educated; commoners who went to hear them or to see comedies performed in the theater might have enjoyed the gestures of orators or actors, or appreciated the stage scenery, but they would have understood practically nothing of the text that they heard.

The dispute marked a turning point. Instead of the old idea of Latin as a fixed artificial language, invented by scholars, humanist analysis based upon the newly available texts rendered visible both the diachronic evolution of Latin and its wide expressive registers. For the first time, language became a subject of historical inquiry. The debate continued over the course of the fifteenth century, engaging many of the most important humanists: Guarino Veronese, Poggio Bracciolini, and Francesco Filelfo taking Biondo's side;[3] while Angelo Decembrio and Lorenzo Valla defended Bruni's position.[4] These scholars had no interest whatsoever in the vernacular, but it is clear that Biondo's thesis opened up new perspectives for Italian literature as well, for if the ancients had written in their own native language (not in a learned construct), there was no reason for the moderns to do any differently. There was, therefore, no reason to maintain that the vernacular and its literature were in any way genetically inferior to Latin. Humanists began to realize that the vernacular too was subject to its own grammatical rules and that all Romance languages were derived from Latin, even if – from Biondo onwards – many of them would always consider this relationship as debased, a sort of poisoned fruit left in the wake of the northern invasions and the fall of the Roman empire.

---

[3] On them, see Celenza (2009) 226–33, 237–40.
[4] On Decembrio, see *ibid.* 225–26.

Leon Battista Alberti was the first to draw more promising conclusions for the vernacular from Biondo's thesis. After recalling the terms of the earlier debate in the third book of his *Libri della Famiglia* [Books of the Family, 1436–37], Alberti justified his championing of the vernacular by asserting the necessity of being understood by all: "and be it as many say that the ancient language provided good authority for all peoples because many learned people wrote in Latin, our language will certainly enjoy a similar fate if [our] scholars would polish and refine it through their study and vigilance."[5] Consistent with this thinking, Alberti wrote a *Grammatichetta* [Basic Grammar] of the vernacular between 1438 and 1441, the first work of its kind, and in Florence he organized the *Certame coronario* in 1441, a vernacular poetry contest dedicated to the theme of friendship meant to emulate the poetic *certamina* [competitions] of the ancients. But neither the *Grammatichetta* nor the *Certame* were particularly successful; they were too far ahead of their time.[6]

Lorenzo Valla was the undisputed protagonist of Latin studies in the mid fifteenth century. Belonging to the first generation of scholars following the initial period of humanist textual recovery, Valla was above all a linguist. His mission was to restore Latin prose to its ancient purity, cleansing it from medieval syntactic irregularities through careful analysis of the language and style – the *usus* – of all extant ancient authors. Valla's most important work in this regard, the *Elegantiae linguae Latinae* [The Properties of the Latin Language], survived as a reference work about Latin morphology and syntax well beyond the fifteenth century. Valla's ideas about the Latin language are expounded in two short texts, the preface to the *Elegantiae* (likely written in Rome in 1448), and an oration given at the University of Rome during the opening ceremony of the academic year 1455–56.[7] The preface to the *Elegantiae* begins with a comparison between empire and language: many peoples have had empires, and some of them lasted longer than the Roman one, but none had spread its language as the Romans did, in an area that extended over the entire Italian peninsula to almost the whole known West and a large part of Africa and Northern Europe. Having brought

---

[5] Alberti (1996).
[6] On Alberti, see Celenza (2009) 222–25; on the *Certame*, see Gorni (1972).
[7] For a comparative study of the two texts, and generally on Valla's ideas on language, see Rizzo (2002) 87–118.

Latin to the provinces, Valla says, was by far a greater and more splendid glory than the political and military supremacy the Romans enjoyed, since through the Latin language the people of the empire learned both liberal arts and laws. He recognizes that Roman dominion over previously independent peoples might have been perceived as a loss of freedom, but he presents the spread of Latin as an enrichment, not the erasure, of local vernacular traditions.[8] Latin was for Valla "a metahistorical language, valid for all time, that can be learned as well by moderns as it was by the ancients ... [it] constitutes for both the most perfect cultural medium available to humankind."[9] Restoring the Latin language to its ancient splendour meant for Valla providing the arts and sciences once again with a virtually inexhaustible linguistic field in which they could take root, spread, and flourish.

The later *Oratio* represents Valla's intellectual will and testament. Here the joint fortunes of Latin and the liberal arts are recounted, but from a slightly different and historically more convincing point of view. Progress in each separate art, writes Valla, depends on a plurality of practitioners, but in order that imitation – the basis of all development – be fostered, all must first share the same language. Valla claims that Rome, after having established its far-reaching dominion, "gave" its language to its subjected peoples. He again resorts to a similitude – here between language and money – to portray this potentially loaded situation: "when Latin came to be adopted as a sort of gold standard, it was then possible for any people to learn anything written by any others and to teach in turn their own things, whereas before they could read only what their countrymen had written."[10] But Valla also signals in the *Oratio* the precipitous decline of learning that ensued upon the end of the empire: "after the Roman empire – on which the Latin language relied – had disappeared, it was unavoidable that the language itself should collapse, and all the liberal arts with it."[11] The indissoluble link between political and military dominion, and the destinies of language and culture which had been left out of the preface to the *Elegantie* are clearly affirmed in the *Oratio*. Valla draws a further distinction based on geography: in Asia and Africa "the Latin language was expelled with the

---

[8] Garin (1952). On Valla's linguistic theories in the *Elegantie*, see Marsh (1979).
[9] Cesarini Martinelli (1980) 62; see also Celenza (2009) 233–36, 241–42.
[10] Valla (1994) 196.   [11] *Ibid.* 198.

empire and all the good arts with it, and the earlier barbarity recovered its authority."[12] In Europe, however, things went differently, the credit for which goes to the Church which defended Latin as the language of Christian religion and ecclesiastical administration, such that the nations of Europe, though liberated from the ancient Roman empire, did not abandon Latin. The Roman curia, where Latin held undisputed sway, was for Valla something akin to a brightly illuminated harbor, where the learned of the world converged. Two issues are here at center-stage: the link between political supremacy and linguistic/ cultural dominion; and the matter of Rome as the *communis patria* [common homeland] of all learned persons. Both would find enormous resonance in the Renaissance.

From a pragmatic point of view, the model of language suggested by Valla was an eclectic one: within the strict boundaries of what had been sanctioned by the *usus* of the ancient prose-writers, Valla did not set a particular scale of values. If Latin was a language created by authors, all writers of Latin, not only ancients but also moderns, contributed to enriching it. This explains the open-mindedness Valla showed about neologisms: what criterion was to be followed for expressing things and notions that had been unknown to the ancient world? It was a highly topical issue, especially for historiographers, and was also discussed by Flavio Biondo. The choice was between the preservation of the purity of ancient Latin – either through adopting circumlocutions or using only words guaranteed by ancient authors (and taking a chance on misunderstanding) – and the use of neologisms, which meant introducing into Latin modern words which inevitably would have sounded crude or new-fangled to purists. Valla had no doubt that the proper choice was the latter.

Another factor makes Valla a key figure in the transition from the first to the second generation of fifteenth-century humanism: he spent the last part of his life as a university professor. The spread of the teaching of rhetoric in Italy was among the greatest successes of the humanist movement, establishing its place alongside the most important disciplines traditionally taught in medieval universities – law, moral and natural philosophy, medicine, and theology – slowly turning the medieval *studia* [universities] into humanist *academiae* [academies].

[12] *Ibid.*

The largest universities eventually employed two or more professors of rhetoric, who taught on the same days but at different times and earned disparate salaries. Universities were thus among the most lively centers of humanist culture during the second half of the fifteenth century. Rhetorical training was most of all a linguistic education, and even when professors elicited discussions of antiquarianism or ancient history their ultimate aim was to teach students how to write in the best Latin style. Significant in this regard are Domizio Calderini's words in an address he delivered at Rome in 1474 on the occasion of the beginning of a course on Cicero's *De oratore*, the high-water mark of the whole curriculum: "We will have labored in vain over the past four years to shed light on unexplained traces of antiquity and most obscure poems unless you have finally managed to express distinctly, with proper words, at length, and to render illustrious through your discourse those things you nurtured thanks to the strength of our minds and your untiring study."[13] The topic was as old as humanism itself, but for Calderini and his colleagues in Italian universities it was an institutional mission, as he affirms in the remainder of his address. Pomponio Leto, who also taught at the Roman university, is still known today for his antiquarian studies, but his Latin philological work is now almost completely forgotten. Eulogies written just after his death by Pietro Marso and Michele Ferno praise Pomponio as *linguae Latinae instaurator maximus* [the greatest restorer of the Latin language], and as the scholar who purified the Latin language from all outside contamination, restoring it to its native land, re-establishing its ancient prerogatives and splendor.[14]

Philologists were most active as university professors in Italy just as the printing press arrived there. Humanists played a leading role in the diffusion of print culture in Italian cities large and small. Many humanist editors considered the new era that opened with moveable type as no less significant than the earlier period of the rediscovery of ancient texts. Just as Poggio and his contemporaries had resuscitated ancient literature, so the printing press, and its editors, preserved this literature for posterity, ensuring that they would never again be lost. Guaranteeing the survival of texts, once again, meant preserving the language in which they were written. In the life of Lucan that he provided as

---

[13] The text is quoted in Campanelli/Pincelli (2000) 158–59.
[14] On the teaching of rhetoric in the Roman *studium* see *ibid.*

an introduction to his edition of the *Bellum Civile* [Civil War] printed in 1469, Pomponio Leto writes that the famous early typographers Sweynheym and Pannartz churned out books "so that the Latin language would not die." Printing produced such a quantity of books and permitted their circulation in ways which would have been inconceivable previously. The effects were multifaceted, not least among which were a renewed interest in Latin vocabulary, an impulse both to explore remote areas of the Latin language and to recover neglected words. The need for reliable texts widened the parameters of humanist Latin and scholars engaged in a competitive effort to avoid multiplying in print the profligate corruption of difficult words already evident in manuscripts. Giovanni Andrea Bussi, bishop of Aleria, who edited many of the principal ancient Latin classics between the end of 1468 and mid-1471 in Rome, meant to append a short dictionary of rare words at the end of the text of his edition of Pliny the Elder's *Naturalis historia* [Natural History] but failed to do so.[15]

Rare words were the preserve of professional philologists whose leading fifteenth-century figure was Angelo Poliziano, unique among his peers for having joined the most sophisticated philological skills with outstanding qualities as an author of prose and verse works in Latin, Italian poetry, and a collection of Greek epigrams.[16] In the first half of the 1470s Poliziano translated Books Four and Five of the *Iliad* into Latin, and his Greek epigrams amply demonstrate the influence of Homer.[17] In addition, while teaching Aristotle's logical and moral philosophy in Florence, Poliziano employed his knowledge of Greek in recuperating ancient philosophical texts, such as the *Enchiridion* by the Stoic Epictetus, and the *Problemata physica* then attributed to Aristotle's Greek commentator Alexander of Aphrodisia. Poliziano's formidable language and philological skills were one of the results of the general recovery of Greek studies in the Latin West that began toward the end of the *Trecento* with the arrival in Florence of Manuel Chrysoloras and received a renewed impetus following the conquest of Constantinople in 1453 by the Ottoman Turks and the consequent exodus of Greek-speaking scholars. In the second half of the fifteenth century, Byzantine

---

[15] See Bussi's 1469 preface to Apuleius in Botfield (1861) 72–73.
[16] See Rizzo (1998); Carlino (2010); and Daneloni (2014).
[17] Poliziano (2002).

émigrés progressively strengthened the study of Greek in Italian humanist schools and universities, a contribution considered decisive for the rediscovery of ancient Roman culture that in its time had appropriated so much of the culture of ancient Greece. Both princes and scholars avidly collected Greek manuscripts, and at the end of the century the Venetian printer Aldus Manutius began to make available a number of Greek classics in handsome printed editions, from Homer to Plato, and Thucydides to Sophocles.[18]

The taste for sophisticated words – recovered through the careful philological analysis of ancient texts and subsequently absorbed into his own literary work – constituted the heart of Poliziano's labors. But his was not only a scholarly ambition: it mirrored a social class that had turned an artistic aesthetic into ideology, using it to portray itself favorably and to legitimize its political supremacy. In the preface to the first *centuria* [one hundred chapters] of his *Miscellanea* (1489), Poliziano defends his philological work by asserting that it is not intended for the masses, and that the skilled use of an elevated lexicon is "never criticized by cognoscenti. It should be unobjectionable to renew words which are already almost obsolete, provided that in so doing these words not *vetustescere* [grow even older] but begin to *veterascere* [be revitalized as they age]."[19] In the spirit of *docta varietas* [learned variety], the practice of juxtaposing words drawn from every era and disciplinary field of ancient Latin with a keen sense for the most recondite makes Poliziano's style as refined as it is difficult, requiring a reader in possession of the same extraordinary culture as the author. But for the tumultuous *Quattrocento* such an exclusive idea of art was bound to give rise to polemics. Poliziano was alarmed to learn in a 1489 letter from Alessandro Cortesi that the language of his Latin translation of Herodian's *Historiae* – a work on which Poliziano had staked his reputation in the *res publica litterarum* [republic of letters] – was being criticized in Rome for its recourse to a vocabulary some there considered obsolete. And in 1493 he had a bitter dispute with the Florentine chancellor Bartolomeo Scala, who accused

[18] On interest in Greek in *Trecento* Italy, see Coccia (2010); and on the subsequent "recovery" of Greek by Italian Renaissance humanists, see Dionisotti *et al.* (1988); Hankins (2003) 273–91; Monfasani (2012); and Brownlee/Gondicas (2013). See Ciccolella/Speranzi (2010) on the diffusion of Greek culture and the study of Near Eastern languages in Italy in the period. And for a catalogue of humanist translations from Greek in the fifteenth and sixteenth centuries, see Cortesi/Fiaschi (2008).
[19] See Rizzo (1998) 87.

him of using *ascita nimium verba et remota* [words too excessively sophisticated and remote].²⁰ Poliziano defended himself by noting that the
distinction between rare and common words might have made sense in
antiquity, when Latin was a living language, whereas in the present,
with Latin vocabulary grounded only on extant ancient texts, the two
categories were equivalent; it was thus the task of the author, drawing on
his taste and cultural preparation, to breathe life into words that had
fallen into disuse through widespread ignorance. But Poliziano also
drew a social distinction between Scala's language – meant to be used
by notaries and those working in the Florentine chancellery, and thus to
be understood by any Latin-literate reader – and his own, an elegant and
elaborate language intended to mold the future ruling class of the city.

Poliziano was hardly alone: his views were shared among a narrow
class of prominent university professors and scholars who represented
the vanguard of late-fifteenth-century humanist culture. They aspired
to establish a modern Latin interwoven with exotic words at the same
time as they sought to colonize disciplinary fields which had previously
proven impervious to humanist Latin. For centuries many disciplines
had successfully employed a Latin vocabulary and syntax quite far from
the polished language of ancient authors that nevertheless served their
purposes. In a famous exchange of letters between Pico della Mirandola
and Ermolao Barbaro in 1485, Ermolao wanted to rescue the language
of philosophy from the ugliness of "Parisian" (or Scholastic) Latin,
arguing the humanist article of faith that truth and beauty should go
hand in hand.²¹ It is, however, important to bear in mind that the
fifteenth century was a period of pronounced multilinguism in Italy,
and with regard to Latin there coexisted a wide range of stylistic levels
and technical languages.²²

Poliziano's model of strenuous Latin scholarship wed to high literary
accomplishment died with him in 1494 as he had had little success in
exporting this lofty standard beyond the Florentine circle of Lorenzo de'
Medici. In contraposition to Poliziano, Bartolomeo Scala expressed a
widespread learned opinion when he argued that Cicero was the only
good model of Latin style, but in so doing Scala reopened a recent
wound. The young Roman humanist Paolo Cortesi had written a dialogue *De hominibus doctis* [Of Learned Men] between 1489 and 1490 in

---

²⁰ See Godman (1998) 125–26.
²¹ See Pico della Mirandola/Barbaro (1998).   ²² See Rizzo (2004).

which he aimed to sketch out a history of fifteenth-century Latin literature, using the style of Cicero as his touchstone. Cortesi succeeded in eliciting from Poliziano a rather short and decidedly cool preface to his dialogue, and buoyed by this coup he subsequently sent to Poliziano a collection of humanist epistles whose distinctive feature was the imitation of Cicero. Poliziano replied with a letter in which he complains about the time he had lost reading the anthology: in his opinion, the aim of imitating only Cicero was a *superstitio*, typical of weak writers, and as for imitation in general he notes that "just as one who cares for putting his foot only in the footprints of others cannot run well, so one who dares not go beyond an established model cannot write well ... it is typical of an impoverished mind to draw nothing from itself, to do nothing other than imitate in any circumstances."[23] Cortesi responded, somewhat ironically, with a defense of the principle of imitation as the basis of all the arts.[24] For Cortesi, imitation is a guarantee against excess and ensures textual harmony, the fundamental requirement of an elegant writer. But while he had clearly wanted the imprimatur of Poliziano's authority to grace his own work, Cortesi can be seen as provoking Poliziano, challenging and to some extent mocking his authority.

The two most distinguished philologists of the beginning of the sixteenth century, Filippo Beroaldo and his student Giovan Battista Pio, took the taste for rare words to extremes, the former producing a huge commented edition of the *Metamorphoses* [Metamorphoses, or The Golden Ass] of Apuleius in 1500, and the latter moving even farther toward the outer limits of late antique literature by concentrating on authors such as Fulgentius and Sidonius Apollinaris. "Apuleianism" had a limited impact, however, as its achievements were widely judged to be both abstruse and ponderous. Texts written in or inspired by Apuleian style are notoriously difficult to read: the admixture of Latin and Italian of the *Hypnerotomachia Poliphili*, published by Aldus Manutius' Venetian press in 1499 is perhaps the best-known example.[25] Cortesi was a late convert to Apuleianism, and his treatise *De cardinalatu*

---

[23] See Dellaneva/Duvick (2007) 4 (also for these texts of Poliziano and Cortesi). On the correspondance between Poliziano and Cortesi, and on the following evolution of Ciceronianism during the first decades of the sixteenth century, see D'Ascia (1991); Monfasani (1999); Dionisotti (2003); and above all, Celenza (2009) 202–12, 241–42. On imitation, see Pigman (1980); and McLaughlin (1995) 692.
[24] See Dellaneva/Duvick (2007) 10.   [25] See Carver (2007) 183–235.

[On the Cardinalate, published in 1510] – a sort of training manual for the perfect Renaissance cardinal, a courtesy book that anticipated in some respects Baldassare Castiglione's *Libro del cortegiano* [Book of the Courtier, 1528] – is a good example of the problems facing the theoreticians of Latin style in the early sixteenth century. In a letter to Cortesi, Raffaele Maffei noted three separate lexical strata in *De cardinalatu*: "familiar words; somewhat obscure words which are nonetheless easily understood through dictionaries; [and a] third kind . . . entirely Apuleian and your own . . . [requiring a powerful] interpreter, without whom [none of] the oracles and soothsayers celebrated by the ancients . . . could have penetrated the meaning."[26]

Cardinal Adriano Castellesi, an influential but eccentric figure in the papal courts of Innocent VIII, Alexander VI, Julius II, and Leo X – he served first as papal nuncio in England, and then as representative of the English crown in Rome – composed a short treatise against "Apuleianism," *De sermone Latino* [On the Latin language, 1514], which serves as a starting point for sketching a history of the Latin language divided into four *tempora* [eras]: *antiquissimum* [most ancient], *antiquum* [ancient], *perfectum* [perfect], and *imperfectum* [imperfect]. Castellesi's aim was to show that ancient authors were already well aware that the age of Cicero represented the zenith of Latin culture, and the model Castellesi proposed therefore makes of Cicero and the entire literature of his contemporaries the *perfectum*; Apuleius and Martianus Capella, not to mention Sidonius Apollinaris and Fulgentius, represent the *imperfectum*, the period of ancient Latin's decline.[27]

The rapid growth of the Italian vernacular in the late fifteenth and early sixteenth centuries required a serious reflection on the space and the role of modern Latin literature. In Rome, Ciceronianism continued to gain ground in literary practice, and an epistolary exchange between Pietro Bembo and the philosopher Giovanni Francesco Pico spells out what was at stake. In a long letter sent to Bembo in 1512, Pico objects to the principle of *imitatio*, noting that ancient authors had avoided it. He makes two strong points. The first, philosophical in character, acknowledges that while it is true – as in Aristotle – that humans have a peculiar tendency to imitate, it is equally true that from birth they already possess instincts and inclinations which cannot be

---

[26] *Ibid.* 264.   [27] On Castellesi's treatise see *ibid.* 265–67.

modified without doing violence to nature. The idea of proper eloquence is created by nature, imprinting on the soul a simulacrum of its beauty, the criterion for judging one's own eloquence and that of others. The subject of imitation must therefore be the *dicendi perfecta facultas* [consummate skill in speaking] that everyone already possesses impressed in the mind, rather than the style of a particular ancient author. The second point is more technical: within the categories of classical rhetoric designated for the composition of an oration – *inventio* [invention], *dispositio* [arrangement], and *elocutio* [style] – there was no place for *imitatio*. Pico's letter contains a further claim for the merits of modern authors, forcefully setting itself against the trend that makes virtue of whatsoever is ancient and vice of everything modern. The weakness of Pico's argument is in its setting out only general principles about the idea and the nature of imitation, rather than rules which could be effectively turned into an alternative practice.

Bembo replied with a letter – actually a short treatise – dated January 1, 1513. He makes an empiricist argument against Pico's neo-Platonism: perfect eloquence is not to be sought in one's soul, but in books and through extended study. That perfect eloquence does actually exist is not, for Bembo, an argument against but rather a confirmation of the necessity to imitate only one model, provided that it is the most perfect one. Rather than Pico's democratizing general principles, Bembo makes it clear that his take on style is a theory of excellence, intended for a chosen few and consistent with a strictly aristocratic idea of art. Platonic ideas are insufficient for Bembo's conception, requiring *exempla* [examples] to give it form: "*imitatio* is entirely understood through the *exemplum* and must be drawn from it."[28] The opinion that all good authors were suitable for imitation leads, for Bembo, to an art that fails to meet two fundamental requirements: coherence and harmony. According to Bembo, the work of art is a single body in which all parts must seamlessly fit together, and *imitatio* is the only criterion that facilitates this achievement. Cicero is acknowledged as the exclusive model for Latin prose and Virgil for poetry, but Bembo also notes that an author need not be enslaved by his model: "First let us set out to imitate the best; then imitate, endeavouring to reach him; finally, once we have reached him, let us direct all our efforts towards surpassing him."[29] Here Bembo

---

[28] Dellaneva/Duvick (2007) 56.   [29] *Ibid.* 80.

establishes the relationship between *imitatio* and *aemulatio* [emulation] which would come to form the core of Renaissance classicism. His letter embodies a concise presentation of Renaissance aesthetics at the same time as it provides irrefutable rules for modern Latin authors that were relatively easy to put into practice. Pico might have had the upper hand in the dispute had its objective been philosophical rather than literary. The differences between friends and foes of Ciceronianism were perfectly encapsulated by Francesco Berni in his anti-Ciceronian *Dialogo contro i poeti* [Dialogue against the Poets] (1526), and by Erasmus in his equally critical *Ciceronianus* [The Ciceronian, 1528], but in the end Bembo's view prevailed during the first half of the sixteenth century, and it had a significant collateral impact on justifications for the Italian vernacular which came to be understood as *la questione della lingua* [the language question].

The first half of the *Trecento* had seen a remarkable maturation of the Tuscan vernacular in the works of the *tre corone* [three crowns] – Dante, Petrarch, and Boccaccio – but no precise rules were provided for its usage, no lexicon was established to aid in its interpretation, and Dante's *De vulgari eloquentia* – the only contemporary attempt to address the language question from a theoretical position – remained incomplete and largely unknown in the period.[30] What did prove to be decisive were the geographic origins of the language employed in this foundational literature, and however differing the conclusions reached at various points in the debate, Tuscany, and Florence in particular, remained the fixed terms around which all subsequent discussion turned. In the "Epistola" Poliziano wrote for the *Raccolta aragonese*, a collection of vernacular poetry Lorenzo de' Medici presented in 1477 to Federico d'Aragona, a canon of primarily Tuscan writers is proposed through adherence to an aesthetic that accommodates the very earliest *Duecento* Sicilian poets and their *Stilnovisti* successors [the practitioners of the "Sweet New Style"] while also criticizing some aspects of Dante's work at the same time that Cino da Pistoia, a contemporary much influenced by Dante, is singled out for praise.[31] Poliziano's "was a

---

[30] For a helpful survey of the parameters of the *questione della lingua*, see Antonelli/Ravesi (2010).

[31] See Poliziano (for Lorenzo de' Medici) in Varese (1955) 989. Bologna (1986) 585, notes "the radical metamorphosis in sensibility operative between the late *Quattrocento* and the early *Seicento* ... a transformation of the term judgment into that of taste."

provocative judgment which placed private taste before what we might call national and monumental value" in daring to reprove the author of the *Commedia*.[32] But this aestheticizing tendency also prepared the way for the inclusion of Lorenzo's own poetry in a collection which focuses on the *Duecento* and *Trecento*, and which despite the presence of the very earliest *Quattrocento* poets situates Lorenzo as Petrarch's heir for his epoch, a politically centripetal gesture making of Florence's effective leader also the vessel through which her literary culture is reinvigorated and her language affirmed as normative.

In his *Comento* to Dante's *Commedia* Cristoforo Landino turned Poliziano's judgment back at him in order to dismiss the non-Tuscan poets Poliziano had sought to elevate above Dante, an effort that while short-changing the *Commedia*'s sources did serve to recognize the *Quattrocento* poets rejected by the *Raccolta* as Dante's successors,[33] just as it provided for the first systematic study of Dante's language, resulting in what amounts to a Florentine politico-cultural manifesto. In Landino Dante's banishment is represented as having extended well beyond the grave by all who had done his poetry damage in both "correcting" and commenting upon it in forms of Italian different from the "Florentine" of the early *Trecento*; now, however, through Landino's stewardship, Dante is finally and truly repatriated, and through his patronage Lorenzo de' Medici is recognized for presiding over the end of the poet's long exile.[34]

Bembo's position with regard to the vernacular first took tangible form during the course of the editorial work he performed for Aldus Manutius' editions of Petrarch's *Rime sparse* (1501) and *Le terze rime di Dante* (1502), an effort that demanded a more exigent standard than Landino had employed with which to redact and collate extant manuscripts and previously printed editions.[35] The radically innovative format of the Aldine Dante is in striking contrast to Landino's 1481 edition of the *Commedia* (a large-scale folio volume in which the commentary on each of its 372 very large pages literally engulfs Dante's tercets), containing only the text of the poem, not a word of commentary,

[32] Tavoni (1992a) 75.

[33] On Landino's response to Poliziano, see R. Cardini (1973) 212–32. Poliziano tempered his differences with Landino following the publication of the *Comento*, given their mutual commitment to promoting Florentine civic culture under Lorenzo's auspices; see Godman (1993) 196–98.

[34] See Landino (2001) 221. For Lorenzo's own views on the language question, see Grayson (1960) 417–20.

[35] On these editions, see Trovato (1994) 79–81.

and printed in a pocket-size – 244 *ottavo* pages – previously unknown for works of *gravitas*. The nexus in these editions of a developing print culture and the urge to "fix" the vernacular in order to reproduce it consistently in print led not only to Bembo's *Prose della volgar lingua* [On the Vernacular Language, 1525] but also to the first vocabularies and grammars, some of which took issue – episodically with some passing success in Italy itself – with Bembist ideology. Bembo – a Venetian aristocrat long resident in Urbino and then in Rome – insisted on linguistic unity in the absence of the political unity of the Italian peninsula, echoing Dante's similar concern in *De vulgari* I.xvi, an effort all the more urgent in the wake of the political disasters that befell Italy in the early decades of the sixteenth century.

Gian Giorgio Trissino's initial contribution to the language question, after his rediscovery and study of the *De vulgari* (perhaps as early as 1513), was to posit for the first time the value of innovation in approaching the issues central to a debate that hitherto had been so preoccupied with precedent.[36] The *Epistola de le lettere nuovamente aggiunte ne la lingua italiana* [Epistle on Letters Newly Added to the Italian Language] was published in Rome in 1524 and addressed to Pope Clement VII, under whose aegis Trissino hoped for "the integral reform of literary, orthographic, and linguistic institutions, a language that would emanate from Rome" and serve as a culturally unifying force authorized by the Italian peninsula's only trans-municipal power (linked, moreover, in Clement with the political and cultural authority of Florence). Trissino's ideas in the *Epistola* are bogged down, however, by his program of introducing into written Italian an incongruous system of Greek vowels in an attempt to better visually reproduce the sound of the language and to mark the vernacular's liberation from Latin (ancient *exempla* are provided only from Greece, as if to suggest that Roman cultural history could be entirely ignored). In the same period Trissino also published his *Sofonisba* (entitled after its female protagonist and written earlier for the papal court of Leo X), the first full-fledged tragedy to appear since the collapse of the ancient world, in

[36] See Trovato (1994) 109. Migliorini (1994) 315 notes that Trissino likely introduced the *De vulgari* to the circle of Florentine intellectuals (among whom was Machiavelli) which met in the enclosed garden of the Rucellai family, the Orti Oricellari, during the time of his initial work on the manuscript. For a brief summary of Trissino's career, see Zatti (1999); the principal study remains Morsolin (1894). For Trissino's works on language, see Trissino (1986).

which the author's ideas about both the Italian lexicon and its spelling are put into provocative practice.[37] Trissino's initial published work constituted a pointed early reaction to Bembo's *Prose*, already widely known through its manuscript circulation prior to publication in 1525, and Bembo's supporters were quick to launch a counter-offensive against Trissino's contrary ideas.

With the publication of Bembo's *Prose*, the theoretical center of vernacular gravity shifted to a form of imitation that sought to impose on Italian the same principles operative in the contemporary promotion of Latin style.[38] Though the dialogic form which Bembo utilizes in the *Prose* allows for opposing points of view, it is always clear that his surrogate in the treatise, his brother Carlo, represents the position that will in the end carry the day. The first two books of the *Prose* were written in Urbino, where Bembo had participated in the court culture cultivated there by Guidobaldo da Montefeltro and memorialized in Castiglione's *Cortegiano* (in which a fictionalized Bembo figures as one of the interlocutors); the third book was composed in Rome, during the years Bembo served at the papal court of Leo X; and between 1522 and 1524 in Padua, Bembo finished and then revised the entire manuscript before returning to Rome after Giulio de' Medici's election to the papacy as Clement VII. Printed in 1525 and dedicated to the pope, the *Prose* ignores the present tense of the book's date of publication and presents itself as a dialogue that had occurred over three days in Venice in 1502, redacted and addressed to Cardinal Giulio de' Medici in 1515. Like the linguistic context of the treatise's principal arguments, this strategy artificially seeks to convey the impression of a seamless narrative, as unmarked by the corruptible passage of time as the language it seeks to promote.

At the outset of the *Prose*, Carlo articulates an idea fundamental to Bembo's perspective when he asserts that "one cannot say that any language lacking writers is really a language" [*Prose* I.xiv, 95].[39] No language can be considered legitimate, therefore, unless it has a written

---

[37] See *ibid*. xiii–xvii, for the close relationship between *Sofonisba* and Trissino's developing vernacular apologetics.

[38] Tavoni (1992b) is the best concise survey of Bembo's work; and Trovato (1994) 111–16 provides a terse analysis of the first edition of the *Prose*. The catalogue of the exhibit dedicated to Bembo in Padua in 2013 provides an excellent introduction to all aspects of the career of this seminal figure in sixteenth-century Italian letters; see Beltramini *et al.* (2013).

[39] All citations of the text are from Bembo (2001).

literature, according to Bembo, a position that both marginalizes the oral aspects of linguistic culture and renders impossible any recognition of the impact of orality on the development of more codified forms of language in writing. Following a discussion of the superiority of Tuscan *voci* [words] over his own Venetian dialect, Carlo goes on to suggest that "being born Florentine in these times is no advantage in writing the Florentine language well" [*Prose* I.xvi, 40], a perspective that serves both to stress the priority of writing an antique Tuscan over speaking it in its contemporary form and to legitimize the fact that though it is a Venetian making the argument, association through birth with the geographical and political coordinates of contemporary Florence have no bearing whatsoever on one's capacity to defend or utilize the illustrious vernacular. Carlo argues further, in fact, that being a non-Tuscan is in itself a great advantage, for "others who are not Tuscans learn the language, beautifully and with grace, through reading excellent books" [*Prose* I.xvi, 40].[40] This suggests that Tuscan is exactly the same kind of 'artificial' language Dante in the *De vulgari* argues that Latin is.

Giuliano, the devil's advocate of the *Prose*, challenges Carlo's position by asserting that it is better to write in the language of one's own time and place than to depend on forms of the language that have passed into history, "because writing, like clothing and arms, must both resemble and accommodate the usage of the time in which one writes; for it is meant to be read and understood by those men who are still alive, not by those who are already dead" [*Prose* I.xvii, 42]. While Giuliano insists on the natural, and thus entirely legitimate, evolution of language, Carlo argues against the proximity of the language of writing and that used by common people [*Prose* I.xviii, 44]. Bembo's surrogate argues that though neither Petrarch nor Boccaccio were contaminated by the common tongue, Dante's mixed language – the *Commedia* having been largely written during the poet's peregrinations in exile from Florence – compromises its suitability for a vernacular paradigm. In the second book of the *Prose*, another of the dialogue's interlocutors, Federigo, notes that "among Dante's works many are serious but lack grace; and among those of Cino [da Pistoia] many are graceful, but lack seriousness." It is only in Petrarch "that both of these parts are

[40] Tuscans themselves, however, took these lessons about their own language from a Venetian reluctantly: see Trovato (1994) 120–21; and about the similar reaction regarding Trissino's efforts to teach Florentines pronunciation, see Trissino (1986) xix–xx.

marvelously resplendent and in such a fashion that one would be hard-pressed to say in which he was the greater master" [*Prose* II.ix, 71]. The evocation of Dante and Cino is a good example of the manifold ways in which the terms of the language question are continually reiterated, for here critical axes of Poliziano's and Landino's arguments are recalled in order to be dismissed.

To conclude his argument at the end of the first book of the *Prose*, Carlo refers his vernacular apologetics back to the Ciceronian golden age of classical Latin, asserting that had Boccaccio and Petrarch followed the examples of their predecessors Dante, Guinizzelli, and Cavalcanti, their contributions to Italian would have amounted to nothing more than those of Seneca, Suetonius, Lucan, and Claudian, writers who strayed from Cicero's paradigmatic example with regrettable results. Bembo "aims at persuading, not defeating, the humanists," in arguing for the legitimacy of the vernacular, "he wants to see a vernacular literature founded on principles analogous, not antithetical, to contemporary Latin literature."[41] But this approach fails to recognize that Latin (even in its contemporary form) and the rapidly developing European vernaculars were different organisms, as Dante clearly acknowledges in *De vulgari* I.i. Bembo presumed a Latin culture in the readers of his defense of the vernacular, and in organizing his valorization of Italian on Latin models he unwittingly perpetuated Flavio Biondo's view of the vernacular as an interloper in the linguistic world.

The *Prose* [I.xiii–xiv, 31–37] is the best available source to reconstruct the *teoria cortigiana* [the eclectic theory of language], since Bembo's dialogue contains an exposition of the ideas of Vincenzo Colli, also known as Calmeta, whose *Della volgar poesia* has survived only in a compendium of it made by Ludovico Castelvetro. Calmeta proposed that the language spoken at the papal court be adopted as the standard for Italian literature, given that it incorporated the regional vernaculars of Italy as well as Spanish and French: a language as cosmopolitan as the Roman curia. The objection to such a language is obvious: it would be prone to anarchy. Calmeta responded, according to Bembo, by drawing attention to ancient Greece, where four different dialects gave life to a common language which did not belong to any one Greek people but had assimilated the qualities of the separate dialects. Castelvetro, in his

---

[41] Tavoni (1992b) 1071.

Giunta al primo libro delle Prose di M. Pietro Bembo [Addition to the First Book of the *Prose* published posthumously in 1572], took a slightly different tack, claiming that Calmeta thought that the Florentine of Dante and Petrarch, refined by the use of the Roman curia, should have been the basis of the language of Italian poetry. The idea that the center for the codification and diffusion of the language could have been Rome was endorsed also by Mario Equicola: he was in favor of a language that could absorb words from every Italian vernacular, polished with a Latinate finish, as was in fact the case in the Roman curia. Equicola claimed to have employed such a language in his *Libro de natura de amore* [Book on the Nature of Love] (written in Latin at the end of the fifteenth century, translated into Italian at the beginning of sixteenth century, but printed only in 1525). Another apparent supporter of the eclectic theory was Baldassare Castiglione, whose *Cortegiano* – a dialogue set in the court of Urbino in 1507 (printed in 1528) – proposed an Italian restrained neither by the archaic language of Petrarch and Boccaccio nor by contemporary Florentine, but grounded in the vernaculars used in the main cities of Italy, especially by the courtly intellectual elites, a language "communal, rich and various, and like a delightful garden full of different flowers and fruits."[42] The strength of the eclectic theory was its attempt to bridge the gap between written tradition and actual usage, aiming at a language that every writer or scholar in Italy could recognize as their own, particularly in the Italian courts which had already promoted a common literary language; its weakness was an innate empiricism, given that the so-called common language was invariably destined to change from city to city, rendering impossible its grammatical and stylistic systemization as Bembo had done for his ideal language, relying on the texts of Petrarch and Boccaccio.

Trissino responded to the *Prose* and to the other polemicists in Bembo's camp with a barrage of texts, six new works in addition to the translation of the *De vulgari* as well as a second edition of the *Epistola*, all published in his native Vicenza in 1529. The tendency already manifest in the earlier edition of the *Epistola*, to advance potentially useful ideas but then fail to work them out with the rigor required to lend them persuasive force, is much in evidence in these later linguistic writings. But as unsuccessful as Trissino's approach proved to be as a

---

[42] Castiglione (1998) I.xxxv, 75–76.

systematic answer to Bembist ideology, a number of issues taken up in his later work did pave the way for alternatives to Bembo's conservative project. Perhaps the most significant of these ideas is expressed in the dedicatory epistle of Trissino's translation of Dante's *De vulgari, De la vulgare eloquenzia* [On Vernacular Eloquence] when he argues that Italian, far from having already reached its zenith, "is still quite young, still growing and gathering strength; and for this reason, it [still] has much need of help."[43] This assertion of the vulnerability of the Italian vernacular is far from the position expressed in the *Prose*, and Trissino's critique of Bembo's approach suggests that Italian is as much in need of being defended from those who would seek to limit its potential as it is of attentive care on the part of others with a more accommodating perspective to ensure that its continuing growth be as fruitful as possible.

In the *Castellano*, Trissino's only concession to the dialogue form usually favored for treatises dedicated to the language question, the principal disputants are Florentine humanists representing two of the city's most prominent families, Giovanni Rucellai (speaking for Trissino) and Filippo Strozzi, thus providing a suitably Florentine patina to the arguments set forth. The dialogue is situated in Rome, at Castel Sant'Angelo where Rucellai had served as warden until the time of his premature death in 1525; and though the Neapolitan Jacopo Sannazaro sits silently through most of the dialogue, his standing as "one of the authors of illustrious non-Tuscan literature [then] most in view" suggests that his presence as another kind of Italian is meant to affirm the broader linguistic limits Rucellai defends.[44] The central question again revolves around what to call the vernacular, and while the argument revisits familiar territory, Trissino demonstrates a keen sense of the historical development of Italian, noting that the *Duecento* Sicilian poets had actually written in Sicilian, not in Tuscan (though that was the form in which most of this poetry first circulated in the north); that Dante acknowledged a Bolognese poet, Guido Guinizzelli, as "padre"; that Dante's and Petrarch's poetry resembles much more the non-Tuscan poets who had preceded them than the "pure" Florentine verse of the *Quattrocento*; and that "among the vocabulary of the first sonnet of Petrarch [in the *Canzoniere*, his Song Album], there is not more

[43] Dante (1529) Ai[v].   [44] Trissino (1986) xxxix.

than one word that is ours [i.e., Tuscan], all the others being common
to other regions of Italy."[45] Trissino's argument for a single Italian
language marked by regional idiosyncrasies might not entirely fit in
terms of the Aristotelian language he employs at length to describe it,
but by exposing the array of Italian voices contributing to even the most
unimpeachable Tuscan literary authority's work – Petrarch's normative
status in the debate remained a constant – Trissino made an important
point lost on those who wished to promulgate a version of Italian remote
from actual usage. Together with his introduction of the *De vulgari* into
the terms of the language question, Trissino's opening up of the possibilities of a vernacular whose scope reached beyond the boundaries of
Tuscany (while clearly, with his Medici connections, remaining rooted
there) reflects his drive for a "diverse and polyvalent future literary
language" rendering possible "the unleashing of all of the potentialities
inherent in language."[46]

Advocates of the Florentine vernacular had an apologist in Niccolò
Machiavelli, although his treatise on the language question, *Discorso
intorno alla nostra lingua* [Discourse on our Language], probably written
in 1524, remained unpublished until the eighteenth century.[47] A polemical text reacting to the ideas of Trissino (though he is never named in it),
the dialogue aims to establish that the language used by the *tre corone* was
decidedly Florentine, not generically Italian. Machiavelli assumes that
all languages are mixed, the crucial difference being "that the language
worthy of a 'nation' is one that manages to convert the words it scav-
enges from other languages into its own, and is so powerful that words
so scavenged do not disorder its nature but, on the contrary, disorder
theirs since it takes from others in such a way as to make it seem its
own."[48] Machiavelli's interlocutor in the dialogue is Dante himself, who
is made to renounce those "errors" in the *De vulgari* that endorse either a
communal or courtly language, admitting that he had in fact written in
Florentine. Other supporters of contemporary Florentine, or Tuscan,
were Lodovico Martelli, who in 1524 published a *Risposta* to Trissino's
Epistola, and Claudio Tolomei, who in his *Cesano* (a dialogue written
between 1525 and the early 1530s – the moment of most intense

---

[45] Il Castellano, in Trissino (1986) 65.
[46] Floriani (1980) 65, writing of Trissino's challenge not only to Bembo's linguistic theory
but also to his idea of working only within accepted genres.
[47] See Machiavelli (1982) xxvi–xxix.   [48] *Ibid.* 50.

engagement in Italy over the language question – but published only in 1555, without the author's consent) dealt with how the vernacular should be named, whether *italiana, lingua di sì*,[49] *cortigiana, fiorentina*, or *toscana*. Tolomei favored the last of these, and in order to counter those who considered the Tuscan language merely an outcome of the anarchy which followed the collapse of the Roman empire he argued that Tuscan retained a great deal of Latin, some Etruscan, and small bits of the languages of the northern invaders. Significantly, Tolomei recognizes that language precedes writing, and he notes that even if writers might thus be considered unessential to language, literature is nevertheless necessary to impart *splendore* [splendor] to the vernacular.

Literature in both Latin and Italian in the later sixteenth century benefitted from the vigorous exchange of ideas represented by their independent *querelles*. Giovanni della Casa's most famous work is the vernacular *Galateo* [A Treatise on Manners] (1558), which enjoyed a considerable success both in Italy and abroad in translation, but he was equally skilled – and exacting – in Latin prose and Italian verse.[50] Between 1550 and 1552 Della Casa wrote a biography of Bembo in which he stigmatized the final period of fifteenth-century humanist culture: Bembo is presented here as the first Latin writer worthy of attention after more than 800 years, he who set free the *purus incorruptusque veterum Romanorum sermo* [pure and incorrupt ancient Roman language] from the fetters of erudition and bad taste for *duri, obscuri, asperi scriptores* [difficult, obscure, and rough writers]. It was a classic case of history written by the winners – and perhaps not surprisingly, Della Casa was the first Italian to compile an Index of Forbidden Books (in Venice, in 1549, though the Venetian republic soon capitulated to the resistance of the book industry so central to its economy) – and the lesson of rigorous classicism embodied by Bembo and Della Casa would long continue to play a crucial role in the linguistic and literary history of Italy. Powerfully and elegantly argued, Bembo's *Prose* proved to be the most widely influential intervention in the *questione della lingua* during the course of the sixteenth century, and even if significant signs of resistance did arise the conservative coordinates of Bembo's treatise set the standard against which later literary,

[49] A distinction Dante makes in *De vulgari* I.viii–x to differentiate the languages of the Italian and Iberian peninsulas from that of France ("*sì*" as opposed to "*oïl*" or "*ouï*").
[50] See Pedullà (2011); and for an English translation, Della Casa (2013).

grammatical, and lexicographical developments throughout Italy were to be measured. But while Bembo's views came to be monumentalized in the first vernacular *Vocabolario degli Accademici della Crusca* [Vocabulary of the Crusca Academicians] in 1612, already the year before – in distant England – John Florio had published *Queen Anna's New World of Words*, the second edition of an Italian–English dictionary which took Italian lexicography into new and uncharted waters in its comprehensive survey of the vernacular as it had developed through the early *Seicento*, unshackled from Latin precedent and the constraints of the *tre corone*.[51]

Acknowledgment

I am particularly grateful to Michael Wyatt for his careful correction of my English text, and for a number of suggestions regarding my treatment of the vernacular *questione della lingua*.

---

[51] See Wyatt (2005) 203–54, and particularly 205–09, 216–17 for a discussion of one of the more interesting "alternative" language theorists, Alessandro Citolini, who had an important impact on the development of Florio's work.

7
___

Publication

In about 1441–43 Leon Battista Alberti, lying in bed in Florence
with a slight fever and surrounded by friends, received from Guarino da
Verona in Ferrara a Latin version of Lucian's *Muscae encomium* [Praise of
the Fly], dedicated to him. Guarino's translation was read aloud and
entertained them all. Alberti proceeded to dictate the text of a *Musca* of
his own, which was written down by those present. Next day a friend
asked Alberti to send a copy to Cristoforo Landino, in order to amuse
him too; and Alberti did so with an accompanying letter – in which he
gave this account of the genesis of his little work.[1]

Alberti's scenario may be a bit too neat to be completely trust-
worthy, but it is based on practices of manuscript and oral diffusion
that were typical of the early Renaissance and would not have seemed
odd or old-fashioned in the sixteenth century. Throughout the period
from 1350 to 1600, handwriting was used by authors for the initial
publication of their works and then by users of texts as a means of
circulating them further. Some authors still dictated their works to an
amanuensis, and some kinds of texts continued to be heard in oral
performance. However, Alberti lived long enough to welcome the
introduction into Italy of the printing press. This new technology
was to alter radically the scale on which some (though not all) books
were made, sold, and read, and hence to some extent the ways in which
works were written. In due course, given both the financial investment
required for this alternative means of reproduction and its power to
diffuse texts more rapidly and (for the reader) more cheaply, the

---

[1] Alberti (1954).

commerce and content of books came to be controlled in ways that Alberti could not have imagined.

Authors who published their works scribally used varying methods, sometimes in combination, according to their circumstances. They could send a work solely to a dedicatee, who might then circulate it further; they could send copies as gifts to favored persons, who might do the same; they could lend a copy for transcription, sometimes endeavoring to control the accuracy of this process by preparing an "archetype" or "original" as a source.[2] Authors often managed the act of publication with care in order to enhance the status of their works in the eyes of patrons and subsequent readers; thus, for example, the poet Antonio Cornazzano had copies transcribed calligraphically on vellum (fine calf-skin), more expensive and durable than paper, and presented them to prominent figures who would, by association, add luster to his writings.[3]

Manuscripts were copied by both professional and amateur scribes, as well of course as by authors themselves. Two surveys of fifteenth-century scribes carried out by Armando Petrucci, using sources such as signed colophons (the information with which scribes sometimes concluded a manuscript), suggest that professionals, who might be clerics or notaries working part-time, tended to be employed when a text was in Latin or when it was to be copied on vellum. However, nearly ninety percent of those who copied manuscripts that contained vernacular texts, or that had a relatively low commercial value, were amateurs writing for themselves, their families, or friends.[4] Nuns copied religious works for their own and other institutions. From a census of 106 humanistic scribes active in later *Quattrocento* Florence, Albinia de la Mare concluded that copying, even for money, was a socially acceptable occupation.[5]

When copyists were remunerated, those who paid them were usually the persons who intended to use the text. Some courts had salaried scribes, but they could commission individual manuscripts. Professional copying was also organized by booksellers or stationers. The best-known example is that of Vespasiano da Bisticci, who sold books in Florence from the 1440s to the late 1470s. The clients who commissioned copying through him included wealthy collectors from Italy and

---

[2] Rizzo (1973) 301–23.
[3] Bruni/Zancani (1992) 53–54, 57–59, 80, 84–86, 105–06, 118–19, and 125–28.
[4] Petrucci (1988) 825–28.   [5] De la Mare (1985) 401–06.

even abroad. Scribes employed by him worked, however, as freelancers, on their own premises.[6] Work was not abundant for professional scribes, and they might have to travel to the larger cultural centers, such as Florence, Rome, or Naples, in search of commissions or more permanent posts.

In the *Trecento* and early *Quattrocento*, the dominant book-hands were forms of what was later called "gothic script."[7] Some letter forms were angular, including a minuscule "g" with a loop below the upper bowl, and consecutive round letters, such as "be" or "do," frequently touched or overlapped. In some versions, "d" was uncial (with the ascender turning to the left), "r" within a word resembled the arabic numeral "2," and "z" had a curved tail. But two humanistic scripts were developed in Florence from just before 1400 and gained ground during the century, especially in literary texts. This reform of handwriting was developed by Poggio Bracciolini and Niccolò Niccoli and supported by an older scholar, Coluccio Salutati. Their formal variety of the script, and the format and layout of the manuscripts in which they used it, were based on manuscripts in Carolingian script from the eleventh and twelfth centuries, though they did not imitate specific models slavishly. The letter-shapes of this script were essentially those of modern roman type (apart from an upright "s," like an "f" without the cross-stroke): thus "d" and "r" were upright and "g" was made with two bowls joined by a stroke. In the 1420s Niccoli developed a humanistic cursive (more rapidly written) script sloping slightly to the right, of a kind that came to be known as italic or chancery. It retained features of the formal script such as upright "d" and "r," but included cursive features such as an "a" formed as "*a*," long "s" and "f" both descending below the line, and round rather than long final "s" in Latin. These hands – used for Latin texts at first but later for the vernacular, too, if the text was of sufficient merit – were taken up and developed by leading calligraphers of the late *Quattrocento* and early *Cinquecento*, for example Bartolomeo Sanvito and Ludovico degli Arrighi.[8]

The manuscripts of men such as these, but also those of humbler professionals and – just as important – of amateur copyists, demonstrate

---

[6] *Ibid.* 417–20; and De la Mare (1986) and (1996).
[7] Casamassima (1960).
[8] On these developments, see Ullman (1960); Wardrop (1963); Casamassima (1964); De la Mare (1973); Petrucci (1995) 169–235; and Zamponi (2004).

that scribal culture thrived even after the invention of printing.[9] Its durability was due to a number of factors. For the publisher of a text, manuscript was quicker and less expensive to use than print as long as only a small number of copies was needed. It was also attractive, in both elite and other circles, precisely because it was more exclusive than print: it allowed texts to be directed to specific readers, who in turn would feel privileged to have access to them. Manuscript allowed greater freedom of content than print, especially with the tightening of controls over publication and reading in the course of the *Cinquecento* (discussed below), and it was more effective in creating and strengthening bonds between those who shared interests and values. Some would have preferred the older medium on aesthetic grounds. This could, particularly in the *Quattrocento*, have been one of the explanations for the not uncommon cases of manuscripts copied from printed books, but such copying must also have occurred simply because a printed text was unavailable for purchase.

Manuscript circulation continued to prove especially attractive for shorter works and for genres that were closely associated with relationships with other people or that were of particular interest to communities and networks of the like-minded, for example members of courts or academies, or supporters of political or religious causes. Such genres included lyric poetry, which was often addressed to other individuals; newsletters, which began to be put together and sometimes sold in the second half of the sixteenth century, and accounts of Italian or foreign states; essays on current politics; works on religion, especially but not only if heterodox; and prophecies, which often straddled the worlds of politics and religion. Those who wished to have texts copied often did this themselves, but scribes, some of them professionals or semiprofessionals, continued to be available to authors and readers who preferred to delegate the task. Print, paradoxically, played a role in the training of expert calligraphers through the production of writing manuals composed for the new medium by practicing scribes and writing masters, although their specimens of scripts were printed from woodblocks rather than moveable metal type.[10]

Some sixteenth-century authors, including major ones, chose to use scribal publication for at least some of their writings. Only three of the

---

[9] For a general survey, see Richardson (2009).   [10] Morison (1990).

works of Niccolò Machiavelli were printed during his lifetime, and only in the case of the *Arte della guerra* [The Art of War] can one be confident that the author gave his blessing to the edition (1521). Most of his works, such as *Il principe* [The Prince], begun in 1513, were first circulated in manuscript; this allowed him to address his often controversial ideas to a particular readership and to use a more informal style. Giovanni della Casa, the leading lyric poet of the mid *Cinquecento* and author of prose works such as *Il Galateo* [A Treatise on Manners], circulated his works only scribally within his close circle. One of the key figures in the movement for spiritual reform during the 1530s was the Spaniard Juan de Valdés; yet in this period the influence of his writings among Italians depended solely on handwritten copies made by and for a network of followers after he reached Naples in 1535.[11]

Alongside scribal reproduction, the technique of making multiple copies of texts with moveable metal type was introduced in Germany around 1450 and then spread to Italy. Presses may have been brought to northern Italy in the early 1460s by itinerant German printers in search of occasional work. The first major undertaking was the press set up by Conrad Sweynheym and Arnold Pannartz in the Benedictine monastery of Subiaco; this produced four editions between 1465 and 1467, three of them containing substantial works aimed at a readership of humanists and clerics. Printing then spread to Rome itself. Another German, John of Speyer, introduced printing to Venice in 1469. After this somewhat hesitant start, printing spread very rapidly to the major Italian cities from the early 1470s, in many cases again thanks to an initial pairing of printers from north of the Alps with Italian finance.[12]

There were strong interrelationships between the production of manuscripts and that of printed books.[13] Handwritten additions had to be made to some early printed books if they were to be fully usable. Printed typefaces imitated three main scripts: at first formal humanistic (or roman) and "gothic," then humanistic cursive (italic); only the specialized "mercantile" hand was not reproduced in print. In the early years, too, the size of printed editions might be cautiously low, just 100 or 200 copies. Some very small, essentially private editions were

---

[11] Lopez, P. (1976) 27–50, 137–42; and Russell (2006).
[12] For an overview of the spread of printing and its effects, see Richardson (1999). For suggestions about the earliest printing in Italy, see Scapecchi (2001).
[13] See especially McKitterick (2003).

published in the *Cinquecento*. However, in general the market for print and confidence in it grew, so that print runs were often 1,000 or even higher.[14]

The investment needed to produce these editions was considerable. The main cost was usually paper, followed by labor (chiefly compositors, proof correctors, and pressmen), types, the press, ink, and so on. Often the initiative for an edition came from a publisher who was not a printer but a bookseller or a businessman with other interests; only some printers financed their own work partly or wholly. The element of risk was increased by fierce competition in some sectors of production. Not surprisingly, many enterprises were short-lived. But by the mid sixteenth century the Italian printing industry had developed to a point where it was renowned throughout Europe. The largest center of book production was Venice, followed at some distance by Rome, Florence, and Milan. Venice had an active intellectual and cultural life; political life in its large state was relatively stable; and its strong economic infrastructure supported both the large capital investments needed for printing and the subsequent distribution and sale of copies over the widest possible area.

In order to be successful, publication in print required a combination of financial acumen and resources, technical skill, and a sense (often provided by collaborators among men of letters) of what would appeal to the reading public, or rather to certain readers, since no single enterprise could cater for all tastes. The foremost example of such achievement from the early *Cinquecento* was Aldus Manutius, who was unusual in being a scholar as well as a printer and (in partnership) a publisher. In Venice, from 1495 to his death in 1515, he printed books that appealed to contemporary learned and cultured tastes and which achieved a lasting reputation as models of typography: his roman types and his italic type (introduced in 1501), cut for him by Francesco Griffo, were much imitated.[15] Aldus' initiatives in scholarly publishing had a strong influence on the leading contemporary Florentine printers, Filippo Giunti and his son Bernardo. But other members of this family established flourishing businesses elsewhere and in other sectors of the market: for instance, Filippo's brother Lucantonio, in Venice, was a printer–publisher who produced renowned liturgical texts, among

[14] The markets of manuscripts and printed books are compared in Bonifati (2008).
[15] Lowry (1979).

other genres; Filippo's nephew Giacomo, in Lyon, specialized in publishing theology, law, and medicine; and Filippo's son Giovanni printed in Spain.[16] The outstanding printer–publisher of the mid *Cinquecento* in Venice, and indeed in Italy, was Gabriele Giolito. Like his father Giovanni, Gabriele was above all a businessman, but he made shrewd use of men of letters who wrote, translated, or edited many of the literary, historical, religious, and other texts that helped him to expand the family firm.[17] Francesco Bindoni and his stepfather Maffeo Pasini in Venice catered ably for a broad readership, offering popular literature as well as treatises and devotional texts. Printers working in Italy also made some remarkable contributions to the technically problematic printing of music, among them Ottaviano Petrucci, who printed in about 1501–20 using multiple-impression methods for staves, notes, and text, and the French musician Antonio Gardano (Antoine Gardane), who around 1538 began to use a single-impression system adopted from the Parisian printer Pierre Attaingnant.[18]

Some Italian writers expressed misgivings about printing. The ethos of print publication was more evidently commercial than that of its scribal equivalent. The printed word could be seen as lowering the standards of writers eager to gain fame, and as giving too many people access to knowledge. In any case, getting into print could be expensive for writers, since they, or someone on their behalf, would often be expected to contribute all or some of the costs. However, print did prove attractive to many authors, for at least three reasons. The first was the possibility, which made a vivid impression on those who first witnessed the process, of producing many copies at speed once type had been set up. Second, print seemed to reproduce texts in a way that seemed more enduring and less prone to the variations that copyists were, accidentally or deliberately, liable to introduce. (In reality, of course, printed texts were still likely to contain errors made by compositors, and copies of the same edition often differed typographically as a result of alterations made during printing.[19]) Third, while writers frequently continued, as in scribal culture, to dedicate their works to prominent figures who might then show them favor, an investment in the printing of an edition could lead to

---

[16] Camerini (1962–63); Pettas (1980), (1997), and (2005).
[17] Bongi (2000); and Nuovo/Coppens (2005).
[18] Lewis (1988–97); Agee (1998); and Boorman (2006).
[19] See, for example, the studies in Fahy (1988) 1–211, 245–70.

some direct financial return from sales. Authors might become parties in contractual agreements with a printer or with a publisher such as a bookseller, although the women who, in due course, wished to see their works in print would normally have had to make arrangements through a male intermediary. Protection against unfair competition could be gained by obtaining from a state a book privilege that prevented others from printing and selling an edition for a fixed period, normally five or ten years. This applied only to the state in question, of course, but privileges issued by the pope were supposed to be effective throughout Christendom.

As was seen earlier, scribal publication was not brought to an end by printing, but writers from the late *Quattrocento* onwards began to make increasingly enterprising use of the press. The importance that the new medium could acquire for them is shown well by the example of Ludovico Ariosto and his great chivalric epic, the *Orlando furioso* [Orlando Gone Mad], conceived – like its predecessor, Boiardo's *Orlando innamorato* [Orlando in Love] – for diffusion in print. When Ariosto came to have the first version printed in 1516, he organized the whole publishing process himself from start to finish, importing paper, obtaining privileges, overseeing printing (by a local press in Ferrara, so that the process would be under his control), correcting proofs, and arranging for distribution. About 1,300 copies were produced, costing 1 *lira* each when bought unbound, as was then normal. In May 1516 Ariosto appeared in Mantua with a chestful of copies that he wanted to have sold, as well as three presentation copies for the ruling Gonzaga family. His income from sales and the benefits bestowed in return for gift copies must have supplemented appreciably his official annual court salary of 240 *lire*. A second edition followed in 1521. For the third, of 1532, Ariosto ordered enough paper for a print run about double that of the first edition. Some copies were printed on vellum for presentation to patrons.[20]

Baldassare Castiglione was at first not so eager to send his masterpiece, *Il libro del cortegiano* [The Book of the Courtier], to the press: he claimed in the dedication that he did not resolve to publish the work by this means until he feared that part of it would be printed by others from a transcription that had fallen into the wrong hands. Then he entered

---

[20] Ariosto (2006); and Fahy (1989).

into negotiations with the Aldine press in Venice in April 1527 for the edition that came to be printed in 1528. After a series of proposals and counter-proposals lasting about a year, the final agreement seems to have been that 2,030 copies would be printed, that the author would pay 35 *ducats* (the cost of paper for 500 copies), and that in return he would receive between 100 and 150 copies, including 30 on larger-sized paper. All his copies would have been used as gifts.[21] The somewhat different approaches of Ariosto and Castiglione illustrate how authors using print could attach varying importance to the traditional role of publication in winning the favor of patrons and peers. However, unless the print run was very small, all print authors now had to attend to the tastes and interests of the wider book-buying public.

The noblewoman Vittoria Colonna did not sanction the editions of her verse that were printed during her lifetime; however, from the late 1540s a few women authors began to take advantage of the opportunities of the press. The courtesan Tullia d'Aragona must have consented to her *Rime* [Poems] being printed by Giolito in 1547. Women of respectable social standing, too, began to use the new medium. Laura Terracina, born of an upper-middle-class Neapolitan family, had eight books of poetry printed from 1548 onwards. Laura Battiferri meticulously prepared her *Primo libro dell'opere toscane* [First Book of Tuscan Poetry], containing 146 poems by her and 41 by male correspondents, for printing in Florence by the Giunti in 1560.[22]

Readers of books had a number of reasons to be grateful for the invention of the printing press. Most obviously, printing brought down the unit price of books considerably, perhaps to one-eighth or more of the price of an equivalent manuscript, although even a printed book would have cost a much higher proportion of someone's income then than it would today. Inventories and catalogues of booksellers suggest that during the fifteenth and sixteenth centuries the quantities of printed books held by publishers and booksellers grew, that the choice of titles available was greater, and that their prices did not rise as much as salaries and other prices. The traditional elementary school texts, used to teach reading and writing in Latin, were stocked in shops in large quantities and at low cost. Although those who owned any books remained a minority of the population and were mainly male, private

---

[21] Quondam (2000a) 32–33, 74–79.
[22] Battiferri degli Ammannati (2006). On the use of print by women poets, see Cox (2008).

collections grew in number and size. In 1501 Aldus Manutius launched his successful and fashionable (and high-priced) series of Latin, Greek, and Italian texts in octavo format (in which the sheet of paper was folded three times); thereafter, formats smaller than folio (in which the sheet was folded only once) came to be used more often even for canonical literary texts, and this tendency made printed books more easily portable, freeing reading from the desktop. As collections grew larger and the books themselves became smaller, so browsing had to be made easier: thus books began to be kept upright rather than stored flat, and to be stored regularly on shelves or in cupboards set against the wall, rather than in chests as was sometimes the case previously.

As for the contents of books, both authors and publishers of printed books in the sixteenth century sometimes took opportunities (which could of course have been lucrative) to produce books for a wider readership, not just for a well-educated, well-to-do, predominantly male elite. One of those who wrote works intended to furnish the elements of literacy and numeracy for the great majority of the population that did not attend school was Domenico Manzoni of Oderzo near Venice, a former teacher of mathematics. In 1546, for instance, he produced a *Libretto molto utile per imparar a leggere, scrivere, et abaco, con alcuni fondamenti della dottrina christiana* [Very Useful Booklet for Learning to Read, Write, and Do Arithmetic, with Some Elements of Christian Doctrine], to be used by parents in teaching their children. The volume included alphabets and prayers that would have been used in learning to read, and woodcut exemplars of handwriting in different scripts. As well as aiding the acquisition of literacy, printing widened its uses by offering a growing range of material for reference and self-instruction. Among them were works that codified good linguistic usage in prose and verse, such as Giovan Francesco Fortunio's *Regole grammaticali della volgar lingua* [Grammatical Rules of the Vernacular] (first edition, 1516) and Francesco Alunno's *Ricchezze della lingua volgare* [Riches of the Vernacular], a dictionary based on the writings of Boccaccio (first edition, 1543). An increasing quantity of translations into Italian from Latin, from Greek via Latin, and (doubtless partly because of Spain's political influence in the peninsula) from Spanish were printed from 1540 onwards.

Because printed texts needed to be made acceptable and attractive to readers whose identity was not known in advance, they could be prepared by an editor, a figure who had no regular professional equivalent in manuscript publication.[23] Editors might be little-known figures, perhaps clerics or schoolteachers who worked occasionally for printers. But some academics and distinguished writers and scholars – such as Pier Vettori in classical literature, or Pietro Bembo, Vincenzio Borghini, and Lionardo Salviati in the vernacular – came to collaborate as editors with publishers. From the mid 1530s, an increasing demand for literature of all kinds in the vernacular led to the rise of figures, sometimes called *poligrafi*, who became well known for their editing and writing in the service of Venetian publishing houses. The pioneers of the 1530s and 1540s were Antonio Brucioli from Florence and Lodovico Dolce from Venice; among those who followed in their footsteps were Lodovico Domenichi from Piacenza and Girolamo Ruscelli from Viterbo.

The work of such men could be important for printers and publishers and for readers alike; hence the prominence that editorial contributions came to receive on some title pages. The reason was essentially the same: editors could make texts more authoritative, more attractive to readers, and hence more saleable. One of their more important and delicate tasks could be to impose on vernacular texts a form of language that would be both widely esteemed and widely readable. In the fifteenth century there was no clear linguistic norm. The Tuscan of the great fourteenth-century authors – mainly Petrarch in verse and Boccaccio in prose – was generally accepted as the basis of the literary language for all Italian authors, but this Tuscan was combined, with inevitably varied results, with influences from the dialects of other regions and from Latin, still the dominant language of high culture. However, partly because the vernacular was being treated more seriously by writers such as Bembo, and partly because printing had created a greater need for a norm, from about 1515 authors and editors began to eliminate non-Tuscan usage and traces of Latinizing influence. Thus when Castiglione decided to have his *Cortegiano* printed in Venice, he made some linguistic revisions in his manuscript and then allowed it to be revised further in Venice; the person chosen for this task by those responsible for the printing was a member of Bembo's circle, Giovan Francesco Valier. Another

---

[23] For what follows, see Trovato (1991); and Richardson (1994).

factor that encouraged revision was the desire, on the part of the growing numbers of users of the literary vernacular, for texts that could be used as models for their own writing. The tendency to impose a uniform vernacular on printed texts helped to consolidate and diffuse among readers a standard literary language, but of course it created problems of authenticity, particularly with prose writing, easier to interfere with than verse. Most editors tended to give less weight to what was objectively correct, in terms of what the author had probably written, and more weight to what in their own time was perceived as correct usage. Yet some precocious examples of relatively sound scholarly practice emerged. One was the 1490 edition of Jacopone da Todi's *Laude* [Songs of Praise]; but naturally most of them concerned the canonical authors Dante, Petrarch, and Boccaccio, beginning with the Petrarch and Dante edited by Bembo and printed by Aldus in 1501 and 1502 respectively.

When editors were preparing vernacular texts that were objects of study and imitation, they might try to help readers to understand and use them – while also guiding their reading in certain directions – by adding paratexts. Some new commentaries were composed for Dante's *Commedia* [Divine Comedy] and for Petrarch's *Rime* [Poems] and *Trionfi* [Triumphs]. From the 1540s onwards, in line with Counter-Reformation tendencies, editors added summaries or glosses that suggested a moralizing or spiritual interpretation of works such as the *Commedia*, the *Decameron*, and the *Orlando furioso*. For texts by Petrarch and Boccaccio, the pre-eminent literary and linguistic models, and for the *Furioso*, also seen by some as worthy of imitation, editors provided guidance for readers and would-be writers in several forms, such as notes or explanations on meaning and usage, glossaries explaining difficult words, lists of the epithets used with certain nouns, indexes, and, where appropriate, rhyming dictionaries.

Several punctuation marks and some diacritic accents were already used in Latin and vernacular manuscripts, but in printed texts the range of punctuation became wider and the use of accents was extended. Thus another function of an editor could be to punctuate the text (as long as the requisite signs were available among the printer's characters) in order to make it more rapidly comprehensible. The first major initiatives taken in this area involved a collaboration between Bembo and Aldus. The comma, the semicolon, and the apostrophe were introduced with some accents in Bembo's Latin dialogue *De Aetna* [On Etna], printed in roman type in 1496, then in the Petrarch and Dante printed in Aldus' new italic type in 1501–02.[24]

Some authors were assisted by editors in the preparation of their work for the press. Thus Domenichi edited Laura Terracina's first book of *Rime* for printing by Giolito in Venice. There was, though, the danger that an author could resent the editor's interventions. Bernardo Tasso (1493–1569), for instance, father of Torquato, authorized Lodovico Dolce to edit his lyric poems for the printing carried out by Giolito in 1555. But in the following year Bernardo wrote to another printer to complain that Dolce had allowed the work to appear full of confusion and errors, and that he had removed some poems, apparently for political reasons.

Editors also compiled anthologies of contemporary vernacular writing. These had their roots in literary tradition and in scribal culture but, especially from the 1540s, collections of letters and of lyric verse became very successful print–publishing phenomena, reflecting the latest literary trends while offering material for imitation. The *Rime diverse di molti eccellentissimi auttori* [Selected Poems by Most Excellent Authors] edited by Domenichi and printed by Giolito in 1545 inspired several similar compilations, including the first anthology of verse by women, the *Rime diverse d'alcune nobilissime et virtuosissime donne* [Selected Poems by Several Most Noble and Virtuous Women] (Lucca: Vincenzo Busdraghi, 1559), also put together by Domenichi.[25]

The power of the press to circulate ideas and information led the Church to try to control it as a means of combating the perceived threat of the Reformation.[26] Steps to establish pre-publication censorship and to list banned books were taken from the second decade of the *Cinquecento* onwards. The Fifth Lateran Council decreed in 1515 that permission to print a book had to be obtained from a representative of the Church. In Venice, it was decided in 1527 that, before a privilege could be issued by the state, a licence had to be granted by three people, one of them a churchman. Such measures were not enforced strictly, but after 1541 sterner ones were introduced in order to prevent the circulation and ownership of heretical books. The Congregation of the Holy Office,

---

[24] On developments over the period, see Mortara Garavelli (2008) 65–137.
[25] On the Giolito *Rime*, see Quondam (2011); and on women writers in the period, see Cox (2008); Cox (2011); and Allonge (2011).
[26] Grendler (1977); Rozzo (1997); Fragnito (2001); and Frajese (2006).

known as the Roman Inquisition, was created in 1542. In 1547 Venice set up a new magistracy, the *Tre Savii sopra eresia* [Three Wisemen against Heresy], to work with the Inquisition. Indexes of prohibited books, or of books prohibited unless expurgated, such as Boccaccio's *Decameron*, were issued by some states (for example, Venice in 1549), by the papacy (notably Paul IV's Index of 1559), and by the Council of Trent (ratified by Pius IV in 1564). Venice decided in 1562 that new works needed an imprimatur before printing. The use of scribal circulation would have allowed a greater degree of freedom than print, though manuscripts, too, were in principle still subject to censorship. All these measures thus led inevitably to restrictions of choice: for readers, for writers, increasingly required to censor themselves in advance, and for the book trade in general. Inspections were made of the stocks of bookshops, consignments of imported books, and the libraries of suspect individuals. Banned books were confiscated and were burned in public. Strange as it may now seem, these included Bibles and some books of devotion in the vernacular, since the papacy considered it too dangerous for ordinary lay people to own them. No Bible in Italian was printed in Italy between 1567 and the translation of Antonio Martini, published in 1769–81.[27]

The reception of the kinds of texts that have been discussed so far depended above all on their actualization in manuscript or in print. However, some texts would also have been heard. Verse was frequently read out loud by one person to another; Torquato Tasso, for instance, was said to have made regular visits to Sperone Speroni in Rome in 1575 in order to read poems to him.[28] Those questioned in Holy Office trials mentioned the reading aloud or even singing of heterodox religious works, perhaps with the purpose of diffusing their message to the illiterate. Lyric poetry was often set to music for performance by one or more voices, and it was sometimes written expressly to be sung. Those who sang verse for others included figures from the social elite such as Isabella d'Este, but Montaigne claimed to have heard shepherdesses singing stanzas from Ariosto's *Orlando furioso* in Tuscany in 1581.[29] The improvisation of vernacular and Latin verses by amateurs and by professional entertainers is well attested, and it was evidently a much appreciated skill, even if performers were suspected at times of having done some preparation in advance. Some extemporized texts

[27] Fragnito (1997) 198 and (2005) 191–213.
[28] Solerti (1895) vol.2, 107.   [29] Montaigne (2003) 1230.

never came to be written down. But texts could move in both directions within an oral–written continuum, and works that began their existence in song or recitation survived in transcriptions that were said to have been made by listeners, either during performance or from memory, and could eventually find their way into print. The voice, the pen, and the printing press all had complementary roles to play in the rich textual world of Renaissance Italy.

Acknowledgment

I am grateful to Neil Harris for his comments on an earlier version of this essay.

8

Verse

Readers today encounter the lyric and heroic poetry of the
Italian Renaissance almost exclusively through the medium of the
book. While the history of both lyric and heroic poems is closely
related to the gradual rise of literacy and the advent of printing in
Italy, we should keep in mind that only a fraction of the Renaissance
audience for these texts accessed them in written form. Verse of
many sorts circulated in medieval and Renaissance manuscripts,
and later in commercially printed editions, but these compositions
reached their widest audience by traveling through the air, in vocal
performance.

Literary history has traditionally looked at lyric, epic, and romance
through the lens of the literary canon, highlighting the transmission of
ancient models and their transformation in the Renaissance to serve the
cultural needs and tastes of early moderns. Another approach, however,
is to view these texts as evidence of practices and to consider the role
they played in social life for their authors, performers, and consumers.
Because they were often recited or sung in company, to pass time after
a meal or on long journeys, they were, in fact, forms of entertainment
and community building for early modern Italians of all classes, both
those who could read and those who could only listen. If we keep in
mind the popularity as well as the sophistication of Renaissance lyric
and heroic poetry we may begin to perceive a past that echoes around
us even today, for our popular songs about love and longing have
deep roots in medieval and Renaissance lyric, while the serial adventures we enjoy in literature, television, and film count among their
important ancestors the jumbo-sized exploits of ancient, medieval,
and Renaissance heroes.

Lyric poetry

An extraordinary quantity of lyric poetry was produced in the Italian fifteenth and sixteenth centuries, by an astonishing array of writers. To a degree that is difficult for us to imagine today, lyric poems were penned, exchanged, sung, and collected by a great number of people in the Renaissance. By the sixteenth century, it had become unremarkable for persons ranging from scholars and artists to merchants and tradesmen to send each other poems addressing a wide number of subjects. There was love poetry, of course, but people also sent simple greetings, thank-you notes, invitations, excuses, and insults in rhyme. Occasional verse abounded, commemorating rulers, military victories, births and deaths. This widespread poetic production and exchange was possible in part thanks to the humanists' commitment to a new program of liberal education and the spread of literacy, but also because lyric poetry had become highly conventionalized, often adhering to themes and words that could be adopted by almost anyone who tried. To understand this vibrant poetic culture, we must look at its sources in medieval Europe and the Mediterranean.

Renaissance Italian love poetry in particular inherited much of its character and flavor from important literary developments of the thirteenth century. In his theoretical treatise, *De vulgari eloquentia* [On Vernacular Eloquence], Dante Alighieri cites a number of crucial Occitan sources for the development of poetry writing in Italian.[1] Beyond these models, literary history has generally acknowledged three important medieval phases for the rise of Italian lyric poetry: the concentration of poets at the multicultural, Sicilian court of Holy Roman Emperor Frederick II between about 1230 and 1250; the development of a courtly and civic lyric idiom in Tuscany identified with Guittone d'Arezzo and his followers in the 1250s and 1260s; and the emergence, beginning in the 1270s, of a theorized strain of poetry founded by the Bolognese Guido Guinizzelli and embraced in Tuscany by Dante and his friends, which Dante dubbed the *dolce stil novo* [sweet new style] in *Purgatorio* 24.[2]

---

[1] These include Aimeric de Belenoi, Aimeric de Peguilhan, Arnaut Daniel, Bertran de Born, Folquetz of Marseilles, Girautz de Borneihl, and Peire d'Alvernhe. He also cites the French Thibaut de Champagne and Gace Brulé (whom he misidentifies as Thibaut).

[2] A recent, and controversial, account of this history aims to establish Padua as the medieval center of a northern Italian literary awakening; see De Vincentiis *et al.* (2010).

Troubadour poets of the twelfth century in numerous locations across Europe had developed intricate metrical forms and (when they wrote love poetry) brilliantly projected the language of war and feudal servitude onto the predicaments of love.[3] The most important forms for these poets were the *canso* [song] and the *tenso* [debate poem], which Italians later took up as the *canzone* and the *tenzone*. Some Troubadour lyric forms (for example, the *alba*, the *serena*, and the *pastorella*) celebrate explicit sexual encounters; but often they figure the beloved as a noblewoman whose beauty and aloofness are an assault on the hapless lover, a man who is also her social inferior and thus can never hope to win her. Italian poets of the thirteenth century took up this theme of adverse love, while also systematizing in specific ways the metric and stanzaic forms they derived from the Troubadours.[4] The imperial notary Giacomo da Lentini, for example, probably invented in Frederick II's court the fourteen-line form known as the sonnet, in which two quatrains develop an argument that is then resolved or concluded in two closely linked tercets. It is perhaps no coincidence that the sonnet, which has been called a poetic syllogism for its analytical concision and power, was crafted by a legal professional.[5] The *dolce stil novo* poets in particular developed a philosophical, quasi-scientific discourse to analyze the experience of love, employing their verses in ambitious investigations of inspiration, memory, and the process of writing. Love appears in their poems as a personified figure who inspires (literally breathes into) the poet's soul and "dictates" what must be written.[6] The lover sighs and "notes" or transcribes in his poetry the symptoms of his experience, studying it as a philosophical, moral, and even physiological problem. His style is sweet because his language

---

[3] Zumthor (1992).

[4] Giulio Ferroni remarks that while Italian lyric continued to circulate orally, the great difference between it and its Occitan predecessors was the "absolute pre-eminence" in the Italian environment of the written text. While the Troubadour poets were also musicians and composed their works in intimate relation to performance, the thirteenth-century Italian poets were literati who "concentrated all their attention on the written word." This pre-eminence of writing, in Ferroni's view, led to both a reduction and a rationalization of metric forms inherited from the previous century, even as musicians continued to set this poetry to music and disseminate it to a broad public; see Ferroni (1992) 73–74.

[5] See Usher (1996), especially 11–12. On the Arabic, Latin, Greek, and Latin elements that contributed to the rise of the first school of vernacular poetry in Italian at Frederick's court, see Mallette (2005).

[6] For a psychoanalytic and philosophical reading of the poetics of the *dolce stil novo*, see Agamben (1993).

harmonizes with the radical, life-altering experience of love, which turns out to be an intellectual as well as a spiritual threshold.

Having followed Love's dictates, the *stil novo* poet shares his verses with like-minded friends, who form an elite community based solely on the fact that they all recognize the absolute value of love. In fact, in their persistent political critique of contemporary class relations, for these poets it is the capacity to love – not an aristocratic bloodline – that constitutes nobility. The object of these poets' amorous attentions is, moreover, not the noble lady of the castle or the shepherd girl about whom the Troubadours had written, and the *stil novo* poet is no knight. He is instead an urban male, whose beloved is an acquaintance glimpsed in a church or walking down the city street, often flanked by protective female friends.[7] The lady for whom the *dolce stil novo* poet yearns is nonetheless unobtainable, for the main interest of these lyrics is not in enjoyment or union, but rather in the destabilizing experience of love and the strenuous project of describing its impact. The culmination of the *stil novo* tradition, Dante reached for the ultimate expression of these effects, spiritualizing his beloved and representing her as an earthly sign of the Christian salvation that awaits the faithful. In his *Vita Nuova*, a book of poems and commentary about his love for Beatrice (literally, "she who blesses"), she figures as nothing less than a heaven-sent miracle in Dante's tracing of his own coming of age through the life and death of his beloved.[8]

This poetic heritage is evident on every page of the most influential book of poems in the Western tradition, the *Canzoniere* [Song Album] of Petrarch. Building on medieval models from the Troubadours to the *dolce stil novo* and bringing to his poetic craft an intense engagement with Roman antiquity, Petrarch worked for much of his adult life on this sequence of 366 poems, also known as the *Rime sparse* [Scattered Rhymes].[9] Read from beginning to end, Petrarch's *Canzoniere* narrates the poet's tormented love for a woman named Laura, whom he barely or

---

[7] On the urban context for Dante's poetry, see Steinberg (2007) 125–44.
[8] Harrison (1988).
[9] Petrarch himself provided another title for the most authoritative manuscript of the work (*Vaticano Latino* 3195): *Rerum vulgarium fragmenta* [Fragments in the Vernacular]. On the thirteenth- and fourteenth-century development of the author-assembled poetry book from the oral poetry cycles of the earlier Middle Ages, see Holmes (2000); and on Petrarch's ongoing process of writing, arranging, and rearranging the poems in his sequence, see Langeli (2010).

never met; his efforts to abandon his futile, earthly obsession with her in order to tend to his own spiritual salvation; and his ambitions to be recognized as a poetic peer to the ancients he so admires. Laura herself becomes the symbol of all the speaker desires. Word play with her name permits Petrarch to evoke the fleeting aura [*l'aura*] of her bodily presence, the *oro* [golden nets] of her hair which entangle his emotions, and the *lauro* [laurel crown] he hopes to win by being named poet laureate of Rome.[10] Like Dante's Beatrice, Petrarch's Laura dies, leaving the bereft lover to cope with memory, mourning, and regret, which become major themes of his lyrics. Petrarch's meticulously crafted individual sonnets, *canzoni*, *sestine*, madrigals, and *ballate*, and his minute attention to the ordering of the poems in this sequence result in a work of intricate musicality and immense psychological power, two sources of the *Canzoniere*'s enduring appeal for modern readers. The poet struggles deeply with his vain desires, repeatedly promising himself and God that he will change, only to return again and again to the exhausting state of ineluctable longing and his own personal shortcomings. The reader is left to decide, in the end, whether the book's final song of devotion to the Virgin Mary provides true resolution to this personal struggle, or whether in fact the *Canzoniere*'s first sonnet, in which the poet declares that he is "in part" a changed man, arches over the entire sequence as an admission of incomplete conversion.[11] The poetic achievements of Dante and Petrarch functioned as models throughout the Italian Renaissance, even as poets also strove to take distance from these two, gigantic predecessors.

In the fifteenth century, Florence became a major poetic center, thanks to the patronage of Lorenzo de' Medici ("the Magnificent"), who ruled the city and was himself a poet. Trained as a humanist and steeped in neo-Platonic philosophy, Lorenzo championed the superiority of Tuscan as a literary language. He wrote playful poems on rustic entertainments like hunting, and bawdy songs for carnival season, but also love sonnets influenced by Dante and Petrarch, and mythological poems inspired by Ovid. Collaborating with the humanist poet and philologist Angelo Ambrogini, known as Poliziano, Lorenzo compiled the earliest known anthology of Italian lyric poetry, the

---

[10] Petrarch was successful in this campaign. In 1341 he became the first since antiquity to be crowned poet laureate of Rome; see, in this volume, Wyatt, "Renaissances," pp. 00–00.
[11] See Freccero (1986).

Raccolta aragonese, and sent it (*c.* 1476) to Frederick of Aragon, son of the King of Naples. Naples itself was another of Italy's important poetic hubs. There, the Abruzzese Serafino Aquilano studied poetry and music, mastering numerous verse forms. Aquilano is best known for his *strambotti,* which he accompanied on the lute for the lords of Urbino, Mantua, and Milan. Another popular musical verse form, the *frottola* was practiced widely but developed most intensely in Naples.[12]

Poetry in the many dialects of Italy thrived in the period, but Renaissance lyric across all of Europe was soon to be vastly dominated by imitations of Petrarch's Tuscan *Canzoniere,* as we may see in countless individual poems (many of which were being set to music and performed) and in the numerous efforts to write sequences telling stories of love and loss as Petrarch had done.[13] In sixteenth-century Italy and elsewhere, this literary phenomenon also gained a distinctly protonational dimension.[14] By 1494, when Italy was invaded by the French, many Italian elites believed it was in the collective interest for the peninsula's separate city–states to unite, if not politically then at least linguistically and literarily, under the banner of a single vernacular. But which of Italy's many regional dialects merited this pan-Italian status – and how Italians might achieve such unification – was matter for debate. Some (following Dante) argued against official adoption of one specific dialect. Traffic among the many Italian courts, they thought, would spontaneously evolve a language comprising the most favored usages in circulation. Since ambassadors and visitors from throughout the peninsula (and the larger world) moved from court to court, according to this argument the shared language for writing in Italy should correspond to the way people spoke in these environments. Others, however, urged a conscious choice for one dialect or another, based not on speech practices but on the literary achievements in those

---

[12] On Aquilano and the *strambotto,* see Calitti (2010) 640–42; for the *frottola,* see Taruskin (2005).

[13] On dialect poetry, see Haller (1999). For the longer trajectory of the Petrarchan lyric sequence, see Greene (1991).

[14] Italy would not become a nation state until 1861, but Petrarchism played a role in various movements toward cultural unity and national identity in the Renaissance, about which see Navarette (1994); Greene (2000); and Kennedy (2003). On Petrarch's exclusion, in favor of Dante, from the nineteenth-century rhetoric of Italian national unity, see Quondam (2004).

languages. Today we recognize these two positions as descriptive and prescriptive approaches to grammar and usage, respectively.[15]

The Venetian poet and literary theorist Pietro Bembo published in 1525 a treatise entitled *Prose della volgar lingua* [On the Vernacular Language], in which he argued for the adoption of fourteenth-century Tuscan for all artistic writing in Italy because Italy's greatest literary works to date had been composed in that language, by Giovanni Boccaccio in prose and by Petrarch in lyric poetry.[16] In 1501, however, Bembo had already done something far more influential in the service of his cause: in collaboration with the innovative Venetian publisher Aldus Manutius, he had overseen the publication of the first pocket-sized edition of Petrarch's *Canzoniere*. The humanist Manutius had been printing elegant editions of Greek classics since the mid 1490s and also published in 1501 his edition of Virgil's *Aeneid*. By printing Petrarch in the same format, he and Bembo implicitly raised this "classic" of medieval Tuscan literature to the same level as the great works of antiquity they so admired. These small-format editions were luxury items, but they (and more economical books emulating them) facilitated the circulation of Petrarch's poems as a handy model. The attractiveness and convenient size of the *Petrarchini* [mini-Petrarchs] permitted readers to carry them about and to enjoy them at leisure. This meant that Petrarch's verses could easily be accessed, recited at social gatherings, and – perhaps most significantly – studied and imitated. Bembo's 1501 commercial innovation thus paved the way for his arguments in the 1525 *Prose*, where he details the rhyme, diction, and formal balance that constitute Petrarch's suitability as a national model. In the meantime, he also published another dialogue, the *Asolani* (1505), in which his characters discuss the nature of love, taking their cues from both Petrarch and the neo-Platonic philosopher Marsilio Ficino. Together, Bembo's writings and his editorial activities advanced a cultural program of enormous scope.

Thanks to Bembo's publications and Manutius' vision as a typesetter and marketer, Petrarchan poetry came to be written and exchanged by many educated Italians of the sixteenth century, male and female. The *Petrarchino*, in fact, may be seen in the hands of numerous portrait-sitters

---

[15] Notably, this debate – known in Italy as the *questione della lingua* [the language question] – aimed at a common language for writing but did not concern itself with uniting speech practices; see Campanelli, "Languages," Chapter 6 in this volume, 155–63.

[16] Dante, whose language was too varied for Bembo's tastes, was conspicuously absent as a model; see *ibid.* 157–58.

of the century. The golden hair and alabaster skin of Petrarch's beloved determined standards of female beauty and were reflected in paintings by artists from Botticelli to Testa.[17] Literate society frequently exchanged sonnets as a form of correspondence; and women first embraced print authorship by marketing their own Petrarchan verses. It takes some effort for us, as modern readers accustomed to value originality and purported uniqueness, to appreciate the high esteem in which Renaissance writers held the skill for Petrarchan imitation. If the term "Renaissance" has any meaning today, however, it must point to a passionate interest in the world of Greco-Roman antiquity. As Italians rediscovered long-lost writings by Cicero and other writers and as they unearthed astonishing examples of ancient Roman sculpture, they responded with deep admiration and longed to match the achievements of a past from which they felt their culture had somehow degenerated. The path to greatness appeared to them to be through historical study and emulation of the best models they could find, but this kind of imitation was competitive as well as admiring. Even when poets chose, on Bembo's advice, a vernacular model to imitate, their hope was not to parrot but to measure up to and even surpass Petrarch, by displaying both their profound acquaintance with his poetry and their ability to rework his themes and forms. This meant, on the one hand, that in the hands of the less gifted, poetry quickly became numbingly predictable and formulaic. On the other hand, severe constraints drove invention and ingenuity, as poets strove for new effects and insights using the limited, if beautiful, precision tools left them by their master and model.

Beginning in the fourteenth century, some humanist educators included elite girls among their pupils, tutoring them separately from their brothers but affording them access to the new, liberal-arts education in ever-growing numbers. By the sixteenth century, the female writer had emerged as an Italian cultural type, closely linked to humanist circles and their vision of cultural progress.[18] Adapting Petrarchan lyric to themes of marital love, moral reflection, and religious devotion, a number of highly accomplished women of the Italian elite published their own lyric collections, Vittoria Colonna, Veronica Gambara, Laura Terracina, Chiara Matraini, and Laura Battiferri among them.

---

[17] See Cropper (1976) and (1986) 175–90, 355–58.
[18] Cox (2008) 64–75, 80–91.

Two learned courtesans, Tullia d'Aragona and Veronica Franco, also emerged as lyric writers within the century, the latter introducing more openly erotic themes into her verses, while the merchant-class musician Gaspara Stampa sang her poetry in the *ridotti* [salons] of Venice.[19] Among their contemporaries, the most celebrated of these women was undoubtedly Colonna, whose first published volume (1538) consisted of love lyrics to her deceased husband. In her subsequent work, Colonna became a leading innovator in spiritual poetry, which gained increasing prominence amid the religious controversies of the Reformation and Counter-Reformation movements.[20]

Across the breadth of the Petrarchan wave, so much poetry was produced in this period that one distinguished literary historian has argued for seeing all Petrarchist lyric as a single macro-text.[21] Such sociological reading illuminates Petrarchism as a cultural phenomenon spanning not just all of Italy, but much of Europe and a number of trans-Atlantic contexts. Given its broad diffusion, Petrarchist verse varied extremely in quality, to the point where its crude practitioners could be satirized in theatrical comedies of the time.[22] Much Renaissance verse was indeed amateur, and though it played an important part in the broad culture of reading, writing, painting, and music-making in Europe, what earned Petrarchism its importance for literary history was the fact that a number of highly gifted poets wrote powerful, technically dazzling lyrics in the Petrarchist mode. Virtually every major poet of the period (including Sannazaro, Ariosto, and Tasso) participated in the culture of Petrarchism as did Bembo himself, yet even in this company the poetic *oeuvre* of Giovanni della Casa merits distinction. Della Casa is best known to non-readers of Italian as the author of the *Galateo*, a book of manners that was widely translated after his death. His lyrics, however, with their jagged, enjambed lines and brooding content, earn him uncontested primacy as the finest lyric poet of the Italian Renaissance.

Poetry was by this time, as noted earlier, also a commercial enterprise. All this interest in reading and sharing rhymes was supported

---

[19] Smarr (1991). On women's poetry and the salon culture of the period, see Robin (2007).
[20] While the earlier *Petrarca spirituale* (1536) of Girolamo Malipiero had rewritten Petrarch's poetry, editing out all references to earthly love, Colonna's spiritual verses constituted the influential foundation of a new genre of Petrarchan *rime spirituali*; see Cox (2008) 71. For more on Colonna, see the introduction to Colonna (2005); and Brundin (2008).
[21] Quondam (1974) 21 and (1991).
[22] For several readings of this satirical vein, see Ruggiero (2006).

(perhaps enabled) by the publication of single-author volumes of lyrics, which had been profitably marketed throughout Italy practically since the arrival of the printing press. The trendsetting Venetian publisher Gabriel Giolito, however, opened a new chapter of literary history in 1545, when he printed the first-ever multi-authored lyric anthology, *Rime diverse di molti eccellentissimi autori* [Assorted Poems by Many Most Excellent Authors]. Competing presses quickly followed suit, and poetic anthologies of all sorts (based on genre, on the authors' cities of origin, on occasions such as weddings and deaths, and even on gender) commanded the Italian printing market for at least the next century.[23] Thus, some seventy years after Lorenzo de' Medici's multi-authored manuscript gift to the prince of Naples, a publishing format was born that still endures today.

Petrarchism was pervasive, but it did not appeal to everyone. Some of the greatest poets of the Italian Renaissance are best described as anti-Petrarchist for their rejection (or lack of awareness) of the tight strictures Bembo placed on would-be versifiers of his time. Among these we must count the artist Michelangelo Buonarroti (1475–1564), who experimented constantly with lyric forms and content, adopting at times a rough and earthy vocabulary much closer to Dante than to Petrarch. Michelangelo's poems are influenced less by formal education than by assiduous reading, both of poetry and of neo-Platonic texts. Jotted on the backs of sketches and scribbled on scraps of bills, they document a literary counterpart to the artworks he was feverishly producing at the time.[24] His sonnets, madrigals, and *capitoli* deal with spiritual and erotic torment; the pains of aging; life's astonishing extremes of beauty, ugliness, joy, and despair; the tensions between devotion and forbidden sin. Quite contrary to the soul-searching Michelangelo was another anti-Petrarchist, the scandalous "Scourge of Princes" Pietro Aretino. In addition to the letters, plays, dialogues, and public slanders that earned him infamy, Aretino wrote sixteen obscene poems known as the *Sonetti lussuriosi* [Salacious Sonnets], each of which served as caption for an engraving depicting a male–female pair copulating in a different position. Aretino shared the space of scandal with the comic poet Francesco Berni, who was so much identified with burlesque genres

---

[23] On the phenomena of the anthology and the female author, see Shemek (2005); also Curran (2005).

[24] On this juxtaposition of text and image, see Barkan (2011b).

that the Italians adopted the playful adjective *bernesque* to designate this late-sixteenth-century mode. Berni's poems are riotously transgressive in their nonsensical exuberance over things that are condemned, debased, or taboo in polite society: from spit and card games to artichokes and the bubonic plague, Berni revels in the crude and the naughty.

Italian Renaissance literature was unquestionably dominated by vernacular poetry that took Petrarch's lyrics as a basic point of reference (either positively or negatively), but two general exceptions to this claim merit our attention. From the fifteenth century survive the works of several poets who wrote in popular forms rather than in the highly literate lyric tradition described above. In Florence, the barber Domenico di Giovanni (known as "Il Burchiello"), for example, wrote humorous and nonsense sonnets familiar to all the city's inhabitants. The Venetian nobleman Leonardo Giustinian was a learned humanist, but he too wrote *ballate*, *strambotti*, and *canzonette* on playful folk themes. Both Giustinian and the Florentine Lucrezia Tornabuoni (as well as numerous anonymous poets) also wrote in the medieval tradition of the spiritual poems called *laude*, lyric compositions based on stories from the Bible. The colorful and evocative lauds sometimes developed into theatrical pieces best known in Italy as the *sacre rappresentazioni* [religious dramas], which were acted out by members of religious confraternities for enthusiastic, popular audiences. In the sixteenth century, the Neapolitan Luigi Tansillo adopted Dante's *terza rima* [an interlocking three-line rhymed stanza] to write advice poems on breast-feeding and on real-estate acquisitions. All of these forms point to a vernacular poetic culture outside the tradition of Petrarchism.

A second exception to the dominance of vernacular Petrarchism was poetry written in Latin by Italian humanists. In the fifteenth century, humanist efforts to emulate ancient literary forms included the commitment to write not only in the genres, but also in the language of these models. Much Latin writing in the Renaissance was in prose, especially philosophical and theological texts, but many poets also produced neo-Latin lyrics, including those best known now for their vernacular production.[25] Those who excelled in these compositions include the Neapolitans Giovanni Pontano, who wrote love lyrics in

---

[25] See Perosa/Sparrow (1979); Bonora (1987); De Robertis (1987) 463–72; and Vecce (1993a) and (1993b).

Latin;[26] and his compatriot Jacopo Sannazaro, who adapted the genre of
Virgil's poems on country life (the *Eclogues*) to the world of fishermen
in his *Eclogae piscatoriae* [Piscatory Eclogues]. The Tuscan Poliziano wrote
many Latin lyrics in addition to the vernacular poem for which he is
most famous, the *Stanze per la giostra di Giuliano di Piero de' Medici* [Stanzas
for the Tournament of Giuliano di Piero de' Medici] which celebrates a
jousting match.[27] A few poets also wrote lyrics in a hybrid language
known as macaronic verse, which mixed the grammar of Latin with
Italian words and syntax much as the humble peasant's supper of
macaroni might mix available ingredients. Most famous of these was
the Mantuan poet Teofilo Folengo, whose *Zanitonella* celebrates the love
of the peasant Tonino for his sweetheart Zanina in a parody of the
courtly love lyric.

The last two great lyric poets of the period were Torquato Tasso
and Giambattista Marino, both of whom represent departures from
Renaissance sensibilities. Tasso, who is best known for his heroic poetry
(see below), was also a lyric poet and a theorist. A profound admirer of
the classics, Tasso was also tormented in his devotion to Counter-
Reformation Catholic orthodoxy. Many of his delicate and troubled
verses inspired early-modern composers such as Monteverdi to set them
to music. The audacious and cosmopolitan Marino's lyrics are wider-
ranging in form, tone, and theme. Though Marino, too, is remembered
for his epic poem (see below), his collection of 400 lyrics was imitated in
Italy and abroad. First published under the title, *Rime* (1602) and then
revised as *La lira* [The Lyre, 1614] these are arranged by mode (amorous,
heroic, lugubrious, sacred, etc.) rather than organized into a narrative
canzoniere. While living in Paris, Marino also wrote a volume of *Epitalami*
[Wedding Poems, 1616] in celebration of the world's court cultures,
and a collection of verses explicating works of art, entitled *La galleria*
[The Gallery, 1620] as well as a book of classical idylls, *La Sampogna* [The
Bagpipes, 1620]. Both Tasso and Marino reflect the shift, which had
been building gradually across the sixteenth century, away from
classicizing Petrarchism toward dramatic and sensual effects that would
emerge powerfully in the seventeenth-century baroque aesthetic.

---

[26] Pontano also composed an extraordinary work in Latin verse, *Urania*, that straddles both
lyric and epic in its effort at explaining the human vis-à-vis astronomical and astrological
reflections situated against an encyclopedic retelling of ancient mythology; see Kidwell
(1991) 131–36.

[27] On Poliziano's Latin verse, see, in this volume, Campanelli, "Languages," 147–49.

Over the course of these developments, we see also significant stylistic and metrical shifts in lyric production, as the sonnet yields to popular, more singable forms such as the madrigal and the *canzonetta*.

Heroic poetry

Heroic adventure poetry, like the lyric, was a social medium through which the educated and privileged classes shared both values and pleasures. Like the lyric, it was rooted in popular, oral sources and performance, and was widely consumed by many non-readers who accessed it not through the eye, but through the ear. If lyric poetry exalted the individual desiring subject and often explored love as a source of creativity, civilization, and personal ennoblement, heroic verse in the Renaissance as in earlier periods focused on collective identities. Many characters of epic and romance were famous for their specific exploits and personalities, but the overarching narratives of the most important of these poems feature mythical stories of foundation and connected powerful patrons to heroic histories by claiming to narrate what those patrons' ancestors had achieved in the wars of ancient Greece and Rome. What these features tell us, beyond the fact that early moderns were fascinated with the ancient past, is that they believed that both history and myth mattered. Their sense of themselves was largely based on heritage, but they felt quite free to project imagined ancestries for themselves in order to further their own ambitions.

Italian heroic poems were wildly popular not only because they instilled collective pride in a gallery of local or "national" heroes to which listeners could feel connected, but also because they were wonderfully entertaining. Within the scope of their larger narratives, these poems indulged a love for adventure, exoticism, fantasy, and erotic intrigue. The heroes of the Trojan War and the later Christian Crusades reappear in poem after poem, like favorite action figures or superheroes whose adventures could always be expanded to include new episodes. Our task as readers of these poems is, therefore, at least twofold: to allow ourselves to be entertained by them, and to discern what "cultural work" they performed.

The Renaissance heroic poem in Italy is a hybrid genre that draws strenuously on four earlier, sometimes overlapping, narrative forms: medieval *chansons de geste* [songs of heroic deeds], medieval romance, ancient epic, and ancient Greek romance. The French *chansons de geste* date to the eleventh and twelfth centuries and are thus roughly contemporary with, or even slightly earlier than, the Troubadour lyrics discussed above. These were epic poems commemorating (and sometimes mocking) the exploits of the French military heroes, most famously Holy Roman Emperor Charlemagne, whose fictional campaign against the Saracens for the conquest of Spain is immortalized in the most renowned of them, the *Chanson de Roland* [Song of Roland]. The origins of the *chansons* are much debated, but it is important to note that in addition to their legendary content, they sometimes seem to allude to chronicled historical events. The medieval French, Anglo-Norman, and Occitan romances (also in verse) are usually sorted into three broad cycles (though there are others). The "Matter of Britain" (Arthurian or Breton cycle) recounts tales of King Arthur and his Knights of the Round Table, their political rivalries, chivalry, and love entanglements; the "Matter of France" derives from the *chansons de geste*; and the "Matter of Rome" narrates stories of the Trojan War, Alexander the Great, and other ancient heroes of the Mediterranean. Important features especially of the later romances are spiritual mystery, supernatural elements, and the theme of courtly love.

The third form to which Italian Renaissance heroic poems are indebted is the ancient epic. Homer's *Iliad* (*c.* 750 BCE) tells the story of the Trojan War (*c.* 1300 BCE) from the perspective of the victorious Greeks, while his *Odyssey* (*c.* 725 BCE) narrates the Greek warrior Odysseus' ten-year journey home after the war and his many encounters along the way. These Greek poems were thoroughly oral in their origins. They had been sung in many variations for centuries before being captured in writing by the shadowy figure we have come to call Homer. Virgil's Latin *Aeneid* (29–19 BCE), on the other hand, is a fundamentally literary creation. Written in the service of Caesar Augustus, it too reaches back to the Trojan War for its material, this time from a distance of twelve centuries, to tell the story of Aeneas, a soldier on the losing (Trojan) side of the conflict, who legendarily fled, voyaged to Italy, and founded the city – and thus the civilization – of Rome. These three ancient epics too (of war, of homecoming, and of foundation) were major sources of material for the Italian adventure poems. Finally, a number of narrative elements and techniques especially in the later Italian poems appear to be indebted to the ancient Greek prose romances of Achilles Tatius Chariton, Xenophon of Ephesus, and Heliodorus, though the history of these works' transmission in early modern Europe still remains largely to be written.

Until the fifteenth century, mergings of the classical and medieval strains of heroic poetry remained relatively limited in Italy. Dante drew directly on the *Aeneid* and indirectly on the Homeric epics for material in his *Commedia* [Divine Comedy], flagging the dangers of romance reading through the pilgrim's encounter with Francesca da Rimini in *Inferno* V. Consistent with his humanist commitments, Petrarch had begun in 1338 to write a Latin epic poem of his own, taking as his hero the Roman general Scipio Africanus; but this work, *L'Africa*, remains incomplete.

The chivalric romances and the *chansons de geste*, on the other hand, were mingling freely, thanks to the *cantastorie* or *canterini*, the popular minstrel singers who appeared regularly in the piazzas and the inns of Italy hoping to be paid for singing episodes from these cycles. The *canterini*, who often sang their verses in dialect, had counterparts in virtually every other culture of the world. Oral, written, and musical realizations of these many poems proliferated in a common space, often overlapping in the piazza or on the page. If, as is now thought, the Old French romances began as written texts, they were popularized by performing improvisers as well as by copyists and eventually flooded the print market. Crossing linguistic borders, the medieval heroic poems spawned new contributions to the corpus also in hybrid dialects. Two of the earliest surviving transcriptions of these in Italy are the fourteenth-century Franco-Italian *Entreé en Espagne* [Entry into Spain] and the *Prise de Pampelune* [The Taking of Pamplona]. There is also converse evidence that strictly literary authors were influenced in their compositional choices by hearing performances of their own verses in public.[28]

Boccaccio had already participated in this borrowing and proliferation. After he adopted the *ottava rima* form for his romances, the *Teseide* (1340) and the *Filostrato* (1347), Italians generally followed his example, standardizing the eight-line stanza with a rhyme scheme of ABABABCC for both spoken and written versions of these tales.[29] If the brevity and the strong formal consistency of lyric poetry opened it to appropriation by amateurs, the scale and the narrative demands of heroic poetry called

---

[28] On this nexus between performed and written poems and between poetry and music, see Haar (1986). On a report of Ariosto's authorial revision based on heard performance, see Shemek (1998) 135 and n. 28
[29] See Alfano (2011a).

for more specialized technicians, whether the product was a written or a vocalized text. Against a cultural backdrop of performances by skilled, "professional" minstrels who roamed from town to town singing heroic verse narrative, several of Italy's most sophisticated and artful poets made literary history by authoring book-length heroic poems.[30] These texts, in turn, were regularly read aloud for groups in courtly and urban settings, thus circling back to the realm of performance.[31]

Luigi Pulci, an impoverished nobleman in the Florence of Lorenzo de' Medici, drew on earlier Tuscan sources to write his explosively satiric, burlesque adventure poem in twenty-eight *cantari* [sung chapters], the *Morgante* [final edition 1483]. Taking his cues from wildly undisciplined popular speech and from his predecessor Burchiello, Pulci snubbed the rarefied philosophical bent of poets in Ficino's neo-Platonic circle. In his loosely structured poem of concatenated episodes, every detail seems to shout Pulci's rejection of such classical values as symmetry, moderation, order, and structural unity. The poem's hero is an invention of Pulci's own, the pagan giant Morgante, a captive of the paladin Orlando (an Italianized Roland), whose combination of enormous strength, docility, and vitality tears across the stanzas of Pulci's poem until the giant perishes from a trivially fatal crab bite. Morgante's sidekick (also a Pulci original), the demi-giant Margutte, dies in a fit of laughter when he spies an ape wearing his boots.[32] The *Morgante* holds tightly onto its popular roots: the poem's epic catalogues and lists are obsessed with food (a favorite theme of the hungry and impoverished); its language is exuberantly local, corporeal, and everyday; and its content baldly parodies high culture.

Pulci's poem presents a narrator who, like the *cantari* of his day, calls out his verses to the crowd in a bustling urban piazza. The next major heroic poem to be produced in Italy would reflect its author's quite different context, with a narrator who poses as a singer at court, eager to

---

[30] The prose chivalric romance *I Reali di Francia* [The Royal House of France] by Andrea da Barberino falls outside the formal parameters of this chapter but bears noting as a key text in the popularization of these tales; the genealogical move of Andrea's text is to connect the French monarchy with the lineage of Charlemagne ("Gostantino").

[31] Beer (1987) 207 notes that "Between the fifteenth and the sixteenth centuries Italian humanists, literary writers, and editors applied themselves to turning the *cantastories'* forms of entertainment into epics, which became printed books, fundamentally tied to reading, whether aloud or silently, and no longer to performance alone."

[32] Pulci's third original creation is the verbose demon Astarotte.

please a group of "gentle" listeners. Matteo Maria Boiardo's *Orlando innamorato* [Orlando in Love, 1494] emerged from the princely court of Ferrara, where the ruling Este lords had been welcoming performers, writers, and books of chivalric poetry for generations. Ferrara was at the time also an intellectual center, with its own university and a strong humanist tradition. These two facets of the Ferrarese scene – the long-standing presence there of both popular chivalric literature and classical learning – positioned Boiardo to merge several traditions in the pages of his unfinished masterpiece of sixty-nine cantos arranged in two books. The first of these fusions is signaled by the title. Though previous poems in the Carolingian cycle had featured the occasional damsel infatuated with Roland, Charlemagne's steadfast Christian soldier had remained impervious to Cupid's arrow. Boiardo effectively overlaid the Breton and Carolingian cycles as no one had done before him, pulling the austere Orlando into a violent passion for Angelica, a princess from Catai (Cathay, Marco Polo's name for China, though Angelica is also described in the later tradition as an "Indian Princess") whose appearance marks the opening of the *Innamorato*, when she arrives in the midst of Charlemagne's camp as the knights celebrate the Feast of Pentecost (the end of the Easter season). Erupting from one romance cycle into another, Angelica upsets a military culture with the illogic of erotic desire, as virtually every knight she encounters wants nothing more than to possess her. Other elements of the Breton cycle invade the Carolingian one along with Angelica, including the magic fountains that trigger either passionate desire or its opposite, thus subjecting Boiardo's characters to the arbitrariness of erotic obsession. Significantly, the chaos of emotional upheaval brought about by this meshing of one narrative cycle with another necessitates the interweaving of multiple plot lines, as characters encounter and lose each other, run into new figures and adventures, and rediscover old friends and foes. This material thus challenges Boiardo to develop an entirely original use of the technique of *interlace*, keeping many plot lines in play, allowing characters and relationships to intersect at key points, and then suspending them to pick up others.

Boiardo's second great convergence was one that he only managed to initiate, but his effort in this direction laid the groundwork for the innovations of his successor, Ludovico Ariosto. In Book Two of the *Innamorato*, Boiardo introduces the "Matter of Rome" into his poem by creating a dynastic ancestor for the Este, giving that character a heroic life of its own.[33] For the humanist Boiardo, a translator of both Latin and Greek texts, the idea of modeling a mythical past for his patrons must have seemed both an irresistible and a logical next step in the development of Italian heroic poetry. His half-Saracen, half-Christian knight, Ruggiero, would meet the female Christian knight, Bradamante. The two would share a destiny in marriage as ancient forebears to the lords of Ferrara, Boiardo thus taking his place in the imperial poetic tradition of Virgil.

Ariosto was, like Boiardo, a court poet and diplomat in the service of the Este. Signaling his sense of connection with Boiardo – literally picking up where the *Innamorato*'s author had left off – but also his drive to innovate, Ariosto entitled his work the *Orlando furioso* [Orlando Gone Mad] and took his title character not only down the road of love on which Boiardo had placed him, but into a totally unhinged realm of jealous frenzy.[34] Ariosto capitalized as no poet before him had on the structural and thematic complexities of the heroic tradition. Fully overlaying the centrifugal structure of romance – its constant proliferation of characters and plot lines and its persistent deferral of narrative resolution – and the linear structure of epic narrative – with its necessary resolution in the foundation of a state or dynasty – Ariosto remarkably works both of these narrative machines at once, even as they pull in opposite directions. Significant space is dedicated in the forty-six cantos of the *Furioso* to the desperate wanderings of characters like Orlando, in movement and pursuit of the things they desire, whether lovers, helmets, horses, or revenge (at least until they change their minds and long for something else), and this constant flux propels the narrative ever outward and away from any stable goal. But Ariosto also binds into this tapestry an overarching, intricate tale of love, loss, betrayal, and final union in marriage for his dynastic heroes, Ruggiero and Bradamante. As Ariosto's characters weigh their (sometimes crazed) personal desires against their sense of public duty, the poem becomes a sustained meditation on the instability of human commitments and the tenuous nature of sanity. Even Ariosto's narrator – who in contrast with those of Pulci and Boiardo is emphatically not a singer but a writer with a

---

[33] See Everson (2001).
[34] Marinelli (1987). For studies of Ariosto that situate it both in its world and also within a series of contemporary critical perspectives, see Ascoli (1987); Javitch (1991); Shemek (1998); Zatti (2006); and Stoppino (2012).

pen in his hand – confesses that he himself is subject to fits of madness, because he, like Orlando, is insane with love. The self-conscious ravings and the political musings of Ariosto's narrator are one of the poem's most strikingly modern features, characteristics which beg the question of connections between these long verse narratives and the modern novels which are in some sense their descendants. The *Furioso* also incorporates other forms, including novellas, lyric poems, and argumentative debate (especially on the questions of women's worth and the value of fidelity in love) in such a wide variety of registers as to suggest the poem's effective participation in the tradition Mikhail Bakhtin identified with the novel.[35]

With Ariosto, the Italian epic of foundation takes shape, wrapped up in the strategies of romance that challenge its own myth-making.[36] Ariosto's openness to this thematic and tonal range, and his generous use of fantasy, erotic adventure, and swiftly moving plots, earned him an unprecedentedly large audience among his contemporaries. Numerous editions and translations into all of the principal European languages well into the eighteenth century guaranteed the poem a long afterlife. The *Furioso* inspired many sequels and spin-offs, keeping alive the adventures of Ariosto's characters. Though the vast majority of these are woefully unequal to their task, one exception is Teofilo Folengo's macaronic comic epic *Baldus* (1521), which also leans heavily on Pulci. Here the protagonist is a peasant hero who is actually – through his mother, Baldina – the grandson of the King of France and – through his father, Guidone – a distant relative of Charlemagne's Rinaldo.[37]

Ariosto's extravagant multiplication of plot lines, characters, and locations, and his vigorous weaving together of the traditional "Matters" of France, Britain, and Rome were the product of a brilliant compositional sensibility largely untroubled by prescriptive theories. Though the successive editions of the *Furioso* published in Ariosto's lifetime (1516, 1521, 1532) increasingly encompass revisions aimed at capturing a "national" readership rather than a regional one by strengthening the

[35] The Russian literary theorist Mikhail Bakhtin (1981) discussed the novel as a literary form under constant renovation and in continuous dialogue with its contemporary audience, contrasting it with the epic which he saw as walled off in an absolute past. Though Bakhtin (remarkably) does not mention Ariosto, postmodern novelists including Italo Calvino and Salman Rushdie clearly look to the *Orlando furioso* for some of their own narrative strategies and tonal choices.

[36] On romance as a strategy rather than a genre or a mode, see Fuchs (2004).

[37] Lazzerini (1992).

poem's epic dimension and following Bembo's Tuscanizing linguistic dictates, the poem moves free of generic "rules" that – just a few years after the its final edition – would put heavy pressure on the production of heroic poetry. Aristotle's *Poetics* (*c.* 335 BCE), which describes the principal features of lyric, tragic, and epic literature, had been translated from Greek into Latin in 1498 by Lorenzo Valla, but a new Latin translation by Alessandro Pazzi in 1536, followed by a corrected translation and influential commentary by Francesco Robortello in 1548, gave the work new vigor. The next generation of narrative poets in Italy took Aristotle's descriptions as regulations to be followed, becoming deeply engaged in theoretical concerns as to the proper composition of epic poetry. Explicitly rejecting the heritage of medieval heroic poetry (which, given its undeniable popularity, was seen as troublingly plebeian), these poets tried their hands at writing texts in the classical epic mode, aiming to produce poems dignified by unity of action and character as well as by epic linearity. Gian Giorgio Trissino's *L'Italia liberata dai Goti* [Italy Freed from the Goths, 1547–54] is one such, as are the *Amadigi* [Amadis, 1560] of Bernardo Tasso, and the *Girone il cortese* [Girone the Courteous, 1548] of Luigi Alamanni. All are generally regarded as failures. But another poet emerged from the thick of these debates to write the last great heroic poem of the Italian Renaissance.

Torquato Tasso too was employed by the Este lords, but his cultural and political moment contrasted significantly with those of his predecessors. Tasso's Italy was a land now worn down by religious strife and foreign political domination. The Protestant Reformation unleashed in 1517 by the German Martin Luther's challenge to papal authority and Catholic doctrine had by this time provoked a Catholic Counter-Reformation that urged orthodoxy not only in religious practices but also in cultural endeavors. The Italy whose 1494 French invasion Boiardo had decried in the last stanzas of his *Orlando innamorato* was now subject to Spanish rule in Milan and Naples, Sicily and Sardinia; and another dreaded enemy, the Turks, had for decades been breaching not only the Mediterranean coastline but also the borders of continental Europe.[38]

Son of the failed epic poet Bernardo Tasso, Torquato was drawn to heroic verse from an early age and wrote a conventional chivalric

---

[38] In 1526, Sultan Suleiman I won the Battle of Mohács and took control of southern Hungary, and in 1529 the Turks made their first attempt to take Vienna.

romance, the *Rinaldo* (1562) as a young man. His historical position and his sensibilities, however, drew him ultimately to a topic of striking contemporary resonance, that of the Christian battle in the First Crusade to retake Christ's tomb in Jerusalem from the Ottomans. Tasso's *Gerusalemme liberata* [Jerusalem Delivered, 1581] casts the Muslims as infidels but also as the embodiments of all that is wrong, in Tasso's view, with romance as a genre. Romance's wandering narrative and its personally motivated, easily distracted heroes become the symbol not only of Islamic "error" but also of the religious splintering and Protestant heresy of Tasso's Europe. In contrast, the epic undertaking that binds the Christian forces under the *Liberata*'s hero Goffredo embodies narrative unity, collective discipline, and Catholic orthodoxy. Tasso was also a theorist. His *Discorsi dell'arte poetica* [Discourses on the Art of Poetry, 1560s] and *Discorsi del poema eroico* [Discourses on the Epic Poem, 1594] lay out his commitment to Aristotelian unity of action, to decorum, and to narrative credibility (verisimilitude), offering a conceptual backdrop against which to understand his poem's radical shift away from romance ambiguity, pluralism, and digression and its striving for oneness – whether literary, spiritual, or ideological. This is not to say, however, that Tasso's poem fully expunges its medieval heritage. Standing in for the magical beasts of romance in Tasso's poem are angels, demons, and Christian miracles, while erotic attraction haunts his poem as a dreadful mystery. Taming (or conquering) the religious, gender, racial, and cultural alterity which had colored so much of the romance tapestry, the *Liberata* nonetheless cultivates an intense fascination with all of these elements, which are perhaps most concentrated in the darkly seductive sorceress Armida, and the racially mixed female pagan knight, Clorinda.

Though Tasso's poem programmatically distances itself from the festive world of the *cantari* and asserts its place in the literary tradition of Virgil's *Aeneid*, the *Gerusalemme liberata* nonetheless enjoyed a significant afterlife in vocal performances of a different sort. From the time of its early editions, Tasso's poem provided subject matter for madrigals, operas, and other musical works by Wert, Monteverdi, Handel, Vivaldi, Gluck, Haydn, Rossini, Brahms, and Dvořák. Ariosto's poem too spawned a large number of operatic versions, including three of Handel's greatest works, *Ariodante*, *Alcina*, and *Orlando*. The most recent of these operas is an *Ariodante* from 1942 by Nino Rota, composer of the film scores for Federico Fellini and the *Godfather* series.

Women did not, to our knowledge, perform as roving *cantari*, but after the mid sixteenth century they produced a number of heroic poems, asserting their increasing presence as both consumers and creators of popular literature. Tullia d'Aragona's *Il Meschino* [The Wretch, 1560] appears to have been the first of these. Based on an earlier, Italian prose text, *Il Meschino* tells the tale of a young nobleman named Guerrino, whose capture by pirates initiates a series of adventure travels in Europe, the Mediterranean, and India as well as to Hell and Purgatory. The unfinished chivalric poem, *Floridoro* (1581) by the Venetian Moderata Fonte features the female knight Risamante, who is cast in a dynastic role as a Medici ancestor and who injects into the poem a theme dear to women of the time, that of wrongfully denied inheritance.[39] The Neapolitan Margherita Sarrocchi narrates in her *Scanderbeide* (1606, 1623) the exploits of a more recent figure, the fifteenth-century Albanian Gjerg (George) Kastrioti (Scanderbeg), who fought against the Turks for the territory of Christian Albania. Lucrezia Marinella's *Enrico, ovvero Bisanzio acquistato* [Henry, or Byzantium Conquered, 1635] takes a cue from both Sarrocchi and Tasso, as it recounts the early-thirteenth-century Fourth Crusade, when Christian forces under the leadership of Venetian doge Enrico Dandolo defeated rebels against the Holy Roman Empire in Constantinople (Byzantium). Echoing her explicitly feminist works, Marinella effectively critiques the heroic genre's gender politics, most visibly in the three uncompromising women warriors she creates. Finally, Barbara Albizzi Tagliamochi wrote a poem based on one character from Virgil's *Aeneid*, the *Ascanio errante* (1640).[40]

Giambattista Marino's long poem, *Adone* [Adonis, 1623] departs in major ways from the cultural sensibilities of the Renaissance. Based on the myth of Venus and Adonis found in Ovid's *Metamorphoses*, *Adone* polemically rejects all the historical and martial elements of epic poetry and focuses instead on a mythological tableau of erotic sensuality. Marino's contemporary Alessandro Tassoni provided the baroque period's other rejection of Renaissance heroic values, in *La Secchia rapita* [The Stolen Bucket, 1624], a twelve-canto poem in which the 1393 war between Bologna and Modena is recounted as a dispute to the death over a pilfered pail.

[39] See Malpezzi Price (2003).
[40] On these works, see Cox (2011) 164–97.

Acknowledgments

My sincere thanks to Margaret Brose, Virginia Cox, Julia Hairston, Jason Jacobs, and Sharon Kinoshita as well as to Michael Wyatt for reading this chapter in draft and improving it through their questions, suggestions, and corrections.

9

Prose

Neither dialogue nor narrative prose fiction had a prominent place in the ancient pantheon of genres, or what today we might call the "literary system," made up of many different kinds of writing. In the West, Greek philosophers and rhetoricians were the first to codify this system, culminating in Aristotle's *Poetics*, which put forward a total theory of literature and its kinds. If classical culture recognized differences between lyric and epic poetry, for instance, or between tragedy and comedy, it is in no small part because there was a general consensus concerning the order of genres. We know, however, from the surviving portion (on tragedy) of the *Poetics*, that both dialogue and narrative prose fiction were given only the briefest consideration by Aristotle: he observes that there is no "common name" for works of this sort composed in "plain language," before turning his attention to the privileged poetic genres, such as epic and tragedy.[1] Nevertheless, the Greeks and Romans wrote dialogues for centuries after Aristotle, and the prose romance flourished in the Hellenistic world. If ancient critics did not know what to make of narrative prose fiction or dialogue, what did it matter? Authors and readers clearly knew a good thing when they saw one, whether or not it was codified by literary authorities, and this situation would endure for almost two millennia. In what follows, I will examine two literary genres whose origins can be traced back to antiquity – the novella and the dialogue – in order to see how the Italian Renaissance approached the transmission and transformation of these

---

[1] For the relevant passage, see Aristotle (1995) 31; and on the importance of Aristotle's *Poetics* in the period, see Procaccioli (2011).

kinds of writing, which seemed to elude critical classification and offer a privileged site for experimentation with the literary system itself.

The novella is the oldest genre of narrative prose written in Italian. Its roots reach deep into the tradition of medieval prose genres, either in neo-Latin or in the vernacular, that precedes it: the devotional *exemplum* [moralizing tale], *argumentum* [theme], *historia* [account], legend, *fabliau* [a brief, often ribald tale], and epistle are among its many sources from the Middle Ages, which in turn are indebted to the practices of prose-writing in late antiquity. Although printing had yet to appear in the West, and although Italian had yet to be codified as a literary language, novella-like narrative fictions – either singly or in collections – circulated among readers on the peninsula in the thirteenth and fourteenth centuries.[2] The episodic stories that these brief texts tell of love, adventure, fortune, faith, laughter, and loss clearly addressed a cultural need not met in religious sermons, courtly love poetry, or other high literary genres of the era. In general formal terms, novellas are fairly brief narrative prose fictional tales that: (i) do not usually represent only historical events or characters; (ii) avoid formulating explicit moral lessons for their readers; (iii) develop plot through linear (not episodic) action; (iv) employ chiefly realistic elements; (v) have protagonists who overcome an obstacle without supernatural assistance, and act on their own autonomous initiative (unlike the fairy tale); (vi) reveal the life of the protagonist through action (unlike the novel); and (vii) provide only a limited number of motives for that action.[3] One collection of tales matching this description achieved such fame that it marked the ascension of the novella to an art form that would change the course of European culture, the *Decameron* (*c*. 1348–53; revised *c*. 1373).

The author of that work, Giovanni Boccaccio, was born in 1313, during the final flourishing of medieval culture (Dante was at the time still at work on his *Commedia*), into a Tuscan merchant family whose ancestral home was in the town of Certaldo, south-west of Florence.[4] Originally destined for a career in banking and commerce, the young Boccaccio instead embraced the humanist study of letters, producing numerous works in medieval prose or verse genres in the 1330s and

---

[2] Still invaluable for an overview of early Italian prose are De Luca (1954); and Segre/Marti (1959).

[3] Bragantini (1998) 158–59; and Papio (2007) vol. 2, 1295.

[4] For the richly informative critical edition of the *Decameron* produced for the 700th anniversary of Boccaccio's birth, see Boccaccio (2013).

1340s that anticipate the themes of his masterpiece. After experiencing the terror and trauma of the Great Plague in Florence in 1348, which decimated the population of the city (more than half of the residents died of the disease) and killed his father, stepmother, and many close friends, Boccaccio turned to the composition of a *libro di novelle* [book of tales] in the vernacular, at a time in which Latin was still the privileged literary language. Without breaking sharply with the culture of the Middle Ages in which its author was steeped, the *Decameron* founds the modern practice of writing narrative prose fiction, and provides one of the first signposts pointing to the incipient Italian Renaissance.[5] Although Boccaccio's book was completed only thirty years after the death of Dante, its effect on the future of European literature was more immediate than that of the Florentine poet's Christian epic: across the continent, the Boccaccian poetics of narrative realism became the gold standard for post-medieval generations of writers who chose to narrate through the shorter forms of prose fiction.

The *Decameron* – and this is perhaps the key trait of the genre of the "book of tales" – employs a *cornice*, a meta-narrative frame, surrounding the collection of one hundred novellas. It not only tells a story about storytelling itself; the artfully composed frame tale is the totalizing device that transforms the *Decameron* into a book rather than a sheaf of scattered novellas.[6] Within the frame, Boccaccio relates that seven young women and three young men met by chance in the church of Santa Maria Novella in Florence during the darkest days of the 1348 epidemic. With the rules of normal social interaction temporarily suspended, they decide to flee the city, which has become a charnel-house, and to meet at a nearby villa in the hills to the north. There the *brigata* [brigade], or company, of young people passes ten idyllic days in pleasant conversation, banquets, and dancing. Each day they gather in the afternoon on a lovely green lawn, where they take turns narrating novellas around a theme chosen by a "king" or "queen" elected for that day by the group (Fridays and Saturdays, however, are reserved for religious observances). The framing device not only confers formal and thematic unity to the tales by creating a closed narrative system, but establishes the fiction that these novellas are a transcription of live performances by real flesh-and-blood individuals speaking in the

---

[5] Battaglia Ricci (2000) 132.   [6] *Ibid.* 137.

language of everyday life.[7] Boccaccio's frame, despite the seemingly edenic nature of its central "brigade in the garden" image, thus favors the historical over the allegorical and the real over the fantastic. If Dante's epic Christian poem employs one hundred cantos to tell the story of one pilgrim's progress from despair to salvation, Boccaccio's one hundred novellas narrate a human rather than divine comedy.[8]

The title of the work refers to the ten days that it takes the group of young men and women to narrate their one hundred tales: indeed, the collection was also often referred to as the *Centonovelle* [One Hundred Novellas]. As the fiction of the frame indicates, Boccaccio is thoroughly self-conscious in the *Decameron* about the process by which his text was produced, and includes meta-literary moments in which the author or a surrogate speaks openly about novella-writing.[9] A further layer of complexity is added, however, by the extremely large number of themes, motifs, and textual models that Boccaccio deploys within this work, as carefully organized as a book of accounts.[10] The author of the *Decameron* tirelessly uses and reuses the repertory of medieval literary genres, looting the lumber-room of almost a thousand years of Western culture: for the novella of Filippo Balducci (at the beginning of the Fourth Day), for instance, the erudite Boccaccio likely drew on sources as varied as a thirteenth-century French *fabliau*, early Italian collections of fables and novellas, a medieval *exemplum*, and possibly other, more ancient texts. The themes or subjects of the ten days, which range from sex to religion, from fortune to deception, are far from unique to the *Decameron*, but are scrutinized in it by the various narrators from many different perspectives, allowing Boccaccio to portray and critique human foibles, vices, hypocrisy, and superstition without recourse to heavy-handed moralism. His book is not just a satire, of course, for the analysis of virtue is central to the tales, many of which emphasize marital fidelity, friendship, and so on. Its many comic moments, moreover, are pointedly counterbalanced by tragedy and romance. At the level of both form and content, then, the *Decameron* proposes a multifaceted vision of existence, always open to experimentation.

Like death itself, sex and love are woven into the very tissue of the tales. The brigade exalts the life-giving powers of *eros* in the eternal struggle with *thanatos* [the "death drive"], which seems to them to be

---

[7] Bragantini (2000) 7–32.   [8] De Sanctis (1871).   [9] Battaglia Ricci (2000) 192.
[10] Mazzacurati (1996) 12.

running amok in Florence and across Europe. Seductions, bed-tricks, adulterous trysts, lascivious monks, lustful nuns, ludicrous cuckolds, merry widows, curious virgins, and cunning lechers are found everywhere in the *Decameron*, in contravention of the rigid social controls concerning sex, love, marriage, and family in fourteenth-century Italy. Culture here cannot overcome nature: sexuality is, in Boccaccio's eyes, an integral part of the human comedy. Despite the observance of graceful good manners by the members of the brigade in the frame narrative, intimate body parts and functions are put on uninhibited display in the tales, especially in those of the Third and Seventh Days. Masetto's smock blows in the wind, "leaving him totally exposed" to the gaze of the abbess (III.1); the hermit Rustico, encountering a beautiful young penitent, experiences "the resurrection of the flesh" (III.10); the amorous Caterina sets her lover's "nightingale singing a great many times" one warm spring night (V.4); Peronella's lover possesses her "as the unbridled stallions cover their mares" (VII.2).[11] Boccaccio's tales show us both men and women who, in a world in flux, freely address their own sexual needs and desires, despite all that laws and institutions do to try to stop them. Throughout the book, this equality between the sexes is captured in the mutual delight that women and men take in consensual sexual congress, celebrating and cherishing *eros* and one another. As Emilia remarks at the end of the novella of Tedaldo (III.7), "they enjoyed their love for a long time. God grant we may enjoy ours." In the *Decameron*, however, a fully realized sexuality is never an end in itself, but rather an integral part of the realism with which Boccaccio paints his great fresco of human life.

Among the many other themes embedded in both frame and tales, two in particular – *fortuna* [fortune] and *ingegno* [wit] – engage in infinite interplay with the theme of love.[12] This interplay is often best captured in the plot device of the *beffa*, an untranslatable Tuscan term referring to a sometimes elaborate (and sometimes cruel) practical joke, prank, or hoax. There are about thirty novellas built around a *beffa* in Boccaccio's collection. A paradigmatic tale with a *beffa* is that of Andreuccio (II.5), who is naively stripped of 500 gold florins by a clever prostitute in Naples: after falling for a cock-and-bull story told to him by the woman, Andreuccio ends up falling naked (through a hole made in the

[11] Boccaccio (1993).   [12] Battaglia Ricci (2000) 161.

floorboards of her house) into a pool of raw sewage lying in the street. Most readers may sympathize with the foolish Andreuccio, but, in the eyes of the brigade, the victim of the *beffa* fully deserves his or her fate, because a character flaw such as jealousy, ingenuousness, or avarice leads the victim to act against his or her own best interests. The *beffa* displays the superior intelligence of the *beffatore* [prankster], who carries it out not only because of the victim's vulnerability, but because fortune presents an opportunity, although sometimes a very slender one, that the *beffatore* can fully exploit by using her or his wits. Florentine mercantile society, one of the cradles of early Western capitalism, highly prized the intelligence to exploit, in one's own best interests, the possibilities presented by a given situation: one had to know how to size up an opportunity and to think quickly on one's feet, or risk becoming in turn the victim of someone else's superior will and wit.[13] Although still in its embryonic phase in the *Decameron*, this secularized world-view would eventually lead to Machiavelli's landmark theory of *virtù* – impersonal fortune versus human intelligence – in *Il Principe* [The Prince].

Boccaccio's followers were numerous. Among the first were the Tuscans Giovanni Sercambi, who composed his *Novelle* [Tales] between 1370 and 1390, and Franco Sacchetti, who wrote – without a frame – the *Trecentonovelle* [Three Hundred Tales] between 1385 and 1392.[14] After the end of the fourteenth century, novellas imitating Boccaccio continued to be produced in Italy either singly (the so-called *novella spicciolata*) or in collections, among which are included Gentile Sermini's *Novelle* (composed *c.* 1424), Lorenzo de' Medici's novellas *Giacoppo* and *Ginevra* (composed prior to 1467–1470), and Giovanni Sabadino degli Arienti's *Le novelle porretane* [Tales [told] at "La Porretta," composed *c.* 1483]. Two works of this genre, however, stand out in the *Quattrocento*, which witnessed the full flowering of Italian humanism. The first of these is the reworking into the *novella spicciolata* form, by the Florentine man of letters Antonio di Tuccio Manetti, of a long-circulating tale about a famous urban *beffa* of the early fifteenth century. *Il grasso legnaiuolo* [The Fat Woodworker, composed in the second half of the century] tells the story of a gullible Florentine artisan who falls victim to an elaborate hoax planned and executed by the architect Filippo Brunelleschi and

---

[13] See Rochon (1975).
[14] For a limited selection of translated tales by Sermini, Lorenzo de' Medici, Bandello, Masuccio, and Grazzini, see R. L. and V. Martone (1994).

his friends, including the sculptor Donatello.[15] The conspirators convince the woodworker, through a series of ruses, that he has inexplicably exchanged identities with someone else in the course of a night's sleep. The guileless artisan becomes the laughing-stock of Florence, and is forced to move far away from the city to avoid further public humiliation. Some critics have seen in Manetti's tale a remarkable anticipation of the theme of loss of identity found in the twentieth-century dramatist Luigi Pirandello's writings. The other key work of the genre in the *Quattrocento* is Masuccio Salernitano's *Il novellino* (1476).[16] This collection of fifty novellas survived the burning of the original manuscript by Church authorities in 1475, and was published posthumously in Naples. The *Novellino* does not follow the model of the *Decameron*: instead of an overarching frame narrative, each tale has its own introduction in the form of a dedicatory epistle, and at the end is followed by a concluding comment by the narrator. This innovation was destined to be influential among subsequent writers working in the genre, for it allowed a more free-form narrative structure for collections of tales. Masuccio's ability to modulate between comic, grotesque, and tragic registers also proved important for the sixteenth-century novellas to follow, as they sought to incorporate an ever-wider range of material.

Any account of the novella in the *Cinquecento* would be incomplete without mentioning the numerous narratives that appeared within chivalric romances composed in verse, such as Cieco da Ferrara's *Mambriano* (1509; 1513) and Ludovico Ariosto's *Orlando furioso* [Orlando Gone Mad, 1516; 1521; and 1532). These intercalated tales, which had already been employed in the late fifteenth century by Matteo Boiardo in his unfinished epic poem *Orlando innamorato* [Orlando in Love, 1482–83; published 1495], are generally told by a narrator involved as a character in the events of the main epic narrative.[17] Some of the novellas are carefully integrated with the plot, themes, and motifs of the body of the poem, while others are virtually autonomous. One need only think, in the case of the *Orlando furioso*, of the tale of Ginevra (V.5–74) for the former, and the tale of Lidia (XXXIV.11–43) for the latter. These chivalric romances, with their extraordinary popularity among the reading public, helped to lead the genre of the novella ever further from the original model established by Boccaccio, opening its borders to a

---

[15] Manetti (1991).   [16] Salernitano (1990).   [17] See Boiardo (1995); and Ariosto (1998).

free-flowing exchange with other narrative forms and structures. With the dramatic growth of printing and the book market, tales began to circulate not only in epics, but in letters, treatises, and dialogues, as well as in collections of fables, mottos, proverbs, parables, and so on.

Overall, the novella faced a mixed reception in sixteenth-century Italy.[18] In the form of the *novella spicciolata*, renowned writers such as Niccolò Machiavelli in *Belfagor* [Belfagor the Arch-Devil, 1518] and Pietro Aretino in *Carte parlanti* [The Talking Playing-Cards, 1543] successfully tried their hand at the genre. The conditions that originally led to the growth of humanism had begun to mutate, however, as a new culture, eventually culminating in the Baroque, began to take shape on the peninsula. The humanist literary aesthetic of *imitatio*, or creative imitation of the works of ancient literature, was increasingly challenged by the explosion of print culture, which vertiginously multiplied the source materials and literary models available to writers, encouraging improvisation and experimentation, while straining the classicizing rules of decorum. Although the Venetian humanist Pietro Bembo, in his influential dialogue *Prose della volgar lingua* [On the Vernacular Language, 1525], proposed a standard Italian prose based on the classical lexical and stylistic example of the *Decameron*, the Boccaccian model simply did not have the same cultural weight as did the Petrarchan one in the *Cinquecento*.[19] The poet's followers – "Petrarchisti" – produced a seemingly infinite number of imitations of the Petrarchan "song album" all across Europe, whereas true sixteenth-century "books of tales" – not just anthologies – with a frame narrative were by comparison fairly few.[20] I limit myself here to a discussion of only the most important of these.[21]

---

[18] For a useful anthology of sixteenth-century Italian tales, see Ciccuto (1982).
[19] On Bembo's theorization of Italian, see Campanelli, "Languages," Chapter 6 in this volume, 156–58.
[20] See Guglielminetti (1984) 1–51.
[21] Among those not discussed here, but nonetheless important for the history of the genre in the Renaissance, see Girolamo Morlini, *Novellae et fabulae* [Novellas and Tales, 1520]; Girolamo Parabosco, *I diporti* [Pleasures, 1552]; Pietro Fortini, *Le giornate delle novelle dei novizi* [Daylight Pastimes of Novices] and *Le piacevoli et amorose notti dei novizi* [Pleasurable and Amorous Nights of Novices] (composed 1555–61 but unpublished until the early seventeenth century; the first complete editions of the two collections appeared only, respectively, in 1988 and 1995); Sebastiano Erizzo, *Le sei giornate* [Six Days, 1567]; Girolamo de' Bargagli, *Dialogo dei giuochi* [Dialogue of Games, 1572] (written 1563–64); Scipione Bargagli, *I trattenimenti* [Entertainments, 1587]; and Celio Malespini, *Ducento novelle* [Two Hundred Novellas, 1609].

The versatile Florentine writer Agnolo Firenzuola's *Ragionamenti d'amore* [Discussions of Love, composed between 1523 and 1525, but published only in 1548] was the first major book of tales to appear in the vernacular in the *Cinquecento*.[22] Although Firenzuola intended to produce a revision of the *Decameron* in six "days" of six novellas each, he completed only the first and part of the second of these in his elegant Tuscan prose that drew on Latin and Italian models, while freely incorporating contemporary usage. Author of works in many genres, including poetry, Firenzuola was the translator of Apuleius' ribald *The Golden Ass*, and published a transcription of an ancient collection of fables from India, the *Panciatantra*. His *Ragionamenti* deploy a wide range of familiar themes – trickery, revenge, wealth, etc. – within the various tales, which are limited solely to the treatment of love. The author includes a lively cast of characters reminiscent of Boccaccio's masterpiece, with an assortment of religious and lay pilgrims of desire, whose couplings and uncouplings are depicted in a language that tends to avoid both lyricism and obscenity. The narration of the tales is inserted in a skillfully composed frame of refined conversations between members of a brigade (three women and three men) in an idyllic country setting. For these fortunate few, governed by their chosen queen Gostanza, the telling of these novellas is preceded by a neo-Platonic discussion of love and the recitation of a poem by each member of the brigade, with a witty *facezia* [motto] to conclude each day. In the *Ragionamenti*, narrative prose fiction blends with other genres such as the dialogue and the lyric, breaking down generic barriers in a process of compenetration and contamination anticipating the direction others will follow.

Another Florentine man of letters, Anton Francesco Grazzini (known by the nickname "Il Lasca"), an outspoken advocate of vernacular realism in literature, was among the founders of one of the city's leading academies, the Accademia della Crusca. Like Firenzuola, he was not only adept at writing in many different genres, but composed a book of novellas in the style of Boccaccio. This singular work, entitled *Le cene* [The Banquets], was left unfinished and unpublished by its author; twenty-two novellas survive, but their date of composition is unknown.[23] In the fiction of the narrative frame, six young women

---

[22] A partial English translation is Firenzuola (1987); the most recent Italian edition is Firenzuola (1993).
[23] Grazzini (1989).

and four young men meet in Florence at the home of a rich young widow named Amaranta over three evenings of Carnival; every evening each one of them tells a story to the gathering of friends. There is no king or queen, however, and the novellas are told in random order. Ten of the tales are *piccole* [very brief], ten are *mezzane* [of medium length], and two are *grandi* [rather longer]. Grazzini's chief compositional concerns in the *Cene* are complicated plot lines and colorful local – often folkloric – language rather than careful characterization. His novellas make extensive use of the *beffa* at the level of both theme and plot, but often with overtones of savagery and sadism unknown in the *Decameron*. The expressionistic effects of these tales, with their graphic and macabre scenes of mutilation (I.2), terror (II.6), madness (I.3), and capital punishment (I.5), seem explicitly designed to subvert the decorum of "high" literature favored by the reigning Medici court. The book of novellas, in Grazzini's hands, becomes a weapon in the cultural war against the enforcement of the genre system and the overly restrictive regulation of the literary and linguistic heritage of Boccaccio.

Giovan Francesco Straparola, author of *Le piacevoli notti* [Pleasant Nights, vol. I, 1550; vol. II, 1553; complete edition 1556], adopted different tactics in this same war.[24] Born in the Po valley, he felt free to take liberties with the entrenched Tuscan model of the "book of tales." According to the fiction of Straparola's frame narrative, a company of ten young women meets on the island of Murano in the Venetian lagoon for thirteen consecutive evenings during Carnival, telling five novellas during every dinner (except for the final night, when thirteen novellas are recounted). The tales are loosely interwoven with dialogues, witty banter, riddles, and other conversational elements that turn *Le piacevoli notti* into a composite, rule-bending, and hybrid text, straddling genres and further weakening the narrative design inherited from the *Decameron*. Moreover, although the *beffa* remains from the Boccaccian model, Straparola introduces into his book an element not previously seen in the Renaissance Italian novella: the folk-tale or fable. Straying from the realism that had long been a part of this tradition, the author includes primordial versions of several literary fairy tales (such as Puss in Boots) in *Le piacevoli notti*, along with

---

[24] No recent English translation exists of the complete work; for the Italian text, see Straparola (2000).

folk-tale narrative devices such as trebling.[25] Because it is no longer bound to the depiction of everyday life (one does not normally talk with a tuna fish), Straparola's book radically expands the potential repertory of themes and plots for the novella, which explains in part its popularity in Europe: numerous translations of *Le piacevoli notti* appeared in the years following its publication.

The Piedmontese nobleman and Dominican friar Matteo Bandello's *Novelle* were first published in 1554 (a posthumous fourth part appeared in 1573), but were certainly written considerably earlier in the century.[26] This was the most important book of tales to appear in Italy since the *Decameron*, but its author's roots were in the social circuit of the northern Italian courts rather than in the mercantile urban society of Tuscany. Like a number of other sixteenth-century collections of novellas, Bandello's worldly and refined masterpiece freely blends narrative prose fiction with dialogues, epistles, treatises, and so on. Following the example of Masuccio in *Il novellino*, Bandello jettisons entirely the Boccaccian frame tale, in favor of an epistle that functions as a preface within each tale. Thus each novella has its own distinctive mini-frame transmitting the residue, or rather, the conclusion of a conversation that subsequently turns into the narration of a tale.[27] No doubt Bandello was deeply influenced, as so many of his contemporaries were, by the conversational model of his close friend Baldassare Castiglione's *Libro del cortegiano* [Book of the Courtier]. Paradoxically, the 214 *Novelle*, when considered as a whole, appear as a collection of letters with tales scattered through them, almost like an extended courtly or civil conversation between prominent, high-ranking members of sixteenth-century Italian society.[28]

The narrators of Bandello's novellas do not inhabit an ideal space in which the rules of daily life are suspended, unlike their Boccaccian counterparts, but rather are immersed in contemporary sixteenth-century society, with all of its inherent contradictions and tensions. Gone too is the careful arrangement of themes typical of the *Decameron*: the *Novelle* are consequently free to engage a far wider and more heterogeneous repertory of storylines and sources, drawing on materials as diverse as classical literary *topoi* and Oriental tales, historical accounts

[25] Propp (1968) 74–75.
[26] Bandello (1990). On the Renaissance novella, see Alfano (2011b).
[27] Bruscagli (1996) 872–73.   [28] *Ibid.* 876.

and chronicles of current events, or proverbs and treatises. Thanks to this new structural and thematic freedom, Bandello's tales seem to move rapidly and effortlessly between disparate registers, from the obscene to the comic to the horrific, allowing plot events to occur in sudden and almost random fashion.[29] Indeed, in the heading for II.9, which retells the story of Romeo and Juliet (adapted from a sixteenth-century *novella spicciolata* by Luigi da Porto), we are told that the star-crossed lovers "morirono con vari accidenti" [died from various chance occurrences].[30] Elsewhere Bandello observes: "my novellas are not governed by continuity of plot, but [are] a mixture of different chance occurrences, which happen to different people in different times and places, and narrated without any order."[31] In short, its hybrid and non-conformist narrative as well as its stylistic qualities place the *Novelle* in the very forefront of sixteenth-century prose fiction in Italy.[32]

Giambattista Giraldi Cinzio, born in Ferrara in 1504, is best known today for experimental tragedies such as *Orbecche* (1541). However, he also authored a book of novellas, *Gli ecatommiti* [The Hundred Tales, 1565], first printed in the Piedmontese city of Mondovì. These 113 tales are set in a frame and divided into ten "days," separated by intermezzos in verse and prose. Most were likely written long prior to publication.[33] In the middle of the collection, before the beginning of the Sixth Day, the author tellingly inserts three unrelated *Dialoghi della vita civile* [Dialogues on Civil Life]. The proem of the *Ecatommiti*, which clearly refers to the *Decameron*, tells the story of a company of ten men and ten women who flee Rome after the traumatic sack of the city in 1527 and the plague that followed it. Traveling by sea to Marseilles, they narrate to one another ten tales each day to pass the time. Giraldi Cinzio, however, does not depict in the *Ecatommiti* an amoral urban society of light-hearted lovers and unscrupulous merchants. His intent, as he explains in the book, is instead to uphold secular and religious authority in Italy while condemning every kind of vice – an ethical

[29] Bragantini (1998) 169.
[30] Bandello's book was translated into French and English in the sixteenth century. Shakespeare, however, seems to have found the story of Romeo and Juliet through an English verse version of Bandello's novella authored by Arthur Brooke, *The Tragicall Historye of Romeus and Iuliet*, 1562; see Prunster (2000).
[31] Cited in Bragantini (1998) 169.   [32] Bragantini (2000) 39.
[33] Giraldi Cinzio seems to have begun work on the collection in 1528. The introduction itself contains ten "extra" novellas, and three more are attached to the conclusion of Days 3 and 5.

project previously unknown in the history of the Renaissance novella. Several of the days are devoted to questions of love, while others consider specific virtues or vices; one is given over to the theme of Fortune, and the last is allotted to tales of chivalry. Employing a style indebted to "high" literary genres, Giraldi Cinzio turns his back on Boccaccian realism, with its focus on everyday life and language. He instead prefers extreme situations of human experience: the tale recounting the downfall of Otello (III.7), for instance, was to become the source of Shakespeare's tragedy. In the final passage of this tale, however, the horrific tortures inflicted on the guilty by the Venetian state are explained by the narrator as "God's revenge for the innocent Desdemona."[34] Religious and secular authority is identified with the divine will itself, undermining the possibility of a tragic interpretation of Otello's actions. The monological Counter-Reformation moralism of the *Ecatommiti* weakens its potential for polyphonic representation as a "book of tales": perspectives are single rather than multiple, unlike the *Decameron*, thus leading to a dead-end in this particular conception of the genre.[35]

Although Boccaccio was celebrated by critics as one of the *tre corone* [three crowns] of Italian literature, together with Dante and Petrarch, the development of the "book of tales" was surprisingly limited in the fifteenth and sixteenth centuries.[36] That Boccaccio's masterpiece was placed by the Inquisition on the Index of Forbidden Books in 1559 (and again in 1564) did not help matters; censored versions, published in Florence in 1573 and 1582, were bowdlerized almost beyond recognition. Most writers in search of prestige and patrons were obliged to turn to "high" genres, such as epic and lyric: indeed, throughout the Renaissance, and beyond it, non-Tuscan writers were more likely to express themselves in verse rather than prose.[37] Despite the intense critical debates of the late Italian Renaissance, we know of only one slender theory of the novella from that era, the Florentine critic Francesco Bonciani's 1574 *Lezione sopra il comporre delle novelle*

---

[34] Curiously, Otello does not here commit suicide, is banished from Venice, and only later is slain by Desdemona's relatives; see Guglielminetti (1986) vol. 1, 349.

[35] Although there exists neither a critical edition of the *Ecatommiti* nor a translation of the entire collection, an English translation of the 'Othello novella' is provided in Bullough (1973).

[36] See Quondam (2000b) 553–55. On the *tre corone*, see Manetti (2003); and Baranski/McLaughlin (2007).

[37] Ordine (1996) 32.

[Instruction on the Writing of Tales].[38] Bonciani argues that the "book of tales" is an essentially hybrid comic genre "that through narration generates joy," but lacks both literary dignity because it is written in prose instead of verse, and moral dignity because of its indecorous comic nature: Boccaccio may have been visited by the muses when inventing his subject matter, but not when writing it down.[39] The *Lezione* relegates the novella to literary limbo, in short, pushing it to the outermost margins of the genre system in Italy, where – with a few exceptions – it would remain for centuries to come.[40]

In no period of Western culture was the writing of dialogues more important than in the Renaissance.[41] "In all the arts and in every kind of knowledge questions can be asked and consequently dialogues can be written," observed Torquato Tasso in his *Discorso dell'arte del dialogo* [Discourse on the Art of the Dialogue, 1585].[42] Between the fifteenth and sixteenth centuries in Italy, as humanism spread, questions were asked about nearly everything, and, not surprisingly, the dialogue offered writers a way to represent both questions and the answers to them. Many of the greatest writers of the age turned to the dialogue: in the fifteenth century, such prominent intellectuals as Leonardo Bruni, Poggio Bracciolini, Lorenzo Valla, Leon Battista Alberti, Cristoforo Landino, Giovanni Pontano, and Marsilio Ficino composed works in this genre, mainly in neo-Latin; in the sixteenth century, Pietro Bembo, Baldassare Castiglione, Pietro Aretino, Sperone Speroni, Torquato Tasso, Leone Ebreo, and Giordano Bruno were among the many who tried their hand at this kind of writing in the vernacular, often with striking results.[43] Hundreds followed their lead. I will limit my inquiry here to only a few of the most innovative dialogues, but readers should keep in mind that thousands of dialogues were produced in the Renaissance on every subject under the sun, from cosmetics to cosmology.

The literary dialogue, composed in prose, is a simulacrum or representation of a conversation. The exchange between speakers embodied in the text may or may not have occurred in real life, but the dialogue is, in any case, not to be confused with that (hypothetical) event: rather, the dialogical text "portrays and comments on the act of communication."[44]

---

[38] Included in Weinberg (1972) vol. 3, 137–65.   [39] See Snyder (1989a) and (1993).
[40] For a general study of the novella in Italy, see Allaire (2003).
[41] See Celenza/Pupillo (2010).   [42] Tasso (1982) 27.   [43] Godard (2001) 8–9.
[44] Cox (1992) 7.

If the dialogue conveys information, like a treatise or a letter, it is also – unlike these – a *fiction* of a scene of speaking involving social interaction through communication.[45] The fictional features of the dialogue may be treated seriously or indifferently by Renaissance writers, who may or may not provide readers with detailed descriptions of the setting or characterizations of the speakers.[46] At least four principal modes of dialogical writing were inherited from antiquity by the Renaissance: expository dialogue; maieutic dialogue; dialogue *in utramque partem* [on both sides (of an issue)]; and satirical dialogue. The first of these represents a didactic process of discovery through dialogical exchange, dominated by a main speaker – usually the author's persona (as Socrates is for Plato) – who formulates doctrinal answers. The second mode is eristic, employing the Socratic method – *ignorantia docta* [learned ignorance] – to bring the writer's doctrines into view through one interlocutor's questioning of others, who must answer yes or no. The third mode involves the testing of ideas in dialogue, in which questions may be asked by all participants in what amounts to dialectical combat with no certain outcome (Plato and, especially, Cicero sometimes wrote in this mode). The fourth, comical-satirical mode of dialogue – whose most important ancient practitioner was Lucian – subverts philosophical decorum, incorporating parody, allegory, and corrosive irony in a carnival of competing voices and styles.[47] Renaissance writers were to employ all of these modes, most memorably those of testing and satire, in their attempts to imitate the ancient models and to break with the heritage of medieval scholasticism.

Renaissance humanists often formed close-knit circles, and this practice is reflected in their dialogical texts: the author of a given dialogue may reappear as a character in a dialogue by another humanist. Among the first dialogues of the *Quattrocento* was Leonardo Bruni's *Dialogi ad Petrum Paulum Histrum* [Dialogues for Pier Paolo Vergerio], likely composed between 1401 and 1408.[48] A leading early Florentine humanist, Bruni translated several Platonic dialogues in the first years of the century, and knew Cicero's dialogues well. Bruni's neo-Latin *Dialogi*, set in Florence, reconstruct a literary debate that took place over two days at Eastertime 1401 between the author, the famed humanist

---

[45] Snyder (1989b) 6.
[46] On the dialogue's relationship to other kinds of prose fiction, see Forni (1992) 215–72.
[47] See Snyder (1989b) 68–70, 84–86.   [48] Bruni (1994); see also Marsh (1980).

Coluccio Salutati (who had preceded him as *Cancelliere*, or Chancellor, of the city of Florence), and some young friends of theirs. In the first day's dialogue, the vernacular works of the so-called *tre corone* (Bruni had translated *Decameron* IV.1 into Latin) are subjected to a scathing critique; the second day, the same three authors are instead liberally praised in a moving palinode. Through dialogue Bruni rejects the culture of medieval scholasticism, which did not allow for such contradictions, embracing instead the principle of argumentation *in utramque partem* – from multiple points of view – that would help to define humanist ideology. With great self-consciousness, he makes the *Dialogi* into a veritable dialogue on dialogue, representing the process of intersubjective exchange as it unfolds: the first and second days serve as counterfoils for one another, leaving the reader to draw his or her own conclusions.

Author of numerous dialogues, Lorenzo Valla was one of the most prominent humanists of the fifteenth century, insistently seeking to discredit medieval scholasticism in both ideological and linguistic terms. His dialogue *De vero falsoque bono* [Of the True and False Good, first published 1431], divided into three books, examines the definition of the true good through a provocative comparison of the Epicurean and Stoic philosophies.[49] Different versions drafted by Valla of his dialogue are set in different venues, with different participants in the discussion (including Leonardo Bruni and Niccolò Niccoli, who also play major roles in Bruni's *Dialogi*). The interlocutors in *De vero* attempt a synthesis of pagan and Christian thought by exploring their mutual dependence on the principle of *voluptas*, the natural human drive for pleasure and happiness. If perpetual happiness is the greatest good, as one speaker contends, then morality is important insofar as it will lead us to this end; otherwise, repression of what is instinctual in human nature can only be harmful to us. Because of the undecidable way in which the dialogue is structured (*in utramque partem*), critics have been unable to ascertain Valla's true position on this topic, although in life he had few qualms about making his opinions known, no matter how controversial or scandalous they may have been. The extraordinary flexibility and openness of this mode of dialogue gives the author room to explore and develop ideas without committing him, or restricting the reader, to a single conclusion.

[49] Valla (1977).

Leon Battista Alberti is today considered one of the supreme polymaths of the Italian Renaissance: architect, humanist, playwright, mathematician, sculptor, cryptographer, and musician, he produced path-breaking work in a number of fields, from the great Tempio Malatestiano in Rimini to a treatise on painting and perspective, *De pictura* (1435). Alberti's *I libri della famiglia* [Books of the Family], composed in four books between 1433 and 1437, is at the vanguard of humanist vernacular dialogue.[50] Set in Padua in 1421, the dialogue involves numerous members of the Alberti family, who have gathered at the bedside of Leon Battista's mortally ill father. Three of these carry most of the conversation: Lionardo is an advocate of humanist learning, Giannozzo is an experienced and practical-minded family leader, and Adovardo occupies the ground between. The Albertis discuss education in the first book, youth and marriage in the second, management of family economic interests in the third, and social interaction with others – from friends to princes – in the fourth. The interlocutors offer, among other things, a vibrant defense of the vernacular as the legitimate heir of the Latin tradition. In much the same way, the text of Alberti's dialogue itself not only imitates the genre inherited from the ancient philosophers and rhetoricians, but transforms it through inclusion of a repertory of pithy sayings, proverbs, aphorisms, textual fragments, etc., assembled by the author after sifting through both ancient and modern literature, so that past and present come together seamlessly. Alberti's *Intercenales* [Dinner Pieces], composed over the course of his lifetime and divided into eleven books, one of which is dedicated to Leonardo Bruni, contains a number of satirical dialogues, fables, and allegories in the irreverent Lucianic mode that lead the genre away from its roots in "pure" inquiry and into the realm of narrative.[51]

The five *Dialogi* (*Charon, Antonius, Actius, Aegidius,* and *Asinus*) by the Neapolitan humanist Giovanni Pontano first appeared between 1491 and 1507, although some were composed earlier in the fifteenth century.[52] The majority of these neo-Latin works are written in the Lucianic mode of satirical dialogue: their author also inserts a considerable amount of verse into the texture of the conversations,

---

[50] Alberti (1969).   [51] Alberti (1987).

[52] *Charon* and *Antonius* are available in English translation together with the original Latin text in Pontano (2012; the others are forthcoming in the same I Tatti Renaissance Library series of neo-Latin literature); for an Italian translation of all five dialogues, see Pontano (1943).

which are – with the exception of *Charon* – set in contemporary Naples. The interlocutors in the dialogues are mostly members of Antonio Beccadelli's "Porticus Antoniana" academy (later to be known as the "Pontaniana," after Pontano himself), although other speakers come and go in the seemingly casual give-and-take of the discussions. As an example of Pontano's dialogical practice in the *Dialogi*, let us consider briefly how the dialogue *Antonius* (Anthony) unfolds in the streets of Naples. Conversation begins with an elegy for the late Sicilian poet Antonio Beccadelli, former leader of the Neapolitan humanists, but quickly shifts gear. Two passers-by are drawn into the discussion: one narrates a ridiculous tale concerning a flatulent bishop, and the other is himself a grotesquely besotted old lecher. Other academicians enter the conversation, and the topics under discussion veer toward grammar and poetry. They are soon joined by a Sicilian, Suppazio, who recounts that he has traveled the length and breadth of Italy in search of a wise man but has failed to find one. Pontano's young son arrives on the scene, looking for his father, and comically describes a fit of jealousy just witnessed at home. A lute-player then comes along and sings four quite different poems; he is followed by a company of street-acrobats, who introduce an epic poem by Pontano (more than 600 hexameters in length), which is then recited – despite interruptions by the street-artists – for the group. Pontano's dissonant satirical works break sharply, in short, with the classicizing practices of earlier humanists writing in Latin, opening the dialogue to interpenetration with other genres, from the novella to Plautine comedy.[53]

A far more harmoniously classicizing project for the dialogue is Bembo's *Gli asolani* [The People of Asolo, 1505], presumably written between 1496 and 1502 (revised edition 1530).[54] The occasion for this vernacular dialogue is the marriage celebration of one of the hand-maidens of the Queen of Cyprus, Caterina Cornaro, resident in Asolo with her court as a guest of the Venetian republic. Three young men and three young women participating in this celebration debate the nature of love over the course of three days. Each of these days centers on a different theme: the first treats amorous misfortune; the second happiness in love; and in the third the young people turn their attention to spiritual love. Bembo's neo-Platonic vision is reinforced by his

---

[53] Kushner (2004) 67.   [54] Bembo (1954) and (1991).

imitation of the dialogical form that Plato had favored.[55] His approach to dialogue is at once conservative and innovative: in linguistic terms, Bembo favors fourteenth-century Tuscan usage (especially Boccaccio's), yet – from the perspective of genre – he freely incorporates verse into his text. *Gli asolani* was enormously popular in the sixteenth century, with at least twenty-six editions printed before 1586. Bembo also was central to the *Cinquecento* debate over literary language, and his hugely influential dialogue in three books, *Prose della volgar lingua* [On the Vernacular Language] was first published in 1525, but composed over the preceding quarter-century.

Despite his claim in the preface that "I was moved ... to write these books of the Courtier ... in but a few days," Castiglione probably began work on *Il libro del cortegiano* in 1507 or 1508, and continued to revise it, layer upon layer, until its publication in 1528, just a year prior to his death in Spain.[56] No dialogue of the sixteenth century was more influential or more widely read than Castiglione's masterpiece, a portrait of the court of Urbino in 1506, before the Italian wars forever altered the cultural energies that fueled the Renaissance. Divided into four books, the dialogue takes place over four evenings in the great palace of Duke Federico da Montefeltro, where a group of courtiers – Castiglione himself is absent on a diplomatic mission to England, but Bembo is present – and high-ranking guests attempt to "form with words a perfect courtier" (XII.1).[57] The genre of dialogue gives crucial support to the author's aims, not only because his neo-Platonism is reflected in this imitation of Platonic dialogue, but because the text always incorporates multiple perspectives on the themes under discussion, which range from the proper use of *sprezzatura* [a sort of knowing nonchalance] to the special relationship between courtier and prince. The *Cortegiano* leaves the interlocutors' arguments largely unresolved or suspended, thus opening the way to a plurality of possible interpretations by readers. In short, dialogical writing problematizes Castiglione's analysis of the perfect courtier while enriching the reader's experience of the courtly debate: it always appears that more could be said, and that it would be possible for the conversation to develop in other, unforeseen directions. At the end of Book Four, for instance, one speaker questions whether women are as capable of divine love as are

---

[55] Paternoster (1998).   [56] See Guidi (2001); and Castiglione (2002) 3.   [57] *Ibid.* 19.

men, but no answer is given because dawn unexpectedly brings the courtiers' all-night conversation to a close.

Il libro del cortegiano was to be read by courtiers, and those aspiring to their ranks, throughout Europe for more than a century: it was truly a pan-European book, translated into numerous languages in the period and appearing in myriad editions.[58] Castiglione's dialogue was followed by Giovanni della Casa's *Galateo* [A Treatise on Manners] and Stefano Guazzo's *Della civil conversazione* [On Civil Conversation, 1574], which became the other two most widely read dialogues on "courtesy" to appear in Renaissance Europe.[59] In Guazzo's dialogue, for example, divided into four books and set in the Piedmontese city of Casale Monferrato, speakers explore together the rules of "honest, praise-worthy and virtuous" conversation in every social situation, whether in public or at home. In its final book one of the participants in the dialogue recounts at length a banquet for ten that incarnates the ideals of social cohesion and *bon ton* underpinning civil conversation. The text is saturated with fragments of moral and ethical wisdom drawn from Guazzo's enormous repertory of classical and humanist learning, which take the form of aphorisms, fables, anecdotes, proverbs, commonplaces, and the like.[60] Although still far from Pontano's hybrid satirical dialogues, *Della civil conversazione* is nonetheless rich in micro-narratives that make the text oscillate between the representation of conversation and narration itself.

Pietro Aretino's *dialoghi puttaneschi*, or whores' dialogues, are known by a number of different names and are composed of two works in one volume, each divided into three days; the *Ragionamento* [Discussion] was likely written in 1529–30, and the *Dialogo* in 1534–36.[61] The protagonist of the *Ragionamento* is Nanna, an aging courtesan, who reflects with her friend Antonia on the three possible life-paths for women in Renaissance Italy – nun, wife, and whore – by dedicating one day's conversation to each of these. Nanna gives a ribald account of the sexual licence of the brides of Christ, the infinite infidelities of married women, and the profitable art of prostitution in sixteenth-century Rome. She concludes that the only logical choice for her own daughter Pippa is to

[58] See Amedeo Quondam's "Introduzione" to his magisterial edition of Guazzo (1993).
[59] On the many non-dialogical qualities of the *Galateo*, see Pugliese (1995) 114–28.
[60] See the critical apparatus to Guazzo (1993).   [61] Aretino (2005).

become a courtesan as well. Thus, in the first two days of the *Dialogo* that follows, Nanna and Pippa discourse together on the proper way to behave for those who practice the world's oldest profession. Covering everything from make-up to home furnishings to social relations, the conversation between the two establishes a *vade mecum* for the aspiring prostitute. Late in the second day, Nanna and Pippa are joined by the girl's godmother and wet-nurse, who (freely citing Aretino's own poetry) the following day return to explain to mother and daughter the fine art of the bawd. By transforming the dialogue into a scandalous portrayal of unbridled female sexuality, Aretino subverts the classicizing norms of elite Renaissance culture, forcing wide open the thematic boundaries of the genre.[62]

Sperone Speroni's *Dialoghi* (1542; revised 1596) display the vast range of topics that could be treated in Renaissance dialogue: language, rhetoric, love, the dignity of women, philosophy, history, literature, and even dialogical writing itself.[63] Speroni was a writer–critic, like so many of his contemporaries on the Italian literary scene from the 1530s onward, and his *Apologia dei dialoghi* [An Apology for Dialogues, 1574] articulates a theory of dialogue as a genre whose main virtue consists in its interweaving of different voices and points of view.[64] Among those joining the contemporary debate over dialogue was the poet–critic Torquato Tasso, most of whose twenty-six *Dialoghi* were completed while their author was still confined, by order of Duke Alfonso II, to an asylum in Ferrara. If, in these dialogues, Tasso treats a wide range of literary, philosophical, and moral topics, from nobility and beauty to household management, in his theory of the genre – the previously cited *Discorso dell'arte del dialogo* – he praises above all the Socratic–Platonic model, both for its tradition of open intellectual inquiry and its literary aesthetic of *enargeia* [vivid description], welding philosophical concepts and poetic figures into a single complex text suspended between conversation and narration, or cognition and fiction.[65]

Neither dialogue nor novella disappear with the end of the Renaissance, but are left to subsist near the margins of early modern Italian literature. The culturally repressive situation in Counter-Reformation Italy did not encourage work in these genres, although several late masterpieces did appear, such as Galileo Galilei's *Dialogo dei massimi*

---

[62] On the dialogue as a weapon in Aretino's literary arsenal, see Buranello (2004).
[63] Speroni (1989b).   [64] Pignatti (2001) 135–37.   [65] Paternoster (2001).

sistemi [Dialogue Concerning the Two Chief World-Systems, 1632], and Giambattista Basile's *Pentamerone* [Pentameron, 1634–36].[66] Perhaps their extraordinary capacity to mimic and to interpenetrate with other kinds of writing eventually led these two prose genres to an impasse: for in the Renaissance, dialogue and novella tend to merge not only with comedy or satire or treatise, but – as we have seen – with each other. They are, in other words, fundamentally intertextual kinds of writing. With historical hindsight it is not difficult for us to see the significance of the fusion of these two genres, which prepares the ground for a new protagonist in Italian literature. Some thirty years after Tasso's death, Francesco Pona's remarkable prose narrative fiction *La lucerna* [The Lantern, 1625], fully embracing the Baroque's freedom from the rules of artistic decorum, embodies not only this admixture of genres, but its greatest descendant: *La lucerna* is at once a satirical dialogue in the tradition of Lucian, a collection of novellas, and – among the very first to be penned by an Italian – a novel.[67]

---

[66] Although Basile's is a collection of fairy-tales rather than novellas, it still employs a frame narrative, division of the tales into "days," and so on; see the introduction in Basile (2007) 12.

[67] Marini (1997) 1012. The first Italian novel to appear in northern Italy – though written during its author's long sojourn in England – was Giovan Francesco Biondi's *Eromena* (1624).

10

Music

In 1581, the historian Francesco Bocchi published a pamphlet against music. He was convinced that the nobility spent too much time pursuing idle musical pleasures. There would have been nothing wrong with this, had it not been for the fact that the ruling elite's immoderate interest in music had caused and continued to cause serious problems. For Bocchi, what may have looked like an innocuous pastime contributed to the civic disengagement that had led to the political decline of Italy and to the subjugation of a large part of its territory to foreign powers. Bocchi was also convinced that the unjustifiably high esteem in which Italians held music was due to what the ancients (and some moderns in the footsteps of the ancients) believed about its extraordinary psychological, metaphysical, and medical properties. Indeed, his essay aimed at demonstrating that music, contrary to common opinion, could not affect the emotional equilibrium of the soul, make the mathematical structure of the universe audible, or move people to noble and heroic actions. His mission was to convince the Italians that music had no such powers.[1]

It is hard to believe that less music would have saved Italy. But Bocchi's analysis is not for this reason less interesting or instructive. That a close observer of Renaissance society should regard the enjoyment of music as a distinctive trait of the aristocratic lifestyle – to the point of becoming a symbol of what had gone wrong in the recent history of Italy – speaks volumes about the role that music had come to play in the centers of cultural and political power. Italian court society, especially

---

[1] Bocchi (1989); see also Gerbino (2007).

in the second half of the century, reveled in a refined musical image of itself, promoting a rich array of musical practices, both public and private.[2] The church fueled a similar artistic escalation, despite, as we shall see, the Council of Trent's call for a more restrained musical approach to liturgical texts. Even outside the direct areas of influence of court and church, the technical advances that allowed the dissemination of polyphonic music in print (starting with Ottaviano Petrucci in 1501) contributed to an unprecedented expansion of musical literacy.[3]

Bocchi was also right in insisting that, for all its merits, classical antiquity had attributed to music an extravagant number of psychological and cognitive functions. The central concepts of Greek musical theory found an elegant synthesis in Boethius' *De institutione musica* [On the Fundamentals of Music] – one of the chief texts through which they reached the medieval manuscript tradition and eventually the humanist laboratory.[4] The Renaissance philological spirit deepened the knowledge of classical sources and set the terms of a somewhat different philosophical agenda. But by the time this body of knowledge became available in the sixteenth century, the world-view of the ancients had already irreversibly conditioned Western musical thought. For a long time, the European elite upheld the ancient belief that music shared with the other mathematical disciplines (arithmetic, geometry, and astronomy) "the task of searching for truth."[5] Since music offered a sounding image of the same mathematical proportions upon which the universe had been built, knowledge of music revealed the order of the universe in an ascending path from sense perception to abstract comprehension. At the same time, music differed from the other mathematical disciplines because "[it] is associated not only with speculation but with morality as well. For nothing is more characteristic of human nature than to be soothed by pleasant modes or disturbed by their opposite."[6] These few sentences summarize the two main strands of ancient musical philosophy (or mythology, depending on one's point of view): the Platonic–Pythagorean investigation on the mathematical

---

[2] On the role of music in Renaissance court culture, see Lorenzetti (2003).

[3] For an account of the impact of print on Italian Renaissance music, see Fenlon (1995); the essays by Carter, Haar, and Feldman in Van Orden (2000); and Bernstein (2001). The activity of the two most important music publishing houses, Gardano and Scotto, is reconstructed in Lewis (1988–97); and Bernstein (1998).

[4] On Boethius and the first millennium of the Christian era, see Bower (2002). For the late fifteenth and sixteenth centuries, see Palisca (1985).

[5] Boethius (1989) 2.   [6] *Ibid.*

proportions infused in the cosmic order, and the credence given to the idea that music could influence human behavior and the general well-being of the soul.

This way of thinking about music is the only true point of historical convergence between classical antiquity and Renaissance Italy. It could not have been otherwise, since neither humanists nor composers could rely on actual examples of ancient music. Almost nothing could be gathered from the fragments of musical notation known in the sixteenth century. Ancient music was an inaudible idea. There has been some debate over the extent to which the classical tradition affected the development of Renaissance music. In any period, musical practices are shaped by a complex interplay of behavioral codes, socially stratified traditions, and patterns of transmission and preservation of specific musical idioms, and the Renaissance is no exception. But the influence of ancient culture becomes visible if we accept the principle that what we think music is affects what we do with it. In the last analysis, this was also Bocchi's view.

The mathematical legacy of Greek musical thought, based on the observation that musical intervals express and can be expressed as numerical ratios, continued to provide music theory with its technical foundation. This tradition reached its apex with Gioseffo Zarlino and with the publication of the first edition of his *Istitutioni harmoniche* [The Fundamentals of Harmony, 1558].[7] But Zarlino's magisterial theoretical architecture is also emblematic of the sixteenth century's proud awareness of the achievements of modern music. Indeed, for Zarlino the highest of these achievements coincided with what is still today considered a distinctive trait of Renaissance music: polyphony, or, to use a term closer to Zarlino's language, harmony, i.e. the simultaneous superimposition of two or more melodic lines. Thus Zarlino used the philosophical and mathematical arsenal refined by the ancients to demonstrate that the moderns possessed a superior knowledge of the laws of harmony, laws that, when properly comprehended on a rational level and correctly applied to musical composition, embodied the immutable laws of the cosmos.[8]

---

[7] Zarlino (1965); only Books Three and Four are available in English translation: see Zarlino (1968) for Book Three; and Zarlino (1983) for Book Four.
[8] On Zarlino's notion of harmony, see Berger (2006).

While for theorists like Zarlino modern counterpoint was the realization of the universal principles of harmony, the practice of musical composition and the social uses associated with it molded themselves to fit a somewhat different image of music. It was the other side of the ancient philosophical meditation, the side concerned with music's ability to interact with the emotional processes of the human soul, that presided over some of the most important and enduring innovations of Italian Renaissance music. At the heart of this conception of musical communication was the madrigal.

The basic, descriptive definition of madrigal – a polyphonic setting, commonly for four, five, or six voices, of a poem in Italian – is useful but insufficient. What does not transpire from it is the variety of social contexts for which different types of madrigal were composed, a variety that in its turn helps explain the extraordinary popularity of the genre. The madrigal served as vocal chamber music for private use, both in the courts of the main ruling families and in the residences of the affluent urban elite. In the second part of century, an increasing interest in vocal virtuosity led to the emergence of a vocal style less and less accessible to non-professional musicians. Concomitantly, courts increasingly vied for the services of renowned singers. Madrigals provided the soundtrack to the imposing ceremonies staged to celebrate dynastic and state events. They could also appear in plays, often as *intermedi* [interludes, often on a mythological theme] between acts, or at the meetings of the numerous academies created in the sixteenth century. A good deal of the poetic production of this period, certainly more than we may be inclined to estimate today, was meant to be enjoyed as song.

In a word, the madrigal was the most ambitious form of musical entertainment in sixteenth-century Italy. Its origins seem to have been Florentine. Although the name did not appear in print until 1530, the new genre had already made headway and gained momentum in the 1520s in the hands of the French composer Philippe Verdelot. He arrived in Florence in 1521, under Medici protection, but his traces are lost after the sack of Rome. Another Franco-Flemish composer, Jacques Arcadelt, took his place in the circles of Florentine musical patronage.[9]

---

[9] See Fenlon/Haar (1988); and Cummings (2004). For an analytical essay on the neo-Platonic underpinnings of the Florentine madrigal, see La Via (2002). The most comprehensive history of the madrigal is still Einstein (1949), to be read, however, in light of more recent scholarship.

The publication of Verdelot's first two books in 1533–34 and Arcadelt's first book in 1538 marked the entrance of the madrigal in the broader market of Venetian printers.

For a genre so closely bound to the contemporary development of Italian poetry, the central role played by foreign composers (however fully Italianized) may come as a surprise. Italians were not totally absent. Bernardo Pisano, Sebastiano Festa, Costanzo Festa, and Francesco Layolle made significant contributions to the nascent madrigal. However, Verdelot's and Arcadelt's position in the history of the genre overshadows, fairly or not, that of their Italian colleagues. Italy had long been importing polyphonists from northern Europe. It is possible that the early patrons of the madrigal continued to regard composers of Franco-Flemish formation as better equipped to meet the stylistic challenge posed by the demand for a new polyphonic repertory in Italian. This trend gradually diminished over the ensuing decades, although Adrian Willaert and Cipriano de Rore still dominated the mid-century madrigal. Even in the second half of the century, when a new generation of Italian madrigalists gained the upper hand, the figure of Giaches de Wert towered from the Gonzaga court in Mantua.

The madrigal, especially in its most ambitious forms, did require significant contrapuntal skills. On the other hand, the level of complexity could vary significantly from piece to piece. While the range of stylistic choices was often a function of the different social uses of the poetry set to music, one of the key features in the development of the polyphonic madrigal was an increasingly self-conscious problematization of the relationship between text and music. The early madrigal – Verdelot's best pieces, for example – tends to display an elegant but simple chordal texture, and, more in general, a stylistic naturalness that probably stemmed from pre-existing musical traditions (most notably the French *chanson*). The Venetian madrigal championed by Willaert a couple of decades later already showed the signs of a complex re-elaboration of the relationship between poetic language and musical style. His only madrigal collection, *Musica nova* [The New Music, 1559], offered a demonstration of what music could achieve when confronted with the depth of Petrarch's poetry (twenty-four of the twenty-five madrigals are settings of Petrarch's sonnets). The result was an unrelenting style of polyphonic declamation whose contrapuntal refinement and sensitivity to the nuances of Petrarch's language continue to puzzle modern scholars. In the same years and with the same sensitivity and technical mastery, Cipriano explored harmonic and textural solutions that were to influence secular music for decades to come.[10] But the search for a more and more effective musical oratory did not stop. Witnesses are Giaches de Wert's combination of declamatory style and multiple-subject counterpoint, Luzzasco Luzzaschi's creative manipulation of texture, Gesualdo da Venosa's bold chromaticism, Luca Marenzio's ineffable melodic elegance and harmonic ingenuity, and Claudio Monteverdi's sense of dramatic urgency.[11] To this day, the madrigal stands as a monument to the Renaissance effort to understand and enjoy the incommensurable affinities binding language and music.

The cultural stimulus for this intensification of musical rhetoric probably came from two sources: the vast socio-literary phenomenon known as Petrarchism, and the ideal of rhetorical persuasion cultivated by sixteenth-century humanists. Underlying both was the theme of music's power to affect psychological and emotional states. The history of the madrigal largely overlapped with that of Petrarchism, albeit not necessarily with Pietro Bembo's restrictive version.[12] They both shared obvious chronological and thematic features. The emergence of the madrigal coincided with the heated linguistic debate of the 1520s, and its poetic language conformed to the new standard of lyric poetry modeled on the experience of the Petrarchist lover. Although poems from Petrarch's *Canzoniere* [Song Album] appeared in the collections of virtually every major composer, the primary function of the madrigal was to give musical voice to the love poetry through which men and women of the educated elite forged their sense of identity as members of a society of kindred spirits. Indeed, the bulk of the poetry set to music belonged to contemporary poets, great and small, at times identifiable but often anonymous. From this point of view, the madrigal made a unique contribution to the Renaissance discourse on love by translating the verbal logic of poetry into musical performances shared as social events.

---

[10] Fundamental for the cultural context of Willaert's and Cipriano's music is Feldman (1995).

[11] On the stylistic trends of the late-sixteenth-century madrigal see Newcomb (1980); Haar (1986) 125–47; and Tomlinson (1987).

[12] See Gerbino (2005). The musical implications of Bembo's poetic theory are discussed in Feldman (1995) 145–55. For an overview and case studies on the relationship between Petrarchism and sixteenth-century music, see the essays by Cecchi, Feldman, La Via, Luzzi, Mangani, Piperno, Sabaino, and Tibaldi in Chegai/Luzzi (2005). The musical expression of Petrarchan notions/perceptions of subjectivity is investigated in Calcagno (2012).

The importance of music as a privileged locus of socialization went beyond mere entertainment. At the beginning of *canzone* 23, Petrarch confessed that *"cantando il duol si disacerba"* [singing makes pain less bitter]. The widespread *topos* of song's therapeutic value against love's wounds (real or fictional) assigned *canto* – in its ambivalent meaning as poetry and song – a special role in the social management of passions, especially within the context of the behavioral codes of the court. As the members of that society learned to understand their own existential condition through habituation to the Petrarchist poetic discipline, music emphasized poetry's double role as a means of communication and spiritual self-medication. Thus, a madrigal existed at the same time as a musical "setting" (i.e. as a form of textual exegesis) and as a sensorial realization of music's power to soothe the love suffering described in the text itself. The preference for expressions of sorrow or even despair was integral to this vision of the role of music and poetry, since it is the pleasure of the lament – to be understood as the pleasure we draw from (simulated) utterances of pain transformed into aesthetic objects – that makes pain less bitter.

Although it is hard to overestimate the influence of Petrarchism, other poetic traditions found a musical outlet in the polyphony of the madrigal. Epic is probably the most important of these traditions. Episodes from Ludovico Ariosto's and Torquato Tasso's chivalric poems were often extrapolated and distributed as musical tableaux. At the end of the century, Battista Guarini's pastoral tragicomedy *Il pastor fido* [The Faithful Shepherd] supplied texts for hundreds of musical compositions.[13] For this reason, the madrigal can be viewed as the litmus paper of the shifting popularity of authors and poetic genres, not only from a purely quantitative standpoint, but also as an indicator of the different social functions that poetry performed in the culture of Renaissance Italy.

There was also a lighter side to Renaissance secular music, both within and outside the stylistic domain of the madrigal. Forms such as the *villanella, villanesca,* and *villotta* might have preserved traces of folk traditions, especially when couched in local dialects, although their ambiguous rusticity may be better understood as a foil for the standard of taste expressed by the urban elite. The terminology is unstable and

---

[13] Studies on the musical reception of individual authors include the trilogy edited by Balsano (1981); Balsano/Walker (1988); and Pompilio (1997).

often reflects regional linguistic cultures. What the three terms have in common is the root in the *villa*, the rural properties economically and politically bound to the urban centers. So, *villanella, villanesca,* and *villotta* evoked the voice of the *villani* [peasants], the humanity who lived *extra moenia* [beyond the city walls]. The most popular type was the *canzone villanesca alla napoletana* [peasant song in the Neapolitan style], for which we also know the time and place of its editorial birth: a collection of fifteen songs published in Naples in 1537 by Giovanni da Colonia.[14] The fact that this repertory often offered a comical reversal of images and situations current in lyric poetry betrays its literary origins, although the nature of the subtle relationship that the genre established with genuine oral traditions remains an open question.

The polyphonic paradigm of Renaissance music and Zarlino's attendant concept of harmony were challenged by a group of Florentine scholars and musicians, at first a small group indeed. In the 1570s, when their ideas were beginning to take shape, such a systematic criticism of polyphony went against the grain of contemporary musical taste. However, the debate sparked by their writings eventually contributed to the erosion of polyphony's cultural standing and to the rise of a new ideal of solo singing. The core of the problem was the perception of an unbridgeable distance between past and present, between the miraculous powers that the ancients had attributed to their music and the modest psychological profile of modern music. However pleasant and gratifying to the ear, polyphony no longer seemed to be able to produce any significant effect on the listener, whether ethical, spiritual, or emotional. What had happened? Why was modern music incapable of touching the human soul the way ancient music had?

These were the questions that Vincenzo Galilei was trying to answer in the early 1570s. And this was also the item of faith, as it were, that Bocchi sought to eradicate, since for him there was no evidence that music ever had such powers, despite what the ancients may have believed. In those years, Galilei was working on a counterpoint treatise. Uncertain about the correct interpretation of some aspects of Greek theory, he contacted the leading expert in the field, the Florentine humanist Girolamo Mei, at the time in Rome in the service of Cardinal Giovanni Ricci. The correspondence between Galilei and Mei is one of

[14] The standard study is Cardamone (1981); see also Cardamone/Corsi (2006). For the later part of the century, see Assenza (1997).

the most famous episodes in the history of Italian Renaissance music. Galilei eventually published his findings and theories (many of which stemmed from his collaboration with Mei) in his 1581 *Dialogo della musica antica et della moderna* [Dialogue on Ancient and Modern Music].[15]

Mei argued that there was a simple explanation for the expressive gap between ancient and modern music: the ancients did not use polyphony. Their music was fundamentally monophonic and geared toward an optimal coordination of musical pitches and speech patterns. It was this unique brand of solo singing that allowed the ancients to maximize the properties of both language and music, fusing them into a powerful instrument of logico-emotional communication. Polyphony did not and could not produce the same effects on the listener because the different melodic lines forming the contrapuntal fabric distorted the words, making them barely comprehensible. Moreover, whatever emotional content each vocal line may have had, it was neutralized by the simultaneous superimposition of the other voices. This does not mean that modern music was not pleasant to the ear. On the contrary, polyphony, according to Mei, was developed precisely with the goal of enticing the sense of hearing into the pleasure of harmony. The problem is that polyphony's is an empty pleasure. Devoid of any meaningful connection with language, the beauty of harmony triggers a pleasure response without content, a pleasure response that should not be confused with the deeper power of ancient song to move the soul to specific affections.

This is what separates human beings from irrational animals. For Mei the historical trajectory that led from logocentric song to contrapuntal refinement marked the victory of the senses over reason. "For nature gave the voice expressly to man not so that he might with its pure sound, like animals which lack reason, express pleasure and pain, but so that, together with meaningful speech, he might suitably express the thoughts of his mind."[16] To give up the uniquely human faculty of language for the pure pleasure of sound means to give up what makes us human: "Thus we could not claim – almost to our shame – to have been born rational; it delights us more to be without intellect and entirely subject to any pleasure whatever than to be truly human

---

[15] Galilei (2003). On the Galilei–Mei correspondence, see Mei (1960); and Palisca (1989).
[16] Letter to Vincenzo Galilei, May 8, 1572, in Mei (1960) 89–122; English translation in Palisca (1989) 72.

beings."[17] Mei's recasting of the opposition between ancient and modern music as reason and sense perception obscured the mathematical and transcendent "reason" of Zarlino's concept of harmony. In its place, he offered the linguistic *logos* of human agency. If we accept his view, music no longer referred to an intelligible reality independent of music (the order of a created universe). Its meaning rested solely on the semantic activity of human communication – although the two positions were not mutually exclusive. Galilei, who had studied with Zarlino, recognized his teacher's error, abandoned the idea that music only delights the sense of hearing with harmony, and embraced Mei's historical reorientation: the proper aim of music is "to lead someone else to the same affections as one's own."[18]

Mei's collaboration with Galilei coincided with one of the highest moments of the humanist investigation into ancient music. But at the same time it laid the foundation for a slow and inevitable deterioration of the polyphonic ideal. The most tangible effects on late Renaissance music were a new emphasis on the expressive properties of the human voice (which was to last well into the Baroque period), and a rekindled interest in the power of music to move the emotions (not in itself a new concept, as already mentioned) through the medium of solo singing. The tenets of this reconfigured value system animated the declarations and polemics that accompanied the birth of opera and the publication of the first collection of accompanied solo songs in 1602. Ottavio Rinuccini, the poet who supplied the poetic texts for Jacopo Peri's and Giulio Caccini's early operas, still breathed the air of this Florentine debate when in the dedication of his libretto for *Euridice* (1600) to Maria de' Medici stated that his and Peri's interest in musical theater was motivated by the desire to "make a simple test of what the song of our age could do."[19] Around 1578, Giovanni de' Bardi, patron of both Galilei and Caccini, addressed to the latter a long essay in which he outlined the principles for a reform of vocal music.[20] Caccini publicly acknowledged his debt to Bardi in the preface to *Le nuove musiche* [The New Music] – the first printed collection of solo songs for voice and basso continuo – with a polemical tract of his own: "At the time

---

[17] *Ibid.* 73.   [18] *Ibid.* 66.
[19] Original text and English translation in Carter (1994) 17.
[20] Bardi (1989). For the cultural context of Bardi's musical patronage, see Gargiulo *et al.* (2000).

that the most excellent *camerata* of the Most Illustrious Signor Giovanni Bardi, Count of Vernio, flourished in Florence, wherein not only a good number of the nobility met, but also the best musicians and clever men, poets, and philosophers of the city, I can truly say, since I attended as well, that I learned more from their learned discussions than I did in more than thirty years of studying counterpoint."[21] For Caccini, Bardi had the merit of recognizing that his brand of solo singing and recitative style was "that used by the ancient Greeks when introducing song into the presentations of their tragedies and other fables."[22] Secular polyphony did not disappear overnight, but the anti-polyphonic movement of the late sixteenth century had come to a full circle. The Renaissance yielded to a new era when the moderns convinced themselves that they had finally unearthed the spirit, if not the sound, of ancient music.

The church indirectly contributed to the flourishing of secular music thanks to the opulent patronage of its officials, especially cardinals born into the high ranks of the Italian nobility. Secular and sacred traditions interacted in forms and contexts which were variously supported or condemned by the ecclesiastical authorities. Religious adaptations of popular songs were absorbed into non-liturgical devotional practices, often in conjunction with the activity of lay confraternities. The *lauda* [simple monodic religious song] tradition in particular shows how the lure of secular music could be effectively reoriented toward spiritual education.[23] More restrictions were imposed on liturgical polyphony, but this did not prevent composers from incorporating secular material even in their majestic settings of the ordinary of the mass. Local ecclesiastical hierarchies sometimes provided a tacitly tolerant environment, until at least the Council of Trent; composers worked miracles of contrapuntal creativity.

If there was an area in which the moderns could celebrate the feats of counterpoint, this was the polyphonic mass and motet. Sacred polyphony represented the highest point of the professionalization of composition – a process that had already started in the Middle Ages. The contrapuntal bravura cultivated in the sacred repertory suggests not only a long-lasting link between liturgical music and the social and institutional prestige of the church, but also a deeper symbolic connection between the mystique of technical complexity and the sacredness

---

[21] Caccini (1998a) 100.   [22] Caccini (1998b) 98.
[23] For a brief history of the *lauda* see Wilson (2001).

of the texts set to music. For the believer in the debt that humankind owed its creator, this was music at its highest and best.

The enormous importance attributed to the polyphonic mass was the natural corollary of a vision of the human condition centered on Christ's sacrifice. Paolo Cortesi, the author of *De cardinalatu*, a conduct manual for cardinals, appropriately called these compositions "sacrificial" or *litatoria* [propitiatory] songs. And because of their unique function as intermediaries between the human and the divine, he placed them at the top of the stylistic hierarchy, bestowing on composers of polyphonic masses the same honor in the social hierarchy. "Wherefore not without cause," Cortesi writes, "does Cardinal Giovanni de' Medici, a man expert in the learned study of musical matters, maintain that no one is to be accounted amongst the leading musicians who is less skilled in the composing of the sacrificial genre. Thus it is for this one thing that they say Josquin the Frenchman stood out among many, because more learning was added by him to the sacrificial kinds of song than is wont to be added by the unskilled zeal of recent musicians."[24] The idea that striving for compositional learning was consistent with the nature of liturgical music and the acknowledgment of the role played by Franco-Flemish musicians are concepts central to both Cortesi's discourse and the history of Renaissance music as we know it today. Examples of contrapuntal virtuosity in the music of Josquin, his contemporaries, and his successors could be easily multiplied. But the most evident demonstration of this mindset – with long-lasting effects in the sixteenth century – is probably the cyclic mass: the polyphonic setting of the *Kyrie, Gloria, Credo, Sanctus*, and *Agnus Dei* (the fixed sung parts of the high mass) as a large-scale complex governed by unifying and structuring musical elements.[25]

Renaissance composers continued to practice the art of *cantus firmus* [fixed song] elaboration as a device through which to generate multiplicity from unity. The unity was guaranteed by a single melody drawn from plainsong or from a secular song – often a French *chanson* – and reiterated in slow-moving note values in each of the five sections of the

---

[24] See Pirrotta (1966) 150; and Kirkman (2001) 8, from which I also draw the English translation.
[25] The literature on the polyphonic mass is vast; for a brief and lucid account see Atlas (2006), and the bibliography cited therein. The historiography of the cyclic mass is discussed in Kirkman (2001) and (2010). On Josquin's masses, see the essays by Blackburn, Planchart, and Bloxam in Sherr (2000) 51–209.

mass ordinary, usually in the tenor. The result was an ingenious set of contrapuntal variations on the same *cantus firmus* as well as a demonstration that variety and unity were not mutually exclusive concepts. A similar technique was employed in what is today known as "paraphrase" mass. The name derives from the observation that the melody chosen as model, rather than being quoted in long and uniform note values, was pre-treated with ornaments and embellishments and freely paraphrased. In this new form the model spread and dissolved into the polyphonic fabric through the contrapuntal technique of imitation. The third type of mass – and the most widespread one – is the so-called "parody" mass. Here the model is not a single melodic line but an entire polyphonic composition, and the mass is conceived as a creative reworking of the model. It would be anachronistic to think that the self-imposed norm of contrapuntal metamorphosis was perceived as a limitation on artistic freedom. Nobody in this period seems to have doubted that it was precisely in the ability to transform pre-existing musical matter into seemingly infinite forms that a composer exercised the best of his ingenuity.

Cantus firmus, paraphrase, and parody do not exhaust the range of mass types in use in Renaissance Italy. They do however point to two important features, or, for some, contradictions. In seeking an appropriate musical idiom for the solemnity of the mass, composers had pushed musical style to a level of complexity that impinged on the integrity and intelligibility of the text. In the second half of the sixteenth century, a renewed emphasis on the centrality of the word turned the display of contrapuntal prowess into a disvalue as some church officials started to replace the equation between sacred rituality and compositional learnedness with the theological primacy of the liturgical text.[26] The second problem concerned the use of secular songs as models for the composition of polyphonic masses. Since the model appeared in the title, the currency of this practice had never been a secret. Thus, for example, Josquin's output includes masses based on Gregorian chant such as the Missa *"Ave maris stella"* (paraphrase of the Vespers hymn for the feasts of the Virgin with elements of *cantus firmus* technique), and the Missa *"Pange lingua"* (paraphrase of the Vespers hymn for Corpus Christi), as well as masses based on secular songs such

---

[26] Doubts, uncertainties, debates, and polemics against sacred polyphony are examined in Wegman (2005).

as the *Missa "L'Ami Baudichon"* (*cantus firmus* from a monophonic chanson), the *Missa "Malheur me bat"* (*cantus firmus* and parody on a three-voice *chanson* by Johannes Martini, or Malcort), and two famous masses on *L'Homme armé*, a popular tune that inspired over forty mass ordinary cycles, from Dufay to Palestrina. Eventually, the wind of reform blew, albeit mildly, on music as well.

Both issues – the intelligibility of the text and the infiltration of secular music – were raised at the Council of Trent in a preliminary document discussed on September 10, 1562. Two recommendations were made: "In those masses where measured music and organ are customary, nothing profane should be intermingled, but only hymns and divine praises ... The entire manner of singing in musical modes should be calculated, not to afford vain delight to the ear, but so that words may be comprehensible to all ..." The text was never approved for publication and the Council's official decrees offered only a generic injunction to avoid "compositions in which there is an intermingling of the lascivious or impure, whether by instrument or voice." As Craig Monson has demonstrated, the problem of textual comprehensibility outlived the Council thanks to the activity of committed reformers such as Gabriele Paleotti and Carlo Borromeo.[27] Borromeo – together with Vitellozzo Vitelli – was appointed at the head of a committee to verify, among other things, that the music sung by the papal choir conformed to the new standards of intelligibility. In his diocese in Milan, Borromeo was able to give a real impulse to the realization of the ideals of a musical reform – at least as he saw them. Some composers joined in the effort. Vincenzo Ruffo, *maestro di cappella* at the cathedral in Milan, responded to the directives of his bishop with the publication of a book of masses in 1570, which can be considered the prototype of the "reformed" genre.[28] A four-voice homophonic declamation freed the liturgical text from the sumptuous intricacies of Franco-Flemish polyphony. But aside from individual actions, the effects of the Council's tenuous pronunci-ation on music were mixed. "The diversity of post-Tridentine music was due partly to this vagueness and flexibility of interpretation and implementation, but also to the fact that much 'sacred' music developed and flourished outside the institution of the Church."[29] On the other hand, it was in this context that the legend of Palestrina as the savior

---

[27] Monson (2002) and (2006).   [28] Lockwood (1970); and Sherr (1984).
[29] Monson (2006) 402.

of sacred polyphony – later followed by the pedagogical codification of his compositional style as model of *stile antico* [old style] and paradigm of church music – took its first steps.[30]

Although abandoned in the preliminary phases of the Council, the language of the 1562 proposal is revealing, all the more so for the reference to the "vain delight to the ear." It is a language that recalls Mei's fear that music devoid of language can make humans similar to irrational creatures deceived by the gratification of sense perception. The thread linking the humanist and the prelate was the problem of reconciling the logos of language with the pure pleasure of sound. There is a slight difference, however, as a sermon by Savonarola revealed as early as 1494: "So that God may always be praised, the *laude* and divine offices of the church were created. But we today have converted these divine praises into something secular, with music and songs that delight the sense and the ear but not the spirit."[31] For some, the purely sensual pleasure of sound as music impoverished the intellect; for others, the spirit. Today, it is difficult not to acknowledge that the compositional splendor of Renaissance sacred polyphony was – and still is – a delight for both the intellect and the senses.

---

[30] See, for example, Garratt (2002).   [31] Macey (1998) 93.

11

Spectacle

The importance of festivity and spectacle to the political, social, and cultural history of early modern Italy has been richly illustrated in recent scholarship.[1] The Renaissance *festa* [festival] arose from a liturgical feast (often one during carnival, from Epiphany to Shrove Tuesday), or from aristocratic milestones such as dynastic weddings, and could include games, races, masques, dancing, plays, pageants, processions, banquets, and jousts. Planning, financing, and producing the *festa* galvanized urban classes and socialized youth; it might be done for "the honor and magnificence of the city" or, when *signori* ruled, affirm their glory and dominance.

Entire city populations witnessed the entries of prelates and sovereigns. French and Spanish conquerors criss-crossed the peninsula between 1494 and 1590, and by the time Pope Julius II entered Rome on Palm Sunday 1506 to celebrate his conquest of Bologna, and Medici pageants marked their repossession of Florence in 1512–13, re-enactments of Roman triumphs had long been fashionable in Italy.[2] The city piazzas witnessed carnival mummery, *cantastorie* [reciters of the deeds of Arthur, Charlemagne, and their knights], and flyting contests like those in Florence's Piazza San Martino – as well as hangings and burnings, at which members of pious confraternities comforted the condemned.

---

[1] The critical literature is extensive, and I provide only a sampling of it here: for Florence, see D. Kent (2000); on Rome, Stinger (1998); Muir (2007) for Venice; and Tuohy (1996) on Ferrara. For a wide-ranging general introduction, D'Ancona (1891) is fundamental; see also L. Zorzi (1977), Attolini (1988), and Clubb (1995). The most important recent collections of sixteenth-century play-texts are Davico Bonino (1977–78) for comedy, and Ariani (1977) for tragedy and pastoral.

[2] Especially after Alfonso of Aragon's entry into Naples in 1443; for triumphs, see Mitchell (1986).

Founder's day celebrations included the *palio* horse-race in Florence on St. John's day, and, as depicted in the Schifanoia palace frescoes for Duke Borso d'Este), the race of the defamed, including Jews and prostitutes, run in Ferrara on the feast of San Giorgio. The Florentine jousts won by Lorenzo and Giuliano de' Medici in 1469 and 1475 were commemorated in verse by Luigi Pulci and by Poliziano, and a 1496 painting of Gentile Bellini records a solemn procession of the Serene Republic of Venice on the feast of San Marco in honor of the True Cross.

Also public were most religious spectacles: the dedication of Florence's cathedral, Santa Maria del Fiore, was officiated on March 25, 1436 by Pope Eugene IV – then resident in the city – with music by Guillaume Dufay that expressed the proportions of the church itself, now complete with Brunelleschi's finished dome. Regular litanies and processions included those on the feast of the Purification of the Virgin, Palm Sunday, and Corpus Christi. When in Florence in 1515–16, Pope Leo X personally led processions. Funerals went beyond prescribed rites to become grandiose spectacles, especially after the Florentine exequies of Michelangelo in 1564.[3]

Confraternities of both youths and adults spent much of their year's income on *feste di quartiere* [neighborhood festivals], including plays performed in churches, or in ancient monuments like the Colosseum in Rome. The humanists Guarino Veronese and Giovanni Aurispa, tutors to Este princes, abetted the recovery of classical drama in the wake of the rediscovery of fourteen comedies by the ancient Roman playwright Plautus by Nicholas of Cusa in 1429 (Aurispa also recovered Donatus' commentary on Plautus' contemporary Terence in 1444): these led to performances in Latin by young aristocrats, a custom taken up also in Rome and Florence. Duke Ercole I of Ferrara fostered translations of ancient Roman comedies that drew crowds into the Este palace courtyard, and imitation of classical plays fueled later Italian drama, both the so-called erudite comedy and the later *commedia dell'arte*. Publio Mantovano's *Formicone*, a 1503 school production in Mantua, is the first known vernacular play to imitate Roman models. Though unknown to the public, enclosed nuns played music and performed plays for their own edification.[4]

---

[3] For the Florence cathedral, see Trachtenberg (2001); on Michelangelo's funeral, see Ruffini (2011).
[4] Humanist performance of Latin texts is discussed in Garbero-Zorzi/Serragnoli (2004); for performances by nuns, see Weaver (2002).

Court spectacles often crystallized around dynastic weddings and coronations, which required banquets, plays, allegorical pageants, and jousts; but Leonardo Bruni's orations at Florence, or Fedra Inghirami's opulent Ciceronian oratory for the curias of Popes Julius II and Leo X were surely court spectacles, as was the sumptuous polyphonic liturgy of the Sistine chapel. In Sicily, an elaborate series of events was staged in Palermo for the 1574 wedding of Anna d'Aragona, daughter of Don Carlo d'Aragona (Prince of Castelvetrano and later Governor of Spanish-controlled Milan) to one of the island's greatest landholders, Don Giovanni Ventimiglia, a full description of which was published in Palermo the same year.[5] Ceremonialists and artist–employees of the Medici Grand Dukes, from the Platonist Giovanni de' Bardi to the flamboyant Bernardo Buontalenti, devised the *intermedi* [shows between acts of plays] that dominated the later sixteenth-century stage. *Naumachie* [mock naval combats], and *sbarre* [mock battles for love inspired by chivalric romance], like that for the Venetian noblewoman Bianca Capello when she married Ferdinando de' Medici in 1546, were held in the courtyard of the Pitti Palace, while other pastoral and romance spectacles lit up the theater in the Boboli gardens behind.[6] Pastoral was the most courtly of genres: the 'satyric' stage type, described in Vitruvius' and Alberti's treatises, was canonized by Sebastiano Serlio in 1545.[7]

The theater was a place for seeing and being seen, *theatrum* or *visorio*, and itself a sight to be contemplated, *spectaculum*. The description of the Roman theater by the second-century Roman architect Vitruvius was interpreted in Alberti's *De re aedificatoria* [On the Art of Building, 1486], in Pellegrino Prisciani's *Spectacula* [On Spectacle, c. 1500], and in editions of Vitruvius' treatise produced by Sulpizio da Veroli (1486), Fra Giocondo (1511), Cesare Cesariano (1521), and Daniele Barbaro (1555, in collaboration with Andrea Palladio). Concomitant, though only loosely related theoretically, was the development of the stage under the influence of artifical perspective, with early perspective painted

---

[5] For the text of the proceedings, as well as an introductory essay on the "scenic" space of Palermo in the sixteenth century, see Martellucci (1992).

[6] For oratory in Rome, see Rowland (1998a). Courtly entertainments are studied in Nagler (1964); and Saslow (1996).

[7] See Serlio (1996–2001) vol. 1, 83–93. On the two most famous pastorals of the period, Tasso's *Aminta* and Battista Guarini's *Pastor Fido*, see Perella (1973); and Stampino (2005).

stage scenes (Pellegrino da Udine's set for the 1508 *Cassaria* [The Cash-box Tale] of Ludovico Ariosto, for example) giving way to backdrops and a raked stage with built scenery, both practicable and not (the 'piazza-plus-street', as in Baldassare Peruzzi's 1531 set for Plautus' *Bacchides* [The Sisters Bacchis]), to the set by Bastiano da San Gallo for Francesco Landi's *Commodo* [Serendipity] staged by Giorgio Vasari in 1539, fur-nished with a mechanically moving sun that measured out the single day of play-time supposedly required by Aristotelian theory.[8]

The nested spaces, social and architectural, of city, piazza, palace, court – all sites receptive to spectacle – focus in turn on the stage as their microcosm and mirror. In his treatise on architecture *De re aedificatoria*, 8.7, Alberti implicitly theorized the theater as the destination of the *via regia*, the "royal road," and thus as the focus of the city. Stage scenes, real or imagined, often included city walls and adjacent rivers in the perspective, as if delimiting civic space. Serlio's inclusion of the house of the *ruffiana* [bawd] in his drawing of the comic stage set preserved the association, going back to the early medieval etymologies of Isidore of Seville, between the theater and prostitution. At the other social extreme, the Medici theater in the Uffizi (1585) crystallized the ruler's position at the focal point of the theatrical space. The idea of the duke's eye as the focal point of visual information was troped by the *corridoio*, the elevated, enclosed walkway stretching from the Palazzo della Signoria to the Pitti Palace: not only could Duke Cosimo I attend spec-tacles unobserved in the Teatrino di Baldracca which connected to the walkway, he could practice surveillance on his subjects. An authentic panopticon, the *corridoio* embodied the ducal gaze in brick and mortar and defined the city as a theater for staging the spectacle of power.

How entangled with larger political events the *festa*, its settings, and its theatrical performances might be in the sixteenth century is sug-gested by the Medicean renewal of the ancient Roman *palilia*, the birth-day of the city, proclaimed after the election in March of 1513 of Giovanni de' Medici as Pope Leo X. Set in September rather than the traditional April, and co-produced by the Tuscan Fedra Inghirami, prefect of the Vatican library, and the Romans Camillo Porzio and Marc' Antonio Altieri, the festival marked the conferral of Roman citizenship on Giuliano, the brother, and Lorenzo, nephew of the pope. Lorenzo

---

[8] For editions of Vitruvius, see Rowland (1998b). The history of perspective stage sets is traced by L. Zorzi (1977); and Pallen in Vasari (1999).

(Giuliano was not present) was borne in triumph to the Capitoline Hill [Roman Capitol], where conferral of citizenship preceded a banquet, a high Mass, and allegorical pageants; on the following day further pageants were followed by Plautus' *Poenulus* [The Wee Carthaginian] in Latin, directed by Inghirami. Giuliano and Lorenzo were hailed as twin heroes like Castor and Pollux, even as the two great civilizing peoples, the Romans and Etruscans, were effectively unified under Medici auspices. The Roman play was performed on the *Campidoglio* hill in a classicizing, though in no sense accurate, "Vitruvian" theater that displayed images of Roman–Etruscan cooperation dating from remote antiquity. The *Campidoglio* itself was imbued with humanist luster after Petrarch's coronation there in 1341, and with political intrigue after the murder of Cola di Rienzo at the site less than a decade later. The hill was to have a distinguished future as the site of Michelangelo's piazza in honor of Emperor Charles V, created in 1544 with a pavement design that suggests the cosmological floor plan of Vitruvius' Roman theater.[9]

On a cultural and political level the renewed feast coopted native Roman traditions. The Medici capture of supremacy in Rome was reflected in Bibbiena's *Calandra* [also known as *Calandria*, or *Calandro* after the comedy's male protagonist], first played in Urbino in February 1513, and then in the Vatican in December 1514 for Isabella d'Este. In the play, separated twins (a boy and girl) make their way to Rome where, after many misprisions they find one another and marry into wealth. That for much of the play the twins bear the name of Lidio suggests their "Etruscan" origin, for the ancestors of the Tuscans had come from Lydia in Asia Minor; this makes the play, a reflection, but also probably a send-up, of Medici, or "Etruscan," acquisitiveness. Bibbiena's play exemplified what came to be known as *commedia erudita*, combining narrative ideas, often drawn from Boccaccio's *Decameron*, with the five-act structure and stock roles of Latin comedy; as such, *Calandra* was seminal for Machiavelli, the later Ariosto, Pietro Aretino, Giordano Bruno, and Giambattista della Porta, among others. Even when played in Urbino, *Calandra* was represented as set in Rome, the *urbs* [city] by antonomasia, and Baldassare Castiglione reported in a letter that its stage set included a temple and a triumphal arch:

---

[9] For the 1513 *Palilia* see Cruciani (1969); Ackerman (1986) and Stinger (1998). On Michelangelo's piazza, see Ackerman (1986).

thus Bibbiena's play fostered the adaptation of stage settings to the specific urban locations of play texts.[10]

In Florence, three kinds of spectacle flourished during the fifteenth century: the elaborate pageants for the feast day of the city's patron, San Giovanni; plays with brief texts drawn from the Bible and the liturgy, also known as "plays in churches" or *feste di quartiere*; and the *sacre rappresentazioni* [religious dramas], composed according to a well-defined pattern by writers close to the Medici, such as Feo Belcari, Piero di Mariano Muzi, and Antonio di Meglio. All three kinds were conceived and produced by the city's confraternities – associations dedicated to singing God's praise in *laudi* [vernacular sacred song], and to the performance of good and charitable works.[11]

Describing the 1454 San Giovanni festival, the vernacular humanist Matteo Palmieri attested to the recent separation – on the orders of Antonino Pierotti (archbishop of Florence, 1446–59) – of the huge procession in which all the city's religious orders participated, from the dramatic pageants which had been viewed the day before the religious procession and a day after the *mostra* [display] of consumer goods by the city's merchants. The *edifici* [pageants] and *rappresentazioni* [plays] were closely related to many of the *sacre rappresentazioni* for which there is manuscript evidence. The pageants epitomized the liturgical year's occasions for religious plays: the Annunciation, Epiphany, Passion–Ascension, Pentecost, and Corpus Christi feasts, enacting the salient steps in salvation history, from creation to the Last Judgment.

The most renowned and enduring of the "plays in churches" were performed in churches in the Oltrarno district: the Annunciation play, done in San Felice in Piazza, was produced by the confraternity of the Annunciate Mary; the Ascension play, in the Church of the Carmine, was produced by the Confraternity of St. Agnes; and the Pentecost play, in the Church of Santo Spirito, was performed by the Confraternity of the Holy Spirit (or of the *Pippione*, the "pigeon"). The 1439 Annunciation play, probably presented in the Servite church of Santa Maria Annunziata, was described by a Russian bishop attending the ecumenical Council of Florence. The production featured an angel in a mandorla-shaped frame lowered from a suspended dome-like "heaven."

---

[10] On *Calandra*, see Dovizi (1985); Padoan (1996); and Martinez (2010).

[11] For texts, see Newbigin (1983) and (1996); for accounts of the city festivals and their plays, see Trexler (1980); and Ventrone (2001).

Upon alighting, the angel spoke to Mary, and bursts of fire signifying the Holy Spirit (conveyed by pitch, or "greek fire") flashed down ropes from the divine throne and overshadowed her. God the Father held a Gospel, signifying Christ, and this inclusion in the play of the three persons of the Trinity reflected how, during the Council, the view of the Latin church that the Spirit proceeded from both Father and Son [*filioque*] had prevailed over the view held by the Eastern church that the Spirit proceeded from the Father alone.[12]

All three plays used pyrotechnics. Along with the others, the Pentecost play was produced during Lent in 1471 to impress Galeazzo Maria Sforza of Milan but resulted in the destruction by fire of the Santo Spirito church. The Ascension play of the Carmine, which ended with a shower of sparks when Christ was pulled by a mechanism up into heaven, was reconstructed by Vasari in 1565, with mediocre results, for the wedding of Francesco de' Medici and Queen Giovanna of Austria. Both the pyrotechnics and the use of machinery, including revolving domes, led Vasari to cite Filippo Brunelleschi as inventor of the mechanisms, though his involvement lacks any documentation. That the cupola of Florence cathedral was still under construction in 1430, and required winches and pulleys of Brunelleschian design, lent plausibility to the attribution.[13]

Sacra rappresentazione defines a corpus of scripted plays, performed by confraternities of youths thirteen to twenty-one years of age. Archbishop Antoninus promoted the genre to impart piety, civic virtue, and loyalty, just as Ciceronian oratory and Latin plays had been used in the ancient world for training in elocution and deportment. The plays follow a determinate pattern, including a call to attention and epilogue recited by an angel, few characters, a reiterated moral message, stage directions in prose, and use of *ottava rima* [eight-line hendecasyllable rhymed stanzas] long associated with the chivalric *cantastorie* and Boccaccio's narrative poems. Later plays add *inframessi* [scenes] with realistic dialogue. Latin drama may have inspired the announcing angel, who resembles the speaking prologue in Plautus – "Silence: listen!" – and the use of stock characters in the *inframessi*.

The known plays are doctrinally sophisticated and suppose a literate audience: Belcari's *Abraam e Isacco* [Abraham and Isaac] draws on biblical

---

[12] See Ventrone (1994); and Newbigin (1996).
[13] For other revivals, see Vasari (1999); for skepticism about Brunelleschi's involvement, see Newbigin (2007).

exegetes Origen and Nicholas of Lyra to produce a "mystical meaning." Belcari's much-admired play, dedicated to Giovanni di Cosimo de' Medici, has as its theme obedience to authority: the word *ubbidienza* [obedience] or its like is used a dozen times in 400 lines. But the plays also reflect Tuscan cultural leadership in the fifteenth century. Dale Kent observed that Brunelleschi's unsuccessful competition panel for the Florence baptistery doors, on the subject of the sacrifice of Isaac, follows Belcari's stage direction for the gesture by the angel that halts Abraham's sacrifice of his son: a striking instance of a homogeneous civic culture in which artistic innovation and a didactic program employing all the arts work closely together.[14] "Plays in churches" brought together talented architects, painters, and engineers: on the rolls of the confraternity of St. Agnes are found, among others, the names of Brunelleschi, Masolino, and Filippo Lippi.[15]

The *sacre rappresentazioni* flourished during the "soft hegemony" of Cosimo the Elder. With the de facto *signoria* [dominion] of Lorenzo (1469–92), cooptation of the political intentions of the genre, as well as of the "plays in churches," progressed apace: jousting sharpened the aristocratic tone of public spectacle, and in 1489 the traditional San Giovanni pageants had to compete with a re-enactment of the triumph of the ancient Roman Aemilius Paullus. The *sacre rappresentazioni* were also eclipsed by saints' plays featuring garish martyrdoms which were simply and inexpensively staged in front of churches.[16]

In their heyday, Florentine *festaiuoli* [festival-arrangers] were famed far and wide. Alfonso of Aragon sent his court singers to Florence in 1451 for a special out-of-season rendition of the Ascension play. Florentines were called to Rome by Cardinal Pietro Riario (Archbishop of Florence, 1473–74) to perform on behalf of Eleonora d'Aragona and her escorts during her nuptial progress toward Ferrara: on successive days the plays of Susanna, Corpus Christi, and five others were performed; seven more were realized as the wedding party passed through Florence. Poliziano's *Orfeo* [Orpheus] play for the Gonzaga (1480, or possibly 1473), adopts formal devices from *sacra rappresentazione* and led to a series of Orpheus plays in Mantua, including one for which Leonardo da

---

[14] Newbigin (1981) provides the fullest reading of *Abraam e Isacco*; see D. Kent (2000) on Brunelleschi's baptistery doors and Belcari's play.

[15] See Barr (1984).

[16] For aristocratic encroachments, see Trexler (1980); for the martyr plays, Newbigin (1997). *Sacre rappresentazioni* were, however, often reprinted.

Vinci designed a mountain that revolved to disclose the cave of Hell. Machiavelli echoed the St. Agnes Company Purification play at the conclusion of his brilliant *Mandragola* [The Mandrake Root].[17]

To consolidate his reputation as the leading classicizing playwright of the time, Ariosto in his last years rewrote for new performances his prose comedies *Cassaria* (1508) and *Suppositi* [Things Supposed, 1509] in the *sdrucciole* verses [blank-verse lines ending with the first of its final three syllables accented] he devised to imitate the iambic verse of ancient Roman comedy. That same year Ariosto premiered a new play, *Lena* [The Bawd], repeated the following year and again in 1532 (this performance in the new, ducal theater within the palace). The playing of *Lena*, which caps Ariosto's direct representation in his plays of Ferrarese places (inns, streets, monuments) and characters (drunks, jesters, officials), is a culminating moment for Ariosto's stagecraft and for Ferrarese theater.[18]

Study of the stage had a long history in Ferrara. Duke Ercole's love of theater moved court humanist Pellegrino Prisciani to write a vernacular adaptation of Alberti's eighth book on show buildings, entitled *Spectacula*, giving a rough account of Vitruvius' theater.[19] The vernacular paraphrase of Vitruvius by Cesariano (1521) was likely meditated during his residence in Ferrara during Ercole's tenure, while accounts of plays translated and staged in the city, from the 1486 *Menechini* to the 1502 performances in honor of Lucrezia Borgia, wife to Alfonso I d'Este, to Ariosto's 1508 *Cassaria*, with a reported perspective stage set, as we saw, have been variously, and inconclusively, interpreted by students of the Renaissance stage.[20]

That the typical Ferrarese stage set should be a view of Ferrara – just as Vasari's permanent stage set in what was the Uffizi theater would represent Florence – was well established in the city's stage buildings, real or imagined, Vitruvian or Peruzzian. Among the depictions of Ferrara in the Schifanoia palace frescoes done for Duke Borso in 1469–70 is an attempt at rendering a complex *scaenae frons* [Vitruvian stage set]: in the April cycle on the east wall of the *Salone dei Mesi*

---

[17] For the activities of *festaiuoli*, see Falletti (1988); for the Orpheus plays, Tissoni-Benvenuti (1986); and on Machiavelli, see Martinez (2010).

[18] For *Lena*, see Ariosto (1964); Larivalle (1982); Plaisance (1982); and Tuohy (1996).

[19] On Prisciani and Ferrarese theater in the late fifteenth century, see Santorio (2013).

[20] On Ferrarese theatricality, see Clubb (2005); and for Cesariano in Ferrara, see Ruffini (1982).

[Hall of the Months], the ducal family – men on horseback and women situated on balconies over the lower "playing space," a street scene where prostitutes, Jews, and wild asses manifest their social degradation – is the domineering spectator and chief object of spectacle. An anonymous drawing made between 1532 and 1550 shows a stage set with buildings in perspective foreshortening on the sides and a backdrop of the city's central piazza flanked by Duomo and Palace, with the Este Castello looming up in the background.[21]

Ercole's other great obsession, architectural planning, also had consequences for the Ferrarese stage set. In *Spectacula*, Prisciani had theorized public spaces as stages by adding the *xystus*, or playing field, to Alberti's list of show places. Such a theatrical use of the city square was familiar, since the area between the cathedral and the Este palace had long been a place for jousts (represented in Schifanoia frescoes now damaged). Ercole increased the square's stage-likeness by having *logge* [arcades] built on the palace side to balance those built along the cathedral nave. In 1499 Prisciani published in his *Historie ferrarienses* [History of the Peoples of Ferrara] a plan of Duke Ercole's *Addizione* [Addition], built after 1492 in response to the invasion of the northern reaches of the city during the Venetian war of 1482–84. With wide rectilinear avenues like the Via degli Angeli, the "Addizione erculea" was designed to facilitate defense, but may also have been intended to appear magnificent, an effect Alberti had attributed to broad streets. Such was the Duke's interest that he would often abandon his beloved chess games to inspect the dredging of the new moats, and some consider him the "architect" of the "Addizione." Thus in the generation preceding Ariosto's, development of the city stage set paralleled that of the city's architectural fabric. A print from 1499 ascribable to Prisciani's circle depicts Ferrara as a scenography: foregrounded is a profile view of the city beyond the Po and behind its walls; but around the checkerboard of the central piazza are recognizable, as stage buildings in perspective, the cathedral and the Este palace, behind which towers the Castello fortress; in the background, as a flat backdrop, is the "Addizione erculea." Dividing the old city from the new, the San Leo gate marks the vanishing point.[22] No wonder that the epic poet Torquato Tasso wrote in his dialogue *Il Gianluca ovvero delle*

[21] On the Ferrarese stage, see L. Zorzi (1977); and Ruffini (1983).
[22] See Bocchi (1982); Tuohy (1996); and Rosenberg (1997).

maschere [Gianluca, or, On Masks, 1586] that the city was "a marvelous and never-before-seen stage set."

The close identification of city and stage, plus the fact that the tax burden for financing the "Addizione" fell on Ferrara's citizens, is the context for Ariosto's *Lena*, a play about prostitution and economic injustice that offers striking opportunities for correlating the dramatic text to the stage set. As the play opens, Licinia – who never actually appears on stage – daughter to wealthy Fazio, is being taught sewing and weaving by Lena, Fazio's kept mistress. The plot revolves around the attempts of Corbolo, clever servant to Flavio, rich Ilario's son, to find the 25 florins needed to bribe Lena so that his master and Licinia can be united. The play begins at Lena's door, and her house, which Fazio had given her in exchange for access to her favors, becomes, as if anticipating Serlio's prescription for comic stages, a focus of the action: critically so when Fazio, calling Lena's bluff after a sharp exchange, puts the house on the market. When Lena jokes acidly in one of the scenes Ariosto added in the play's final redaction (V.11) – scenes crucial to sharpening the comedy's economic focus – about front and back entrances used for access to her body, the house's doors again come into play.[23]

As the former governor of the Garfagnana – a wild and mountainous Este territory situated between the Apuan Alps and the western Appenines – from 1522 to 1525, Ariosto understood public finance, and he touches again and again in the play on the devices and instruments that manage civic debt.[24] Corbolo's race to find the sum Flavio needs yields an inventory of locations and institutions where Ferrarese credits and debits are tallied: from Jewish pawnshops to corrupt game-wardens selling on the black market wildfowl they are sworn to preserve for the Duke's pleasure (II.3). The seriousness of Ariosto's theme of exploited labor emerges in the implied comparison of Lena's complaints to the braying of asses as they turn millstones (II.3). The same problem, and its gendered nature, is implicit in the chat between Ilario, Flavio's father, and Egano, a Ferrarese landholder, in which they regret that

[23] Windows and doors appear in contemporary representations of Ferrarese prostitution; see Ghirardo (2005). The eroticizing of doors and windows was part of the Italian *novella* tradition (see Boccaccio, *Decameron* VII.1–8).

[24] A reference in the play (III.3) to "*il libro dell'uscita*" [debit-book], may testify to use of double-entry bookkeeping, a practice attested in Italy from the late thirteenth century but only codified into a system by Luca Pacioli in 1494. On Ariosto's economic savvy, see Looney (2010).

unlike their dray animals their wives cannot be sold or rented for hire, or even traded or used as gifts (III.2). These very oxen, the men complain, are periodically requisitioned by the duke for dredging the ditches that surround the city: the contours of the "Addizione erculea" itself. The episode knits the exploitation of women to an instance of the Ferrarese propertied classes disadvantaged by ducal pretensions to a magnificence beyond its purse.

Rather than deploying multiple plots, *Lena* achieves its complications by staging interlocking quarrels over cash, chattels, and real estate. The quest for the essential 25 florins requires that Corbolo leave Flavio's clothing as security for a loan; and the threat of imminent repossession of Lena's house by Fazio brings out creditors who hasten to reclaim goods held within the house by Lena's compliant husband Pacifico. Among these is Bartolo's wine-barrel, Flavio's hiding place after he finally gains admission to Lena's house and in which he is transferred to the house of Fazio, thus granting him unexpected access to Licinia. But the most important property is the house itself – standing, of course, for Lena's prostituted body – which Fazio, in his spiteful decision to sell the house, has professionally measured in order to assess its value, typifying an economy in which prices are calculated "*fino ad un piccolo*" [to the last cent] (III.9).

The *pertica* [measuring-rod] used for the purpose emerges as the instrument not only of an oppressive economic rationality, but – since the surveyor Torbido jokes about its use as a whip – of an authority that imposes discipline through force. The *pertica* was indeed a standard distance measure in Ferrara, which had historically relied on its surveyors in channeling the branches of the Po that ran through its territory, and it was used in measuring out the "Addizione." Along with other Ferrarese places, Ercole's addition appears in the play when Lena sends her maidservant to the Mirasole district on a fool's errand in order to prevent discovery of Flavio (IV.9): the itinerary was well known to Ariosto, whose house was on Via Mirasole, one of the most rectilinear blocks in the neighborhood. Signed with this personal touch, Ariosto's last play dissects the imbalances of the Ferrarese money economy as it is framed by the rationalized perspective grid of the high Renaissance stage set.

Before Ariosto's theater was destroyed by fire in 1533, it probably hosted at least one performance by the actor and playwright known as Ruzante (*Vaccaria* [The Cowherd] in 1532). Born as the illegitimate

Angelo Beolco to a Paduan physician, Ruzante was educated and employed by his father, and established his reputation as the character who recurs in his plays now as a country rustic, now as a clever servant. By the playwright's own testimony, the name Ruzante means frolicking – even sexually – with humans or animals, a term twice attested in Boccaccio's *Decameron* (VIII.10.27, for instance). Beolco's early works were *mariazi* [dialogue wedding plays] and dramatic orations written and delivered in *pavan*, a theatrical version of Paduan dialect. The dialogues *Parlamento* [The Parliament] and *Bilora* [The Peasant Bilora] (1529) reflect the ravaged rural economy wrought by the War of the League of Cognac, which pitted France and Venice against the Holy Roman Empire. Ruzante later adopted the conventions of five-act regular comedy relying on classical models: *Anconitana* [The Woman from Ancona, 1534–35] is set in Padua with a plot that develops the same-sex erotic confusion of the Ricciardetto and Fiordispina episode of Ariosto's *Orlando furioso* [Orlando Gone Mad] (XXV.25–70). Here the characters of the romantic comedy plot speak Tuscan; the servant Ruzante and his cronies speak *pavan*, Venetians their own dialect; every character of note bears a literary name from Boccaccio, Ariosto, or Pietro Bembo's dialogues on love, the *Asolani* [The People of Asoli, 1505, 1530].

Beolco long enjoyed the patronage of the would-be Venetian patrician Alvise Cornaro whose loggia in Padua, built in 1524, sported five Doric bays forming a *scaenae frons* [stage-front] in a style echoing the façade of Palazzo Farnesina in Rome, and served as a site for performances of Beolco's works. Although Beolco refers to specific stage sets in the prologues to *Fiorina* [entitled for its female protagonist] (set in Chioggia, near Venice) and *Vaccària* (set in Padua), it was long asserted that he took scant interest in scenography. But Dersofi has argued that the fifteen songs in *Anconitana*, and its theme of recovered human harmony, should be correlated with the 1534 inauguration of Cornaro's musical perform-ance space, the Odeon, built next to the loggia. If so, the last play of Ruzante's career as dramatist – he continued acting until his death in 1539 – was marked by the institution of a space for musical spectacle.[25]

Ruzante's use of characterization through dialect and jargon became a major trend of regular comedy as the genre responded to Pietro Bembo's decree, in his dialogue *Prose della vulgar lingua* [On the Vernacular

---

[25] See Dersofi in Ruzante (1994). On Ruzante, see Padoan (1970); and Ferguson (2000). For texts of the plays, see Ruzante (1970).

Language, 1525], that the Tuscan idiom of Petrarch for verse and Boccaccio for prose should be the ruling Italian literary language. Born in Arezzo, the satirist and polygraph Pietro Aretino proudly wielded his own version of Tuscan, and his plays draw much of their energy from his simultaneous contestation of and adaptation to Bembo's prescriptions. *Cortegiana* [The Courtesan], first written in 1525, but known through the revised 1534 printed edition, is a satire on courtiership set in an early *Cinquecento* papal Rome where all is for sale: strategically aimed at Castiglione's *Cortegiano* [The Courtier], which circulated before its publication in 1528, the title implies that courtiers are little better than whores; Rome itself is *coda mundi*, "the world's tail."

Like Ruzante, Aretino turned to traditional models of comedy for his later *Ipocrito* [The Hypocrite], *Talanta* [The Courtesan Talanta] (both published in 1542), and *Filosofo* [The Philosopher] (1546). *Talanta*, Aretino's only play known to have been performed in his lifetime, is also set in Rome. The title character is a *cortigiana onesta*, a high-status courtesan. She generates the action of the comedy by obtaining, from competing suitors, a young moorish slave boy and a slave girl – actually twins whose disguises reverse their genders – who are beloved by the daughter and son of Talanta's same two suitors. In the end, Talanta is paid for the slaves, and reconciled with a third suitor. Though flat as a character, she personifies Rome as a *lupanar*, a den of thieves and prostitutes, a role that supports Cairns' allegorical reading of her as Erasmus' Folly, the courtesan–idol of suitors who represent the Vices: thus the playwright's strategy of utilizing licentious material for moralizing purposes would be justified. Aretino's plays update the old prejudice about the theater as a venue for pimping, but more productively, Aretino's "mixed" vernacular marked by dialect, mocks and resists the purist aesthetic of Bembo's *Prose*.[26]

The 1542 Venice performance of *Talanta* by the amateur *Compagnia della calza* [Company of the Sock and Buskin] of the Accademia dei Sempiterni, featured a stage set designed by Giorgio Vasari, the Grand Duke Cosimo de' Medici's minister of culture – as he is fulsomely advertised within the play itself (I.3). According to Cairns, the set depicted a perspectival scene containing the chief Roman monuments (they are

---

[26] On Aretino, see Cairns (1995); and Waddington (2004).

enumerated in a boasting letter by Vasari, and at *Talanta* I.3) – imagined as seen through the Arch of Titus, thus placing the stage and audience within an implied Forum. Anticipated by a quick tour of Roman sites given to the dupe Maco in Aretino's earlier *Cortegiana* (II.3), the staged particulars of *Talanta* – in the wake of Bibbiena's Rome and Ariosto's Ferrara – mark a high point in the explicit interrelation of comic action with a specific urban stage set.

Over half a century after Ariosto's theater in Ferrara burned to the ground, another theater sought to become a principal site of Italian spectacle. On the last Sunday of Carnival and on Shrove Tuesday (March 3) 1585, beginning in the early afternoon, an audience of some 1,000 people from all over northern Italy crowded into the semi-oval *cavea* [a semi-elliptical, tiered seating area, as in ancient Greek and Roman theaters] of the newly built Teatro Olimpico in Vicenza. Comforted with refreshments and soothed by artificial scents which disguised the odors ensuing from the absence of privies, the audience awaited the 7:30 curtain of Sophocles' *Edippo tiranno* [Oedipus the King], translated into Italian by the Venetian patrician Orsatto Giustiniani. Given the assembly of ideas and talent that it represented, and its cultural significance for Italy at the end of the Renaissance and on the threshold of the Baroque era, the evening was monumental in every sense.

Staging *Edippo* in a theater built specifically for the purpose, the Vicenzan Accademia Olimpica registered a number of triumphs. The architect Andrea Palladio's stab at a "correct" recreation of the ancient Vitruvian theater was realized. Sophocles' play had been cited by Aristotle in his *Poetics* as perfect in its tragic form, and thus for the academic culture of the later sixteenth century *Edippo* was the embodiment of a literary art bound by rules (which would subsequently constrain the imagination of Italy's greatest late-sixteenth-century man of letters, Torquato Tasso). The production engaged the chief theatrical talents of the day, including the Ferrarese Angelo Ingegneri and Battista Guarini, author of the pastoral masterpiece *Il pastor fido* [The Faithful Shepherd], composed during the period of the theater's construction (1580–85). Celebrated amateur actors participated: the Verati, father and daughter, played Tiresias and Jocasta, and Oedipus was played by the half-blind playwright Luigi Groto. Music for the choruses was furnished by Andrea Gabrieli, organist of St. Mark's cathedral in Venice; his homophonic music written for the sake of textual intelligibility helped advance understanding of ancient Greek music, anticipating the experiments of the Florentine *Camerata* – a group of accomplished amateur musicians, including Vincenzo Galilei (father of Galileo, the astronomer) – at the end of the century which led to the birth of modern opera. All this was achieved by an academy of Vicentine aristocrats consisiting of fewer than a hundred members, thanks in large part to the leadership provided by the princely leader of the Academy, Leonardo Valmarana, who counted among his assets cordial relations with the imperial Hapsburgs. The triumph was architectural, dramatic, literary, critical–theoretical, dramaturgical, cultural, and even political, for the event was correctly perceived as reflecting the Academy's nostalgia for the greatness of the Holy Roman Empire under Charles V (the Venetian *podestà* [magistrate] who governed Vicenza, cognizant of the event's ideological resonances, boycotted the performance).[27]

That the play was performed at all was remarkable. It would not have been possible had not Valmarana himself guaranteed financing when the academicians failed to meet their subscription obligations. The decision to offer a play was made in 1579, but it was not until May 1584, when construction of the theater was well advanced, that *Edippo* was finally selected. The original idea of staging a voguish pastoral had encouraged academician Fabio Pace, a physician, to write *Eugenio*, a pastoral drama. But Ingegneri and Guarini vetoed Pace's effort and suggested the more dignified tragic genre, which pleased status-hungry academicians, so Giustiniani's translation was solicited after other suggested tragedies were rejected. The delayed selection meant that the theater had to be modified so that it would represent Thebes, a task assigned to the Vicenzan architect Vincenzo Scamozzi – Palladio's successor, and his rival – who was engaged to invent the backstage perspectives, and probably to modify the Vitruvian façade in order to present a seven-gated Thebes, as in ancient epic.

The original design of the theater was the fruit of Palladio's study of ancient theaters at Rome, Pola (now in Istrian Croatia), Verona, and Vicenza itself, supplemented by his collaboration with Daniele Barbaro on the 1556 edition of Vitruvius. Palladio had consolidated

---

[27] Contemporary accounts are reprinted in Gallo (1973); for the theater's history, see Gordon (1980); Mazzoni (1998); and Jossa (2011).

his idea of the ancient Roman stage for productions of Alessandro Piccolomini's comedy *Amor costante* [Constancy in Love] in 1561, and Giangiorgio Trissino's *Sofonisba* [entitled after its female protagonist] (written 1515) in 1562, the first Italian tragedy to follow Aristotle's presumed rules for the genre; both plays were mounted by the Olympians in the Vicenza *Palazzo della Ragione*, or Basilica, itself built to Palladio's design. If the 1595 illustrations of these performances now in the vestibule of the Olimpico are accurate, Palladio's stage included a Vitruvius-inspired *scaenae frons* with a central royal arch (but not, as in the Olimpico, breaking the entablature into the second storey), with lateral *hospitalia* [apertures] and perspectives placed behind them. In accordance with Palladio's drawings of ancient theaters, the earlier stage-fronts have an attic storey with panels for sculpture in low relief. The counterparts to these panels as realized in the Olimpico depict the labors of Hercules, and directly above the central arch of the completed theater is the claim of the Olympians to have achieved the work by dint of *virtute ac genio* [virtue and genius]; above, in the attic storey, is the Virgilian motto of the academy, *hoc opus hic labor est* [this is the work, this the hard task], and the illustration of a chariot race in a classical Roman amphitheater: a typology of for-show buildings is probably implicit.

Dominant in all Palladio's concepts of the *frons scaenae* was the central triumphal arch, with winged victories in the spandrels, flanked by double pairs of detached columns; the façade was articulated with alternating segmented and pedimented aedicules for portrait statues of individual academicians. Alberti had recommended the triumphal arch for approaches to the city forum and as a model for the theater building, and the arch was a prominent motif in Palladio's later commissions, such as the lateral façade of the loggia for the rebuilt Venetian *Capitanato* [Captaincy General] of Vicenza in 1572, celebrating the victory over the Turks at Lepanto (1571). In light of the Virgilian quotation chosen by humanist physician Elio Belli in 1556, the triumphal architectural motif, alluded to the academy's own achievement, for *hoc opus* can refer to the theater building itself. But the academicians only grudgingly allowed the name of the theater's designer to be inscribed above the central arch. Discovered and trained by the Vicentine humanist Giangiorgio Trissino, the Paduan stonecutter Andrea di Pietro della Gondola, later Palladio, had been a founding member of the Academy in 1550, but by 1580 (the year prior to

Palladio's death) the founding meritocratic ideal of the *olimpici* had yielded to Vicenzan aristocratic pretensions.

The heroic virtues trumpeted by the Olimpico stage-front were, especially at the first performance, frankly imperialist in flavor: in Giustiniani's *Edippo*, Thebes is repeatedly presented as an "imperial" city. Vicenza billeted emperor Maximilian's troops at the time of League of Cambrai against Venice in 1509, and in 1532 the city professed its allegiance to Charles V. He, along with his son Philip II of Spain, had processed in effigy with the empress Mary of Austria, Charles' daughter and consort of Maximilian II of Hapsburg, during her entrance into Vicenza in 1581, where she was Valmarana's guest, an event memorialized in an inscription over the portal to the Valmarana Palladian town palace. The imperial image was in fact built into the fabric of the Olimpico itself. In a pose favored by Charles V (as in Titian's *Victory at Mühlberg*, 1551), an equestrian statue was placed over a small triumphal arch framing the vanishing point of Scamozzi's perspectives; directly opposite, in the niche reserved for the Prince of the Olympians at the center of the peristyle framing the semi-elliptical *cavea* for the audience, was a statue of Valmarana with the features of the legendary Emperor: a specter from an idealized feudal past presiding over the theater's visual axis and the royal arch of Palladio's *scaenae frons*. Along with perfume, the nostalgia for empire was heavy in the air of the Olimpico as the 1585 carnival drew to a close. But as if in tune with nascent Baroque aesthetics, the theater itself was of transient utility, and until the modern era only occasionally hosted events of any kind, although a performance of Tasso's tragedy *Re Torrismondo* [King Torrismondo] is documented in 1618.

Giordano Bruno published *Il candelaio* [The Candle-Bearer] in 1583. The title alludes to the sodomitic proclivities of one of its protagonists, but also refers to the candle of philosophy – borne by Bruno himself – the only hope of escape into light from the dark labyrinth of false values represented in the play (the nod to Dante is unmistakable; in his next vernacular work, *La cena degli ceneri* [The Ash Wednesday Supper], Bruno gave the contours of Dante's Hell to early modern London). Dialectically comic and "Democritean" in contrast to Bruno's characteristic melancholy – his motto, *in tristitia hilaris, in hilaritate tristis* [in sadness good cheer, in good cheer sadness] appears on the title page of the play's 1583 edition, published in Paris – the theatrical satire here continues and deepens

Aretino's, but also draws on Ariosto and Bibbiena – *Candelaio* is a near-anagram for *Calandro* – in its bid to exhaust the form of learned comedy with its surfeit of introductory material and seventy-five scenes.[28]

In its dedication to an unidentified Morgana, Bruno suggests that the play's complex, protean plot mirrors the incessant transformations of the natural world. Lust, greed, and pedantry – each afforded its own subplot, typical character, and its own rhetoric or jargon – are pilloried in order to cleanse the world of sterile rhetoric in poetry, ossified Aristotelianism in philosophy, and – at the dawn of the scientific revolution – bogus practices such as alchemy and dark magic. Both the multiple plot – Bruno alludes to the *gran tela*, the "great weave" of Ariosto's interlaced narrative, in the Argument and in V.11 – and the linguistic cornucopia can be seen to reflect Bruno's ideas, explicit in the preface to the play, of a "generative" artificial memory based on the relation of universals to singulars and worked out in his treatise *De umbris idearum* [The Shadow of Ideas, 1582–83]. This intellectual background also helps to explain the imaginary space where the play's action unfolds.

Bruno's Prologue has the play occurring overnight in the Seggio del Nilo district of Naples. Contemporary maps show that the Via del Nilo of Bruno's day corresponded to the ancient *decumanus*, or axis of the city (the modern Spaccanapoli), so Bruno appears to have adapted the concept of the typical Renaissance stage set of piazza plus street(s), here focused on the very heart of the city, near where Bruno resided as a Dominican friar in 1560–70. The Seggio del Nilo itself – typically a seigneurial palace serving as the *seggio* [seat] of the local council of nobles – Bruno presents as the center of a network of theft, prostitution, and the arbitrary power of the patrols which roam the night-time streets of Spanish Naples. In the play, the role of official *sbirri* [cops] is usurped by ruffians and cutpurses who become moral agents and humble the adulterous Bonifacio, bind the acquisitive Bartolomeo, and flagellate the pedant Marfurio. Bruno has thus assimilated Ariosto's diagnosis of Ferrarese corruption as well as Vasari's concept of the *Talanta* stage as a prospect on Rome, and he has enlarged them: not only does Bruno

---

[28] Never performed in Bruno's lifetime, *Candelaio* has had a number of successful modern stagings. On the play, see Ferrone (1973); Pesca-Cupolo (1999); and Phillips-Court (2011). On Bruno and Ariosto, see Bolzoni (2000).

enumerate Neapolitan neighborhoods notorious for prostitution, but he declares state-fostered prostitution to be the rule in Rome and Venice as well – implicitly, in all Italy (V.18).

The Neapolitan Giambattista della Porta, born in 1535, was from his early years a celebrated natural philosopher and magus: he claimed to have written his *Magiae naturalis* [Natural Magic] at age fifteen, and published it when he was twenty-three. In his sixteen known comedies, Della Porta refreshed learned comedy by importing the mixture of genres and moods deployed in the Ferrarese Giambattista Giraldi's mid-century experiments with pastoral tragicomedy and *tragedia a lieto fine* [tragedies with happy endings]. Thus in the late, sober tragicomedy *Duoi fratelli rivali* [Two Rival Brothers, 1596], an indirect source for Shakespeare's *Much Ado about Nothing*, two noble brothers, Ignazio and Flaminio, court the modestly born Carizia; when not chosen, Flaminio accuses Carizia of wantonness. The slander appears to kill her, but the rivals are spared a fratricidal duel by the good offices of the Salernitan governor and the unexpected return of Carizia, who finally marries the right brother. Della Porta stages the extremes both of Petrarchan devotion and of the inflammatory Spanish honor codes that by the 1590s were an almost obligatory theatrical topic in Aragonese Naples. The play is more stilted on the page than Della Porta's earlier comedies, though leavened by the parasitic servants whose slapstick rhapsodies on their own gluttony reflect improvised comedy.[29]

Ruzante's "character," Aretino's "mixed" style, along with virtuosic Venetian *buffoni* [clowns] like Zuan Polo, heralded the emergence at mid-century of professional acting companies. In what is better called, at least during its earlier years, *commedia all'improvviso* (or *commedia di zanni*) [improvised comedy], scenarios usually drawn from extant plays, such as *Calandra*, along with repertories of phrases, proverbs, and narrative texts provided material for skilled players who formed companies in Florence, Padua, Mantua, Naples, and Venice, criss-crossing Italy as they performed in courts and theaters (more often than in public squares). The cult of the performer offered scope not only for *zanni* [lower-class clowns, often servants] like Ser Maphio who led a company of eight actors, beginning in 1545, and Tristano Martinelli (the original Harlequin, who divided his time between the Gonzaga court in Mantua and

---

[29] For Della Porta's biography and comedies, see Clubb (1968); and Della Porta (1980) for the text of *I duoi fratelli rivali*.

those of Kings Henri IV and Louis XIII of France), or Francesco Andreini, famous as Capitan Spavento; but also for virtuosic female players such as Flaminia Romana, Vittoria Piissimi, and Isabella Andreini. Thanks to Isabella and her father, the Gelosi became a leading troupe, and played in Paris in 1571 and 1577; when Isabella died in childbirth in 1605 she had achieved fame, prosperity, and social status. Language barriers created by foreign touring – to France, England, Spain, the Netherlands, even Scandinavia – pushed players in the direction of the physical comedy identified with *commedia dell'arte*, but in Italy comedy, farce, pastoral, tragedy, and tragicomedy as well as mythological *intermezzi* were the rule. At the Medici wedding of Grand Duke Ferdinando with Christina of Lorraine in 1589, in Vasari's permanent Medicean theater within what is now the Uffizi, and amid Francesco Buontalenti's innovative movable scenography, Vittoria Piissimi in the comedy *La cingana* [The Gypsy] was pitted against Isabella Andreini, who went sensationally mad on stage in her signature piece, *La pazzia di Isabella* [Isabella's madness].

As political absolutism gained strength in Florence, Naples, Milan, and papal Rome, the public eye turned to grandiose entries, processions, and funerals. Italy's theatrical spectacle in the *Seicento* took the form of Medicean *intermedi*, the *commedia di zanni*, and the new genre of opera, conceived in Florence in 1599 by the antiquarian musical theorists of the *Camerata*, but subsequently promoted especially in Venice, where it was performed in public theaters for paying audiences.[30]

---

[30] For the *commedia dell'arte* and virtuosic actors, see Henke (2002); Ferrone (2006); and Andreini (2009). On Venetian opera, see Heller (2003) and (2007); and Muir 2007.

12
___

Philosophy

The Renaissance has often been regarded as a period lacking in major philosophical achievements, frequently reduced to nothing more than a transition between late medieval and early modern thought, far from the speculative heights of Thomas Aquinas and William of Ockham, and irrelevant for the Scientific Revolution of Galileo Galilei and Isaac Newton.[1] In *The Individual and the Cosmos in Renaissance Philosophy* the German philosopher Ernst Cassirer lamented the limited attention scholars had given Renaissance philosophy, accusing Jacob Burckhardt of having excluded "philosophy ... from his observation field," and having completely ignored philosophical thought while constructing his "great portrayal of Renaissance civilization."[2] The German scholar Paul Oskar Kristeller reaffirmed the same view years later, reproving Burckhardt and his followers for giving Renaissance philosophy less attention than the artistic and literary achievements of the period in concentrating their studies more deeply on religious and political history.[3] In recent decades, close collaboration between philosophical and philological research and growing attention to the transmission of culture in both manuscript and printed form have finally established the study of Renaissance philosophy as a field unto itself, allowing for a new understanding of the old problem of the

---

[1] For significant studies of philosophy in the period, see Kristeller (1979); Schmitt *et al* (1988); Copenhaver/Schmitt (1992); Kraye/Stone (2000); Kraye (2002); Hankins (2007); and Hankins/Palmer (2008).
[2] Cassirer (1963) 3.
[3] Kristeller (1964) 2. In reviewing Kristeller's work for the *New York Review of Books* in November 1964, Frances Yates still labeled Renaissance philosophy "something of a no-man's-land in the history of thought"; the text was republished in Yates (1983) 73–76.

transition between medieval and modern thought.[4] By now scholars have widely recognized that the Renaissance recovery of classical antiquity played a critical role in opening new philosophical horizons and in changing the Scholastic curriculum of medieval universities. As the Italian scholar Eugenio Garin underlined on more than one occasion, the return of the ancient philosophers deeply transformed the very image of philosophy and the philosopher himself: "Just as philosophy broke sharply with the past, recognizing no 'book' or 'author' as its spokesman, and blazed new trails and forged new alliances, so too the philosopher refused barriers or predetermined paths and was open to the active life and intensely involved in the moral and political world, in humandkind, and its existence."[5]

Plato and the Italian Renaissance

Though Aristotle did remain at the center of university study into the heart of the seventeenth century, his predominance began to be questioned through the recovery of Platonic and Hellenistic philosophies. Humanists became consistently less inclined to crown Aristotle the *auctor* [authority] par excellence, Dante's "master of those who know" (*Inferno* IV.131), and they began to view Aristotelianism as only a moment, albeit of great importance, in the long history of ancient philosophy. In the early Renaissance, Petrarch gave voice to this rising conviction in affirming his preference for Plato. It is important to remember, however, that Petrarch did not call for an outright rejection of Aristotle; on the contrary, he prescribed a direct reading of the original Greek in response to his own Scholastic opponents. Petrarch was convinced that the philosopher from Stagira could not be considered the exclusive source of human understanding, and that Plato was often preferable given that his content could be more easily Christianized, as Augustine and the Church fathers had already recognized:

> Plato was praised by princes and nobles, and Aristotle by the entire populace ... Plato and the Platonists ascended higher in divine

---

[4] See Blair (2003). The study of Renaissance philosophical manuscripts was established by Paul O. Kristeller's fundamental work, *Iter Italicum* (1963–97).
[5] Garin (1991). On what "philosophy" meant in the Renaissance, see especially Vasoli (1987); and Copenhaver/Schmitt (1992). On the different approaches taken by Kristeller and Garin in the study of Renaissance philosophy, see Hankins (2003) 591–615; and Celenza (2004). On Garin, see Ciliberto (2011).

matters, but neither he nor his followers could achieve the goal they sought. Still, as I said, Plato came closer. No Christian will doubt this, especially if he is a faithful reader of Augustine's works. Even the Greeks, despite their present ignorance of letters, do not disguise the fact, and follow in the footsteps of their ancestor by calling Plato 'divine' and Aristotle 'daemonic.'[6]

Petrarch's Platonism, as is often noted, constituted an important intellectual premise for the Renaissance recovery of Plato, which took place in Italy through the renewal of the study of Greek. The renewed interest in Plato was the result of contact between Italian humanists and erudite Byzantines, Manuel Chrysoloras among them. In the first decades of the fifteenth century, Leonardo Bruni, who had left the study of law in favor of the Greek language after meeting Chrysoloras in Florence, undertook Latin translations of several complete Platonic dialogues, including the *Phaedo*, the *Gorgias*, the *Apology of Socrates*, the *Crito*, the *Epistles*, and parts of the *Phaedrus* and the *Symposium*.[7] Despite these early efforts it was only Marsilio Ficino, in the late fifteenth century, who truly succeeded in placing Plato at the center of Renaissance philosophical culture. In 1484 Ficino published in Florence the first integrated Latin translation of Plato's works, an edition that would remain the means of access to Platonic thought up to the eighteenth century. In the late 1450s Ficino had taken up the study of Greek at the suggestion of both his teacher Cristoforo Landino and his patron Cosimo de' Medici. His work on the Platonic writings represented the application of his Greek in an attempt to arrive at a full understanding of the original sources of the Platonic tradition, a task that occupied him for decades. Cosimo had assembled an impressive collection of Greek manuscripts, and it was long thought that he also established an academy in Florence dedicated to the study of Plato, with Ficino as its head. But while Ficino's intimacy with the Medici would certainly have afforded him privileged access to their extraordinary library, care must be taken in delineating the particular forms through which Platonic scholarship in Florence came to be expressed.[8]

During these years Ficino had furthermore absorbed several other philosophical traditions, beginning with Aristotelianism, known not

---

[6] Petrarca (2003) 326–27.   [7] Hankins (1990) and (2003).

[8] See Hankins (2004) 219–72; and Celenza (2010a). For a critical examination of the recent scholarship on Ficino, see Allen *et al.* (2002); and Gentile/Toussaint (2006).

only through Scholastic mediation, but also through the Latin translations of Leonardo Bruni. In the same period Ficino also encountered the
Asclepius, a text that would be decisive for his interpretation of Platonism and became the means through which Ficino arrived at the *Corpus
hermeticum* [Hermetic Corpus], a text he translated into Latin in 1463.
Ficino's Latin translation was immediately rendered into Italian by his
friend Tommaso Benci, thus contributing to the diffusion of Hermetic
doctrine beyond the narrow confines of elite culture. Ficino held that
the author of the *Corpus hermeticum*, the Egyptian theologian Hermes
Trismegistus, was the founder of the *prisca theologia* [ancient theology],
a body of knowledge thought to have been conserved for centuries
through Orphic hymns, Chaldaic oracles, and Pythagorean maxims
before reaching Plato and the neo-Platonists. Major Renaissance philosophers and intellectuals, from Nicolaus de Cusa to Lefèvre d'Étaples,
John Dee to Giordano Bruno, shared Ficino's interpretation, and the
relationship between Platonism and Hermeticism became an essential
component of early modern European philosophy.[9] It was only in
1616 that the Huguenot philologist Isaac Casaubon challenged the
authenticity of the *Corpus*, pointing out its late and discontinuous revisions from the second and third centuries CE, thus dissolving the myth
of the *prisca theologia*.[10]

Though not published until 1482, Ficino finished writing the
Theologia platonica de immortalitate animorum [Platonic Theology on
the Immortality of Souls] in 1474, a work that sought to confirm the
perfect coexistence of Christianity, Platonism, and *prisca theologia*.[11]
The conceptual nucleus of the *Theologia platonica* was focused on the
doctrine of the immortality of the soul. Ficinian thought was based
upon the notion that the soul was configured as a *copula*, an insoluble
"bond" between the many levels of the "great chain of being," squeez-
ing together the sensible and the intelligible, the finite and the infinite,
time and eternity. For humankind, always inferior to the gods but
blessed with an immortal soul, these ontological levels were entwined
with more significant consequences. The human condition was characterized by an insuperable conflict between the aspiration toward God
and truth, and the desire for earthly pleasures. Emblematic of this

[9] On Hermeticism, see the classic studies by Yates (1964); Garin (2006); and the
'Introduction' to Copenhaver (1992) xiii–lxi.
[10] Grafton (1991).   [11] Ficino (2001–03).

tragic condition was the philosopher, who like all those "born under Saturn" – Ficino notes in *De vita libri tres* [The Three Books of Life] – is condemned to a melancholic temperament, continuing to oscillate between the search for the eternal and the infinite on one side, and madness on the other.[12]

Very closely connected to the *Theologia platonica* was *De Christiana religione* [On the Christian Religion], that Ficino published in Italian (1474) and in Latin (1476). Despite the fact that the second part of the work was conventionally conceived as an articulation of the errors of Jews and Muslims, *De Christiana religione* was quite far from traditional models of Christian apologetics and sheds light on Ficino's original religious ideas. Any reference to the institutional structure and hierarchy of the church, for example, is entirely absent from the work. Already years before, working on the vernacular translation of Dante's *Monarchia*, Ficino had affirmed the necessity of a universal monarch granted to the Roman people "sanza mezo del Papa" [without the mediation of the Pope].[13] In the late fifteenth century the old Florentine anticlerical tradition was nourished by new religious upheaval that preceded the Reformation. It is thus not surprising that Ficino closely followed the anti-establishment preaching of Girolamo Savonarola, a figure who would attract the attention of many Florentine intellectuals in those years, including Niccolò Machiavelli.[14]

Savonarola's prophetic message also deeply inspired Ficino's friend Giovanni Pico della Mirandola, another – though distinctly independent – figure in the development of Florentine Platonism. Giovanni Pico's close relationship with Ficino and the philosophical circle linked to Medici patronage did not stop him from composing a long commentary on Girolamo Benivieni's *Canzone de amore* [Song of Love] as part of a longer commentary on the *Symposium* and in open competition with Ficino. This commentary, never completed, made multiple references to an endeavor in which Pico was invested until the late 1480s. The idea was to gather a council in Rome that might proclaim a universal *concordia* [harmony] and a *pax philosophica* [philosophical peace] among the many intellectual traditions, different in appearance but convergent in their affirmation of a single universal truth. In December of 1486 Pico published the celebrated *Conclusiones sive Theses DCCCC*

---

[12] Ficino (1989) 112–21.   [13] Shaw (1978) 328.
[14] See Vasoli (1999); and Edelheit (2008).

[Conclusions, or 900 Theses] in Rome.[15] The first 400 theses were dedicated to the many traditions of philosophical thought, while the remaining 500 presented Pico's own philosophical ideas. As an introduction to the *Theses*, Pico composed one of the most celebrated texts of the Renaissance, the posthumously titled *Oratio de hominis dignitate* [Oration on the Dignity of Man], a work that drew a great deal of attention in the twentieth century with regard to the philosophical debates surrounding the notion of "humanism."[16] Pico's *Theses* were immediately condemned by Innocent VIII as heretical, forcing the philosopher to escape to Paris, where he would remain until diplomatic mediation on the part of Lorenzo de' Medici allowed him to return. The *Oratio* evoked many of the central themes of Renaissance philosophy, returning to the ongoing discussion on human dignity that had occupied a number of humanists, from Coluccio Salutati to Leonardo Bruni, from Poggio Bracciolini to Giannozzo Manetti. Ficino too had lingered over the question, and he came to assign the human soul a privileged position in the hierarchy of being. Working within this tradition, Pico nonetheless added a clear metaphysical framework, based on a vast philosophical literature that combined Platonism and Scholasticism, hermeticism, Kabbalah, and Arabic philosophy. In contrast to all other living beings conditioned to behave according to their own natures, humans, Pico asserted with a citation from the Hermetic *Asclepius*, were not tied to any particular nature. They were instead completely free to choose at will their own fates, the rationale for their ontological primacy.[17]

Pico's position on human dignity explains, at least in part, his polemic against the judiciary astrology contained in the *Disputationes adversus astrologiam divinatricem* [Disputations against Divinatory Astrology], completed in 1494 by his nephew Giovanni Francesco Pico and published posthumously in 1496. Giovanni Pico carefully distinguished mathematical astrology, which studies the movement of the stars, from false astrology, which he judged to be entirely incompatible with the Christian religion. Ficino had earlier expressed his own opposition to astrology, publishing the *Disputatio contra iudicium astrologorum* [Disputations against the Judgment of Astrologers] in 1477, in which he differentiated between the proper

---

[15] See Farmer (1998).
[16] Toussaint (2008). For the text of Pico's oration, with an English translation and commentary, see Pico (2012).
[17] See Pico della Mirandola (1948) 225.

and improper uses of astrology. Both Ficino and Pico had thoroughly absorbed astrological doctrines, and, as has been often observed, Renaissance philosophy would be difficult to understand without reference to the great importance astrology had in the fifteenth and sixteenth centuries up to Girolamo Cardano and Tommaso Campanella.[18] Indeed, the very idea of a rebirth of antiquity, the awareness of the *renovatio* [renewal], was formulated by humanists with typical astrological concepts, extended from the astral world to the history of religions and civilizations, both marked by the cyclical alternation between dawn and dusk.[19]

Despite the rebirth of Platonism, Aristotle's primacy in the university curriculum was not seriously challenged until the seventeenth century. In comparison to Aristotelian treatises, Platonic dialogues were not considered sufficiently systematic, nor particularly useful for teaching. Nonetheless, in the late sixteenth century, attempts were made to introduce Platonism in Italian universities. In 1592 Pope Clement VIII called Francesco Patrizi to Rome to teach Platonic philosophy. In the dedication to his most important work, the *Nova de universis philosophia* [New Philosophy of the Universe], published in 1591, Patrizi had directly attacked Aristotelianism, claiming that Peripatetic philosophy was manifestly in conflict with Christianity. In agreement with Ficino, he taught that Platonism was the result of the *prisca theologia* founded by Hermes Trismegistus and thus represented a philosophical doctrine more harmonious with Catholicism. But Patrizi's philosophical project resulted in a resounding failure as the *Nova de universis philosophia* was condemned by the Congregation of the Index in 1594 and Patrizi failed to complete a new edition of the work before his death in 1597. By the last years of the century the inquisitorial actions of the Counter-Reformation had already begun to expand beyond the prosecution of heresy and religious dissent to the control of philosophical and scientific culture.[20] The pontificate of Clement VIII, which contemporaries had expected to favor philosophical renewal in Italy, produced instead a brutal attack on the *libertas philosophandi* [freedom to philosophize] with the Index of Prohibited Books of 1596. Among the most famous victims of the Clementine pontificate was Giordano Bruno, arrested in Venice in 1592 and executed in Rome in 1600 after a lengthy trial.

---

[18] On Cardano and astrology see especially Grafton (1999); and on Campanella, see Ernst (2010).

[19] Garin (1976).

[20] On the impact of the Counter-Reformation on Italian philosophy, see L. Firpo (1970); and Ricci (2008).

Renaissance Aristotelianisms

The Renaissance revival of Greek studies contributed not only to the rebirth of Platonism, but also to a new approach to the study of Aristotle. In contrast to the Platonic *corpus*, the majority of Aristotelian works were well known and had been used in Europe from the beginning of the thirteenth century, but humanism promoted the study of Aristotle in the original Greek and produced new, more faithful, Latin translations. For Angelo Poliziano, Aristotle's Scholastic interpreters and Arabic commentators were unreliable because of their ignorance of Greek and Latin. The work of Leonardo Bruni was crucial to this renewal in the early fifteenth century. After having initially translated several Platonic dialogues, Bruni dedicated himself completely to Aristotelian texts, realizing a number of translations between 1416 and 1438, including the Latin versions of the *Nicomachean Ethics*, *Politics*, and *Oeconomica*, a work today considered spurious. In line with the intellectual tendencies of "civic humanism," Bruni argued harshly against academic Aristotelianism, which focused largely on Aristotle's books of physics, metaphysics, and logic. He claimed that Aristotelian ethics and politics were much more pertinent for civil life and for the education of the Florentine republic's ruling class.[21] In his *Isagogicon moralis disciplinae* [Introduction to Moral Philosophy], drafted between 1421 and 1424 and deeply indebted to Aristotle's *Nicomachean Ethics*, Bruni reaffirmed the idea of an intimate relationship between active and contemplative life, between the duty to serve the state and the study of Greek and Roman literature.[22] In the preface to his translation of Aristotle's *Politics*, dedicated to Pope Eugene IV, Bruni condemned medieval translations and articulated the objectives of his new approach to Aristotle: "What could I possibly do that would be more meritorious than to make it possible for my fellow citizens, first of all, and then for others who use Latin but are ignorant of Greek, to read the text of Aristotle, not *via* the enigmas and nonsense of absurd and false translations, but face to face as he wrote it in Greek?"[23]

As Bruni's translations indicate, Aristotelianism was far from being in decline during the Renaissance and on the contrary it proved to inspire major philosophical debates.[24] The foremost Aristotelian philosopher

---

[21] On the notion of "civic humanism" see Hankins (2000).
[22] Bruni (1987a).   [23] Bruni (1987b) 163.   [24] Schmitt (1983).

of the Italian Renaissance, Pietro Pomponazzi, was not, however, a humanist in any conventional sense of the term. He entirely rejected the view that Poliziano and Bruni had held, asserting that there was no direct connection between philosophical study and knowledge of Greek. According to Sperone Speroni's *Dialogo delle lingue* [Dialogue on Languages], Pomponazzi even proposed a translation of Aristotle into Lombard dialect so as not to waste time learning classical languages.[25] Nonetheless, Pomponazzi's distaste for the Aristotle of the humanists did not drive him closer to the Aristotle of the Scholastics; rather, Pomponazzi employed an innovative interpretation of the Peripatetic tradition, in stark contrast to the traditional Scholastic approach. In his most famous work, *De immortalitate animae* [On the Immortality of the Soul], published in 1516, Pomponazzi maintained that, contrary to the theses of Thomas Aquinas, it was impossible to demonstrate the immortality of the soul through Aristotelian philosophy. Ficino had already discussed the theme thoroughly in his *Theologia platonica*, using instead the concepts of Platonic philosophy to prove that, as the mediator between the eternal and the temporal, the human soul was indeed immortal. *De immortalitate animae* confronted Ficino directly, criticizing him as well as undermining Pico's conception of *dignitas hominis*. According to Pomponazzi, humankind had a specific and determined position in the cosmos, and could not in any way acquire another nature. The matter remained at the forefront of Pomponazzi's thought for many years. He knew that the issue was not exclusively exegetic, but rather a much larger philosophical question about the relationship between faith and reason, and more directly, Christian doctrine and Aristotelian philosophy. During the Fifth Lateran Council, in 1513, Leo X had issued the papal bull *Apostolici regiminis* [Apostolic Rule], addressing the doctrine of the immortality of the soul and declaring it dogma. Teachers of philosophy were subsequently prohibited from contradicting the doctrine in their lessons, but Pomponazzi directly challenged the conciliar decree when he affirmed that both the soul and the body were material and mortal. Although *De immortalitate animae* concluded with a profession of faith in favor of the Christian doctrine of the immortality of the soul, the work was burned publicly in Venice and formed the subject of a violent debate among philosophers and theologians, including Pomponazzi's

---

[25] Speroni (1989a) 191–92.

former student Gasparo Contarini and his former colleague Agostino Nifo, famous for his Latin translation of Machiavelli's *Prince*. Despite the controversy, Pomponazzi managed to maintain his position in Bologna, mostly thanks to the help of his friend Pietro Bembo, who enjoyed the confidence of Pope Leo X.[26]

In the second part of *De immortalitate animae*, Pomponazzi developed several important reflections on moral philosophy, which responded to the objections put forth by Nifo and others. Particularly important was the objection that considered the mortality of the soul an attack on the foundation of morality, since without fear of punishment or hope of reward in the afterlife, there would be no more incentive for virtuous behavior. To contest this assumption, Pomponazzi reinterpreted elements of Stoic philosophy through Aristotelian categories, a strategy he would employ again in his *De fato, de libero arbitrio et de praedestinatione* [On Fate, Free Will, and Predestination], completed in 1520 but never published in the period.[27] The mortality of the soul, he argued, had nothing to do with the existence, or destruction, of morality. Virtue had no need for recompense, as its reward was manifest in its exercise, just as vice itself implied its very punishment.[28]

Yet, according to Pomponazzi, this idea could be put into practice only by philosophers who align their own conduct with the Stoic ethic of self-sufficient virtue. For the common person, the persuasive force of religion, with its promise that the immortal soul would be rewarded or punished in the afterlife, created the necessary motivation for virtuous acts. Religion had a fundamental role as a social constraint, indispensable for the majority of men who, like children, were considered incapable of independent rational behavior. It was thus impossible to reveal the rational truth to the masses without undermining their convictions based on religious dogma. Ficino's own plan for a philosophical religion, a Christianity free of superstition reconfigured through Platonism, was in Pomponazzi's eyes not only utopic, but actually dangerous to the social order.[29] The difficulty of reconciling religious orthodoxy with the content of Aristotle's *libri naturales* forced Pomponazzi to address several theological problems. In 1518, lecturing on Aristotle's *Physics*, he focused on the problem of the origin of life, reconfiguring it

[26] Pine (1986).
[27] For a modern edition and Italian translation of the text, see Pomponazzi (2004).
[28] See Pomponazzi (1948) 375.   [29] See Pomponazzi (1999) lxvii–lxxxv.

in exclusively naturalist terms, independent from creationist doctrine. Commenting on the interpretation formulated by the Arabic commentator Ibn Sina (Avicenna) in *De diluviis* [On Floods], Pomponazzi discussed the doctrine of spontaneous generation, arguing that both animal and human life had its origins not from copulation between male and female but from spontaneous generation, as a result of the action of the sun on matter. This materialistic explanation of the origin of life drew much attention in the Renaissance also beyond the restricted world of academic culture. As Carlo Ginzburg has noted, even the Friulian miller Menocchio, tried by the Inquisition in the last years of the sixteenth century, was convinced that life originated in matter without the necessity of divine intervention, as worms from cheese.[30]

While Pomponazzi had tried to explicate Aristotle's philosophy without accommodating it to Christian theology, in the late sixteenth century ecclesiastical censorship progressively restricted the intellectual freedom of Italian universities. The establishment of the Roman Inquisition in 1542 and the Indexes of Prohibited Books produced profound effects in Italy in both religious life and philosophical culture. Pomponazzi's *De naturalium effectuum causis sive de incantationibus* [On the Causes of Natural Effects or On Incantations] was placed on the Index of Parma in 1580 and again on the Papal Index in 1596. With Antonio Possevino's *Bibliotheca selecta* [Select Library], published first in 1593, the intellectual elites of the Counter-Reformation reaffirmed forcefully the inseparability of Aristotelianism and Catholic truth, condemning without reservation philosophical approaches not supplemented by Christian revelation.[31] Attempts at philosophical renewal were harshly opposed even when they did not openly challenge orthodoxy. Such was the case of Bernardino Telesio, whose major work, *De rerum natura iuxta propria principia* [On the Nature of Things According to its Own Principles], was placed on the Index in 1596.[32] For this reason anti-Aristotelian polemic became ingrained within the most innovative Italian philosophers. In *De la causa principio et uno* [On the Cause, Principle, and Unity], Giordano Bruno countered Aristotelianism with the "wisest Telesio Cosentino,"[33] and Tommaso Campanella presented Telesio as the harbinger of a new philosophy that had finally defeated Aristotle,

---

[30] Ginzburg (1980).   [31] On Possevino's philosophical ideas, see Ricci (2008).
[32] *Ibid.* 221–58, 377–89; on Telesio, see Bondì (1997).
[33] Bruno (2000b). On Bruno and philosophy, see Gatti (2002).

"tyrant of human intellects."[34] In opposing Scholastic Aristoteliansim, both Bruno and Campanella fought for the principle of intellectual freedom, endorsing the astronomical discoveries and openly defending the ideas of Nicolaus Copernicus and Galileo Galilei.[35]

The recovery of Hellenistic philosophies: Epicureanism and Stoicism

In his De immortalitate animae, Pomponazzi had argued for the mortality of the soul, referring to the Stoic doctrine of self-sufficient virtue in order to distance himself clearly from Epicurean philosophy. According to a medieval tradition still alive in the Renaissance Epicureanism was criticized for its conviction of the mortality of the soul, the principal reason for which Dante placed Epicurus and his followers, "who make the soul die with the body," in Hell (Inferno X.14–15). Cristoforo Landino interpreted these verses of the Commedia with a further condemnation of Epicurus as the one who had located human happiness in earthly pleasures, considering the Epicurean ethic as more suitable for beasts than humans. And yet Landino did not simply repeat the traditional denunciation of Epicureanism; rather, he revealed a clear understanding of Epicurean physics, according to which the soul died with the body because the two were both composed of atoms and thus destined to dissolve and die.[36] The traditional view of Epicureanism evolved considerably during the Renaissance as a result of the recovery of two ancient texts: the first was Lucretius' De rerum natura [On the Nature of Things], rediscovered by Poggio Bracciolini in 1417, and destined to make a huge impact in the following centuries;[37] and the second, the Lives and Opinions of Eminent Philosophers of Diogenes Laertius, translated from Greek into Latin by Ambrogio Traversari in 1433. The Lives circulated widely in manuscript form before its publication in 1472, establishing the basis for the rediscovery of Hellenistic philosophies.[38] Ficino used the Lives to outline a new, more accurate image of Epicurus,

[34] Campanella (1998) 278–79.
[35] Bruno (2000c) esp. 25–26, for the praise of Copernicus; and Campanella (2006). On Renaissance philosophy and early modern science, see Gatti (1999); and on Bruno in general, see Rowland (2008).
[36] Landino (2001) vol. 2, 579–81.
[37] See Prosperi, V. (2004) and (2007); A. Brown (2010); and Passannante (2011).
[38] See Gigante (1988).

differentiating his doctrine of happiness as absence of pain from that of Aristippus and the Cyrenaic school that identified happiness with earthly pleasures. In his youth Ficino had been profoundly influenced by Epicureanism, which he encountered through Lucretius.[39] Traces of Epicurean thought can be found in his *Symposium* commentary, a work that exercised enormous influence on sixteenth-century literary and philosophical works such as Baldassare Castiglione's *Il Cortegiano* [The Courtier] and Giordano Bruno's *Gli eroici furori* [The Heroic Frenzies].[40] In his *Theologia platonica*, however, Ficino condemned unhesitatingly "those two ungodly figures, Lucretius and Epicurus," who did nothing but "roil our current discussion – on the immortality of the soul – not with any cogent argument, but with their usual clamor."[41]

By the end of the sixteenth century, the traditional condemnation of Epicureanism began to be actively questioned and atomistic physics played an important role in the Scientific Revolution. Strongly influenced by Lucretius, Bruno outlined his discovery of the infinite universe largely drawing on Democritus and Epicurus while criticizing the Aristotelian cosmology of the finite world.[42] Leaving aside customary criticism of Epicurean thought, Bruno recommended a more careful reading of Diogenes Laertius' *Lives*, pursuing a course similar to that of Pierre Gassendi's *De vita et moribus Epicuri* [The Life and Morals of Epicurus], published in 1647, which marked the definitive entry of Epicurus into early modern philosophy.[43]

In contrast to the polemic surrounding Epicurean philosophy, Stoicism met with a generally warm welcome in the Italian Renaissance. It had been transmitted to the medieval period through the writings of Seneca and Cicero, and it became a central part of Petrarch's *De remediis utriusque fortunae* [Remedies for Fortune Fair and Foul], a text that contributed significantly to renewed Renaissance interest in Stoic thinking.[44] Several humanists shared Petrarch's admiration for the Stoic ethic. In his *Isagogicon moralis disciplinae*, Bruni betrayed an obvious sympathy for the austere and severe morality of the Stoics: "Zeno and his followers, the Stoics ... said nothing was good except what was of moral worth, and in moral worth, they maintained, the happy life lay."[45]

---

[39] See Kristeller (1937) vol.1, cxxxix, and vol. 2, 7–11.   [40] See Ficino (1985).
[41] Ficino (2001–06) vol. 3, Bk. X, 6; and vol. 1, Bk. III, 162–63.   [42] Bruno (2000d) 317.
[43] Bruno (2000e) 859.   [44] On the revival of Stoicism, see Kraye (2004).
[45] Bruni (1987a) 271.

Stoicism continued to provoke new interest throughout the fifteenth century, culminating in the Latin version of Epictetus' *Enchiridion* [Manual], realized by Poliziano.[46]

Lorenzo Valla's *De voluptate* [On Pleasure], a work published only after a lengthy genesis in the 1440s, proved to be of great importance in the debates over the ethical doctrines of Hellenistic philosophies.[47] In direct conflict with the Stoic ethic, Valla harshly criticized the idea that virtue coincided with the highest good and was a reward in itself. Not even the Stoics had been virtuous for virtue's own sake, he argued, but rather for glory and profit. For Valla, the Epicurean ethic – which supported the search for pleasure in synchrony with a virtuous life – was preferable not only for its realism, but also because it accorded with Christian doctrine, asserting that virtue would be remunerated in the next life.[48] The reading of Epicurean thought as elaborated in Valla's *De voluptate*, and the belief in a basic harmony between Christianity and Epicureanism, was reaffirmed in the sixteenth century by Erasmus of Rotterdam in the dialogue "Epicureus" contained in his *Colloquia*: "no one better deserves the name of Epicurean than the revered founder of Christian philosophy."[49]

Ancient skepticism and Renaissance doubt

As in the case of Epicureanism, the Renaissance recovery of ancient skepticism depended largely upon Diogenes Laertius' *Lives*, the ninth book of which was dedicated to the beginning of Greek skepticism and in particular its founder Pyrrho of Elis. But the humanists also learned about skeptical philosophy through Cicero's *Academica*, a text known in the medieval period through Augustine's *Contra Academicos* [Against the Academicians].[50] Petrarch possessed a manuscript of the *Academica* and in the course of his battle against Scholasticism employed several skeptical strategies. He argued, for instance, that one should never follow the opinion of a philosophical school without having first examined all other available positions. Petrarch thus suggested that the emphasis should be on *ratio* rather than *auctoritas*, giving more credit to truth

---

[46] See Kraye (2001).   [47] See Valla (1977).   [48] *Ibid.* 267.
[49] Erasmus (1969) 731 (the translation is mine).
[50] Schmitt (1972). For a detailed examination of the wide impact of skepticism on Renaissance philosophy see Popkin (2003); and Paganini/Maia Neto (2010).

than to a philosophical sect, even in the case of Aristotelianism: "I believe that Aristotle was a great man and a polymath. But he was still human and could therefore have been ignorant of some things, or even of many things."[51] In the fifteenth century skepticism attracted the attention of many humanists, including Valla, Poliziano, and Francesco Filelfo, who shaped the first humanist understanding of Sextus Empiricus. Prior to the publication in the 1560s of Sextus' works, the *Outlines of Pyrrhonism* and *Against the Professors*, by the French humanist and printer Henri Estienne in Paris, there had been little direct engagement with Pyrrho's ideas (which were practically unknown in the Middle Ages).[52] A major exception was, however, Gianfrancesco Pico della Mirandola, nephew of Giovanni Pico, whose works he published in 1496. Gianfrancesco Pico had been attracted in his youth to Savonarola's preaching and he attributed his initial impulse to translate the writings of Sextus into Latin to Savonarola himself. Later, he dedicated a hagiographical biography, the *Vita Savonarolae*, to the Dominican friar. In his *Examen vanitatis doctrinae gentium et veritatis Christianae Disciplinae* [Examination of the Vanity of Pagan Learning and the Truth of Christian Teaching], published in 1520, Gianfrancesco interpreted skepticism with a strong apologetic tone in order to question the certainties of pagan philosophy and to promote instead the absolute certainty he believed to be guaranteed by Christianity.[53]

In the religious crisis that erupted with the Reformation, skepticism also provided arguments to defend religious tolerance and cultural variety. Skeptical criticism of philosophical and religious dogma proved to be a significant intellectual resource in the battle of religious dissidents against the intolerance of both old and new orthodoxies. In direct conflict with John Calvin and in defense of the heretic Miguel Serveto, executed in Geneva in 1553, the French humanist and theologian Sebastian Castellio turned to the arguments of Sextus Empiricus to formulate a tenacious defense of religious freedom in his *De arte dubitandi et confidendi ignorandi et sciendi* [On the Art of Doubting and Believing, Ignoring and Knowing]. No one could be so sure of a religious truth as to justify the killing of another human being: it is unjust and contrary to Christian morality, Castellio argued, to condemn as heretics those who simply do not share our religious beliefs.[54] A few

[51] Petrarca (2003) 264–65.   [52] See Cao (2001); and Nauta (2006).
[53] See Cao (2007).   [54] On Castellio, see Guggisberg (2003).

decades later, Pyrrhonism became an essential point of reference also for Michel de Montaigne's *Essais*. Urged by the new geographical horizons opened by the American discoveries, Montaigne's skepticism put in doubt the very notions of civility and barbarism, arguing that "each man calls barbarism whatever is not his own practice."[55]

With Montaigne's *Essais*, skepticism established itself definitively as an important philosophical current in early modern Europe. Among Italian philosophers, Bruno had a particular interest in skeptical thought, although he was also one of its harshest critics. Many pages of his *Cabala del cavallo pegaseo* [The Kabbalah of Pegasus] seem to emerge directly from a reading of Sextus Empiricus. Bruno made a careful distinction between Academic skepticism, which entirely negated the possibility of certain knowledge, and Pyrrhonian skepticism, which instead preferred to suspend judgment, aware of the limits of human reasoning.[56] Several decades later, in the *Discours de la méthode* [Discourse on Method], René Descartes declared that he had defeated once and for all the doubts of the skeptics, "who only doubt for the sake of doubting," by establishing a truth "so certain and so assured that all the most extravagant suppositions brought forward by the Skeptics were incapable of shaking it."[57] Nevertheless, the intellectual crisis generated by the Renaissance recovery of ancient skepticism continued to stimulate debates in the seventeenth and eighteenth centuries, notably in Pierre Bayle and David Hume, playing an important role in the development of early-modern philosophy.[58] In the preliminary discourse to the *Encyclopédie*, a summa of eighteenth-century knowledge published in Paris from the 1750s onwards, Denis Diderot and Jean d'Alembert saw in the Renaissance the start of the intellectual revolution that would generate the Enlightenment.

Acknowledgments

I would like to thank Ann Blair, Rita Sturlese, and Michael Wyatt for their comments and criticism on previous versions of this essay.

---

[55] Montaigne (2003) 185; and Maclean (1996).
[56] Bruno (2000f), 699–714. On Bruno's view of skepticism, see Meroi (2006) 203–16.
[57] Descartes (1996), 19–21. On Descartes and the skeptics, see Broughton (2002).
[58] Popkin (2003).

13
—————

Religion

Perhaps the Renaissance is in crisis.[1] But the religion of the Italian Renaissance finds itself in excellent health in historical studies. Ground-breaking new research, textual editions, and scholarly exchanges proliferate. Problems posed by nineteenth-century historians who challenged the Medieval-to-Modern historiographical continuum through the introduction of the intermediate period of the Renaissance continue to be debated. The question of religion is particularly alive in scholarship dedicated to this period, but the first problem to address is whether one should speak of the religion of the Italian Renaissance, or of the religion of Italians in the age of the Renaissance. Two aspects of the matter are intertwined and difficult to disentangle: first, the way in which the Renaissance as a cultural movement involved with the rediscovery of pagan antiquity elaborated its own particular idea of religion, one that engaged with and disputed the conceptualization of medieval Christianity and the authority of the Church; and second, the general evolution of Italian religious life in the period traditionally designated as the age of the Renaissance. We must bear in mind, therefore, intellectual developments relative to religion on the part of single individuals or small groups, and the ways in which those developments came to be welcomed or rejected by others. These matters necessarily meet in the Church as an institution, and in the religion of the peoples of Renaissance Italy.

Translation by Michael Wyatt.
[1] Jurdjevic (2007) 241: "Since the 1970s, intellectual historians in general and Renaissance historians in particular have perceived a state of crisis, fragmentation and isolation in the larger enterprise of intellectual history"; see also Engammare et al. (2003).

Two elements are peculiar to the Italian situation: the presence of the papacy at the heart of the Italian peninsula and at the seat of the ancient Roman empire; and the fact that religion was the principal unifying factor in a region torn asunder by numerous and deep political divisions. A fundamental subject of recent studies has been how religious differences were resolved and reformed with the consolidation of the Catholic Church following the Council of Trent and the subsequent religious unification of Italy. The most significant period of these divisions extends from the Black Death of 1348 through the Council of Trent (concluded in 1563) to the inquisitorial prosecutions of the late sixteenth and early seventeenth centuries, the most famous of which was the trial of Galileo Galilei. The initial phase of this era came to be called the "Renaissance" by historians such as Jules Michelet and Jacob Burckhardt in the nineteenth century, while Leopold von Ranke suggested the phrase "Age of the Counter-Reformations" for the concluding period. The singular form of this latter term, "Counter-Reformation," entered into common use but has been the subject of considerable recent debate.[2]

In the course of the century and a half that has passed since the beginning of this discussion, historical inquiry dealing with the relations between the Church and the religion of the Italian peoples in the Renaissance has developed along various lines. In addition to the conflicts between Catholics and Protestants complicated in Italy by the problematic process of political unification of the peninsula (to which the papacy's political maneuvering made its own unique contribution), one undisputed fact turned out to be decisive: the movement in sixteenth-century Italy from a period of extraordinary cultural and artistic plenitude to one of greatly diminished prestige, and indeed (according to some) of real and serious decline.

Accounts of the causes, forms, and duration of this decline have been many and continue to be rearticulated. But the judgment formulated by nineteenth-century liberal Protestant historiography was unequivocal: Italy was considered the cradle of the Counter-Reformation, dominated by the Inquisition, intolerant, and superstitious. And while cultural historiography of the Renaissance celebrated Italy as a space of intellectual and artistic creativity, the promoter of great individuality, it nevertheless

---

[2] Jedin (1999); O'Malley (2000); and A. Prosperi (2001).

acknowledged that Italy in this period was a declining star with respect to its earlier and highest achievements, when the peninsula had exercised unparalleled cultural influence over all of Europe.

The importance of a history of Italian religious practices and doctrine, and of the power of ecclesiastical institutions over the lives of individuals, was underscored by two significant texts which stand at the origin of this discussion and established the divergent lines along which subsequent historical research has developed. Von Ranke, the great Prussian Lutheran historian, in his *Die römischen Päpste* [History of the Popes, 1834–36] asked why the reforms of Luther had not taken hold in the Roman Church; his answer was that the papacy managed to stay on its feet and emerged reinvigorated specifically because of its confrontation with Luther. But the Swiss Burckhardt's famous work, *Die Kultur der Renaissance in Italien* [The Civilization of the Renaissance in Italy, 1860], argues that an individualistic religion and a sort of modern rationalism combined in Renaissance Italy to affirm a religious skepticism typical of modern man. Burckhardt was the first to situate individualism in relation to religious sentiment and to place the disengagement from belief in the church and the afterlife at the center of Renaissance culture. According to Burckhardt, individualism and disbelief are the defining characteristics of the relation between modern man and religion, positions affirmed in Italy between the fourteenth and sixteenth centuries, two hundred years before the rest of Europe. But because of their early appearance, Burckhardt argues that these attitudes were weakly held and prone to revision in the face of the inevitable offensive strategies of traditional religion.

The question of the Church as institution is also of central importance. The governance of religious life, and the elaboration and transmission of religious knowledge were – before the Reformation – the exclusive domain of the Church, a hierarchical structure ordered by its own code of law and the standard-bearer of a theology that presented itself as unassailable orthodox truth. Every new idea had to pass through the controlling optic of the institutional Church.

As the other chapters in this volume demonstrate, the Renaissance in Italy was a complex phenomenon that belonged to no single individual, group, line of thinking, or development.[3] That the Renaissance Church

---

[3] Gliozzi (1977); Kelly-Gadol (1977); and Mignolo (1997).

was a major player in these currents – for both good and ill – is confirmed not only by the voluminous collections of ecclesiastical history dedicated to the topic "Renaissance Church," but also by the indispensable place in that history of a pope such as the quintessentially Renaissance prince Leo X (Giovanni de' Medici, second son of Lorenzo the Magnificent, reigned 1513–21), and the importance of an institution such as the papal court – in Avignon, early in the period under consideration, but more importantly in Rome, after the papacy's fifteenth-century restoration there – where the most significant Renaissance artists and its greatest intellectuals operated, from Petrarch to Pietro Bembo, Simone Martini to Raphael and Michelangelo.

But well beyond papal patronage, there was also the reality of the Church as an institutional power that reacted to the ideas of the Renaissance. When Pico della Miradola proposed his 900 theses and gave shape to a central Renaissance religious idea – the reconciliation of philosophy with theology, Hebrew Kabbalah, ancient wisdom, and Christian truth – the church's condemnation marked the definitive defeat of the project. The ban on Pietro Pomponazzi teaching the philosophical idea of the mortality of the individual soul, and on other philosophers advocating hypotheses in conflict with theology (enacted by the Fifth Lateran Council, 1512–17) anticipated the developments which would lead Giordano Bruno to trial and execution, and to the condemnation of the heliocentric thesis of Galileo in 1632 by the Roman Inquisition. These were dramatically significant moves through which the Church slammed shut the door on the freedom of philosophers and on the new mathematical and astronomical sciences. In these exemplary cases the Church was decisive in preventing new intellectual discoveries from becoming a part of the general culture of Italy in the period and beyond.

The Church kept a close eye on preaching. Ecclesiastical authorities were particularly preoccupied with establishing the limits of intellectual freedom, submitting it to the restrictive template of religious orthodoxy. This concern took on an urgency during the period of the Renaissance for several reasons: the wide diffusion of moveable-type printing, the tensions provoked by the various religious conflicts of the Reformation (some of which extended well into Italian territories), and the growth and centralization of new political powers throughout Europe. An important chronological and thematic distinction to bear in mind is that the elaboration of Renaissance religious ideas occupied a central position in the history of the period from the fifteenth to the sixteenth centuries, while the problem of how to govern the religious life of European society was made manifest from the sixteenth century onward, at the time of the Protestant Reformation and the Catholic Counter-Reformation (or, as now designated by some, the Catholic Reformation). The latter guaranteed the continuity of ecclesiastical institutions, the elaboration and diffusion of orthodox theological doctrine, and the fight against heresy. But at the same time there were pervasive and persistent elements of novelty, ruptures of historical continuity: epidemics, wars, and movements of reform and revolt.

Papacy and Church

The most significant change on the stage of Italian public life had to do with the papacy. At the time of the plague that devastated Europe in 1348, its seat was in Avignon, and the men called in this period to the Chair of Peter were French ecclesiastics. Earlier Italian popes – beginning with Gregory VII (reigned 1073–85), Innocent III (reigned 1198–1216), and Dante's nemesis Boniface VIII (reigned 1294–1303) – had effected a "papal revolution" in asserting the prerogatives of the papacy above all other earthly powers, and upon this foundation of the supreme authority of the pope was constructed the doctrine of his infallibility. The transfer of the papacy to Avignon – what to the religious sensibility of Italians seemed like a form of exile and imprisonment – the "Avignon Capitivity" – did nothing to impede the evolution of the papal court and curia into enormously complex and wealthy structures. The resulting spectacle of power and riches provoked the criticism of Petrarch and provided a rationale for the violent denunciations of the pauperists (the so-called "radical" friars) within the Franciscan tradition. Meanwhile in Rome, the ephemeral experiment of a return to ancient models of republican government played itself out in the tribuneship of Cola di Rienzo (1347–51), and local lords sought to establish themselves in the territories hitherto controlled by the ancient patrimony of St. Peter, creating widespread feudal anarchy. But in the absence of the pope, the Italian mission of the Spanish Cardinal Egidio Albornoz expanded papal dominion over the peninsula with the conquest of Bologna in 1364, just as Holy Roman imperial power was diminishing in Italy. Episcopal jurisdiction in the northern Po valley – a region already largely subject to the power of the great local monasteries – enlarged the area for the consolidation of temporal papal power over nascent nobility such as the Este of Ferrara. The impassioned plea of St. Catherine of Siena urging the pope to return to Rome is an extraordinary document that bears witness to an unbroken Italian religious consciousness that continued to find in the papacy an indissoluble key to the unity of the Italian peninsula.[4]

That return occurred only after the conclusion of the Western Schism (1378–1417) which by its end had seen three separate but contemporary claimants to the papal office, and followed upon the rise of conciliarism – which claimed the superior authority of Church councils over any single pope – at the Councils of Constance (1414–18) and Basel (1431–49). The presence of simultaneous popes and the resulting conflicts that lacerated ecclesiastical institutions mark the lowest point to which papal authority ever sank. But beginning with the papacy of the Roman Otto Colonna (Martin V, reigned 1417–31) there was a renewal of papal power that grew exponentially over the course of the fifteenth century, both in Italy and in relation to other European powers. Tied to the affirmation of the power of the pope as sovereign of the Church's territories was a strategy of bilateral relations with the sovereigns of other states.[5] Concordats were the means through which the papacy consolidated its reascent: in exchange for the alliance of European princes, these sovereigns were granted political and financial advantages, such as depositing church tithes in their own state treasuries and the nomination of candidates to ecclesiastical offices. The agreement reached by Leo X and the French King Francis I in 1516 would govern relations between the French church and the papacy until the time of the French Revolution. Papal relations with the sovereigns of the emerging Catholic dynasties of the Iberian peninsula became especially strong in this period. Special powers were conceded to the kings of Portugal, and to the kings of Castile and Aragon, among which were the creation of Inquisitorial tribunals controlled by the crown, and rights as patrons of their respective state churches through which they were able to control the ecclesiastical administration of their colonial dominions in the Americas and East Indies.

[4] See Tylus (2009).   [5] See Prodi (2002).

At the same time, the Papal States – which extended over much of the terrritory of central Italy – were consolidating their power, seeking to establish a centralized administrative authority against the separatist tendencies of local aristocratic lines and *signorie* [dominions] while expanding its territorial dimensions in an ambitious program aimed at extending papal rule over the entire Italian peninsula. The principal instrument of this political program was papal nepotism, realized in two distinctly diverse forms: "major nepotism" which characterized the papacy from the middle of the fifteenth through the middle of the sixteenth centuries – from Pius II (Enea Silvio Piccolomini, reigned 1458–64) to Paul III (Alessandro Farnese, reigned 1534–49) – consisting in the creation of hereditary titles for the children and relatives of popes; and "minor nepotism" which involved the delegation of papal political affairs to the figure of the cardinal nephew as secretary of state. The political moves of the most famous papal offspring, Cesare Borgia, led to the physical elimination of local lordships in Emilia and Romagna and the formation there of a solid papal dominion, subsequently consolidated by the warrior pope Julius II (Giuliano della Rovere, reigned 1503–13). This political enlargement of the Papal States was among the chief causes of instability in the system of Italian states and served as the justification for the invitation extended to the French King Charles VIII on behalf of still-independent states to invade the peninsula in 1494, initiating the long period of Italian wars that ended only with the Peace of Cateau-Cambrésis in 1559. The conflict between Julius II and the Republic of Venice (1508–09) served to block the growth of the Venetian state at the same time that it prevented the papacy from dominating control of Italy. According to the well-known diagnosis of Niccolò Machiavelli, the papacy failed to unite the peninsula and saw to it that no other power would be in a position to do so.

The transformation of the papal office into the sovereign of a territorial state was accelerated by the need of the papal administration to furnish itself with adequate new financial resources capable of substituting those compromised by the various concordats reached with other European authorities. The process of affirming this new face of the papacy as equal parts territorial sovereign and titular possessor of powers over the universal Church occurred through the creation of a central structure in which the various forms of that power found institutional expression: the Papal Chancellery – involved in the redaction of letters and the regulation of correspondence with its envoys (nuncios), and with sovereigns, republics, and city–states – assumed a considerably new importance. The simultaneous expansion of the office of the Datary – whose authority rested in registering appeals to the papacy through fixing the date of their reception – played a decisive role in the concession of benefices. The pope was their de facto proprietor and had the right to dispose of them as possessions [Dominus beneficiorum]. Aspirants to bishoprics, abbies (and their attendant incomes), or even the job of a simple parish priest, were required to address their appeals and pay the accompanying fees to these administrative arms of the Church. And those guilty of performing abortions, incest, offenses against an ecclesiastic, and many other "confidential" sins which a confessor was not permitted to erase were obligated to deal with the Roman Penitential Tribunal. The system of Roman tribunals consequently saw a significant evolution. Papal financial exigencies and Roman judicial activity thus operated in a vast arena, to the detriment of local churches and feeding the conviction that in Rome anything at all could be obtained at a price.

As a result, a complex movement of ideas and initiatives developed which was aimed at reform, as a return to the evangelical purity of the early Church. Among the celebrated interpreters of this season of reform were the Dominican Fra Girolamo Savonarola, and the founders of new religious orders as well as the reformers of already established ones:[6] Fra Matteo Bascio (Capuchin Franciscans), Fra Antonio Maria Zaccaria and Fra Battista da Crema (Barnabites), and Ignazio di Loyola (Jesuits). Pious women gave rise to spiritual circles and religious congregations – Santa Caterina Vigri da Bologna (Clarissans) and Angela Merici (Ursulines) – while laymen were active in confraternities and in charitable works, such as the Genoese notary Ettore Vernazza and the Compagnia del Divino Amore [Company of Divine Love]. But there were also reforming ecclesiastics involved in the government of religious orders: Gerolamo Seripando, Father General of the Augustinians; dioceses: Pietro Barozzi, bishop of Padua, Gian Matteo Giberti, bishop of Verona, and Carlo Borromeo, archbishop of Milan; as well as those responsible for the political stewardship of the Church: cardinals Gasparo Contarini and Giovanni Morone.

A decisive turning point came with Pope Paul III's nomination of a commission charged with elaborating proposals for the reform of

---

[6] On the baffling array of religious orders in Italy in the period, see Gotor (2011a).

ecclesiastical institutions [*Consilium de emendanda ecclesia*, 1537], and then with the convocation of a council that would meet periodically in Trent, in Bologna, and again in Trent from December 1545 through December 1563. The failure of the dialogue with Protestants strongly encouraged by Emperor Charles V but considered particularly dangerous in Rome marked the defensive realignment of the Church through the creation of the Roman Congregation of the Holy Office of the Inquisition (or, simply, Holy Office) in 1542, an *annus horribilis* or *mirabilis* – depending on one's vantage point – that witnessed a series of clamorous events which would permanently alter the religious climate of the Italian peninsula and beyond. The very first actions of the Holy Office were aimed at tamping down dissent, and among them was the censorship of the fundamental text of Italian reformed religious thinking, the *Trattatello utilissimo del beneficio di Cristo crocifisso* [Most Useful Treatise on the Benefit of Christ Crucified], published anonymously in Venice, in 1542. Also in that same year, the most famous preacher of the moment, Bernardino Ochino, Father General of the Capuchin Franciscans, was summoned to Rome but fled instead to Geneva, declaring that he no longer wished to "preach Christ from behind a mask."[7] Soon after, another prominent preacher sympathetic to reformed concerns, Pietro Martire Vermigli, the Augustinian prior of San Frediano in Lucca, also chose exile in the face of the Roman Church's instransigence. Both Ochino and Vermigli were later to spend several years in England, and they left their mark on the Anglican Church, then only in its infancy.

The case of Pier Paolo Vergerio – nuncio in the 1530s to the Hapsburg Prince Ferdinand I (and hence a Catholic mediator in Lutheran territories) and later bishop of Capodistria – was somewhat different in that he sought to defend himself from charges of heresy brought by the Venetian arm of the Inquisition, a process initiated by the humanist bishop Giovanni della Casa. Vergerio attempted to take his case to the conciliar fathers meeting at Trent, but given that he had not been absolved of his purported "errors" he was denied access to the council in whose preparations he had taken an active role. By 1549, Vergerio too went into exile, first in the Italian Protestant region of the Grigioni and finally in Germany.

[7] On both the extraordinary diffusion of the *Beneficio di Cristo* throughout Europe in the period and the figure of Ochino, see Gotor (2011b).

From this moment on the physionomy of the papacy and Church changed decisively; moral rigor and doctrinal intransigence were the models imposed by the Church's hierarchy. The example was set by figures such as Gian Pietro Carafa – later Paul IV (reigned 1555–59), but earlier the co-founder, with Gaetano de Thiene, of the Order of the Theatines, as well as an ardent supporter of the Inquisition – and his favored collaborator, Michele Ghislieri, Inquisitor General and later Pius V (reigned 1566–72). Whatever lingering suspicions attended the powerful idea that the authority of a church council might supersede that of the pope, the decrees of the Council of Trent were ratified by a papacy that made itself their exclusive interpreter and centralized in Rome the task both of investing them with their true significance and ensuring their application. Concomitantly, the opening of new global horizons with the "discovery" of America and the birth of new colonial empires provided a stong incentive for the religious conquest of the indigenous peoples of the West and East Indies. The same spirit of evangelical rigor led to the return of Italian bishops to their own dioceses – many of them long resident elsewhere – often accompanied by members of the Jesuit order and by priests trained in their seminaries. From the encounter between this renewed Church and a population inclined toward traditional forms of religion – "magical" practices deeply embedded in folklore – arose a series of "missions" within Italian territories, periodic efforts at religious revitalization aimed at inculcating devotion and instructing the faithful through the dedicated use of confession as an intimate dialogue with a spiritual father. Italian religion thus began to assume its modern character.

Religious practices

A world in the course of extraordinary economic and cultural develop-ment was upended by the plague of 1348. Given the contemporary absence from the peninsula of the two principal medieval authorities, the Holy Roman Emperor and the papacy, the organization of Italian political power was then in the hands of communal authorities that evolved into oligarchic structures which had a strict relationship with the organization of religious life. Important religious rites were sol-emnly celebrated in the principal church of the city rather than in the cathedral, and the bishop was a central figure in the oligarchy together with the great ruling families. For this reason, the pope preferred to lean on the religious orders of Franciscans and Dominicans – unbounded as they were by territorial constraints – whose friars conducted cycles of sermons, administered the annual sacramental confession, and conducted inquisitorial investigations in order to root out heresy.[8] It was against this clerical class that the critique of lay literati was directed: Dante Alighieri launched a severe attack against the "papal revolution" of the age of Innocent III and Boniface VIII, appealing to the authority of the Holy Roman Emperor; and when Petrarch railed against ecclesiastical corruption, his particular target the papal curia in Avignon. But it was in Giovanni Boccaccio that Italian vernacular literature found its perfect lay expression: the *Decameron*, a cycle of one hundred novellas, gave voice to a widely held anticlericalism that both criticized and derided the hypocrisy evident in the breach between official preaching and the actual behavior of friars. Boccaccio's themes came to be re-elaborated in subsequent Italian vernacular collections of novellas, from Franco Sacchetti to Matteo Bandello, but widespread as was this form of anticlericalism, it was strikingly disengaged from any reforming gesture with regard to religious doctrine or to the Church as institution, limiting itself simply to a critique of the incongruity between religious ideals and the reality of clerical conduct. Only in the wake of Luther's Reformation did anticlericalism come to be considered dangerous, and at that point Boccaccio's text was subjected to painstaking censure through which all mention of clergy and religious orders was eliminated.[9]

The papacy's initial reaction to Luther's "protest" was rather unfocused. Only after the Sack of Rome in 1527, when the *lanzichenecchi/Landsknechten* [soldiers, for the most part, from the German-speaking lands of the Holy Roman Empire] carved the name of Luther into the Renaissance frescoes of the Vatican, was there a shift in strategy. Bishops and cardinals such as Marcello Cervini, Gian Matteo Giberti, Gasparo Contarini, Giovanni Morone, Ercole Gonzaga, and Vittore Soranzo were widely recognized for the care they took in the administration of their dioceses. Reforming decrees with regard to both ecclesiastical discipline

---

[8] With the decrees of the Fourth Lateran Council in 1215, Pope Innocent III had established a mechanism for the control of orthodoxy through inquisitorial tribunals, and he imposed the obligation on every Christian to make a confession at least once a year, at Easter. In exchange for their "collaboration," the Franciscans and Dominicans were granted a series of special privileges by the papacy. On the central role of preaching for Catholic reform, see Michelson (2013).

[9] See Niccoli (2006).

and the care of souls were elaborated and enacted by the Council of Trent, among which were the obligation for bishops to be resident in their dioceses and to make regular pastoral visits to the parishes under their jurisdiction. Models of the "good bishop" and "good parish priest" were delineated and held up for emulation. The parish became the essential territorial component of a new architecture of religious life based upon the supervision and education of parishioners on the part of a clergy newly subject to acquiring a cultural preparation equal to its duties and expected to maintain a rigorous standard of personal moral conduct.

The Holy Office was organized following the paradigm of the Spanish *Inquisición*. Directly presided over by the pope, the Holy Office coordinated the work of all inquisitors active in the Catholic world, and particularly those in Italy, collecting information and sending directives with regard to investigations and trials already under way; in the most significant cases, the accused were brought to Rome in chains in order to be tried there. Information-gathering was carried out in strict collaboration with the network of confessors: penitents at their annual confession were first of all obligated to respond to questions about their knowledge of the reading of forbidden books or other heretical errors, theirs or those of others. Whoever repented and/or spontaneously exposed their erring companions was guaranteed impunity. It was thus thanks to a priest from the Marche, Don Pietro Manelfi, that an extended network of radical heretics – Anabaptists and anti-Trinitarians, who had organized a secret council in Venice in order to discuss their ideas – was discovered in 1551.

But the most ferocious conflict played itself out at the heart of the Italian ecclesiastical body: in the late 1540s, Gian Pietro Carafa, cardinal prefect of the Holy Office, opened an investigation against the English Cardinal Reginald Pole for his ties to the group of so-called *spirituali* [evangelicals], readers of the *Beneficio di Cristo* and the writings of the Spanish theologian Juan de Valdés.[10] When Carafa was elected pope as Paul IV in 1555 (reigned through 1559) he launched an offensive against the most prominent members of the *spirituali*: Vittoria Colonna, the poet and friend of Michelangelo; Giulia Gonzaga; Cardinal Morone; the *protonotario apostolico* [apostolic protonotary, a papal honorific] Pietro Carnesecchi; and the poet Marcantonio Flaminio. Carafa did not live

---

[10] For the impact of Valdés on the religion of Italians in this period, see Crews (2008).

long enough, however, to bring the initiative to fruition; his successor, Pius IV (Giovanni Angelo de' Medici, reigned 1559–65), absolved Morone, and Pole had by then already died after having returned to England to aid Queen Mary Tudor in re-establishing Catholic religion there.

With the election of Pius V the battle was on again: Carnesecchi was extradited to Rome, tried and executed; and Vittore Soranzo, bishop of Bergamo, was investigated for opinions he had disseminated in his diocese.[11] Smaller Italian states were not spared. In Mantua, resistance to the Dominican inquisitors on the part of the ruling Gonzagas and their allies among the local aristocracy were rebuffed, and Cardinal Carlo Borromeo conducted a special mission to the territory that concluded with a series of auto-da-fés. There were other such rulings in Faenza, where the entire city council was stripped of its mandate and put on trial, and its most prominent member, Camillo Regnoli, was executed with his wife. In Ferrara, the Duchess Renée de France, consort of Ercole II d'Este,[12] protected Protestant refugees (she had hosted the young John Calvin, disguised, in 1536), but she was unable to shield the Faentine Calvinist Fanino Fanini – an artisan turned popular preacher – from the death sentence he received in 1549, a case that had a wide resonance in Italy and beyond. The matter was taken up in a brief polemical text written by the ex-Benedictine exile Francesco Negri and in an extended discussion among other Italians concerned about the reform of the Church as to whether it was licit to simulate conformity while hiding one's true convictions, or whether martyrdom was preferable. Such simulation had been condemned by Calvin, who accused those who practiced it of behaving like Nicodemus, the Pharisee who went to hear Christ's teaching under the cloak of night in the Gospel of John 3:1–21. Calvin's position made a victim of the Venetian jurist Francesco Spiera, who after having publicly abjured his reformed inclinations became convinced that he had committed an unpardonable sin and was condemned to eternal damnation; his tormented conscience brought on a physical collapse that led to his death in 1548, provoking a heated debate among would-be Italian reformers. The legitimacy of simulation – "Nicodemism" – was sustained by another ex-Benedictine monk, the Sicilian Giorgio Rioli ("il Siculo"), who was put on trial and executed in Ferrara in 1551.

---

[11] On these trials, see M. Firpo/Marcatto (1998); and M. Firpo/Pagano (2004).
[12] See Belligni (2012).

The road to exile thus inevitably opened up for a number of prominent Italians sensitive to the need for reform. The Neapolitan aristocrat
Galeazzo Caracciolo, Marquis of Vico, related through marriage to Gian
Pietro Carafa, fell under the influence of Valdés and fled to Geneva,
where he established a close relationship with Calvin. The young
Ferrarese humanist Olimpia Morata – one of the most promising scholars
of Greek and Latin antiquity in the circle of Renée de France in Ferrara, and
also a correspondent of several of the leading lights of the Reformation –
abandoned Italy after marrying a Protestant German doctor, and spent
the remainder of her short life privately teaching ancient languages in
Heidelberg. Two cities were especially known as bastions of heresy and
were consequently hard hit by repression: Modena and Lucca. Giovanni
Morone was bishop of Modena from 1529 through 1550, the period of
the greatest penetration of reformed ideas in Italy; his diocese was
considered by some Roman authorities to be a hotbed of objectionable
religious ideas and practices – particularly among women – and Morone
was eventually constrained to leave its administration in more trusted
orthodox hands before then being submitted to Roman incarceration
and a trial by his fellow cardinals that exonerated him only in 1559.[13]
Lucca – the "infected city" whence Vermigli had gone into exile – refused
to admit an Inquisition tribunal, opting rather for a local court that
operated in such a way as to allow many of its citizens a means for
escaping to northern cities such as Geneva, from where they they managed, nevertheless, to maintain contacts with their families and businesses.[14] In 1543, Pietro Perna, a Dominican and follower of Vermigli's,
left Lucca for Basel, where he became that city's most distinguished
printer of the later sixteenth century, publishing important Reformation
authors, as well as Greek and Latin classics and contemporary Italian
authors. A number of the exiles for *religionis causa* [religious motives] were
important conduits of Italian Renaissance culture to the foreign cultures
which welcomed them. Without John Florio, son of the anti-Trinitarian
pastor Michelangelo, English culture of the late sixteenth and early
seventeenth centuries might look very different to us today.[15]

Basel and Geneva served as the initial havens for many Italians
escaping religious persecution at home, but not all of these exiles
willingly embraced the rigors of Calvinism. In the face of Calvin's fierce

[13] On Modena, see M. Firpo (2008); and on Morone's trial, see M. Firpo (1981–95).
[14] See Adorni-Braccesi (1994).   [15] See Yates (1934); Tedeschi (2000); and Wyatt (2005).

control of religious orthodoxy, Lelio Sozzini, for example, sought to dislodge Protestant certainties by posing uncomfortable questions about the foundations of predestination and salvation itself. The most radical wing of the Italian exiles, those defined by Delio Cantimori as "heretics" insofar as they refused any form of ecclesiastical communion whatsoever, nurtured convictions that were hostile to infant baptism and the doctine of the Trinity, interpreting religion instead as a matter of severe moral conduct and imitation of Christ's example rather than as a set of doctrines.[16] But the trial and execution of the Spanish anti-Trinitarian Miguel Servet in Geneva in 1553 elicited a harsh protest on the part of Italian exiles in Switzerland and elsewhere. The humanist Celio Secondo Curione, the most prominent member of the Italian community in Basel, wrote a treatise in response to Serveto's case, *De amplitudine beati regni Dei* [On the Fulness of the Blessed in the Kingdom of God, 1554], in which he challenges the notion of predestination and argues for an understanding of salvation that is considerably more accommodating than any of the prevailing orthodoxies, Protestant or Catholic, would have it. Other Italian exiles such as Matteo Gribaldi, Mino Celsi, and Fausto Sozzini defended the principles of tolerance and freedom of religion. The anti-Trinitarian ideas defended by Sozzini traveled with him to Poland where they gave life to a religious tradition that anticipated the later developments of Anabaptism and Unitarianism – a Christian religion reduced to its barest essentials – that would subsequently, in Holland, have a profound impact on developments which would later contribute to the Enlightenment. The Florentine "heretic" Francesco Pucci, in more than two decades of itinerancy that took him to France, Switzerland, England, Holland, Germany, and Poland expressed in his *Forma d'una republica catholica* [Form of a Catholic Republic, 1581] many of the principles – a Pelagian dismissal of original sin, the contestation of all forms of institutional-ized religion, the project for a council that would put a definitive end to all religious divisions – that would lead to his condemnation by the Roman Inquisition, and his execution in Rome in 1597.[17]

---

[16] Cantimori (2002).

[17] On Pucci, and indeed on the whole phenomenon of Italians active in the reformed world outside of Italy, see Caravale (2011); and see Biagioni *et al.* (2011) for concise biographical sketches of the principal Italian "heretics." For the debate that took place in the Roman curia in the years following the conclusion of the Council of Trent with regard to the legitimacy of executing heretics, see Catto (2012).

In Italy the Inquisition proceeded apace with its systematic control of the religious convictions and practices of Italians, while the task of disseminating orthodox doctrine and verifying the behavior of the laity fell to bishops and to the religious orders, old and new. A new phase of the religious history of the Italian peninsula was thus inaugurated, and from this moment forward the idea that the unity of the peninsula had been achieved – if not at the political level at least in terms of religion – gained considerable traction. The equivalence between "Italian" and "Catholic" seemed settled, and relationships of reciprocal support were established between the Roman Church and the various Italian states. The pope was accordingly considered the repository of unique spiritual and temporal powers, among which those which authorized the designation of Cosimo I de' Medici as Grand Duke of Tuscany in 1569, a reward both for Cosimo's zealous support of the Inquisition and the personal attention he had dedicated to the religious obedience of his Tuscan subjects. But was the orthodoxy of the peninsula's population such a closed case? And how deeply had the Tridentine reform of Catholicism entered into the actual religion of Italians?

The discovery of the survival of an ancient culture made up of magical practices and pagan cults in southern Italy recounted by Carlo Levi in his autobiographical novel *Cristo si è fermato a Eboli* [Christ Stopped in Eboli, 1945] suggests one response to these questions and inspired the anthropological research of Ernesto de Martino, dedicated to the religious life of the Italian south in the twentieth century, as well as the historical investigations of Carlo Ginzburg into religious beliefs alive in the oral culture of the Italian sixteenth century and its ancient origins.[18] In his effort to grasp the differences of class, culture, and geography which constitute the overall design of what we now consider "religion," Ginzburg proposed that the separate categories of folklore, magic, and religion might best be used to delineate the components of Italian religion prior to Catholic unification in the wake of Trent.[19] But this is an argument that has elicited strong criticism in a Catholic historiography that has always considered the religion of Italians as fundamentally faithful to Roman Catholicism, even as it distinguishes between officially "orthodox" and "popular" religion, the latter a degraded and simplified version of the former.

---

[18] See Ginzburg (1966) and (1980).   [19] See Ginzburg (1972).

Renaissance culture and Church reform

Italian cultural elites that believed in the ideal of a unified Italian peninsula had a paradoxical relationship with the Church: through economic
dependence via the system of ecclesiastical benefices which supported
many of them; but also in taking a critical, even oppositional stance due
to the rebirth of interest in ancient religion, and also – as we have seen –
because of the diffusion of reformed religious ideas among them.

The economic recovery following the crisis of the Black Death in 1348
led to a tremendous intellectual and artistic flowering in the principal
mercantile cities and the princely courts of Italy. But the division of
the peninsula into a number of small states attracted the attention of
European monarchies keen on expansion and opened a period of Italian
wars (1494–1530) that ended only with the confirmation of Hapsburg
imperial authority. This political crisis drove Italian cultural elites to
Rome, attracted by the patronage of a papacy possessed of a multifaceted
power – religious, political, economic – and the proprietor of a vast international web of ecclesiastical benefices. But if Ludovico Ariosto – author
of Renaissance Italy's greatest long poem, *Orlando furioso* [Orlando Gone
Mad] – vainly sought a bishopric from his old friend, Leo X, another
poet and cultural arbiter, Pietro Bembo, spent the last years of his life
as a cardinal.[20] Within the space of only a few decades in the sixteenth
century, as critical voices and calls for Church reform were silenced,
Italian literary society accepted the protection of the Church and
welcomed the Index of Forbidden Books.[21]

But the cultural efflorescence that preceded this crisis had been
extraordinarily rich. New forms of religious thinking and analysis had
made great headway in Italian cities, in the universities of Padua and
Bologna, in courts, and in mercantile centers engaged in traffic with the
Mediterranean world and with northern Europe. The rebirth of ancient
paganism in Italian learned culture and in particular in fifteenth-
century Florence dominated the research of Aby Warburg and his circle
of twentieth-century Renaissance scholars, a return to the themes and
values of the ancient world investigated through the study of incono-
graphic sources. Warburg taught his students to recognize the emergence in the Renaissance of figurative forms of expression, of a sense of
life and reality fixed by the artistic language of antiquity, and to these

---

[20] See Dionisotti (1967); and M. Firpo (2011).   [21] See Fragnito (2001).

he gave the name *Pathosformeln* [pathos-evoking form]. For a culture
fascinated with the rediscovery of antiquity, to capture images of life
in movement – as in Botticelli's *Birth of Venus*, and in the family scenes
painted by Domenico Ghirlandaio – or to represent the mutability of
human experience, artists appropriated ancient images and forms, and
in so doing displaced the iconographic tradition of medieval Christian
culture. The Florentine merchant Filippo Sassetti's 1488 will specified,
for instance, that the feminine figure of ancient Fortune should grace
his tomb in order to signify the linkage in his life and work with the
risks of commerce and navigation. Here, within the context of mercantile culture, we see the penetration of that same figure of Fortune that so
influenced the world-view of contemporary politicians and historians
and would subsequently contribute so significantly to the weakening
and later annulment of the basic tenets of the Christian vision. It had
already been some time since Italian chroniclers and civic historians
had set aside the narrative scheme beginning with Adam and Eve and
ending with the Universal Judgment, and analysis of historical and
political change came increasingly to occupy center-stage, focusing on
human action and individual agency but also evoking the dark forces
that pagan culture had identified with fate and sought to presage
through astrology. In a famous passage in *Il principe* xxv, Niccolò
Machiavelli conceives political struggle as the conflict between human
energy and intelligence, *virtù*, and the unpredictable mutation of reality
dominated by chance, *fortuna*. But among the forces that threatened the
free exercise of individual *virtù* for the contemporaries of Machiavelli
was the power of the stars, a refutation of Christian prophecy as both
warning and invitation on the part of a paternal God and the apparent
endorsement of astrology as the decoding of an immutable future
written in the heavens.

The rebirth of ancient astrology was an important phenomenon that
left its traces in both philosophical thinking and in everyday attitudes:
the reading of horoscopes and the consultation of astrologers at decisive
moments became common practice. The pictorial representation of con-
stellations was a common feature of aristocratic homes, and one of the
most famous of these – studied by Warburg – is the fresco cycle painted
for the Este lords of Ferrara in their summer palace, the Schifanoia.[22]

[22] See Warburg (1999).

The culture of astrology provoked a sharply negative reaction on the part of theologians who asserted the paternal providence of the Christian God against the power of the stars and defended human free will over astral determinism.

The most heated conflict between religious authorities and the new ideas and preferences that gave the Renaissance its distinctive character took place over books, the fundamental Renaissance instrument of information and the critical element in the acclerated diffusion of intellectual exchanges among all literate social classes. An early task of Renaissance book culture was the "liberation" of ancient texts from their "imprisonment" in monastic libraries, according to the language employed by passionate humanist scholars such as Poggio Bracciolini. It is difficult now to reconstruct the enormous impact a text as radical as *De rerum natura* [On the Nature of Things] of Titus Carus Lucretius would have had on its Renaissance readers, but the allure of its elegant poetry so closely tied to a powerful defense of a materialistic vision of life posed no small problem for its Renaissance circulation.[23] Plato too was an author long sought after – apart from the *Timaeus*, authentic Platonic ideas had been little known to medieval culture – and his thinking came to take pride of place in the religious and philosophical questions of the Renaissance, a process in which Marsilio Ficino and the circle of Platonic scholars he cultivated in Florence played a decisive role.[24]

The reaction of traditional theological culture to these new themes and interests was harsh, above all among Dominicans, the religious order most responsible for the elaboration and defense of religious orthodoxy. The Florentine Dominican Giovanni Dominici challenged the Chancellor of the Florentine Republic Coluccio Salutati in his 1405 *Lucula noctis* [Nocturnal Firefly], openly criticizing the reading of pagan authors approved by Salutati and other humanists, even if the polemic was still framed at this point from within the Christian tradition. Ancient stylistic models in a culture that remained decidedly Christian continued to pervade the various writings of the Florentine elite in the fifteenth century, as the *Zibaldone quaresimale* [Commonplace Book, begun in 1457 and added to over thirty years] of Giovanni Rucellai – the wealthy Florentine merchant who commissioned the façade of the

---

[23] See V. Prosperi (2004) and (2007).
[24] For both Plato and Lucretius in the Renaissance, see Pirillo, "Philosophy," Chapter 12 in this volume, 261–66, 271–72.

Church of Santa Maria Novella – bears witness. The designer of this façade was Leon Battista Alberti, who imported ancient models into Renaissance architectural culture, demonstrating in sacred buildings in Mantua (the Church of Sant'Andrea) and Rimini (the Tempio Malatestiano) how ancient design elements – some of them actually recycled from Roman monuments – could serve a new Christian aesthetic.

But together with the political and military crisis of the first several decades of the sixteenth century there were ample reasons for a profound discrediting of both the Church and the papal court. In his *Discorsi* [Discourses] I.xii, Machiavelli writes that "due to the wicked example of that [papal] court, Italy has lost all devotion and religion ... we Italians, therefore, [owe it] to the Church and its priests for having become a wicked people, entirely deprived of religion." The initial diffusion in Italy of news about Luther's protest was joined to the reading of texts of Desiderius Erasmus, stimulating widespread interest and empathy at the time but whose traces remain for the most part only in the records of Inquisitorial trials. The reforming impetus aroused by these northern European voices gave fleeting rise to the idea of an Italian religion free of intolerance, nurtured by a merciful God, open to all, and indifferent to institutions and dogma.[25] It was to such attitudes, shared by a large part of the Italian population, that ecclesiastical institutions then turned their attention: bishops, parish priests, and members of religious orders dedicated to the "care of souls" – to the administration of the sacraments and disciplinary control, work carried out with renewed vigor following the reforms promoted by the Council of Trent; and the commissioners and vicars of the Roman Inquisition, charged with controlling the othodoxy of opinion and conduct. Missionaries comprised a third phalanx of this "reformed" Church, traveling the rural and mountainous areas of the Italian peninsula with the same evangelical spirit that animated those who went to Christianize the "savage" peoples of the "Indies," and due to their work a renewed Catholicism established critical alliances with the needs and traditions of the Italian popular world in forms that continue to be studied and debated.[26]

One thing is certain: while magical practices and devotions continued to animate the religious life of the popular classes, doctrinal dissent, initially widespread in Italian cities, disappeared almost

[25] See Seidel Menchi (1987).   [26] See A. Prosperi (2009).

entirely by the end of the sixteenth century. The execution of Giordano Bruno – with his occult interests and his belief in unbridled intellectual freedom – in Rome's Campo de' Fiori on February 17, 1600 symbolically brought to a close the long season of Renaissance culture. Italy had by then been reconquered by the Catholic Church, even if a few intrepid souls still died for their heretical ideas. The vast majority of Italians accepted the Tridentine form of Catholicism, and the extensive control exercised by parish priests and local missionaries through preaching and confession encouraged conformism.

Sir Edwin Sandys, an English traveler to Venice who established close ties to the Servite Fra Paolo Sarpi there in the 1590s, was quite critical of the situation he found in Italy: his *Relation on the State of Religion* (1605) describes Italians as welcoming, pious, and well-behaved, but also as corrupted by clerical education.[27] Thanks to Roman directives, they heard Mass and other prayers in a language incomprehensible to all but a select cultural elite, religious ignorance favored superstition, and in place of Christ they worshipped Mary and the saints. Sandys was struck most of all by the effects of confession. The clergy pardoned each individual sin, even actual crimes – the distinction between the two was effectively blurred – at the price of a few prayers repeated mechanically, and in so doing actually encouraged immorality and delinquency. The censorship of books prevented Italians from knowing the ideas of other Christian confessions, and the propaganda of the friars fomented diffidence and hatred for dissidents. Sarpi collaborated with Sandys and added several chapters of his own to the work, first published in English (in England, though apparently without the author's consent). Translated into Italian by Sarpi and Fulgenzio Micanzio, the text was not, however, published in Italy as the "War of the Interdict" exploded in 1605 between the Republic of Venice and Pope Paul V (Camillo Borghese, reigned 1605–21). Sarpi dedicated all of his energies to defending the right of the state to adjudicate delinquent priests and to govern local matters related to church and religion. For a brief period it seemed that Venice would have to break with Rome entirely, and during this time the island republic counted enormously on the support of the French King Henri IV and the German Protestants, but in the end Venice preferred a settlement with Rome. Sarpi was subsequently

[27] On Sandys, see Rabb (2004).

marginalized, and barely escaped an attempt on his life widely believed at the time to be a Jesuit plot. With the assassination of Henri IV in 1610 and the aggressive re-emergence of Catholicism in Germany the hopes invested in Venice as "portal of the Gospel in Italy" were dashed. The work of Sandys and Sarpi was published in Italian in Geneva in 1625 thanks to Giovanni Diodati,[28] the celebrated Lucchese Biblical scholar whose Italian translation of the Bible had also been published in Geneva in 1603 – the first Italian translation to be based on the sacred text's original languages, and the only Bible available to Italians in their own language (it was reprinted well into the nineteenth century) before the Catholic translation of Antonio Martini (1769–81).

But in Italy a triumphant Catholicism conquered the population, spawning new forms of devotion and artistic expression. Its vitality by the late sixteenth century was such that it has recently been redefined as the moment of "Catholic Renewal."[29] Papal patronage transformed the city of Rome and made it the center of Catholic devotion with the exploration of the catacombs and the newly coined emphasis on the pope as "Holy Father."[30] The Basilica of St. Peter's in its second incarnation mandated by Julius II and built over the course of much of the sixteenth century with the collaboration of the period's greatest artists, was initially financed thanks to the selling of the indulgences which had precipitated the Lutheran crisis. When the basilica was completed, pilgrims could read on its façade a dedication to the Apostle Paul signed by Paul V,[31] member of the powerful Borghese family and bearer of a double title: spiritual head of the worldwide Catholic Church, and political leader of the Papal States. These powers permitted the pope to exercise far-reaching control over the consciences of Catholics but also made him a major player among the political leaders of his time, above all with regard to the other Italian states. The strict web of client relationships which effectively made the pope their head clarifies the particular character of the nexus between the Catholic papacy and Italy that was established in this period and that has since been defined with a specific term: hegemony.

---

[28] For both the original text and its Italian translation, see Sandys/Sarpi (1969). Sarpi's polemical history of the Council of Trent, *L'istoria del concilio tridentino*, was first published in London in Italian (1619), and then in Latin (1620) and English (1620) translations there; it was immediately condemned by the Inquisition and placed on the Index.
[29] See Hsia (2005).   [30] See Rusconi (2010).   [31] Reinhard (2009).

14

Political cultures

The instinct to connect the Renaissance and modernity has been nowhere more resilient than in the realm of political culture. For much of the twentieth century, the apparent connection was broad and included more than politics. It seemed evident in many different areas of human activity: in literature, the visual arts, and economics, for example, but also in more domestic contexts such as family structure and identity.[1] Repeated waves of revision, however, have challenged and often refuted that connection in recent decades, but it persists stubbornly in analyses of Renaissance politics. In the most influential studies, the Renaissance was a fundamentally political phenomenon, a moment in which creative intellectuals asked penetrating questions about the purpose of political life and the nature of political legitimacy, and in which actual Renaissance regimes took the first steps, for better or worse, towards the modern state.[2] Furthermore, many of those arguments influentially posited political developments as the principal catalyst for the vibrant intellectual culture of the Italian peninsula between 1350 and 1550.[3] And although the valence and understanding of "modern" often changes, Renaissance political culture always manages to remain a direct interlocutor with it.[4]

---

[1] For assessments of this historiographical tradition and challenges to it, see Muir (1995); the essays by Gouwens, Findlen, Bouwsma, Grafton, and Starn in "AHR Forum" (1998); and Jurdjevic (2007).
[2] For the original statement and pan-Italian synthesis, see Burckhardt (2002); for the Renaissance as a key moment in the formation of the modern state, see Chabod (1958); Mattingly (1988); Kirshner/Molho (1996); and Muir (2002). And for the most recent and comprehensive study of the full range of political expression in all parts of Renaissance Italy, see Gamberini/Lazzarini (2012).
[3] Bouwsma (1968); Baron (1988); and Witt (2000).   [4] Yoran (2007).

Simply put, Renaissance political theorists spoke about politics in ways that differed from transalpine settings because the Italian context itself was different. The emergence of autonomous communes in medieval Italy was an unprecedented phenomenon that defied defensible explanation in terms of existing political thought. In medieval Europe, legitimate power derived from popes or emperors, then monarchs or princes – all understood as particular variations on the universal model of monarchy. Scholastic political thought, derived from Aquinas, generally concentrated on questions of monarchy: the rights and obligations of monarchs, the limits of monarchical authority, and their relationship to the Roman papacy.[5] In early medieval Italy, the central and northern city–states owed theoretical obedience either to the popes in Rome or the Holy Roman Emperors in Vienna. But as the major European rivalry between popes and emperors left the two superpowers increasingly exhausted, the already largely de facto self-governing urban towns of central and northern Italy proclaimed themselves sovereign entities, throwing off even the theoretical obedience that would have otherwise bound them into the more universal conceptions of power prevailing elsewhere in Europe.

The consolidation of independent communes across central and northern Italy in the mid thirteenth century coincided with the rediscovery and translation of Aristotle's *Politics*, a text that provided the early structure and style of city–state political culture. Prior to its rediscovery, there was simply no text in the western European political canon capable of describing or analyzing, let alone legitimating, the Italian setting. Through the *Politics*, however, the Italian city–states began to find a conceptual voice and guide. Aristotle wrote about politics and humanity's inherent tendency to organize itself around urban political communities, and he did so in strictly secular terms, a crucial distinction for the newly independent communes living in the shadow of papal Rome. In Aristotle, the communes found arguments for humanity's instinct for political association, the ideal of the common good, the notion of distributive justice, and the theory of the mixed constitution. Furthermore, Aristotle's arguments were philosophically rigorous but did not require the implicit overarching Christian superstructure that monarchy, empire, and papacy

[5] Rubinstein (1979) 183–85.

required. And the regional and structural parallels between the Italian city–states and those of classical antiquity only increased the impact of the *Politics*.[6]

Certainly not all Renaissance political thought was republican. On the contrary, by 1400 most of the formerly independent communes had fallen under signorial, or one-man, rule, the result of chronic factional rivalries, oligarchic coups from within, and mercenaries from without. By the period considered in this chapter, roughly 1400–1550, the remaining major self-governing republics of Florence, Venice, Genoa, and Siena were the exception rather than the rule. And certainly not all Renaissance political thought was Aristotelian. But whether an apologist of princely government such as Antonio Loschi or an apologist of communal government such as Leonardo Bruni, the inability of Italian political theorists to insert the regimes they defended into the universal hierarchies of feudal and monarchical Europe led them to use Aristotelian categories, if not strictly Aristotelian arguments.

In general, the political culture of the Renaissance addressed the two preponderant constitutional forms of the Italian city–states, signorial rule and republican self-government. This chapter will examine two major examples of each: monarchical Naples and ducal Milan, the two most powerful princely states, and republican Venice and Florence, the two most powerful republics. A first point of qualification at the outset is that between those two poles there was considerable regional and temporal variation. As we shall see, politics in monarchical Naples differed in structure, form, and substance from politics in Milan, just as Florentine republicanism differed from Venetian, for example; but even within individual city–states there was often considerable change. Milan, primarily a princely state, underwent a tumultuous and brief republican revival, while Florence, primarily a republican state, was eventually transformed into an enduring princely state. And even during its republican phase, the nature of Florentine politics changed considerably between the fourteenth and fifteenth centuries. And it is beyond the scope of this chapter even to begin to encapsulate Roman political culture. Rome hardly compared to any other Renaissance state since it was simultaneously heir to the universal imperial legacy of ancient Rome, a sprawling urban city–state, temporal overlord of much

---

[6] *Ibid*. 184; for the medieval origins of theories of Renaissance self-government, see Rubenstein (1942); and Najemy (2004).

of central Italy, the central stage of European diplomacy, and the spiritual and administrative center of Christendom and the church.[7]

Two important points do apply to the political cultures of most city–states. The first is that the political life of the city–states was notably volatile, and this relatively ubiquitous condition informed the style and substance of their political cultures.[8] During the two centuries preceding the Renaissance, the political narrative of Italy's urban communes was a struggle for dominance between various forces: laboring artisanal classes, prosperous merchants, old aristocracies, and predatory mercenaries eager to install themselves as princes of the cities that had hired them. Although in the major city–states, republican and signorial, the political setting had stabilized considerably around elite dominance by 1400, the lessons of history taught those in power not to take their ascendancy for granted nor to assume that it required no explanation. Given the absence of any universally recognized theoretical or canonical answer to the question of who ought to be in power, Renaissance political elites were particularly receptive to the notion that politics in the absence of other authorities could be legitimated by culture.

The second and related point is that humanism became the dominant voice of politics throughout the peninsula. Renaissance regimes may not have been "works of art" in the Burckhardtian sense, but political anxiety did lead Renaissance rulers in despotisms and republics alike to devise cultural legitimations of their dominance and to patronize artists and intellectuals to build support for their regimes. With surprising uniformity, political elites turned to humanists and humanism to describe, interpret, and defend their political world.

As a result, there was a certain consistency in the assumptions of Renaissance political thought. Some humanists championed monarchy, some championed the rule of aristocratic oligarchies, and others outright republican rule, but even in the midst of contrasting arguments they shared a number of axioms about politics.

It was once held that the two quintessentially "modern" features of Renaissance political thought were its realism and secularism. As we shall see in more detail, the Renaissance political imagination only

---

[7] On Rome see D'Amico (1983); Stinger (1998); Signorotto/Signorotto (2002); and Prosperi, "Religion," Chapter 13 in this volume, pp. 280–83, 297.
[8] This Burckhardtian point is also evident in Lubkin (1994); Martines (1998); and Najemy (2004).

rarely engaged the political, economic, and social realities of politics, though it certainly reflected those realities. But humanist political thought was consistently secular. Human factors, rather than a Christian providential scheme, determined the outcome of events. This conviction did not always or necessarily make their analyses deeper or more coherent than earlier models that privileged divine will, but by removing the providentialist framework, they implicitly advanced the view that the purpose of politics was secular and immediate. Humanists also tended to focus on the reform of individuals, particularly the ruling elite, rather than on the reform of institutions, whether legal, constitutional, or economic. And humanists in republics and princedoms alike celebrated the active life and the pursuit of honor and glory in the political arena, which necessitated a general re-evaluation of the religious ideals of contemplation and humility, which pushed Renaissance political thought that much further from the Christian template evident elsewhere in Europe.[9]

The ubiquitous embrace of humanist political thought was in part the result of the relative smallness of the peninsula with its consequent permanent diplomatic contact between states. As humanism became the fashionable mode of intellectual inquiry in centers like Florence and Venice, rulers across the peninsula increasingly hired humanists to serve in their chanceries, to draft legations, and to serve as court intellectuals and propagandists, and many humanists were permanently itinerant, serving at courts and republics throughout the peninsula.[10] But there is perhaps an additional, more structural reason why humanism might have become the dominant political voice during the Renaissance. As we shall see in further detail, humanism tended to speak about politics in ideal terms; it was concerned with the qualities of ideal rulers, ideal citizens, the common good, and the collective subordination of private to public interest. It was predicated on a positive view of human nature, on the conviction that with the right upbringing and education political actors, whether rulers, subjects, or citizens, could attain wisdom, prudence, and virtue. Drawing heavily on the political culture of classical antiquity, humanism described the political arena with the classicizing aesthetics of order, symmetry, and harmony.

---

[9] Hankins (1996).   [10] Kristeller (1961); and Witt (1982).

One of the crucial limitations of humanist political thought, however, was precisely its insistence on those aesthetics. It was reluctant to describe and make sense of politics as it was most often actually conducted – by republican factions, by self-serving *condottieri* [mercenary military leaders], by court cabals, and by princes who frequently fell short of the humanist ideal. Only after the outbreak of the Italian wars of the sixteenth century did thinkers like Niccolò Machiavelli and Francesco Guicciardini begin to elaborate a political theory based on a bleaker assessment of human nature and on the axiomatic assumption that internal divisions and quarrels were an unavoidable feature of political life. But for most of the Renaissance, the more idealistic humanist interpretation of politics prevailed – not, however, in spite of the gulf between its ideals and the more hard-nosed power politics of the city–states, but because of it. The Renaissance obsession with the harmonious politics of selfless individuals may well have been the last residue of anxiety about the improvised *ad hoc* origins of the city–states and the fear of social discord.

Naples

Naples was the only formal monarchy of the Italian peninsula. As an established and relatively old monarchical state, the political narrative of Neapolitan history was less volatile than those of the northern princedoms, though it too underwent several changes of dynasty. Between 1268 and 1442, Naples was part of the Angevin empire. After the conquest of the region by the Aragonese king Alfonso V, Naples became part of a Mediterranean Aragonese empire until 1503. In 1504, as a result of the Italian wars of the early sixteenth century, the monarchy fell to the Spanish Hapsburgs, in whose possession it remained until the early eighteenth century. And each of Naples' successive rulers – Angevin, Aragonese, and Hapsburg – had to face periodic baronial revolts and challenges to their rule.[11]

The political culture of Naples during the Renaissance was particularly influenced and shaped by its Aragonese rulers – notably Alfonso I (Vth of Aragon), who began a sustained campaign to classicize the city. Alfonso expanded its streets to their older and larger Roman breadth,

[11] Marino (1999).

restored the visual icons and imagery of its classical past, sponsored numerous architectural building projects conceived around the new aesthetic principles of humanism, and hired as his advisers and apologists humanists such as Lorenzo Valla and Antonio Beccadelli.[12]

Neapolitan humanism emphasized the benevolent cultural and social dimensions of Aragonese rule, praised monarchy in general, and instructed its Aragonese sovereigns to adhere to the idealized prince of the *speculum principum* [mirror for princes] genre found elsewhere in Italy. In Angelo Catone's Neapolitan panegyric of 1474, for example, he drew particular attention to the abundance of learned men in the city – he put the number at 300 – as evidence of the political virtue of its rulers. Similar sentiments were expressed by Loise de Rosa, Constantine Lascaris – who prepared for Alfonso a list of famous Greek philosophers of Calabrian origin – and Giovanni Pontano, who pointed to the exceptional efflorescence of literature, science, and scholarship in the 1490s.[13] Giovanni Brancati praised Alfonso's son Ferrante for founding a public school in Naples, building a hospital for plague victims, and repairing the city's ports, which in distinctly secular urban fashion he declared "deserved more praise than a temple to God."[14] Giuniano Maio praised the aesthetics of the recently completed renovation of the city's walls and more importantly still the safety and security citizens thereby acquired.

Maio's praise of the restored wall was merely one instance of the larger connection frequently made between the institution of monarchy and the pacific consequences of security and stability. Maio went on to connect the wall renovations with the larger and still more praiseworthy pacific strategy of Ferrante, who had ruled the kingdom for thirty years with peace and stability.[15] Francesco Bandini, a Florentine exile, wrote a similar panegyric about Ferrante's rule, stressing the city's political stability, material prosperity, and intellectual communities, all of which he argued were the result of Ferrante's reputation for justice and the rule of law; he further argued that such ideals were difficult to attain in faction-ridden and divisive republics such as Florence.[16]

In *De obedientia* [On Obedience, 1470], Giovanni Pontano elaborated more conceptually on the superiority of monarchical to republican government. Pontano argued that the rule of a single man inherently inclined towards peace, stability, and concord, while republican self-rule

---

[12] *Ibid.* 278.   [13] Bentley (1987) 198–201.   [14] *Ibid.* 199.
[15] *Ibid.* 199–200.   [16] *Ibid.* 198.

intrinsically tended towards factional strife and discord, since public office would always be manipulated towards the pursuit of self-centered private interests. Pontano argued by analogy: just as a single deity rules the universe and a single monarch bee rules the hive, so a single monarch should rule the state. Only in a monarchy, Pontano maintained, could individuals live in true freedom, defined as living according to the dictates of reason, in obedience to the rule of law, and in observation of one's social responsibilities to family and community.[17]

By far the most common form of political writing in Renaissance Naples, however, were analyses of the proper character and conduct of the ideal prince.[18] In their writing on princely conduct, Neapolitan humanists generally expressed ideas consistent with the genre elsewhere in Italy, stressing the inculcation of individual virtue, impartial justice, and wise ministers. Pontano's *De principe* [On the Prince] of 1468, written for Alfonso, insisted on the importance of listening to wise counsel, earning the loyalty of servants and subjects, and promoting only the most moderate, wise, and committed subjects to offices of authority.[19] Writing to Ferrante in praise of his conquest of Apulia, Antonio Beccadelli (or Panormita) urged Ferrante to employ ministers that were "just, chaste, and moderate men of virtue" and to lead by example, cultivating the qualities of humanity, generosity, gratitude, kindness, and justice.[20] To Ferrante's grandson, Ferrandino, Pontano stressed the necessity of dispensing justice fairly, issuing serious, impartial, and swift verdicts. In keeping with the earlier emphasis on the beneficent effects of princely rule, Pontano also reminded Ferrandino that maintaining the most strict discipline with his army was crucial, particularly to ensure that his military forces did not prey on the civilian population.[21] Elisio Calenzio wrote that justice was "the prince of all virtues, the signal companion of the gods and of men, the ornament of all princes, the fortress of all cities and estates."[22]

The *speculum principum* genre identified a specific set of character traits which the wise prince should consistently attempt to inculcate. Pontano exhorted Ferrandino to conduct himself in public with authority and dignity and to maintain both the love and fear of his subjects. He should

---

[17] *Ibid*. 201.   [18] On this genre in Italy, see Stacey (2007).
[19] Bentley (1987) 206.   [20] *Ibid*. 204.   [21] *Ibid*. 205.
[22] *Ibid*. 220; for partial English translations of Giovanni Pontano, Il Platina, and Giuniano Maio, see Kraye (1997) vol. 2, 69–112.

always attempt to maintain a reputation for justice, liberality, and clemency – crucial for winning popular support for his rule – and should consistently display moderation and self-control – crucial for overcoming the unforeseen challenges of fickle fortune. Pontano elaborated at length on the quintessential princely attribute of majesty. For Pontano, Maio, and other humanists, majesty was a human quality, subject like the other virtues to cultivation and practice. Majesty was indispensable for the promotion of the monarch's reputation and glory but was acquired only with difficulty and care. A majestic prince displayed caution, gravity, and consistency, privileged hearing over speech, maintained composure, and always kept his true thoughts and feelings private.[23]

Milan

Milan was larger and more powerful than the petty despotisms of Mantua, Ferrara, or Urbino, for example, but in terms of broad political themes, it is not an atypical example.[24] Like Naples, it underwent three major dynastic changes during the Renaissance.

The city won *de facto* [effective] independence from the emperor in the twelfth century, but by the thirteenth century had fallen under the control of the Visconti family. Their regime emerged in the late fourteenth century with the triumph of Giangaleazzo over rival family members. Giangaleazzo and then in turn each of his two sons ruled Milan until 1447, when his youngest son Filippo Maria died without a male heir. In 1447, a coup led by patrician oligarchs established a short-lived republican experiment – the Ambrosian republic, after the city's patron saint – which ended three years later, the result of chaotic rule from within and external pressure from without. The republic was toppled by Francesco Sforza, one of the most capable mercenary captains of the Renaissance and the husband of Filippo Maria's daughter Bianca Maria. In the aftermath of the suppression of the republic, Francesco Sforza subsequently proclaimed himself duke. The Sforza ruled the city until the early sixteenth century, when during the Italian wars it became subject briefly to France and then in 1535 became part of the Spanish Hapsburg empire.[25]

---

[23] Bentley (1987), 206; and Kraye (1997) 109–13.
[24] But see the cautionary remarks of Lippincott (1989).   [25] Lubkin (1994).

The political culture surrounding both the Visconti and Sforza houses most often took the form of historical writing, often by humanists working in the ducal chancery. In this respect, Milanese political culture typified patterns in other northern cities ruled by fledgling houses which commissioned historical writing that attempted to legitimate their newly won authority. Most of the new princes of the Renaissance lacked the lineage and venerable political traditions to make *de jure* [by right] claims to power and hence refashioned such claims in the form of historical narratives that demonstrated through the ruler's illustrious and martial deeds an implicit *de facto* right to rule.

As in most other city–states, republican and princely, Giangaleazzo staffed his chancery with humanists and they provided the tone and style of Milanese political writing. Chancery humanists in Milan viewed history in political terms and that conviction resulted in novel forms of historical narrative – purely secular, devoid of providential schema, rooted in transformative individual action, and thoroughly political in tone and substance.[26] In general, their histories focused on the recent past and presented Milanese history as a struggle between the forces of order and chaos. Chancery humanists interpreted Giangaleazzo's rise to power in Milan as the necessary and welcome suppression of divisive factionalism by order. As Giangaleazzo began an ambitious campaign to expand his power beyond Lombardy, Milanese historians lent their pens to his army by elaborating the argument that Milan was performing the same function of suppressing chaos and factionalism for northern Italy that Giangaleazzo had earlier provided for Milan.

For example, Giovanni Manzini wrote a neo-Senecan tragedy (perhaps never completed, it does not survive) that narrated Giangaleazzo's defeat of the Della Scala in 1387, presenting Giangaleazzo as an ideal example of a prince equally virtuous in arms and letters.[27] The humanist Antonio Loschi wrote *Achilles*, an epic in which the embattled Visconti represent order locked in combat with capricious fortune, the ostensible source of Italian divisiveness and discord. In response to

---

[26] Ianziti (1998) 8, 15. Humanists writing outside of the political setting of chanceries and courts tended to view history in moral terms. They wrote exemplary history, narratives that related stirring *exempla* of heroic action and glory in an effort to inspire their readers to strive for virtue; and their choice of subject matter was almost always culled from antiquity – as Petrarch put it in his defense of Italy, "What else, then, is all history if not the praise of Rome?" See Petrarch (2003) 417.

[27] Ianziti (1998) 237.

Florentine propaganda that characterized the Visconti in sharply tyrannical terms as enemies of liberty, Loschi praised peace as more important than liberty, which he argued meant little more in practical terms than factional rivalries, political turbulence, and a state of systemic urban danger.[28] To Loschi and Manzini's connection between the Visconti and order, Uberto Decembrio added the familiar humanist connection between legitimate rulers and the cultural vibrancy of their regimes. In *De republica* [On the Republic], a dialogue dedicated to Filippo Maria Visconti, Decembrio exalted the cultural primacy of classical Milan, a period in which the city boasted an illustrious list of poets and philosophers. Following the collapse of the Roman empire, the cultural life of Milan entered into a period of silence and stagnation rescued only in recent years by the Visconti, whose patronage of the *studium* [university] and library of Pavia had restored the city's ancient intellectual primacy.[29]

Francesco Sforza's claim to Milan was considerably more dubious than that of the Visconti. Visconti rule in Milan may have been unstable, but the family had long been dominant in Milanese and Lombard politics before Giangaleazzo established a formal duchy. Francesco Sforza, by contrast, was neither Milanese nor Lombard, but a Tuscan-born mercenary with no formal or even recognizably legitimate claims to the duchy of Milan. He had led Milanese forces against Venice for the Visconti, then besieged and toppled the Ambrosian republic that followed Filippo Maria Visconti's death in 1447, and installed himself as duke. Unsurprisingly, he faced considerable challenges to his rule. The emperor, still the city's theoretical overlord, refused to acknowledge Sforza's *de facto* possession of the city, who hence had to rule without an externally recognized title in the midst of considerable hostility from the traditional Milanese aristocratic elite.[30]

It is a revealing detail that the transition from Viscontean to Sforzean rule occasioned no significant change in the style or substance of Milanese political culture. To establish his rule, Francesco had to engage in the practical labor of diplomacy – for example establishing an alliance with Cosimo de' Medici and the Florentine republic, formerly a bitter foe – and patronage, dispensing money, favors, and jobs to the city's political elite. But in conceptual terms, when presenting the nature of

---

[28] *Ibid.* 238.   [29] *Ibid.* 240.   [30] *Ibid.* 15–16.

his rule and his claims to the duchy, Francesco essentially continued the tradition of historical composition already established. Sforzean histories, like their Viscontean predecessors, elided issues of historical origins, were thoroughly secular in narrative structure and framework, and were catalyzed by the transformative individual power of the ruler. To use Gary Ianziti's term, the histories written under Francesco and subsequent Sforza were "an invented political culture," an implicit claim to power based on the deliberate exclusion of tradition at the expense of exceptional individual merit.

Lodrisio Crivelli, a humanist chancery official, wrote several orations in defense of Sforza that took the familiar form of Milanese politics as a struggle between order and chaos. He dwelt at length on the chaos and failures of the Ambrosian republic, its moral and financial bankruptcy, and the belated return of concord and peace that followed Francesco's suppression of the republic. He then elaborated on Francesco's capability as a military leader and his successes against Venetian encroachment from the east, recently renewed after the collapse of the Visconti, painting in broad strokes an image of Sforza as the self-proclaimed and self-made savior of the city from internal strife and foreign conquest.[31] In challenge after challenge, conquest after conquest, Sforza's individual *virtus* – understood as skill, power, and ability – determines the outcome of events, rather than any transhistorical scheme. Nor is divine approval, explicit or implicit, ever invoked as evidence of Sforza's right to the city of Milan, only Sforza's abundant skill and the beneficial consequences for the Milanese of his triumphs. Similarly structured historical works were written by other chancery humanists such as Cicco Simonetta and by court humanists such as Giorgio Merula and Francesco Filelfo.[32]

Venice

Humanism was no less central to Venetian political culture during the Renaissance, though its principal contribution was the rearticulation and reinterpretation of pre-existing political themes and axioms. Unlike most northern Italian city–states for whom the previous two centuries had been highly mutable, Venice began life as a free city, was formally recognized as such by popes and emperors, and had a proud

---

[31] *Ibid*. 238.   [32] Rabil (1988) 251.

tradition of independence already centuries old by the beginning of the Renaissance. As a result, the principal themes and arguments of Venetian political culture were already largely formed by the early Renaissance, though they were restated by Venetian humanists in influential and original ways.

Venice also constituted an exception in that the key figures of its political culture did not emerge from the chancery, a pattern clearly evident in Milan, Naples, and Florence, but were instead drawn from the ranks of the political elite. As a result, Venetian humanism was "not particularly successful" as an intellectual movement, in the words of its most authoritative historian, but was remarkably successful and pervasive as a political phenomenon.[33] Humanism became the principal language and conceptual vocabulary through which the Venetian aristocratic political elite defended its hegemony, the political institutions of the republic, and the consequent culture of order, hierarchy, and harmony.

The government of republican Venice consisted of a series of councils presided over by an elected ducal figure known as the *doge*. The office of the *doge* was the symbolic center of the Venetian government, but in political terms dogal power was sharply circumscribed by an elaborate network of councils that initiated policy. The Venetian patriciate was defined by membership in the Great Council, the body that initiated laws and administered the electoral process that staffed the republic's various offices. In 1297, the Council decreed that membership would henceforth remain restricted within families of the current council, a decision that defined and limited the Venetian nobility in legal and political terms. Although excluded families did occasionally gain subsequent entrance into the council, the *serrata* [locking-out] of the council effectively limited full citizenship and the right to active political participation to roughly 200 families and roughly 1,500 men at any one time. The two other major councils were a Senate that administered diplomacy and mainland territorial government, and the Council of Ten that investigated treason, sedition, and other political crimes.

Politics in all Renaissance city–states were faction-ridden and tumultuous – even more so in republican settings like Venice and Florence – and hence considerable distance prevailed between the manner in

---

[33] King (1988) vol. 1, 210.

which political goals and policies were actually pursued and the language of civism and selflessness that claimed to describe them. But the contrast between political practice and political ideal was nowhere greater than in Venice, which generated a political culture that historians have labeled the "myth of Venice" but that could equally be described as a fantasy of order and harmony.

The myth of Venice began as an answer to the question of the source of the Venetian republic's longevity. What had enabled the Venetian republic to survive for centuries upon centuries when the lessons of history suggested – particularly to humanistically inclined patricians reflecting on antiquity – that all political communities and especially republics rose and fell in cycles?

Unlike the view evident in the secular histories prevalent in Milan and the northern princedoms, the Venetians embraced a providential outlook, arguing in the first instance that Venice's longevity revealed a special place in the divine plan. Bernardo Giustiniani classicized the city's origins, fusing the providential Christian elements with the best elements of Roman antiquity. In his narrative, Venice was settled by a select group of virtuous Romans, inspired and led by God during the last days of the Roman empire to the safety of the lagoon.[34] The significance of the city's founding lay not only in the revelation of the hand of God in Venetian history, but also in the historical fact that Venice was the first republic founded after the rise of Christianity. The stability and prosperity of the republic also had a substantial constitutional component, but it too had divine origins. In the words of the Vicentine humanist Giangiorgio Trissino (Vincenza was then a Venetian tributary), "anybody who starts considering attentively the marvellous constitution and the divine laws of this Republic, must conclude that they are not the fruit of human intellect but have been sent by God."[35]

The most influential analysis of the Venetian constitution was Gasparo Contarini's *De magistratibus et republica Venetorum* [On the Civil Officers and Republic of the Venetians]. Contarini began by dispensing with the traditional argument that monarchy was the best form of government by pointing to the lessons of history, from which he concluded that all monarchies eventually and inevitably lapse into tyranny.

[34] Muir (1981).   [35] Finlay (1980).

Hence, considered from the broadest possible perspective, republics are superior forms of political organization. As a member of the patrician class himself (he would later become a cardinal), Contarini unsurprisingly privileged the aristocratic, oligarchical style of republicanism that prevailed in Venice. A government of all the people, Contarini, argued, would lead to chaos since the multitude is neither capable nor fit to govern.[36]

Within his general conviction about the aristocratic dominance of republican politics, however, lay a more nuanced Aristotelian and Polybian view of the need for a balance of power between various social groups, a "mixed constitution." The Venetian constitution distributed power between a ducal figure or *doge*, the Senate, and the Great Council, reflecting respectively monarchical, aristocratic, and popular elements. Venetians steadfastly championed the classical conviction that such mixed regimes benefitted from the advantages of each of its component parts, such as the stability of monarchy or the wisdom of aristocracy, while avoiding their perils, such as the potential for chaos in democracy or the potential for tyranny in monarchy.[37] In the famous formulation of J. G. A. Pocock, Venetians "mechanized" virtue, relocating it from the individual citizen to the complex interlocking parts of the Venetian constitution.[38]

The sense of a harmonious, balanced, and ordered state transcended precise questions of constitutional configuration, moreover, and permeated Venetian political culture in general. Contarini elaborated on the "mixed" dimension of Venetian policies and sensibilities: the government balanced martial and pacific policies, when necessary engaging in war with force, conviction, and success but maintaining in general a policy of peace and respect for one's neighbors; the army was balanced by periodically recruiting citizen soldiers but augmenting them with hired auxiliary forces; and the social composition of the city's councils was balanced by permitting young patricians on some of them but stipulating that only elder statesmen serve in the most important offices, protecting against the domination of councils by factional or family groupings.

In addition to the tradition of cultural and constitutional balance, Venetian political writers praised the humility and anonymity of

---

[36] Gilmore (1973) 431.   [37] *Ibid.* 430–32.   [38] Pocock (2003) 272–332.

Venetian patrician culture, viewed as a crucial component in the republic's success in transcending the mundane yet pernicious and pervasive problems that politics in other cities seemed inevitably to generate. Venetian thinkers argued that the absence of factionalism and self-interest was the result of a larger culture that privileged the collective over the individual. Unlike the republics of antiquity that boasted foundations by stirring individuals of exceptional virtue such as Solon in Athens, Lycurgus in Sparta, and Romulus and Numa in Rome, Venice was founded by groups of unidentified refugees and ruled by committees outside the control of single individuals. Contarini emphasized that in Venice "there are to be found few monuments to our ancestors, though at home and abroad they achieved many glorious things to the advantage of their homeland. There are no tombs, no statues, no naval spoils, no enemy flags, after so many great battles."[39] In such a political climate, Venetians liked to believe, patricians naturally inclined away from excessive ambition, factional maneuvering, and corruption.

Of course the realities of Venetian politics were often the inverse of the myth – politicians jockeyed for influence, power, and the pursuit of factional advantage as openly in Venice as in Florence, if not more so, and in general, public life was violent.[40] As we have seen in princely contexts such as monarchical Naples and ducal Milan, political turbulence, predatory neighbors, and challenges to fledgling dynasties produced a classicizing political language that stressed the order, harmony, and cultural and social benevolence of the regimes in power. In republican contexts, which by definition implied more political instability and more challenges to those in power by those excluded from the regime, the need for stability, security, and predictability generated a yet more exaggerated vision of politics as rational, measured, and fundamentally selfless. Venetians were no more faithfully described by the myth than Alfonso of Aragon by his humanist chancellors and advisors. But languages of politics and their contexts are always closely linked, and hence the myth of Venice and the vision of a grandly rational and ordered republic reveal both the priorities Venetian politicians aspired to and more precisely still the kinds of conditions and values they felt conferred legitimacy.

[39] Finlay (1980) 35.   [40] On Venice, see *ibid.* 197–221; and Ruggiero (1980).

Florence

Like Venice, republican Florence consisted of a series of councils. At the apex sat the *Signoria*, an executive council of eight elected *Priori* [priors] drawn from the city's four neighborhoods (San Giovanni, Santa Croce, Santa Maria Novella, and Santo Spirito), presided over by a ninth formal figurehead, the *Gonfaloniere di Giustizia* [the standard-bearer of justice]. The priors were formally advised by two councils, the twelve *Buonomini* [good men; made up of elder members of the community] and the sixteen *Gonfalonieri* [standard-bearers; four for each neighborhood], and informally advised by committees formed of ex-priors, usually distinguished senior politicians. War and wartime diplomacy were administered by a separate council, the *Dieci della Guerra* [Ten of War], while the prosecution of crime and keeping of the peace were entrusted to the *Otto di Guardia e Balìa* [Eight of Public Safety]. Service varied from two months (*Signoria* and *Otto di Guardia*), to three (*Buonomini*), four (*Gonfalonieri*), or six months (*Dieci della Guerra*, though in their case sometimes extended to a full year). The right to full citizenship and active political participation was limited to members of the city's guilds, the merchant, industrial, and artisanal core of the city. Membership in the guilds, however, was not circumscribed and hence political life in Florence was considerably more dynamic and socially fluid than in Venice. In Venice, politics often took the form of struggles within the patriciate whereas in Florence politics often became a competition between various groups and classes for political power and control of the government itself.

The political culture of Renaissance Florence underwent three discrete stages. During the late thirteenth and fourteenth centuries, the Florentine government was dominated by a corporate, guild-based republicanism that was relatively inclusive of the city's various social groups. Consistent with patterns across the peninsula, the late fourteenth and fifteenth centuries witnessed a sharp turn away from the broad-based regimes of the Middle Ages towards an aristocratic and oligarchic concentration of power around wealthy elites. In Florence, this process began in earnest after the suppression of the Ciompi, a wool-workers' revolt in 1378 that briefly and radically enlarged the social composition of the Florentine government. From 1380 to 1530, an oligarchic elite, after 1534 led by the Medici family, held sway over Florentine politics. The Medici-dominated oligarchy faced several challenges to their rule, most of them unsuccessful, though the family was expelled from the city in 1494 and a more inclusive popular republicanism championed by the charismatic friar Girolamo Savonarola briefly prevailed until 1498. After 1530 and the final republican uprising, the Medici returned to the city as formal princes, establishing themselves as dukes and transforming republican traditions into a ducal court culture.[41]

Humanism became the dominant voice of Florentine republican culture in tandem with the consolidation of power by the city's oligarchic elite. Although in intellectual terms, Florentine humanism transcended its political context, becoming a sophisticated philological and philosophical movement in its own right, in political terms its vision of politics implicitly championed the recent triumph of the elite families over the guild republic, providing the vocabulary and axioms of their ideology.

This was in part a natural consequence of humanist intellectual priorities. Sustained study of classical languages and engagement with classical texts required wealthy patrons who valued those pursuits and were willing to pay for them – far more likely to be found among the city's aristocratic houses than within the city's industrial guild community – and as a result humanists ensured that their pursuits met the needs of their patrons. But the political content of Florentine humanism was also in part an inevitable result of the connection, as elsewhere, between the movement and the chancery. Throughout the fifteenth and early sixteenth centuries, Florence's chancellors were the city's leading humanists, and its diplomatic and ambassadorial functions made the chancery a lucrative and reliable source of employment for anyone with a humanist education. Since the purpose of the chancery in general was to provide ideological and intellectual support for the government's policies and decisions, it followed naturally that Florentine humanism, even outside of formal chancery activities, tended to provide ballast for elite dominance of the republic.

Like their counterparts in ducal Milan and monarchical Naples, Florentine humanists defended the legitimacy of their regimes in cultural terms. Humanist praise of Florentine cultural energy, unlike those in Milan and Naples, however, had a distinctly republican connotation

---

[41] On the persistence of republican traditions at the Medici court, however, see Jurdjevic (2008); and Baker (2013).

because one of the axioms of Florentine republicanism was that intellectual creativity flourished best under conditions of political liberty. Leonardo Bruni and Poggio Bracciolini articulated this conviction most clearly, drawing on classical historians to argue that Roman culture reached its apogee during the republic and began sharply to decline after the rise of the Caesars. They celebrated Florentine culture broadly conceived – its arts, letters, wealth, constitution, and tradition of liberty – but also in ways that typically dovetailed with elite rule. For example, fifteenth-century Florentine republicanism praised the active life, particularly in terms of the full political participation exercised by increasingly few citizens, and praised commercial wealth – the key component of the elite's power – as a central safeguard of the republic.

A particularly key text in the formation of Florentine republican ideology was the Florentine chancellor Leonardo Bruni's *Laudatio florentinae urbis* [Praise of the City of Florence, 1403–04, re-elaborated in 1430]. Bruni's text – in many ways as distant from Florentine political realities as the myth of Venetian harmony and concord – featured a binary vision of Florentine politics featuring a strong, central, sovereign state and disinterested public-servant citizens: "[h]ere are outstanding officials, outstanding magistrates, an outstanding judiciary, and outstanding social classes. These parts are so distinguished so as to serve the supreme power of Florence, just as the Roman tribunes used to serve the emperor."[42]

Just as fear of social and political discord in Venice led to a republicanism that stressed harmony and stability, so too in Florence did fear of factionalism and popular challenges to elite rule lead to the elevation of obedience and humility as quintessential political virtues. As a result, Bruni and other humanists such as Coluccio Salutati, Poggio Bracciolini, and Matteo Palmieri tended to portray the republic as an extended patrician family, in which women and children gratefully and passively accepted the benevolent rule and authority of fathers and senior males. Bruni wrote: "[t]herefore, under these magistracies this city has been governed with such diligence and competence that one could not find better discipline even in a household ruled by a solicitous father. As a result, no one has ever suffered any harm, and no one has ever had to alienate property except when he wanted to ..."[43] Bruni

---

[42] Bruni (1978) 141, 169.   [43] *Ibid.* 159.

made clear that Florentine paternal rule, although hierarchical, was nevertheless representative and consistent with the common good because "in Florence the majority view has always been identical with the best citizens."[44]

At the turn of the sixteenth century, however, Florentine political culture took a sharp turn away from the classicizing aesthetics of order, symmetry, and concord that prevailed elsewhere, and here Florentine thought constituted a striking, original, and innovative exception. The two most profound political thinkers of the sixteenth century, Machiavelli and Guicciardini, wrote against the backdrop of the invasion of Italy in 1494, in which Florence effectively became a powerless pawn in the violent battle for supremacy in Italy between the Germanic Hapsburg and French Valois dynasties. In such a desperate context, both thinkers recognized the need for a political theory that directly engaged the problems of politics as actually conducted, rather than hoping to influence political actors through visions of ideal political culture. And both thinkers' most sustained works of political analysis were republican. Guicciardini shared the elitism of earlier humanist republicanism, anchoring his blueprint for the city in an aristocratic and oligarchic senate composed of the city's eldest families, balanced – but crucially, not ruled – by a quasi-princely figure at the apex and a representative popular council underneath.

Machiavelli's republicanism was more radical. He rejected outright the widespread Renaissance assumption that individuals were capable of improvement and perfection and made that rejection the centerpiece of his political theory. In *Il principe* [The Prince] and *I discorsi* [The Discourses], his formal analyses of – respectively – princely and republican governments, Machiavelli accepted that conflict was an inevitable and permanent feature of political life. As a result, wise rulers should attempt to control, manage, and direct that conflict rather than attempt the utopian task of eradicating the conditions that generated it. He further deviated from the widespread elitist pattern of fifteenth-century political culture by squarely locating the strength and stability of regimes, princely and republican, in the people rather than the aristocracy. He argued that wise rulers, whether princes or republican leaders, should ally with the people, whose political ambitions were limited,

---

[44] *Ibid.* 158.

to offset the power of aristocracy, whose traditions of pre-eminence and wealth naturally inclined them to seize power and establish a tyrannical oligarchy. Implicit in that specific recommendation was his larger and more shocking conviction that, contrary to the preceding two centuries' insistence on concord and harmony, political conflict in the right circumstances could be beneficial to a regime. Throughout the *Discorsi*, Machiavelli argued that Roman class conflict between senators and plebeians, because channeled in political and institutional directions, became the crucial ingredient in the dynamism and martial power of Rome.

What should we conclude about the modernity – or in less loaded terms, the legacy and impact – of Renaissance political cultures?

Any response to this question must stress the plurality of ideas and contexts in these cultures. The city–states of the Renaissance are singularly resistant to generalization. However much the general cultures of France, England, and Spain may have differed, their political cultures had major features in common – they all more or less adhered to the feudal system, had monarchs at the apex of government, and believed themselves to belong to a universal Christian political community. As we have seen, there was little such uniformity in Italy: some states were monarchies and others fledgling princely states, neither with established claims to rule nor traditions of rule that dated back further than a few generations, while other regimes were self-governing republics with considerable variation in social composition. Renaissance political thought tended to displace discussion of the timeless and transcendent aspects of politics with socially and temporally contextual analyses – to take the most extreme example, a sacred principle of the Venetian self-image was precisely that it applied only to them and existed nowhere else in Europe. Hence, the local variation in Renaissance political culture was at least as significant, if not more so, than the principles and themes that tended to prevail across the political spectrum, one of the reasons the period has proved so consistently fascinating for historians of political thought.

In terms of the common themes and developments, however, Burckhardt may have been right: the most distinctive and influential features of Renaissance political culture were related to the relative newness of Renaissance regimes, their instability and consequent anxiety, and their temporal fragility. The Renaissance city–states were an exceptionally successful example of the power of culture – often "invented" – to lend ballast to new regimes, to mask political tensions, and to privilege particular political principles without raising divisive, indeed often explosive, constitutional questions outright. And more particularly, the Renaissance city–states showed how influentially classical culture could be brought to bear on contemporary political arenas. The language of civism and education in classical languages that until recently prevailed in the Western world were a direct by-product of that success. Political insecurity of course had a dark side, and the Renaissance city–states also provided a precedent and model for the intrusive modern state, as eager to monitor the thought and beliefs as well as the actions of its citizens.[45]

But in the broadest terms, the significance of Renaissance political culture lay in transmitting to Europe new choices in political ideology and vocabulary, alternative "visions," to use Quentin Skinner's image, of political community and legitimacy.[46] The European seventeenth century was also a notably volatile and violent period convulsed by civil and religious wars, and by regicide that inspired a longing for harmony, symmetry, and order similar to that of the Renaissance. And although the solutions – ideal and practical – in post-Reformation Europe differed from those of the Renaissance, its influence periodically resurfaced and often did so during moments of intense political and ideological conflict. The mercenary-turned-prince Albrecht von Wallenstein, for example, who for a time was the key arbiter of the religious question during the Thirty Years War (1618–48), was a self-styled Renaissance prince who projected his sudden rise to authority in European affairs as the product not of blood, but of exceptional individual virtue. For radical republicans such as Oliver Cromwell and James Harrington in England, Italy's republican city–states provided ideological inspiration as well as the power of historical precedent for the overthrow of monarchy. In Switzerland and France in the late seventeenth and eighteenth centuries, thinkers like Rousseau began to develop a systematic republican alternative to the oldest and strongest monarchical state in Europe, and they did so with their eyes squarely fixed on Florence and Venice, with Machiavelli as their guide. All such developments required ideological and historical counter-arguments to the political claims upon which traditional monarchical and aristocratic authority rested, and Renaissance political culture furnished excellent examples of both.

[45] Zorzi, A. (1988); and Rocke (1996).   [46] Skinner (2002) vol. 2, x–xi.

15

Economies

As events in recent years remind us, we live in an increasingly international world. Dense and growing networks of economic exchange, political interactions, and cultural influences link us to people and events in faraway places. We may not know their names or very much about their cultures and societies, yet they have the ability to change our lives in fundamental ways. In this environment, consumerism has paradoxically become a way to embrace globalism as well as to seek protection from it. Some consumers see shopping as a way to connect with people in distant lands and to improve standards of living throughout the world. Others see it as a means to fulfill a patriotic duty by shunning foreign products and thereby increase the demand for domestic goods. While both approaches are likely to have less impact than their adherents believe because of our limited ability to affect internal conditions in distant lands and because of the overwhelming internationalization of production at all levels, both attitudes reflect a heightened awareness of the importance of consumerism in modern society and the making of the modern world.

Not surprisingly, the works of scholars of the Renaissance, with their concerns about consumerism and the place of Renaissance Italy in the larger world, reflect this environment. In the last decade or so, we have seen a spate of books and articles focusing on the relationship between the international world of trade in the Renaissance and the world of goods and consumption practices on the one hand, and the emergence of a new world of art, ideas, attitudes, and values on the other. Some recent examples that explore the different sides of these relationships are Richard Goldthwaite's *Wealth and the Demand for Art in Italy: 1300–1600*, Lisa Jardine's *Worldly Goods: A New History of the Renaissance*, Rosamond

E. Mack's *Bazaar to Piazza: Islamic Trade and Italian Art, 1300–1600*, Jerry Brotton's *The Renaissance Bazaar: From the Silk Road to Michaelangelo*, Evelyn Welch's *Shopping in the Renaissance: Consumer Cultures in Italy, 1400–1600*, and Paola Lanaro's *At the Centre of the Old World: Trade and Manufacturing in Venice and the Venetian Mainland, 1400–1800*.[1]

Among these books, only the first and last are by economic historians. Yet all the others, written by art historians and literary scholars, also begin from the mostly implicit premise that the structure of the economy and economic activities not only impacted the material culture of Renaissance Italy and affected the world of goods, from high art to everyday objects, but also affected the attitudes and values of the consumers who commissioned them, purchased them, used them, traded them, and discarded them. While these authors differ in their judgments about the degree of change that took place in consumption patterns, what these patterns reveal about consumers, and how they relate to the emergence of modern consumer societies, all believe that the important qualitative changes that took place in the material life of people in Renaissance Italy, in their attitudes and values, and in how these were expressed in the realm of high culture and everyday life, were related in fundamental ways to changes in economic life and economic structures.[2]

By linking the economic world to the world of high culture and broader cultural attitudes,[3] scholars have returned in some ways to connections first raised half a century ago by Robert Lopez in a lecture delivered at a symposium on the Renaissance held at the Metropolitan Museum of Art and subsequently expanded several times for publication.[4] Lopez, whose ideas developed in the aftermath of the Great Depression of the 1930s, asserted that after a period of prosperity and economic growth up to the middle of the fourteenth century, Italy entered a long period of economic depression and stagnation, both in

---

[1] Goldthwaite (1993); Jardine (1996); R. E. Mack (2001); Brotton (2002); Welch (2005); and Lanaro (2006).

[2] Welch, for example, questions Goldthwaite's suggestion that the "Renaissance consumer revolution" prefigured consumer developments in eighteenth-century London or Paris; see Jardine (1996) 14.

[3] By cultural attitudes I refer here rather deliberately but loosely to the term *mentalités* used by historians of the Annales school, though one needs to be aware of the problematics of the term; see Hunt (1986).

[4] See R. S. Lopez (1953) for the full version of his initial reflections on the matter; and R. S. Lopez/Miskimin (1962) for his final revision.

overall and in per capita trends, that led the wealthy elites of Renaissance Italy to invest in art.[5] Their investments in culture, he claimed, stemmed directly from the lack of opportunities for successful investments in conventional economic actitivies. In short, the cultural Renaissance was the product of a downturn in the economy that lasted well over a century.

Yet while the scholars of consumer cultures implicitly share with Lopez a sense that the economic and cultural worlds are linked, the linkages they reveal through the goods and credit traded and the social groups involved in trading activities run in the opposite direction from what Lopez posited in his depression thesis. The world they bring to their readers is that of Renaisance Italy as a large bazaar, overflowing with a multiplicity of goods produced outside of Europe as well as within, and available for purchase, indeed, affordable for purchase by different classes of buyers who would not have been part of the market if they could not have purchased the goods offered. In this, they are – without necessarily realizing it – in agreement with the consensus that has emerged among economic historians of Renaissance Italy in the last several decades.

The depression thesis was challenged first in the 1960s by Carlo Cipolla, one of the great economic historians of Italy.[6] While he agreed with Lopez that the volume of overall economic activity declined, that the economy of Italian states declined relative to those of northern Europe, that the woolen cloth industry, which was the single most important industry in the late Middle Ages, contracted in many cities, and that the average size of Italian banking firms shrank, the decline, he argued, was not absolute since it was lower than the drop in population stemming from the 1348 Black Death and subsequent waves of plague. On a per capita basis, therefore, the people of Renaissance Italy had a higher standard of living than their predecessors because there were fewer people with whom they had to share the material wealth left by previous generations, because the survivors could command higher wages, and because the agricultural economy needed to support urban

---

[5] R. S. Lopez (1953) 423, 425: "It seems necessary to conclude that the per capita volume of international trade suffered a substantial decline during the first seventy years of the *Quattrocento*. Further, it seems likely that the decline was general to Western Europe … Italy, the earliest and most brilliant center of the artistic Renaissance, felt the impact of the economic recession most heavily … [it] fell harder because it had climbed higher."

[6] R. S. Lopez/Miskimin (1962); R. S. Lopez (1964); Miskimin (1964); and Cipolla (1964).

life produced a larger surplus than before. The reason for the latter was that with a smaller population, marginal lands could be abandoned in favor of more productive areas and more consolidated agricultural holdings, thereby making agricultural production more efficient, increasing agricultural yields, reducing the price of foods, and releasing more disposable income for other purchases. With their new-found wealth, individuals could now buy better and more varied foods, clothing, furniture, and other products than they could have purchased before, thus supporting the diversification of the economy.

Cipolla was joined by Gino Luzzatto, another leading economic historian of Italy, who also conceded that Italy's place in the European economy changed during the Renaissance and that by the end of the sixteenth century it no longer enjoyed unrivalled primacy, but that "to use the word 'decline' in the further sense, of an absolute fall in the volume and value of production and exchange, would be wholly unjustified."[7] Losses in some areas, he argued, were more than made up for in others – new industries developed, manufacturing spread to different cities, new trade networks emerged, and banking recovered from its mid-fourteenth-century slump.

These were for many years among the few voices making such arguments. More common were lamentations about the recurrence and persistence of "crises" from the mid fourteenth to the mid seventeenth century, the "refeudalization" and "involution" of the Italian economy and Italy's "failed transition" to modern capitalism. The sense of stagnation and lost opportunities was summarized most tellingly in the theme of a conference, subsequently published as a book entitled *Failed Transitions to Modern Industrial Society: Renaissance Italy and Seventeenth-Century Holland*.[8] The views most commonly held in the 1960s and 1970s were encapsulated in Ruggiero Romano's *Tra due crisi: l'Italia del Rinascimento* and in his contribution to the massive *Storia d'Italia*, published by Einaudi. For Ruggiero, the central problem of the Italian economy was not that of quantitative decline, but of the failure of imagination and of nerve. Caught between crises, the elites of the peninsula, according to him, did not pursue those transformations that led the rest of Europe to modern capitalism. Instead, they became a

---

[7] Luzzatto (1961) 142; this argument was seconded in greater detail for Venice by Rapp (1976).

[8] Krantz/Hohenberg (1975).

parasitic class that blocked change. Aided by the techniques of commercial capitalism developed in the late Middle Ages and driven by the acquisitive and exploitative mentality of the counting house, they exploited those below them more ruthlessly than ever while abandoning commerce, banking, and manufacturing in favor of the purchase of feudal rights and government offices, speculation in government bonds, and the exploitation of peasants. The Italian Renaissance, Ruggiero believed, was marked by "refeudalization," an anomalous and negative break from the path towards modernization that put Italy on a different trajectory from that of northern Europe – a trajectory from which it would not begin to emerge until the eighteenth century and whose consequences it would take even longer to shed.[9] Across the English Channel, Philip Jones agreed with this view. In a famous essay, "The Legend of the Bourgeoisie," he wrote that "in its march toward capitalism, Italy either stopped in mid-road or regressed toward feudal capitalism."[10]

In recent decades, the tide has turned away from these debates. The concept of "refeudalization" has been discredited.[11] Most economic historians have come to agree with the view that there was, in fact, no depression in the Renaissance, and that the period was marked by greater continuity with the past and the present, as well as by greater innovation, linking it more closely to a similarly resourceful past and future than was possible with the depression thesis. This conception of the Renaissance has had several consequences. It has led to the extension of the term "Renaissance" to a much longer period, lasting from about 1300 to about 1600–30, which may not correspond to the term as used in political or cultural history, thus adding to the difficulties of periodization that have always bedeviled the "Renaissance." It has also meant discarding the terms "crisis" and "depression" for the whole period, and to their application, if at all, to smaller, transitory events and to trends with limited repercussions.[12]

Economic historians have arrived at these views through work on detailed aspects of the economy, ranging from the outlook and practices of different types of merchants, to changes in particular industries and agriculture, to fiscal policies and their effects, rather than through efforts to test the depression thesis itself. In some ways this makes the

---

[9] Romano (1971) and (1974).   [10] Jones (1978) 363.
[11] See, for example, Malanima (1980).   [12] Franceschi (2004) 125; and Alfari (2013).

case for overarching prosperity stronger because it is built on many foundations. This approach also has the advantage of enriching our understanding of the economies of Renaissance Italy and gives us a better sense of their complexities. Scholars now know more about regional and temporal economic differences and their interactions; they have a better understanding of the variety of technical innovations that took place and the limits that economic forces put on their spread; and they know more about the distribution of wealth among different segments of society and the opportunities and limits this put on economic growth.

Evidence of what has been gained can be seen most clearly in the chapters on economic matters in the recent multi-volume work, *Il Rinascimento italiano e l'Europa*. Overseen by two economic historians, and a multidisciplinary committee of scholars, this series, which is likely to have an important influence on the historiography of the Renaissance for many years to come, eschews an encyclopedic and synthetic approach in favor of overlapping essays on techniques of production, commerce, mercantile cultures, and, among other topics, changes in consumption habits. These essays explore the Renaissance in all its richness and contradictions, revealing a period of economic vitality and innovation that lasted from the early fourteenth to the seventeenth century despite the occasional downturns that one would expect in any economy over such a long stretch.[13]

Turning then to a few of these topics to see what has changed in the recent decades of economic history, let us begin by looking at studies that touch on the values, attitudes, and practices of Italian merchants. In the 1950s and 1960s Armando Sapori charged that the generous, courageous, visionary, educated, and heroic merchants of the Middle Ages, who "brought civilization everywhere and opened the way to future progress," were followed by miserly, quarrelsome, small-minded, and backwards-looking merchants who dominated the economy of the Renaissance and contributed to its problems.[14] For Sapori, the wealthy

---

[13] Fontana/Molà (2005–10); this broad periodization emerges clearly in the volumes dealing with history and historiography – Fantoni (2005); production and techniques – Braunstein and Molà (2007); and commerce and mercantile culture – Franceschi *et al.* (2007). Goldthwaite (1989) had earlier noted the broader arc of the Renaissance for economic history and the difficulties of fitting it into periodizations for other aspects of history. For an earlier, more limited chronology – 1400–1570 – see Tenenti (1988); and for an extended treatment, Ferguson (1963) 55–71.

[14] Sapori (1955) vol. 1, 619–52, especially, 643–46; (1955) vol. 3, 557–78; and (1970) 38.

merchant of Prato, Francesco di Marco Datini, exemplified the new type. This depiction was vigorously challenged at the time by Federico Melis, whose scholarship centered on using the voluminous Datini archives to show the innovative qualities of Renaissance business techniques and the man whose businesses used many of them.[15] Fortunately, non-specialists could steer clear of Sapori's overly critical portrayal and Melis' excessively complimentary one by turning to other sources. Many were introduced to the world of Renaissance merchants by Iris Origo's engaging book, *The Merchant of Prato: Francesco di Marco Datini, 1335–1410*, and by Frederic Lane's, *Andrea Barbarigo, Merchant of Venice, 1418–1449*.[16] Together, these books – one written by a gifted writer and amateur historian, and the other by one of the leading economic historians of his time – enable us to obtain both a glimpse and a healthy but realistic respect for how individual entrepreneurs who operated at the highest levels of the international economy met the risks that came their way, seized new opportunities when they could, diversified their portfolios to reduce risks, and innovated business practices. Though written half a century ago, both books are still classics and among the best introductions to the subject, particularly when supplemented by some of the essays on mercantile practices and attitudes written by Frederic Lane and Raymond de Roover. Lane's work on usury and its effects on the economic thought and practices of Renaissance merchants, and De Roover's work on the emergence and evolution of the bill of exchange as a credit instrument as well as his extended work on the risk-minimizing organization of the Medici bank, are especially helpful for tracing the introduction of economic innovations in the Renaissance and what they tell us about the mentalities of international merchants and bankers.[17]

More recently, the works of two other authors have extended our views about the sources and diffusion of innovative practices in the mercantile economy. The first is Paul Marshall's study of the small and local merchants of Prato. Looking at the account books of artisans and shopkeepers, ranging from cheesemakers to paper manufacturers,

---

[15] Melis (1962).

[16] Lane (1944); and Origo (1957). Melis savaged Origo's book in a lengthy review, which Robert Lopez characterized as "merciless but not unwarranted" – see Melis (1959); and R. S. Lopez (1961).

[17] De Roover (1963) 108–41 and (1974); and Lane (1966). On the bill of exchange, also see Mueller (1997).

Marshall reveals the very deep roots that the capitalist economy had sprouted by the last half of the fourteenth and first decade of the fifteenth century. The widespread use of account books, the extension of credit, the existence of commercial trust reinforced by social networks, the diversification strategies adopted to limit liability, and the willingness to take risks by contravening religious prohibitions against certain commercial practices, all suggest that the spread of capitalism did not necessarily depend on or flow exclusively from large international firms.[18]

Using a very different approach, John Padgett arrived at similar conclusions. His protagonists, however, are not small artisans and shopkeepers but small bankers from the middle strata of society. Padgett's study of "the invention" of a new form of economic organization and its relationship to the transformation of the elite in Renaissance Florence argues that in the late fourteenth century, Florentines "invented" a new form of business organization that reduced the risks of doing business, vastly expanded the possible reach of individual organizations, and in the end transformed the political elites of Florence. This new business organization consisted of a set of legally autonomous companies linked either through one entrepreneur or a small number of partners who had a financial interest in all of them. In effect, this new partnership system, which enlarged the scope of business while limiting risk, was what De Roover called a holding company. It was used by the Datini and the Medici banks and by many others as it spread from Florence to other parts of Tuscany and beyond. The impetus for this system, according to Padgett, came from the small domestic bankers in the *arte del cambio* [the Money-Changing Guild, one of the seven principal professional guilds in Florence] who in the aftermath of the Ciompi revolt of 1378 found themselves in a strengthened position. Whether scholars in the long run will accept the more controversial aspects of this thesis regarding the social origins and the transformative effects of this partnership system, both for the economy and for the political structure of Florence, remains to be seen.[19] There is no doubt, however, that this form of organization spread rapidly among important business firms in the late fourteenth

---

[18] Marshall (1999).
[19] Padgett (2001), including the critical commentary of G. Besharof and A. Greif; and Padgett/McLean (2006).

and early fifteenth centuries and that until the greater spread of *accomandita* [limited liability partnerships] in the sixteenth century remained a prevalent method to expand the capital available to them while limiting their risk.[20]

Innovations such as those noted above, flexibility in the face of changing economic conditions, and relentless entrepreneurship enabled Italians to dominate international commerce and banking from the fourteenth to the end of the sixteenth century. While there was fierce competition for being in the top rank, the leading competitors taking turns from the fourteenth to the end of the sixteenth centuries were Genoa, Venice, Florence, and Milan. Ships laden with precious cargoes of luxury goods and spices from the Middle East and Asia as well as raw materials from other parts of Europe stopped in at the ports of the first two cities, where they were unloaded for local sale or further distribution elsewhere in Italy. Caravans of goods made in Florence, Milan, and other cities made their way through overland routes or to the coasts for export to the rest of the world. Money and credit from Italian bankers fueled these transactions as well as others, creating a complex network that tied many Italian towns and their hinterlands to the rest of Europe and the world.[21]

Yet despite this abundance of trade, for which there is a great deal of evidence,[22] one of the questions that has arisen is whether the size and prosperity of the international market was limited, indeed, seriously reduced by a bullion scarcity that gripped all of Europe, including Italy, from the 1370s to the 1470s, when the resurgence of German silver mines temporarily eased the shortage. The cause given for this dearth – especially severe, it has been claimed, in 1395–1415 and 1457–64 – was that bullion was being siphoned to the Levant because European products were not in sufficient demand to meet the sophisticated consumer tastes of the Levantine public. The luxury goods that Europeans wished to purchase from the Levant, therefore, would have been paid for

[20] Legislation on *accomandita* began in 1408, but its greatest use occurred in the sixteenth century; for the debate about *accomandita* and the possibility that it may have had different uses over several centuries, see Carmona (1964); Malanima (1982a) 132–37; and Melis (1991) 170–78.

[21] Superb recent books that highlight the embeddedness of the economies of Italian cities in the international market and their innovative responses to changing conditions are Lanaro (2006); and Goldthwaite (2009).

[22] On the extent of international trade in specific major cities, see Heers (1961); Lane (1973); Sella (1979); Mainoni (1982); and Goldthwaite (2009).

primarily through coins and bullion, and these, it has been thought, were increasingly in short supply both because of the imbalance of trade and because European mines were depleted, given the level of mining technology available at the time.[23] This thesis has come under critical scrutiny in recent years on several grounds, including the difficulties of calculating the money supply from scarce mint data, determining coin depletions due to wear and accidental losses, and taking sufficient account of the use of credit mechanisms. Most importantly, it has been criticized from the point of view of economic theory on the grounds that Europe could not have suffered a balance-of-payments deficit and a bullion shortage simultaneously.[24] The scarcity, if any, might well have been less severe in Italy because of the uneven integration of European markets, the greater use of credit in Italy than elsewhere, and the fact that so much of Europe's gold and silver was funneled through the hands of Italian merchants and bankers. Gold coins, for example, seem to have been abundant in fifteenth-century Florence.[25] Some evidence points to short-term shortages of bullion due to government actions rather than to its flow outside of Europe. Monetary policy is difficult enough to calibrate well in our own day, and at times Renaissance governments, even when trying to act prudently, inadvertently contributed to hoarding or to the flight of coins and bullion to other European cities.[26] Finally, Italian sources, including those of convents – where large quantities of silver and gold thread were made – reveal that fourteenth- and fifteenth-century fashions in clothing made abundant and increasingly extravagant use of gold and silver – big silver buckles, gold buttons, silver and gold threads woven into silk, and so on.[27] The growing taste for luxury goods among Italian consumers may have contributed to the scarcity of bullion in other parts of Europe.

What Italians wore, how they decorated their homes, and what they purchased raises the question of what was produced in Renaissance Italy. Italian Renaissance elites made most of their wealth from international trade and banking, but they and others further down the

---

[23] Day (1978); and Spufford (1988).
[24] Sussman (1998); and Epstein (2000) who supports Sussman's critique.
[25] Goldthwaite, cited in Munro (1983).
[26] For examples, see the accessible introductions to monetary history by Cipolla (1982) and (1989); in addition, see Lane/Mueller (1985) and Mueller (1997) 288–340, excellent references for very complex subjects, but not for the faint-hearted.
[27] Frick (2002); Killerby (2002); Stuard (2006); and Strocchia (2009) 111–51.

social hierarchy also invested in manufacturing and artisanal work, a significant part of the economy that had both cultural and economic repercussions. In the late Middle Ages, the economies of many Italian cities, favored by their geographic position, depended primarily on international trade and banking. While most had some small-scale manufacturing activities and were regional economic hubs, few were major manufacturing centers. Milan, to be sure, was an important center for metallurgy and textiles, Lucca had a virtual monopoly on the production of silk cloth, and Florence, which had a large woolen cloth industry, focused much of its effort on the high-quality refinishing of cloth produced in England rather than locally. But after the demographhic and social upheavals of the mid fourteenth century, manufacturing spread to many more centers, some even in rural areas; products in previously established industries became more specialized and diversified so as to appeal to different types of customers, new products were introduced, and technical innovations improved their quality while making them more affordable. The textile industries, which were the largest in pre-modern Europe, are a case in point, as can be observed from changes in the production of all types of cloth – cotton, wool, and silk, but particularly the latter two – from the second half of the fourteenth through the sixteenth century.[28]

In response to changed market conditions after the later fourteenth century, the woolen cloth industry in Italy became more distinctively bifurcated. There were two markets: one for cheap, rough cloths, often produced in small towns and rural villages, and destined for purchase by peasants and the urban poor; the other for medium- and high-quality cloths produced for the middle and upper classes of Italy, other parts of Europe, and the Middle East. Woolen cloth production for this second market grew in certain cities, such as Venice, where industry had previously been subordinate to commerce; it grew in other cities, such as Milan, where woolen cloth production had been significant for centuries;[29] it spread as an export industry in Lucca, Vicenza, Verona,

---

[28] For a summary of the textile sector in these centuries and a useful bibliography, see Dini (1990). Recent work has also emphasized the importance of cotton cloth for the spread of rural industry, the consumption patterns of less affluent classes, and the links of Italian cotton cloth production to international trade with Europe, South East Asia, and the New World via the import of raw cotton and the export of finished cloths; see Mazzaoui (2009).

[29] Pullan (1968); Mainoni (1983) vol. 2, 575–84; and Cozzi/Knapton (1986).

Padua, and other parts of the Veneto; and it even developed in the small towns of Umbria and the Marche, such as Norcia, which had previously produced only rough peasant cloths for local consumption. To be sure, because of keener competition after the population decline of the mid fourteenth century, production collapsed in some places, most notably perhaps in Siena, which had already experienced earlier difficulties because of water shortages. The industry also shrank in absolute numbers in Florence, where Florentines responded to the changed market conditions by abandoning the refinishing of English cloths and taking up instead the production of high-end luxury cloths made from the finest English wool. For several decades these cloths were highly successful in international markets, meeting the European elite's demand for luxury products. But when conditions for the industry changed yet again because of newly imposed barriers to obtaining raw materials and accessing markets in England and Flanders, Florentine entrepreneurs changed course again. With wool imported from Spain and the Abruzzo, they began to produce lighter cloths of medium quality and price that found a ready market among middle-class buyers, primarily in the Levant but also elsewhere in Europe until the third quarter of the sixteenth century. In short, the ability to understand and find new markets as well as to adapt to and shape demand helped the Florentine woolen cloth industry remain a major player in international markets throughout the Renaissance. In their assessments of the Florentine and other Italian woolen cloth industries scholars in recent decades have emphasized that these kinds of adaptive transformations were the key to their survival.[30]

The Italian silk industry faced fewer challenges during the period. With greater wealth in the hands of the upper strata of society and with no competition yet from other European sources, Italian producers had an uncontested field for the expansion of the industry. Indeed, its growth made up for losses that occurred in the woolen cloth industry. Silk cloth production grew significantly in many cities, but especially in Florence, Genoa, Lucca, Milan, Venice, and Naples. Because of the high level of skill needed to make these cloths and the high cost of materials used – not just silk but also silver and gold threads, expensive dyes, and so on – this was very much an urban-based industry. By the 1560s the

---

[30] The Florentine woolen cloth industry in particular has been the subject of much debate; see the excellent studies by Hoshino (1980) and (1983); and Franceschi (1993).

silk industry employed around 20,000 full- and part-time workers in Milan and even more in Venice, while a few decades later, it accounted for the employment of 20,000 people in Florence and 25,000 in Bologna.[31] Silk cloth, even more than woolens, seemed to release the potential for the creative adaptations of producers to rapidly changing fashions. Satins and damasks, velvets and tabbies, embroidered with precious metals or not, woven with favorite designs, silk was made into ribbons and stockings, caps, belts, and gowns, furniture covers, and ornamental banners. Possible designs, textures, and uses were endless, and Italian producers were eager to oblige. Indeed, they extended the market by introducing silk cloths that mixed high-quality silk thread with waste thread and other products such as flax, wool, and cotton into the weave so as to make these cloths more affordable to less wealthy consumers. Before long, different cities also specialized in different types of silk cloths for different sectors of the market. Contemporary observers commented on these phenomena at times with admiration but sometimes with censure as they tried to regulate the production and uses of silk cloth in vain efforts to maintain easily discernible social hierarchies.[32]

Historians have tended to concentrate on textiles in pre-modern societies because they were, after all, the most important industries. But one of the distinguishing characteristics of the Italian economy in the Renaissance was the spread and evolution of other industrial activities which were stimulated by and in turn reinforced the emergence of a consumer-oriented society. As recent work has shown, one of those industries was glassmaking, and it became a major industry in Renaissance Venice because of the growing demand for moderately priced luxury goods. Renaissance consumers prized the beauty of glass, its ability to imitate more costly materials, the skill of artisans who made it into objects of beauty, and the multiple forms and uses of such objects. Glassmaking is an ancient art, so the Venetians were not the only or the first glassmakers in Italy, but by means of technological and organizational innovations they refined its manufacture into a high art while allowing its producers to make an increasing quantity of objects

[31] Molà (2000) 16, which includes an extensive bibliography, is an excellent source of information on the silk industry not just in Venice but in other areas as well; see also Goodman (1983) vol.1, 327–41; Franceschi (1995); and Molà et al. (2000).
[32] Molà (2000) 89–106.

for a growing market that reached further down the socio-economic scale, so that by the late eighteenth century production was twice what it had been in the late sixteenth century, when historians until recently thought the industry had reached its height.[33]

From the point of view of economic history, the importance of glassmaking is not confined to its role as a high-end consumer product. The industry had strong already well-established ties to other economic activities – the importation of soda-rich ash from the Levant, the transportation of wood for furnaces, and the manufacture of molds; but it was also forward-looking, and among its most important Renaissance innovations would be the manufacture of eyeglasses. Recent scholarship shows that this thirteenth-century invention was produced in rather large quantities by the fifteenth century, when Florence became a center of the industry, making them in sufficient quantity to meet local as well as foreign demand. Because they were fairly inexpensive, costing about the same as the daily wage of an unskilled worker, eyeglasses became ubiquitous and undoubtedly contributed to the increased production of the Renaissance economy by extending the working life of its participants.[34]

Two other interrelated industries that deserve attention are paper manufacturing and printing. The importance of the former for the development of the latter has been noted by most historians of printing, and it goes without saying that both were crucial for Renaissance education and the diffusion of writing in print. Papermaking was introduced into Italy in the last half of the thirteenth century and spread to Fabriano, Colle Val d'Elsa, Pescia, Genoa, and Verona. More often than not, because of its need for large buildings and a good supply of clean running water, the industry was located in medium or smaller towns. But it also flourished best when these locations were not too far from large cities such as Venice, which became important sites for the printing industry after the mid fifteenth century.[35]

The establishment of papermaking in smaller regional centers raises an important issue for economic historians of Renaissance Italy: the creation and evolution of economic regions. Papermaking was not, of

---

[33] McCray (1999); and Trivellato (2006) 165.
[34] In the 1460s, when an unskilled construction worker could expect to make about 8.5 soldi daily, a cheap pair of eyeglasses cost about 6.8 soldi; see Ilardi (2007) 98.
[35] Cavaciocchi (1992).

course, the only economic activity to develop a symbiotic relationship with related activities in large cities. The silk cloth industry, a quintessentially urban activity, also created important linkages to rural areas. By the sixteenth century, large parts of the Italian countryside saw the cultivation of mulberry trees whose leaves were used to feed the silkworms that produced thread for the urban industry. By means of sericulture, which was largely carried out by women and children who could not find sufficient employment in other agricultural tasks, peasant families could now reap additional income.[36] In addition, by the seventeenth century, the countryside would also see the introduction of large water-powered silk-throwing mills that in the preindustrial era revolutionized the production of silk, first in Italy and then in other parts of Europe.[37]

Among the questions that emerge from recent studies of such complementary activities is to what extent did they represent natural economic relationships? Or were they, instead, the result of protectionist policies of centralized governments? And, regardless of the answers to the previous questions, did they contribute to or stifle economic growth? The political/economic regions that emerged in the Renaissance were larger than those of the late Middle Ages and they created opportunities for greater integration through the abolition of trade barriers, the improvement of transportation networks, and the emergence of greater competition that might spur efficiencies, the production of better products at lower prices, and hence an improvement in the region's competitive position vis-à-vis other regions of the Italian peninsula or beyond. Whether this actually occurred or not, or whether it occurred to a greater degree in some regions than in others, has been a matter of considerable debate in recent years. For Stefan Epstein, the most successful integration took place in two rather different economies, those of Sicily and Lombardy: in the former, Epstein claims that cities allied with the monarchy and helped to promote good government at the level of the central bureaucracy and in state finances; in the latter, because Milan was not sufficiently strong to subdue its regional rivals within the state, its "backwardness" resulted in the long run in a more pluralistic region that contributed to economic growth. In Tuscany, however, Florence subdued its rivals and there were no other urban powers to

---

[36] J. C. Brown (1982).   [37] Poni (1976).

check its vested political and economic interests; in Epstein's view, this dominant city was therefore free to exploit and limit the economic activities of its subject areas, thereby curbing long-term economic development.[38] A different and in some ways opposing view of the limits to the further economic development of Tuscany has been forwarded by Paolo Malanima, who argues that the structure of rural and urban sectors as well as that of the urban hierarchies had become so interwined and had adapted so closely to one another and to the economic system of Tuscany as a whole that they resulted in a path dependence that blocked receptiveness to new opportunities. The very adjustments that contributed to the successes of the fifteenth and sixteenth centuries became the source of problems in the seventeenth.[39] Yet a third view arises from the work of Elena Fasano Guarini, Giorgio Chittolini, Edoardo Grendi, and others on Italian state formation in the Middle Ages and the early modern period. Taking the microhistorical approach of N. B. Harte and K. G. Ponting in *Cloth and Clothing in Medieval Europe*, these historians come to the conclusion that the territorial states of premodern Italy consisted largely of clusters of overlapping and diverse centers of power and jurisdiction: the dominant city, regional towns, and rural communities in actual practice retained a great deal of autonomy. In the absence of strong central bureaucracies and effective enforcement mechanisms, these entitities jostled with each other in order to do what they pleased as often as possible. In this respect, Tuscany was no different from the other Italian states. Guarini *et al.* suggest that positing simple "center–periphery" dichotomies obscures rather than clarifies the realities on the ground. When trying to account for the decline of the woolen textile industry in a town like Prato in the Florentine state, for example, one must look first to the strictly economic disadvantages that such a town suffered when trying to compete on the international market rather than simply attributing the decline to Florentine legislation. And for every Prato there may have been a Padua, whose woolen textile industry grew just as that of Venice, which exercised dominion over Padua, declined.[40]

One last set of issues that has emerged in the economic literature about Renaissance Italy focuses on the distribution of wealth in society, which factors might have affected it, and whether when we are looking

---

[38] Epstein (1993) and (2000).   [39] Malanima (1982b).
[40] Guarini (2003) and (1986); and Demo (2006).

at the emergence of consumer society we are really talking about a very small proportion of the population. Unsurprisingly, accurate and comprehensive data are not available. Scholars sometimes cite the uneven distribution of wealth evident in various Renaissance fiscal surveys to make the point that wealth distribution was badly skewed. But we must remember that in all societies wealth distribution tends to be spread more inequitably than income and that the wealth declared in fiscal documents follows certain computational rules and permissible exclusions that render them imperfect reflections of reality. Hence when we learn from the Florentine *catasto* [fiscal record], for example, that the top 1% of households owned over 25% of both the declared gross wealth and the net taxable wealth of the city, that the bottom 14% had no declared wealth, or that an additional 16% had neither declared nor taxable wealth, we should not be surprised since these figures do not look very different from those in some of the most economically advanced modern societies. From the 1980s to the mid 1990s the richest 1% of Americans, for example, owned between 33% and 40% of the total wealth of the nation while the poorest 40% owned less than 1% and the figures since then have become even more lopsided.[41]

Such comparisons between very different economies and different fiscal regimes, however, do not get us any closer to understanding the living conditions of most people in Renaissance Italy. Of greater value are studies such as those conducted by Richard Goldthwaite, Charles de La Roncière, and Giuliano Pinto on wages and prices of grain as well as baskets of consumables. These show that workers from the mid fourteenth century to the end of the fifteenth were relatively well off compared to previous times, and that their conditions eroded in the sixteenth century as growth in population, a concomitant decline in wages, and rising prices caught workers in a vise.[42]

But we should also keep in mind that most people lived close to the margins of subsistence, even in the best of times. Several bad harvests, an epidemic that disrupted trade or food supplies, and warring armies could bring disaster very quickly.[43] Historians have demonstrated the frequency with which such catastrophic events punctuated the lives of

---

[41] Herlihy/Klapisch-Zuber (1985); the raw data are available online at http://www.stg. brown.edu/projects/catasto/overview.html; see also Goldthwaite (2009) 560–67.
[42] Goldthwaite (1980) 435–43 and (2009) 568–82; De la Roncière (1981); and Pinto (1981).
[43] Caferro (1998) and (2008).

people, particularly in the early part of the Renaissance. Disruptions such as these, rather than low living standards in ordinary times, may have been the fuel for some of the worker uprisings that occurred in Italy in the late fourteenth century. Having become accustomed to better food, better shelter, and occasionally having a bit of disposable income with which to buy extra clothing or a household item, some may have joined the revolts for fear of losing what had been gained.

In conclusion, we can point to the many aspects of the economic history of Renaissance Italy explored by historians in recent decades that have, among other things, enabled us to gain a keener understanding of the complex relationship between demographic and economic factors, including its effects on the standard of living; that have given us richer documentary evidence about the economic interactions among different regions of the Italian peninsula, particularly those between the south and the north; that have expanded our knowledge of trade relations between Italy, the Levant, and other parts of Europe; and that have given us a more nuanced sense of the connections between the patterns of production and consumption.[44] While there were many questions left to explore and many which we may never be able to answer, the scholarship of recent years shows that Italy had dynamic and vital economies that met difficult challenges creatively and in doing so contributed to the beginnings of modern consumer societies.

---

[44] Among the more interesting directions of scholarship in recent decades are efforts to explore the connections between northern and southern Italy as well as the non-Italian powers that influenced them, and the creation of new demographic databases to examine the resilience of Italian regional economies in the face of war, famine, and plague; see Abulafia (1977); Marino (1988); Epstein (1989); Calabria (1991); and Alfari (2013).

16

Social relations

Renaissance families were institutions that defied easy character-ization because they were continually influenced by the particular social, cultural, and geographic context in which they evolved. Uncovering the dynamic relationships between household organization and social strategies, between cherished ideals and local realities, and between gender norms and everyday life reveals that the meaning of family in this period varied between women and men, the poor and the wealthy. Privileging the male line, legal norms and cultural values accentuated the power of fathers and husbands while simultaneously reducing the rights of those persons in positions of legal dependency: daughters, wives, and widows. In order to remedy difficult socio-economic and demographic circumstances, or in order to consolidate wealth and attain power and status, individuals sorted out their rights and privileges, playing out their conflicts through the multifaceted relationships that women and men negotiated within and in relation to the family. The Renaissance family was a dynamic enterprise suspended between the complexities of shifting legal norms and practices.

Exploring the Renaissance family: sources and methodological frameworks

The women and men of Renaissance Italy were keenly aware of the crucial role that family played in their lives. As the primary unit of biological and social reproduction, the family provided for its members' material needs, supervised their morality, shaped their future and their identity, created memory, and ultimately preserved and perpetuated status and power. In an age of demographic disasters and economic instability Renaissance humanists, unsure about the survival of fathers and their ability to provide advice to future generations, wrote treatises about family life, household management, and marriage. Inspired by the classical tradition, they produced images of family and marriage which idealized familial relationships as the building block of concord between women and men, as necessary for the preservation of the bloodline, and as the utmost expression of domestic order but also of public harmony, the heart of "civilization."[1] Wealthy merchants, land-owners, and professionals as well as middling groups recorded their thoughts about the importance of marriage alliances for preserving property, maintaining status, increasing political influence, and assur-ing the continuity of their lineages in letters, account books, and family diaries or *ricordanze*, as the Florentines called them.[2] They had frequent recourse to notaries to seal matrimonial alliances, to select heirs, and to devolve property; they also appealed to civil and ecclesiastical courts to settle marital and family disputes. Municipal and centralized govern-ments, recognizing the significance of order and stability in family and state, drew up detailed legislation which protected family wealth, promoted matrimony, and imposed moral norms. The extensive private and public writing of the period has inspired several generations of Renaissance scholars to study family as a distinct field of inquiry. Drawing on the innovative techniques of historical demography and economic analysis, social anthropology, and historical sociology, as well as cultural theory and gender studies, these scholars have disclosed uncharted aspects of family life and have raised novel and important questions about family make-up, the role of marriage and dowry in women's and men's lives, and how kinship was constructed.

The family included but was not limited to the household, which consisted of the domestic residential group formed by all those who lived under the same roof. Cyclically this group could alternate between the smaller nuclear unit of parents and children and the extended group formed by elderly parents, married adult children and their offspring, and joint-fraternal families of brothers. Servants and appren-tices were also part of the household. The family, or *casa* as the

---

[1] Alberti (1969); and Barbaro (1978).
[2] Philips (1987); Brucker (1991); Branca/Murtha (1999); Ciappelli (2000); and Philip/Caferro (2001). Prior to 1500 Florentines produced most of the approximately 500 surviving *ricordanze*; few were produced or have survived in other Italian cities, and in the case of Venice only one remains, for which see Grubb (1994).

Florentines called it, comprised the kinship group which varied in its configuration according to how kinship was interpreted. Kinship ties were formed through the principle of descent, both agnate (through paternal ancestors) and cognate (via the maternal line). But while agnatic kinship was vertical and patrilineal, favoring the male line from fathers to sons, cognate kinship was horizontal and bilateral, and it included both women and men. The family could encompass individuals related by blood ties which included all lateral branches sharing a common surname or connected by a common ancestor, but it might also embrace individuals related by marriage.

The main tool of family organization was marriage. An economic and political contract as well as a social and public event, marriage was a complex phenomenon. In 1436, the humanist Leonardo Bruni praised marriage as "the fundamental union, which by multiplication makes the city [. . .]."[3] The result of careful calculations based on dowry practices and inheritance patterns, marriage aimed at protecting and reinforcing status and power through supporting the survival of family and community rather then the needs of the individuals involved. According to canon law, marriage was a sacrament that required only the consent of the couple to be wed, but senior members of the household – fathers or, in their absence, other male kin and sometimes mothers – normally made such calculations and rarely invited the participation of those most directly concerned, particularly among the upper classes. Affection and friendship as well as financial cooperation might develop between husbands and wives, but marriage choices did not depend on romantic love. The spiritual aspect of marriage emphasized by the Church did not diminish parental authority, but it did leave open the possibility for individuals to challenge that authority if they had been forced by their families to marry against their will.

The fragmented geography of the Italian peninsula combined with shifting population trends and economic developments to support a varied landscape of family and household configurations. The villages, towns, and cities of the Italian peninsula shared common traditions of law, language, religion, and customs, but the socio-economic systems of the Italian states differed in fundamental ways. In the center and north, advanced urbanization fostered a complex and often volatile economy

---

[3] Herlihy/Klapisch-Zuber (1985) 130.

grounded on commercial and industrial activities; in the south, fewer cities and *latifundi* [large agrarian estates] led to household economies centered on farming and agricultural production. Between the fourteenth and sixteenth centuries, these environmental characteristics were exacerbated by recurring famines and frequent epidemics which led to high mortality and fluctuating demographic trends. In the same period, numerous wars triggered by the aggressive expansionist politics of the larger Italian cities and foreign states affected public and private finances. By the sixteenth century republican and princely governments alike had erected the institutional foundations of their regional states by transforming disjointed and divided territorial units into more unified and centralized political entities, a Europe-wide trend. Towns, cities, and rural villages were grouped together as peripheral and centralized bureaucracies were expanded, and permanent military structures were established and reorganized. The administrative and judicial prerogatives of municipal governments and local elites passed under the political control of central rulers, though reforms often coexisted with enduring local autonomy. Demographic fluctuations, wars, and political change threatened the survival of family lines with high mortality rates and low life expectancy, challenging the economic standing of rich and poor alike by disrupting trade and agricultural production, unsettling traditional structures of hierarchy and authority. These developments also intensified the efforts by both states and heads of households to discipline family life and individual behavior with the intent of preserving the peace and maintaining social order. Perpetuating social exclusiveness and political stability by balancing financial resources with the preservation of the patrilineage became the central consideration of wealthy urban elites, while poor rural families endeavored to develop creative strategies of survival.

The structures of family and household and the meaning of kinship were class-, time-, and place-specific, but their narrative is also the product of three interconnected and mutually supportive historiographical perspectives. The first contends that household composition, marriage patterns, and kinship ties were shaped under the impact of demographic and socio-economic trends as well as by political factors; the family was thus seen to be a tight and congruent space characterized by the shared identity and solidarity of its members. A second approach introduces gender to redefine categories such as "family" and "kinship" which had previously taken for granted a dominant male subject, consequently rendering more visible all those on what had been considered the margins.[4] In this light, family and kinship appear in all their ambiguity and contradictions, as a space of entrenched gender inequality that while it expanded privileges for some, also produced subordination for others. The third perspective builds on the previous ones but shifts the functionalist model and the "inequality" approach by examining the interactions and conflicts that guided decision-making processes. Here family is viewed as the space where women and men negotiated their relations, enacted their conflicts, and represented themselves in constant dialogue with existing legal norms, everyday practices, and shifting historical circumstances.

Families and households in two urban contexts: Florence and Venice

Most research on Renaissance families has privileged the urban setting of prominent cities such as Florence and Venice and their upper classes, given the abundance of information preserved about them. The particular abundance and exceptionality of the Florentine documents has disclosed uncharted aspects of family life: household composition, the age at marriage of daughters and sons of both the wealthy and the poor, death and fertility rates, and life expectancy as well as the strategies regulating kinship ties and marriage alliances. Such research also created a model of Italian family and household configurations that long claimed the Florentine family as the norm.

Between the mid fourteenth and mid fifteenth centuries, the combination of demographic fluctuations and commercial wealth affected household size and marriage practices of urban families across the social spectrum.[5] The commercial organization of the urban economy discouraged young men from either the wealthy or middling classes from setting up their own families too early in life. Low pay for apprentices and the need to accumulate enough capital to set up an independent business delayed marriage among artisans. Careers in commerce, banking, and the professions took even longer to secure financial

[4] On gender and the social meaning attached to sexual difference, see J. C. Brown/Davis (1998); Pomata (2002a) and (2002b); and Outram (2006).
[5] On demographic fluctuations in the fourteenth century, see Cipolla (1962); and Herlihy/Cohn (1997).

independence at an early age, so much so that men married later, in their late twenties or early thirties and often did not marry at all. Demographic pressures, bachelorhood, late age at marriage, and the consequently shrinking pool of available, marriageable men shortened male reproductive rates and lowered birth rates. To compensate for these potentially disastrous outcomes for the size and prosperity of households, women tended to marry young. These trends were most pronounced among the wealthy. In Florence, rich men married fourteen- to sixteen-year-old girls who were at least twelve years their junior; and the wealthier women were, the younger they married, while the opposite was true of men. A notable result of these tendencies was a large number of small, unstable, and truncated households in towns and cities across north-central Italy. In the early fifteenth century there were 3.8 persons per household in Florence, 3.5 in Bologna, and 3.7 in Verona, a trend that was reversed only later in the century when an uptick in the population led to households of 4.8 persons in Florence and 5.2 in Verona.[6]

Not only the size but also the composition of households changed as a consequence of demographic movement and the organization of commercial wealth in Italian cities and towns. The significant age difference that separated husbands from wives led to households that at different stages of the life cycle contained older fathers whose mean age of around forty years was sometimes twice that of the mother, a factor contributing to a high number of widows.[7] In Florence, between the late fourteenth and early fifteenth centuries, one in every four women was a widow, in contrast to one in ten in the countryside. Widowers instead represented only 4% of the male population. Following a trend evident also in Venice, very few Florentine widows remarried.[8] Two-thirds of women were widowed before the age

---

[6] Demographic studies require availability of serial documentations such as tax records and parish registers – baptisms, marriages, and deaths – which are incomplete or lacking for many Italian regions and became more regular and reliable only during the seventeenth century as a consequence of the post-Tridentine reforms. The Florentine *catasto* – the most detailed tax records produced by any government in the fifteenth century – supplemented with the distinctively Florentine *ricordanze*, opened new methodological possibilities with important implications for understanding the internal dynamics of family and household, and the socio-economic and demographic factors affecting them. The demographic analysis of about 60,000 Tuscan households listed in the *catasto* and undertaken by Herlihy/Klapisch-Zuber (1985) in the 1970s represents the peak of Renaissance demographic studies.

[7] *Ibid.* 202–31, 248; and Chojnacki (2000) 244–56.   [8] *Ibid.* 98.

of twenty, but remarriage prospects steadily declined as women aged and only 11% of widows between thirty and thirty-nine ever remarried. In contrast, between 75% and 100% of widowers took a second wife before the age of sixty.[9] These marriage patterns preserved the social stability of the wealthy classes in dangerous times but aggravated further the recurring demographic strains of the period. The great age difference that separated husbands from wives together with the disparity in women's and men's opportunities for remarriage draws attention to patterns of gender inequality in wealthy urban households. In the process of accommodating and supporting commercial wealth and coping with demographic decline, social practices gave fathers and husbands enormous control over their households and wives. Strategies of marriage alliances intended to preserve the patriline further relegated women to older male authority, in particular with regard to the management and transmission of the family's wealth.[10]

In the complex and multilayered socio-political context of commercial and highly competitive Italian Renaissance cities which were often beset by rivalries and factionalism, marriage alliances were instrumental in consolidating power and in creating indispensable financial, political, and emotional support networks among the ruling classes.[11] In the words of the fifteenth-century Florentine humanist and patrician Matteo Palmieri, the great Florentine families "encompass a good part of the city, whence, being related by marriage, they charitably assist each other, conferring ... advice, favors, and assistance which ... result in benefit, advantage and abundant fruits."[12] Because the stability of family and state, and hence political power, was dependent on the large networks that linked together kin, friends, and neighbors, marriage alliances were responsible for the preservation and the distribution of family and wealth. But favorable marriage alliances hinged on the dowry, the amount of wealth that a woman brought into her husband's family. "He who takes a woman wants cash," wrote the renowned Florentine widow Alessandra Macinghi Strozzi to her son in 1447, and

---

[9] Herlihy/Klapisch-Zuber (1985) 211–21.
[10] Kelly-Gadol (1977) was one of the first scholars who offered a critical evaluation of the position of women during the Renaissance.
[11] On marriage patterns among ruling classes see Goldthwaite (1968); F. W. Kent (1977); Klapisch-Zuber (1986); Fabbri (1991); and Chojnacki (2000) 27–75.
[12] Cited in Molho (1994) 223.

this was the case across all social ranks.[13] At the same time, marriages were planned with the intent of minimizing loss of wealth through dowries and inheritance.

In the economically prosperous self-governing cities of north-central Italy, statutory law introduced in the thirteenth century abolished the ancient Roman legal tradition of daughters and sons sharing equal inheritance rights.[14] The dotal wealth that a woman brought into her marriage, although originally designated as women's share of her family's property, in reality sanctioned the exclusion of women from property rights.[15] In the following centuries the law further strengthened paternal authority, not only by enforcing patrilineal transfers of property, but also by restricting what women could inherit and on whom they could bestow their wealth. Only through marriage or entry into a convent did women obtain their dowries, and these consisted of a cash sum that was much smaller than the value of property that remained in the male line. In addition, even if dowries legally belonged to women through marriage they were placed under the management of male kin, and even then widowed women were not always able to distribute them according to their own wishes.[16]

The difference in women's and men's freedom of action within the household highlights a critical dimension of the arrangement of marriages chiefly among wealthy urban elites: how the interplay between individual lives and collective behavior oriented the choices that families made to protect status, preserve lineage, and assure the orderly administration and preservation of the family patrimony. This is most evident in Renaissance Florence, where gender differences with regard to the freedom of action within the household were most extreme. The inheritance calculations of the wealthy Florentine elite celebrated the superiority of the patrilineage (agnatic kinship) by favoring sons over daughters, even if there were no direct male heirs. Because the responsibility for the preservation and the distribution of wealth was incumbent upon men, fathers bore a primary role in

[13] Strozzi (1997) 31; and Crabb (2000).
[14] Hughs (1978); Herlihy (1976); and Chojnacki (2000) 76–94.
[15] Kirshner (1978); and Kuehn (1991) 197–222.
[16] On property law and the degree of women's control over their dowries in Florence, see Kirshner (1991); Kuehn (1991) 238–57; and Chabot (1998). On Venice, see Bellavitis (1998); Chojnacki (2000) 132–52, 169–82; and Guzzetti (2002) 431–73. A broader geographic prospective is offered by Sperling (2007).

carrying the bloodline and legitimately transmitting the lineage. Conversely, a woman's duty was to generate and perpetuate the family line, but women were linked to their children and husbands not through the bloodline but through the social agreement sealed with the marriage contract.[17] If this contract was broken by the husband's death, widows often found themselves at the center of a complicated predicament, pressured by the interests of two kinships and supported by neither. Nevertheless, the observation of the humanist Ludovico Dolce that women "rejoice at the death of their husbands as if they had been freed from the heavy yoke of servitude" may well have reflected a widespread sentiment among Florentine widows whose new-found status relieved them of frequent childbearing and procured for them a certain degree of autonomy.[18] But often they had no choice, as the case of Tancia Bandini, daughter of a Florentine notary, shows. In 1448, two years after her wedding, Tancia's husband died. Twenty years old and childless, she tried to resist her family's remarriage plan by entering a convent and, with the help of a notary, donating a large part of her dowry worth 300 florins to her mother. Tancia's father was not deterred by his daughter's aspiration to independence. Unable to recover the first dowry, he provided her with another of the same amount and a month after entering the nunnery Tancia was remarried to a silk merchant.[19]

Different ways of calculating who inherited and who controlled wealth might have prevented the dispersion of the family patrimony but also led to different ways of determining gender hierarchy within the household. The dowry system and considerations of marriage alliances imposed paternal authority over daughters by curbing relationships between mothers and children. A wealthy Florentine woman, once married, owed complete devotion to her marital lineage in preference to her father and brothers, and in the case of remarriage she was obligated to forsake all previous commitments even to her children from the earlier marriage. Widows could remain in their deceased husband's household and live with their children, but if young their natal families often reclaimed them and their dowries in order to create newly profitable marriage alliances. If a widow obeyed her father and left her

---

[17] Klapisch-Zuber (1986) 213–60.
[18] Cited in Herlihy/Klapisch-Zuber (1985) 610; see also Klapisch-Zuber (1986) 261–81; and Calvi (1998).
[19] Chabot (1999a).

marital family, however, she became a "cruel mother" because she was constrained to abandon her children – they belonged to the father's lineage – preventing them from inheriting her dowry, which instead passed to the children of her second marriage. This is what happened in 1389 to Madonna Isabetta Sassetti whose brothers promptly remarried her soon after she became a widow, forcing her to leave behind three small boys even if in his will the deceased husband had named her their guardian.[20] Grown-up children and kin voiced their resentment when widows left their marital households: an indignant merchant commented in 1417 that his widowed sister-in-law "left the house [with a dowry of 900 *fiorini*] and left her children on the straw, with nothing";[21] and in 1469 one Florentine orphan bitterly asserted that he and his siblings had been left "without a father (and in effect motherless), and we haven't anybody else in the world and have been abandoned by everybody."[22]

Husbands imposed their authority in day-to-day relationships with their wives by restricting the role of mothers within the household. In fifteenth-century Florence, for example, the common practice of hiring wet-nurses was in part a response to demographic considerations, since it was believed that a woman's fertility increased if she did not nurse.[23] It was the father, however, who selected wet-nurses – a telling action that further deepened the legal separation between mothers and children while enforcing paternal authority over both children and wife. Likewise the practice of naming children by exclusively selecting names from the patriline reinforced and preserved the memory of the agnatic line.[24] Legal impediments as well as everyday cultural practices have influenced recent depictions of urban patrician women as "passing guests" in both their natal and their marital families who had no role in the construction of kinship ties and family memory, their lineage beginning and ending with them. But the law could not single-handedly protect the male line and could not totally take away women's rights concerning inheritance, especially when they had no close male kin.

To be sure, while Italian Renaissance families predominantly celebrated patrilineage and the agnatic line, women and men were also very

---

[20] Klapisch-Zuber (1986) 117–31, especially 123–24.
[21] Bec (1969).
[22] Cited in F. W. Kent (1977) 36; the orphan was Bartolo di Strozza Rucellai.
[23] Klapisch-Zuber (1986) 132–64.   [24] *Ibid.* 283–309.

much aware of the importance of cognate and affine (in-law) ties, which were created through women and their marriages. In Venice, marriage and inheritance patterns similar to those in Florence led to a different outcome. In contrast to the weak bargaining position of their Florentine counterparts, Venetian women played a crucial role in boosting the financial well-being of their families. But the law did not in itself secure women's relative freedom of action over their dowries, and Venetian women's bargaining power in the decision-making process must thus be understood within the broader political and cultural context in which it was performed.

Political traditions, in particular membership in the Great Council – the city's principal ruling body – created a deep collective identity among the Venetian patriciate, with a profound impact on the marriage practices of the island republic.[25] A tight network of endogamous marriage alliances (those within the narrow confines of one's city) shielded the unequal distribution of wealth within the Venetian patriciate, prevented the entrance of newcomers, and strengthened patricians' awareness of sharing common political and family interests. Dowries came to represent a vital instrument to protect the patriciate as well as an essential form of revenue aimed at safeguarding its social exclusiveness and served to further the interests of both lineages. Through their dowries, women played a supportive social role in creating bilineal kinship alliances. The dowry system granted Venetian women some independent control over their dotal and non-dotal assets, whether they married, entered convents, or remained single, and this relative power generated in women a new sense of legitimacy as contributors, together with their husbands and fathers, to the continuity and success of their families. In this way, Venetian women secured and augmented daughters' dowries, promoted the careers of sons, invested in family businesses, and loaned money to needy kin. In Venice, mothers promoted the well-being of both lineages, but in the process they also negotiated advantageous benefits for themselves and for other female relatives, such as arranging marriages for women at an older age – thus narrowing the age difference between husbands and wives – and bargaining with male householders about their children's futures. Not only did Venetian women bring into their marital families major economic

---

[25] See Labalme *et al.* (1999); and Chojnacki (2000), especially 53–75.

assets in the form of dowries, but as mothers they also became crucial agents in protecting the integrity of the patriline.[26]

The power of culture and class ideologies

Clearly, demographic and socio-economic constraints as well as environmental factors affected the everyday life of individuals and their families across place and class, severely limiting their choices and opportunities. But these factors were also complicated by the expectations of cultural values, by shifting political circumstances, and by gender and class ideologies. Redirecting the focus away from utilitarian planning and strategies of survival to cultural values and the gendered perspective that guided the decision-making process reveals a complex landscape of family relations in which both male and female agency as well as ensuing negotiations over power play a considerable role. Over the course of the fifteenth century in the large urban centers of north-central Italy, the financial and political standing of the wealthy classes was in transition as urban elites reoriented some of their commercial and banking interests toward land investment in the face of significant political changes. These shifts had their impact on family life as well. Marriage alliances contributed to and reflected the development of an aristocratic consciousness among the wealthy families of the large urban centers of central and northern Italy, delineating them as socially separate and superior from the rest of society.

Ruling elites in Italian cities had long shaped laws and public documents to reflect the interests of fathers and husbands. The early age at which daughters of wealthy families first married – certainly an outcome of the high mortality rate – was also strongly influenced by cultural attitudes regarding the nature of women. A comparison between the declarations of Florentine heads of households in the *catasto* [fiscal record] and birth dates recorded in the *Monte delle doti* [a government-controlled dowry fund] has shown, for example, that fifteenth-century Florentine fathers regularly falsified the age of unmarried daughters in order to make them appear younger. For Italian Renaissance society, women's and men's reputations were tied to the honor, status, and power of their

---

[26] Turchi (1998); Chojnacki (2000) 115–52; and Hacke (2004). Aristocratic women in Rome and Naples also enjoyed considerable rights over their dowries and contributed to the advancement of their families, for which see Ago (1992); and Astarita (1992).

families. Humanistic rhetoric argued that the honor of one's family resided both in male civic service and in the purity and chastity of daughters and wives. For this reason, marriage customs were strongly influenced by the widespread ideological consensus that women should be excluded from public life, relegated to the home, and kept there under the strict control of men. An important means to ensuring female personal virtue and the purity of the family line was to marry daughters off very young, when they were presumably more malleable and less subject to corrupting passions or prone to developing questionable reputations. "Take her as a child," advised the Florentine merchant Giovanni Morelli in his *ricordanze*, "if you wish to be happy with her, that she might be healthy and whole."[27] A daughter who at age eighteen was still unmarried might have suggested some financial or political predicament and hence jeopardized the reputation of her family. In falsifying their daughters' ages, Florentine fathers not only asserted the unblemished purity of these girls but also affirmed the long-standing reputation of their lineage, thereby improving the chances for negotiating advantageous and honorable marriages for the family.[28] Cultural considerations based on the idea that older men were better prepared to take on the responsibility of domestic life also determined the late age at which men married. The Venetian Francesco Barbaro argued that by marrying at the age of thirty-seven men would have fathered healthier children, and other humanists wrote that marrying too early in life hindered men's growth.[29]

In a society where marrying off a daughter was of utmost importance and where the wealth of a wife was praised as much as her purity and chastity, it is not surprising that making advantageous and powerful marriages depended on the ability of families to provide their daughters with large dowries. By the mid fifteenth century increased competition between wealthy families with young girls of marriageable age drove up the value of dowries to unprecedented levels. Wealthy Florentine and Venetians again displayed different legal practices that nevertheless produced similar behavior. In 1425, to keep up with inflation and to fulfill budding aristocratic aspirations, the Florentine republic established the *Monte delle doti* with the intent of guaranteeing ready accessibility to large

[27] Cited in Herlihy/Klapisch-Zuber (1985) 210.
[28] Molho (1988).   [29] See Chojnacki (2000) 185–205.

amounts of cash when needed, and to facilitate the most profitable marriages.[30] During the same period, the Venetian government, fearing financial ruin among the patriciate, sought to pass legislation intended to halt the financially disastrous rise in the value of dowries. The 1420 law which determined the maximum value of dowries at 1,600 ducats, however, was persistently ignored by wealthy Venetian families. Just a few years after the law was passed, the patrician brothers Jacopo and Girolamo Gabriel suffered no consequences for each receiving dowries amounting to 2,500 ducats. The dowry was the utmost expression of aristocratic taste and aspiration, and the higher it was the more lavish and elaborate the wedding ceremony. Although it was in the courts of Ferrara, Milan, Mantua, and Naples that the magnificence of wedding ceremonies was first celebrated as one of the "duties" of the wealthy prince, even in republican cities humanists such as the Venetian Barbaro praised the extravagant nobility of wedding processions. A century later, in 1535, a new Venetian law increased the maximum value of dowries to 4,000 ducats.[31] The subsequent increase in the price of dowries signaled not simply a response to the laws of supply and demand, it epitomized the pretensions to nobility of urban newcomers.

By the sixteenth century, however, the dynastic ideals and patrimonial patterns of both the new urban aristocracies and the older nobility put great strains on family finances, further emphasizing the male line and the inalienability of patrimony at the expense of women, a succession policy that particularly favored primogeniture. In Venice, Florence, and other cities of the center-north of the Italian peninsula patricians tried to avoid dispersing family patrimonies by limiting marriages and maintaining family wealth in just one line, that of the son (not necessarily the first born) destined to marry. The majority of available young girls married in the early fifteenth century, but the increase in the price of dowries and the indivisibility of wealth limited both women's and men's marriage choices and consigned many women to convents against their will. Between the fifteenth and the mid sixteenth centuries in Florence the number of convents grew from twenty-six to forty-seven and the number of nuns in each institution more than doubled; by 1552 one-eighth of the female population lived in convents.

---

[30] Kirshner/Molho (1978); and Molho (1994).
[31] Queller/Madden (1993); and Chojnacki (2000) 58, 71. On wedding ceremonies, see D'Elia (2002).

By the early seventeenth century – left with no other opportunity but *clausura forzata* [forced claustration] – more than one-half of Florentine and Venetian women were nuns.[32] Similarly, in the sixteenth century, more than half of the men from Florentine affluent families remained bachelors, while in Milan at least 50% of men from the same class gave up marriage. Bachelorhood was also common in the Tuscan countryside and among artisans in Turin. As the seventeenth century approached, the unmarried state offered men opportunities of leadership within the domestic unit and, often, access to prestigious professional and public positions rather then relegating them to a life of suffering and exclusion.[33] Alberto Verna, a bachelor from Turin, became chief surgeon at the San Giovanni Hospital, and having acted as provider and protector to some of his brother's children he left them sole heirs of the large patrimony he had amassed. He also trained one of his nephews in the medical profession, and following in his uncle's footsteps this nephew became chief surgeon in the same hospital.[34]

In southern Italian territories, unlike the principal center-north cities, aristocratic families embraced consanguineous marriages (through blood relatives) in order to strengthen their threatened position and close ranks. By the fifteenth century, the Sicilian nobility had established closed social and political ties with the ruling Aragonese monarchy through military favors and exogamous marriage alliances (those outside the confines of one's place of origin). In this way they created kinship ties across multi-generational lines throughout the island, increased their landholdings, and expanded their local sphere of influence. By the early sixteenth century, however, dynastic disputes over the southern kingdoms combined with the rise of new wealthy urban elites to challenge the privileges of Sicilian nobles. Legal regulations which prevented the restitution of the dowry to the wife's family further threatened the barons' stability and led to a drastic shift from exogamous to endogamous and consanguineous marriages. Marriage exchanges such as those of the counts of Cammarata became customary: in 1503, Margherita Abatellis Branciforte, daughter of the third Count of Cammarata, first married her paternal uncle and subsequently a first cousin; years later, Gaetana Maria Branciforte

---

[32] For Florence, see Trexler (1994); J. C. Brown (1994); and Strocchia (2009). For Venice, see Sperling (1999); and for other Italian cities, Baernstein (1994). On forced claustration, see Zarri (1980); and Medioli (1991).
[33] Litchiefield (1969); and Cavallo (2008).   [34] *Ibid*. 390–92.

Moncada, daughter of the ninth Count of Cammarata, also married an uncle, her mother's brother. Marriage alliance among cousins and between uncles and nieces and aunts and nephews sustained the otherwise endangered political and social stability of the old Sicilian nobility.[35]

Marriage alliances, however, did not always protect or define social exclusivity and instead at times revealed factionalism and dissent. Among Florentine merchants and bankers who worked and resided in Rome, for example, marriage alliances were visible domestic expressions of their native city's deeply factionalized politics, at least until the establishment of the Medici Grand Duchy in the 1530s. During the earlier part of the fifteenth century, Florentines selected endogamous marriages as a strategy to protect their status and preserve their collective "national" identity abroad. By choosing marriage partners from within the community of Florentine conationals, fathers protected the economic interests and cultural heritage of their families. But by the late fifteenth and early sixteenth centuries successful Florentine immigrants combined such endogamous marriages with more profitable and socially advantageous alliances with the Roman nobility linked to the papal curia. The second wife of Antonio Altaviti, a prosperous Florentine banker in Rome, was Clarenza Cybo, the niece of Pope Innocent VIII. But in 1511 Antonio's son, Bindo, married the Florentine Fiammetta Soderini, niece of both Piero, *il Gonfaloniere* [the Standard-Bearer, or effective leader] of the Florentine republic, and Cardinal Francesco Soderini. The young Altaviti's marriage was significant because it epitomized the domestic expression of Florentine factionalism, embodying both his family's anti-Medicean political sentiments and their sponsorship, together with other Roman nobles, of the Florentine republican regime of 1494–1512, and in particular of Piero Soderini's leadership during that period.[36]

Through tight family connections, interpersonal loyalties, and kinship networks the wealthy constructed class solidarity and fashioned

[35] Motta (1983); and Delille (1985) 242–75.
[36] Fosi/Visceglia (1998). On internal conflicts among patrician families see Ruggiero (1980); and Kuehn (1982) and (2008). In the territory of Fontanabuona, south of Genoa, kinship networks sustained local political factions and helped organize peripheral resistance to the Genoese state, for which see Raggio (1990).

an aristocratic identity. Marriage alliances and preservation of the bloodline were crucial components in the success of urban elites because marriage, lineage, and property guaranteed the exercise of power and justified privilege. In the course of the sixteenth century, the elaboration of new aristocratic principles and self-fashioning paralleled the arrangement of carefully calculated marriages according to endogamous and homogamous alliances (within one's class) which were centered on the honor of the family, the reputation of the lineage, political heritage, and financial success.

Families in the countryside

Factoring in poorer rural families shifts the focus from marriage planning and preservation of the lineage to strategies of survival aimed at addressing land scarcity and lack of labor power. Here women and men were closer in age at first marriage and, at least in relation to their urban counterparts, both married at a later age and tended to remarry frequently. But rural families throughout Italy, like center-north urban elites, fashioned diverse social and cultural responses to precarious economic conditions and low life expectancy, with important implications for family dynamics and power relationships.

The familial practices of small peasant landowners in both north and south often reveal the same male preferences that placed wealthy urban women under the authority of their husbands. The survival strategies of small- and medium-sized peasant proprietors of Campania, in the Kingdom of Naples, kept household size small while at the same time increasing family wealth by tapping into resources external to the community. Although property was equally divided among sons, scarcity of landed wealth and efforts to keep property undivided encouraged young men to migrate to neighboring regions and to renounce their hereditary claims, at least temporarily. These patterns not only reduced the pool of marriageable men but encouraged them not to marry at all. Instead, women who married did so at a later age, remarried infrequently, and often not at all. Low birth rates, which put at risk the biological continuity of their lineages, were a subsequent outcome of these marriage arrangements but strategic intermarriages within a preferred group of families, not necessarily consanguineous, fostered a circular movement of dowries which in the short run enabled daughters to marry more frequently, even if their fathers were short on cash. In the long run these matrimonial strategies concentrated the property of those families close to extinction in the hands of surviving patrilineages with which the former were connected by marriage ties.[37]

In contrast to the unequal position of husband and wife among the small landholders of Campania, some other rural women and men shared the constraints and successes of marriage decisions, and often their interpretation of kinship was broader, including both maternal and paternal kin. In Puglia – also in the Kingdom of Naples – where large estates dominated, the economic stability and biological continuity of rural wage-earners was achieved through marriage patterns that entailed women and men close in age at first marriage, frequent remarriage, and high birth rates. Mobile wage-earners employed on the large ecclesiastical and noble estates planned exogamous marriages – particularly of daughters – which hinged on practices of property devolution which favored both daughters and sons, and on dowries in real property rather than cash so as to appeal to a supply of young male laborers needed for agricultural activities. Women married preferably outside the community but, contrary to custom, brought husbands into their natal households.[38] By creating multiple and overlapping households of sisters, brothers, and brothers- and sisters-in-law, the rural workers of Puglia collectively saw themselves as integral to reinforcing horizontal kinship ties of bilateral lineages (both maternal and paternal) and affinal (in-law) relationships linked by mutual trust and solidarity, shared labor power, and economic cooperation. Similar construction of kinship existed among the villagers in the mountainous regions of the diocese of Como in northern Italy: in villages "narrowed" there by high mortality, small dowries and consanguineous partners assured the short-term survival of families.[39] This suggests that at least among some rural families, both in the north and the south, arrangements to address the critical demographic and socio-economic circumstances of the times involved the collective and individual efforts

---

[37] Delille (1985) 161–95.
[38] See Eisenach (2004) 67–75 for similar cases among the middling groups of Verona where husbands often moved into the home of their wives' family for one year or more before they settled on their own.
[39] Merzario (1981). On marriage patterns among the peasants who lived in the lowlands and in the mountains near Florence see Cohn (1998) 174–96. On consanguinity, see Pomata (1994).

of both women and men. Collective planning not only assured the survival of families but also implied social and cultural responses that led to an idea of kinship that fused the idea of lineage with friendship, sociability, and socio-economic solidarity.

Provincial families in a century of change

The power dynamics realized through marriage, family, and kinship shaped class solidarity, constructed gender politics, and fomented dissent; they also produced regional integration and assimilation. Over the course of the sixteenth century, provincial middling groups identified the means with which to expand and consolidate local interests and, crucially, defend their rights in marriage alliances, property transfers, and kinship networks. In the process, they became key players in the development of pre-national regional states.

As agents of regional integration these groups pursued a combination of endogamous and exogamous alliances, but unlike their wealthy counterparts in the principal cities – Florence and Venice in particular – they were not as preoccupied with the patriline. While endogamous marriages for daughters consolidated wealth within municipal confines, the intermarriage of sons and daughters with other middling families between towns shaped the social identity of regional middling groups. Arranging advantageous marriages of as many sons and daughters as possible with other provincial families became the ambition of lesser elites. During the fifteenth century, little distinguished the marriage exchanges of Tuscan provincial sons from those of daughters. Both intermarried with families of similar standing and professions from within their own communities, but also with those from Florence and other smaller cities and towns such as Arezzo, Pescia, Pietrasanta, Montevarchi, and Borgo San Sepolcro. Interregional marriages guaranteed the defense of social prerogatives and fostered a collective identity defined by mutual professional choices, similar financial interests, and shared connections with centralized rulers. A dowry system of land-wealth and land-rents, and an inheritance policy based on a more equal distribution of the family patrimony among all sons supported the matrimonial exchanges that connected middling elites and linked provincial towns to emerging regional states. Additionally, in many provincial towns across central and northern Italy, policies of property transfers across generations were flexible, and it was not uncommon for fathers to favor daughters over distant kinsmen such as nephews or cousins and to bequeath daughters dowries in real estate rather than cash. These practices guaranteed the preservation and transmission of wealth and the continuity of lineages either through the male or female lines, revealing an understanding of kinship that was bilateral and celebrated – as in the case of the peasant families of Puglia – both the maternal and paternal bloodlines.[40]

In the smaller Tuscan municipalities it was not uncommon for the ancestral line of a family close to extinction to be carried on by women. In Poppi, this practice was echoed in the writing of Niccolò Lapini, a local historian who, in the early seventeenth century, recognized two maternal lineages as carriers of both family honor and memory. The inclusion of the maternal lineage was also symbolically strengthened and prolonged through the use of given names. Parents often named their first-born son after the maternal grandfather while girls were given the female derivatives of either the maternal or paternal grandfather's name. If names were viewed as property at that later time in Poppi – unlike fifteenth-century Florence – the wife participated in this possession together with her husband.[41]

But in the course of the seventeenth century, the ideology grounded on concepts of grandeur and exclusivity elaborated by urban aristocracies also redefined provincial families within a new regional context. Shifts in the decision-making process came to entail a policy of succession that favored primogeniture and the male line with disregard for the contribution of women to the family ethos. Together, middling elites and centralized authorities reinforced a decentralized political structure that promoted a localized system of male privilege.

Mapping the limits of the patriline: other voices, alternative views

How could family be a source of identity and solidarity when its power structures and decision-making processes were so unequal? Whose interests and stability did marriage protect? Though legal norms and cultural practices constrained women and men alike, rules could be bent and different forms of agency could be devised to maneuver

---

[40] Studies on provincial societies include J. C. Brown (1982); Angiolini (1987); Grubb (1988) and (1996); Cohn (1992); Ferraro (1993); Benadusi (1996); and Eisenach (2004).

[41] Benadusi (1996) 184–85.

creatively around the structures of patriarchy in order to promote individual self-interest and even occasionally the interests of the family.

Recent studies have shown the limits of what was thought to be within or outside the acceptable social norms of marriage, kinship, and family relationships in Renaissance Italy. These limits were tested time and again by a variety of factors, among them same-sex relationships and marital separations, which generated a more elastic understanding of paternal authority than contemporary prescriptive literature and earlier research on marriage suggest.

Because the continuity and stability of the patriline were deemed crucial not only for the success of the family but also of the state, contemporary moralists and republican governments in the late fourteenth and first half of the fifteenth centuries initiated efforts to regulate sexual behavior and public morality. In their incendiary sermons attacking male same-sex relationships, preachers such as the influential Franciscan friar Bernardino of Siena mobilized broad pre-existing social and political concerns about the biological annihilation of family lines and the political instability of urban ruling groups that might result from such extinctions. They also galvanized public opinion, blaming the devastating natural disasters of the times on men who engaged in sex considered "against nature" and incapable of procreation (sodomites). "O my lads," Bernardino blasted in one of his sermons, "if you want to exterminate your city and motherland, I tell you, keep on being sodomites; I tell you, if you want her to be exterminated, then don't give up your sodomizing."[42] By the early fifteenth century, in line with moralists' propaganda, the republican governments of several central and northern cities passed repressive measures to discipline sexuality. Special judiciary commissions were established in Venice (1418), Florence (1432), and Lucca (1448) with the unprecedented intent to police and prosecute male-to-male relationships.[43]

In Florence, the *Ufficiali di notte* [Officers of the Night] incriminated over 17,000 men for sodomy between 1432 and 1502 (some 3,000

[42] Mormando (1999) 130.
[43] For Venice, see Ruggiero (1989); and for Florence, Rocke (1996). J. C. Brown (1986) examines same-sex practices in a provincial Tuscan convent; and Rocke (2003) extends the discussion to encompass sexual norms and ideals as well as a range of unauthorized sexual practices. There is as yet no full-scale account for the Italian context of alternatives and challenges to marriage and the family in this period, but the essays in Milner (2005) provide a useful survey of the margins of Italian social life; and those in Cestaro (2004) 1–116 offer readings of early modern literary texts that represent same-sex relations.

were actually convicted), the year when the magistracy was abolished. A number of factors contributed to the high number of such "reports" in the seventy years this court existed, but two were particularly telling: the late age at which men married in Florence, and the large number of men who remained bachelors (as discussed above). In Renaissance Florence, same-sex relationships had been an important stage of many young men's sexual experience during adolescence and the long period of bachelorhood prior to marriage, though there were also individuals who engaged in same-sex practices throughout their lives. While most men reported to the *Ufficiali di notte* were (presumably) unmarried and under thirty-five, there were also cases of married men whose engagement in sodomy was facilitated by practices that followed a particular model: men eighteen and older taking the "active" role and adolescents the "passive" one.[44] These patterns undoubtedly complicated and destabilized heterosexual marriages, creating conflicts and tensions between young wives constrained into forced unions by family interests and the homoerotic orientations of their older husbands.

Although affection and friendship might develop between husbands and wives, many marriages were not successful and marital separations were far more common than the prescriptive literature on marriage suggests. By studying the detailed ecclesiastical court records of marital litigations, scholars have recently questioned the improbable uniformity of marriage practices in Renaissance society, pointing instead towards their convolution.

Women occupied a leading role in resisting patriarchal authority by testing both the influence of family on their marriage choices and husbands' presumed responsibility to control them. While upper-class women were less likely to abandon an unhappy relationship because of the burden imposed on them by concerns about family honor and property, women of the middling and lower ranks voiced their discontent about lack of spousal support, marital violence, and sexual dysfunction by bringing their stories to court. Municipal and ecclesiastical institutions and sympathetic judges as well as kinsmen, friends, and servants sometimes facilitated restraining husbands who had misbehaved. On occasion, even though the Church considered marriage an indissoluble tie, canonical authorities went so far as to annul these women's

---

[44] Rocke (1996).

marriages. Most of all, beyond these women's court cases stood divergent ecclesiastical and secular conceptions of marriage, in particular the reaffirmation by the Council of Trent in 1563 of the right of the bride and groom to consent or not to marriage regardless of parental wishes and family interests.

In the eyes of the Church, the bride's or groom's lack of consent at the time of marriage was a decisive factor both for obtaining marital separation and for sealing marital pre-agreements based on reciprocal consensus. Underage girls, often orphans, were forced into marriages that were never consummated. The motive behind these marriages was often financial but in all cases these young girls were the victims of broader schemes of deceit and exploitation. In other instances, working-class women went to court to fight husbands who refused to recognize the legal validity of their private promises (or clandestine marriage) to each other. These premarital agreements, based on reciprocal consensus and often sealed by consummation, acquired the same validity as a formal marriage promise recognized by the broader community. Frequently involving exchanges between wealthier men and lower-status women, these relationships circumvented the pressure of marriage calculations, the formality of marriage contracts, and the burden of dowry exchanges dictated by kin, providing these women the possibility for socio-economic mobility.[45] Through these means, women performed their self-determination before civil and ecclesiastical courts and in the process proposed different expectations of marriage, motherhood, and kinship that further reveal the complexity and multiformity of family in the period.

Women were also actively engaged in assuring the well-being of their children. Renaissance merchants celebrated the mutual love between father and son, but women were equally vocal in praising maternal love. "The bond of maternity," wrote the Venetian poet Moderata Fonte at the end of the sixteenth century, "outweighs those of marriage or filial obligation."[46] Most mothers were not just "visitors," and they were rarely "cruel"; indeed they regularly played the role of crucial mediators between maternal and paternal lineages. Last wills and testaments

---

[45] On marital litigations, see Ferraro (2001); on illegitimacy, Kuehn (2002); and on clandestine marriages, Brucker (1986); Ferrante (1996); Seidel Menchi/Quaglioni (2001); Eisenach (2004); Sperling (2004); and Hacke (2004).

[46] Fonte (1997), 68; and Jacobson Schutte et al. (2001).

suggest that women who remarried, such as the seventeenth-century Florentine Maddalena Nerli Tornabuoni, often circumvented statutes that prevented them from transmitting their dowries to children from their deceased husbands and instead distributed their wealth equally among all children from their first and second marriages.[47] It was not only the legal *inclusion* of women in the management of property, as in the case of the Venetian patriciate, that empowered them. The legal *exclusion* of women from family wealth also gave widowed mothers a new-found role as financially disinterested intermediaries between the patriline and its children.[48] Seventeenth-century Tuscan women petitioned government institutions in charge both of protecting orphans and widows and of dealing with family quarrels over civic matters – the *Magistrato dei pupilli* [Magistracy of Wards] and the *Magistrato supremo* [the principal Magistracy for Arbitration] – calling upon the Grand Dukes to intervene to resolve perceived injustices or challenge the unfairness of legal conventions. In their petitions, widowed mothers whose husbands had died without leaving a will asked to be allowed to supervise their children's material well-being and to be protected against unsupportive relatives, including uncles, cousins, and grandfathers. Both women and magistrates relied on the argument that mothers alone (when they did not remarry and have other children) could assure their children a love that was free from pecuniary concerns, "impartial" and "pure."[49]

In the process of claiming their wealth, reclaiming their dowries from insolvent husbands, and suing male kin over inheritance, women gave form to a legal culture that helped them shape their own social position and redress perceived imbalances. In their wills, women of all classes – property-less servants, peasants, and artisans; or members of urban lesser elites – negotiated the conventional social and legal norms that defined their relationships within the households where they resided, challenged restrictions, and contested gender-based assumptions about themselves and those around them: fathers, sons, and masters. Women from elite and middling groups transmitted newly self-aggrandizing and self-preserving family values and participated in shaping a new familial ideology. But

---

[47] Calvi (1992); see also Chabot (1999b).
[48] Kirshner (1985); Chojnacki (2001); and Guzzetti (2002).
[49] On guardianship, Kuehn (1991) 212–37; Calvi (1994); Benadusi (2009); and Castiglione (2009a). On the crucial role of mothers in Roman noble families, see D'Amelia (2001).

they acted on their own perceptions of collective and individual family memory and of kinship. In her last will and testament of 1609, Elisabetta Taglieschi, who had moved to Borgo San Sepolcro upon her marriage, specified the quality and quantity of objects to furnish a chapel that her heirs were asked to build to commemorate and house her remains: candles of different sizes, silver torches and chalices, and embroidered altar-cloths were to be emblazoned with her paternal family name and its coat of arms. Acting on their own perceptions of public life, Elisabetta and other provincial women like her gendered public space and the rules of admission into it. To justify this public presence and deflect criticism about it, these women bestowed honor and prestige to the families into which they had married but also symbolically legitimized the public presence of their natal family – a presence made all the more essential for women who originally came from other towns.[50]

Renaissance "family" was not an abstract all-encompassing concept independent of gender and class, and domestic life was not a single and confined ideal that inevitably created a shared identity and the solidarity of its members. Instead "family" was a set of cultural constructs supported by a variety of processes: the multifaceted product of individuals – women and men, rich and poor – who shared a wide array of interests and agendas contingent on shifting circumstances, legal norms, and cultural practices. In their efforts to address the socio-economic and demographic challenges of the period in which they lived, consolidating or increasing wealth and property, and in perpetuating or attaining power and status, individuals sorted out their rights and privileges, playing out their conflicts within the family and through the dynamic process of male and female agency. The interaction between individuals, households and families, on the one hand, and socio-economic pressures, political transformations, and cultural conflicts, on the other, reveals the complexity of family as a social institution. Through family, marriage, and kinship ties the state guaranteed social order, families pursued their interests, wealthy elites perpetuated their privileges, fathers imposed their authority, and women pursued both their own self-interest and the interests of the family. In certain respects, family was a repressive and hierarchical body

---

[50] Benadusi (1998). On women's role in shaping familial identities, see Strocchia (1989); for the case of Rome, see Castiglione (2009b).

wherein men had authority over women through the control of family wealth and the management of the household. Despite inequalities and imbalances, however, family was also the space where women's agency was played out. Marriages could be broken and dissolved, laws could be adjusted, and the boundaries of what was normal and licit could be put to the test. The interaction between individuals, families, and institutions reveals the complexity of family affairs and shifts the analytical perspective to how women and men in a constant dialogue with existing legal norms and cultural practices constructed family in their own minds and behavior.

17

Science and medicine

One of the most famous scientific achievements of early Renaissance Italy was the "planetarium" or "astrarium" of Giovanni Dondi. Meticulously planned and built between 1365 and about 1380, while Dondi was for the most part professor of medicine at the university of Padua, this precisely engineered clockwork mechanism tracked not only the time of day and the feasts of the Christian calendar, but also the positions of each of the planets in the zodiac. As Dondi described in his *Tractatus astrarii* [Treatise on the Astrarium], the instrument served both practical and theoretical ends. On the one hand, it facilitated the casting of horoscopes, since it allowed the user to determine planetary positions without what Dondi called "tedious calculations." On the other hand, because its elaborate system of gears and dials was configured to reflect the equants, deferents, and epicycles of Ptolemaic planetary models, it proved that those models were not necessarily only geometrical hypotheses but might correspond to physical reality – a topic of long-standing debate among medieval astronomers. As Dondi put it, if human ingenuity could construct such a device artificially, using ordinary matter, then the Creator could put a similar one in place in the heavens "more easily, more perfectly, and with even fewer contradictions."[1]

Although Dondi is best known as the designer and builder of the astrarium, his interests ranged broadly across the phenomena of the natural world. He taught medicine at the universities of Padua, Pavia, and (briefly) Florence, and he treated a range of patients, including the

---

[1] G. Dondi (2003) 40, 42. For the lives and work of Giovanni Dondi and his father Jacopo, see Pesenti (1992a) and (1992b). Despite occasional errors (cf. Pesenti, 1992a), the most useful treatment in English is Bedini/Maddison (1966).

humanist Petrarch and the household of Giangaleazzo Visconti, Lord of Pavia, whom he also served as court astrologer. In addition, he worked on natural philosophical topics related to his two principal fields of interest, medicine and the science of the stars. His treatise *De fontibus calidis agri patavini consideratio* [On the Hot Springs of the Paduan Countryside] proposed a novel explanation for the heat of the region's natural spas, arguing that this probably arose from the proximity of an underground heat source like that found in volcanoes, rather than the presence of underground deposits of sulfur, as proposed by his father, Jacopo Dondi, also a master of medicine, who had written on the same subject.[2] Jacopo's and Giovanni's interest in this topic reflected the family's ownership of a salt-works near Abano, where they extracted salt from local hot springs and sold it under a privilege granted by the Lord of Padua, Francesco Carrara.

The diversity of Dondi's scientific activities reflects the broad range of topics and approaches that constituted the literate study of the natural world in late-fourteenth-century Italy, which is how we will define science for the purposes of this chapter.[3] While Dondi's interests may look miscellaneous to modern eyes, they were in fact closely related, organized around his university training in the three linked disciplines of medicine, natural philosophy, and the science of the stars which formed the curricular core of the faculties of arts and medicine at Italian universities throughout the Renaissance period. It was through astral science – embracing both positional astronomy and judicial astrology – that Dondi's academic interests intersected with the mechanical arts; in addition to designing the famous astrarium, he seems to have been involved in the artisanal work of its production, to judge from his repeated use of first-person verbs, such as "I soldered," "I fabricated," and "I engraved." We find a similar involvement in the design and fabrication of machines and instruments, military, observational, and horological, on the part of other Italian physicians of the fourteenth century, including Dondi's older contemporary, Guido of Vigevano, court doctor to the household of Philip VI of France. In addition to a spectacularly illuminated work on anatomy, dedicated to his patron in

---

[2] G. Dondi (1553) 94[r]–108[v]; and J. Dondi (1557) 109[r–v].
[3] Study of the orally transmitted knowledge of empirical healers, midwives, gardeners, and so forth, while also important, is still in its infancy; see Park (1998); and Green (2008) 291–301.

1345, Guido compiled his *Texaurus regis Francie* [Treasury of the King of France, 1335], which illustrated his designs for machines ranging from siege towers to a paddle-wheeled submarine.[4]

As these examples show, understanding the landscape of natural knowledge in Renaissance Italy requires casting off anachronistic assumptions regarding what did or did not constitute science at the time. Throughout the Renaissance period, science and medicine embraced a range of activities, some of which – for example, judicial astrology, alchemy, and various forms of natural magic – are no longer considered intellectually respectable. Yet no history of Renaissance science can ignore these forms of natural knowledge, which became more, rather than less, central to disciplines such as medicine and natural philosophy over the course of the fifteenth and early sixteenth centuries. It is equally important to look beyond the world of the universities. These were indeed vibrant centers of scientific and medical training and speculation, but since their curricula were organized around the study and production of texts, they created more than their share of written documentation, unjustly upstaging other sites of natural inquiry, such as courts, monasteries, households, or urban workshops in the historical record.[5] Indeed, many university masters worked in one or more of these non-academic sites. Not only did professors of astrology and medicine like Giovanni Dondi deal on a daily basis with the complicated and messy world of clients and daily practice, but many of them were immersed in the commercial and technical culture of their time – witness the Dondi family salt-works and Dondi's astrarium, which drew on the skills and techniques of artisans engaged in Padua's well-developed metalworking industry.

Similarly, Dondi's long-standing connection with the court of Giangaleazzo Visconti, to which he carted the astrarium in 1381 and where he spent the last eighteen years of his life, exemplifies the important part played by princely patronage in Italian scientific culture of the period. Courts were not only significant centers of astrological and medical practice but also an important market for the expertise of alchemists, who experimented with novel medical remedies and consulted on metallurgical issues related to coinage, and engineers, skilled in the construction of everything from canals and fortifications to

---

[4] See Luzzi/Vigevano (1926); and White (1975).
[5] See Newman (2004) 228; and in general Smith (2009).

machines for use in festivals and pageants. Princes and courtiers were also the principal market for the rare but stunning scientific manuscripts, skillfully illustrated by local painters, which decorate the pages of modern histories of Renaissance science. Examples from Dondi's immediate environment include not only his own *Tractatus astrarii*, but also the extraordinary *Serapione Herbario Volgare* also known as the *Carrara Herbal*, made for Francesco Carrara, Lord of Padua in the years around 1400, and the famous *Tacuinum sanitatis* [Handbook of Health] manuscripts commissioned by Giangaleazzo Visconti for his friends and relatives, with their lovely paintings of plants, spices, and other foodstuffs from the studio of Giovannino dei Grassi.[6]

The variety and originality of scientific activity increased significantly in fourteenth-century Italy, compared to most other parts of Europe. Causes include its geographical position at the crossroads of Byzantine, Greek, Arabic, and Latin culture; its relatively high levels of urbanization; and the sheer multiplicity of sites that fostered the understanding and manipulation of nature. Italy's host of city–states and principalities, together with their courts, universities, markets, and workshops, provided a wealth of opportunities for cross-fertilization and collaboration across a wide spread of activities, from the speculations of academic natural philosophers to the sale of natural ingredients for medical remedies to the fabrications of skilled artisans. Regional competition within this welter of courts and cities encouraged a high degree of mobility on the part of these (mostly) men, while relatively high levels of male literacy meant that at least some of the expertise of the latter two groups found its way into textual form. These conditions produced a scientific culture of remarkable vibrancy and diversity throughout the Renaissance period, even as the jumble of city–states and principalities morphed into fewer, larger, mostly princely territories.

While retaining these basic features over the course of the Renaissance, Italian scientific culture was by no means static, and it underwent important changes between the late fourteenth and the late sixteenth centuries. These changes were gradual: at no point was there a marked rupture between tradition and new ways of understanding and representing the natural world. Rather, we see the cumulative effects of broader intellectual and cultural shifts, including the humanist endeavor

---

[6] See Hoeniger (2006).

to rethink and expand the heritage of classical antiquity through the discovery of previously unknown texts and the renewed study of known ones; the development of printing as a new technology for the dissemination of knowledge; and the great expansion of geographical knowledge associated with the European voyages of exploration.

The parts of this story that belong to the late fifteenth and sixteenth centuries, after the diffusion of printing, are reasonably well known and many of them have already been described in some detail by historians.[7] The science and medicine of the later fourteenth and early fifteenth centuries, however, is largely *terra incognita*, its traces buried in countless manuscripts in Italian libraries and archives, which have yet to be read, let alone studied and assimilated into the historical narrative. If the many unpublished and understudied humanist texts of this period constitute, in the words of Christopher S. Celenza, a "lost Italian Renaissance," the same is true to an even greater degree of scientific manuscripts, both Latin and vernacular, which are more numerous by far than humanist ones and offer even richer opportunities for exploration.[8]

The learning of the schools

One reason for the remarkable flourishing of scientific ideas and interests in Renaissance Italy was the characteristic organization of its universities, where – in contrast to northern European institutions – a single faculty housed medicine and the "arts." The latter included arithmetic, geometry, grammar, and logic, usually taught as preparatory to the more advanced disciplines of natural philosophy and astrology, which were studied both for their own sake and as propedeutic to medical training and practice. In addition, in Italy, unlike northern Europe, few universities devoted significant resources to theology, which was an alternative site of natural philosophical speculation. This institutional arrangement privileged the study of nature in general and medical studies in particular by concentrating them in a single large and powerful faculty.[9]

The universities of Bologna and Padua were the most influential sites of scientific study in the late fourteenth and fifteenth centuries,

---

[7] For an excellent introduction, see Grafton (1992).

[8] Celenza (2004). The otherwise invaluable I Tatti Renaissance Library series of translations and editions of neo-Latin texts has yet to include a single scientific work.

[9] Siraisi (1973) 9–10 and 143–71; see also Grendler (2002), especially 267–92, 408–29.

and the 1405 statutes of the university of Bologna give a good general sense of the curricula of Italian faculties of arts and medicine.[10] Natural philosophy was based on the works of Aristotle and devoted to the study of the general principles that governed the universe as a whole (Aristotle's *Physics*), as well as the causes and nature of change in the various regions of the universe, including the celestial, aerial and terrestrial realms (*On the Heavens, Meteorology, On Generation and Corruption*). A parallel course of study focused on the nature of life and the physiology of living creatures, vegetable and animal (including human), through lectures on Aristotle's *On the Soul*; more limited topics were explored in shorter works such as *On Sense and Sense Objects* or *On Respiration*. These readings in turn provided the theoretical basis for medicine, as did a separate course of study of astral science (usually called "astrology"), which was mathematically oriented and taught through a range of Greek, Arabic, and Latin authorities; astrology was an important supplementary tool for physicians, since the motions and relative positions of the planets were strongly thought to influence the terrestrial world, including the human body and the plants and minerals that were its principal therapeutic agents.

This was the educational system that shaped the work of scholars and practitioners like Giovanni Dondi, and it meant that, like Dondi, many professional natural philosophers and almost all professional astrologers, whose horoscopes and judgments guided the activities of princes, cathedral chapters, municipal governments, and private individuals, had medical training. There were rare but important exceptions to this rule: masters whose first commitment was to logic and philosophy, such as Paulus Venetus, or to the cluster of mathematical disciplines sometimes called the "middle sciences," such as Biagio Pelacani da Parma. These sciences addressed number and extension only as manifested in material objects, thereby straddling the mathematical/physical divide. Thus Biagio supplemented his studies of astrology with work on the mathematics of *perspectiva* [vision], music, and statics (the "science of weights"), and he even argued that – setting aside theology – the mathematic disciplines, rather than philosophy, were the highest, most universal, and most certain forms of human science.[11]

---

[10] English translation (occasionally incomplete) in Thorndike (1975) 279–85; Latin original in Malagola (1888) 213–324.

[11] See Vescovini (1979) 9–17. On the middle sciences, see Gagné (1969).

A second, related characteristic of Scholastic science in Italy was its orientation toward practice. This focus on practice had a great deal to do with the importance attributed to astrology and, especially, medicine in Italian universities. While the natural philosophy curriculum was theoretical in orientation throughout, focused on the general causes of natural phenomena, studied deductively, rather than on the particulars of those phenomena, instruction in astrology and medicine had a strong practical bent. In addition to astrological theory – the geometry of celestial motions, the nature of celestial influences – students in the former learned to use tables and instruments; these allowed them to cast horoscopes, compile almanacs, and advise on issues such as time-keeping and the calendar.

In medicine, likewise, as the 1405 Bologna statues show, the morning and afternoon lectures focused on theoretical matters, studied for the most part through the works of Hippocrates and Galen, while evening instruction in all four years of the medical degree was devoted to "Prac-tica," taught through intensive study of the third book of the *Canon* of Ibn Sina (Avicenna); this was a compendium of illnesses organized by the affected organ, starting from the head and moving downward to the genitals, together with their symptoms, etiology, and treatment. A further index of the status accorded to medical practice was the fact that surgery was a university discipline, taught through Latin lectures on the works of Galen, Ibn Sina, Al-Razi (Razes or Rhazes), and the mid-thirteenth-century Italian surgeon Bruno of Longoburgo.[12] Thus while the vast majority of Italian surgeons were, as in northern Europe, taught by apprenticeship, there was a significant, learned surgical elite, skilled in surgical principles and their practical application, which had no counterpart in northern Europe.

The urgency of practical concerns in medicine relative to natural philosophy is reflected in the proliferation of genres of medical writing related to practice in Latin and the vernacular: manuscripts devoted to the commentaries, *questiones*, and ceremonial addresses of academic instruction were outnumbered by pharmacopeias, herbals, regimens of health, *practicae* (on the model of the third book of Ibn Sina's *Canon*), *consilia* (advice on individual cases), and, especially, recipes, known as

---

[12] Thorndike (1975) 284–85. On the rise of surgery as a learned discipline in Italy, see McVaugh (2006). For an excellent overview, see Siraisi (1990b), which while not focused on Italy contains a great deal of fourteenth- and fifteenth-century Italian material.

experimenta. The last were ubiquitous. One finds clusters of therapeutic recipes attributed to famous physicians, such as a manuscript of the *Experimenta* of Giovanni Dondi dating from 1453.[13] More common by far, however, are the recipes physicians and laypeople entered individually in the margins or the blank pages of manuscripts; these testify to the thriving practice of exchanging and collecting recipes from disparate sources, both oral and written.

The attention given to medical practice should not, however, obscure the fundamentally bookish nature of scientific study in Italian universities – a feature it shared with European universities in general. After all, even surgery was taught through lectures commenting on the works of classical and medieval writers. The same was true of the course in practical medicine, which focused on Ibn Sina's *Canon*, although there is scattered evidence that medical students shadowed more senior physicians or interned in hospitals for the sick poor.[14] The canon of texts and authors represented in the curriculum of the faculty of arts and medicine defined simultaneously a system of knowledge and practice and a community of expert practitioners, their legitimacy sanctioned by their possession of a university degree.[15] The result was an approach to knowledge that remained conservative and backward-looking, at least on the surface, even – or especially – when novelties were being proposed.

A case in point is the introduction of human dissection as a regular and required part of medical training in fourteenth-century Italian universities.[16] This was a striking innovation: because human dissection had not (with very few exceptions) been practiced in ancient or medieval Islamic culture, there were no authoritative texts suitable for the teaching of this field. The void was filled by a new treatise intended to accompany the dissection of a cadaver in the classroom and completed *c.* 1316 by Mondino de' Liuzzi, professor of medicine at the university of Bologna. Far from claiming to replace the authority of earlier texts with first-hand observation, however, let alone to reveal new truths about the human interior, Mondino drew most of his information from Greek and Arabic medical writers, most notably Galen and Ibn Sina. Rather than using the dissected cadaver to correct their errors,

---

[13] Pesenti (1992a) 101. On *experimenta*, see Agrimi/Crisciani (1990); and Crisciani (2004).
[14] Park (1985) 58–64.
[15] See Agrimi/Crisciani (1988), especially 5–20; and Crisciani (1990).
[16] See Park (1994); and French (1999) 8–72. For the relevant provision of the 1405 statutes of the university of Bologna, see Thorndike (1975) 283–84.

he treated it as a visual aid intended to help students remember and assimilate the anatomical information contained in older texts. Many of his descriptions, including most famously the purported seven cells of the human uterus, reflect earlier textual tradition, supplemented and shaped by the dissection of animals, and stand in stark contrast to what his students might actually have seen. Dondi, too, in his *Tractatus astrarii*, did not emphasize the originality of his achievement but described his instrument as intended to confirm the planetary models of the "ancients," inspired by and conceived in "imitation" of the work of the thirteenth-century astronomer Campanus of Novara.[17]

Despite their allegiance to their predecessors, Scholastic writers did, of course, recognize the existence of progress, especially in the area of practice. Although the theoretical principles of most of the sciences had been conclusively established by the ancients – meteorology being a recalcitrant exception[18] – the multiplicity and contingency of particular phenomena did not lend itself to exhaustive description and analysis. But the vagaries of medical, astrological, and meteorological practice, reinforced by the demands of the market for remedies and forecasts, pushed their practitioners to develop new therapies and refined techniques. This process can be seen throughout the later Middle Ages, in new practices such as the keeping of weather diaries, treatments for wounds that aimed to discourage suppuration, and the increasing use in pharmacy of distillation, a technology imported from Islamic lands. More dramatically, the appearance of plague, which made its first post-classical appearance in 1347 and returned regularly in devastating epidemics over the course of the next three centuries, pushed physicians to develop new drugs, such as the alchemical remedy of "potable gold," or to resurrect more esoteric ones, notably poison antidotes.[19] The widespread mortality in plague epidemics also forced practitioners to develop novel ideas concerning the causes of illness that ran against the traditional emphasis on the complexional constitution of individual patients. Nonetheless, the tendency was to present these changes as

---

[17] J. Dondi (2003) 39–40.
[18] Meteorology was studied in the context of both natural philosophy and astrology. On the latter, see Jenks (1983); on the former, Martin (2011) 21–37. Renaissance meteorology was much more broadly defined than its modern counterpart and include a broad range of phenomena in addition to weather, including aurorae, comets, and earthquakes, all thought to be produced by celestial influences.
[19] Jacquart (1990); and Crisciani/Pereira (1998).

incremental and cumulative, rather than major discoveries. At best they were presented as supplementing existing knowledge, and they achieved authority only by being integrated into the intellectual system established by earlier texts.

By the middle of the fifteenth century, however, there were signs that sense experience was beginning to gain ground as an alternative source of authority, albeit in a slow and tentative way. This reflected in part the increasing diffusion of alchemical ideas and techniques, which never managed to penetrate the university curriculum but flourished in non-academic contexts, most notably at court and in the workshops of pharmacists and metalworkers. Alchemy provided an alternative, non-Scholastic epistemology, which emphasized the interrelatedness of theory and practice, and a theory of matter and its transformations that could be reconciled with Aristotelian ideas but that emphasized different kinds of cause.[20] But one also finds new appeals to autoptic experience to challenge traditional explanations in university disciplines such as medicine, meteorology, and the science of the stars. One example, which straddled the first two fields, is the burgeoning literature on hot springs and thermal baths, to which Dondi's De fontibus was an early contribution, but where Dondi had relied largely on theoretical reasoning based on a few cases, early fifteenth-century physicians such as Ugolino of Montecatini and Michele Savonarola developed extensive research programs based on direct experience. They traveled from spa to spa, grilling local physicians and other residents of the area about the medicinal properties of each spring, collecting samples of their waters for analysis by distillation, and carefully noting their temperature, taste, and smell.[21]

The best-known example of this kind of work, which used autoptic experience to test and supplement material found in earlier texts, relates to the science of the stars. One of the prime movers was Cardinal Bessarion, who had brought with him a Greek manuscript of Ptolemy's Almagest (c. 150 CE) when he fled to Italy from Constantinople in 1453. Invited to Bessarion's court to produce a reliable summary and updated version of this work, the German astronomer Johannes Regiomontanus made a series of observations of eclipses, conjunctions, comets, and planetary positions in Rome and Viterbo, and found his results to disagree with those predicted by the Alfonsine tables (based on the

[20] Crisciani (2001) 9–31 and (2004).   [21] Park (1999).

geometrical models in the *Almagest*). During the first half of the 1460s, Regiomontanus was part of a lively astronomical scene focused on the universities of Ferrara, Padua, and Bologna, and although Regiomontanus never developed an alternative model of the heavens to Ptolemy's geocentric system of eccentrics and epicycles, this project was ultimately completed by a young Polish scholar, Nicolaus Copernicus, who had studied astrology at the university of Bologna and was probably familiar with Regiomontanus' criticisms of the *Almagest*.[22]

Cinquecento: medicine and the sciences

Just as the varied scientific activities of Giovanni Dondi and the multiple sites in which he worked provide a point of entry into fourteenth- and fifteenth-century Italian scientific culture, so the pursuits and career of Girolamo Fracastoro (1478–1553), another Paduan-trained physician with astronomical interests, show the ways in which that scientific culture had changed by the first half of the sixteenth century.[23] Fracastoro practiced medicine in the service of political, military, and religious leaders such as the mercenary captain Bartolomeo d'Alviano, and Pope Paul III, who appointed him as *medico condotto* [salaried physician] to the Council of Trent. Like Dondi, Fracastoro's interests were literary as well as scientific, but the tenor of literary studies had changed over the course of the century and a half that separated the two men; rather than the early, morally and religiously inflected humanism shared by Petrarch and Dondi, Fracastoro participated in a mature humanist culture focused on the edition and interpretation of ancient texts newly available in the original Greek or in neo-Latin translations made from Greek texts established according to the rules of the new philology. Thus Fracastoro's strategy, unlike Dondi's, can be understood as a humanist effort to return to the actual words of the ancient fathers of Greek medicine and astronomy, adopting them as models for new research.

Fracastoro's *Homocentrica sive de stellis* [Homocentric Spheres, or On the Stars] reflects this new approach. Printed in Venice in 1538 by the Giunta press and dedicated to Pope Paul III (Alessandro Farnese), the *Homocentrica*, a cosmological treatise, was paired with *De causis criticorum dierum per ea quae in nobis sunt* [On the Causes of Critical Days Analyzed

---

[22] Shank (2008) 11–15.   [23] On Fracastoro, see Pastore/Peruzzi (2006).

through the Features of Our Body], a medical one. The training that underpinned these linked works had its roots in Fracastoro's training at the university of Padua, which continued to support a strong tradition of mathematical and astronomical teaching in addition to medical study, as it had in Dondi's day, and which increasingly attracted students from northern Europe as well as Italy. One such student was Copernicus himself, who enrolled in the faculty of arts and medicine at the same time as Fracastoro, having previously worked with the astronomer Domenico Maria da Novara, professor at the university of Bologna, and earned a doctorate in canon law at the university of Ferrara in 1503.[24] Fracastoro's and Copernicus' studies culminated in very different ends, however. Copernicus, like Dondi before him, worked in the mathematical tradition of Ptolemaic astronomy, ultimately replacing Ptolemy's earth-centered system of planetary eccentrics and epicycles with one centered on the sun; his De revolutionibus orbium coelestium [On the Rotations of the Heavenly Spheres], published in Nuremberg in 1543, five years after Fracastoro's Homocentrica, and also dedicated to Paul III, clashed with the geocentric cosmology defended by the Church and ultimately led in 1616 to the condemnation of Copernican innovations by the Roman Congregation of the Index.[25]

Fracastoro's project was quite different from Copernicus' and, in many ways, more radical (if less successful). Rejecting Ptolemy's complicated system of eccentric circles and epicycles, which aimed for the closest possible fit between these geometric constructions and the observed positions of the heavenly bodies,[26] Fracastoro followed the lead of Alessandro Achillini and Giovambattista Amico, scholars also associated with the universities of Padua and Bologna. Inspired by Aristotle and his Averroist commentators and working in a philosophical rather than a mathematical vein, these men proposed a simplified system of homocentric spheres which sacrificed conformity to the apparent movement [apparentia] of the stars for a unified and harmonious model organized around simple and uniform circular motions.[27] Fracastoro's Homocentrica, as its title suggests, argued that this cosmological system best accounted for the natural phenomena of the sublunary world.

[24] See Nardi (1958) 170; Knox (2002); and Shank (2008).
[25] See Granada/Tessicini (2005) 431–32 and (2008) 22.
[26] Peruzzi (1995); and Granada/Tessicini (2008) 31–33.
[27] Fracastoro (1538) 1^{r–v}.

De causis criticorum dierum was equally radical in the arena of medical astrology, calling for wholesale rejection of the theory of "critical days," which proposed a causal relation between the movement of the stars and the ebb and flow of disease and which lay at the heart of the medieval medical tradition, itself saturated by Ptolemaic and Arabic astrological theory.[28] In the third book of his *De diebus decretoriis* [On Decisive Days], Galen elaborated mathematical calculations and astronomical observations that had allowed Arabic and Latin interpreters of the Middle Ages and Renaissance to establish complex interconnections between the motion and appearance of stars and critical stages of diseases.[29] Against this idea, Fracastoro argued that the moon and other "planets" do not affect the trajectory of disease through their movement, appearance, or emanations. It is rather the movement of humors and differences in complexion and temperament within the body that cause changes in the health of patients and determine their various outcomes. By eliminating this cornerstone of contemporary medical theory, Fracastoro laid himself open to criticism by eminent astrologers and colleagues, including Andrea Turini, Michelangelo Biondo, and Luca Gaurico,[30] whose attacks recall the *post-mortem* controversies regarding Giovanni Pico della Mirandola following the posthumous publication of his *Disputationes adversus astrologiam divinatricem* [Disputations against Divinatory Astrology] in 1496.[31]

Fracastoro's writing on epidemic disease, like his writing on medical astrology, received its impulse from the movement of medical humanism, then centered in Rome, Padua, Venice, and Ferrara, committed to the philologically informed reading of ancient medical texts. This permitted for the first time in millennia an informed reading of the Greek texts of Galen and Hippocrates – published by the Aldine press in Venice, in 1525 and 1526 respectively – and the Latin translations made from them contributed to the development of a modern medical–scientific language. In the hands of medical humanists these studies gave learned physicians intellectual and literary tools to deal with new diseases and new scientific, technological, and geographic discoveries. In Fracastoro's poem *Syphilis sive morbus gallicus* [Syphilis or the French Disease, 1530],

---

[28] See Jouanna (1992) 474–79.
[29] Galen (1825) III.9, 930–33; Garofalo (2003); Langermann (2008); and Cooper (2011).
[30] Turini (1542); Biondo (1544); and Gaurico (1546).
[31] Pico della Mirandola (1946–52); Broecke (2003); Bacchelli (2008); and Bertozzi (2008).

for example, ancient mythology encounters the New World in the person of the shepherd Syphilus, who, having insulted the sun-god of Hispaniola (now Haiti), is inflicted with the disease that today bears his name but that was called the "French disease" by sixteenth-century Italians. This illness appeared in Europe toward the end of the fifteenth century and soon came to be blamed on sailors from Christopher Colombus' expeditions after their return to Spain from the New World, where the disease had been witnessed as endemic.[32] From Spain, the disease spread to Naples, transported by the Spanish fleet tasked with defending that city from the French troops of Charles VIII in 1494, and was further diffused by the French army as it made its way back up the Italian peninsula (hence the Italian name for it).[33] Its first appearance in medical writing dates from 1495, when it was described by military doctors among the troops that fought at the battle of Fornovo. By the middle of the sixteenth century, Italian physicians had produced a vast medical literature analyzing the origin of the French disease itself, the problem of whether and how it was possible for new diseases to arise, and the prospect that other diseases besides those already described by ancient medicine could continue to appear in Europe. While some physicians wondered if syphilis had already existed in antiquity under another name, most medical writers agreed quickly on both its American origin and its sexual transmission, which differentiated it from other forms of epidemic disease, which were attributed to corruption of the air by both terrestrial and astrological causes.[34]

While Renaissance physicians referred to a range of diseases – syphilis, typhus, diarrhea – as "pestilence" or "epidemic," the most famous and terrifying among all of them was what we now identify as plague. While plague had ravaged early medieval Italy, it had since died out, only to return in the great epidemic of 1347–51, sometimes referred to by historians as the Black Death; radiating from the Italian ports of southern Italy and Genoa, this spread fear throughout the peninsula and ultimately killed a vast swath of the European population; other epidemics recurred at more or less regular intervals through 1720–22.[35] As noted above, the

---

[32] On voyages to the New World, see Fiorani, "Mapping and voyages," Chapter 3 in this volume.
[33] The critical literature on syphilis is considerable, but for essential overviews see Quétel (1986); and Arrizabalaga *et al.* (1997).
[34] See Sudhoff/Singer (1925); and Fracastoro (1984) 11–15.
[35] On plague, see Mollaret (1980); Benvenuto (1996); Eckert (1996); Bos *et al.* (2011a) and (2011b).

arrival of plague pushed doctors to seek explanations and treatments for epidemic diseases by interrogating ancient medical knowledge anew. The theory that dominated medical discussions of the topic in the fourteenth and fifteenth centuries focused on the model of pestilential fever, inherited from the Arabic medical writer Ibn Sina (Avicenna), whose *Liber canonis*, as we have already mentioned, dominated the Italian medical curriculum in the area of therapeutics. According to this theory, the air could be "corrupted" by putrid vapors (pestilential seeds) emanating from unburied cadavers, rotting mounds of refuse, swamps, and so on, as well as by the conjunctions of certain planets (to say nothing of divine wrath). Depending on their individual complexions, as well as the *aptitudo patientis* [lifestyle or predisposition of the patient], people in an afflicted region were more or less susceptible to the disease.[36] These ideas pervade the vast literature of plague *consilia* (short treatises offering brief explanations and therapeutic advice) churned out by university masters and municipal physicians, as well as better-known authors such as Marsilio Ficino (1433–99) and Symphorien Champier (1471–1538).[37]

Fracastoro's contribution to this literature was typically ambitious and informed by reading Galen's own work, notably *De differentiis febrium* [On the Differences among Fevers], rather than treatises by medieval Arabic writers such as Ibn Sina. In *De sympathia et antipathia rerum liber unus. De contagione, contagiosis morbis et curatione libri III* [One Book on Sympathy and Antipathy in Things. Three Books on Contagion, Contagious Diseases, and their Cure, 1546], dedicated to Alessandro Farnese (a nephew of Paul III), Fracastoro built on Galen's idea of pestilential seeds spread through the air. In it he elaborated his celebrated theory of the *seminaria* [seeds] and the three modes of transmission: through direct contact, *fomes* [tinder] or an intermediary, and indirect contact.[38] Against Galen, however, he argued the patient is not responsible for becoming ill because of his regimen or lifestyle: the *aptitudo patientis* in Galen's *De differentiis febrium* is substituted by Fracastoro with the *aptitudo materiae* [fitness or predisposition of the material], in other words an affinity or correspondence of substances between contagious *seminarium* [seed] and the body of the patient.

---

[36] Galen (1824) I.6, 289–91; Avicenna (1527) IV.1.4.1, 325ᵛ.
[37] See Champier (1522) X.1, 49ᵛ–50ᵛ; and Ficino (2007).
[38] The bibliography on Fracastoro and contagion is enormous, but useful points of departure are Nutton (1983) and (1990).

In this way, Fracastoro elaborated a medical theory that stopped short of negating Galenism, while profoundly remaking ancient medicine through etiological research dedicated to contagious diseases as a class – De contagione analyzes among others plague, syphilis, rabies, and fevers – thanks to two elements essential to the formation of the Renaissance doctor: the study of natural philosophy and the clinical practice of medicine. De sympathia et antipathia rerum is a text in which the doctor–physicus [natural philosopher][39] studies the manifestation of natural phenomena (from magnetic attraction to pregnancy, the action of the suckerfish, and the repulsion of oil and water, to cite only a few examples) which permit him to understand how contagions function. The study of natural philosophy thus goes hand in hand with the practical experience of the doctor. In particular, for Fracastoro clinical experience demonstrates that among the thousands afflicted by a given epidemic, many enjoyed good health and led virtuous lives with regard to exercise and diet; contemporary adherents of Galen, such as the university professor Giambattista da Monte (1498–1551), would therefore do well to follow their master in relying on the use of both reason and experience rather than mere book-learning.[40]

The dedication of De sympathia and De contagione to Alessandro Farnese is hardly surprising, given that the cardinal was famous for his patronage, and Fracastoro was the official doctor of the Council of Trent. Other doctors also dedicated medical works to Farnese, such as shown by the first edition of Girolamo Mercuriale's De arte gymnastica [On the Art of Exercise, 1569] (the second edition, in 1573, was dedicated the Holy Roman Emperor Maximilian).[41] Yet while Fracastoro downplayed the role played by regimen in preserving health, at least in the case of contagious illness, Mercuriale reinforced it. In light of the renewed interest in formal physical exercise all but forgotten with the decline of the Roman empire, Mercuriale proposed a prophylactic and therapeutic alternative to traditional medical remedies, which he claimed often resulted in deceiving or even killing patients. In place of these, Mercuriale identified physical exercise as an alternative remedy in complete harmony with Galenic principles, which acknowledged in "regimen" the

---

[39] On the physicus and the relationship between natural philosophy and medicine, see Bylebyl (1990); Blair (2006); and Cook (2006).
[40] Fracastoro (1930) II.3, 76–82.   [41] See Mercuriale (2008)

path to sound health. Games played with balls, different forms of dance, wrestling, boxing, running, jumping, discus-throwing, weight-lifting, swimming, horsemanship, and the multiform use of the voice (reading aloud, singing, modulations exercises) are among the sports analyzed in *De arte gymnastica* in keeping with ancient recommendations and counter-indications regarding health and well-being.

Whereas Mercuriale's detailed promotion of the medical utility of exercise marked a significant innovation relative to medieval medical knowledge, the analysis of thermal baths that constitutes the greater part of the first book of his treatise corresponds to a long-standing Italian tradition, in which Dondi and his father had both participated; like many other branches of Renaissance medicine, this one brought together medical and natural philosophical concerns.[42] Tommaso Giunta's 1553 collection of over seventy earlier texts, *De balneis omnia* [All Extant Books on Therapeutic Baths], testifies to this rich, uninterrupted tradition, as demonstrated by the numerous ancient, medieval (Arabic–Latin), and Renaissance sources that fill the index to the volume. Giunta explains in the introduction to the collection that his objective in making available such a wide range of writing on balneotherapy was to promulgate knowledge about how to correct humoral defects using the health-giving thermal springs that a beneficent God caused to flow from the earth. Precisely because such waters are free and do not pose the hazards of other medical remedies they can obviate recourse to iron that cuts, fire that burns, the prescription of hunger or thirst, bitter juices, or bloodletting.[43]

A number of Italian Renaissance balneologists used alchemical methods to analyze the composition and properties of the waters of the springs they studied. The Swiss doctor Paracelsus (1493–1541) is an indispensable point of reference for alchemical medicine in the sixteenth century, though scholars have only recently begun to shed light on the diffusion of his ideas in Italy. Paracelsus had his greatest impact there in the second half of the century, as attested by the patronage of Italian princes who assured protected spaces for the spread of the ideas of the "Luther of doctors," as had already occurred elsewhere in

---

[42] On hot springs, see Boisseuil/Nicoud (2010); and Boisseuil/Wulfram (2012).

[43] Giunta (1553) 2ʳ; on Giunta's collection, see Stefanizzi (2011). Note that we have adopted the spelling "Giunta" in use in American library catalogues, though "Giunti" is the form used in Italy.

Europe.[44] Exemplary in this sense is the dedication with which Adam von Bodenstein – editor of dozens of Paracelsus' works – addressed *De tartaro* [On Tartar, 1563] to Grand Duke Cosimo I de' Medici. Cosimo had earlier invited Luca Ghini to join the faculty of the University of Pisa, where he founded its famous botanical garden, followed soon thereafter by one in Florence. Cosimo also instituted the laboratory known as *La Fonderia* [The Foundry] for distillation and other alchemical experiments in Florence.[45] Medicine and alchemy found fertile ground in their encounter with pharmacopeia, as demonstrated by figures such as Angelo Forte, the author of works of alchemy, magic, astrology, and medicine; active in Venice in the middle decades of the sixtenth century, Forte collaborated with the herbalist Sabba di Franceschi, and the doctor Leonardo Fioravanti (1518–88), who included remedies obtained through distillation in his *Secreti medicinali* [Medical Secrets, 1561].[46] The work of these authors was hardly isolated, as shown by the publishing success of the book of medical recipes, *Secreti del reverendo donno Alessio Piemontese* [Secrets of the Reverend Don Alessio Piemontese, 1555]; this best-seller – it appeared in more than ten separate Italian editions within a decade, and in French (1557) and English (1569) translations – was written by the polymath Girolamo Ruscelli (d. 1566), whose wide-ranging interests encompassed vernacular philology, editing contemporary literary works (Ariosto, Ludovico Dolce, Vittoria Colonna), military engineering, and the foundation of the Neapolitan Accademia Segreta, the first experimental scientific society in Europe.[47]

The debate provoked by these new forms of knowledge with respect to Galenism must be understood within the larger context we have aimed to elaborate throughout this chapter. While Paracelsian medicine dramatically recast knowledge of the human body, the causes of disease, and the remedies that should be used to treat them, the impulse for renewal made itself felt even at the heart of orthodox Galenism with regard to method, diagnosis, pathology, and therapeutics. Our brief glance at Fracastoro drew attention to this ferment, but other Renaissance doctors such as Girolamo Cardano (1501–76) or Giovanni Argenterio (1513–72) also demonstrate how the notion of *experimenta* [empirically attested

[44] See Clericuzio (2005) and (2008).
[45] See Perifano (1997); Clericuzio (2008) 375–76; and Kieffer (2012) 381–419.
[46] See Palmer (1985); Clericuzio (2008) 374–75; and Eamon (2010).
[47] See Clericuzio (2008) 377–81, and the bibliography cited therein.

remedies] combined with direct knowledge of the earth's natural resources (minerals, metals, herbs, and the like) to ground a new way of conceiving of medicine and health.[48] The integration of medical knowledge within the domain of philosophical knowledge, on the one hand, and natural history, on the other, was pushed to its limits by these *physici*: the authority of the ancients was no longer sufficient for an era in which new diseases such as the French disease, contact with newly discovered lands, and technological innovations allowed doctors to widen the range of their expertise while also measuring themselves against other scientific disciplines.

Giovanni Filippo Ingrassia is a telling case in point, and not only for the history we have aimed to outline here but also for the still largely unwritten history of the Italian south in the period of the Renaissance.[49] Ingrassia was born in either 1510 or 1512 into a well-to-do family in what is now the province of Enna in Sicily, and through tutors he received a humanist education in Latin and Greek letters before passing on to the (private) study of medicine in Palermo. Ingrassia subsequently traveled to continue his medical studies first in Padua and Ferrara from 1532 to 1534, and finally in Bologna, where he received his doctorate in medicine and philosophy in 1537. Thus his formation took place in the thick of the enormous challenge to medical and scientific ideas posed by the work of Paracelsus, Vesalius, Fracastoro, Copernicus, and others, and the combination of a critical eye to received knowledge and a keen sense of the necessity of clinical observation that Ingrassia learned in northern universities and took back with him to Sicily was to have a significant impact on both the practice and teaching of medicine there and in the wider Kingdom of Naples. Given the official roles that he filled as professor of medicine and anatomy in Naples and later in Messina, as *Protomedicato generale* [Chief Public-Health Officer] first of Palermo and then of the entire Kingdom of Sicily, and as *Publico lettore di medicina teorica e pratica* [Public Reader in Theoretical and Practical Medicine] there, it would be difficult to overestimate the impact Ingrassia had on the development of a medical infrastucture as efficacious in Sicily as anywhere on the peninsula; in fact, his *Constitutiones protomedicales* [Protomedical Regulations, 1564] were a

---

[48] On these authors, see Siraisi (1990a) and (1997); and Clericuzio (2008) 373–74.
[49] For a summary of Ingrassia's career, see Preti (2004); for a fuller treatment, based on archival evidence and concise readings of each of Ingrassia's works, see Marchese (2010).

blueprint for public-health legislation. Ingrassia's management of the ferocious plague that devastated Italy in 1575–76 was such that out of a population of almost 100,000 there were only some 3,000 victims in Palermo, while 50,000 died in Venice (population 190,000), where Girolamo Mercuriale and and his colleagues had seriously underestimated the scope of the pandemic.[50] The treatise that Ingrassia published in the wake of this crisis, *Informatione del pestifero et contagioso morbo* [Knowledge of the Pestilent and Contagious Disease, 1576], extended Fracastoro's theory of the *seminaria* in identifying transmission via fomites and through actual contact, and in proposing a strategy of isolating the infected and destroying the contagion-bearing agents and their host environments in order to block the spread of the disease (the text was translated into Latin after Ingrassia's death, published in Nuremberg in 1583, and gained a wide European readership).[51] Ingrassia was the first to demonstrate – in a 1548 dissection at the Ospedali dei Incurabili in Naples – that the human brain could host tumors, and he subsequently published *De tumoribus praeter naturam* [On Swellings Contrary to Nature, 1552]; while he gave this work the same title as Galen's work on tumors, it contained a rigorous classification of the phenomenon linked to a critique of the orthodoxies of academic medicine – this, a constant in all of Ingrassia's writing – drawing on his extensive clinical and pedagogical experience. Ingrassia was the first to distinguish chickenpox from scarlet fever; he successfully argued for the drainage of swamps surrounding Palermo in order to fight malaria; and in his *Methodus dandi relationes pro mutilatis, torquendis* [...] [Method for Giving Reports on behalf of the Mutilated and Tortured], written between 1569 and 1578, he effectively invented the field of forensic medical ethics, addressing the ethical implications of medical practitioners increasingly involved as witnesses in judicial proceedings.

Ingrassia's efforts to balance the written tradition of ancient medicine with the contemporary practice of medicine – he compiled a monumental commentary on Galen's *De ossibus* [On Bones] in 1546–53 – were seconded by Gabriele Falloppio, the noted doctor/anatomist who taught in the universities of Ferrara, Pisa, and Padua between 1547 and 1562, carrying on the tradition he inherited from his predecessors and teachers, Andrea Vesalius and Realdo Colombo. But if dissections such

---

[50] See Nutton (2006) and Palmer (2008).   [51] See Ingrassia (2005).

as those described by Mondino in the early fourteenth century and discussed above did not displace ancient textual authorities, the situation changed over the course of the sixteenth century. The errors of the ancients – above all Galen – had to be corrected, as Vesalius did in *De humani corporis fabrica* [On the Fabric of the Human Body, 1543]. But the errors of contemporaries and colleagues also required emendation, as Falloppio reminded Vesalius: just as Vesalius had taken Galen to task for having mistaken the uterus of a cow for that of a woman, thus creating a chimera in his treatise *De uteri resectione* [On the Dissection of the Uterus],[52] according to Falloppio Vesalius' mistake consisted in associating *sinus* [sinuosity] and the uterine cervix.[53] It is no coincidence that the female body offered sixteenth-century anatomists the opportunity both for polemicizing and collaborating with their colleagues in the construction of new medical knowledge, given that the exploration of the female body and its secrets had been at the center of the earliest anatomical studies and of Vesalius' work.[54] But medical interest in women's diseases and the female body had been a constant since antiquity, as attested by medieval obstetrical and gynecological treatises and the proliferation of texts dealing with women's medicine and pregnancy from the late fourteenth century on.[55] Physicians could thus complement the practices of other healthcare practitioners in Renaissance society, expanding the therapeutic marketplace. The *physicus* formulated diagnoses and recommended therapies based on the study of the body's constitution, but it was surgeons and barbers, obstetricians and midwives, herbalists and pharmacists who looked after everything that concerned the body's limbs and organs performing therapeutic interventions on them. These various possibilities for sixteenth-century patients (as for their early Renaissance counterparts) were vast, so much so that *Collegi* [medical guilds] and *Protomedicati* [public-health officials] sought (with very little success) to regulate and oversee the healthcare market in which doctors, surgeons, and pharmacists participated. Over the course of the sixteenth century, well-being became an affair of state and court, in which public authority and professional expertise collaborated in order to prevent the spread of

---

[52] Vesalius (1543) V.15, 532. On Vesalius and *De humani corporis fabrica*, see Vesalius (2014).
[53] Falloppio (1606) 53.
[54] See Park (2006).   [55] See King (2007); and Green (2008).

contagious disease, provide the best hospital care, and protect citizens from unauthorized practioners.[56]

Both continuity and innovation characterized the medical and scientific culture of Renaissance Italy. The permeability of scientific and philosophical knowledge represented a significant element of continuity between antiquity, the Middle Ages, and the Renaissance: Giovanni Dondi, professor of medicine at the University of Padua, constructed his "planetarium" in the late fourteenth century, while Girolamo Fracastoro published a series of medical, astronomical, philosophical, and literary texts in the middle of the sixteenth century. But the persistence of certain medical and scientific arguments came face to face with the arrival of new, often lethal, diseases such as syphilis and plague, and with the discovery of new technologies, worlds, and cultures which necessitated a wholesale renewal of learning and the search for new ways to reconceptualize the healing and experimental professions. Over the course of the sixteenth century, a number of ancient ideas – such as regimen or contagion – required readjustment in light of the experience of doctors and scientists working in the wake of the latest discoveries. At the same time, however, anatomical studies and the growing specialization of medical learning – gynecology, thermal, and gymnastic medicine, to name only a few – show that the continuing dialogue with antiquity, the renovation of learning, and collaboration within the scientific community fostered a new understanding of the natural world in the period of the Renaissance. Beginning in the second half of the sixteenth century, the fruits of Renaissance discovery and rediscovery examined in this volume were seized upon and further developed by the likes of Galileo Galilei, Johannes Kepler, and William Harvey, who took the work of dialogue with tradition and renewal of knowledge of the natural world in entirely new, and – for traditionalists – unwelcome directions.

Acknowledgment

We would like to thank Michael Wyatt for his translation of Concetta Pennuto's contribution to this essay, and for his attentive editing of the resulting final text.

---

[56] See Conforti (2008) and the bibliography cited therein.

Bibliography

Abulafia, D. (1977). *The Two Italies: Economic Relations between the Norman Kingdom of Sicily and the Northern Communes.* Cambridge
  (2004). 'The South', in Najemy (ed.) 208–25
  (2005). 'The Diffusion of the Italian Renaissance: Southern Italy and Beyond', in Woolfson (ed.) 27–51
Ackerman, J. S. (1986). *The Architecture of Michelangelo.* Chicago
  (1994). 'The Regions of Italian Renaissance Architercture', in Millon/Lampugnani (eds.) 319–47
  (2000). 'Imitation', in A. Payne, A. Kuttner, and R. Smick (eds.), *Antiquity and Its Interpreters* 9–16. Cambridge
Aconcio, G. (2011). *Trattato sulle fortificazioni* (ed. P. Giacomini). Florence
Adams, N. (1998). 'Pienza', in Fiore (ed.) 314–29
  (2002). 'L'architettura militare in Italia nella prima metà del *Cinquecento*', in Bruschi (ed.) 546–61
Adams, N. and Nussdorfer, L. (1994). 'The Italian City, 1400–1600', in Millon/Lampugnani (eds.) 205–31
Adorni-Braccesi, S. (1994). *'Una città infetta': la repubblica di Lucca nella crisi religiosa del Cinquecento.* Florence
Agamben, G. (1993). *Stanzas: Word and Phantasm in Western Culture.* Minneapolis
Agee, R. J. (1998). *The Gardano Music Printing Firms, 1569–1611.* Rochester NY
Ago, R. (1992). 'Giochi di squadra: uomini e donne nelle famiglie nobili del XVII secolo', in M. A. Visceglia (ed.), *Signori, patrizi e cavalieri in Italia centro-meridionale nell'età moderna* 256–64. Rome
Agosti, G. (1990). *Bambaia e il classicismo lombardo.* Turin
  (1995). 'Su Mantegna, 5 (Intorno a Vasari)', *Prospettiva* 80.61–89
Agostinelli, M. and Mariano, F. (1986). *Francesco di Giorgio e il Palazzo della Signoria di Jesi.* Jesi
Agrimi, J. and Crisciani, C. (1988). *Edocere medicos: medicina nei secoli XIII–XV.* Naples
  (1990). 'Per una ricerca su *experimentum–experimenta*: riflessione epistemologica e tradizione medica (secoli XII–XV)', in P. Janni and I. Mazzini (eds.), *Presenza del lessico greco e latino nelle lingue contemporanee* 9–49. Macerata
'AHR Forum: The Persistence of the Renaissance' (1998). *American Historical Review* 103.50–124

Alberti, L. B. (1954). *Opuscoli inediti: Musca, Vita S. Potiti* (ed. C. Grayson). Florence
  (1966a). *On Painting* (trans. J. R. Spencer). New Haven
  (1966b). *L'architettura [De re aedificatoria]* (ed. and trans. G. Orlandi, comm. P. Portoghesi). Milan
  (1969). *The Family in Renaissance Florence [I libri della famiglia]* (trans. R. N. Watkins). Columbia SC
  (1987). *Dinner Pieces [Intercenales]* (trans. D. Marsh). Binghamton NY
  (1988). *On the Art of Building In Ten Books* (trans. J. Rykwert, N. Leach, and R. Tavernor). Cambridge MA
  (1996). *Grammatichetta e altri scritti sul volgare* (ed. G. Patota). Rome
Alfano, G. (2011a) 'Una forma per tutti gli usi: l'ottava rima', in Irace *et al.* (eds.) 31–57
  (2011b) 'La voce e l'inchiostra: la novella del Rinascimento', in Irace *et al.* (eds.) 70–75
Alfari, G. (2013). *Calamities and the Economy in Renaissance Italy: The Grand Tour of the Horsemen of the Apocalypse.* London
Allaire, G. (2003). *The Italian Novella.* New York
Allen, M. J. B., Rees, V., and Davies, M. (eds.) (2002). *Marsilio Ficino: His Theology, His Philosophy, His Legacy.* Leiden
Allonge, G. (2011). 'Le scrittrici nella prima età moderna', in Irace *et al.* (eds.) 119–26
Ambrosini, A. (2000). 'Fuori contesto: testimonianze dai centri minori', in R. P. Ciardi and A. Natali (eds.), *Storia delle arti in Toscana: il Cinquecento* 189–210. Florence
Ames–Lewis, F. (1986). *The Draftsman Raphael.* New Haven
  (2000). *The Intellectual Life of the Early Renaissance Artist.* New Haven
Ames-Lewis, F. and Wright, J. (1983). *Drawing in the Italian Renaissance Workshop.* London
Andreini, G. B. (2009). *Love in the Mirror / Amor nello specchio* (ed., trans., and intro. J. R. Snyder). Toronto
Angiolini, F. (1987). 'Il ceto dominante a Prato', in E. Fasano Guarini (ed.), *Prato, Storia di una città* 343–427. Florence
Antonelli, G., Picchiorri, E., and Ravesi, M. (2011). 'L'emergere delle letterature dialettali', in Irace *et al.* (eds.) 293–99
Antonelli, G. and Ravesi, M. (2010). 'La questione della lingua nel *Cinquecento*', in De Vincentiis *et al.* (eds.) 739–49
Aretino, P. (2005). *Dialogues* (trans. R. Rosenthal). Toronto
Argan, G. C. (1984). *Classico anticlassico: il Rinascimento da Brunelleschi a Bruegel.* Milan
Ariani, M. (ed.) (1977). *Il teatro italiano: la Tragedia del Cinquecento*, 2 vols. Turin
Ariosto, L. (1964). *Tutte le Opere*, vol. 4: *Commedie* (eds. A. Casella, G. Ronchi, E. Varasi) ix–xlix. Milan
  (1998). *Orlando furioso* (trans. G. Waldman). Oxford
  (2006). *Orlando furioso secondo la princeps del 1516* (ed. M. Dorigatti). Florence
Aristotle, Longinus, and Demetrius (1995). *Poetics* (ed. and trans. S. Halliwell, W. H. Fyfe, and D. C. Innes). Cambridge MA
Arnaldi, F. N. (1974). 'Camilliani (della Camilla), Francesco', DBI: www.treccani.it/enciclopedia/francesco-camilliani_%28Dizionario_Biografico%29/
Arrizabalaga, J., Henderson, J., and French, R. (1997). *The Great Pox: The French Disease in Renaissance Europe.* New Haven
Ascoli, A. R. (1987). *Ariosto's Bitter Harmony: Crisis and Evasion in the Italian Renaissance.* Princeton
  (2008). *Dante and the Making of a Modern Author.* Cambridge

Asor Rosa, A. (ed.) (1992). *Letteratura italiana: le opere*, vol. 1: *Dalle origini al Cinquecento*. Turin

Assenza, C. (1997). *La canzonetta dal 1570 al 1615*. Lucca

Astarita, T. (1992). *The Continuity of Feudal Power: The Caracciolo di Brienza in Spanish Naples*. Cambridge

Astengo, C. (2007). 'The Renaissance Chart Tradition in the Mediterranean', in Woodward (ed.) 174–262

Atlas, A. W. (2006). 'Music for the Mass', in J. Haar (ed.), *Renaissance Music: Music in Western Europe, 1400–1600* 101–129. New York

Attolini, G. (1988). *Teatro e spettacolo nel Rinascimento*. Bari

Avicenna (1527). *Liber canonis*. Venice

Bacchelli, F. (2008). 'Appunti per la storia del testo delle *Disputationes adversus astrologiam divinatricem*', *Dianoia* 13.141–59

Baernstein, P. R. (1994). 'In Widow's Habit: Women between Convent and Family in Sixteenth Century Milan', *Sixteenth Century Journal* 25.787–807

Baker, A. (ed.) (1984–89). *Greek Musical Writings*, 2 vols. Cambridge

Baker, N. (2013). *The Fruit of Liberty: Political Culture in the Florentine Renaissance, 1480–1550*. Cambridge MA

Bakhtin, M. M. (1981). 'Epic and Novel', in M. Holquist (ed.), *The Dialogic Imagination: Four Essays, by M. M. Bakhtin* 3–40. Austin

Baldacci, O. (1993). *Atlante colombiano della grande scoperta*. Rome

Ballon, H. and Friedman, D. (2007). 'Portraying the City in Early Modern Europe: Measurement, Representation and Planning', in Woodward (ed.) 680–704

Balsano, M. A. (ed.) (1981). *Ariosto, la musica, i musicisti: quattro studi e sette madrigali ariosteschi*. Florence

Balsano, M. A. and Walker, T. (eds.) (1988). *Tasso, la musica, i musicisti*. Florence

Bambach, C. C. (1999). *Drawing and Painting in the Italian Renaissance Workshop: Theory and Practice, 1300–1600*. New York

Bandello, M. (1990). *Novelle* (ed. E. Mazzali). Milan

Baranski, Z. G. and McLaughlin, M. (eds.) (2007). *Italy's Three Crowns: Reading Dante, Petrarch and Boccaccio*. Oxford

Barbaro, F. (1978 [*c.* 1414–15]). 'On Wifely Duties', Pt. 2 of *De re uxoria*, in B. Kohl and R. Witt (eds.), *The Earthly Republic: Italian Humanists on Government and Society* 189–228. Philadelphia

Bardi, G. (1989). 'Discorso mandato a Giulio Caccini detto romano sopra la musica antica e'l cantar bene', in Palisca (ed.) 90–131

Barkan, L. (1999). *Unearthing the Past: Archaeology and Aesthetics in the Making of Renaissance Culture*. New Haven

  (2011a). 'La voce di Michelangelo', in Irace *et al.* (eds.) 374–79

  (2011b). *Michelangelo, a Life on Paper*. Princeton

Baron, H. (1988). *The Crisis of the Early Italian Renaissance: Civic Humanism and Republican Liberty in an Age of Classicism and Tyranny*. Princeton

Barr, C. (1984). 'Music and Spectacle in the Confraternity Drama of Fifteenth-Century Florence: The Reconstruction of a Theatrical Event', in T. Verdon and J. Henderson (eds.), *Christianity and the Renaissance: Image and Religious Imagination in the Quattrocento* 176–204. New York

Barzman, K. (2000). *The Florentine Academy and the Early Modern State: The Discipline of Disegno*. Cambridge

Basile, G. (2007). *Giambattista Basile's The tale of tales, or, Entertainment for little ones* (trans. N. L. Canepa). Detroit

Battaglia Ricci, L. (2000). *Boccaccio*. Rome

Battiferri degli Ammannati, L. (2006). *Laura Battiferra and her Literary Circle: An Anthology* (ed. and trans. V. Kirkham). Chicago

Battistini, F. (2003) *L'industria della seta nell'età moderna*. Bologna

Baxandall, M. (1963). 'A Dialogue on Art from the Court of Leonello d'Este: Angelo Decembrio's *De politia litteraria* Pars LXVIII', *Journal of the Warburg and Courtauld Institutes* 26.304–26

(1972). *Painting and Experience in Fifteenth Century Italy: A Primer in the Social History of Pictorial Style*. Oxford

Bec, C. (ed.) (1969). *Libro degli affari proprii di casa de Lapo Niccolini de' Sirrigatti*. Paris

Bedini, S. A. and Maddison, F. R. (1966). 'Mechanical universe: the Astrarium of Giovanni de' Dondi', *Transactions of the American Philosophical Society* 56.1–69

Beer, M. (1987). *Romanzi di cavalleria: il 'Furioso' e il romanzo italiano del primo Cinquecento*. Rome

Belhoste, J. F. (2007). 'Nascita e sviluppo dell'artiglieria in Europa', in Braunstein/ Molà (eds.) 325–43

Bellavitis, A. (1998). 'Patrimoni e matrimoni a Venezia nel *Cinquecento*', in Calvi/ Chabot (eds.) 149–60

Belligni, E. (2012). *Renata di Francia (1510–1575): un'eresia di corte*. Turin

Belloni, G. and Drusi, R. (eds.) (2007). *Umanesimo ed educazione*, vol. 2 of Fontana/Molà (eds.). Treviso

Beltramini, G., Gasparotto, D., and Tura, A. (2013). *Pietro Bembo e l'invenzione del Rinascimento*. Venice

Bembo, P. (1954). *Gli asolani* (trans. R. B. Gottfried). Bloomington

(1991). *Gli asolani* (ed. G. Dilemmi). Florence

(2001). *Prose della volgar lingua, L'editio princeips del 1525 riscontrata con l'autografo Vaticano latino 3210* (ed. C. Vela). Bologna

Benadusi, G. (1996). *A Provincial Elite in Early Modern Tuscany: Family and Power in the Creation of the State*. Baltimore

(1998). 'Equilibri di potere nelle famiglie toscane tra *sei* e *settecento*', in Calvi/ Chabot (eds.) 78–92

(2009). 'La madre e il granduca: stato e famiglia nelle suppliche al Magistrato Supremo', in A. Bellavitis and I. Chabot (eds.), *Famiglie e poteri nell'Italia medievale e moderna* 397–415. Rome

Beneš, C. E. (2011). *Urban Legends: Civic Identity and the Classical Past in Northern Italy, 1250–1350*. University Park PA

Benigni, P. and Ruschi, P. (1980). 'Il contributo di Filippo Brunelleschi all'assedio di Lucca', in F. Borsi (ed.), *Filippo Brunelleschi, la sua opera e il suo tempo* vol. 2, 517–33

Benson, P. J. and Kirkham, V. (eds.) (2005). *Strong Voices, Weak History: Early Women Writers and Canons in England, France, and Italy*. Ann Arbor

Bentley, J. H. (1987). *Politics and Culture in Renaissance Naples*. Princeton

Benvenuto, G. (1996). *La peste nell'Italia della prima età moderna: contagio, rimedi, profilassi*. Bologna

Benzoni, G. (1992). 'Tra centro e periferia: il caso veneziano', in G. Benzoni and M. Bernego (eds.) (1992), *Studi veneti offerti a Gaetano Cozzi* 97–108. Venice

(1995). 'Dal centro alla periferia: qualche spunto ai fini di un fondale per Jacopo Bassano', in *Atti dell'Istituto Veneto di Scienze, Lettere ed Arti, Classe di Scienze Morali, Lettere ed Arti* 153.1–27

Berenson, B. (1895). *Lorenzo Lotto: An Essay in Constructive Art Criticism*. New York

Berger, K. (2006). 'Concepts and Developments in Music Theory', in Haar (ed.) 304–28

Bernini Pezzini, G. (1985). *Il fregio dell'arte della guerra nel Palazzo Ducale di Urbino*. Rome

Bernstein, J. (1998). *Music Printing in Renaissance Venice: The Scotto Press (1539–1572)*. New York

(2001). *Print Culture and Music in Sixteenth-Century Venice*. New York

Berrigan, J. R. (1990). 'A Tale of Two Cities: Verona and Padua in the Late Middle Ages', in C. Rosenberg (ed.), *Art and Politics in Late Medieval and Early Renaissance Italy 1250–1500* 67–80. South Bend IN

Bertozzi, M. (ed.) (2008). *Nello specchio del cielo: Giovanni Pico della Mirandola e le Disputationes contro l'astrologia divinatoria*. Florence

Besharov, G., and Greif, A. (2001). 'Comments and Further Thoughts on "Organizational Genesis, Identity, and Control: the Transformation of Banking in Renaissance Florence,"' in J. E. Rauch and A. Casella (eds.) 259–69.

Beyer, A. (2000). *Parthenope: Neapel und der Süden der Renaissance*. Munich

Biagioni, M., Duni, M., and Felici, L. (2011). *Fratelli d'Italia: riformatori italiani nel Cinquecento*. Turin

Biffi, M. (2002). *La traduzione del 'De architectura' di Vitruvio dal ms. II.I.141 della Biblioteca Nazionale Centrale di Firenze*. Pisa

Biondo, M. (1544). *De diebus decretoriis, et crisi eorumque verissimis causis in via Galeni, contra Neotericos Libellus*. Rome

Birnbaum, M. D. (2003). *The Long Journey of Gracia Mendes*. Budapest

Black, R. (1995). 'The Donation of Constantine: A New Source of the Concept of the Renaissance', in A. Brown (ed.), *Languages and Images of Renaissance Italy* 51–85. Oxford

(2001). *Humanism and Education in Medieval and Renaissance Italy: Tradition and Innovation in Latin Schools from the Twelfth to the Fifteenth Century*. Cambridge

(2004). 'Education and the Emergence of a Literate Society', in J. Najemy (ed.) 18–36

(2007). *Education and Society in Florentine Tuscany: Teachers, Pupils and Schools c. 1250–1500*, vol. 1. Leiden

Blair, A. (2003). 'Historiens de la philosophie et des sciences', in M. Engammare, M. M. Fragonard, A. Redondo, and S. Ricci (eds.), *L'étude de la Renaissance nunc et cras* 107–14. Geneva

(2006). 'Natural Philosophy', in Park/Daston (eds.) 365–416

Bober, P. P. and Rubinstein, R. (1987). *Renaissance Artists and Antique Sculpture: A Handbook of Sources*. London

Bobis, L. (2000). *Une histoire du chat: de l'Antiquité à nos jours*. Paris

Boccaccio, G. (1993). *The Decameron* (trans. G. Waldman and ed. J. Usher). Oxford

(2011). *Genealogy of the Pagan Gods / Genealogia deorum gentilium*, vol. 1 (trans. J. Solomon). Cambridge MA

(2013). *Decameron* (eds. A. Quondam, M. Fiorilla, and G. Alfano). Milan

Bocchi, F. (1982). 'La terranova da campagna a città', in Quondam/Papagno (eds.) vol. 1, 167–92

(1989). 'Discorso ... sopra la musica, non secondo l'arte di quella ma secondo la ragione alla politica pertinente', in *Due scritti intorno alla musica nel principato mediceo di Cosimo I e Francesco I* (ed. F. Perruccio) 83–109. Naples

Bock, N. (2008a). 'Center or Periphery? Artistic Migration, Models, Taste and Standards', in L. Pestilli, I. D. Rowland, and S. Schütze (eds.), *'Napoli è tutto il mondo': Neapolitan Art and Culture from Humanism to the Enlightenment* 11–36. Pisa

(2008b). 'Patronage, Standards, and *Transfert Culturel*: Naples between Art History and Social Theory', *Art History* 31.574–97

Boethius (1989). *Fundamentals of Music* (trans. C. Bower and ed. C. Palisca). New Haven

Boiardo, M. (1995). *Orlando innamorato* (trans. C. S. Ross). Oxford

Boisseuil, D. and Nicoud, M. (eds.) (2010). *Séjourner au bain: le thermalisme entre médecine et société (XIVe–XVIe siècle)*. Lyon

Boisseuil, D. and Wulfram, H. (eds.) (2012). *Die Renaissance der Heilquellen in Italien und Europa von 1200 bis 1600: Geschichte, Kultur und Vorstellungswelt / Il Rinascimento delle fonti termali in Italia e in Europa dal 1200 fino al 1600: storia, cultura e immaginario*. Frankfurt am Main

Bologna, C. (1986). 'Tradizione testuale e fortuna dei classici italiani', in A. Asor Rosa (ed.), *Letteratura italiana*, vol. 6: *Teatro, musica, tradizione dei classici* 445–928. Turin

Bologna, F. (1969). *I pittori alla corte angioina di Napoli, 1266–1414*. Rome

(1982). *La coscienza storica dell'arte italiana*. Turin

(2000). 'Tanzio a Roma, sugli Altopiani Maggiori d'Abruzzo e a Napoli', in *Tanzio da Varallo: realismo, fervore e contemplazione in un pittore del Seicento* 33–41. Milan

Bolzoni, L. (1993). 'Le città utopiche del Cinquecento italiano', *L'asino d'oro* 4.64–81

(2000). 'Note su Bruno e Ariosto', *Rinascimento* 40.19–43

Bomford, D., Dunkerton, J., Gordon, D., and Roy, A. (eds.) (1989). *Art in the Making: Italian Painting before 1400*. London

Bondì, R. (1997). *Introduzione a Telesio*. Rome

Bongi, S. (2000 [1890–97]). *Annali di Gabriel Giolito de' Ferrari da Trino di Monferrato stampatore in Venezia*, 2 vols. Mansfield Centre CT

Bonifati, G. (2008). *Dal libro manoscritto al libro stampato: sistemi di mercato a Bologna e a Firenze agli albori del capitalismo*. Turin

Bonora, E. (1987). 'Poeti latini', in Sapegno (ed.) 283–96

Boorman, S. (2006). *Ottaviano Petrucci: Catalogue Raisonné*. New York

Boorsch, S. (2004). 'The Case of Francesco Rosselli as the Engraver of Berlinghieri's *Geographia*', *Imago Mundi* 56.152–69

Bora, G., Kahn-Rossi, M., and Porzio, F. (eds.) (1998). *Rabisch: il grottesco nell'arte del Cinquecento – l'Accademia della Val di Blenio, Lomazzo e l'ambiente milanese*. Milan

Borsi, F. (1977). *Leon Battista Alberti* (trans. R. G. Carpanini). Oxford

Borsook, E. (1980). *The Mural Painters of Tuscany*. Oxford

Bos, K. I. *et al.* (2011a). 'A Draft Genome of *Yersinia pestis* from Victims of the Black Death', *Nature* 478.506–10

(2011b). 'Corrigendum', *Nature* 480.278

Botero, G. (2012). *On the Causes of the Greatness and Magnificence of Cities* (trans. G. M. Symcox). Toronto

Botfield, B. (ed.) (1861). *Praefationes et epistolae editionibus principibus auctorum veterum praepositae*. Cambridge

Bouwsma, W. (1968). *Venice and the Defence of Republican Liberty: Renaissance Values in the Age of the Counter-Reformation*. Berkeley

Bowd, S. (2010). 'General Introduction', in *Renaissance? Preceptions of Continuity and Discontinuity in Europe c. 1300–c. 1550* 1–8. Leiden

Bower, C. (2002). 'The Transmission of Ancient Music Theory into the Middle Ages', in T. Christensen (ed.), *The Cambridge History of Western Music Theory* 136–67. Cambridge

Bragantini, R. (1998). 'Alcune economie della narrazione cinquecentesca', in G. M. Anselmi (ed.), *Dal primato allo scacco: i modelli narrativi italiani tra Trecento e Seicento* 153–70. Rome

(2000). *Vie del racconto: dal 'Decameron' al 'Brancaleone'*. Naples

Branca, V. and Murtha, B. (eds.) (1999). *Merchant Writers of the Italian Renaissance*. New York

Braudel, F. (1972). *The Mediterranean and the Mediterranean World in the Age of Philip II*. New York

Braunstein, P. and Molà, L. (eds.) (2007). *Produzione e tecniche*, vol. 3 of Fontana/Molà (eds.). Treviso

Brioschi, F. and Di Girolamo, C. (eds.) (1993). *Manuale di letteratura italiana: generi e problemi*. Turin

Broecke, S. van den (2003). *The Limits of Influence: Pico, Louvain, and the Crisis of Renaissance Astrology*. Leiden

Brotton, J. (1997). *Trading Territories: Mapping the Early Modern World*. London

(2002). *The Renaissance Bazaar: From the Silk Road to Michelangelo*. Oxford

(2006). *The Renaissance: A Very Short Introduction*. Oxford

Broughton, J. (2002). *Descartes's Method of Doubt*. Princeton

Brown, A. (2010). *The Return of Lucretius to Renaissance Florence*. Cambridge MA

Brown, C. M. (1976). '"Lo insaciable desiderio nostro de cose antique", New Documents for Isabella d'Este's Collection of Antiquities', in C. H. Clough (ed.), *Cultural Aspects of the Italian Renaissance: Essays in Honour of Paul Oskar Kristeller* 324–53. New York

Brown, D. A. (1993). 'The Pentimenti in the Feast of the Gods', in J. Manca (ed.), *Titian 500: Studies in the History of Art* 289–99. Washington DC

Brown, J. C. (1982). *In the Shadow of Florence: Provincial Society of Renaissance Pescia*. New York

(1986). *Immodest Acts: The Life of a Lesbian Nun in Renaissance Italy*. New York

(1994). 'Monache a Firenze all'inizio dell'età moderna: un'analisi demografica', *Quaderni storici* 85.117–152

(2005). 'Gender', in Woolfson (ed.) 177–92

Brown, J. C. and Davis, R. C. (eds.) (1998). *Gender and Society in Renaissance Italy*. London

Brown, P. F. (1996). *Venice and Antiquity: The Venetian Sense of the Past*. New Haven

Brownlee, M. S. and Gondicas, D. (eds.) (2013). *Renaissance Encounters: Greek East and Latin West*. Leiden

Brucker, G. (1986). *Giovanni and Lusanna: Love and Marriage in Renaissance Florence*. Berkeley

(ed.) (1991). *Two Memoirs of Renaissance Florence: The Diaries of Buonaccorso Pitti and Gregorio Dati*. Prospect Heights IL

Brundin, A. (2008). *Vittoria Colonna (1490–1547) and the Spiritual Poetics of the Italian Reformation*. Aldershot

Bruni, L. (1978). *Panegyric to the City of Florence* (trans. R. Witt), in R. Witt and B. Kohl (eds.), *The Earthly Republic: Italian Humanists on Government and Society* 173–74. Philadelphia

(1987a). *Isagogicon moralis disciplinae* (trans. J. Hankins), in Griffiths *et al.* (eds. and trans.) 267–92

(1987b). 'Preface' to Bruni's translation of Aristotle's *Politics* (trans. J. Hankins), in Griffiths *et al.* (eds. and trans.) 162–64

(1994). *Dialogi ad Petrum Paulum Histrum* (ed. S. U. Baldassarri). Florence

Bruni, R. L. and Zancani, D. (1992). *Antonio Cornazzano: la tradizione testuale.* Florence

Bruno, B. (2000a). *Dialoghi filosofici italiani* (ed. M. Ciliberto). Milan

(2000b). *De la causa principio et uno*, in Bruno (2000a) 161–296

(2000c). *Cena de le Ceneri*, in Bruno (2000a) 1–155

(2000d). *De l'infinito, universo e mondi*, in Bruno (2000a) 299–454

(2000e). *De gl'heroici furori*, in Bruno (2000a) 753–960

(2000f). *Cabala del cavallo pegaseo*, in Bruno (2000a) 673–750

Bruscagli, R. (1996) 'La novella e il romanzo', in E. Malato (ed.), *Storia della letteratura italiana*, vol. 4: *Il primo Cinquecento* 835–907. Rome

Bruschi, A. (ed.) (2002). *Storia dell'architettura italiana: il primo Cinquecento*. Milan

Bullough, G. (ed., and trans.) (1973). *Narrative and Dramatic Sources of Shakespeare*, vol. 7: *Major Tragedies* 239–52. London

Buranello, R. (2004). 'Pietro Aretino between the *locus mendacii* and the *locus veritatis*', in D. Heitsch and J. F. Vallée (eds.), *Printed Voices: The Renaissance Culture of Dialogue* 95–112. Toronto

Burckhardt, J. (2002). *The Civilization of the Renaissance in Italy* (trans. S. G. C. Middlemore). New York

Burioni, M. (2010). 'Vasari's Rinascità: History, Anthropology, or Art Criticism?', in A. Lee, P. Péporté, and H. Schnitker (eds.), *Renaissance? Perceptions of Continuity and Discontinuity in Europe, c. 1300–c. 1550* 115–27. Leiden

Burke, P. (1987). 'Language and Anti-Languages in Early Modern Italy', in *The Historical Anthropology*. Cambridge

(1987). *The Historical Anthropology of Early Modern Italy*. Cambridge

(1999). *The Italian Renaissance: Culture and Society in Italy*. Princeton

(2005). 'Decentring the Italian Renaissance: The Challenge of Postmodernism', in Milner (ed.) 36–49

Burns, H. (1998). 'Leon Battista Alberti', in Fiore (ed.) 114–65

(2010). 'Castelli travestiti? Ville e residenze di campagna nel Rinascimento italiano', in Calabi/Svaduz (eds.) 465–545

Bury, M. (2001). *The Print in Italy 1550–1560* 121–70. London

(1990). 'The Medical Meaning of *Physica*', in McVaugh/Siraisi (eds.) 16–41

Caccini, G. (1998a). 'Preface' to *Le nuove musiche*, in Strunk/Treitler (eds.) 99–109

(1998b). 'Preface' to *L'Euridice composta in musica in stile rappresentativo*, in Strunk/Treitler (eds.) 97–99

Caciorgna, M. and Guerrini, R. (2005). '*Imago urbis*: la lupa e l'immagine di Roma nell'arte e nella cultura senese come identità storica e morale', in B. Santi and C. M. Strinati (eds.), *Siena e Roma: Raffaello, Caravaggio e protagonisti di un legame antico* 99–118. Siena

Caferro, W. (1998). *Mercenary Companies and the Decline of Siena*. Baltimore

(2008). 'Warfare and Economy in Renaissance Italy, 1350–1450', *Journal of Interdisciplinary History* 39.167–209

(2011). *Contesting the Renaissance*. Malden MA

Cagliotti, F. (2007). 'Desiderio da Settignano: Profiles of Heroes and Heroines of the Ancient World', in *Desiderio da Settignano: Sculptor of Renaissance Florence* 87–101. Washington

Cairns, C. (1995). 'Teatro come festa scenografia per la Talanta del 1542', in *Pietro Aretino nel Cinquecentenario della Nascita: Atti del convegno di Roma–Viterbo–Arezzo (28 settembre–1 ottobre 1992), Toronto (23–24 ottobre 1992), Los Angeles (27–29 ottobre 1992)* vol. 1, 231–43

Calabi, D. and Svalduz, E. (eds.) (2010). *Luoghi, spazi, architetture*, vol. 6 of Fontana/Molà (eds.). Treviso

Calabria, A. (1991). *The Cost of Empire: The Finances of the Kingdom of Naples in the Time of Spanish Rule.* Cambridge

Calcagno, M. P. (2012). *From Madrigal to Opera: Monteverdi's Staging of the Self.* Berkeley

Calitti, F. (2010). 'In morte di Serafino Aquilano', in De Vincentiis *et al.* (eds.) 640–45

Calvi, G. (1992). 'Maddalena Nerli and Cosimo Tornabuoni: A Couple's Narrative of Family History in Early Modern Florence', *Renaissance Quarterly* 45.312–39

(1994). *Il contratto morale: madri e figli nella Toscana moderna.* Rome

(1998). 'Reconstructing the Family: Widowhood and Remarriage in Tuscany in the Early Modern Period', in Dean/Lowe (eds.) 275–96

Calvi, G. and Chabot, I. (eds.) (1998). *Le ricchezze delle donne, diritti patrimoniali e poteri familiari in Italia (XIII–XIX secc.).* Turin

Camerini, P. (1962–63). *Annali dei Giunti.* Florence

Camerota, F. (2006). *La prospettiva del Rinascimento: arte, architettura, scienza.* Milan

Campanella, T. (1998). 'Al Telesio Cosentino', in *Le poesie.* (ed. F. Giancotti) 278. Turin

(2006). *Apologia pro Galileo* (ed. M. P. Lerner and trans. G. Ernst). Pisa

Campanelli, M. and Pincelli, M. A. (2000). 'La lettura dei classici nello Studium Urbis tra Umanesimo e Rinascimento', in L. Capo and M. R. Di Simone (eds.), *Storia della Facoltà di Lettere e Filosofia de 'La Sapienza'* 93–195. Rome

Campbell, S. J. (2004). 'Mantegna's Triumph: The Cultural Politics of Imitation *all'antica* at the court of Mantua, 1490–1530', in S. J. Campbell (ed.), *Artists at Court, Image-Making and Identity, 1300–1550* 91–106. Boston

(2008). 'Vasari's Renaissance and its Renaissance Alternatives', in J. Elkins and R. Williams (eds.), *The Art Seminar: Renaissance Theory* 47–69. New York

(2009). 'Renaissance Naturalism and the Jewish Bible: Ferrara, Brescia, Bergamo 1520–1540', in H. Kessler and D. Nirenberg (eds.), *Judaism and Christian Art* 291–327. University Park PA

Campbell, S. J. and Milner, S. (eds.) (2004). *Artistic Exchange and Cultural Translation in the Italian Renaissance City.* Cambridge

Campbell, T. (1987). 'Portolan Charts from the Late Thirteenth Century to 1500', in Harley/Woodward (eds.), 371–463

Cantimori, D. (2002). *Eretici italiani del Cinquecento, e prospettive di storia ereticale italiana del Cinquecento* (ed. A. Prosperi). Turin

Cao, G. M. (2001). 'The Prehistory of Modern Scepticism: Sextus Empiricus in Fifteenth-Century Italy', in *Journal of the Warburg and Courtauld Institutes* 64.229–79

(2007). *Scepticism and Orthodoxy: Gianfrancesco Pico as a Reader of Sextus Empiricus, with a Facing Text of Pico's Quotations from Sextus.* Pisa

Caraci Luzzana, I. (1996–99). *Amerigo Vescuppi*, 2 vols. Rome

Caravale, G. (2011). *Il profeta disarmato: l'eresia di Francesco Pucci nell'Europa del Cinquecento.* Bologna

Cardamone, D. (1981). *The Canzone Villanesca alla Napolitana and Related Forms, 1537–1570*. Ann Arbor

Cardamone, D. and Corsi, C. (2006). 'The Canzone Villanesca and Comic Culture: The Genesis and Evolution of a Mixed Genre (1537–1557)', *Early Music History* 25.59–104

Cardini, F. (2006). 'Le bombe intelligenti di Sigismondo: umanesimo e arte della guerra tra Medioevo e Rinascimento', in Valturio 9–17

Cardini, R. (1973). *La critica del Landino*. Florence

Carlino, A. (2010). 'Angelo Poliziano e la nuova filologia', in De Vincentiis *et al.* (eds.) 586–91

Carlsmith, C. (2010). *A Renaissance Education: Schooling in Bergamo and the Venetian Republic, 1500–1600*. Toronto

Carminati, M. (1994). *Cesare da Sesto 1477–1523*. Milan.

Carmona, M. (1964). 'Aspects du capitalisme Toscan aux XVI et XVII siècles: les sociétés en commandite à Florence et à Lucques', *Revue d'histoire moderne et contemporaine* 11.81–108

Carpo, M. (2003). 'Drawing with Numbers: Geometry and Numeracy in Early Modern Architectural Design', *Journal of the Society of Architectural Historians* 62.448–69
  (2009). 'Architecture: The Rise of Technical Design and the Fall of Technical Memory in the Renaissance', in A. M. Busse Berger and M. Rossi (eds.), *Memory and Invention: Medieval and Renaissance Literature, Art, and Music* 23–36. Florence

Carter, T. (1994). *Composing Opera: From Dafne to Ulisse Errante*. Kraków

Carver, R. H. F. (2007). *The Protean Ass: The Metamorphoses of Apuleius from Antiquity to the Renaissance*. Oxford

Casamassima, E. (1960). 'Litterae gothicae: note per la storia della riforma grafica umanistica', *La Bibliofilìa* 62.109–43
  (1964). 'Lettere antiche: note per la storia della riforma grafica umanistica', *Gutenberg-Jahrbuch* 13–26

Casey, E. (1993). *Getting Back into Place: Toward a Renewed Understanding of the Place-World*. Bloomington

Cassani, A. G. (2005). 'Alberti a Rimini, il Tempio della buona e della cattiva fortuna', in G. Grassi and L. Patetta (eds.), *Leon Battista Alberti Architetto* 153–209. Florence

Cassirer, E. (1963). *Individual and the Cosmos in Renaissance Philosophy* (trans. M. Domandi). New York

Cassirer, E., Kristeller, P. O., and Randall, J. H. (eds.) (1948). *The Renaissance Philosophy of Man*. Chicago

Castelnuovo, E. and Ginzburg, C. (2009). 'Symbolic Domination and Artistic Geography in Italian Art History' (trans. M. Currie and intro. D. Gamboni), *Art in Translation* 1.5–48

Castiglione, B. (1998). *Il libro del Cortegiano* (ed. W. Barberis). Turin
  (2002). *The Book of the Courtier: The Singleton Translation* (ed. D. Javitch). New York

Castiglione, C. (2009a) '"To Trust is Good, but Not to Trust is Better": An Aristocratic Woman in Search of Social Capital in Seventeenth Century Rome', in N. A. Eckstein and N. Terpstra (eds.), *Sociability and its Discontents: Civil Society, Social Capital, and their Alternatives in Late Medieval and Early Modern Europe* 149–70. Turnhout

(2009b). '*Mater litigans*: Mothering Resistance in Early Eighteenth-Century Rome', *Historical Reflections* 35.6–27

Catto, M. (2012). *Cristiani senza pace: la chiesa, gli eretici e la guerra nella Roma del Cinquecento*. Rome

Cavaciocchi, S. (ed.) (1992). *Produzione e commercio della carta e del libro (secc. XIII–XVIII)*. Florence

Cavallo, S. (2008). 'Bachelorhood and Masculinity in Renaissance and Early Modern Italy', *European History Quarterly* 38.375–97

Cazort, M. (1996). *The Ingenious Machine of Nature: Four Centuries of Art and Anatomy*. Ottawa

Celenza, C. S. (2004). *The Lost Italian Renaissance: Humanists, Historians, and Latin's Legacy*. Baltimore

(2005). 'Petrarch, Latin, and Italian Renaissance Latinity', *Journal of Medieval and Early Modern Studies* 35.509–36

(2009). 'End Game: Humanist Latin in the Late Fifteenth Century', in W. Verbaal, Y. Maes, and J. Papy (eds.), *Latinitas Perennis*, vol. 2: *Appropriation and Latin Literature* 201–42. Leiden

(2010a). 'Platone in villa', in De Vincentiis *et al.* (eds.) 431–37

(2010b). 'Filologia sacra: da Erasmo a Valla e ritorno', in De Vincentiis *et al.* (eds.) 668–72

Celenza, C. S. and Pupillo, B. (2010). 'La rinascita del dialogo', in De Vincentiis *et al.* (eds.) 341–47

Cellini, B. (1967). *Treatises on Goldsmithing and Sculpture* (trans. C. R. Ashbee). New York

Cennini, C. (1960). *The Craftsman's Handbook: Il Libro dell'Arte* (trans. D. V. Thompson, Jr.). New York

Cesarini Martinelli, L. (1980). 'Note sulla polemica Poggio-Valla e sulla fortuna delle *Elegantiae*', *Interpres* 3.29–79

Cesera, M. (2004). 'Lascaris, Costantino', in DBI: www.treccani.it/enciclopedia/costantino-lascaris_%28Dizionario_Biografico%29/

Ceserani, G. (2012). *Italy's Lost Greece: Magna Graecia and the Making of Modern Archaeology*. Oxford

Cestaro, G. P. (2003). *Dante and the Grammar of the Nursing Body*. Notre Dame IN

Chabod, F. (1958). 'Y-a-t'il un état de la Renaissance?' in *Actes du colloque de la Renaissance* 57–74. Paris

Chabot, I. (1998). 'La loi du lignage: notes sur le système successoral florentin (XIVe/XVe–XVIIe siècles)', *Clio, Histoire, Femmes et Société* 7.51–72

(1999a). 'Lineage Strategies and the Control of Widows in Renaissance Florence', in S. Cavallo and L. Warner (eds.), *Widowhood in Medieval and Early Modern Europe* 127–44. Harlow

(1999b). 'Seconde nozze e identità materna nella Firenze del tardo Medioevo', in S. Seidel Menchi, A. J. Schutte, and T. Kuehn (eds.), *Tempi e spazi della vita femminile nella prima età moderna* 493–523. Bologna

Chambers, D. S. (1971). *Patrons and Artists in the Italian Renaissance*. Columbia SC

Chambers, D. S., Pullen, B., and Fletcher, J. (eds.) (1992). 'Working Practice, Technique, and Style of Life', in *Venice: A Documentary History 1450–1630* 434–42. Oxford

Champier, S. (1522). *De generibus febrium [. . .]*, in *Practica nova [. . .]*. Venice

Chegai, A. and Luzzi, C. (eds.) (2005). *Petrarca in musica*. Lucca

Chojnacki, S. (2000). *Women and Men in Renaissance Venice: Twelve Essays on Patrician Society*. Baltimore

(2001). 'Getting Back the Dowry: Venice, *c.* 1360–1530', in Jacobson *et al.* (eds.) 77–96

Chong, A. (2005) 'Gentile Bellini in Istanbul: Myths and Misunderstandings', in A. Chong and C. Campbell (eds.), *Bellini and the East* 98–105. London

Christian, K. W. (2010). *Empire without End: Antiquities Collections in Renaissance Rome, c. 1350–1527.* New Haven

Ciappelli, G. (2000). 'Family Memory: Functions, Evolution, Recurrences', in G. Ciappelli and P. L. Rubin (eds.), *Art, Memory and Family in Renaissance Florence* 26–38. Cambridge

Ciccolella, F. and Speranzi, D. (2010). 'Le lingue orientali e la cultura greca', in De Vincentiis *et al.* (eds.) 438–47

Ciccuto, M. (ed.) (1982). *Novelle italiane: il Cinquecento.* Milan

Ciliberto, M. (2011). *Eugenio Garin: un intellettuale del Novecento.* Rome

Cipolla, C. M. (1962). *Economic History of World Population.* London
   (1964). 'The Economic Depression of the Renaissance?', *Economic History Review* 16.519–24
   (1982). *The Monetary Policy of Fourteenth-Century Florence.* Los Angeles
   (1989). *Money in Sixteenth-Century Florence.* Berkeley

Ciracono, S. (2007). 'Trasmissione tecnologica e sistemi idraulici', in Braunstein/Molà (eds.) 439–56

Clarke, G. (1996). 'The Palazzo Orsini in Nola: A Renaissance Relationship with Antiquity', *Apollo* 144.44–50
   (2002). 'Vitruvian Paradigms', *Papers of the British School at Rome* 70.319–46

Clarke, K. (1999). *Between Geography and History: Hellenistic Constructions of the Roman World.* Oxford

Clericuzio, A. (2005). 'Chemical Medicine and Paracelsianism in Italy (1550–1650)', in M. Pelling and S. Mandelbrote (eds.), *The Theory and Practice of Reform* 59–79. Aldershot
   (2008). 'La critica della tradizione: chimica, farmacologia spagirica e medicina paracelsiana', in Clericuzio/Ernst (eds.) 367–88

Clericuzio, A. and Ernst, G. (eds.) (2008). *Le scienze*, vol. 5 of Fontana/Molà (eds.). Treviso

Clubb, L. G. (1968). *Giambattista della Porta, Dramatist.* Berkeley
   (1995). 'Italian Renaissance Theatre', in J. Russell Brown (ed.), *The Oxford Illustrated History of Theatre* 107–41. Oxford
   (2005). 'Staging Ferrara: State Theatre from Borso to Alfonso II', in Looney/Shemek (eds.) 345–63

Coccia, E. (2010). 'Il greco, la lingua fantasma dell'Occidente medievale', in De Vincentiis *et al.* (eds.) 252–57

Cocke, R. (2001). *Paolo Veronese: Piety and Display in an Age of Religious Reform.* Burlington VT

Coffin, D. R. (2004). *Pirro Ligorio: The Renaissance Artist, Architect, and Antiquarian.* University Park PA

Cohen, J. M. (ed.) (1969). *The Four Voyages of Columbus.* New York

Cohn, S. K. (1992). *The Cult of Remembrance and the Black Death: Six Renaissance Cities in Central Italy.* Baltimore
   (1998). 'Marriage in the Mountains: The Florentine Territorial State, 1348–1500', in Dean/Lowe (eds.) 174–96

Cole, B. (1983). *The Renaissance Artist at Work: From Pisano to Titian*. New York

Cole, M. (2002). 'The Demonic Arts and the Origin of the Medium', *The Art Bulletin* 84.621–40

Colonna, V. (2005). *Sonnets for Michelangelo* (ed. and trans. Abigail Brundin). Chicago

Columbus, C. (1989). *The 'Diario' of Christopher Columbus's First Voyage to America* (eds. O. Dunn and J. E. Kelly, Jr.). Norman OK

Conforti, C. and Hopkins, A. (eds.) (2002). *Architettura e tecnologia: acque, tecniche, e cantieri nell' architettura rinascimentale e barocca*. Rome

Conforti, M. (2008). 'Chirurghi, mammane, ciarlatani: pratica medica e controllo delle professioni', in Clericuzio/Ernst (eds.) 323–39

Conley, T. (2007). 'Early Modern Literature and Cartography', in Woodward (ed.) 401–11

Connell, S. (1988). *The Employment of Sculptors and Stonemasons in Venice in the Fifteenth Century*. New York

Connors, J. (1995). 'The Seated Sublime', *New York Review of Books* www.nybooks.com/articles/archives/1995/feb/16/the-seated-sublime/

Connors, J. and Dressen, A. (2010). 'Biblioteche: l'architettura e l'ordinamento del sapere', in Calabi/Svalduz (eds.) 199–228

Cook, H. J. (2006). 'Medicine', in Park/Daston (eds.) 407–16

Cooper, G. M. (2011). 'Galen and Astrology: A Mésalliance?', *Early Science and Medicine* 16.120–46

Copenhaver, B. P. (1992). *Hermetica: The Greek Corpus Hermeticum and the Latin Asclepius in a New English Translation*. Cambridge

Copenhaver, B. P. and Schmitt, C. B. (1992). *Renaissance Philosophy*. Oxford

Cortelazzo, M. and Zolli, P. (1979). *Dizionario etimologico della lingua italiana*, 6 vols. Bologna

Cortesi, M., and Fiaschi, S. (2008). *Repertorio delle traduzioni umanistiche a stampa: secoli XV–XVI*. Florence

Cosgrove, D. (1992). 'Mapping New Worlds: Culture and Cartography in Sixteenth-Century Venice', *Imago Mundi* 44.65–89

(1993). *The Palladian Landscape: Geographical Change and Its Cultural Representations in Sixteenth Century Italy*. University Park PA

(1999). 'Introduction: Mapping Meaning', in D. Cosgrove (ed.), *Mappings* 1–23. London

(2003). 'Globalism and Tolerance in Early Modern Geography', *Annals of the Association of American Geographers* 93.852–70

Cox, V. (1992). *The Renaissance Dialogue: Literary Dialogue in Its Social and Political Contexts– Castiglione to Galileo*. Cambridge

(2008). *Women's Writing in Italy, 1400–1650*. Baltimore

(2011). *The Prodigious Muse: Women's Writing in Counter-Reformation Italy*. Baltimore

Cox, V. and Ferrari, C. (eds.) (2012). *Verso una storia di genere della letteratura italiana: percorsi critici e 'gender studies'*. Bologna

Cozzi, G. and Knapton, M. (1986). *La repubblica di Venezia nell'età moderna: dalla guerra di Chioggia al 1517*. Turin

Crabb, A. (2000). *The Strozzi of Florence: Widowhood and Family Solidarity in the Renaissance*. Ann Arbor

Crews, D. A. (2008). *Twilight of the Renaissance: The Life of Juan de Valdés*. Toronto

Crisciani, C. (1990). 'History, Novelty, and Progress in Scholastic Medicine', in McVaugh/Siraisi (eds.) 118–39

(2001). *Il papa e l'alchimia: Felice V, Guglielmo Fabri e l'elixir*. Rome

(2004). '*Experientia* e *opus* in medicina e alchimia: forme e problemi di esperienza nel tardo Medioevo', *Quaestio (Yearbook of the History of Metaphysics)* 4.149–73

Crisciani, C. and Pereira, M. (1998). 'Black Death and Golden Remedies: Some Remarks on Alchemy and the Plague', in A. P. Bagliani and F. Santi (eds.), *The Regulation of Evil: Social and Cultural Attuitudes to Epidemics in the Late Middle Ages* 7–39. Florence

Cropper, E. (1976). 'On Beautiful Women: Parmigianino, "Petrarchismo" and the Vernacular Style', *The Art Bulletin* 58.374–94

(1986). 'The Beauty of Woman: Problems in the Rhetoric of Renaissance Portraiture', in M. W. Ferguson, M. Quilligan, and N. J. Vickers (eds.), *Rewriting the Renaissance: The Discourses of Sexual Difference* 175–90. Chicago

Crosby, A. W. (1997). *The Measure of Reality: Quantification and Western Society, 1250–1600*. Cambridge

Crouzet-Pavan, E. (2007). *Renaissances italiennes, 1380–1500*. Paris

Cruciani, F. (1969). *Il teatro del Campidoglio e le feste romane del 1513*. Milan

Cummings, A. (2004). *The Maecenas and the Madrigalist: Patrons, Patronage, and the Origins of the Italian Madrigal*. Philadelphia

Curran, B. (2007). *The Egyptian Renaissance: The Afterlife of Ancient Egypt in Early Modern Italy*. Chicago

Curran, S. (2005). 'Luisa Bergalli's Componimenti poetici (1726)', in Benson/Kirkham (eds.) 263–86

Cyriac of Ancona (2003). *Later Travels* (eds. and trans. E.W. Bodnar and C. Foss). Cambridge MA

D'Amelia, M. (2001). 'Becoming a Mother in the Seventeenth Century: The Experience of a Roman Noblewoman', in Jacobson Schutte *et al.* (eds.) 223–44

D'Amico, J. (1983). *Renaissance Humanism in Papal Rome: Humanists and Churchmen on the Eve of the Reformation*. Baltimore

D'Ancona, A. (1891). *Origini del teatro italiano*, 2 vols. Rome

D'Ascia, L. (1991). *Erasmo e l'umanesimo romano*. Florence

D'Elia, A. (2002). 'Marriage, Sexual Pleasure, and Learned Brides in the Wedding Orations of Fifteenth-Century Italy', *Renaissance Quarterly* 55.379–433

D'Ercole, F. (1999). 'Segni del rinascimento nella Puglia cinquecentesca: la figura e le opere di Giangiacomo dell'Acaya', *Quaderni dell'Istituto di Storia dell'Architettura* 33.21–34

Dacos, N. (1986). *Le logge di Raffaello: maestro e bottega di fronte all'antico*, 2nd edn. Rome

(1994). 'Italian Art and the Art of Antiquity', in *History of Italian Art* (trans. E. Bianchini and C. Dorey) vol. 1, 113–213. Cambridge

Dal Co, F. (1998). *Storia dell'architettura italiana: il secondo Cinquecento*. Milan

Dal Poggetto, P. (2003). *La Galleria Nazionale delle Marche e le altre Collezioni nel Palazzo Ducale di Urbino*. Rome

Dalché, P. G. (2007). 'The Reception of Ptolemy's *Geography* (End of Fourteenth to Beginning of the Sixteenth Century)', in Woodward (ed.) 285–364

Daneloni, A. (2014). 'Poliziano (Angelo Ambrogini)', in S. Gentile, F. Bausi, J. Hankins, and M. Campanelli (eds.), *Autografi dei letterati italiani: il Quattrocento*, 295–329. Rome

Dante Alighieri (1529). *De la volgare eloquenzia* (trans. G. Trissino). Vicenza

Davico Bonino, G. (ed.) (1977–78). *Il teatro italiano: la commedia del Cinquecento*, 3 vols. Turin

Davies, M. (1995). *Aldus Manutius: Printer and Publisher of Renaissance Venice*. London

Day, J. (1978). 'The Great Bullion Famine of the Fifteenth Century', *Past and Present* 79.3–54

DBI [*Dizionario biografico degli italiani*] (1960–). www.treccani.it/biografie/

De Divitiis, B. (2007). *Architettura e committenza nella Napoli del Quattrocento*. Venice
  (2008). 'Building in Local *all'antica* Style: The Palace of Diomede Carafa in Naples', *Art History* 31.505–22

De Franco, L. (1995). *Introduzione a Bernardino Telesio*. Soveria Mannelli

De la Mare, A. C. (1973). *The Handwriting of Italian Humanists*. Oxford
  (1985). 'New Research on Humanistic Scribes in Florence', in A. Garzelli (ed.), *Miniatura fiorentina del Rinascimento 1440–1525: un primo censimento* vol. 1, 393–600. Florence
  (1986). 'Vespasiano da Bisticci e i copisti fiorentini di Federico', in G. C. Baiardi, G. Chittolini, and P. Floriani (eds.), *Federico di Montefeltro: lo stato, le arti, la cultura*, vol. 3: *La cultura* 81–96. Rome
  (1996). 'Vespasiano da Bisticci as Producer of Classical Manuscripts in Fifteenth-Century Florence', in C. A. Chavannes-Mazel and M. M. Smith (eds.), *Medieval Manuscripts of the Latin Classics: Production and Use* 167–207. Los Altos Hills

De la Roncière, C. (1981). 'La condition des salariés à Florence au XIVe siècle', in *Il Tumulto dei Ciompi* 13–40. Florence

De Luca, G. (ed.) (1954). *Prosatori minori del Trecento*. Milan

De Mambro Santos, R. (2012). *Timeless Renaissance: Italian Drawings from the Alessandro Maggiori Collection*. Seattle

De Marchi, A. (2002). 'Viatico per la pittura camerte', in A. De Marchi and M. Giannatiempo López (eds.), *Il Quattrocento a Camerino: luce e prospettiva nel cuore della Marca* 51–68. Milan
  (2005). 'Fra Carnevale, Urbino and the Marches: An Alternative View of the Renaissance', in K. Christiansen (ed.), *Fra Filippo Lippi to Piero della Francesca: Fra Carnevale and the Making of a Renaissance Master* 67–97. New York

De Maria, B. (2010). *Becoming Venetian: Immigrants and the Arts in Early Modern Venice*. New Haven

De Robertis, D. (1987). 'I Latini', in Sapegno (ed.) 463–72

De Roover, R. (1963). *The Rise and Decline of the Medici Bank, 1397–1494*. Cambridge MA
  (1974). *Business, Banking, and Economic Thought in Late Medieval and Early Modern Europe*. Chicago

De Sanctis, F. (1871). *Storia della letteratura italiana*, vol. 2. Naples

De Vincentiis, A., Luzzatto, S., and Pedullà, G. (eds.) (2010). *Atlante della letteratura italiana*, vol. 1: *Dalle origini al Rinascimento*. Turin

Dean, T. and Lowe, K. J. P. (eds.) (1994). *Crime, Society, and the Law in Renaissance Italy*. Cambridge
  (eds.) (1998). *Marriage in Italy, 1300–1650*. Cambridge

Delille, G. (1985). *Famille et propriété dans le Royaume de Naples (XVe–XIXe siècle)*. Rome

Della Casa, G. (2013). *Galateo, or the Rules of Polite Behavior* (intro. and trans. M. F. Rusnak). Chicago

Della Porta, G. (1980). *I duoi fratelli rivali / The Two Rival Brothers* (trans. L. G. Clubb). Berkeley

Dellaneva, J. (ed.) and Duvick, B. (trans.) (2007). *Ciceronian Controversies*. Cambridge MA

Demo, E. (2006). 'Wool and Silk: The Textile Urban Industry of the Venetian Mainland (15th–17th Centuries)', in Lanaro (ed.) 217–43

Dempsey, C. (1980). 'Some Observations on the Education of Artists in Florence and Bologna during the Later Sixteenth Century', *The Art Bulletin* 62.552–69

(1992). *The Portrayal of Love: Botticelli's Primavera and Humanist Culture at the Time of Lorenzo the Magnifico*. Princeton

(2000). *Annibale Carracci and the Beginnings of Baroque Style*, 2nd edn. Florence

Descartes, R. (1996). *Discours de la méthode / Discourse on Method,* in *Discourse on Method and Meditations on First Philosophy* (ed. D. Weissman, trans. E. S. Haldane and G. R. T. Ross). New Haven

Di Pasquale, S. (2002). *Brunelleschi: la costruzione della cupola di Santa Maria del Fiore*. Venice

Di Teodoro (2002). 'L'architettura idraulica negli studi di Leonardo da Vinci: fonti, tecniche costruttive e macchine da cantiere', in Conforti/Hopkins (eds.) 259–77

Dini, B. (1990). 'L'Industria tessile italiana nel tardo medioevo', in S. Gensini (ed.), *Le Italie del Tardo Medioevo* 321–59. Pisa

Dionisotti, A. C., Grafton, A., and Kraye, J. (eds.) (1988). *The Uses of Greek and Latin: Historical Essays*. London

Dionisotti, C. (1967). *Geografia e storia della letteratura italiana*. Turin

(2003). *Gli umanisti e il volgare fra Quattro e Cinquecento*. Milan

(2003). *Raffaello, Baldassar Castiglione e la 'Lettera a Leone', con l'aggiunta di due saggi raffaelleschi*. San Giorgio di Piano

Dolza, L. (2007). '*Utilitas et delectatio*: libri di tecniche e teatri di macchine', in Braunstein/Molà (eds.) 115–43

Dondi, G. (1553). *De fontibus calidis agri patavini consideratio*, in Giunta (ed.) 94^r–108^v

(2003). *Tractatus astrarii* (ed. and trans. E. Poulle). Geneva

Dondi, J. (1553). *De causa salsedinis aquarum*, in Giunta (ed.) 109^{r-v}

Doti, G. (2008). 'Mariano di Iacopo (detto Taccola o Archimede da Siena)', in DBI: www.treccani.it/enciclopedia/mariano-di-iacopo_%28Dizionario-Biografico%29/

Dovizi, B. (1985). *La Calandra, commedia elegantissima per Messer Bernardo Dovizi da Bibbiena* (ed. G. Padoan). Padua

Eamon, W. (2010). *The Professor of Secrets: Mystery, Medicine, and Alchemy in Renaissance Italy.* Washington DC

Eckert, E. A. (1996). *The Structure of Plagues and Pestilences in Early Modern Europe: Central Europe, 1560–1640.* Basel

Edelheit, A. (2008). *Ficino, Pico and Savonarola: The Evolution of Humanist Theology 1461/2–1498.* Leiden

Edelstein, B. (2004). '"Acqua viva e corrente": Private Display and Public Distribution of Fresh Water at the Neapolitan Villa of Poggioreale as a Hydraulic Model for Sixteenth-Century Goardeus', in Campbell/Milner (eds.) 187–220

Edgerton, S. Y. (1991). *The Heritage of Giotto's Geometry: Art and Science on the Eve of the Scientific Revolution*. Ithaca NY

Edson, E. (2007). *Mapping Time and Space: How Medieval Mapmakers Viewed their World*. London

Einstein, A. (1949). *The Italian Madrigal*, 3 vols. Princeton

Eisenach, E. (2004). *Husbands, Wives, and Concubines: Marriage, Family, and Social Order in Sixteenth-Century Verona*. Kirksville MO

Elkins, J. and Williams, R. (2008). *Renaissance Theory*. New York

Engammare, M., Fragonard, M. M., Redondo, A., and Ricci, S. (eds.) (2003). *L'étude de la Renaissance nunc et cras, Actes du colloque de la Fédération internationale des sociétés et Instituts de la Renaissance*. Geneva

Epstein, S. A. (1989). 'The Textile Industry and the Foreign Cloth Trade in Late Medieval Sicily (1300–1500): A "Colonial relationship"?', *Journal of Medieval History* 15.141–83

(1993). 'Town and Country: Economy and Institutions in Late Medieval Italy', *Economic History Review* 46.453–77

(1996). *Genoa and the Genoese*. Chapel Hill

(2000). *Freedom and Growth: The Rise of States and Markets in Europe, 1300–1750*. London

(2001). *Speaking of Slavery: Color, Ethnicity, and Human Bondage in Italy*. Ithaca NY

Erasmus, D. (1969). *Epicureus*, in *Opera omnia*, ordo I, tome 3, 720–33. Amsterdam

Ernst, G. (2010). *Tommaso Campanella: The Book and the Body of Nature* (trans. D. L. Marshall). Dordrecht

Everson, J. E. (2001). *The Italian Romance Epic in the Age of Humanism: The Matter of Italy and the World of Rome*. New York

Fabbri, L. (1991). *Alleanza matrimoniale e patriziato nella Firenze del '400*. Florence

Fagiolo, M. (2007). 'Caprarola: la rocca, il palazzo, la villa', in *Vignola, l'architettura dei principi* 107–51. Rome

Fagliari Zeni Buchicchio, F. T. (2002). 'Palazzo Farnese a Caprarola', in R. J. Tuttle, B. Adorni, C. L. Frommel, and C. Thoenes (eds.), *Jacopo Barozzi da Vignola* 210–33. Milan

Fahy, C. (1988). *Saggi di bibliografia testuale*. Padua

(1989). *L'Orlando furioso del 1532: profilo di una edizione*. Milan

Falletti, C. (1988) 'Le feste per Eleonora d'Aragona da Napoli a Ferrrara (1473)', in R. Guarino (ed.), *Teatro e culture della rappresentazione: lo spettacolo in Italia nel Quattrocento* 121–40. Bologna

Falloppio, G. (1606). *Institutiones anatomicae*, in *Opera genuina omnia. Tomus I.* 1–36. Venice

Fanelli, V. (1979). 'Angelo Colocci e Cecco d'Ascoli', in *Ricerche su Angelo Colocci e sulla Roma cinquecentesca* 182–205. Vatican City State

Fantoni, M. (ed.) (2005). *Storia e storiografia*, vol. 1 of Fontana/Molà (eds.). Treviso

Fara, A. (1997). *Leonardo e l'architettura militare*. Florence

Farago, C. J. (1995). *Reframing the Renaissance: Visual Culture in Europe and Latin America, 1450–1650*. New Haven

Farbaky, P. and Waldman, L. A. (2011). *Italy and Hungary: Humanism and Art in the Early Renaissance*. Milan

Farmer, S. A. (1998). *Syncretism in the West: Pico's 900 Theses (1486) – The Evolution of Traditional Religious and Philosophical Systems, with Text, Translation and Commentary*. Tempe AZ

Feigenbaum, G. (1993). 'Practice in the Carracci Academy', in Lukehart (ed.) 58–76

Feldman, M. (1995). *City Culture and the Madrigal in Venice*. Berkeley

Fenlon, I. (1995). *Music, Print and Culture in Early Sixteenth-Century Italy*. London

Fenlon, I. and Haar, J. (eds.) (1988). *The Italian Madrigal in the Early Sixteenth Century: Sources and Interpretation*. Cambridge

Ferguson, R. (2000). *The Theatre of Angelo Beolco (Ruzante): Text, Context and Performance*. Ravenna

Ferguson, W. K. (1963). *Renaissance Studies*. London ON

Ferrante, L. (1996). 'Marriage and Women's Subjectivity in a Patrilinean System: The Case of Early Modern Bologna', in M. J. Maynes, A. Waltner, B. Soland, and U. Strasser (eds.), *Gender, Kinship, Power: A Comparative and Interdisciplinary History* 115–29. New York

Ferraro, J. (1993). *Family and Public Life in Brescia, 1580–1650: The Foundation of Power in the Venetian State*. Cambridge

(2001). *Marriage Wars in Late Renaissance Venice*. New York

Ferrente, S. (2010). 'Latino lingua materna', in De Vincentiis *et al.* (eds.) 335–39

Ferrone, S. (1973). 'Il Candelaio, scienza e letteratura', *Italianistica* 2.518–43

(2006). *Arlecchino: vita e avventure di Tristano Martinelli attore*. Rome

Ferroni, G. (1992). *Profilo storico della letteratura italiana*. Turin

Ficino, M. (1985). *Commentary on Plato's Symposium on Love [De amore]* (trans. S. R. Jayne). Dallas

(1989). *Three Books on Life [De vita libri tres]* (eds. and trans. J. R. Clark and C. V. Kaske). Binghamton NY

(2001–3). *Theologia platonica / Platonic Theology*, (eds. J. Hankins and W. Bowen, trans. M.J.B. Allen and J. Warden), 6 vols. Cambridge

(2007). *Consilio contro la pestilentia*, in *Medicina e filosofia in Marsilio Ficino* (ed. and trans. T. Katinis) 159–210. Rome

Filarete (1972). *Trattato di Architettura* (eds. A. M. Finoli and L. Grassi), 2 vols. Milan

Findlen, P. (1998). 'Possessing the Past: The Material World of the Italian Renaissance', *American Historical Review* 103.83–114

Findlen, P. and Gowens, K. (1998). 'The Persistence of the Renaissance', *American Historical Review* 103: 51–54

Finlay, R. (1980). *Politics in Renaissance Venice*. New Brunswick

Fiorani, F. (2005). *The Marvel of Maps*. New Haven

Fiore, F. P. (1998a). 'The *Trattati* on Architecture by Francesco di Giorgio', in Hart/ Hicks (eds.) 66–85

(ed.) (1998b). *Storia dell'architettura italiana: il Quattrocento*. Milan

Fiore, F. P. and Tafuri, M. (1993). *Francesco di Giorgio architetto*. Milan

Firenzuola, A. (1987 [1889]). *Tales of Firenzuola* (trans. Anonymous). New York

(1993). *Opere* (ed. A. Seroni). Florence

Firpo, L. (1970). 'The Flowering and Withering of Speculative Philosophy: Italian Philosophy and the Counter Reformation – The Condemnation of Francesco Patrizi', in E. Cochrane (ed.), *The Late Italian Renaissance* 266–84. London

(1971).'Botero, Giovanni', in *DBI*: www.treccani.it/enciclopedia/giovanni-botero_%28Dizionario-Biografico%29/

Firpo, M. (ed.) (1981–95). *Il processo inquisitoriale del Cardinal Giovanni Morone*, 6 vols. Rome

(2006). 'Lorenzo Lotto and the Reformation in Venice', in R. K. Delph, M. M. Fontaine, and J. J. Martin (eds.), *Heresy, Culture, and Religion in Early Modern Italy: Contexts and Contestations* 21–36. Kirksville MO

(2008). *Riforma protestante ed eresie nell'Italia del Cinquecento: un profilo storico*. Rome

(2011). 'Il cappello rosso di Pietro Bembo', in Irace *et al.* (eds.) 58–63

Firpo, M. and Marcatto, D. (eds.) (1998). *I processi inquisitoriali di Pietro Carnesecchi, 1557–1567*, 4 vols. Vatican City State

Firpo, M. and Pagano, S. (eds.) (2004). *I processi inquisitoriali di Vittore Soranzo (1550–1558)*, 2 vols. Vatican City State

Fleck, C. A. (2008). 'The Rise of the Court Artist: Cavallini and Giotto in Fourteenth Century Naples', *Art History* 31.460–83

Fletcher, S. (ed.) (2012). *Roscoe and Italy: The Reception of Italian Renaissance History and Culture in the Eighteenth and Nineteenth Centuries*, Aldershot

Floriani, P. (1980). 'Trissino, la questione della lingua, la poesia', in N. Pozzi (ed.), *Atti del Convegno di Studi su Giangiorgio Trissino* 53–66. Vicenza

Folin, M. (ed.) (2011). *Renaissance Italy: Art, Culture and Politics, 1395–1530*. Woodbridge

Fontana, G. (1984). *Le macchine cifrate di Giovanni Fontana: con la riproduzione del Cod. Icon. 242 della Bayerische Staatsbibliothek di Monaco di Baviera e la descrittazione di esso e del Cod. Lat. Nouv. Acq. 635 della Bibliothèque Nationale di Parigi* (eds. and trans. E. Battisti and G. Saccaro Battisti). Milan

Fontana, G. L. and Molà, L. (gen. eds.) (2005–10). *Il Rinascimento italiano e i'Europa*, 6 vols. Treviso

Fonte, M. (1997). *The Worth of Women* (ed. and trans. V. Cox). Chicago

Forni, C. (1992). *'Il libro animato': teoria e scrittura del dialogo nel Cinquecento*. Turin

Fosi, I. and Visceglia, M. A. (1998). 'Marriage and Politics at the Papal Court in the Sixteenth and Seventeenth Centuries', in Dean/Lowe (eds.) 197–224

Fracastoro, G. (1538). *Homocentrica: Eiusdem de causis criticorum dierum per ea quae in nobis sunt*. Venice

(1930). *De contagione et contagiosis morbis et eorum curatione, libri III* (ed. Wilmer Cave Wright). New York

(1984). *Fracastoro's 'Syphilis'* (ed. and trans. G. Eatough). Liverpool

Fragnito, G. (1997). *La Bibbia al rogo: la censura ecclesiastica e i volgarizzamenti della Scrittura (1471–1605)*. Bologna

(ed.) (2001). *Church, Censorship and Culture in Early Modern Italy* (trans. A. Belton). Cambridge

(2005). *Proibito capire: la Chiesa e il volgare nella prima età moderna*. Bologna

Frajese, V. (2006). *Nascita dell'Indice: la censura ecclesiastica dal Rinascimento alla Controriforma*. Brescia

Franceschi, F. (1993). *Oltre il 'Tumulto': i lavoratori fiorentini dell'arte della lana fra Tre e Quattrocento*. Florence

(1995). 'Florence and Silk in the Fifteenth Century: The Origins of a Long and Felicitous Union', *Italian History and Culture* 1.3–22

(2004). 'The Economy: Work and Wealth', in Najemy (ed.) 124–44

Franceschi, F., Goldthwaite, R. A., and Mueller, R. C. (eds.) (2007). *Commercio e cultura mercantile*, vol. 4 of Fontana/Molà (eds.). Treviso

Francescutti, E. (2011). 'Annunciazione', in G. C. F. Villa (ed.), *Lorenzo Lotto* 128–30. Milan

Freccero, J. (1986). 'The Fig Tree and the Laurel: Petrarch's Poetics', *Diacritcs* 5.34–40

French, R. K. (1999). *Dissection and Vivisection in the European Renaissance*. Aldershot

Frick, C. C. (2002). *Dressing Renaissance Florence: Familes, Fortunes, and Fine Clothing*. Baltimore

Frick, C. C., Biancani, S., and Nicholson, E. S. G. (eds.) (2007). *Italian Women Artists: From Renaissance to Baroque*. New York

Fuchs, B. (2004). *Romance*. New York

Fusco, L. (1982). 'The Use of Sculptural Models by Painters in Fifteenth-Century Italy', *The Art Bulletin* 64.175–94

Gagné, J. (1969). 'Du quadrivium aux scientiae mediae', in *Arts libéraux et philosophie au Moyen Âge* 305–54. Montreal

Galen (1821–33). *Opera omnia* (ed. C. G. Kühn), 20 vols. Leipzig
  (1824). *De differentiis febrium*, in *Opera omnia*, vol. 7, 273–405
  (1825). *De diebus decretoriis*, in *Opera omnia*, vol. 9, 769–941
Galilei, V. (2003). *Dialogo della musica antica et della moderna* (trans. C. Palisca). New Haven
Gallo, A. (1973). *La prima rappresentazione al teatro Olimpico, con i progetti e le relazioni dei contemporanei.* Milan
Galluzzi, P. (1991). *Prima di Leonardo: cultura delle macchine a Siena nel Rinascimento.* Milan
  (1996). *Renaissance Engineers from Brunelleschi to Leonardo da Vinci.* Florence
  (2002). 'Gli ingegneri del Rinascimento, artefici di un nuovo linguaggio: il disegno', *Notiziario dell'Università degli Studi di Firenze* 25.27–31
Gamberini, A. and Lazzarini, I. (2012). *The Italian Renaissance State.* Cambridge
Garbero-Zorzi, E. and Serragnoli, D. (2004). 'Lo studio e lo spettacolo in Ferrara estense', in J. Bertini (ed.), *Gli Este a Ferrara: una corte nel Rinascimento* 307–29. Milan
Gardini, N. (1997). *Le umane parole: l'imitazione nella lirica europea del Rinascimento da Bembo a Ben Jonson.* Milan
  (2010). *Rinascimento.* Turin
Gargiulo, P., Magini, A., and Toussaint, S. (eds.) (2000). *Neoplatonismo, musica, letteratura nel Rinascimento: i Bardi di Vernio e l'Accademia della Crusca.* Prato
Garin, E. (ed.) (1952). *Prosatori latini del Quattrocento.* Milan
  (1965). *Italian Humanism: Philosophy and Civic Life in the Renaissance* (trans. P. Munz). Oxford
  (1976). *Lo zodiaco della vita: la polemica sull'astrologia dal Trecento al Cinquecento.* Rome
  (1991). 'The Philosopher and the Magus', in E. Garin *et al.* (eds.), *Renaissance Characters* (trans. L.G. Cochrane) 123–53. Chicago
  (2006). *Ermetismo del Rinascimento* (pref. M. Ciliberto). Pisa
Garofalo, I. (2003). 'Note sui giorni critici in Galeno', in N. Palmieri (ed.), *Rationnel et irrationnel dans la médecine ancienne et médiévale: aspects historiques, scientifiques et culturels* 45–58. Saint-Étienne
Garratt, J. (2002). *Palestrina and the German Romantic Imagination: Interpreting Historicism in Nineteenth-Century Music.* Cambridge
Gaston, R. W. (ed.) (1998). *Pirro Ligorio Artist and Antiquarian.* Milan
Gatti, H. (1999). *Giordano Bruno and Renaissance Science.* Ithaca NY
  (2002). *Giordano Bruno: Philosopher of the Renaissance.* Aldershot
Gaulin, J. L. (2007). 'Trattati di agronomia e innovazione agricola', in Braunstein/Molà (eds.) 145–63
Gaurico, L. (1546). *Super diebus decretoriis, quos etiam Criticos vocitant, Axiomata [. . .].* Rome
Geerts, W., Paternoster, A., and Pignatti, F. (eds.) (2001). *Il sapere delle parole: studi sul dialogo latino e italiano del Rinascimento.* Rome
Gehl, P. F. (1993). *A Moral Art: Grammar, Society, and Culture in Trecento Florence.* Ithaca NY
  (2008). *Humanism for Sale: Making and Marketing Schoolbooks in Italy, 1450–1650* www.humanismforsale.org/text/
Gentile, S. and Toussaint, S. (eds.) (2006). *Marsilio Ficino: fonti, testi, fortuna.* Rome
Gerbino, G. (2005). 'Florentine Petrarchismo and the Early Madrigal: Reflections on the Theory of Origins', *Journal of Medieval and Early Modern Studies* 35.607–28
  (2007). 'Skeptics and Believers: Music, Warfare, and the Political Decline of Renaissance Italy according to Francesco Bocchi', *The Musical Quarterly* 90.578–603
Ghiberti, L. (1998). *I commentarii* (ed. L. Bartoli). Florence

Ghirardo, D. (2005). 'Marginal Spaces of Prostitution in Renaissance Ferrara', in Looney/Shemek (eds.) 87–128

Gigante, M. (1988). 'Ambrogio Traversari interprete di Diogene Laerzio', in G. C. Garfagnini (ed.), *Ambrogio Traversari nel VI centenario della nascita* 367–459. Florence

Gilbert, C. E. (ed.) (1980). *'The Patron Speaking', in Italian Art, 1400–1500: Sources and Documents* 105–42. Evanston

Gilmore, M. (1973). 'Myth and Reality in Venetian Political Theory', in J. R. Hale (ed.), *Renaissance Venice* 431–44. Totowa NJ

Ginzburg, C. (1966). *I benandanti: Stregoneria e culti agrari tra Cinquecento e Seicento*. Turin
    (1972). 'Folklore, magia, religione', in R. Romano e Corrado Vivanti (eds.), *Storia d'Italia*, vol. 1: *I caratteri originali* 603–76. Turin
    (1980). *The Cheese and the Worms: The Cosmos of a Sixteenth-Century Miller* (trans. J. and A. Tedeschi). Baltimore

Giordano, L. (1998). 'On Filarete's *Libro architettonico*', in Hart/Hicks (eds.) 51–65

Giunta, T. (ed.) (1553). *De balneis omnia quae extant apud Graecos, Latinos, et Arabas [. . .]*. Venice

Glasser, H. (1977). *Artists' Contracts of the Early Renaissance*. New York

Gliozzi, G. (1977). *Adamo e il Nuovo Mondo: la nascita dell'antropologia come ideologia coloniale – Dalle genealogie bibliche alle teorie razziali (1500–1700)*. Milan

Godard, A. (2001). *Le dialogue à la Renaissance*. Paris

Godman, P. (1993) 'Poliziano's Poetics and Literary History', *Interpres* 13.110–209
    (1998). *From Poliziano to Machiavelli: Florentine Humanism in the High Renaissance*. Princeton

Goldthwaite, R. A. (1968). *Private Wealth in Renaissance Florence: A Study of Four Families*. Princeton
    (1980). *The Building of Renaissance Florence: An Economic and Social History*. Baltimore
    (1989). 'Introduction' to 'Recent Trends in Economic History', *Renaissance Quarterly* 42.760
    (1993). *Wealth and the Demand for Art in Italy, 1300–1600*. Baltimore
    (2009). *The Economy of Renaissance Florence*. Baltimore

Gombrich, E. (1966a). *Norm and Form: Studies in the Art of the Renaissance*. London
    (1966b). 'The Renaissance Concept of Artistic Progress and Its Consequences', in Gombrich (1966a) 1–10
    (1966c). 'The Style *all'antica*: Imitation and Assimilation', in Gombrich (1966a) 122–28
    (1976). 'The Form of Movement in Water and Air', in *The Heritage of Apelles: Studies in the History of Art* 39–56. Oxford

Goodman, J. (1983). 'Tuscan Commercial Relations with Europe, 1550–1620: Florence and the European Textile Market', in *Firenze e la Toscana dei Medici nell'Europa del '500* vol. 1, 327–41. Florence

Goody, J. (2010). *Renaissances: The One or the Many?* Cambridge

Gordon, D. J. (1980). 'Academicians Build a Theater and Give a Play', in S. Orgel (ed.), *The Renaissance Imagination: Essays and Lectures by D.J. Gordon* 247–65. Berkeley

Gorni, G. (1972). 'Storia del Certame Coronario', *Rinascimento* 12.135–81

Gotor, M. (2011a). 'Gli ordini religiosi in Italia (XIII–XX secolo)', in Irace *et al.* (eds.) 188–97

(2011b). 'Un bestseller maledetto, un uomo in fuga: il *Beneficio di Cristo* e Bernardino Ochino', in Irace *et al.* (eds.) 65–69

Grafton, A. (1977). 'On the Scholarship of Politian and its Context', *Journal of the Warburg and Courtauld Institutes* 40.150–88

(1991). 'Protestant versus Prophet: Isaac Casaubon on Hermes Trismegistus', in *Defenders of the Text: The Traditions of Scholarship in an Age of Science, 1450–1800* 145–61. Cambridge

(1992). *New Worlds, Ancient Texts: The Power of Tradition and the Shock of Discovery.* Cambridge MA

(1999). *Cardano's Cosmos: The Worlds and Works of a Renaissance Astrologer.* Cambridge MA

(2000). *Leon Battista Alberti: Master Builder of the Italian Renaissance.* New York

Grafton, A. and Jardine, L. (1986). 'Women Humanists: Education for What?', in *From Humanism to the Humanities* 29–57. Cambridge MA

Granada, M. A. and Tessicini, D. (2005). 'Copernicus and Fracastoro: The Dedicatory Letters to Pope Paul III, the History of Astronomy, and the Quest for Patronage', *Studies in History and Philosophy of Science* 36.431–76

(2008). 'Cosmologia e nuova astronomia', in Clericuzio/Ernst (eds.) 21–45

Grassi, G. and Patetta, L. (2005). *Leon Battista Alberti architetto.* Florence

Grayson, C. (1960). 'Lorenzo, Machiavelli, and the Italian Language', in E. F. Jacob (ed.), *Italian Renaissance Studies: A Tribute to the Late Cecilia M. Ady* 410–32. London

Grazzini, A. (1989). *Le cene* (ed. E. Mazzali). Milan

Green, M. H. (2008). *Making Women's Medicine Masculine: The Rise of Male Authority in Pre-Modern Gynaecology.* Oxford

Greene, R. (1991). *Post-Petrarchism: Origins and Innovations of the Western Lyric Sequence.* Princeton

(2000). *Unrequited Conquests: Love and Empire in the Colonial Americas.* Chicago

Grendler, P. F. (1977). *The Roman Inquisition and the Venetian Press, 1540–1605.* Princeton

(1989). *Schooling in Renaissance Italy: Literacy and Learning, 1300–1600.* Baltimore

(ed.) (1999). *Encyclopedia of the Renaissance*, 6 vols. New York

(2002). *The Universities of the Italian Renaissance.* Baltimore

(2006). 'Humanism: Ancient Learning, Criticism, Schools and Universities', in A. Mazzocco (ed.), *Interpretations of Renaissance Humanism* 73–95. Leiden

Grieco, A., Rocke, M., and Superbi, F. G. (eds.) (2002). *The Italian Renaissance in the Twentieth Century.* Florence

Griffiths, G., Hankins, J., and Thompson, D. (eds. and trans.) (1987). *The Humanism of Leonardo Bruni.* Binghamton NY

Grubb, J. (1988). *Firstborn of Venice: Vicenza in the Early Renaissance State.* Baltimore

(1994). 'Memory and Identity: Why Venetians Didn't Keep *ricordanze*', *Renaissance Studies* 4.375–87

(1996). *Provincial Families of the Renaissance: Public and Private Life in the Veneto.* Baltimore

Guarini, E. F. (1986). *Prato: Storia di una città.* Prato

(1995). 'Center and Periphery', in J. Kirshner (ed.), *The Origins of the State in Italy 1300–1600* 74–96. Chicago

(2003). 'Geographies of Power: The Territorial State in Early Modern Italy', in Martin (ed.) 89–103.

Guazzo, S. (1993). *La civil conversazione* (ed. A. Quondam), 2 vols. Modena

Guggisberg, H. R. (2003). *Sebastian Castellio 1515–1563: Humanist and Defender of Religious Toleration in a Confessional Age* (trans. B. Gordon). Aldershot

Guglielminetti, M. (1984). *La cornice e il furto: studi sulla novella del '500*. Bologna

(ed.) (1986). *Il tesoro della novella italiana*, 2 vols. Milan

Guidi, J. (2001). 'Les différentes rédactions du *Livre du Courtisan*', in P. Grossi and J. C. D'Amico (eds.), *De la politesse à la politique: Recherches sur les langages du 'Livre du Courtisan'* 19–30. Caen

Guidi Bruscoli, F. (2007). *Papal Banking in Renaissance Rome: Benvenuto Olivieri and Paul III, 1534–1549*. Farnham

Guillouët, J. M. (2009). 'Les transferts artistiques: une notion opératoire pour l'histoire de l'art médiéval?' *Histoire de l'Art* 64.17–25

Gulizia, S. (2006–09). '(S)omnia ostendere: Folengo e Bruno a Venezia', *Quaderni folenghiani* 6–7.113–34

Günther, H. (1994). 'The Renaissance of Antiquity', in Millon/Lampugnani (eds.) 259–305

Guzzetti, L. (2002). 'Dowries in Fourteenth-Century Venice', *Renaissance Studies* 16.429–73

Haar, J. (1986). *Essays on Italian Poetry and Music in the Renaissance, 1350–1600* 125–47. Berkeley

(ed.) (2006). *European Music 1520–1640*. Woodbridge

Hacke, D. (2001). '"Non lo volevo per marito: in modo alcuno": Forced Marriages, Generational Conflicts, and the Limits of Patriarchal Power in Early Modern Venice, c. 1580–1680', in Jacobson Schutte *et al.* (eds.) 203–21

(2004). *Women, Sex, and Marriage in Early Modern Venice*. Aldershot

Haines, P. (ed.) (2009). *The Years of the Cupola, 1417–1436* http://duomo.mpiwg-berlin.mpg.de/home_eng.html

Hale, J. (1965). 'The Early Development of the Bastion: An Italian Chronology, c. 1450–1534', in J. R. Hale, J. R. L. Highfield, and B. Smalley (eds.), *Europe in the Late Middle Ages* 466–94. London

(1985). 'Girolamo Maggi: A Renaissance Scholar and Military Buff', *Italian Studies* 60.31–50

Hall, B. S. (1997). *Weapons and Warfare in Renaissance Europe*. Baltimore

Haller, H. W. (1999). *The Other Italy: The Literary Canon in Dialect*. Toronto

Hammer, W. (1944). 'The Concept of the New or Second Rome in the Middle Ages', *Speculum* 19.50–62

Hankins, J. (1990). *Plato and the Italian Renaissance*, 2 vols, Leiden

(1996). 'Humanism and the Origins of Modern Political Thought', in J. Kraye (ed.), *The Cambridge Companion to Renaissance Humanism* 118–41. Cambridge

(ed.) (2000). *Renaissance Civic Humanism: Reappraisals and Reflections*. Cambridge

(2003). *Humanism and Platonism in the Italian Renaissance*, vol. 1: *Humanism*. Rome

(2004). *Humanism and Platonism in the Italian Renaissance*, vol. 2: *Platonism*. Rome

(ed.) (2007). *The Cambridge Companion to Renaissance Philosophy*. Cambridge

Hankins, J., and Palmer, A. (2008). *The Recovery of Ancient Philosophy in the Renaissance: A Brief Guide*. Florence

Hanning, R. W. (2010). *Serious Play: Desire and Authority in the Poetry of Ovid, Chaucer, and Ariosto*. New York

Harley, B. and Woodward, D. (eds.) (1987). *The History of Cartography*, vol. 1: *Cartography in Prehistoric, Ancient, and Medieval Europe and the Mediterranean*. Chicago

Harrison, R. P. (1988). *The Body of Beatrice*. Baltimore

Hart, V. and Hicks, P. (eds.) (1998a). *Paper Palaces: The Rise of the Architectural Treatise*. New Haven

(1998b). 'Serlio and the Representation of Architecture', in Hart/Hicks (eds.) 140–57

Harvey, P. D. A. (1987). 'Local and Regional Cartography in Medieval Europe', in Harley/Woodward (eds.) 464–501

Haskell F. and Penny, N. (1981). *Taste and the Antique*. New Haven

Headley, J. (2008). *The Europeanization of the World: On the Origin of Human Rights and Democracy*. Princeton

Heers, F. (1961). *Gênes au XVe siècle: civilisation méditerranéenne, grand capitalisme, et capitalisme populaire*. Paris

Helas, P. and Wolf, G. (2009). 'The Shadow of the Wolf: The Survival of an Ancient God in the Frescoes of the Strozzi Chapel (S. Maria Novella, Florence) or Filippino Lippi's Reflection on Image, Idol and Art', in M. W. Cole and R. Zorach (eds.), *The Idol in the Age of Art: Objects, Devotions and the Early Modern World* 133–58. Aldershot

Heller, W. B. (2003). *Emblems of Eloquence: Opera and Women's Voices in Seventeenth-Century Venice*. Berkeley

(2007). 'Venice's Mythic Empires: Truth and Verisimilitude in Venetian Opera', in V. Johnson, J. F. Fulcher, and T. Ertman (eds.), *Opera and Society in Italy and France from Monteverdi to Bourdieu* 34–52. Cambridge

Henke, R. (2002). *Performance and Literature in the Commedia dell'Arte*. Cambridge

Herlihy, D. (1976). 'The Medieval Marriage Market', *Medieval and Renaissance Studies* 6.3–27

Herlihy, D. and Cohn, S. K. (1997). *The Black Death and the Transformation of the West*. Cambridge MA

Herlihy, D. and Klapisch-Zuber, C. (1985). *Tuscans and Their Families: A Study of the Florentine Catasto of 1427*. New Haven [abridgement of Herlihy/Klapisch-Zuber (1978). *Les Toscans et leurs familles: une étude du catasto florentin de 1427*. Paris

Hersey, G. L. (1973). *The Aragonese Arch at Naples, 1443–1475*. New Haven

Heydenreich, L. H. (1996). *Architecture in Italy, 1400–1500* (rev. P. Davies). New Haven

Hoeniger, C. (2006). 'The Illuminated *Tacuinum Sanitatis* Manuscripts from Northern Italy, ca. 1380–1400: Sources, Patrons, and the Creation of a Pictorial Genre', in J. A. Givens, K. M. Reeds, and A. Touwaide (eds.), *Visualizing Medieval Medicine and Natural History, 1200–1550* 51–81. Aldershot

Hollingsworth, M. (2004). *The Cardinal's Hat: Money, Ambition and Housekeeping in a Renaissance Court*. London

Holmes, O. (2000). *Assembling the Lyric Self: Authorship from Troubadour Song to Italian Poetry Book*. Minneapolis

Hoshino, H. (1980). *L'arte della lana in Firenze nel basso medioevo*. Florence

(1983). 'The Rise of the Florentine Woollen Industry in the Fourteenth Century', in N. B. Harte and K. G. Ponting (eds.), *Cloth and Clothing in Medieval Europe* 184–204 London

Howard, D. (2000). *Venice and the East: The Impact of the Islamic World on Venetian Architecture 1100–1500*. New Haven

(2011). *Venice Disputed: Marc'Antonio Barbaro and Venetian Architecture, 1550–1600*. New Haven

Hsia, R. Po-chia (2005). *The World of Catholic Renewal 1540–1770*. Cambridge

Hub, B. (ed.) (2009). *Architettura e umanesimo: nuovi studi su Filarete*. Milan

Hughes, A. (1986). '"An Academy for Doing." II: Academies, Status and Power in Early Modern Europe', *Oxford Art Journal* 9.50–62

Hughs, D.O. (1978). 'From Brideprice to Dowry in Mediterranean Europe', *Journal of Family History* 3.262–96

Humfrey, P. (1997). *Lorenzo Lotto*. New Haven

(2001). 'L'importazione di dipinti veneziani a Bergamo e nelle sue valli, da Bartolomeo Vivarini a Palma il Vecchio', in F. Rossi (ed.), *Bergamo: L'altra Venezia – Il Rinascimento negli anni di Lorenzo Lotto 1510–1530* 43–49. Milan

Hunt, L. (1986). 'French History in the Last Twenty Years: The Rise and Fall of the Annales Paradigm', *Journal of Contemporary History* 21.215–18

Hunter, G.K. (1991). Review of Kerrigan/Braden (1989), *Shakespeare Quarterly* 42.379–80

Ianziti, G. (1981). *Il Tumulto dei Ciompi: un momento di storia fiorentina ed europea*. Florence

(1998). *Humanistic Historiography under the Sforzas*. Oxford

Ilardi, V. (2007). *Renaissance Vision: From Spectacles to Telescopes*. Philadelphia

Ingrassia, G. F. (2005). *Informatione del pestifero et contagioso morbo* (ed. L. Ingaliso). Milan

Irace, E., Luzzatto, S., and Pedullà, G. (eds.) (2011). *Atlante della letteratura italiana*, vol. 2: *Dalla Controriforma alla Restaurazione*. Turin

Jacobson Schutte, A., Kuehn, T., and Seidel Menchi, S. (eds.) (2001). *Time, Space, and Women's Lives in Early Modern Europe*. Kirksville MO

Jacquart, D. (1990). 'Theory, Everyday Practice, and Three Fifteenth-Century Physicians', in McVaugh/Siraisi (eds.) 140–60

Jardine, L. (1996). *Worldly Goods: A New History of the Renaissance*. London

Javitch, D. (1991). *Proclaiming a Classic: The Canonization of 'Orlando furioso.'* Princeton

Jedin, H. (1999). 'Catholic Reformation or Counter-Reformation', in D.M. Luebke (ed.), *The Counter-Reformation: The Essential Readings* 19–46. Oxford

Jenks, S. (1983). 'Astrometeorology in the Middle Ages', *Isis* 74.185–210

Jones, P. (1978). 'Economia e società nell'Italia medievale: la leggenda della borghesia', in R. Ruggiero and C. Vivanti (gen. eds.), *Storia d'Italia: annali*, vol. 1: *Dal feudalesimo al capitalismo* 187–372. Turin

Joost-Gaugier, C. L. (2009). *Pythagoras and Renaissance Europe: Finding Heaven*. Cambridge

Jossa, S. (2011). 'Al teatro con Palladio', in Irace *et al.* (eds.) 275–81

Jouanna, J. (1992). *Hippocrate*. Paris

Jurdjevic, M. (2007). 'Hedgehogs and Foxes: The Present and Future of Renaissance Intellectual History', *Past and Present* 195.241–68

(2008). *Guardians of Republicanism: The Valori Family in the Florentine Renaissance*. Oxford

Kallendorf, C. W. (ed. and trans.) (2002). *Humanist Educational Treatises*. Cambridge MA

(2013). 'Virgil in the Renaissance Classroom: From Toscanello's *Osservazioni* [...] *sopra l'opere di Virgilio* to the *Exercitationes rhetoricae*', in *The Classics in the Medieval and Renaissance Classroom* (eds. J.F. Feros, J.O. Ward, and M. Heyworth), 309–28. Turnhout

Karrow, R. (1993). *Mapmakers of the Sixteenth Century and their Maps: Bio-bibliography of the Cartographers of Abraham Ortelius*. Chicago

Kauffmann, T. (2004). *Toward a Geography of Art*. Chicago

Kelly-Gadol, J. (1977). 'Did Women Have a Renaissance?', in R. Bridenthal, C. Koonz, and S. Stuard (eds.), *Becoming Visible: Women in European History* 175–203. Boston

Kemp, M. (1987). '"Equal excellences": Lomazzo and the Explanation of Individual Style in the Visual Arts', *Renaissance Studies* 1.1–26

(1999). 'Making It Work: The Perspective Design of the Gubbio Studiolo', in Raggio/Wilmering (eds.) 169–77

Kennedy, W. J. (2003). *The Site of Petrarchism: Early Modern National Sentiment in Italy, France, and England*. Baltimore

Kent, D. (2000). *Cosimo de' Medici and the Florentine Renaissance: The Patron's Oeuvre*. New Haven

Kent, F. W. (1977). *Household and Lineage in Renaissance Florence*. Princeton

Kerrigan, W. and Braden, G. (1989). *The Idea of the Renaissance*. Baltimore

Kidwell, C. (1991). *Pontano: Poet and Prime Minister*. London

Kieffer, F. (2012). Ferdinando I de Médicis (1587–1609) et les Offices: création et fonctionnement de la Galleria dei lavori, unpublished PhD dissertation. CESR, Université François-Rabelais, Tours

Killerby, C. K. (2002). *Sumptuary Law in Italy 1200–1500*. Oxford

King, H. (2007). *Midwifery, Obstetrics and the Rise of Gynaecology: The Uses of a Sixteenth-Century Compendium*. Farnham

King, M. (1988). 'Humanism in Venice', in A. Rabil (ed.), *Renaissance Humanism: Foundations, Forms, and Legacy* vol. 1, 209–34. Philadelphia

Kirkman, A. (2001). 'The Invention of the Cyclic Mass', *Journal of the American Musicological Society* 54.1–47

(2010). *The Cultural Life of the Early Polyphonic Mass: Medieval Context to Modern Revival*. Cambridge

Kirshner, J. (1978). *Pursuing Honor while Avoiding Sin*. Milan

(1985). 'Wives' Claims against Insolvent Husbands in Late Medieval Italy', in S. Wemple and J. Kirshner (eds.), *Women of the Medieval World* 256–303. Oxford

(1991). '"Maritus Lucretur Dotem Uxoris Sue Premortue" in Late Medieval Florence', *Zeitschrift der Savigny-Stiftung für Rechtsgeschichte* 108.111–55

Kirshner, J. and Molho, A. (1978). 'The Dowry Fund and the Marriage Market in Early Quattrocento Florence', *Journal of Modern History* 50.403–38

(eds.) (1996). *The Origins of the State in Italy, 1300–1600*. Chicago

Klapisch-Zuber, C. (1986). *Women, Family, and Ritual in Renaissance Italy*. Chicago

Knox, D. (2002). 'Ficino and Copernicus', in Allen *et al.* (eds.) 399–418

Krantz, F. and Hohenberg, P. M. (1975). *Failed Transitions to Modern Industrial Society: Renaissance Italy and Seventeenth-Century Holland*. Montreal

Kraye, J. (ed.) (1996). *The Cambridge Companion to Renaissance Humanism*. Cambridge

(ed.) (1997). *Cambridge Translations of Renaissance Philosophical Texts*, 2 vols. Cambridge

(2001). 'L'interprétation platonicienne de l'*Enchiridion* d'Épictète proposée par Politine: philologie et philosophie dans la Florence du XVème siècle, à la fin des années 70', in F. Mariani Zini (ed.), *Penser entre les lignes: Philologie et philosophie au Quattrocento* 161–77. Paris

(2002). *Classical Traditions in Renaissance Philosophy*. Aldershot

(2004). 'Stoicism in the Renaissance from Petrarch to Lipsius', in H. W. Blom and L. C. Winkel (eds.), *Grotius and the Stoa* 21–45. Assen, Netherlands

Kraye. J. and Stone, M. W. F. (eds.) (2000). *Humanism and Early Modern Philosophy*. London

Kristeller, P. O. (1937). *Supplementum ficinianum*, 2 vols. Florence

(1961). 'The Humanism Movement', in *Renaissance Thought: The Classic, Humanist, and Scholastic Strains* 3–23. New York

(1963–97). *Iter Italicum*, 6 vols. (and 4 index vols.). London

(1964). *Eight Philosophers of the Renaissance*. Stanford

(1979). *Renaissance Thought and Its Sources* (ed. M. Mooney). New York

Kroegel, A. G. (2005). 'Quando il centro usa prudenza e la periferia osa: l'iconografia dell'Immacolata Concezione in Emilia e nelle Marche', in Periti (ed.) 215–53

Krohn, D. (2004). 'Between legend, history and power politics: the Santa Fina Chapel in San Gimignano', in S. J. Campbell and S. Milner (eds.), *Artistic Exchange and Cultural Translation in the Italian Renaissance City* 246–72. Cambridge

Kruft, H. W. (1994). *A History of Architectural Theory from Vitruvius to the Present* (trans. R. Taylor, E. Callander, and A. Wood). London

Kuehn, T. (1982). *Emancipation in Late Medieval Florence*. New Brunswick

(1991). *Law, Family, and Women: Toward a Legal Anthropology of Renaissance Italy*. Chicago

(2002). *Illegitimacy in Renaissance Florence*. Ann Arbor

(2008). *Heirs, Kin, and Creditors in Renaissance Florence*. Cambridge

Kushner, E. (2004). *Le dialogue à la Renaissance: histoire et poétique*. Geneva

La Via, S. (2002). 'Eros and Thanatos: A Ficinian and Laurentian Reading of Verdelot's "Sì lieta e grata morte"', *Early Music History* 21.75–116

Labalme, P. H., Sanguineti White, L., and Carroll, L. (eds.) (1999). 'How to (and How Not to) Get Married in Sixteenth-Century Venice (Selections from the Diaries of Marin Sanudo)', *Renaissance Quarterly* 52.43–72

Ladis, A. and Wood, C. (eds.) (1992). *The Craft of Art: Originality and Industry in the Italian Renaisssance and Baroque Workshop*. Athens GA

Lanaro, P. (ed.) (2006). *At the Centre of the Old World: Trade and Manufacturing in Venice and the Venetian Mainland, 1400–1800*. Toronto

Landino, C. (2001). *Comento sopra la Commedia* (ed. Paolo Procaccioli), 4 vols. Rome

Lane, F. C. (1944). *Andrea Barbarigo, Merchant of Venice, 1418–1449*. Baltimore

(1966). *Venice and History: The Collected Papers of F. C. Lane*. Baltimore

(1973). *Venice: A Maritime Republic*. Baltimore

Lane, F. C., and Mueller, R. C. (1985). *Money and Banking in Medieval and Renaissance Venice*, vol. 1: *Coins and Money*. Baltimore

(1987). *Money and Banking in Medieval and Renaissance Venice*, vol. 2: *Coins and Moneys of Account*. Baltimore

Langeli, A. B. (2010). 'Scrivere, riscrivere, trascrivere: la genesi del *Canzoniere*', in de Vincentiis *et al.* (eds.) 241–51

Langermann, Y. T. (2008). 'The Astral Connections of Critical Days: Some Late Antique Sources Preserved in Hebrew and Arabic', in A. Akasoy, C. Burnett, and R. Yoeli-Tlalim (eds.), *Astro-Medicine: Astrology and Medicine, East and West* 99–117. Florence

Larivalle, P. (1982). 'Spazio scenico e spazio cittadino ne *La Lena*', in Quondam/Papagno (eds.) vol. 1, 257–78

Lazzerini, L. (1992). 'Baldus di Teofilo Folengo', in Asor Rosa (ed.) 1033–64. Turin

Lee, A. (2012). *Petrarch and St. Augustine: Classical Scholarship, Christian Theology, and the Origins of the Renaissance in Italy*. Leiden

Leonardo da Vinci (2001a). *Leonardo on Painting: An Anthology of Writings by Leonardo da Vinci, with a Selection of Documents Relating to his Career as an Artist* (trans. M. Kemp). New Haven

(2001b). *Delle acque* (ed. M. Schneider). Palermo

Leone de Castris, P. (1986). *Arte di corte nella Napoli angioina*. Florence

(2001). *Polidoro da Caravaggio: l'opera completa*. Napoli

Lewis, M. S. (1988–97). *Antonio Gardano, Venetian Music Printer 1538–1569: A Descriptive Bibliography and Historical Study*, 2 vols. New York

Liddell, H. G., and Scott, R. (1996). *A Greek–English Lexicon* (eds. H. Stuart Jones and R. McKenzie). Oxford

Lightbown, R. (1986). *Mantegna: With a Complete Catalogue of the Paintings, Drawings, and Prints.* Berkeley

(2004). *Carlo Crivelli.* New Haven

Ligorio, P. (2005). *Libro di diversi terremoti* (ed. E. Guidaboni). Rome

Lippincott, K. (1989). 'The Neo-Latin Historical Epics of the North Italian Courts: An Examination of "Courtly Culture" in the Fifteenth Century', *Renaissance Studies* 3.416–28

Litchiefield, R. B. (1969). 'Caratteristiche demografiche delle famiglie patrizie fiorentine dal sedicesimo al diciannovesimo secolo', in C. A. Corsini (ed.), *Saggi di Demografia Storica* 19–34. Florence

Lockwood, L. (1970). *The Counter-Reformation and the Masses of Vincenzo Ruffo.* Vienna

Loconte, A. (2008). 'The North Looks South: Giorgio Vasari and Early Modern Visual Culture in the Kingdom of Naples', *Art History* 31.438–59

Lomazzo, G. P. (1973–75). *Scritti sulle arti* (ed. R. P. Ciardi), 2 vols. Florence

(1993). *Rabisch* (ed. D. Isella). Turin

Long, P. O. (2001). *Openness, Secrecy, Authorship: Technical Arts and the Culture of Knowledge from Antiquity to the Renaissance.* Baltimore

Looney, D. (2009). 'The Beginnings of Humanistic Oratory: Petrarch's *Coronation Oration*', in V. Kirkham and A. Maggi (eds.), *Petrarch: A Critical Guide to the Complete Works* 131–40. Chicago

(2010). *My Muse Will Have a Story to Paint: Selected Prose of Ludovico Ariosto.* Toronto

Looney, D. and Shemek, D. (eds.) (2005). *Phaethon's Children: The Este Court and Its Culture in Early Modern Ferrara.* Tempe AZ

Lopez, P. (1976). *Il movimento valdesiano a Napoli.* Naples

Lopez, R. S. (1953). 'Hard Times and Investment in Culture', in *The Renaissance: A Symposium.* New York

(1961). Review of Iris Origo, *The Merchant of Prato, Speculum* 36.447–49

(1964). 'The Economic Depression of the Renaissance?', *Economic History Review* 16.525–27

(1976). *Il movimento valdesiano a Napoli: Mario Galeota e le sue vicende col Sant'Uffizio.* Naples

Lopez, R. S., and Miskimin, H. A. (1962). 'The Economic Depression of the Renaissance', *Economic History Review* 14.408–26

Lorenzetti, S. (2003). *Musica e identità nobiliare nell'Italia del Rinascimento: educazione, mentalità, immaginario.* Florence

Lotz, W (1995). *Architecture in Italy, 1500–1600* (intro. D. Howard). New Haven

Lowry, M. (1979). *The World of Aldus Manutius: Business and Scholarship in Renaissance Venice.* Oxford

Lubkin, G. (1994). *A Renaissance Court: Milan under Galeazzo Maria Sforza.* Berkeley

Lucco, M. (2006). *Antonello da Messina: l'opera completa.* Milan

Luchs, A. (1995). *Tullio Lombardo and Ideal Portrait Sculpture in Renaissance Venice, 1490–1530.* Cambridge

Lukehart, P. M. (ed.) (1993a). *The Artist's Workshop.* Washington

(1993b), 'Delineating the Genoese Studio: *giovani accartati* or *sotto padre*?' in Luke-hart (ed.) 37–57

Lummus, D. (2012). 'Boccaccio's Hellenism and the Foundation of Modernity', *Mediaevalia* 33.101–67

Luzzatto, G. (1961). *An Economic History of Italy: From the Fall of the Roman Empire to the Beginning of the Sixteenth Century.* London

Luzzi, M. de' and Vigevano, G. da (1926). *Anatomies de Mondino dei Luzzi et de Guido de Vigevano* (ed. E. Wickersheimer). Paris

Macey, P. (1998). *Bonfire Songs: Savonarola's Musical Legacy.* Oxford

Machiavelli (1982). *Discorso intorno alla nostra lingua* (ed. P. Trovato). Padua

Mack, C. R. (1987). *Pienza: The Creation of a Renaissance City.* Ithaca NY

Mack, R. E. (2001). *Bazaar to Piazza: Islamic Trade and Italian Art, 1300–1600.* Berkeley

Mackenney, R. (2005). *Renaissances: The Cultures of Italy, c. 1300–c. 1600.* Basingstoke

Maclean, I. (1996). *Montaigne philosophe.* Paris

Mainoni, P. (1982). *Mercanti lombardi tra Barcellona e Valenza nel basso medioevo.* Bologna

   (1983). 'L'attività mercantile e le casate milanesi nel secondo Quattrocento', in *Milano nell'età di Ludovico il Moro* vol. 2, 575–84. Milan

Malagola, C. (ed.) (1888). *Statuti della università e dei collegi dello Studio bolognese.* Bologna

Malanima, P. (1980). 'L'economia italiana fra feudalesimo e capitalismo: un esempio di crescita sbilanciata', *Società e storia* 7.141–56

   (1982a). *La decadenza di un'economia: l'industria di Firenze nei secoli XVI–XVII.* Bologna

   (1982b). 'Industrie cittadine e industrie rurali nell'età moderna', *Rivista storica italiana* 94.155–97

Mallette, K. (2005). *The Kingdom of Sicily, 1100–1250: A Literary History.* Philadelphia

Malpezzi Price, P. (2003). *Moderata Fonte: Women and Life in Sixteenth-Century Venice.* Madison NJ

Malvasia, C. C. (2000). *Malvasia's Life of the Carracci* (trans. and comm. A. Summerscale). University Park PA

Manetti, A. (1991). *The Fat Wood-Worker* (trans. R. L. and V. Martone). New York

Manetti, G. (2003). *Vite di Dante, Petrarca e Boccaccio* (ed. S. U. Baldassarri). Palermo

Marchese, A. G. (2010). *Giovanni Filippo Ingrassia.* Palermo

Marchi, A. and Valazzi, M. R. (2012). *La città ideale, l'Utopia del Rinascimento a Urbino tra Piero della Francesca e Raffaello.* Milan

Mariano, F. (1993). *Jesi, città e architettura: forme e tipologie dalle origini all'Ottocento.* Milan

Marinelli, P. V. (1987). *Ariosto and Boiardo: The Origins of the Orlando Furioso.* Columbia MO

Marini, Q. (1997). 'La prosa narrativa', in E. Malato (ed.), *Storia della letteratura italiana,* vol. 5: *La fine del Cinquecento e il Seicento* 989–1056. Rome

Marino, J. (1988). *Pastoral Economics in the Kingdom of Naples.* Baltimore

   (1999). 'Naples', in Grendler (ed.) vol. 4, 276–79

Marsh, D. (1979). 'Grammar, Method, and Polemic in Lorenzo Valla's *Elegantiae*', *Rinascimento* 19.91–116

   (1980). *The Quattrocento Dialogue: Classical Tradition and Humanist Innovation.* Cambridge MA

Marshall, P. (1999). *The Local Merchants of Prato: Small Entrepreneurs in the Late Medieval Economy.* Baltimore

Martellucci, G. (1992). *Le nozze del Principe: Palermo città e teatro nel Cinquecento.* Palermo

Martin, C. (2011). *Renaissance Meteorology from Pomponazzi to Descartes.* Baltimore

Martin, J. J. (2003). *The Renaissance: Italy and Abroad*. London

Martines, L. (1998). *Power and Imagination: City–States in Renaissance Italy*. Baltimore

Martinez, R. L. (2010). 'Comedian, Tragedian: Machiavelli and Traditions of Renaissance Theater', in J. Najemy (ed.), *The Cambridge Companion to Machiavelli* 206–22. Cambridge

(2011). 'Etruria Triumphant in Rome: Fables of Medici Rule and Bibbiena's *Calandra*', *Renaissance Drama* 36–37.67–96

Martone, R. L. and Martone, V. (eds. and trans.) (1994). *Renaissance Comic Tales of Love, Treachery and Revenge*. New York

Mattingly, G. (1988). *Renaissance Diplomacy*. New York

Maxwell, R. (2007). *The Art of Medieval Urbanism: Parthenay in Romanesque Aquitaine*. University Park PA

Mazzacurati, G. (1996). *All'ombra di Dioneo: tipologie e percorsi della novella da Boccaccio a Bandello*. Florence

Mazzaoui, M. F. (2009). 'The First European Cotton Industries: Italy and Germany 1100–1800', in G. Riello and P. Parthasarathi (eds.), *The Spinning World: A Global History of Cotton Textiles, 1200–1850* 63–88. Oxford

Mazzocco, A. (1993). *Linguistic Theories in Dante and the Humanists: Studies of Language and Intellectual History in Late Medieval and Early Renaissance Italy*. Leiden

Mazzoni, S. (1998). *L'Olimpico di Vicenza: un teatro e la sua 'perpetua memoria'*. Florence

McCray, W. P. (1999). *Glassmaking in Renaissance Venice: The Fragile Craft*. Aldershot

McKitterick, D. (2003). *Print, Manuscript and the Search for Order, 1450–1830*. Cambridge

McLaughlin, M. (1995). *Literary Imitation in the Italian Renaissance: The Theory and Practice of Literary Imitation in Italy from Dante to Bembo*. Oxford

McVaugh, M. R. (2006). *The Rational Surgery of the Middle Ages*. Florence

McVaugh, M. R., and Siraisi, N. G. (eds.) (1990). *Renaissance Medical Learning: Evolution of a Tradition. Osiris*, ser. 2, vol. 6.

Medioli, F. L. (1991). *'Inferno monacale' di Arcangela Tarabotti*. Turin

Mei, G. (1960). *Girolamo Mei (1519–1594): Letters on Ancient and Modern Music to Vincenzo Galilei and Giovanni Bardi* (ed. C. Palisca). Rome

Mele, G. (2012). 'A Geometrical Analysis of the Layout of Acaya', *Nexus Network Journal* 14.373–89

Mele, V. and Senatore, F. (2011a). 'Baronial Courts', in Folin (ed.) 401–3

(2011b). 'The Kingdom of Naples: the Durazzo and Aragonese families (1381–1501)', in Folin (ed.) 377–400

Melis, F. (1959). 'A proposito di un nuovo volume: *Il mercante di Prato*', *Economia e storia* 6.737–63

(1962). *Aspetti della vita economica medievale*. Siena

(1991). *L'azienda nel medioevo*. Florence

Mercuriale, G. (2008). *De arte gymnastica* (ed. C. Pennutto, trans. V. Nutton). Florence

Meroi, F. (2006). *Cabala parva: la filosofia di Giordano Bruno fra tradizione cristiana e pensiero moderno*. Rome

Merzario, R. (1981). *Il paese stretto: strategie matrimoniali nella diocesi di Como, secoli XVI–XVIII*. Turin

Michelson, E. (2013). *The Pulpit and the Press in Reformation Italy*. Cambridge MA

Migliorini, B. (1994). *Storia della lingua italiana*. Turin

Mignolo, W. (1997). *The Darker Side of the Renaissance: Literacy, Territoriality, and Colonization*. Ann Arbor

Milanesi, M. (1984). *Tolomeo sostituito: studi di storia delle conoscenze geografiche del XVI secolo*. Milan

Millon, H. A., and Magnago Lampugnani, V. (eds.) (1994). *The Renaissance from Brunelleschi to Michelangelo: The Representation of Architecture*. London

Milner, S. (2004). 'The Politics of Patronage: Verrocchio, Pollaiuolo, and the Forteguerri Monument', in Campbell/Milner (eds.) 221–35

(ed.) (2005). *At the Margins: Minority Groups in Premodern Italy*. Minneapolis

Miskimin, H. (1964). 'The Economic Depression of the Renaissance?', *Economic History Review*. 16.528–29

Mitchell, B. (1986). *The Majesty of State: Triumphal Progresses of Foreign Sovereigns in Renaissance Italy (1494–1600)*. Florence

Molà, L. (2000). *The Silk Industry of Renaissance Venice*. Baltimore

Molà, L., Mueller, R., and Zanier, C. (eds.) (2000). *La seta in Italia dal Medioevo al Seicento: dal baco al drappo*. Venice

Molari, L. and Molari, P. G. (2006). *Il trionfo dell'ingegneria nel fregio del palazzo ducale d'Urbino*. Pisa

Molho, A. (1988). 'Deception and Marriage Strategy in Renaissance Florence: The Case of Women's Ages', *Renaissance Quarterly* 41.193–217

(1994). *Marriage Alliance in Late Medieval Florence*. Cambridge MA

Mollaret, H. H. (1980). 'Presentazione della Peste', in *Venezia e la peste 1348/1797* 11–17. Venice

Monfasani, J. (1999). 'The Ciceronian Controversy', in G. P. Norton (ed.), *The Cambridge History of Literary Criticism*, vol. 3: *The Renaissance*, 395–401. Cambridge

(2012). 'The Greeks and Renaissance Humanism', in D. Rundle (ed.), *Humanism in Fifteenth-Century Europe*, 31–78. Oxford

Monson, C. (2002). 'The Council of Trent Revisited', *Journal of the American Musicological Society* 55.1–37

(2006). 'Renewal, Reform, and Reaction in Catholic Music', in Haar (ed.) 401–21

Montaigne, M. de (2003). *The Complete Works of Montaigne: Essays, Travel Journal, Letters* (trans. D. Frame). New York

Monte, A. (1996). *Acaya: una città–fortezza del Rinascimento meridionale*. Lecce

Morelli, R. (2007). 'La foresta industriale', in Braustein/Molà (eds.) 457–78

Morison, S. (1990). *Early Italian Writing-Books: Renaissance to Baroque* (ed. N. Barker). Verona

Morlino, L. (2010). 'La letteratura francese e provenzale nell'Italia medievale', in De Vincentiis *et al.* (eds.) 27–40.

Mormando, F. (1999). *The Preacher's Demons: Bernardino of Siena and the Social Underworld of Early Renaissance Italy*. Chicago

Morsolin, B. (1894). *Giangiorgio Trissino*. Florence

Mortara Garavelli, B. (ed.) (2008). *Storia della punteggiatura in Europa*. Bari

Mosco, G. F. (2009). *L'architettura del Rinascimento e il tempo dell'artista Vespasiano Genuino dopo 'Lepanto'*. Tuglie

Motta, G. (1983). *Strategie familiari e alleanze matrimoniali in Sicilia nell'età della transizione (secoli XIV–XVII)*. Florence

Mozzoni, L. (ed.) (2009). *Lorenzo Lotto e le Marche: per una geografia dell'anima*. Florence

(2011). 'Deposizione', in V. Garibaldi and G. C. F. Villa (eds.), *Lorenzo Lotto e le Marche* 62–72. Milan

Muccillo, M. (1997). 'Fontana (de Fontana, de la Fontana), Giovanni (Antonio, Jacopo)', in *DBI*: www.treccani.it/enciclopedia/fontana-giovanni-antonio-jacopo_%28Dizionario-Biografico%29/

Mueller, R. (1997). *The Venetian Money Market: Banks, Panics, and the Public Debt*. Baltimore

Muir, E. (1981). *Civic Ritual in Renaissance Venice*. Princeton

(1995). 'The Italian Renaissance in America', *American Historical Review* 100.1095–118

(2002). 'Governments and Bureaucracies', in Ruggiero (ed.) 107–23

(2007). *The Culture Wars of the Late Renaissance: Skeptics, Libertines, and Opera*. Cambridge MA

Munro, J. (1983). 'Summaries of Workshops: Medieval Monetary Problems: Bimetallism and Bullionism', *Journal of Economic History* 43.294–98

Murrin, M. (1994). *History and Warfare in Renaissance Epic*. Chicago

Nagel, A. and Wood, C. S. (2010). *Anachronic Renaissance*. New York

Nagler, A. M. (1964). *Theater Festivals of the Medici 1539–1637*. New Haven

(2002). 'Political Ideas', in Ruggiero (ed.) 384–402

(2006). *A History of Florence, 1200–1575*. Oxford

Najemy, J. M. (ed.) (2004). *Italy in the Age of the Renaissance*. Oxford

Nardi, B. (1958). *Saggi sull'aristotelismo padovano dal secolo XIV al XVI*. Florence

Nauta, L. (2006). 'Lorenzo Valla and Quattrocento Scepticism', *Vivarium* 43.375–95

Navarrete, I. (1994). *Orphans of Petrarch: Poetry and Theory in the Spanish Renaissance*. Berkeley

Newbigin, N. (1981). 'Il testo e il contesto dell' Abramo e Isac di Feo Belcari', *Studi e problemi di critica testuale* 23.13–37

(ed.) (1983). *Nuovo corpus di sacre rappresentazioni fiorentine del Quattrocento*. Bologna

(1996). *Feste d'Oltrarno: Plays in Churches in Fifteenth-Century Florence*, 2 vols. Florence

(1997). 'Agata, Apollonia and Other Martyred Virgins: Did Florentines Really See These Plays Performed?', *European Medieval Drama* 1.77–100

(2007). '"L'occhio si dice che è la prima porta": Seeing with Words in Florentine *sacra rappresentazione*', *Mediaevalia* 28.1–22

Newcomb, A. (1980). *The Madrigal at Ferrara, 1579–1597*, 2 vols. Princeton

Newman, W. R. (2004). *Promethean Ambitions: Alchemy and the Quest to Perfect Nature*. Chicago

Niccoli, O. (2006). *Rinascimento anticlericale*. Rome

Nicolini, F. (1925). *L'arte napoletana del rinascimento e la lettera di Pietro Summonte a Marcantonio Michiel 157–76*. Naples

Nova, A. (1994). *Girolamo Romanino*. Turin

Nuovo, A. and Coppens, C. (2005). *I Giolito e la stampa nell'Italia del XVI secolo*. Geneva

Nuti, L. (1994). 'The Perspective Plan in the Sixteenth Century: The Invention of a Representational Language', *Art Bulletin* 76.105–28

Nutton, V. (1983). 'The Seeds of Disease: An Explanation of Contagion and Infection from the Greeks to the Renaissance', *Medical History* 27.1–34

(1990). 'The Reception of Fracastoro's Theory of Contagion: The Seed that Fell among Thorns?', in McVaugh/Siraisi (eds.) 196–234

(2006). 'With Benefit of Hindsight: Girolamo Mercuriale and Simone Simoni on Plague', *Medicina e Storia* 9.5–19

O'Malley, C. D. (1964). *Andreas Vesalius of Brussels, 1514–1564*. Berkeley

O'Malley, J. (2000). *Trent and All That: Renaming Catholicism in the Early Modern Era*. Cambridge MA

O'Malley, M. (2005). *The Business of Art: Contracts and the Commissioning Process in Renaissance Italy*. New Haven

Omaggio a Lorenzo Lotto (1984). *Atti del convegno Jesi-Mogliano, 4–6 dicembre 1981, Notizie da Palazzo Albani* 13. Urbino

Ordine, N. (1996). *Teoria della novella e teoria del riso nel Cinquecento*. Naples

Origo, I. (1957). *The Merchant of Prato: Francesco di Marco Datini, 1335–1410*. New York

Outram, D. (2006). 'Gender', in Park/Daston (eds.) 797–817

Paci, G. and Sconocchia, S. (eds.) (1998). *Ciriaco d'Ancona e la cultura antiquaria dell'umanesimo*. Reggio nell'Emilia

Pacioli, L. (2009, facsimile of 1498 ms.). *De divina proportione*. Sansepolcro, Arezzo

Padgett, J. F. (2001). 'Organizational Genesis, Identity and Control: The Transformation of Banking in Renaissance Florence', in Rauch/Cassella (eds.) 211–57.

Padgett, J. F., and McLean, P. D. (2006). 'Organizational Invention and Elite Transformation: The Birth of Partnership Systems in Renaissance Florence', *American Journal of Sociology* 111.1463–568

Padoan, G. (1970). 'L'Anconitana tra Boccaccio, Bibbiena e Ariosto', *Lettere italiane* 22.100–5

(1996). *L'avventura delle commedia rinascimentale*. Padua

Paganini, G. and Maia Neto, J. R. (2010). *Renaissance Scepticisms*. Dordrecht

Pagliara, P. N. (1988). 'Vitruvio da testo a canone', in Settis, S. (ed.), *Memoria dell'antico nell'arte italiana* vol. 3, 5–85. Turin

Palisca, C. (1985). *Humanism in Italian Renaissance Musical Thought*. New Haven

(ed.) (1989). *The Florentine Camerata: Documentary Studies and Translations*. New Haven

Palmer, R. (1985). *Pharmacy in the Republic of Venice in the Sixteenth Century*, in A. Wear, R. K. French, and I. M. Lonie (eds.), *The Medical Renaissance of the Sixteenth Century* 100–17. Cambridge

(2008). 'Girolamo Mercuriale and the Plague of Venice', in A. Arcangeli and V. Nutton (eds.), *Medicina e cultura nell'Europa del Cinquecento* 51–65. Florence

Panciera, W. (2007). 'La polvere da sparo', in Braunstein/Molà (eds.) 305–21

Panofsky, E. (1965). *Renaissance and Renascences in Western Art*, 2nd edn. Stockholm

Paolucci, A. (ed.) (2010). *Il Tempio Malatestiano a Rimini / The Tempio Malatestiano in Rimini*, vol. 1: *Atlante/Atlas*, vol. 2: *Testi/Texts*. Modena

Papio, M. (2007). 'Novella', in G. Marrone and P. Puppa (eds.), *Routledge Encyclopedia of Italian Literary Studies* vol. 2, 1295–300. New York

Park, K. (1985). *Doctors and Medicine in Early Renaissance Florence*. Princeton

(1994). 'The Criminal and the Saintly Body: Autopsy and Dissection in Renaissance Italy', *Renaissance Quarterly* 47.1–33

(1998). 'Stones, Bones, and Hernias: Surgical Specialists in Fourteenth- and Fifteenth-Century Italy', in R. French (ed.), *Medicine from the Black Death to the French Disease* 110–30. Farnham

(1999). 'Natural Particulars: Epistemology, Practice, and the Literature of Healing Springs', in A. Grafton and N. G. Siraisi (eds.), *Natural Particulars: Nature and the Disciplines in Renaissance Europe* 347–67. Cambridge MA

(2006). *Secrets of Women: Gender, Generation, and the Origins of Human Dissection*. New York

Park, K. and Daston, L. (eds.) (2006). *The Cambridge History of Science*. Cambridge

Partridge, L. (1970). 'Vignola and the Villa Farnese at Caprarola, Pt. 1', *The Art Bulletin* 52.81–87

Passamani, B. (1979). 'La coscienza della romanità e gli studi antiquari tra Umanesimo e Neoclassicismo', in *Brescia romana: materiali per un museo* vol. 2, 5–17. Brescia

Passannante, G. (2011). *The Lucretian Renaissance: Philology and the Afterlife of Tradition*. Chicago

Pastore, A. and Peruzzi, E. (eds.) (2006). *Girolamo Fracastoro fra medicina, filosofia e scienze della natura*. Florence

Paternoster, A. (1998). *Aptum: retorica ed ermeneutica nel dialogo rinascimentale del primo Cinquecento* 99–145. Rome

(2001). 'I *Dialoghi* di Torquato Tasso e l'*ethos* dei personaggi', in Geerts *et al.* (eds.) 159–74

Patetta, L. (1987). *L'architettura del Quattrocento a Milano*. Milan

Payne, A. A. (1999). *The Architectural Treatise in the Italian Renaissance: Architectural Invention, Ornament, and Literary Culture*. Cambridge

Pearson, C. (2011). *Humanism and the Urban World: Leon Battista Alberti and the Renaissance City*. University Park PA

Pedullà, G. (2010). 'L'età di Padova', in De Vincentiis *et al.* (eds.) 2–127

(2011). 'Giovanni della Casa e il bon ton dell'umanista', in Irace *et al.* (eds.) 136–43

Percival, W. K. (2004). *Studies in Renaissance Grammar*. Aldershot

Perella, N. J. (1973). *The Critical Fortune of Battista Guarini's 'Il pastor fido'*. Florence

Perifano, A. (1997). *L'alchimie à la cour de Côme Ier de Médicis: Savoirs, culture et politique*. Paris

Periti, G. (ed.) (2005). *Emilia e Marche nel Rinascimento: l'identità visiva della 'Periferia'*. Bologna

Perosa, A. and Sparrow, J. (eds.) (1979). *Renaissance Latin Verse: An Anthology*. Chapel Hill

Pertile, L. (1973). 'Montaigne in Italia: arte, tecnica e scienza dal *Journal* agli *Essais*', *Saggi e ricerche di letteratura francese* 12.49–92

Peruzzi, E. (1995). *La nave di Ermete: la cosmologia di Girolamo Fracastoro*. Florence

Pesca-Cupolo, C. (1999). 'Oltre la scena comica: la dimensione teatrale bruniana e l'ambientazione napoletana del Candelaio', *Italica* 76.1–17

Pesenti, T. (1992a). 'Dondi dall'Orologio, Giovanni', in DBI: www.treccani.it/enciclopedia/giovanni-dondi-dall-orologio_%28Dizionario-Biografico%29/

(1992b). 'Dondi dall'Orologio, Iacopo', in DBI: www.treccani.it/enciclopedia/iacopo-dondi-dall-orologio_%28Dizionario-Biografico%29/

Petrarca, F. (1955). *The Coronation Oration*, in E. H. Wilkins (trans.), *Studies in the Life and Works of Petrarch* 300–13. Cambridge MA

(2003). *De sui ipsisus et multorum ignorantia / On His Own Ignorance and That of Many Others*, in F. Petrarca, *Invectives* (ed. and trans. D. Marsh) 222s–363. Cambridge MA

Petrina, A. (2010). '"With his Penne and Langage Laureate": The Symbolic Significance of the Laurel Crown', *Studi petrarcheschi* 23.161–85

Petrucci, A. (1985). 'Potere, spazi urbani, scritture esposte: proposte ed esempi', in *Culture et idéologie dans la genèse de l'état moderne* 85–97. Rome

(1988). 'Pouvoir de l'écriture, pouvoir sur l'écriture dans la Renaissance italienne', *Annales: Économies, Sociétés, Civilisations* 43.823–47

(1995). *Writers and Readers in Medieval Italy: Studies in the History of Written Culture* (ed. and trans. C. M. Radding). New Haven

Pettas, W. A. (1980). *The Giunti of Florence: Merchant Publishers of the Sixteenth Century*. San Francisco

(1997). 'The Giunti and the Book Trade in Lyon', in *Libri, tipografi, biblioteche: ricerche storiche dedicate a Luigi Balsamo*, vol. 1, 169–92 Florence

(2005). *A History & Bibliography of the Giunti (Junta) Printing Family in Spain 1526–1628*. New Castle DE

Pfister, L., Savenije, H. H. G., and Fenicia, F. (2009). *Leonardo's Water Theory: on the Origin and Fate of Water*. Wallingford

Philip, J. and Caferro, W. (2001). *The Spinelli of Florence: Fortunes of a Renaissance Merchant Family*. University Park PA

Philips, M. (1987). *The Memoir of Marco Parenti: A Life in Medici Florence*. Princeton

Phillips-Court, K. (2011). *The Perfect Genre: Drama and Painting in Renaissance Italy*. Aldershot

Piccolpasso, C. (1980). *The Three Books of the Potter's Art* (trans. R. Lightbown and A. Caiger-Smith). London

Pico della Mirandola, G. (1946–52). *Disputationes adversus astrologiam divinatricem* (ed. Eugenio Garin), 2 vols. Florence

(2012). *Oration on the Dignity of Man: A New Translation and Commentary* (eds. and trans. F. Borghesi, M. Papio, and M. Riva). Cambridge

Pico della Mirandola, G. and Barbaro E. (1998). *Filosofia o eloquenza?* (ed. F. Bausi). Naples.

Pigafetta, A. (2007). *The First Voyage around the World, 1519–1522: An Account of Magellan's Expedition* (ed. T. J. Cachey Jr.). Toronto

Pigman, G. W. III (1980). 'Versions of Imitation in the Renaissance', *Renaissance Quarterly* 33.1–32

Pignatti, F. (2001). 'Aspetti e tecniche della rappresentazione nel dialogo cinquecentesco', in Geerts *et al.* (eds.) 115–40

Pilliod, E. (2001). *Pontormo, Bronzino, Allori: A Geneology of Florentine Art*. New Haven

Pine, M. L. (1986). *Pietro Pomponazzi: Radical Philosopher of the Renaissance*. Padua

Pinto, G. (1981). 'I livelli di vita dei salariati cittadini', in *Il tumulto dei Ciompi* 161–98. Florence

Pirrotta, N. (1966). 'Music and Cultural Tendencies in Fifteenth-Century Italy', *Journal of the American Musicological Society* 19.127–161

Plaisance, M. (1982). 'Lo spazio ferrarese nelle due prime commedie dell'Ariosto', in Quondam/Papagno (eds.) 247–55

Pocock, J. G. A. (2003). *The Machiavellian Moment: Florentine Political Thought and the Atlantic Republican Tradition*. Princeton

Poliziano, A. (2002). *Liber epigrammatum graecorum*, (ed. F. Pontani). Rome

Pollak, M. D. (2010). *Cities at War in Early Modern Europe*. Cambridge

Pomata, G. (1994). 'Legami di sangue, legami di seme. Consanguineità e agnazione nel diritto romano', *Quaderni storici* 86.299–334

(2002a). 'Gender and the Family', in *Short Oxford History of Italy: Early Modern Italy 1550–1796* (ed. John Marino) 69–86. Oxford

(2002b). 'Knowledge-freshening Wind: Gender and the Renewal of Renaissance Studies', in Grieco *et al.* (eds.) 173–192

Pompilio, A. (1997). *Guarini, la musica, i musicisti*. Lucca

Pomponazzi, P. (1948). *On the Immortality of the Soul* [*De immortalitate animae*] (trans. J. H. Randall), in Cassirer *et al.* (eds.) 280–381

(1999). *Trattato sull'immortalità dell'anima* (ed. V. P. Compagni) lxvii–lxxxv. Florence

(2004). *Il fato, il libero arbitrio e la predestinazione* (ed. R. Lemay and trans. V. P. Compagni). Turin

Pon, L. (2004). *Raphael, Dürer and Marcantonio Raimondi. Copying and the Italian Renaissance Print*. New Haven and London

Poni, C. (1976). 'All'origine del sistema di fabbrica: tecnologia e organizzazione produttiva dei mulini di seta nell'Italia settentrionale (sc. XVII–XVIII)', *Rivista Storica Italiana* 88.444–97

Pontano, G. (1943). *I dialoghi* (ed. C. Previtera). Florence

(2012). *Dialogues*, vol. 1 (ed. and trans. J. H. Gaisser). Cambridge MA

Popkin, R. (2003). *The History of Scepticism from Savonarola to Bayle*. Oxford and New York

Preti, C. (2004). 'Ingrassia, Giovanni Filippo', in DBI: http://www.treccani.it/enciclopedia/giovanni-filippo-ingrassia_%28Dizionario_Biografico%29/

Previtali, G. (1989). *La fortuna dei primitivi dal Vasari ai neoclassici*. Einaudi

Procaccioli, P. (2011). 'La diffusione della *Poetica* di Aristotele nel *Cinquecento*', in Irace *et al.* (eds.) 170–74

Prodi, P. (2002 [1982]). *Il sovrano pontefice. Un corpo e due anime: la monarchia papale nella prima età moderna*. Bologna

Propp, V. (1968, rev. edn.). *Morphology of the Folktale* (trans. L. Scott, ed. L. A. Wagner, intro. A. Dundes). Austin TX

Prosperi, A. (2001). *Il Concilio di Trento: una introduzione storica*. Turin

(2009). *Tribunali della coscienza. Inquisitori confessori missionari*. Turin

Prosperi, V. (2004). *'Di soavi licor gli orli del vaso': la fortuna di Lucrezio dall'Umanesimo alla Controriforma*. Turin

(2007). 'Lucretius in the Renaissance', in S. Gillespie and P. R. Hardie (eds.), *The Cambridge Companion to Lucretius* 214–26. Cambridge

Prunster, N. (trans. and ed.) (2000). *Romeo and Juliet before Shakespeare: Four Early Stories of Star-Crossed Love*. Toronto

Ptolemy (2000). *Ptolemy's Geography. An Annotated Translation of the Theoretical Chapters* (eds. and trans. J. L. Berggren and A. Jones). Princeton

Pugliese, O. (1995). *Il discorso labirintico del dialogo rinascimentale*. Rome

Pullan, B. (1968). 'The Rise and Fall of the Venetian Woollen Cloth Industry', in *Crisis and Change in the Venetian Economy* 88–105. London

Queller, D. and Madden, T. (1993). 'Father of the Bride: Fathers, Daughters, and Dowries in Late Medieval and Early Renaissance Venice', *Renaissance Quarterly* 46.685–711

Quétel, C. (1986). *Le mal de Naples. Histoire de la syphilis*. Paris

Quondam, A. (1974). *Petrarchismo mediato. Per una critica della forma 'antologia'*. Rome

(1991). *Il naso di Laura. Lingua e poesia lirica nella tradizione del Classicismo*. Modena

(2000a). *Questo povero Cortegiano: Castiglione, il libro, la storia*. Rome

(2000b). '"Limature di Rame": qualche riflessione sulla novella nel sistema del classicismo', in G. Albanese, L. Battaglia Ricci, and R. Bessi (eds.), *Favole parabole istorie: le forme della scrittura novellistica dal medioevo al rinascimento* 543–56. Rome

(2003). 'Lo sguardo dell'altro. *Renaissance in Italy* di John Addington Symonds', in *L'Italia fuori d'Italia: tradizione e presenza della lingua e della cultura italiana nel mondo* 369–446. Rome.

(2004). *Petrarca l'italiano dimenticato*. Milan

(2011). 'Il pubblico della poesia', in Irace *et al.* (eds.) 79–86

Quondam, A. and Papagno, G. (eds.) (1982). *La corte e lo spazio: Ferrara estense*, 3 vols. Rome

Rabb, T.K. (2004). 'Sandys, Sir Edwin (1561–1629)', *Oxford Dictionary of National Biography*, www.oxforddnb.com/view/article/24650

Rabil, A. (1988). 'Humanism in Milan', in A. Rabil (ed.), *Renaissance Humanism: Foundations, Forms, and Legacy* vol. 3, 235–63. Philadelphia

Raggio, O. (1990). *Faide e parentele: lo stato genovese visto dalla Fontanabuona*. Turin

Raggio, O. and Wilmering, A.M. (eds.) (1999). *The Gubbio Studiolo and its Conservation*, vol. 1: *Federico da Montefeltro's Palace at Gubbio and its Studiolo*; vol. 2: *Italian Renaissance Intarsia and the Conservation of the Gubbio Studiolo*. New York

Ramusio, G. B. (1970). *Navigationi e viaggi: Venice 1563–1606*, 3 vols. (intro. R. A. Skelton and comm. G. B. Parks). Amsterdam

Rapp, R. T. (1976). *Industry and Ecnomic Decline in Seventeenth-Century Venice*. Cambridge MA

Rauch, J. E. and Casella, A. (eds.) (2001). *Networks and Markets*. New York

Reinhard, W. (2009). *Paul V. Borghese (1605–1621)*. Stuttgart

Reinhardt, V. (2004). *Il Rinascimento in Italia*. Bologna

Ricci, M (2001). *L'architettura a Bologna nel Rinascimento (1460–1550): centro o periferia?* Bologna

Ricci, S. (2008). *Inquisitori, censori, filosofi sullo scenario della Controriforma*. Rome

Richardson, B. (1994). *Print Culture in Renaissance Italy: The Editor and the Vernacular Text, 1470–1600*. Cambridge

(1999). *Printing, Writers and Readers in Renaissance Italy*. Cambridge

(2009). *Manuscript Culture in Renaissance Italy*. Cambridge

Richardson, C.M., Woods, K.W., and Franklin, M.W. (eds.) (2007). *Renaissance Art Reconsidered: An Anthology of Primary Sources*. Malden MA

Rizzo, S. (1973). *Il lessico filologico degli umanisti*. Rome

(1998). 'Il latino del Poliziano', in V. Fera and M. Martelli (eds.), *Agnolo Poliziano poeta scrittore filologo* 83–125. Florence

(2002). *Ricerche sul latino umanistico*. Rome

(2004). 'I latini dell'umanesimo', in G. Bernardi Perini (ed.), *Il latino nell'età dell' umanesimo* 51–95. Florence

Roberts, S. (2013). *Printing a Mediterranean World: Florence, Constantinople, and the Renaissance of Geography*. Cambridge MA

Robin, D. (2007). *Publishing Women: Salons, the Presses, and the Counter-Reformation in Sixteenth-Century Italy*. Chicago

Rochon, A. (ed.) (1975). *Formes et significations de la 'beffa' dans la littérature italienne*, 2 vols. Paris

Rocke, M. (1996). *Forbidden Friendships: Homosexuality and Male Culture in Renaissance Florence*. Oxford

(2003). 'Gender and Sexual Culture in Renaissance Italy', in Martin (ed.) 139–58

Romano, R. (1971). *Tra due crisi: l'Italia del Rinascimento*. Turin

(1974). 'La storia economica: dal secolo XIV al Settecento', in *Storia d'Italia*, vol. 2: *Dalla caduta dell'Impero romano al secolo XVIII* 1811–931. Turin

Romer, F. E. (1998). *Pomponius Mela's Description of the World*. Ann Arbor

Rosenberg, C.M. (1997). *Este Monuments and Urban Development in Renaissance Ferrara*. Cambridge

Rossi, F. (2001). 'Immagine e mito di Venezia: commitenza artistica e progetto politico a Bergamo', in F. Rossi (ed.), *Bergamo: l'altra Venezia–il Rinascimento negli anni di Lorenzo Lotto 1510–1530* 23–35. Milan

Rossi, M. (2006). *Le fila del tempo: il sistema storico di Luigi Lanzi*. Florence

Rowe, C. and Satkowski, L. G. (2002). *Italian Architecture of the Sixteenth Century*. New York

Rowland, I. D. (1995). 'Feast of Pliny', *New York Review of Books* www.nybooks.com/articles/archives/1995/may/11/feast-of-pliny/

(1998a). *The Culture of the High Renaissance: Ancients and Moderns in Sixteenth-Century Rome*. Cambridge

(1998b). 'Vitruvius in Print and in Vernacular Translation: Fra Giocondo, Bramante, Raphael and Cesare Cesariano', in Hart/Hicks (eds.) 105–22

(2002). 'Vitruvius and Technology', in Conforti/Hopkins (eds.) 244–57

(2008). *Giordano Bruno: Philosopher/Heretic*. New York

(2009). 'The Passions of Palladio', *New York Review of Books* www.nybooks.com/articles/archives/2009/dec/17/the-passions-of-palladio/

(2010). 'Representing the World', in R. Bod, J. Maat, and T. Weststeijn (eds.), *The Making of the Humanities*, vol. 1: *Early Modern Europe* 84–105. Amsterdam

Rozzo, U. (ed.) (1997). *La censura libraria nell'Europa del secolo sedicesimo*. Udine

Rubin, P. L. (1995). *Giorgio Vasari: Art and History*. New Haven

Rubin, P. L., and Wright, A. (1999). *Renaissance Florence: The Art of the 1470s*. London

Rubinstein, N. (1942). 'The Beginnings of Political Thought in Florence: An Essay in Medieval Historiography', *Journal of the Warburg and Courtauld Institutes* 5.198–227

(1979). 'Le dottrine politiche nel Rinascimento', in M. Boas Hall (ed.), *Il Rinascimento: interpretazioni e problemi* 181–237. Rome

Ruffini, F. (1982). 'Linee rette e intrichi: il Vitruvio di Cesariano e la Ferrara teatrale di Ercole I', in Quondam/Papagno (eds.) vol. 2, 365–430

(1983). *Teatri prima del teatro: visioni dell'edificio e della scena tra Umanesimo e Rinascimento*. Rome

Ruffini, M. (2011). *Art without an Author: Vasari's Lives and Michelangelo's Death*. New York

Ruggiero, G. (1980). *Violence in Early Renaissance Venice*. New Brunswick

(1989). *The Boundaries of Eros: Sex Crime and Sexuality in Renaissance Venice*. Oxford

(ed.) (2002). *A Companion to the Worlds of the Renaissance*. Oxford

(2006). *Machiavelli in Love: Sex, Self, and Society in the Italian Renaissance*. Baltimore

Rundle, D. and Petrina, A. (2013). *The Italian University in the Renaissance*, special number of *Renaissance Studies*

Rusconi, R. (2010). *Santo Padre: la santità del papa da san Pietro a Giovanni Paolo II*. Rome

Russell, C. (2006). *Giulia Gonzaga and the Religious Controversies of Sixteenth-Century Italy*. Turnhout

Rutkin, D. (2010). 'Mysteries of Attraction: Giovanni Pico della Mirandola, Astrology and Desire', *Studies in History and Philosophy of Biological and Biomedical Sciences* 41.117–24

Ruvoldt, M. (2004). *The Italian Renaissance Imagery of Inspiration: Metaphors of Sex, Sleep, and Dreams*. Cambridge

Ruzante [Angelo Beolco] (1970). *Teatro* (ed. L. Zorzi). Turin

(1994). *L'Anconitana/The Woman from Ancona* (ed. and trans. N. Dersofi). Berkeley

Rybczynski, W. (2002). *The Perfect House: A Journey with the Renaissance Master Andrea Palladio*. London

Rykwert, J. (1998). 'Theory as Rhetoric: Leon Battista Alberti in Theory and Practice', in Hart/Hicks (eds.) 33–50

Sabbadino, C. (2000). *Il sistema laguna a metà Cinquecento: opere scelte pubblicate nel 450° della morte* (ed. P. G. Tiozzo Gobetto and intro. S. Ciriacono). Venice

Salernitano, M. (1990). *Il novellino* (eds. L. Settembrini and S. S. Nigro). Milan

Salomon, X. (2009). 'The Remains of Piety: Veronese's Petrobelli Altarpiece', in *Paolo Veronese: The Petrobelli Altarpiece* 59–101. Milan

Sandys, E. and Sarpi, P. (1969 [1625]). *Relatione dello stato della religione e con quali dissegni et arti è stata fabricata e maneggiata in diversi stati di queste occidentali parti del mondo, tradotta dall'inglese del Cavaliere Edoino Sandis in lingua volgare con aggiunte notabili*, in P. Sarpi, *Opere* (eds. G. Cozzi and L. Cozzi) vol. 1, 295–330. Milan

Sanson, H. (2011). *Women, Language, and Grammar in Italy.* Oxford

Santorio, A. (2013). 'Pellegrino Prisciani e la pratica teatrale alla corte d'Este di Ferrara', *Engramma* 107 www.engramma.it/eOS/

Sapegno, N. (ed.) (1987). *Storia della letteratura italiana.* Milan

Sapori, A. (1955). *Studi di storia economica (secoli XIII-XIV-XV)*, 3 vols. Florence
(1970). *The Italian Merchant in the Middle Ages.* New York

Saslow, J. M. (1996). *The Medici Wedding of 1589: Florentine Festival as Theatrum Mundi.* New Haven

Scafi, A. (2006). *Mapping Paradise: A History of Heaven on Earth.* Chicago

Scapecchi, P. (2001). 'Subiaco 1465 oppure [Bondeno 1463]? Analisi del frammento Parsons-Scheide', *La Bibliofilìa* 103.1–24

Schmitt, C. B. (1972). *Cicero Scepticus: A Study of the Influence of the 'Academica' in the Renaissance.* The Hague
(1983). *Aristotle in the Renaissance.* Cambridge MA
(1984). *The Aristotelian Tradition and Renaissance Universities.* London

Schmitt, C. B., Skinner, Q., Kessler, E., and Kraye, J. (eds.) (1988). *The Cambridge History of Renaissance Philosophy.* Cambridge

Schofield, R. (1992). 'Avoiding Rome: An Introduction to Lombard Sculptors and the Antique', *Arte Lombarda* 100.29–44.

Schultz, B. (1985). *Art and Anatomy in Renaissance Italy.* Ann Arbor

Scott, J. W. (1986). 'Gender: A Useful Category of Historical Analysis', *American Historical Review* 5.1053–75

Segre, C. and Marti, M. (eds.) (1959). *La prosa del Duecento.* Milan

Seidel Menchi, S. (1987). *Erasmo in Italia, 1520–1580.* Turin

Seidel Menchi, S. and Quaglioni, D. (eds.) (2001). *Matrimoni in dubbio: unioni controverse e nozze in Italia dal XIV al XVIII secolo.* Bologna

Sella, D. (1979). *Crisis and Continuity: The Economy of Spanish Lombardy in the Seventeenth Century.* Cambridge MA

Serlio, S. (1996–2001). *Sebastiano Serlio on Architecture* (eds. and trans. V. Hart and P. Hicks). New Haven

Seta, C. de (1994). 'The Urban Structure of Naples: Utopia and Reality', in Millon/ Lampugnani (eds.) 349–71

Settis, S. (ed.) (1984–86). *Memoria dell'antico nell'arte italiana.* Turin
(ed.) (2007). *Il Palazzo Schifanoia a Ferrara.* Modena

Shank, M. H. (2008). 'L'astronomia nel Quattrocento tra corti e università', in Clericuzio/ Ernst (eds.) 3–20

Shaw, P. (1978). 'La versione ficiniana della Monarchia', in *Studi danteschi* 50.289–408

Sheard, W. S. and Paoletti, J. T. (1978). *Collaboration in Italian Renaissance Art.* New Haven

Shearman, J. (1992). *Only Connect: Art and the Spectator in the Italian Renaissance*. Princeton

Shelby, L. R. (1975). 'Mariano Taccola and his Books on Engines and Machines', *Technology and Culture* 16.466–75

Shell, J. (1998). 'Leonardo and the Lombard Traditionalists', in *The Legacy of Leonardo: Painters in Lombardy 1490–1530* 65–93. Milan

Shemek, D. (1998). *Ladies Errant: Wayward Women and Social Order in Early Modern Italy*. Durham NC

(2005). 'The Collector's Cabinet: Lodovico Domenichi's Gallery of Women', in Benson/Kirkham (eds.) 239–62

Sherr, R. (1984). 'A Letter from Paolo Animuccia: A Composer's Response to the Council of Trent', *Early Music* 12.75–78

(ed.) (2000). *The Josquin Companion*. Oxford

Shils, E. (1975 [1961]). 'Center and Periphery', in *Center and Periphery: Essays in Macrosociology* 3–17. Chicago

Shirley, R. (1983). *The Mapping of the World: Early Printed World Maps, 1472–1700*. London

Signaroli, S. (2009). *Maestri e tipografi a Brescia, 1471–1519: l'impresa editoriale dei Britannici fra istituzioni civili e cultura umanistica nell'Occidente della Serenissima*. Brescia

Siraisi, N. G. (1973). *Arts and Sciences at Padua: The Studium of Padua before 1350*. Toronto

(1990a). 'Giovanni Argenterio and Sixteenth-Century Medical Innovation: Between Princely Patronage and Academic Controversy', in McVaugh/Siraisi (eds.) 161–80

(1990b). *Medieval and Early Renaissance Medicine: An Introduction to Knowledge and Practice*. Chicago

(1997). *The Clock and the Mirror: Girolamo Cardano and Renaissance Medicine*. Princeton

Skinner, Q. (2002). *Visions of Politics*, 3 vols. Cambridge

Smarr, J. L. (1991). 'Gaspara Stampa's Poetry of Performance', *Journal of the Rocky Mountain Medieval and Renaissance Association* 12.61–84

Smith, C. (1992). *Architecture in the Culture of Early Humanism: Ethics, Aesthetics, and Eloquence 1400–1470*. Oxford

Smith, P. H. (2009). 'Science on the Move: Recent Trends in the History of Early Modern Science', *Renaissance Quarterly* 62.345–75

Snyder, J. R. (1989a). 'The Last Laugh: Literary Theory and the Academy in Late Renaissance Florence', *Annals of Scholarship: Metastudies in the Humanities and Social Sciences* 6.37–55

(1989b). *Writing the Scene of Speaking: Theories of Dialogue in the Late Italian Renaissance*. Stanford

(1993). 'Riso, beffa e potere: la poetica della novella di Francesco Bonciani dell'Accademia degli Alterati', in *La novella italiana: atti del convegno di Caprarola, 19–24 settembre 1988* 939–55. Rome

Solerti, A. (1895). *Vita di Torquato Tasso*, 3 vols. Turin.

Somaini, F. (2012). *Geografie politiche italiane tra Medio Evo e Rinascimento*. Milan

Sperling, J. (1999). *Convents and the Body Politic in Late Renaissance Venice*. Chicago

(2004). 'Marriage at the Time of the Council of Trent (1560–70): Clandestine Marriages, Kinship Prohibitions, and Dowry Exchange in European Comparison', *Journal of Early Modern History* 8.67–108

(2007). 'Dowry or Inheritance? Kinship, Property, and Women's Agency in Lisbon, Venice and Florence (1572)', *Journal of Early Modern History* 11.197–238

Speroni, S. (1989a). *Dialogo delle lingue*, in *Opere* (ed. M. Pozzi) vol. 1, 166–201. Rome

(1989b [1740]). *Opere* (anastatic reprint). Manziana

Spufford, P. (1988). *Money and Its Use in Medieval Europe*. Cambridge

Stacey, P. (2007). *Roman Monarchy and the Renaissance Prince*. Cambridge

Stampino, M. G. (2005). *Staging the Pastoral: Tasso's Aminta and the Emergence of Modern Western Theater*. Tempe AZ

Starn, R. (2007). 'A Postmodera Renaissance', *Renaissance Quarterly* 60.1–24

Stefanizzi, S. (2011). *Il 'De balneis' di Tommaso Giunti, 1553: autori e testi*. Florence

Steinberg, J. (2007). *Accounting for Dante: Urban Readers and Writers in Late Medieval Italy*. Notre Dame IN

Stevenson, J. (2005). *Women Latia Poets: Language, Gender, and Anthority, from Autiquity to the Eighteenth Century*. Oxford

Stinger, C. (1998). *The Renaissance in Rome*. Bloomington

Stoppino, E. (2012). *Genealogies of Fiction: Women Warriors and the Dynastic Imagination in 'Orlando furioso.'* New York

Strabo (1917–32). *The Geography of Strabo*, 8 vols. (trans. H. L. Jones). London

Straparola, G. F. (2000). *Le piacevoli notti* (ed. D. Pirovano). Rome

Strocchia, S. (1989). 'Remembering the Family: Women, Kin, and Commemorative Masses in Renaissance Florence', *Renaissance Quarterly* 42.635–54

(2009). *Nuns and Nunneries in Renaissance Florence*. Baltimore

Strozzi, A. (1997). *The Selected Letters of Alessandra Strozzi* (ed. and trans. H. Gregory). Berkeley

Strunk, O. and Treitler, L. (1998, rev. edn). *Source Readings in Music History*, vol. 4. New York

Stuard, S. M. (2006). *Gilding the Market: Luxury and Fashion in Fourteenth-Century Italy*. Philadelphia

Stussi, A. (1994). *Lingua, dialetto, e letteratura*. Turin

Sudhoff, K. and Singer, C. (1925). *The Earliest Printed Literature on Syphilis Being Ten Tractates from the Years 1495–1498, in Complete Facsimile with an Introduction and other Accessory Material*. Florence

Summers, D. (1981). *Michelangelo and the Language of Art*. Princeton

(2003). *Real Spaces: World Art History and the Rise of Western Modernism*. London

Sussman, N. (1998). 'The Late Medieval Bullion Famine Reconsidered', *Journal of Economic History* 58.126–54

Taccola, M. (1972). *Mariano Taccola and his Book De ingeneis* (eds. F. D. Prager and G. Scaglia). Cambridge MA

Tafuri, M. (2006). *Interpreting the Renaissance: Princes, Cities, Architects* (trans. D. Sherer). New Haven

Talignani, A. (2005). 'La Cappella Montini nella Cattedrale di Parma: un unicum di forme, colori ed epigrafi nella "periferia"', in Periti (ed.) 119–81

Tallon, A. (2006). *L'Europe de la Renaissance*. Paris

Talvacchia, B. (2005). 'Raphael's Workshop and the Development of a Managerial Style', in M. B. Hall (ed.), *The Cambridge Companion to Raphael* 167–85. Cambridge

Taruskin, R. (2005). *The Oxford History of Western Music* vol. 1, 694–701

Tasso, T. (1982). *Dialogues* (trans. C. Lord and D. A. Trafton). Berkeley

Tavernor, R. (1998). *On Alberti and the Art of Building*. New Haven

Tavoni, M. (1984). *Latino, grammatica, volgare: storia di una questione umanistica*. Padua

(1992a). *La storia della lingua: il Quattrocento*. Milan

(1992b). 'Le prose della volgar lingua', in A. Asor Rosa (ed.) 1065–88

Tedeschi, J. (2000). *The Italian Reformation of the Sixteenth Century and the Diffusion of Renaissance Culture: A Bibliography of the Secondary Literature* (ca. *1750–1997*). Modena

Tenenti, A. (1988). 'Il mercante e il banchiere', in E. Garin (ed.), *L'uomo del Rinascimento* 203–36. Bari

Terlizzi, F. P. (2010). 'L'istruzione superiore tra Medioevo e Rinascimento', in De Vincentiis *et al.* (eds.) 258–75

Testori, G. (1975). *Romanino e Moretto alla Cappella del Sacramento*. Brescia
    (1995). *La realtà della pittura* (ed. P. C. Marani). Milan

Thomas, A. (1995). *The Painter's Practice in Renaissance Tuscany*. Cambridge

Thorndike, L. (1975). *University Records and Life in the Middle Ages*. New York

Tissoni-Benvenuti, A. (1986). *L'Orfeo del Poliziano, con il testo critico dell'originale e delle successive forme teatrali*. Padua

Tolias, G. (2007). 'Isolarii, Fifteenth to Seventeenth Century', in Woodward (ed.) 263–84

Tomlinson, G. (1987). *Monteverdi and the End of the Renaissance*. Berkeley

Toussaint, S. (2008). *Humanismes, antihumanismes: de Ficin à Heidegger*, vol. 1: *Humanitas et rentabilité*. Paris

Trachtenberg, M. (1983). 'Review of H. Saalman, *Brunelleschi: The Cupola of Santa Maria de Fiore*', *Journal of Architectural Historians* 42. 292–97.
    (1997). *Dominion of the Eye: Urbanism, Art, and Power in Early Modern Florence*. Cambridge
    (2001). 'Architecture and Music Reunited: A New Reading of Dufay's *Nuper rosarum flores* in the Cathedral of Florence', *Renaissance Quarterly* 54.741–75
    (2010). *Building in Time: From Giotto to Alberti and Modern Oblivion*. New Haven

Travaini, L. (2007). 'Zecche e monete', in Braunstein/Molà (eds.) 479–509

Trexler, R. C. (1994). 'Celibacy in the Renaissance: The Nuns of Florence', in *Dependence in Context in Renaissance Florence* 343–72. Binghamton NY
    (1980). *Public Life in Renaissance Florence* 223–61. New York

Trissino, G. (1986). *Scritti linguistici* (ed. A. Castelvecchi). Rome

Trivellato, F. (2006). 'Murano Glass, Continuity and Transformation (1400–1800), in Lanaro (ed.) 143–83

Trovato, P. (1991). *Con ogni diligenza corretto: la stampa e le revisioni editoriali dei testi letterari italiani (1470–1570)*. Bologna
    (1994). *Storia della lingua: il primo Cinquecento*. Bologna

Tuohy, T. (1996). *Herculean Ferrara: Ercole d'Este, 1475–1505, and the Invention of a Ducal Capital*. Cambridge

Turchi, L. (1998). 'L'eredità della madre: un conflitto giuridico nello stato estense alla fine del *Cinquecento*', in Calvi/Chabot (eds.) 161–85

Turini, A. (1542). *Hippocratis et Galeni defensio adversus Hieronymum Fracastorium, de causis dierum criticorum*. Rome

Tuttle, R. J. (1998). 'On Vignola's *Rule of the Five Orders of Architecture*', in Hart/Hicks (eds.) 199–218

Tylus, J. (2009). *Reclaiming Catherine of Siena: Literacy, Literature and the Signs of Others*. Chicago

Ullman, B. L. (1960). *The Origin and Development of Humanistic Script*. Rome

Usher, J. (1996). 'Poetry', in P. Brand and L. Pertile (eds.), *The Cambridge History of Italian Literature* 5–27. Cambridge.

Valla, L. (1977). *On Pleasure/De voluptate* (trans. A. K. Hieatt and M. Lorch, intro. M. de Panizza Lorch). New York

(1994). *Orazione per l'inaugurazione dell'anno accademico 1455–1456* (ed. S. Rizzo). Rome

(2007). *On the Donation of Constantine/De falso credita et ementita Constantini donatione declamatio* (ed. and trans. G. W. Bowersock). Cambridge MA

Valturio, R. (2006). *De re militari* (ed. P. Delbianco), 2 vols. Milan

Van Orden, K. (ed.) (2000). *Music and the Cultures of Print*. New York

Varese, C. (ed.) (1955). *Prosatori volgari del Quattrocento*. Milan

Vasari, G. (1960). *On Technique* (trans. L. S. Maclehose). New York

(1996). *Lives of the Painters, Sculptors and Architects* (trans. C. du C. de Vere), 2 vols. London

(1999). *Vasari on Theatre* (ed. and trans T. A. Pallen). Carbondale IL

Vasoli, C. (1988). 'The Renaissance Concept of Philosophy', in Schmitt *et al.* (eds.) 57–74

(1999). 'Savonarola, Ficino e la cultura filosofica fiorentina del tardo Quattrocento', in *Quasi sit Deus, Studi su Marsilio Ficino* 301–19. Lecce

Vecce, C. (1993a). 'La poesia latina: il classicismo rinascimentale', in Brioschi/Di Girolamo (eds.) 256–62

(1993b). 'Il latino e le forme della poesia umanistica', in Brioschi/Di Girolamo (eds.) 438–62

(2006). 'Scuola e università a Napoli nel Rinascimento', in L. Gargan and M. P. Mussini Sacchi (eds.), *I classici e l'università umanistica* 649–71. Messina

Ventrone, P. (1994). 'L'eccezione e la regola: le rappresentazioni del 1439 e la tradizione fiorentina delle feste di quartiere', in P. Viti (ed.), *Firenze e il concilio del 1439* vol. 1, 409–35

(2001). '"Una visione miracolosa e indicibile": nuove considerazioni sulle feste di quartiere', in E. G. Zorzi and M. Sperenzi (eds.), *Teatro e spettacolo nella Firenze dei Medici: Modelli dei luoghi teatrali* 39–51. Florence

Vergani, R. (2007). 'L'attività mineraria e metallurgica: argento e rame', in Braustein/Molà (eds.) 216–33

Verrazzano, G. da (1970). *The Voyages of Giovanni da Verrazzano, 1524–1528* (ed. L. C. Wroth). New Haven

Vesalius, A. (1543). *De humani corporis fabrica*. Basel

(2014). 'The Fabric of the Human Body': *An Annotated Translation of the 1543 and 1555 Editions of 'De Humani Corporis Fabrica Libri Septem'* (eds. and trans. D. H. Garrison and M. H. Hart). Basel

Vescovini, G. F. (1979). *Astrologia e scienza: la crisi dell'aristotelismo sul cadere del Trecento e Biagio Pelacani da Parma*. Florence

Vespucci, A. (1992). *Letters from a New World* (ed. L. Formisano and trans. D. Jacobson). New York

(2012). *Amerigo Vespucci: le lettere*. Florence

Vignola [Giacomo Barozzi da] (1985). *Regola delli cinque ordini d'architettura* (ed. M. W. Casotti), in *Trattati di architettura* vol. 5, pt. 2 (eds. E. Bassi *et al.*) 499–577. Milan

Visceglia, M. A. and Signorotto, G. (eds.) (2002). *Court and Politics in Papal Rome*. Cambridge

Vitruvius (1999). *Ten Books on Architecture* (trans. and comm. I. D. Rowland, comm. T. N. Howe, and illus. M. J. Dewar). Cambridge

Wackernagel, M. (1981). *The World of the Florentine Renaissance Artist: Projects and Patrons, Workshop and Art Market* (trans. A. Luchs). Princeton

Waddington, R. B. (2004). *Aretino's Satyr: Sexuality, Satire and Self-Projection in Sixteenth-Century Literature and Art.* Toronto

Walsham, A. (2011). *The Reformation of the Landscape: Religion, Identity, and Memory in Early Modern Britain and Ireland.* Oxford

Warburg, A. (1999). 'Pagan–Antique Prophecy in Words and Images in the Age of Luther', in *The Renewal of Pagan Antiquity: Contributions to the Cultural History of the European Renaissance* (trans. D. Britt) 597–697. Los Angeles

Wardrop, J. (1963). *The Script of Humanism: Some Aspects of Humanistic Script, 1460–1560.* Oxford

Warnke, M. (1993). *The Court Artist: On the Ancestry of the Modern Artist.* Cambridge

Warr, C. and Elliott, J. (eds.) (2010). *Art and Architecture in Naples, 1266–1713: New Approaches.* Chichester

Wazbinski, Z. (1987). *L'Accademia Medicea del Disegno a Firenze nel Cinquecento: idea e instituzione*, 2 vols. Florence

Wear, A., French, R. K., and Lonie, I. M. (eds.) (1985). *The Medical Renaissance of the Sixteenth Century.* Cambridge

Weaver, E. (2002). *Convent Theatre in Early Modern Italy: Spiritual Fun and Learning for Women.* Cambridge

Wegman, R. (2005). *The Crisis of Music in Early Modern Europe, 1470–1530.* New York

Weil-Garris, K. and D'Amico, J. F. (1980). 'The Renaissance Cardinal's Ideal Palace: A Chapter from Cortesi's *De cardinalatu*', *Memoirs of the American Academy in Rome* 35.45–119, 121–23

Weinberg, B. (ed.) (1972). *Trattati di poetica e retorica*, 4 vols. Bari

Weisinger, H. (1943). 'Renaissance Theories of Revival in the Fine Arts', *Italica* 20. 163–70

Weiss, R. (1969). *The Renaissance Discovery of Classical Antiquity.* Oxford

Welch, E. (1997). *Art and Society in Italy, 1350–1500.* Oxford

(2005). *Shopping in the Renaissance: Consumer Cultures in Italy, 1400–1600.* New Haven

White, L. (1975). 'Medical Astrologers and Late Medieval Technology', *Viator* 6.298–301

Whitfield, C. and Martineau, J. (eds.) (1982). *Painting in Naples, 1606–1705: From Caravaggio to Giordano.* Washington

Wilson, B[lake]. (2001). 'Lauda', in *The New Grove Dictionary of Music and Musicians* (eds. S. Sadie and J. Tyrrell) vol. 14, 367–74. London

Wilson, B[ronwen]. (2005). *The World in Venice: Print, the City and Early Modern Identity.* Toronto

Wisch, B. and Ahl, D. C. (2000). *Confraternities and the Visual Arts in Renaissance Italy: Ritual, Spectacle, Image.* Cambridge

Witt, R. G. (1982). 'Medieval "Ars Dictaminis" and the Beginnings of Humanism: A New Construction of the Problem', *Renaissance Quarterly* 35.1–35

(2000). *'In the Footsteps of the Ancients': The Origins of Humanism from Lovato to Bruni.* Leiden

(2012). *The Two Latin Cultures and the Foundation of Renaissance Humanism in Medieval Italy.* Cambridge

Woodward, D. (1987). 'Medieval Mappaemundi', in Harley/Woodward (eds.) 286–370

(2001). 'Starting with the Map: The Rosselli Map of the World, *ca.* 1508', in D. Woodward, C. Delano-Smith, and C. D. K. Yee (eds.), *Approaches and Challenges in a Worldwide History of Cartography* 71–90. Barcelona

(ed.) (2007). *The History of Cartography*, vol. 3: *The Renaissance.* Chicago

Woolfson, J. (1998). *Padua and the Tudors: English Students in Italy, 1485–1603*. Cambridge
  (ed.) (2005). *Palgrave Advances in Renaissance Historiography*. Basingstoke
  (2013). 'Padua and English Students Revisited', in Rundle/Petrina (eds.) 572–87
Wyatt, M. (2005). *The Italian Encounter with Tudor England: A Cultural Politics of Translation*.
  Cambridge
Yates, F. A. (1934). *John Florio: The Life of an Italian in Shakespeare's England*. Cambridge
  (1964). *Giordano Bruno and the Hermetic Tradition*. London
  (1983). *Renaissance and Reform: The Italian Contribution*. London
Yoran, H. (2007). 'Florentine Civic Humanism and the Emergence of Modern Ideology',
  History and Theory 46.326–44
Zaggia, M. (2003). *Tra Mantova e la Sicilia nel Cinquecento*, 3 vols. Florence
Zampetti, P. (1988). *Pittura nelle Marche*, vol. 1: *Dalle origini al primo Rinascimento*.
  Florence
Zampetti, P. and Sgarbi, V. (eds.) (1980). *Lorenzo Lotto, Atti del convegno internazionale di
  studi per il V centenario della nascita, Asolo 18–21 settembre 1980*. Venice
Zamponi, S. (2004). 'La scrittura umanistica', *Archiv für Diplomatik, Schriftsgeschichte,
  Siegel- und Wappenkunde* 50.467–504
Zaninelli, S. (ed.) (1995). *Scritti teorici e tecnici di agricoltura*, vol. 1: *Dal Quattrocento alla
  fine del Seicento*. Milan
Zarlino, G. (1965). *Le istitutioni harmoniche*. New York
  (1968). *The Art of Counterpoint* (trans. G. Marco and ed. C. Palisca). New Haven
  (1983). *On the Modes* (trans. V. Cohen and ed. C. Palisca). New Haven
Zarri, G. (1980). 'Monasteri femminili e città (secoli XV–XVIII)', in *Storia d'Italia: Annali*
  9.357–429
Zatti, S. (1999). 'Trissino', in Grendler (ed.) 171–72
  (2006). *The Quest for Epic: From Ariosto to Tasso* (trans. S. Hill and D. Looney). Toronto
Zorzi, A. (1988). *L'amministrazione della giustizia penale nella repubblica fiorentina: aspetti e
  problemi*. Florence
Zorzi, L. (1977). *Il teatro e la città: saggi sulla scena italiana*. Turin
Zorzi, L. and Sperenzi, M. (2001). *Teatro e spettacolo nella Firenze dei Medici: Modelli dei
  luoghi teatrali*. Florence
Zumthor, P. (1992). 'Courtly Love Lyric', in *Toward a Medieval Poetics* (trans. P. Bennett)
  143–93. Minneapolis

Index